=

ONLY

CHRISTOPHER MARLOWE
AND
EDWARD ALLEYN

A.D. WRAIGHT

ADAM HART (Publishers) Ltd
CHICHESTER · SUSSEX · ENGLAND

By the same author
in collaboration with Virginia F. Stern:
IN SEARCH OF CHRISTOPHER MARLOWE
First published 1965
Reissued February 1993

First published in 1993 by
ADAM HART (Publishers) Ltd
London SE27 9HG
England

© A.D. Wraight 1993

A Catalogue Record of this title
is held at the British Library

ISBN 1 897763 00 X

Typeset and produced by Woodfield Publishing Services
Fontwell, Sussex, England
Printed and bound in England by Bookcraft (Bath) Ltd

TO THE BOYS

OF

DULWICH COLLEGE

and all those

associated with

ALLEYN'S FOUNDATION

Tamburlaine in his chariot.

Orcanes: O thou that sway'st the region under earth,
And art a king as absolute as Jove,
Come as thou didst in fruitful Sicily,
Surveying all the glories of the land,
And as thou took'st the fair Proserpina,
Joying the fruit of Ceres' garden-plot,
For love, for honour, and to make her queen,
So, for just hate, for shame, and to subdue
This proud contemner of thy dreadful power,
Haling him headlong to the lowest hell.

The Second Part of Tamburlaine the Great, Act IV, Sc.3, 11. 32–42

*Photograph by Nobby Clark for the National Theatre production of **Tamburlaine the Great**, 1976, directed by Sir Peter Hall.*

CONTENTS

List of Illustrations

Acknowledgements

This book has had a more than usually long gestation period. Retrospectively, I wish to express my sincere appreciation to the then Librarian and Archivist of Dulwich College Library, Mr W.S. Wright, for his kindly assistance when I first conducted this research in the 1960's. More recently I have been extremely fortunate to have the solicitous attention of his successor, Dr Jan Piggott, whose erudition and infectious delight in handling ancient manuscripts has made my final visits to the College a memorable pleasure. Nothing was too much trouble for him, whether arranging for photographs to be taken of the manuscripts, or the hunting down, in a moment of blissful serendipity, an historic photograph of the Dulwich College cricket team circa 1903 with the College buildings in the background, just as I had wanted. I was thrilled, too, to be introduced to the superb leather-bound Scolar Press facsimile of the Alleyn Papers published in 1977, produced under the dedicated hand of Dr. R.A. Foakes, to whom all who study these papers must for ever be grateful. A copy is, of course, in the British Library's Manuscript Department, but I had not discovered its existence. I covet a copy. Also I wish to extend my thanks to the Assistant Librarian, Mr Austin Hall, for his ever ready help.

Inevitably, I am greatly indebted to the works of G.F. Warner, William Young, W.W. Greg and R.A. Foakes and R.T. Rickert on the Alleyn Papers. Without their pioneering studies mine would never have reached completion. Whilst for Marlowe, it is especially to John Bakeless' work on *Tamburlaine*, and to C.F. Tucker Brooke and Allison Gaw that I have turned for essential assistance in writing this book. To a very large extent it is also their work that is here, and I am deeply conscious of my debt.

My acknowledgements are also due to Hanspeter Born on whose thorough study of the anonymous play *A Knack to Know a Knave* I have largely based mine; and to the late Peter Alexander, from whose works I have quoted extensively to argue my case.

My especial gratitude is extended to my generous friend and mentor, Dr Virginia F. Stern, for her unfailing encouragement and timely help in drawing my attention to D. Allen Carroll's paper on *"Greene's "Vpstart Crow" Passage: A Survey of Commentary"* (1985) which provided, in a nutshell, all I could have asked for in the presentation of the long history of academic argument and controversial opinion on this subject; and for finding time from her own busy research to read my manuscript critically and meticulously to correct my errors. I want also warmly to thank my friend, Michael Rowett, for his indispensable assistance in providing translations of the archaic Latin texts of Marlowe's sources for *Tamburlaine* and the Latin "gobbets", as he cheerfully called them; and Dr Wolfgang Deninger for his kindness in going to great lengths to procure for me a rare copy of Allison Gaw's thesis, now long out of print and of inestimable value to me in this study. To my many friends and the members of my family who have given me much appreciated encouragement, have listened patiently, and given moral support to bring this extended research finally to its culmination I am ever grateful.

A.D. WRAIGHT

Note on the printing of manuscripts

For Henslowe's Diary I am indebted to R.A. Foakes' and R.T. Rickert's transcripts in their edition of *Henslowe's Diary* (Cambridge, 1961) which has been of invaluable assistance. Where these worn papers are concerned two heads are certainly better than one! The only difference in printing these extracts *verbatim et literatim* in this book is in the interpretation of the final 's' and 'es' as a symbol, which has been discarded in favour of using the normal 's' of the type-face.

Otherwise, Henslowe's 'er' at the end of the months of September to December is rendered 'ȝ'. In all texts cited such Elizabethanisms as 'yᵉ' and 'wᵗ' or 'wᵗʰ', or 'per" as 'p̱' and 'ment' and its variants as 'n̄' or 'm̄' have been retained.

The works of W.W. Greg and William Young in transcribing the Alleyn Papers have been gratefully consulted.

Preface

The inspiration for researching and writing this book was triggered off many years ago when I was working on a biography of Christopher Marlowe for his quatercentenary, shared with Shakespeare in 1964. In my reading then I came across an exciting thesis, *The Origin and Development of 1 Henry VI: In Relation to Shakespeare, Marlowe, Peele and Greene* by Allison Gaw, published in 1926 by the University of Southern California where Professor Gaw was Chairman of the Department of English; therefore not a recent work, but having undoubted revolutionary implications for Shakespearean and Marlowan studies. I make no apology for resuscitating it here in a chapter devoted to this outstandingly coherent and impressive research, which seems to have been totally passed over.

Gaw's work represents the most thorough textual assessment of *1 Henry VI* that has ever been conducted, and highlights Edward Alleyn's close involvement in a theatrical partnership with Christopher Marlowe for the original production of *1 Henry VI*, or *harey the vj* as Henslowe recorded it in his *Diary*, which was played at the newly refurbished Rose theatre on Bankside on 3rd March 1591/2. This intriguing glimpse of the two dominant figures of the Elizabethan theatre in a unique collaboration led to my research on the Alleyn Papers in the archives of Dulwich College, near to my home. Research on Edward Alleyn has lain fallow for decades despite the existence of this rich store of letters and documents in these archives, including his *Diary*, kept meticulously for five years from 1617, which throws much light on Alleyn's character. The famous theatrical *Diary* of his step-father-in-law, Philip Henslowe, and other related documentation were admirably re-edited in 1961 by R.A. Foakes and R.T. Rickert, but that specifically concerning Alleyn has remained untouched since W.W. Greg paid it partial attention in 1908. This study sets out to fill the gap of our superficial acquaintance with Alleyn. He was a remarkable man who played many parts, both on the stage and in his life.

What has emerged from this fresh look into the Alleyn Papers is a complete reassessment of Edward Alleyn's importance to our study of this period. As a result, some erroneous assumptions that have grown unchecked through neglect of this important historic documentation, have been toppled. Chief of these is the entrenched belief that Robert Greene was attacking Shakespeare under the homophonous guise of 'Shake-scene' in his libellous and vituperous *Groatsworth of Wit* Letter, written in September 1592 when Greene lay dying in penury. This famous Letter, together with the entire autobiographical *Groatsworth of Wit* moralizing tale to which it is appended and to which it bears an integral relationship, are here scrupulously re-examined in conjunction with each other and the historical background relating to Alleyn and his business dealings with Greene. This is the first time that a comprehensive, critical study in such depth has been conducted since Thomas Tyrwhitt came up with his suggested identification in 1778 that 'Shake-scene' was Greene's satirical allusion to Shakespeare as a rival practising actor-playwright in London in 1592. Debate about this apparent and most important discovery waxed hot for many years. What could Greene have been accusing Shakespeare of in such opprobrious terms? So hot, that in 1928 J.S. Smart was moved to exclaim in exasperation:

'This passage from Greene has had such a devastating effect on Shakespearean study that we cannot but wish it had never been written, or never discovered.'[1]

The opposing camps in the Shakespearean academic world have now been reconciled by the clamping of silence on the debate, led by Peter Alexander's establishment of a 'new orthodoxy' which accepts the 'Shake-scene' homophony as a historical fact that must no longer be questioned. With the ease of swallowing a soft icecream it has slipped into received Shakespearean dogma. The subject is dormant, if not moribund. I feel I should apologise for raising this spectre again, fraught with anomalies as it is, but it seems to be my fate to venture where angels fear to tread. My research shows that Greene's barbs were aimed at the great 'Shake-scene' and minor playwright, Edward Alleyn, (a 'Shake-scene' being an Elizabethanism for an actor) and not against William Shakespeare, who, so far as the evidence shows, was wholly unknown to Greene and was probably not yet in London. Thomas Tyrwhitt's error has proved a major tragedy for Shakespearean scholarship, diverting the efforts of generations of able scholars into sterile fields which, despite much admirably assiduous research expended, have produced nothing that can be called solid evidence to illuminate Shakespeare's early emergence. All remains in the realm of hypothesis. But so attractive has Tyrwhitt's spurious identification been that an academic blind eye has been discreetly turned to the glaring inconsistencies of Greene's bitter, anguished accusations against his hated 'Shake-scene' in order to permit the establishment of the Shakespeare-'Shake-scene' identification to take root as a historical fact, and not a Tyrwhittian myth—a shaky hypothesis that fits Shakespeare 'as ill as a raven's croak would fit a lark', as I had suggested in my quatercentenary biography of Marlowe.* There I had briefly summarized Allison Gaw's thesis, and had tentatively suggested that Edward Alleyn was the authentic 'Shake-scene' of Greene's *Groatsworth of Wit*.

Owing to pressure of other work, my research of Alleyn and his relationship with both Greene and Marlowe was abandoned for more than twenty years; but since in all this time no one took up the challenge posed by my brief airing then of Dr Allison Gaw's revolutionary thesis, I can only be grateful for the opportunity eventually to fulfil the obligation to complete what was left unsubstantiated. My research on Marlowe has remained an abiding passion. Once tasted, he is not a study easily dropped. His complex personality and intellectual depth intrigued me the more I became intimately aware of his genius through acting in his plays under the auspices of the Marlowe Society of London, dedicated to the production of the plays of Marlowe and the Elizabethan dramatists whom he influenced, including Shakespeare. This experience brought insight into Marlowe's outstanding genius as a dramatist (often underestimated) which has been a precious revelation, enhancing my understanding beyond desk study.

Marlowe, as a dramatist and poet of power and superb, innovative artistry, was a bold trend-setter of literary fashion – never an imitator, as Peter Alexander falsely presents him. He remains today a controversial and deeply misunderstood figure. This study presents him in the pre-eminent position he held historically, when the great burgeoning of dramatic development of the English renaissance took place; a turbulent time of exciting, intellectual stimulus in which he was inextricably swept up. Marlowe was the 'Morning Star' and catalyst of the Elizabethan dramatic explosion, who reigned in London's theatre-loving heart virtually without rival, hailed by Greene in 1592 as 'Thou famous gracer of Tragedians', and by George Peele as 'Marley the Muses darling' in 1593; whereupon we have the first evidence of Shakespeare's emergence as a consummate poet with his 'Venus and Adonis', but not yet as a dramatist. Shakespeare was clearly a late developer, and those who attempt to prove otherwise can do so only by ousting Marlowe – either by ignoring his existence and his tremendous influence on his contemporaries, or by diminishing him. And this will not do.

---

*A.D. Wraight and Virginia F. Stern: *In Search of Christopher Marlowe* (1965, London and New York).

Recent books on Marlowe have tended increasingly to propagate a malignant view of his personality, based solely on the slanders of his enemies and ignoring the dangerous historical context of the contemporary, political climate which was torn by fierce inter-denominational religious conflict. These perverted estimations have resulted in what amounts almost to a campaign of fashionable character-assassination that takes no account of the testimonies of his friends, all of them eminent and cultured people. This book is a timely step towards the honest rehabilitation of Marlowe as the poetic genius without whom the unique Elizabethan dramatic effusion would not have developed, or certainly not in the way in which it did, and to whom Shakespeare owed an inestimable artistic debt.

It is thanks to Alleyn's charitable foundation, where the Alleyn Papers were carefully preserved, that Henslowe's invaluable theatrical *Diary* has survived, for it was kept there with other personal memorabilia. We know nothing of the Globe or of Burbage's company, whose records have all perished, but of the Rose we have fascinating day-to-day detail. This makes it unquestionably the most important theatre of the time for us, for it is our sole model of an Elizabethan theatre both in its material remains, since its foundations have recently been fortuitously uncovered during building excavations on Bankside, as well as in its extant theatrical records. Through the mass of documentation in the Alleyn Papers, it has become a living theatre, providing us with the indispensable knowledge of the theatrical practices of the period. We know how it was run, what plays were performed, and by which companies, and can follow its financial vicissitudes over a period of some five years from February 1591/2 when Edward Alleyn joined Henslowe and married his step-daughter, becoming a co-owner of the theatre, as the evidence presented suggests, in addition to being the leading actor-manager of the resident company. There is absolutely no foundation for the theory that the Rose was not a typical theatre of the time. On the contrary, it is a true example of an Elizabethan theatrical establishment, for the rival theatre proprietors and their companies imitated each other in a jealous emulation. It may be assumed as a logical deduction that Burbage's company also dealt in brokerage of plays of the period, and it is possible that some of the Lord Chamberlain's actors, besides Shakespeare and Ben Jonson, who transferred from Henslowe to Burbage, would also have tried their hand at writing plays, for my research shows that the Lord Admiral's Men were a scribbling crew of actors, who wrote plays as well as acting in them, foremost of whom was Edward Alleyn himself. He was an ambitious young man who aspired to emulate 'his betters' in writing plays in blank verse. Greene was complaining with bitter scorn of Alleyn's playwriting activities when he wrote sarcastically that he 'supposes he is as well able to bombast out a blanke verse as the best of you, and beeing an absolute *Iohannes fac totum* is in his owne conceit the onely Shake-scene in a countrey'. Note that the *name* that Greene chose for his hated actor-playwright was *'Iohannes fac totum'*, whereas 'Shake-scene' is not *Italicized* as was the printers' style for all proper nouns, so that this latter term is merely a descriptive common noun for a great actor, a well-known Elizabethan term.

The discovery of Alleyn as a minor playwright of the time seals his eligibility as Greene's *bête noire*, the 'vpstart Crow' of his *Groatsworth* Letter, beyond possible doubt for this is supported by undeniably strong evidence concerning their lives and their business relationship. The case for Edward Alleyn as Greene's 'Shake-scene' is presented alongside the orthodox case for Shakespeare, so that the reader may judge which is the historical truth in this important matter.

Edward Alleyn's importance has been masked by these erroneous assumptions. Through their letters and extant memoranda we are made vividly aware of the personalities of 'Father Hinchlowe' as Henslowe was called by the actors, and his 'sonne' Edward Alleyn, the latter the dominant partner in their joint theatrical ventures by virtue not only of his great histrionic talent, but even more by his organizing ability and his undoubted financial acumen, which far exceeded that of his bumbling step-father-in-law. This reassessment of the evidence concerning the relationship of Edward Alleyn and the theatre proprietor Philip Henslowe reveals their partnership in a completely new light, with their roles reversed according to previously held opinion. Heretofore, it had always been assumed that Henslowe had taken the young Edward Alleyn under his wing when he married his step-daughter, and that he had taught his 'sonne' Edward his financial and business expertise. This notion is a fallacy. Before the advent of Alleyn, the Rose was not a remarkably successful theatre. It was Alleyn who made it so. Henslowe was almost pathetically dependent on Alleyn, both emotionally and in his business affairs, which foundered into debt and embittered confrontation with the actors when Alleyn retired and left him to manage his theatrical business alone.

The relationship of Henslowe and Alleyn presents a most interesting psychological study, which would merit further pursuit into the years beyond the scope of this book, which ends with Alleyn's final, second retirement from the stage after he had built his own theatre, the Fortune. His success seems to have remained undimmed by the emergence of the Burbage-Shakespeare rivalry during Elizabeth's reign, for Alleyn was no lightweight to be knocked off his pedestal even by challengers of such quality.

He bowed out in great style in a leading role at the magnificent celebrations for King James's accession, which marked the end of the plague of 1603–4, in order to devote himself henceforth to the foundation of his charitable institution that has grown into one of England's most prestigious public schools, Dulwich College.

Tamburlaine:	Zenocrate, the loveliest maid alive,
	Fairer than rocks of pearl and precious stone,
	The only paragon of Tamburlaine;
	Whose eyes are brighter than the lamps of heaven,
	And speech more pleasant than sweet harmony;
	That with thy looks canst clear the darkened sky,
	And calm the rage of thundering Jupiter;
	Sit down by her, adorned with my crown,
	As if thou wert the empress of the world.

The First Part of Tamburlaine the Great
Act III, Sc 3 11.117–125

Photograph by Nobby Clark for the National Theatre production
*of **Tamburlaine the Great**, 1976, directed by Sir Peter Hall.*

XV

I   *The Triumph of Tamburlaine*

QUEEN ELIZABETH II officially opened London's long awaited National
Theatre on the South Bank of the Thames on 25th October 1976, when
the auditorium of the Olivier Theatre resounded to the glorious blank
verse of the first masterpiece by the twenty-three-year-old Christopher
Marlowe, M.A., his *Tamburlaine the Great*. This historic revival of both
The First Part and *The Second Part of Tamburlaine* played in tandem
to packed houses. It was an inspired choice for the inaugural production
of our National Theatre, and it took London by storm just as it had the
playgoers in the reign of Queen Elizabeth I in 1587, a fact which surprised
many modern academic critics whose views of Marlowe's genius are now
under review.

This was the first revival in modern times of the complete *Tamburlaine
the Great* on the professional stage. *The First Part of Tamburlaine* had
been presented a quarter of a century before with Sir Donald Wolfit
playing Tamburlaine in the production by Sir Tyrone Guthrie at the Old
Vic, when it was equally acclaimed a *tour de force*. The revival in 1976
of the two separate plays in sequel proved beyond doubt that Marlowe's
spectacular dramatization of this Asiatic conqueror's exploits still holds
as much appeal today as it did four hundred years ago. Audiences who
knew nothing of Marlowe's genius came away ecstatic, feeling they had
discovered a new playwright whose poetic and dramatic powers were
reminiscent of Shakespeare.

The enthusiastic reception given to Sir Peter Hall's magnificent
production of the whole of *Tamburlaine* is the final answer to those
scholars who have relegated most of Marlowe's works, apart from his
Edward the Second and *Doctor Faustus* which have been revived from
time to time, to the academician's study desk as fitter subjects for literary
criticism than live performance. The post war years have seen a steadily
increasing revival of his other plays on the boards, which has provided
an opportunity to reassess him as a dramatist in the context for which his
work was created. The vitality of Marlowe's dramatic work is now being
put to the test, and with each revival it is reasserted as valid theatrical
entertainment of superb artistry for modern audiences just as much as it
was for his contemporaries.

The celebration of the quatercentenary of Marlowe's birth in 1964, the
same year as Shakespeare's, brought the revival on our professional stage

of *The Jew of Malta*, long considered to be of no interest to modern audiences. This satirical tragi-comedy and *Tamburlaine the Great* remained the most abidingly popular of all his dramas with Elizabethan playgoers. At one leap his reputation was established together with that of the young Elizabethan actor who was the interpreter of Marlowe's heroes and anti-heroes, Edward Alleyn. *Tamburlaine the Great, The Jew of Malta* and *Doctor Faustus* – three widely contrasted plays – have linked the names of Christopher Marlowe and Edward Alleyn, acclaimed as the most outstanding actor of his day, together indelibly in our dramatic history for these plays provided Alleyn with leading roles to which his particular histrionic talents were ideally suited. It was as though these two, playwright-poet and actor, had been born for this moment in our dramatic history to complement each other and usher in the splendid Renaissance of English drama, which was to rise to its peak of perfection in the glorious maturity of Shakespeare.

The twenty-one-year-old Edward Alleyn, young in years, but old in experience, for Fuller tells us 'He was bred a Stage-player',[1] after a youth spent touring the country had returned home to London where he had been born, to become the leading actor of the Lord Admiral's Men, and make his debut on the London stage just in time to star in Marlowe's *Tamburlaine the Great*. The young and lusty Alleyn, tall of stature and long-limbed, with a voice that could thunder 'to move storms' or 'roar as gently as any sucking dove',[2] was also highly intelligent, and his arresting interpretation of Marlowe's dominant hero, the Scythian Tamburlaine, immediately made him the darling of the theatre-goers. He followed this with equal acclaim in the role of that great anti-hero, Barabas, in Marlowe's 'black comedy' *The Jew of Malta*. This role remained a favourite with the groundlings, and was the most played of his Marlovian repertoire. Alleyn obviously excelled in it, so much so, that following his final retirement from the stage it was never played again, until revived after his death, in Heywood's production at the Cockpit in 1633, from which we derive our only printed edition of this much mutilated play. The performance was introduced by an apologetic prologue from Heywood's pen on behalf of the apprehensive Thespian who was stepping into the shoes of the great Edward Alleyn, Richard Perkins –

> who doth personate
> Our Jew this day, nor is it his ambition
> To exceed, or equall, being of condition
> More modest; this is all that he intends,

(And that too, at the vrgence of some friends)
To proue his best, and if none here gaine-say it,
The part he hath studied, and intends to play it.[3]

To his success in *Tamburlaine* and *The Jew of Malta*, Alleyn added the
role of Marlowe's most personal creation, *Doctor Faustus*, the tormented,
questioning intellectual who aspired to encompass all knowledge and gain
universal power, and sold his soul to the Devil to satisfy his ambition
through the dark power of necromancy. Faustus is the epitomy of
Renaissance Man, and it was, I believe, Alleyn's personal favourite among
the great roles Marlowe gave him, the one with which he could also most
truly identify for he chose it, significantly, for his last performance at his
early retirement when aged thirty-one,[4] from which he was recalled by
Queen Elizabeth to play until the end of her reign,[5] bowing out for the
second and final time soon after King James came to the throne.

It was in these three great roles that Alleyn dominated the Elizabethan
stage for at least a decade, and the first of these, Tamburlaine, made
undoubtedly the greatest impact. The year of its appearance was 1587,
a portentous year in sixteenth century England, when the preparations for
the great Armada of Spain were moving threateningly apace. The Queen
of Scots' head fell in February of that year and this spurred on the leaden-
footed colossus, King Philip II, to rouse himself at last and decide that
the Great Enterprise was to go ahead – and that with all speed. Suddenly
the orders from the Escurial poured forth with impatience, for ships,
provisions, armaments, soldiers and sailors to be made ready and organized
– by tomorrow if possible! His Most Catholic Majesty had uncharacteristically thrown caution to the winds and his urgent exhortation was
to make all ready to attack England. When Marlowe's all-conquering
hero, *Tamburlaine*, whose historical personage had saved Christendom
from the Turks, burst upon the English stage, it seemed that he was the
embodiment of the self-confidence and high aspirations for victory of the
English nation in its moment of greatest challenge and danger.

The valour of every Englishman in the audience must have instantly
doubled at Tamburlaine's stirring words with which he woos the Persian
Theridamas, 'captain of a thousand horse', to desert the effete Persian
King Mycetes and join with himself to carve out kingdoms with their
swords.

> *Tamburlaine.* I hold the Fates bound fast in iron chains,
> And with my hand turn Fortune's wheel about;

And sooner shall the sun fall from his sphere
Than Tamburlaine be slain or overcome.
Draw forth thy sword thou mighty man-at-arms,
Intending but to raze my charméd skin,
And Jove himself will stretch his hand from heaven
To ward the blow, and shield me safe from harm.
See, how he rains down heaps of gold in showers,
As if he meant to give my soldiers pay!
The First Part of Tamburlaine Act I, Scene 2, 11.173-182

In dramatizing the story of Tamburlaine's extraordinary rise to power Marlowe took an Asiatic character from fourteenth century history. Tamburlaine began life as a Scythian shepherd, but by virtue of his aspiring ambition attained the empery of large tracts of Asia. The humble origin of Tamburlaine must have given him enormous appeal for the groundlings. In the above scene Tamburlaine had artfully displayed the gold and treasure his band of warriors had just captured, to impress Theridamus.

If thou wilt stay with me, renowned man,
And lead thy thousand horse with my conduct,
Besides thy share of this Egyptian prize,
Those thousand horse shall sweat with martial spoil
Of conquer'd kingdoms and of cities sack'd:
Jove sometimes maskéd in a shepherd's weed;
And by those steps that he hath scal'd the heavens
May we become immortal like the gods.
Join with me now in this my mean estate,
(I call it mean, because, being yet obscure,
The nations far remov'd admire me not,)
And when my name and honour shall be spread
As far as Boreas claps his brazen wings,
Or fair Böotes sends his cheerful light,
Then shalt thou be competitor with me,
And sit with Tamburlaine in all his majesty.
Act I Scene 2, 11.187-208

Naturally Theridamas succumbs and remains Tamburlaine's loyal companion-at-arms following him to high fortune. In the minds of his audience Marlowe's Tamburlaine may also have stirred thoughts of their

4

admired, popular hero, Drake, and his piratical exploits to seize ship-loads of Spanish gold and treasure, for throughout this play there is a recurrent emphasis on fabulous treasure, jewels and shining gold.

In taking the history of Tamburlaine's meteoric rise to power, riches and fame through his irresistible military prowess as the subject of his drama, Marlowe had picked a winning card. But above all it was the magnificent poetic style in which the play is couched that won the hearts of his audiences and made the experience of *Tamburlaine* more thrilling than anything they had hitherto known.

Tamburlaine the Great is the work of a young poet who has found his own highly individual and unmistakable voice in the dramatic idiom which was the catalyst for his unique genius, which was to set the style for the entire epoch of Shakespearean drama. Marlowe was a born poet, but it was the drama of human affairs with its aspiring ambition and jealousy, its cruelty and pity, its emotional anguish and joy, its love and hatred, and the innumerable facets of good and evil, that inspired his Muse, drawing immortal strains of poetry from his soul – a soul that was in love with beauty of sound and sight.

When we recall what the young Marlowe's background and training were, we see why those fine sensibilities with which he was endowed to make him a potential poet and dramatist should have blossomed to attain so early a near perfection beyond that of any of his contemporary co-writers in the 1580s, the self-styled 'University Wits', who wrote poems, plays, novels, satires, every kind of literature in order to make a precarious living, hoping always to gain the influential patronage which was their life-line – John Lyly, George Peele, Robert Greene, Thomas Nashe, Thomas Lodge; and the outsider Thomas Kyd, the ambitious son of a scrivener who had never made it to the university but succeeded in climbing aboard the theatrical band-waggon with considerable popular success with his *Spanish Tragedy*. None of these talented men had enjoyed a childhood of such rare advantage to a budding poet as Marlowe had been favoured with by Fate.

Of few writers can it be more truly said, 'the child is father of the man.'[6] Peele named him 'The Muses Darling',[7] and it seemed as though he had been specially chosen by those goddesses and set down in Canterbury, the eldest son of a cobbler; a gifted and musical child, who had the rare opportunity to become a choirboy in the ancient Cathedral of the Archbishop, the Primate of England who stands in rank second only to the monarch, in whose great church the Anglican service, reflecting the Elizabethan spirit of compromise, retained much of the beauties of the

Catholic ceremonial and ritual splendour. Here, nurtured by the beauty of sound and sight which his mind absorbed daily, the young Marlowe's poetic genius blossomed.

Marlowe was exceptionally blessed in gaining admittance under a scholarship to the King's School at Canterbury, where he was exposed to the influence of the classical authors, whom Elizabethan pedagogues in their wisdom offered to their pupils as exemplars for style and content, as well as for the learning of Latin and Greek. Subsequently he sharpened and refined his appreciation of the classics in the practice of translating the Latin poets Ovid and Lucan while at the University of Cambridge; and when he eventually turned his attention to dramatic composition, his developing poetic talent led him by selection and discrimination, finally almost unerringly, to fashion a blank verse incomparably more sophisticated and subtle than any heretofore, which pleased his sensitive ear.

It is the sheer beauty of Marlowe's blank verse that still captivates us today, when we are familiar with Shakespeare's yet more sophisticated development of this medium, as it must, with even greater impact, have delighted the audiences for whom he wrote, who had never heard the like before. Drama had certainly been presented to them always and traditionally in verse; from the doggerel of the mystery plays to the rhyming couplets and quatrains, or the mixtures of metres and different rhyming patterns, and even the few examples of plays that had already appeared in a blank verse which was monotonously regular, unvariedly ten-syllabic, as in Norton's and Sackville's *Gorboduc*. But there was little resemblance between even the most polished of the early Elizabethan dramas and the sound of the infinitely more refined poetic language of *Tamburlaine*, with its splendid pace and lyricism, which fell on the playgoers' ears like a new and wondrous kind of verbal music.

Marlowe took the steady decasyllibon of blank verse as it then existed, which Bakeless has likened to 'a procession of wooden soldiers marching in columns of five',[8] and he proceeded to transform it. Professor Oliphant has summed it up simply:

'he was the first to give that verse life and movement, to break up its stately regularity by varying the stresses and distributing the pauses, by adding a syllable here and there, by carrying on the sentence from line to line, instead of having each line severely end-stopped. Kyd had moved timidly in this direction; but Marlowe went forward with giant strides, careless of what anyone might think or say. He really created our blank verse; but he did not carry it to perfection. Shakespeare, Beaumont,

Milton perfected what he had originated; but his remains the glory of creation.'[9]

Marlowe's youthful energies were spent in the glory of creation. His genius ensures that he would, as he matured, have brought the medium of his creation to that perfection we recognize in Shakespeare. There are those who have elected to question this, but, as Oliphant has remarked, 'It is as stupid as it is unfair to set Shakespeare's achievement against Marlowe's; to set the product of six years of work against the product of a quarter of a century....It is, of course, easy to say, and is said, that Shakespeare's was the mind of greater capacity for development; but that is sheer guesswork.'[10]

The critics of the old school, who grow hot under the collar at Professor Bakeless's reference to their idol Shakespeare as Marlowe's 'pupil', are emphatically dismissed by Dr Oliphant, who speaks as one of an unprejudiced school whose eager minds view Marlowe in all his daring innovation as the original genius of the ferment of the Elizabethan literary age. In his day critics were trenchant, vociferous and ardently partisan, for the contemporary interest in literary style was probably more intense than at any time in our history. Marlowe faced the critics of his own time, and he answered them with a nonchalant disregard. He had ears only for the voice of his Muse.

It was Marlowe's particular blend of mellifluous blank verse and skilfully stage-crafted drama that inspired the contemporary effusion of blank verse dramatic composition and breathed new life and vigour into the Elizabethan theatre; and of all his plays this effect was at its most intoxicating in *Tamburlaine*. In this, his first great work, if not perhaps his earliest play, the fusion of poet and dramatist is strikingly evident, if not yet fully balanced. Whether he is writing a speech of invective, or describing battles, or deeds of cruelty and horror, or expressing the languishment of love, Marlowe's words have a musicality that enchants our ears and makes us want to listen. His fellow dramatists were not slow to learn the trick from him, and Shakespeare brought the same cadences to perfection. But their master and teacher for all, from Greene to Shakespeare, was only this young poet-dramatist who had been nurtured first in Canterbury and then in Cambridge. He created the model which they all used after him, and when this new type of drama was first displayed to view and hearing, it produced a resounding echo. The model, though not perfect, was undoubtedly great. It proclaimed its author as a genius.

There has probably never been a more significant premiére than that of *Tamburlaine the Great*, for the impact it made on our dramatic literature, and on the style and format of theatrical production, is almost incalculable. The immediate response was the spawning of numerous imitations, none as good as the original. Like a comet blazing through the skies, the fiery young creator of *Tamburlaine* sparked fire in others, and proceeded on his way trailing his satellites after him. This was to continue throughout Marlowe's all too brief career, for he dashed off one type of play, to turn aside to try his hand in yet another genre, always setting the trend which others followed. He never ceased experimenting and varying his themes in the extraordinarily wide-ranging choice of subjects for his dramas, for above all Marlowe was a daring and restless innovator. It was as though he sensed he would not have long enough to essay all he wanted to accomplish in the vast field of human drama. No one has assessed his contribution to our dramatic literature and the quality of his rare, unfinished genius more perceptively than John Bakeless in this passage from his two-volume critical biography, *The Tragicall History of Christopher Marlowe:*

'Though he was the leading playwright of his day, Marlowe had not yet caught his stride. He used a form once – and dropped it. He did not produce a series of classical plays, all in the same style, like Lyly, who preceded him; nor pour out comedy upon comedy, history upon history, tragedy upon tragedy, like his pupil from Stratford, who succeeded him. Nor did he live long enough to go over his earlier handiwork, as Shakespeare did, retouching rough portraiture....Marlowe's reputation rests wholly on the work of his 'prentice hand. He lived to do no other; and what he did, he did almost without models. He was making straight the path – or at least developing a technique – for a greater than himself. Nothing sets the sheer genius of the man so far beyond cavil or dispute as the way in which his plays, one by one – each in its own separate and unrepeated genre – are caught up and the formula of each developed by other hands...'[11]

This restlessness betokens a somewhat precocious genius, developing probably quite early in youth, perhaps when the Latin plays performed at the King's School in Canterbury could have given scope for dramatic versification to a gifted pupil.

There is evidence in his work that Marlowe was stimulated by a keen interest in history, for which his Canterbury childhood would have provided early inspiration. In taking as his hero for his first great dramatic work the almost legendary figure of the Scythian shepherd who rose to become the conqueror of many Asiatic nations, Marlowe had chosen a historical warrior, living from 1336 – 1405, whose conquests had excited interest throughout Europe. As news of his almost incredibly victorious progress in empire-building percolated into Europe, came also apprehension lest he spear-head his attacks ever further westward, until it was realized with relief and admiration that he had turned the threat of the Turkish military might away from Europe, and by his conquests had created a balance of power beneficial to the western nations. With this vital interest in 'Turkish Affairs', histories on the life of the great Mongol warrior-king were being published from the early 1500s, some of which Marlowe read and used as the source for his play; so that the fame of Tamburlaine had to some extent preceded his arrival on the stage in Marlowe's epoch-making drama, and this probably added to the excitement with which the play was hailed.

Marlowe was faced with the problem, how to present this great all-conquering warrior with requisite force and dramatic power to make him credible on stage. The qualities of dramatist and poet were instinctive in him, and out of their fusion was born the brilliant style of his 'mighty line' to express what Tamburlaine represented. From the first Marlowe knew what he wanted to create, and what his aim was – to uplift the drama to a new height of excellence. The Prologue to The First Part of *Tamburlaine the Great* announces it:

> From jigging veins of rhyming mother wits
> And such conceits as clownage keeps in pay,
> We'll lead you to the stately tent of war,
> Where you shall hear the Scythian Tamburlaine
> Threatening the world with high astounding terms,
> And scourging kingdoms with his conquering sword.
> View but his picture in this tragic glass,
> And then applaud his fortune as you please.

It is a clear statement of intent, and in it we discern that he himself recognized that his conquering hero spoke in 'high astounding terms' for this was the style of the man. Much criticism from his envious contemporaries down to our day has been levelled at Marlowe's indulgence in rant, but this was, I believe, a conscious and deliberate, indeed, an inspired invention for *Tamburlaine*; for how else could he express the nature of this character in his dramatization? In performance on the stage it does not strike one as rant, but is the entirely credible way for this character to speak. Dr Oliphant has also pointed out that it is a part of *Tamburlaine* which does not pertain to all Marlowe's works. 'It was deliberately employed to tickle the palates of the groundlings', he suggests.[12] But it is also far more significantly Marlowe's interpretative realization of the strident, bombastic nature of Tamburlaine himself, with his vaunting ambition and huge self-confidence.

Probably Oliphant had never experienced *Tamburlaine* in performance, when he would have appreciated that the rant is an intrinsic *dramatic* component of this character and of this drama, and not merely a device for catching the ear and the popular vote of the groundlings, though it also achieved that objective. But it has not been remarked elsewhere that Marlowe indulges in unrestrained use of this high-flown style in *Tamburlaine the Great* in order to express the extravagant persona of this almost super-human, fiery, warrior empire-builder, and that this was a deliberate dramatic convention which he later discarded.

It is not in the magniloquence of Tamburlaine's rant that the essential Marlowe, the soul of the poet, is to be found, but rather in the famous passage which contains his apostrophe to Beauty. Here Tamburlaine muses on his beloved Zenocrate, daughter of the Soldan of Egypt, whose armies are opposing the Scythian conqueror's might, so that Zenocrate is torn between her love for Tamburlaine and dreadful fear for her father's life. In these lines Marlowe, the philosophical thinker and classical scholar, blends with his passionate feeling for beauty to find expression in one of the most lyrical soliloquys ever written.

> Ah, fair Zenocrate! – divine Zenocrate!
> Fair is too foul an epithet for thee,
> That in thy passion for thy country's love,
> And fear to see thy kingly father's harm,
> With hair dishevell'd wip'st thy watery cheeks;
> And, like to Flora in her morning's pride,
> Shaking her silver tresses in the air,
> Rain'st on the earth resolvéd pearl in showers,
> And sprinklest sapphires on thy shining face,
> Where Beauty, mother to the Muses, sits,
> And comments volumes with her ivory pen,
> Taking instruction from thy flowing eyes;
> Eyes, when that Ebena steps to heaven,

In silence of thy solemn evening's walk,
Making the mantle of the richest night,
The moon, the planets, and the meteors, light;
There angels in their crystal armours fight
A doubtful battle with my tempted thoughts
For Egypt's freedom and the Soldan's life,
His life that so consumes Zenocrate;
Whose sorrows lay more siege unto my soul
Than all my army to Damascus walls;
And neither Persia's sovereign nor the Turk
Troubled my senses with conceit of foil
So much by much as doth Zenocrate.
What is beauty, saith my sufferings, then?
If all the pens that ever poets held
Had fed the feeling of their masters' thoughts,
And every sweetness that inspir'd their hearts,
Their minds, and muses on admiréd themes;
If all the heavenly quintessence they still
From their immortal flowers of poesy,
Wherein, as in a mirror, we perceive
The highest reaches of a human wit;
If these had made one poem's period,
And all combin'd in beauty's worthiness,
Yet should there hover in their restless heads
One thought, one grace, one wonder, at the least,
Which into words no virtue can digest.
But how unseemly is it for my sex,
My discipline of arms and chivalry,
My nature, and the terror of my name,
To harbour thoughts effeminate and faint!
Save only that in beauty's just applause,
With whose instinct the soul of man is touched;
And every warrior that is rapt with love
Of fame, of valour, and of victory,
Must needs have beauty beat on his conceits:
I thus conceiving, and subduing both,
That which hath stoop'd the chiefest of the gods,
Even from the fiery-spangled veil of heaven,
To feel the lovely warmth of shepherds' flames,
And march in cottages of strowed reeds,

Shall give the world to note, for all my birth,
That virtue solely is the sum of glory,
And fashions men with true nobility.

The First Part of Tamburlaine the Great,
Act V, Sc.1. 11.135-190.

Marlowe's musical ear created the beautiful blank verse which is his legacy to Shakespeare. Even when the situation he depicts is ugly or cruel, his words are never ugly, but reach us illumined with the quality of his bright intelligence and ringing with the musicality of his well-tuned ear trained from his youth as a choirboy of Canterbury Cathedral. In *Tamburlaine* every name has been selected for its musical resonance and rhythm – Zenocrate, Usumcasane, Techelles, Theridamas, Ortygius, Bajazeth, Menaphon, Meander, Cosroe, Mycetes, Ceneus, Zabina, Anippe, Ebea, Almeda, Olympia, Sigismund, Philemus, Calyphas, Amyras, Celebinus, some of them taken from historical sources, some adapted, some of his own invention.[13] He must have revelled in the euphony of these names, which lend their sonorities to this most poetic of all Marlowe's dramatic works. For in *Tamburlaine* the poet is in the ascendant, but the dramatist was emerging on swift and sure pinions to join him in balanced unity. Critics who have only studied Marlowe at their study desks in bookish isolation from the stage, tend to underestimate him as a dramatist, but every performance of his plays on the boards only serves to confirm how brilliant his gifts as a playwright are. *Tamburlaine* on stage is not just a one-man performance of a great ranting warrior surrounded by characterless stooges, as some critics have suggested. The lion's share of lines is properly given to him, but even the smallest part is etched in with a delineation of character which the actor can take hold of to make the person portrayed live in the memory of the playgoer. Techelles, for instance, one of Tamburlaine's closest companions from the beginning of the play, when his fortune had not yet brought him power, has hardly more than fifty lines in the whole of *The First Part*, which runs to fully five acts, but some of those lines are a gift to an actor. The first four words he speaks in the play establish what sort of young man this is. When Tamburlaine, with his band of men has just waylaid the caravan of the Egyptian princess, Zenocrate, seizing her treasure and her person, he falls headlong in-love at the first sight of her and launches impetuously into an outrageously extravagant speech of lavish promises to the lovely Egyptian princess – but it is Techelles' laconic comment that puts its stamp on the scene.

Tamburlaine. Zenocrate, lovelier than the love of Jove,
Brighter than the silver Rhodope,
Fairer than whitest snow on Scythian hills,
Thy person is more worth to Tamburlaine
Than the possession of the Persian crown,
Which gracious stars have promis'd at my birth.
A hundred Tartars shall attend on thee,
Mounted on steeds swifter than Pegasus;
Thy garments shall be made of Median silk,
Enchas'd with precious jewels of mine own,
More rich and valurous than Zenocrate's;
With milk-white harts upon an ivory sled
Thou shalt be drawn amidst the frozen pools,
And scale the icy mountains' lofty tops,
Which with thy beauty will be soon resolv'd:
My martial prizes, with five hundred men,
Won on the fifty-headed Volga's waves,
Shall we all offer to Zenocrate.
And then myself to fair Zenocrate.
Techelles. What now! in love?
Tamburlaine. Techelles, women must be flattered!
But this is she with whom I am in love.

The First Part of Tamburlaine the Great,
Act I, Sc.2.11.87-108

There are no cardboard figures peopling his stage, even when the lines they are given are few. What he achieves with an economy of writing is remarkable, for latent within the poet is a fine understanding of human emotions, motivation, moods, tempers – in a word, character. The suggestion often made by critics is that Tamburlaine is a dominant character, well realised, but that he is surrounded by subordinate characters 'who seem his mere shadows' – the 'bloodlessness' of these other characters is 'one of Marlowe's faults'.[14] This is uninformed criticism from a great scholar which is repeated by others *ad nauseum*, and derives from a lack of dramatic imagination. In Tamburlaine we have the whining Mycetes, a craven-hearted king who surrounds himself with sycophants, not one of whose speeches could be mistaken for anyone else's so adroitly has Marlowe captured the character of the man. Here in a delightful scene the effete King Mycetes is portrayed with his favourite Meander. They have been discussing the defection of Theridamas with his thousand horse to the camp of Tamburlaine, which has annoyed Mycetes no end. Meander is consoling him with fanciful and foolish stratagems by which they can easily defeat Tamburlaine, when a spy enters to report that they have espied the forces of Tamburlaine.

> *Spy.* An hundred horsemen of my company,
> Scouting abroad upon these champion plains,
> Have view'd the army of the Scythians;
> Which make report it far exceeds the king's.
> *Meander.* Suppose they be in number infinite,
> Yet being void of martial discipline,
> All running headlong after greedy spoils,
> And more regarding gain than victory,
> Like to the cruel brothers of the earth,
> Sprung of the teeth of dragons venomous,
> Their careless swords shall lance their fellows' throats
> And make us triumph in their overthrow.
> *Mycetes.* Was there such brethren, sweet Meander, say,
> That sprung of teeth of dragons venomous?
> *Meander.* So poets say, my lord.
> *Mycetes.* And 'tis a pretty toy to be a poet.
> Well, well, Meander, thou art deeply read;
> And having thee, I have a jewel sure.
> Go on, my lord, and give your charge, I say;
> Thy wit will make us conquerors to-day.
> *Meander.* Then, noble soldiers, to entrap these thieves
> That live confounded in disorder'd troops,
> If wealth or riches may prevail with them,
> We have our camels laden all with gold,
> Which you that be but common soldiers
> Shall fling in every corner of the field;
> And, while the base-born Tartars take it up,
> You, fighting more for honour than for gold,
> Shall massacre those greedy-minded slaves;
> And, when their scatter'd army is subdu'd,
> And you march on their slaughter'd carcasses,
> Share equally the gold that bought their lives,
> And live like gentlemen in Persia.
> Strike up the drum, and march courageously:
> Fortune herself doth sit upon our crests.

Mycetes. He tells you true, my masters; so he does.
Drums, why sound ye not when Meander speaks?

I Tamburlaine, Act II Sc.2. 11.39-75

Meander's oh so clever ruse does not work with Tamburlaine's soldiers, of course, but Mycetes hangs on his favourite's words and defers to all his suggestions. These are cleverly observed characters, and the play is full of them, each a sharply defined individual as living in his way, or hers – for there are some well drawn women characters in *Tamburlaine* – as the great Scythian conqueror himself. Else would this play not succeed on the boards as it undoubtedly does. By contrast with the petulant, weakly Mycetes, Marlowe gives us the portrait of a splendid Eastern potentate in the Soldan of Egypt, the father of Zenocrate, who is naturally furious that his daughter has been captured by this Scythian upstart, and Marlowe implies that it is not lack of valour in his heroine's father that eventually results in his military defeat, but the fault of his 'faint-hearted' troops.

> *Soldan.* Awake, ye men of Memphis! hear the clang
> Of Scythian trumpets; hear the basilisks,
> That, roaring, shake Damascus' turrets down!
> The rogue of Volga holds Zenocrate,
> The Soldan's daughter, for his concubine,
> And, with a troop of thieves and vagabonds,
> Hath spread his colours to our high disgrace,
> While you, faint-hearted base Egyptians,
> Lie slumbering on the flowery banks of Nile,
> As crocodiles that unaffrighted rest
> While thundering cannons rattle on their skins.
> *Messenger.* Nay, mighty Soldan, did your greatness see
> The frowning looks of fiery Tamburlaine,
> That with his terror and imperious eyes
> Commands the hearts of his associates,
> It might amaze your royal majesty.
> *Soldan.* Villain, I tell thee, were that Tamburlaine
> As monstrous as Gorgon prince of hell,
> The Soldan would not start a foot from him.
> But speak, what power hath he?
> *Messenger.* Mighty lord,
> Three hundred thousand men in armour clad,

Upon their prancing steeds, disdainfully
With wanton paces trampling on the ground;
Five hundred thousand footmen threatening shot,
Shaking their swords, their spears, and iron bills,
Environing their standard round, that stood
As bristle-pointed as a thorny wood;
Their warlike engines and munition
Exceed the forces of their martial men.
Soldan. Nay, could their numbers countervail the stars,
Or ever-drizzling drops of April showers,
Or wither'd leaves that autumn shaketh down,
Yet would the Soldan by his conquering power
So scatter and consume them in his rage,
That not a man should live to rue their fall.

I Tamburlaine Act IV Scene 1.11.1-36

The fiery opening of this scene well illustrates Marlowe's dramatic powers. His vivid imagery depicting crocodiles 'slumbering on the flowery banks of Nile' invokes the Eastern scene; but it is interesting to note that his 'ever-drizzling drops of April showers' and his picture of autumn leaves betrays him as an Englishman whose experience of the weather was probably limited to the temperate climate of Western Europe.

Tamburlaine is a very well constructed play. The strong, sure framework of Marlowe's dramatic technique is that of an instinctive dramatist who understood stage-craft with the sensitive insight of the artist, varying his scenes, building his climaxes with an unerring sense of what would 'work' for his audience, holding their attention from the prologue to the end. *Tamburlaine* 'shows us the dramatic creativeness of Marlowe. The measure of his might is the greatness of his dramatic design', wrote E.H.C. Oliphant, remarking that 'even more marked than the creation of the Marlovian blank verse is the originality of his drama; and it is no less an indication of the possession of genius. His first play was novel not merely in its verse, but also in its dramatic qualities.'[15]

In this statement Oliphant puts his finger on the three aspects of Marlowe's genius which made him the leading light, the bright 'Morning Star', of the age of Shakespearean drama: his development of English blank verse, his dramatic power, and his essential originality.

16

A Dramatist of History

Marlowe's first encounter with the history of his hero, Tamburlaine or Tamerlane, could have been as early as his fifteenth year when he entered the King's School. His Headmaster was then the scholarly John Gresshop, who owned a well-furnished private library which might have been made available to a bright boy with a keen interest in history. It was in the best tradition of dedicated schoolmasters of that day to offer personal help and encouragement to further their ablest pupils, and all the evidence we have on Marlowe indicates that he was given preferential treatment throughout his education and was the kind of impressive lad who attracted patronage. In Dr Gresshop's library Marlowe might have read Philip Lonicer's *Chronicorum Turcicorum* and Thomas Fortescue's *The Foreste*, both containing histories of Tamerlane.[16] These could have aroused his interest so that the seed lay long in his mind maturing.

It is all but certain that Marlowe must have written *The First Part of Tamburlaine* while still at Corpus Christi College, Cambridge, where he was for six and a half years studying, ostensibly to enter the Anglican Church. At Corpus Christi he was fortunate to have had available in the library a store of books which afforded him almost all the historical background he needed for his dramatization of the life of Tamburlaine. Every student of Marlowe must be indebted to Dr Bakeless's invaluable and definitive study of the sources used for his dramatic works. He has shown that among the literary treasures of Archbishop Parker's bequest of books and manuscripts to his old college, Corpus Christi or Bene't Hall as it was then known, were four works detailing the history of Tamburlaine, some of them repetitive of each other but giving useful factual background.[17] These source books were: Pope Pius's *Asiae Europaeque elegantiss. descriptio* (1574); Baptista Fulgotius's *Exemplorum Libri IX* (1578); Baptista Ignatius's *De Origine Turcarum Libellum* bound together in the second edition with Petrus Perondinus's *Vita magni Tamerlanis* (1556).

Paulus Jovius's *Turcicarum Rerum Commentarii* had been in Corpus Christi's library[18] for some time, and Jovius's *Shorte Treatise upon the Turkes' Chronicles* had appeared in an English translation in 1546 and might well have been available to Marlowe elsewhere, and he would obviously have been keenly seeking information on Tamburlaine wherever it might be found. Philip Lonicer's *Chronicorum Turcicorum*, possibly first read at the King's School, was a source he used for, as Bakeless has shown,[19] he closely follows Lonicer's account in *The Second Part of Tamburlaine,* Act III Scene 1. He seems also to have used John Shute's translation from the Italian of Andrew Cambine's *Turkish affares* published as part of *Two Very Notable Commentaries* (1562) and Antonius Bonfinius's *Rerum Vngaricvm Decades Qvatvor* (1581).[20]

From these books Marlowe could have obtained the basis of his dramatization of the historical Tamerlane's life to which he adhered closely.

He may have based his description of Tamburlaine's appearance on what is stated in Jovius's *Elogia virorum bellica virtute illustrium* (1578), although he improved on it to make his hero considerably more appealing. The excerpts from Jovius and other Latin authors are here given in an English translation. Jovius tells us:

> *Tamerlane had a grim face, always menacing, with deep-set eyes; his body was enormous, with strong muscles so as to be brawny in appearance.[21]*

Marlowe's Tamburlaine is presented essentially following the historical source above being 'large of limbs, his joints so strongly knit' with great 'breadth of shoulders' and 'His arms and fingers long and sinewy' and his eyes are described as 'piercing instruments of sight'. A stunning description of Tamburlaine as Marlowe visualized him is given by Menaphon at the beginning of Act II.

> *Menaphon.* Of stature tall, and straightly fashioned
> Like his desire, lift upwards and divine;
> So large of limbs, his joints so strongly knit,
> Such breadth of shoulders as might mainly bear
> Old Atlas' burden; twixt his manly pitch,
> A pearl, more worth than all the world, is placed,
> Wherein by curious sovereignty of art
> Are fixed his piercing instruments of sight,
> Whose fiery circles bear encompassed
> A heaven of heavenly bodies in their spheres,
> That guide his steps and actions to the throne,
> Where honour sits invested royally;
> Pale of complexion, wrought in him with passion,
> Thirsting with sovereignty and love of arms;
> His lofty brows in folds do figure death,
> And in their smoothness amity and life;
> About them hangs a knot of amber hair,
> Wrapped in curls, as fierce Achilles' was,

On which the breath of Heaven delights to play,
Making it dance with wanton majesty;
His arms and fingers, long, and sinewy,
Betokening valour and excess of strength,
In every part proportioned like the man
Should make the world subdued to Tamburlaine.
Cosroe. Well hast thou portrayed in thy terms of life
The face and personage of a wondrous man.
                                  I Tamburlaine Act II Scene 1.11.7-32

Marlowe's portrait of Tamburlaine deliberately departs from the Mongol warrior of history to give us an idealized Englishman with his 'knot of amber hair' – in the Elizabethan romantic convention men always had amber hair, women were golden-haired. The real Tamer-lane was also reputed to have been lame, but this disability in his hero Marlowe discards. I have previously suggested, following Eleanor Grace Clarke, that the portrait of Tamburlaine may have been partly inspired by his admiration for Sir Walter Raleigh who is reputed to have had 'that awful ascendency in his aspect over other mortalls', and arriving at the Court 'a bare gentleman' had 'gotten the Queen's ear in a trice'[22] to become her favourite on whom she lavished wealth and power second to none. Raleigh's campaign in Ireland under Lord Grey had given him a fearsome reputation for ruthlessness in battle comparable to Tamburlaine's, for he mercilessly slaughtered the 400 Spaniards and Italians who had made common cause with the Irish rebels when he captured Fort Del Ore, so that he arrived back in England in 1581 figuratively dripping blood from the boggy fields of Ireland.[23] Perhaps it was Marlowe's admiration for Raleigh that gave him the entrée to Raleigh's 'little academie' or School of Night, for he puts into the mouth of Tamburlaine words that reflect the aspiring minds of these ardent seekers after knowledge infinite:

Nature that fram'd us of four elements
Warring within our breasts for regiment,
Doth teach us all to have aspiring minds:
Our souls, whose faculties can comprehend
The wondrous architecture of the world,
And measure every wandering planet's course,
Still climbing after knowledge infinite,
And always moving as the restless spheres,
Will us to wear ourselves, and never rest,

Until we reach the ripest fruit of all,
That perfect bliss and sole felicity,
The sweet fruition of an earthly crown.
I Tamburlaine, Act II, Scene 7, 11. 18-29

The concept is neatly turned at the end to fit Tamburlaine's earthly aspirations, but the beginning and inspiration of the speech is surely to be seen as his private tribute to Raleigh, who led his group of esoteric seekers after knowledge to adventure with him in the realms of the mind.

Marlowe deliberately gives us a romanticized figure of a man, an idealized Tamburlaine to match his lovely Zenocrate, who, in despite of herself, falls deeply in love with her captor – who treats her most chivalrously and honourably – and she confesses that she longs to 'live and die with Tamburlaine!' She waxes ecstatic thinking of him, echoing Dido in her passion for AEneas:

> *Zenocrate.* As looks the sun through Nilus' flowing stream,
> Or when the Morning holds him in her arms,
> So looks my lordly love, fair Tamburlaine;
> His talk much sweeter than the Muse's song
> *I Tamburlaine* Act III Scene 2, 11.47-50

recalling Dido's –

> Instead of music I will hear him speak.
> *Dido Queen of Carthage* Act III Scene 1, 1.89

The passionate romanticism of Marlowe, which is so evident in his lovers, whether men or women characters, has been noted appreciatively by A.W. Ward: 'The element in which as a poet he lived was passion; and it was he who first inspired with true poetic passion the form of literature to which his chief efforts were consecrated.'[24]

Jovius provided also a vital clue to Tamburlaine's mind, his concept of himself, as 'Ira die ego sum & orbis vastitas' (I am the wrath of god and the desolation of the world),[25] which is the extraordinary personal conviction that animated this man. Marlowe puts this into Tamburlaine's mouth in *The First Part of Tamburlaine*:

> I that am term'd the Scourge and Wrath of God,
> The only fear and terror of the world,
> Act III Scene 3, 11.44-5

20

and he reaffirms it in *The Second Part*:

> There is a God, full of revenging wrath,
> From whom the thunder and the lightning breaks,
> Whose scourge I am, and him will I obey.
>
> Act V Scene 1, 11.181-183

Fulgotius is one of several historians who give details of Tamburlaine's spectacularly cruel treatment of Bajazeth, the Sultan of the Turks, whom he defeats and takes prisoner.

> *He shut up Baiazetes (Sultan Bayezid) in a cage, whom he dragged with him, thus set up on a chariot, wherever he himself went, using him as a footstool to make it easier for him to mount his horse.*[26]

It was a terrible retribution exacted for Bajazeth's proud challenge to the Scythian upstart's military prowess of which Marlowe makes full dramatic use.

> *Bajazeth.* Now shalt thou feel the force of Turkish arms,
> Which lately made all Europe quake for fear.
> I have of Turks, Arabians, Moors, and Jews,
> Enough to cover all Bithynia:
> Let thousands die: their slaughtered carcasses
> Shall serve for walls and bulwarks to the rest;
> And as the heads of Hydra, so my power,
> Subdu'd, shall stand as mighty as before:
> If they should yield their necks unto the sword,
> Thy soldiers' arms could not endure to strike
> So many blows as I have heads for thee.
> Thou know'st not, foolish hardy Tamburlaine,
> What 'tis to meet me in the open field,
> That leave no ground for thee to march upon.
>
> *I Tamburlaine* Act III Scene 3, 11.134-147

Marlowe makes Tamburlaine's conquest of the Turks the dramatic climax of the play, and Bajazeth, their Emperor, as symbol of this conquest, is the major male part opposite Tamburlaine. The battle for supremacy between the two great military leaders is given highly original treatment in the scene juxtaposing the Turkish Empress Zabina and Zenocrate, who

21

is wearing Tamburlaine's crown for him while he goes off to fight, in earnest that she will become his empress, and the battle rages as the two ladies indulge in a verbal battle worthy of two Billingsgate fishwives! This elevation of Zenocrate to a position as the ardent protagonist of her martial husband-to-be may have its origin in the influence his favourite wife exerted over the historical Tamburlaine, for Bakeless quotes from Heinrich von Efferhen's book of sermons published in 1571, which gives this information, here rendered in an English translation from the Latin:

> *Incited by the ill-considered request of the leading men of Asia,*
> *and of his wife, he took up arms to fight a war against Baiazete.*[27]

Bakeless comments: 'Such a passage certainly makes it possible that other stories of the sort were afloat at the time. The books of the period bear further witness to a lively and general interest in this mysterious Asiatic conqueror, who had in such welcome manner relieved the pressure of the Turks.'[28] His discovery of Marlowe's sources has laid bare the dramatist's method of creating his drama from the carefully garnered data of the historians.

We see that the extreme cruelty of the treatment of Bajazeth as a caged animal, and Tamburlaine's use of him as his footstool, emanate not from Marlowe, but from his historical sources, as also the manner of Bajazeth's death when the tormented emperor, unable to bear his degradation longer, beats out his brains against the iron bars of his cage. The half-crazed Zabina follows him in this suicide. It is Marlowe who moves us to pity when Zenocrate, having herself felt the pangs of fear for her father's life as she awaits the outcome of the battle between Tamburlaine and the Egyptians, and thus, knowing suffering, is finally touched by the death of Zabina and Bajazeth. To express her pity Marlowe uses a technique that is very like the mourning elegy of Tamburlaine in *The Second Part of Tamburlaine* over the dying Zenocrate.

> *Zenocrate.* Earth, cast up fountains from thy entrails,
> And wet thy cheeks for their untimely deaths;
> Shake with their weight in sign of fear and grief!
> Blush, heaven, that gave them honour at their birth,
> And let them die a death so barbarous!
> Those that are proud of fickle empery
> And place their chiefest good in earthly pomp,

Behold the Turk and his great emperess!
Thou, that in conduct of thy happy stars,
Sleep'st every night with conquest on thy brows,
And yet wouldst shun the wavering turns of war,
In fear and feeling of the like distress,
Behold the Turk and his great emperess!
Ah, mighty Jove and holy Mahomet,
Pardon my love! Oh, pardon his contempt
Of earthly fortune and respect of pity;
And let not conquest, ruthlessly pursu'd,
Be equally against his life incens'd
In this great Turk and hapless emperess!
And pardon me that was not mov'd with ruth
To see them live so long in misery!
Ah, what may chance to thee, Zenocrate?

I Tamburlaine Act V Scene 1, 11.349-373

This formula with its poetic, echoing refrain is typical of early Marlowe, which he uses at moments of great emotional intensity in his characters, when mourning the dead, or when a ritual having a religious element is taking place.[29] Even the final line, an emotional denouement, is a trick of technique he repeats in both speeches. (See page 41).

Pope Pius echoes Tamburlaine's historic treatment of the vanquished Turkish Emperor, and he further gives 'innumerable details which Marlowe expanded in his play', Bakeless tells us.[30] The most important of these are in the following extract given here in an English translation.

Tamerlane a Parthian by birth ..... stood out among his own people for nimbleness of both mind & body so that in short time he became the ruler of many nations ..... Pazaites (Baiazites) the lord of the Turks ..... he captured alive, shut in a cage as though he were a wild beast, and carried around throughout Asia ..... Soldanus (Sultan) of Egypt whom he defeated in war he drove back to Perlusum ..... In sieges of cities, on the first day he would make use of a white tent, on the second a red, the third a black: those who surrendered to him sitting in a white one came to be spared. Red colour signified death for the heads of households: black meant the destruction of the town, and all things in it to be reduced to ashes. There is a story of a certain crowded city, which had foreborne to surrender on the first day; when all the boys and girls went out dressed in white and

*carrying olive branches before them to soothe the general's anger:
he ordered them all to be trampled on by the cavalry and pulverized,
their city to be captured and burnt ..... he left behind two sons to
be the successors of his kingdom.*[31]

This is brilliantly dramatized at the siege of Damascus when the virgins
of the city are sent all dressed in white to plead with him for mercy, and
Tamburlaine (so the stage direction reads) appears *'all in black and very
melancholy'*.

> *Tamburlaine.* What, are the turtles fray'd out of their
>   nests?
> Alas, poor fools, must you be first shall feel
> The sworn destruction of Damascus?
> They knew my custom; could they not as well
> Have sent ye out when first my milk-white flags,
> Through which sweet Mercy threw her gentle beams,
> Reflexed them on their disdainful eyes,
> As now when fury and incensed hate
> Flings slaughtering terror from my coal-black tents,
> And tells for truth submission comes too late?
> *First Virgin.* Pity, O pity, sacred emperor,
> The prostrate service of this wretched town;
> And take in sign thereof this gilded wreath,
> Whereto each man of rule hath given his hand,
> And wish'd, as worthy subjects, happy means
> To be investors of thy royal brows
> Even with the true Egyptian diadem!
> *Tamburlaine.* Virgins, in vain you labour to prevent
> That which mine honour swears shall be perform'd.
>   (*Drawing his sword*)
> Behold my sword; what see you at the point?
> *First Virgin.* Nothing but fear and fatal steel, my lord.
> *Tamburlaine.* Your fearful minds are thick and misty
>   then,
> For there sits death; there sits imperious Death,
> Keeping his circuit by the slicing edge.
> But I am pleas'd you shall not see him there;
> He now is seated on my horsemen's spears,
> And on their points his fleshless body feeds.

Techelles, straight go charge a few of them
To charge these dames, and shew my servant Death,
Sitting in scarlet on their armed spears.
Virgins. O, pity us!
Tamburlaine. Away with them, I say, and shew them
   Death!

The First Part of Tamburlaine Act V Scene 1, 11.64-120

This piteous scene is the prelude to Tamburlaine's famous apostrophe to Beauty in his long soliloquy on Zenocrate, providing the perfect contrast in dramatic tension, in which Marlowe reveals his masterhand as a dramatist.

Both Fulgotius and Ignatius confirm the exact numbers of horsemen – a thousand – and foot soldiers – five hundred, which the opposing forces of Theridamas and his Persians and Tamburlaine possess respectively.[32] Marlowe is particular about such details to lend his play historical verisimilitude, although he is prepared to take poetic licence with historic facts where this is necessary to advance the dramatic viability of his play, for he has an infallible instinct for what makes good theatre. For instance, Bakeless has shown in his exhaustive study of Marlowe's use of his sources that the scene in which Orcanes, King of Natolia, and Sigismund, King of Hungary, swear by their respective godheads, Mahomet and Christ, to keep their 'truce inviolable' is based on the text of Bonfinius's *Rervm Vngaricvm Decades Qvatvor* (1581) which Marlowe seems to have studied closely, but uses his material selectively.

The Turks demand an oath from the king at the Eucharist...Finally, there is agreement on both sides that our people should swear on the Gospel, they on the Koran. So they set down in writing, in the same terms but in two languages, the conditions of peace and they vowed that these would be maintained and kept unbroken between them, with a most solemn oath to each other.[33]

Marlowe dramatizes this in a scene which begins with bombastic military challenges between the two kings, but ends in concluding a truce because they are both aware that Tamburlaine is fast advancing on them, whom they must face in the field together or both be vanquished. Orcanes hands Sigismund a sword as symbol of war or peace between them – a Marlovian touch here repeated in *The Second Part of Tamburlaine.*

Sigismund. Then here I sheathe it, and give thee my hand

Never to draw it out, or manage arms
Against thyself or thy confederates,
But, whilst I live, will be at truce with thee.
Orcanes. But, Sigismund, confirm it with an oath,
And swear in sight of heaven and by thy Christ.
Sigismund. By Him that made the world and sav'd my
   soul,
The Son of God and issue of a maid,
Sweet Jesus Christ, I solemnly protest
And vow to keep this peace inviolable!
Orcanes. By sacred Mahomet, the friend of God,
Whose holy Alcoran remains with us,
Whose glorious body, when he left the world,
Clos'd in a coffin mounted up the air,
And hung on stately Mecca's temple-roof,
I swear to keep this truce inviolable!
Of whose conditions and our solemn oaths,
Sign'd with our hands, each shall retain a scroll,
As memorable witness of our league.
Now, Sigismund, if any Christian king
Encroach upon the confines of thy realm,
Send word, Orcanes of Natolia
Confirm'd this league beyond Danubius' stream,
And they will, trembling, sound a quick retreat;
So am I fear'd among all nations.
Sigismund. If any heathen potentate or king
Invade Natolia, Sigismund will send
A hundred thousand horse train'd to the war,
And back'd by stout lanciers of Germany,
The strength and sinews of the imperial seat.

> *The Second Part of Tamburlaine the Great,*
> Act I, Sc.2, 11.50-79

And after some more boastful promises from Orcanes in which the sonorous names of Natolia and Trebizon are rolled off the tongue in the richly poetic vein which Marlowe relishes throughout this masterpiece, they go off to banquet and carouse in celebration of their truce.

Despite his oath made in the name of Christ, Marlowe's Hungarian king, Sigismund, breaks the truce, and yet again Bonfinius supplies the historical source from which Marlowe probably drew his facts for this episode, although here Bonfinius is writing about a later Hungarian king, Ladislaus, who in 1443 had concluded a truce with the Turkish emperor, Amurath II, (the treaty of Szedin) which he was persuaded to break by the papal legate, Cardinal Julian, and launch an attack on the unsuspecting Turks.[34] But their ruse was not successful for Amurath retreated and regrouped his armies to counter-attack and kill the perfidious Ladislaus and the Cardinal. This piece of poetic justice Marlowe seizes upon and transposes into the time of Tamburlaine to apply to the contemporaneous King Sigismund of Hungary, replacing Cardinal Julian with two Lords of Buda and Bohemia who put Cardinal Julian's arguments to Sigismund. Thus Bonfinius's report in translation:

Julian in a timely speech said: If any of you Proceres, perhaps may marvel because I am going to speak about rescinding the peace and breaking faith: Let him first understand that I am going to discuss with you nothing today other than about observing the treaty....In these distressing circumstances hasty counsel may impel us: having made a peace with the Turkish infidel, that we should break the solemn word of the faithful and rescind the sacred deed entered into with the supreme Pontiff and allied Princes before the treaty.[35]

With subtle arguments of political and military opportunism Marlowe skilfully dramatizes the scene.

> *Sigismund.* Now say, my lords of Buda and Bohemia,
> What motion is it that inflames your thoughts,
> And stirs your valours to such sudden arms?
> *Frederick.* Your majesty remembers, I am sure,
> What cruel slaughter of our Christian bloods
> These heathenish Turks and pagans lately made
> Your highness knows, for Tamburlaine's repair
> That strikes a terror to all Turkish hearts,
> Natolia hath dismiss'd the greatest part
> Of all his army, pitch'd against our power
> Betwixt Cutheia and Orminius' mount,
> And sent them marching up to Belgasar,
> Acantha, Antioch, and Caeserea,
> To aid the kings of Soria and Jerusalem.
> Now, then, my lord, advantage take thereof,
> And issue suddenly upon the rest;

That, in the fortune of their overthrow,
We may discourage all the pagan troop
That dare attempt to war with Christians.
Sigismund. But calls not, then, your grace to memory
The league we lately made with King Orcanes,
Confirm'd by oath and articles of peace,
And calling Christ for record of our truths?
This should be treachery and violence
Against the grace of our profession.
Baldwin. No whit, my lord; for with such infidels,
In whom no faith nor true religion rests,
We are not bound to those accomplishments
The holy laws of Christendom enjoin;

But Sigismund is not so easily persuaded and the discussion continues.

Frederick. Assure your grace, 'tis superstition
To stand so strictly on dispensive faith,
And, should we lose the opportunity
That God hath given to venge our Christians' death,
.....
And scourge their foul blasphemous paganism,
So surely will the vengeance of the Highest,
And jealous anger of his fearful arm,
Be pour'd with rigour on our sinful heads,
If we neglect this offer'd victory.

The Second Part of Tamburlaine the Great
Act II, Sc. 1, 11.1-59

With Machiavellian persuasiveness they win Sigismund over, and he attacks Orcanes, but (as happened to the perfidious Ladislaus of history) Marlowe presents his audience with moral justification for the Christian king's defeat at the hands of Orcanes (Amureth II). For the scene in which Orcanes rages over this perfidy by the Christian king, challenging Christ's divinity, Marlowe once again has his authority from Bonfinius.

Now, O Christ, if you are God (as they say, and we are not suffering from delusions), turn away your wrongs and mine, I beseech you: and to those who have not yet professed your holy Name pronounce the penalty for broken faith.[36]

Marlowe dramatizes this in a passionate outburst by Orcanes.

> *Enter a* Messenger
> *Messenger.* Arm dread sovereign, and my noble lords!
> The treacherous army of the Christians,
> Taking advantage of your slender power,
> Comes marching on us, and determines straight
> To bid us battle for our dearest lives.
> *Orcanes.* Traitors, villains, damned Christians!
> Have I not here the articles of peace
> And solemn covenants we have both confirm'd,
> He by his Christ, and I by Mahomet?
> .....
> Can there be such deceit in Christians,
> Or treason in the fleshly heart of man,
> Whose shape is figure of the highest God?
> Then, if there be a Christ, as Christians say,
> But in their deeds deny him for their Christ,
> If he be son to everliving Jove,
> And hath the power of his outstretched arm,
> If he be jealous of his name and honour
> As is our holy prophet Mahomet,
> Take here these papers as our sacrifice
> And witness of thy servant's perjury!
> > (*He tears to pieces the articles of peace.*)
> Open, thou shining veil of Cynthia,
> And make a passage from th'empyreal heaven,
> That he that sits on high and never sleeps,
> Nor in one place is circumscriptible,
> But everywhere fills every continent
> With strange infusion of his sacred vigour,
> May, in his endless power and purity,
> Behold and venge this traitor's perjury!
> Thou, Christ, that art esteem'd omnipotent,
> If thou wilt prove thyself a perfect God,
> Worthy the worship of all faithful hearts,
> Be now reveng'd upon this traitor's soul
> And make the power I have left behind
> (Too little to defend our guiltless lives)
> Sufficient to discomfit and confound

The trustless force of those false Christians!
To arms, my lords! on Christ still let us cry:
If there be Christ, we shall have victory.
                    II Tamburlaine Act II, Sc.2, 11.24-64

With his depleted forces Orcanes is then victorious, and the perjured
Sigismund staggers wounded onto the stage to die, crying –

Let the dishonour of the pains I feel
In this my mortal well-deserved wound
End all my penance in my sudden death!
And let this death, wherein to sin I die,
Conceive a second life in endless mercy!
                    II Tamburlaine Act II, Sc.3 11.5-9

In Marlowe's works the questioning mind that holds the mirror to
man's sinful nature comes to rest always in moral justice and while
venturing into unorthodox beliefs returns at last to orthodoxy. This is as
true of Marlowe as it is of Raleigh, who was also accused of atheism but
lived to refute it.

Bakeless' invaluable research into the astonishingly extensive range of
Marlowe's historical sources in compiling his material for *Tamburlaine*
has been a revelation.

'The study of Marlowe's sources for *Tamburlaine* is of particular
importance because it definitely reverses the view of his mind and
character which has been generally accepted for three centuries.
Detailed, minute, even trifling though the necessary investigation
may be, it is rewarded in the end by a new understanding of the mind
of a very great poet. It shows Marlowe as something more than an
impetuous youth with a gift for poetry. It shows him as a careful
writer who bases work of the purest poetic beauty on an elaborate
and careful study of all available materials.'[37]

The research of Dr Bakeless has provided these sources, here given as
Englished excerpts from the original Latin texts from Bakeless, whose
scholarly mind makes no concessions to the latter day students whose
Latin is rusty or non-existent, alas. His great work on Marlowe is
consequently and regrettably to some extent beyond the reach of many
readers, for practically every ancient document he quotes is in its Latin
original. A reprint of this classic work with translations would be timely.

Olympia   Take pity of a lady's ruthful tears,
That humbly craves upon her knees to stay,
And cast her body in the burning flame,
That feeds upon her son's and husband's flesh.

Theridamas   Madam, sooner shall fire consume us both
Than scorch a face so beautiful as this,
In frame of which Nature hath showed more skill
Than when she gave eternal chaos form,
Drawing from it the shining lamps of heaven.

The Second Part of Tamburlaine
Act III, Sc. 4 11.69–77

*Photograph by Nobby Clark for the National Theatre production
of **Tamburlaine the Great**, 1976, directed by Sir Peter Hall.*

Bonfinius is only one of a dozen authors, tracked down by Bakeless and Ethel Seaton[38], whose books were available in print and were possible sources for Marlowe's historical research for *Tamburlaine*, for the facts and episodes he dramatizes are all there scattered through the pages of these source books. I have quoted in particular the scenes based on Bonfinius because these are concerned with religion and reflect the theological arguments which have been attributed to Marlowe as being entirely his own. Bakeless has demonstrated that this is a fallacy, for they are in fact based on his historical sources – a detail which was evidently obscured to the critics of Marlowe's own time as well as ours until Bakeless' fascinating research into his sources revealed the true situation. As he himself has commented:

'The oath of Amurath (Orcanes in Marlowe's play) is a good illustration of the way in which the study of sources sometimes throws light upon an author's mind. This passage has long been supposed to illustrate Marlowe's "atheistic" leanings and has been pointed out as an example of the sort of blasphemy about which Richard Baines bore tales to the authorities. But when the 'blasphemy' turns out to be merely a vivid bit of history, we see that it is merely one more instance of the selective skill with which Marlowe has sifted the material in his sources.'[39]

This evidence shows that his main aim in researching his material was to supply his dramatic Muse with the stuff from which effective drama could be created. His eclectic taste was catholic in its foraging, and his long years of study had made him a disciplined and dedicated seeker after knowledge, drawing his inspiration from the rich fount of human history in which he found the endless variety that stimulated his art. His theme is humanity, which he interprets preferring to base his portraits on real people whose lives his poetry lifts into the sphere of dramatic art.

Man's violence and cruelty have ever been popular subjects for what we deem entertainment, from the gory horror stories of ancient Greek tragedy to our own day when violence on the television screen occupies the highest proportion of all our viewing of drama. The self-avowed gentle Kyd chose to wallow in the dramatized cruelty of his popular revenge play, *The Spanish Tragedy*, only slightly less horrific than *Titus Andronicus*. *Tamburlaine the Great* has cruelty in full measure, but here again Marlowe's historical source provided him with the evidence for this in the life of the real Tamburlaine, who was a monster of cruelty, curiously combined in a man who reverenced learning and in some respects possessed an aspiring mind even as Marlowe depicts him. It was a tension of opposites that held great attraction for him.

Marlowe's interest in the Mongol conqueror may have been first aroused through some traveller's tale told in his Canterbury boyhood, for all Europe had been agog with his exploits for the past hundred years. Henry IV of England, Charles VI of France and Henry III of Spain had each sent ambassages to his court, anxious to maintain cordial relations with so victorious a conqueror.[40] Tamburlaine, Tamerlane or Timur the Lame, hence Timur-lane, for he had one lame leg (a physical defect Marlowe chooses to ignore) had lived from 1336 to 1405, and led his nomadic hordes to overrun large tracts of Asia, carving himself an empire which stretched from the Volga to India, and included Persia, Turkey and Egypt. His capital was Samarkand, near Bokhara (now in Uzbekistan in Asiatic USSR) lying on what was known as the 'silk road', for merchants with Median silk travelled this route to Europe, and situated in the foothills about 150 miles north of the Afghanistan border where the mountains of the Hindu Kush rear their snowy peaks. At least two intrepid Europeans who penetrated as far as his court at Samarkand had written marvellous accounts of what they saw there, one of which was still in manuscript in Marlowe's time – that by the Bavarian Johann Schiltberger whose Latin manuscript was translated into German and edited by Professor Karl Friedrich Neumann in 1859 and finally Englished by Commander J. Buchan Telfer, R.N. as *The Bondage and Travels of Johann Schiltberger (1396-1427)*[41]. The other was the report of the Spaniard Ruy Gonzales de Clavijo, the ambassador of Henry III of Castille and Leon, who visited the court of Timur in 1403. This was printed in 1582 and could therefore have been available to Marlowe,[42] Clavijo's account of the splendour of Timur's court, and the richness of the jewels he saw adorning the emperor's clothing and furnishings of his palace, would have interested Marlowe greatly. There are also accounts of Timur's ghastly cruelty to those who displeased him, with which he enjoyed demonstrating his despotic power to visitors. By this time, almost at the end of his life, the Mongol emperor had developed a passion for splendid architecture and conceived the ambition to make Samarkand the most beautiful city in the world. He lavished art work in porcelain and turquoise and jade on his Palace of Heart's Delight, which was made of white marble, employing Chinese and Persian artists, and he brought in scholars to supervise his libraries and run his academies of philosophy, mathematics and science. The historical Timur developed into a demoniacal, almost schizophrenic personality, and some of this Marlowe may have heard about if he did not read it, for in *The Second Part* Tamburlaine becomes a despotic, megalomaniac following the death of his beloved Zenocrate, without whose gentle restraining influence he descends into the sheer obsession of unending bloody conquest, making impossible demands to satisfy his lust for ostentatious power; just as the real Timur, in his craze for building his perfect city, had newly-erected mosques torn down if something in the design displeased him and ordered that they be rebuilt in ten days on pain of death to the frenzied builders.

Tamburlaine is indeed a remarkable psychological study of a power-crazed tyrant, such as we have seen even in our own day in Hitler, in whom cruelty also came increasingly to the fore. Anyone who has visited the Plötzensee Memorial in West Berlin must be struck by the parallel. This tragic shrine to the victims of the Third Reich whose plot to assassinate Hitler was discovered, commemorates their terrible punishment with cruel deaths, their bodies strung up on meat hooks suspended from a steel beam. The meat hooks are still there, but the floor is fragrant with the flowers placed freshly always in tribute to the brave men who pitted themselves against this latter-day tyrant, who was far worse than Marlowe's Tamburlaine for he lacked the saving grace of personal bravery and only strutted arrogantly without ever participating in the turmoil of war.

Tamburlaine excited admiration as well as awe and horror. He was, in his rise from obscurity, cast in the heroic mould and the general interest in him was reflected in a proliferation of books, many of which were available to Marlowe. But none of these afforded him any historical basis for the love story of Tamburlaine and Zenocrate, which is the central thread of Marlowe's drama. This presents us with a most curious and interesting puzzle.

As Dr Bakeless' extensive research on Marlowe's historical sources has shown, the story of Tamburlaine's great love for Zenocrate, with which Marlowe underpins his drama and supplies the human emotional element that lifts his warlike theme onto another level, is the one piece lacking in his available sources.[43] Only the most cursory references are made to Tamerlane's wife by the historians whose books were in print in Marlowe's time, and they give the number of his sons as two. Of these historians Perondinus is the most informative and he is very brief.

He married the daughter of some Bactrian prince (ruler) by whom according to all authorities he had begotten two children, in no way

compared to Tamerlane in military valour and good fortune, which
we have seen confirmed later at the conclusion of the campaign.[44]

Marlowe expands the sons to three, one of whom is the cowardly
Calyphas ('in no way compared to Tamerlane in military valour') while
the other two are as warlike and cruel as their father. But the beautiful
Egyptian Princess, Zenocrate, whom Tamburlaine first captures and then
falls in love with and marries, seems, so far as we may judge from the
contemporary history books, to have been Marlowe's original creation.
This, however, is modified when we learn that the historic Timur did, in
fact, have a favourite wife (being an eastern potentate he had not one,
but several wives) whom he had captured and then married, and 'whom
he especially loved; who, like Zenocrate, shared many of her husband's
perils and adventures in the field; and who died when he was in the midst
of his career of conquest,' as Bakeless tells us.[45] This information is
contained in the *Mulfuzat Timury,* or the *Memoirs of Timur* which are
believed to have been written by Timur himself. Several copies of this
Persian manuscript exist, and one of these of 457 pages was 'brought to
England from India in 1784, among the papers of Major William Davy,
of the Honourable East India Company's Service, who had for twelve
years been interpreter to Sir Robert Baker, commander-in-chief in Bengal.'[46]
Bakeless relates this fascinating story, and how Davy's copy was eventually
translated into English in 1829 by Major Charles Stewart.[47]

Johan Schiltberger whose manuscript was nearer home, in Heidelberg,
tells a variant tale of Tamerlane's love for a favourite wife who broke his
heart by being unfaithful to him with one of his vassals, who managed
to escape with tribute stolen from Tamerlane. He had his wife beheaded,
but was so smitten with grief that he sickened and died. In both
Schiltberger's version and the *Mulfuzat Timury* the beloved wife was
much younger than Timur and presumably very lovely.

In the *Mulfuzat Timury* the princess he captured and whom he treated
chivalrously was at that time 'big with child [and] safely delivered of a
daughter in that desert',[48] and it was this daughter who became his much
loved wife.

The historians on whom Marlowe based his narrative were themselves
only partly true to history, and they tended to look to each other's books
as authoritative sources which were quoted and requoted. A character like
Tamburlaine invited legend, and the interest in his exploits and his
extraordinary person had been so wide-spread over so many years that
it is surprising that the drama he created is as near to the true history of

this exotic conqueror. Marlowe's care in researching his facts and using his sources faithfully, skilfully and discriminatingly is commendable. His inspired use for dramatic purpose of the love story of Tamburlaine and Zenocrate, as the stuff whereby he weaves the warp that holds the play together, shows his unerring instinct in creating his dramatic framework. How he came to divine the truth which is shadowed in his version of Tamburlaine's love for 'divine Zenocrate', the beautiful princess who was captured and became his much-loved wife, who accompanied him on his conquering exploits, and who died leaving him desolate, we shall probably never know. But we should not forget that Walsingham's spy ring stretched as far as Turkey, and if Marlowe thus early in his espionage career did not penetrate so far, there is a possibility that he was able to talk with some who did, and who may have known of the *Mulfuzat Timury*.[49]

What also emerges from a study of *Tamburlaine* is Marlowe's keen interest in warfare and in military techniques. His quotation from Paul Ive's *The Practise of Fortification*, then still in manuscript unless an earlier edition had existed – which, when published, was dedicated to Sir Francis Walsingham, for whom Ive also worked as an agent – testifies to Marlowe's appreciation of the development of practical expertise in warfare. If he had not been granted opportunities for foreign travel as an agent, in which some danger, excitement and adventure were inherent, one feels he might well have enlisted for a spell of military experience abroad, and we have evidence that he fought against the Armada.[50]

In sixteenth century Western Europe there was almost continual war going on somewhere, and usually not very far away. In interims of peace the memory of war and the consciousness of the danger of renewed conflict were ever present. In such a society men's warlike qualities and skills are highly prized.

In Marlowe's Tamburlaine, his qualities of dauntless courage, physical prowess, sublime self-confidence and his vaunting ambition expressed in his skill at arms, his passionate, fiery temperament – and even his ruthless cruelty to his enemies, which is matched by his loyalty to his friends – were deemed admirable. Had not Raleigh and Macworth in Ireland pitilessly massacred the Irish, Spaniards and Italians at the siege of Fort Del Ore at Smerwick? Such ruthlessness could be justified in contemporary eyes by personal bravery in the perpetrators. And Raleigh was outstandingly brave and reckless of his own life. A commander who faced danger and hardship with his men was unstintingly admired, even when he was an enemy – like the Duke of Parma, the brilliant Spanish commander in the

Netherlands who personally led his soldiers into the thick of the fighting. It was the dare-devils like Drake, the fool-hardy, dashing young Earl of Essex, the valorous Henry of Navarre whose personal heroism saved the day for his hard-pressed Huguenot army more often than not, who were the darlings beloved by all. It was the age that bred men like Sir Richard Grenville, whose fanatically courageous sea-fight against the Spaniards, pitting his fleet of seven against the combined might of fifty-three Spanish galleons, some three times the tonnage of his little 'Revenge', made him a legend. When finally taken prisoner, the Spaniards' admiration for his courage earned him gallant treatment at their hands, which his proud spirit scorned. He crushed the wine glass they offered him and chewed and swallowed the glass under his captors' incredulous eyes, choosing death rather than submission even as their honoured prisoner. This was the temper of the age.

In choosing Tamburlaine for his hero Marlowe was doing no more than presenting his audience with their martial idol as a dramatic character – a great, invincible warrior who had all the attributes of the popular soldier-heroes they admired, but writ larger, and resounding through the auditorium in the new-minted poetic splendour of the music of his 'mighty line'.

II *A Great Theatrical Partnership*

WITH *TAMBURLAINE THE GREAT* Christopher Marlowe and Edward Alleyn would first have come to know each other with more than mere acquaintance, for this triumphant play must have drawn the aspiring dramatist, new-come from Cambridge, and the ambitious young actor-manager, who had fairly recently risen to the head of his company, into an especially close collaboration. Their joint success in the play was probably a somewhat heady experience! Mutual admiration and liking would, I believe, have engendered warmth in their business relationship from the start.

Alleyn, the younger man by two years, was self-educated, his 'school' having been the touring company, but he venerated learning and would have admired Marlowe the more for his humble origin as a cobbler's son who had attained to a Master of Arts, and he undoubtedby recognized his genius as a dramatist – one, moreover, who had an inborn sense of theatrical craftsmanship. This innate, vivid response to the art of drama on a grand scale was their common meeting ground – the place where, one might say, they spoke the same dramatic language. This compatibility of dramatic understanding made possible a theatrical partnership that dominated the Elizabethan stage for the next six years in which Marlowe wrote those roles which, in his day, were synonymous with Alleyn.

It must have been with a surge of admiration flushed with exultant expectancy that Marlowe realized on meeting Alleyn that here was the very man who seemed born to create the role of the warlike Tamburlaine, an extraordinary actor to meet this extraordinary challenge. Edward Alleyn was young, vigorous, intelligent, experienced and immensely talented as an actor, and he was built on the large scale physically and vocally that Tamburlaine demanded. Fuller tells us that 'He was the *Roscius* of our age, so acting to the life, that he made any part (especially a Majestick one) to become him.'[1] There are many contemporary accolades that bear this out. The tremendous impact that the performance of *The First Part of Tamburlaine the Great* made on Elizabethan audiences must have owed something, at least, to Edward Alleyn who interpreted the role and gave it the lustre of his special histrionic genius.

The conjunction of these two, Marlowe the dramatist, and Alleyn the actor, each supreme in his field at this time, was a remarkable coincidence that ensured the success of *Tamburlaine* at a level which few plays can have reached. Marlowe's wondrous verbal music, his passages of lyricism alternating with the high astounding terms of his warrior's 'mighty line' were not the whole story. What he gave his audiences essentially was *drama*, the tension of conflicting forces and emotions, a dazzling story of an out-topping hero-figure, barbarous and cruel, but also strangely moving in his moments of humanity, in a superbly stage-crafted play, and, to spice it the more, he added some outrageous spectacles that were caviare to the general. In *The First Part* he had featured the caging of the defeated Turkish emperor, Bajazeth, which he drew from historical sources on Timur (from Pope Pius and Baptista Fulgotius already quoted) whom he kept like a wild beast and carted around with him, using him for a footstool; until the desperate man can stand his degradation no longer and beats out his brains against the iron bars of his cage, followed by the demented Zabina. In Marlowe's hands this is the very stuff of cathartic drama. One can imagine the mounting excitement with which Edward Alleyn and the players of the Lord Admiral's Men must have read Marlowe's script in a tavern over wine, as was their custom. Alleyn's experienced judgement would immediately have told him this was a winner, for the ingredients of Marlowe's play were tailor-made for popular appeal. *The First Part* presents the youthful Tamburlaine rising from his lowly status to achieve astonishing military glory and power together with his band of loyal companions, who are all elevated to kingship with him in his ascendant fortunes. Tamburlaine cries exultantly:

> Is it not brave to be a king, Techelles! –
> Usumcasane and Theridamas,
> Is it not passing brave to be a king,
> And ride in triumph through Persepolis?
> *I Tamburlaine* Act II, Sc. 5, 11.51–54

The love story of his wooing of Zenocrate is the theme that underlies the warlike scenario, ending in the restoration of her defeated and captured father to his throne at the magnanimous hands of conquering Tamburlaine, and his marriage to Zenocrate. Tamburlaine is shown as a ruthless conqueror who abides by his own cruel edicts when besieging a town (the white tent of mercy on the first day of surrender, the red tent of bloody retribution on the second day, and the black tent of utter destruction on the third day), but he is a young man moved by love and loyalty, and is not without some saving graces which endeared him to the public. *The First Part* is superb value as drama, and it offered also the kind of high-light of barbarity that the Elizabethan audiences revelled in. The problem for Marlowe was how to follow up this success, with its spectacular treatment of Bajazeth, so that his audiences would not be disappointed.

It has hardly been appreciated by modern scholars that *Tamburlaine* was a momentous theatrical event. His first audiences had responded ecstatically to the 'passionate touch' of the new dramatist who fashioned a play that held their interest from prologue to the last word of the last scene, when they 'clapper-clawed' resoundingly and shouted for more, and they must needs be satisfied. In short time was conjured from Marlowe's pen the swiftly written sequel of this two-part drama, triumphantly announced by the Prologue:

> The general welcomes *Tamburlaine* receiv'd,
> When he arrived last upon the stage,
> Have made our poet pen his Second Part.

What is impressive in Marlowe's characterization of Tamburlaine now is the way he shows his hero to be aging. After the death of Zenocrate, which is the emotional climax of the play, he descends into unrelieved barbarous cruelty and a mad power-lust that make him almost pitiable, for he has nothing else to live for. He is a study in self-destructive *hubris*, and as such *Tamburlaine* compares with some of the great Greek tragedies, horror piled upon horror, the blood-lust of the two callow youths, his warlike sons, appearing especially grotesque. Finally Tamburlaine himself stares death in the face, though defiant to the end in his mortality. Here Marlowe indulges his passion for geography as Tamburlaine, having called for a map of the world, names the countries his dying hand traces on the map, and bewails over and again –

> And shall I die, and this unconquered?
> Act V, Sc.3 1.151

Marlowe sees to it that his hero exits in fine style. But the greatest passage in this play is surely Tamburlaine's magnificent threnody at the death of Zenocrate, making a moving dramatic contrast to the blood and thunder of the rest of the play that follows. It is a passage in which Alleyn would have held his audience spellbound.

Tamburlaine. Black is the beauty of the brightest day;
The golden ball of heaven's eternal fire,
That danc'd with glory on the silver waves,
Now wants the fuel that inflam'd his beams;
And all with faintness, and for foul disgrace,
He binds his temples with a frowning cloud,
Ready to darken earth with endless night,
Zenocrate, that gave him light and life,
Whose eyes shot fire from their ivory bowers,
And temper'd every soul with lively heat,
Now with the malice of the angry skies,
Whose jealousy admits no second mate,
Draws in the comfort of her latest breath,
All dazzled with the hellish mists of death.
Now walk the angels on the walls of heaven,
As sentinels to warn th'immortal souls
To entertain divine Zenocrate:
Apollo, Cynthia, and the ceaseless lamps
That gently look'd upon this loathsome earth,
Shine downwards now no more, but deck the heavens
To entertain divine Zenocrate:
The crystal springs, whose taste illuminates
Refinéd eyes with an eternal sight,
Like triéd silver run through Paradise
To entertain divine Zenocrate:
The cherubims and holy seraphims,
That sing and play before the King of Kings,
Use all their voices and their instruments
To entertain divine Zenocrate;
And, in this sweet and curious harmony,
The god that tunes this music to our souls
Holds out his hand in highest majesty
To entertain divine Zenocrate.
Then let some holy trance convey my thoughts
Up to the palace of th'empyreal heaven,
That this my life may be as short to me
As are the days of sweet Zenocrate. –
Physicians, will no physic do her good?

II Tamburlaine Act II, Sc.4.11.1–38

41

The swift contrasting descent from the sublime to the pathetic query to the physicians is a trick Marlowe developed which is also found in Shakespeare, as here in *King Lear's* powerfully moving heartcry –

> No, no, no life!
> Why should a dog, a horse, a rat have life.
> And thou no breath at all? Thou'lt come no more,
> Never, never, never, never, never.
> Pray you undo this button.
>
> Act V. Sc.1. 11.305–9

While Marlowe knew well the tastes of his fellow countrymen which would make the choice of such a subject as Tamburlaine, whose spectacular success in war was matched by his cruelty, a popular entertainment, he was never satisfied merely to entertain. The Elizabethans were inured to cruelty, bloodshed and death, but when Marlowe paints scenes of human cruelty he does so to evoke a response which finally recoils from this. He does not pander to sadism as, for instance, Nashe does in *The Unfortunate Traveller, Or The Life of Jacke Wilton* (1594). In this Marlowe stands aside from most of his contemporaries. The blood-bath of *Tamburlaine* acts like a powerful cathartic panacea to the soul, for he holds up a cruel conqueror for our admiration only finally to reduce him to a man who is maddened by his bloodlust. A colossus with feet of clay wading in blood, to arouse our pity. The civilizing influence in *Tamburlaine* is the lovely Zenocrate, and when she dies we hear echoes of Othello's forlorn cry –

> But I do love thee; and when I love thee not
> Chaos is come again.
>
> Act III Sc.3. 11.92–3

Othello depends on Desdemona for his sanity: Tamburlaine without Zenocrate is almost a madman. Zenocrate's remorse and pity for the death of the tormented Bajazeth and Zabina invite us to pity, not to gloat. Mycetes expresses the terrors of war feelingly in his outburst –

> Accurs'd be he that first invented war!
> They knew not, ah, they knew not, simple men,
> How those were hit by pelting cannon-shot
> Stand staggering like a quivering aspen-leaf

Fearing the force of Boreas' boisterous blasts!
The First Part of Tamburlaine Act II Sc.4 11.1–5

Mycetes is, of course, not a heroic figure but a weak, effete and cowardly king; but Tamburlaine's war-hating third son Calyphas in *The Second Part of Tamburlaine* is a more complex character, a dissenter against war of courage and conscience who is almost modern. He finds war 'dangerous' yet he is not really a coward – his dislike of warfare is deeply grounded on personal distaste for violence and an intellectual contempt for those who indulge in war. He calls his warlike brothers fools who are 'more childish-valorous than manly-wise' and afraid to be stigmatized as cowards. One of them confesses he is partly motivated by fear of their father's anger should they fail to strive to emulate him in military prowess. 'I would not bide the fury of my father', exclaims Amyras marvelling at Calyphas's foolhardiness. But Calyphas has integrity and a cool courage of his own. He tells his brothers:

> I know, sir, what it is to kill a man;
> It works remorse of conscience in me.
> I take no pleasure to be murderous.
> *II Tamburlaine* Act IV Sc.1 11.27–29

When Celebinus taunts him as a coward who shames their house, Calyphas answers derisively:

> Go, go, tall stripling, fight you for us both,
> And take my other toward brother here,
> For person like to prove a second Mars.
> 11. 33–35

He tells Perdicas, with whom he plays at cards while the battle rages:

> They say I am a coward, Perdicas, and I fear as little their
> taratantaras, their swords, or their cannons as I do a naked
> lady in a net of gold, and, for fear I should be afraid would
> put it off and come to bed with me.
> Act IV Scene 1. 11.66–69

When Tamburlaine returns he is beside himself with rage that Calyphas has not joined the battle and seeks him crying, 'But where's this coward

43

villain, not my son, But traitor to my name and majesty?' Calyphas utters not a word in his self-defence but silently suffers himself to be stabbed to death by his enraged father, like a sacrificial lamb. There is a deeper significance here – even a symbolism, which critics have missed. *Tamburlaine the Great*, the most bloodthirsty of all Marlowe's plays, is not merely about blood and conquest. Like all great works of art it speaks to us at many levels.

We are constantly told that one of Marlowe's main faults is that he cannot create rounded characters in his subordinate parts – a poor judgement which rather evinces lack of imagination or lack of dramatic experience in the critics who state it. The three sons of Tamburlaine are anything but 'bloodless' puppets, and the contrast between the two 'childish-valorous' brothers and the character of Calyphas who defies his father presents a telling foil to the gigantic portrait of Tamburlaine.

The lust for power is man's most heinous and universal sin. It underlies the worst crimes that humanity has committed. Man's cruelty to his fellow man is but a facet of it. From infancy man is born with an over-plus of *will* – the will to have his own way – to dominate others. Infantile tantrums are the first expression of it, and the civilizing process is mainly concerned with subduing this inborn human trait and teaching us to defer to others, and to care for those outside ourselves. A hard lesson to learn. This Marlowe perceived intuitively, and his plays are deeply concerned with the human condition in which the lust for power is such a dominant force creating mayhem and misery. Marlowe is essentially a religious thinker. In his cycle of tragedies featuring a great central character, *Tamburlaine the Great*, *The Jew of Malta*, *Doctor Faustus*, *The Massacre at Paris*, these men epitomize the lust for power in one form or another. They are both superhuman in the intensity of their will and desire, and intensely human. They are not puppets, they are hugely alive – 'giants in crime, in passion, in pomp of utterance, in extravagance of imagination, in the magnificence of their ambitions. Their overmastering emotions are lusts – of wealth, of power, of glory, or knowledge.'[2]

These are all facets of the lust for power, to fulfil the ambitions of infantile self-will, which only the full-grown soul can master. This is the theme of great drama deriving directly from ancient Greek tragedy. Marlowe uses it to hold up the mirror to man's nature. Although he turned aside from the church, the drama had its origin in religious and moral teaching, and he developed this grand tragic theme to the height of his dramatic power to show us characters tainted with *hubris* – and of these *Tamburlaine* is the progenitor.

44

The Westgate, Canterbury.   *Photograph by Tony Whitcomb*

Whilst Marlowe uses the dramatic medium to raise the consciousness of his audiences, he remains ever the complete entertainer – there is no hint of inhibition in his approach to effective theatrical entertainment to draw his audiences in. The huge success of *The First Part of Tamburlaine* clamoured to be matched, and in writing *The Second Part* it seems he had not been able to find anything in his sources so spectacularly cruel as Tamburlaine's treatment of Bajazeth, so he introduced from his own imagination the hanging of the Governor of Babylon in chains on the city walls, where he was shot to death. The origin of this piece of sensational barbarism recalls the experience of Marlowe's boyhood.[3] Elizabethan Canterbury was a city totally environed by its ancient wall, admitting entry only through its six twin-towered gates, and rearing above its

45

ramparts were twenty watch-towers giving it the appearance of a fortified citadel. The massive Westgate, which still stands today, also served as a prison, and when the three gibbets in the city were already occupied with their gruesome burdens, a condemned wretch would be hanged on the wall from the condemned cell on the upper floor of the Westgate prison.

In *The Second Part of Tamburlaine*, following the siege of Babylon – a walled city like Canterbury – Tamburlaine orders the defiant Governor of the city to be shot to death in a spectacular variant of the hanging on the wall that the boy Marlowe might have witnessed at Canterbury's Westgate. When he is condemned, the Governor tries to buy his life by offering to tell Tamburlaine where he has hidden the city's gold, naming the place as 'Against the *western gate* of Babylon'[4] – an autobiographical touch typical of Marlowe – but having disclosed this information Tamburlaine nevertheless has him put to death, so as not to cheat the groundlings of their spectacle, for Alleyn would doubtless have bargained for that!

This incident had catastrophic consequences in a performance of the play reported by Philip Gawdy in a letter to his father written from London on 16th November 1587, which has helped to date the performance of *The Second Part* to no later than early November 1587.[5] In this letter Philip Gawdy describes just such an incident in which a player was shot at in a play being performed by the Lord Admiral's Men, which led to an accident wherein a child and a woman 'great with chyld' were killed when the bullets were mis-aimed and hit the audience, a man also being sorely hurt in the head.[6] The Gawdys were a Norfolk family and fortunately this letter has survived among the family correspondence. There can be no reasonable doubt that the play referred to was Marlowe's *Tamburlaine*, though Philip Gawdy himself had not been present to witness the accident at this performance, and his description suggests that the victim was tied to a stake rather than to the wall, but the circumstances all point to *The Second Part of Tamburlaine* as the play referred to. Seemingly the play was not banned as a result of this catastrophe. The Elizabethans were sanguine about life and death.

People being what they are, this tragic mishap probably only served to increase the fame and popularity of the play. Cruelty was part of Timur's nature, but such spectacular dramatic scenes of cruelty no doubt show Marlowe here deliberately playing to the gallery – and the groundlings – and it was this instinct for showmanship, which he shared with that brilliant showman Edward Alleyn, that gave added impetus to the phenomenal success of *Tamburlaine*. The foregoing incident was sensational enough, one might think, but evidently Alleyn had felt more was required to match, and, if possible, to out-do Bajazeth in his cage. Bakeless has shown that nowhere in any of Marlowe's sources is there a precedent for the most sensational spectacle in the whole of *Tamburlaine*, which Marlowe now introduced in the *Second Part* – the harnessing of Tamburlaine's conquered kings as horses to pull his chariot. This it is which gave the Elizabethans the catch-word that caught their imagination and was repeated again and again in the plays and literature of the next seven decades. Tamburlaine as he whips his 'horses' roars –

> Holla, ye pamper'd Jades of Asia!
> What, can you draw but twenty miles a day?
> Act IV Sc.3 11.1–2

Bakeless himself has given us the clue as to the possible origin of this idea in an unwittingly inspired aside when discussing Marlowe's sources for *Tamburlaine*.

'These books could have given him practically everything...everything except the kings as chariot horses (these appear in no source, and bear all the earmarks of a stage manager's inspiration).'[7]

The stage manager, of course, was none other than Edward Alleyn, who was basking in the sunshine – or rather, the star-shine – of his acclaim as Tamburlaine, and was vitally interested to ensure that the sequel would continue the momentum of success. We can well imagine that in the writing of the *Second Part* there would have been a deal of keen discussion between Marlowe and his actor-manager, for whose acting prowess and expertise in stage-craft he would have had great respect for all his youth. Marlowe had found that the dramatic material in the life of Timur would yield another play, and he probably showed each act newly-written to Alleyn and would have listened to his comments or advice. Taking Bakeless' inspired hint, I believe it was Alleyn who suggested the idea of using the kings as chariot horses, which Marlowe accepted as hilarious! and from his pen flowed the scene depicting the mad charioteer Tamburlaine from whose throat came the bellow which so delighted audiences that it became the most quoted quotation from any play ever written – 'Holla, ye pamper'd Jades of Asia!'

The notion that Marlowe took this spectacle seriously is impossible to credit. It verges on the burlesque which he later used as a foil for tragedy in *The Jew of Malta*, and his larger-than-life hero Tamburlaine, half-crazed after the death of Zenocrate, recalls Herod as a monstrous figure of fun in the mystery plays he had probably seen at Canterbury. Much has been written about Marlowe's 'grim humour' without qualifying what is meant by this. Marlowe's humour is in the same tradition as such popular television and radio shows as Monty Python's Circus, Private Eye, and the Goon Show and its descendants, and much else in British comic entertainment – he has a fine sense of the ludicrous!

Edward Alleyn had had a long experience of acting in the provinces with touring companies whose repertoires included many old-style plays. One of these, written as long ago as 1566 by George Gascoigne, was the tragedy *Jocasta*, translated from an Italian adaptation of Euripedes; a play well suited for acting before provincial audiences by a touring company. There is good reason to believe that Alleyn would have known it; perhaps he even acted the part of Jocasta himself as a transvestite boy-player, as this was a tragic part which would have given him scope as a 'tragedienne'. The play had been originally written for performance at Gray's Inn by Gascoigne and his fellow Grayan, Francis Kinwelmarshe. In the dumb show preceding the play, Gascoigne, who was a bit of a wag, had introduced a chariot drawn by four kings as a symbolic spectacle.

'The argument of the Tragedie' (or prologue) is presented by *Fortunatus Infaelix*. Then follows: 'The order of the dumme shewes and Musicke before every Acte.'

Firste, before the beginning of the first Acte, did sounde a dolefull and straunge noyse of violles, Cythren, Bandurion, and such like, during the whiche there came in uppon the Stage a King with an Imperial crown uppon his head, very richeley apparelled: a Scepter in his righte hande, a Mounde with a Cross in his lefte hande, sitting in a Chariote very richly furnished, drawne in by four Kinges in the Dublettes and Hosen, with Crownes also upon their heades. Representing unto us Ambition, by the historie of Sesostres, *king of* Egypt, *who beeing in his time and reigne a mightie Conquerour, yet not content to have subdued many princes, and taken from them their kingdomes and dominions, did in like maner cause those Kinges whome he had so overcome, to draw in his Chariote like Beastes and Oxen, thereby to content his unbrideled ambitious desire. After he had beene drawne twyce about the Stage, and retyred, the Musicke ceased, and* Jocasta *the Queene issued out of hir house, beginning the first Acte...*[8]

48

The play is written in effective but monotonously regular blank verse when we compare it with Marlowe's, but George Gascoigne was an accomplished poet and in his day a well known literary figure who cut a dash. He was a friend of the youthful Walter Raleigh; a soldier-poet, such a one as Marlowe would have admired, but he was already dead and in his grave ten years before *Tamburlaine* was written. This dumb show is the only precedent known of the use of kings as chariot-horses prior to *Tamburlaine*. Marlowe uses not four kings as horses, but two, keeping the other two captive kings in reserve to replace the original two when they are winded, as Tamburlaine explains to his son, that 'cruel brat' who asks to have a similar coach drawn for him by the spare kings.

> *Amyras.* Let me have coach, my lord, that I may ride,
> And thus be drawn by these two idle kings.
> *Tamburlaine.* Thy youth forbids such ease, my kingly boy:
> They shall to-morrow draw my chariot,
> While these their fellow-kings may be refresh'd.
>
> Act IV Sc.3 11.27–31

The stage direction at the beginning of the scene reads:

> *Enter* Tamburlaine, *drawn in his chariot by the* Kings of Trebizon *and* Soria, *with bits in their mouths, reins in his left hand, and in his right hand a whip with which he scourgeth them.*

This episode made such an impression – and, as was surely intended by Marlowe, was greeted as hilarious entertainment – that it set a fashion. The numerous quotations in plays of the succeeding decades assume that audiences know exactly what is being referred to. It became the longest running in-joke of the theatre ever written!

If imitation is the sincerest form of flattery, both Marlowe and Alleyn must have been delighted at the way in which dramatists seized upon the most spectacular scenes in *Tamburlaine* blatantly to imitate them. Thomas Lodge lost no time in reproducing Tamburlaine's coach-horses to present these as sheer triumphant theatrical spectacle in his tragedy *The Wovnds of Ciuill War*, published in 1594, hence obviously on the boards long before that date, which was also performed by the Lord Admiral's Servants, probably with Edward Alleyn in the role of Scilla.

Actus tertius
Enter Scilla *in triumph in his chare triumphant of gold, drawen by four Moores, before the chariot: his colours, his crest, his*

captaines, his prisoners: Arcathius, Mithridates *son,* Aristion,
Archelaus, *bearing crownes of gold, and manacled. After the
chariot, his soldiers bands,* Basillus, Lucretius, Lucullus:
besides prisoners of diuers Nations, and sundry disguises.

> *Scilla.* You men of Rome, my fellow mates in Armes,
> Whose three yeares prowesse, pollicie, and warre,
> One hundreth three score thousand men at Armes
> Hath ouerthrowne and murthered in the field:
> Whose valours to the Empire hath restorde,
> All Grecia, Asia, and Ionia.

Lodge is obviously making a bid to emulate the triumph of *Tamburlaine,*
choosing a Roman general with a reputation for ruthlessness.

> *Scilla.* Tut my *Lucretius,* fortunes ball is tost,
> To forme the storie of my fatall powre:
> Rome shall repent, babe, mother, shall repent,
> Aire weeping clowdie sorrowes shall repent,
> Wind breathing many sighings shall repent,
> To see those stormes concealed in my brest,
> Reflect the hideous flames of their vnrest:[9]

Lodge's blank verse is no match for Marlowe's mightly line, but he
goes one better in his stage business with four moors to drag his chariot
instead of two kings, thus harking back to the four in *Jocasta,* the play
from which Alleyn, I believe, rather than Marlowe lifted the idea. After
Tamburlaine took London by storm, the immediate imitations spawned
were the outrightly plagiaristic Greene's *Alphonsus,* Lodge's *Wounds of
Civil War* and the anonymous play *The Wars of Cyrus,* but of the extant
plays written in the early 1590s there is hardly one which does not contain
some reference to *Tamburlaine*; among these, the anonymous *George a
Green, Soliman and Perseda* and *The Troublesome Reign of King John.*[10]
Selimus has this passage in dreary, uninspired blank verse:

> For Fortune never shew'd herself so cross
> To any prince as to poor Bajazet,
> That woeful emperor first of my name,
> Whom the Tartarians locked in a cage
> To be a spectacle to all the world,

Tamburlaine.   Holla, ye pampered jades of Asia!
What! can ye draw but twenty miles a day,
And have so proud a chariot at your heels,
And such a coachman as great Tamburlaine,
But from Asphaltis, where I conquer'd you,
To Byron here, where thus I honour you?
The horses that guide the golden eye of heaven,
And blow the morning from their nostrils,
Making their fiery gate above the clouds,
Are not so honoured in their governor
As you, ye slaves, in mighty Tamburlaine.

II Tamburlaine Act IV, Sc.3 11.1–11

Photograph by Nobby Clark for the National Theatre production of
both parts of **Tamburlaine the Great**, *1976, directed by Sir Peter Hall.*

Was ten times happier than I am.
For Tamburlaine the scourge of nations,
Was he that pull'd him from his kingdom so;
But mine own sons expel me from the throne;[11]

We see in these excerpts how far superior Marlowe's poetic and dramatic gifts are. Peele's *The Battle of Alcazar* (played 1591 or before, printed 1594) is shot through with the influence of *Tamburlaine* and directly invokes him:

> Conuey *Tamberlaine* into our Affrike here,
> To chastice and to menace lawfull kings,
> *Tamberlaine* triumph not, for Thou must die.[12]

The impact Alleyn made in the title role also doubtless contributed to this constant recollection of the play. As Tucker Brooke has commented: 'The tremendous figure which Alleyn made when he played the title-role was long remembered. The *Black Book's* comparison (1604) of the spindle-shank spiders stalking over Nashe's head "as if they had been conning of *Tamburlaine*" is pictorial enough.'[13]

Thomas Dekker, who was Alleyn's friend, furnished a steady flow of plays for Alleyn's new theatre, the Fortune, as from 1600 when it opened, and he never lets *Tamburlaine* alone. In his *Old Fortunatus* he seems intent on flattering Alleyn with a remembrance of his most famous role upon his return to the stage after his first early retirement to play again on his own boards. Here Old Fortunatus, having lost his way, has fallen asleep and is awakened by a vision of the goddess Fortune.

(Enter) Fortune. *After her, four* Kings *with broken crowns and sceptres, chained in silver gyves and led by her. The foremost enter singing.* Fortune *takes her chair, the* Kings *lying at her feet so that she treads on them as she ascends to her seat.*

> *Presently* Fortunatus *wakes:*
> Oh, how am I transported? Is this earth?
> Or blest Elysium?
> *Fortune*: Fortunatus, rise.
> .....
> Thou canst not stir, unless I be thy guide.

I the world's empress am, Fortune my name.
.....
Thou shalt be one of Fortune's minions:
Behold these four chained like Tartarian slaves,
These I created emperors and kings,
And these are now by basest underlings:
This sometime was a German emperor,
Henry the Fifth, who being first deposed,
Was after thrust into a dungeon,
And thus in silver chains shall rot to death.
This Frederick Barbarossa, Emperor
Of Almaine once: but by Pope Alexander
Now spurned and trod on when he takes his horse,
And in these fetters shall he die his slave.
This wretch once wore the diadem of France,
Lewis the meek, but through his children's pride,
Thus have I caused him to be famished.
Here stands the very soul of misery,
Poor Bajazet, old Turkish Emperor,
And once the greatest monarch in the East;
Fortune herself is said to view thy fall,
And grieves to see thee glad to lick up crumbs
At the proud feet of that great Scythian swain,
Fortune's best minion, warlike Tamburlaine:
Yet must thou in a cage of iron be drawn
In triumph at his heels, and there in grief
Dash out thy brains.

                                        Act I, Sc.1.

Dekker's *Shoemaker's Holiday* (1594) also refers to *Tamburlaine* in
Act V, iv, and when he joined with John Marston to write *Satiromastix*
(1602), in the full flood of the war of the theatres, they parody Marlowe's
theatrical triumph with gusto:

Dost stampe, mad *Tamburlaine*, dost stampe?[14]

and they make fun of Tamburlaine's 'bloody flag'

What, dost thou summon a parlie, my little drumsticke?
'tis too late; thou seest my red flag is hung out.[15]

For inevitably the caricaturists took over, and the 'Jades of Asia' and innumerable references to *Tamburlaine* in this vein of satirical comedy recur throughout the prolific drama of the period for the next seventy years! There is no reason to suppose that Marlowe would have resented the imitation of his work or the numerous parodies which drew gales of laughter from successive audiences. There is nothing to suggest that he took himself and his dramatic successes that seriously. As a noted wit, Marlowe certainly possessed a lively sense of humour and delighted in the ridiculous. Shakespeare's recollection by his swash-buckling Pistol felicitously captures exactly this sense of the ridiculous:

> These be good humours indeed! Shall pack-horses
> And hollow pamper'd jades of Asia,
> Which cannot go but thirty mile a-day,
> Compare with Caesars, and with Cannibals,
> And Trojan Greeks?[16]

Day and Chettle enhance their comical scene in *The Blind Beggar of Bednall Green* (1600) by parodying *Tamburlaine* when the braggadoccio Swash is invited to watch a fight between the protagonists Tamberlayn the Great and the Duke of Guyso, and Swash in his excitement exclaims:

> I'll murther your *Tamberlayn* and his Coach-horses![17]

Marston's historical drama *Antonio and Mellida* (1602) pokes fun with –

> Rampum scrampum, mount tuftie *Tamburlaine*!
> What rattling thunderclappe breakes from his lips?[18]

After the war of the theatres, once more reconciled with Ben Jonson, in collaboration with Chapman, they wrote the delightful *Eastward Hoe* (1605) in which Quicksilver appears 'unlac'd, a towell about his necke, in his flat Cap, drunke', and cries:

> Eastward Hoe; *Holla ye pampered Iades of Asia*;[19]

Samuel Rowlands in *The Life and Death of John Leyden* (1605) capitalized on his audiences' recollection of what was one of their greatest theatrical experiences:
> Haue you not heard that *Scythian Tamburlaine*

Was earst a Sheepheard ere he play'd the King?
First ouer Cattell hee began his raigne,
Then Countries in subiection hee did bring:
And Fortunes fauours so mayntain'd his side,
Kings were his Coach-horse when he pleas'd to ride.[20]

Edward Sharpham's *The Fleire* (1607) blatantly quotes the famous lines:

Holla, holla ye pampred Iades of Asia,
And can you draw but twentie miles a day?[21]

Beaumont and Fletcher in *The Coxcomb* (1612) are still parodying
Tamburlaine with delight –

Weehee, My pamper'd jade of Asia[22]

and in *Women Pleased* (1620) the joke is not played out yet – with a slight
variant:

Away, thou pamper'd jade of vanity.[23]

Massinger's *Believe as You List* (1631) has a character who is a crazy
priest with Tamberlainesque ambitions:

Then by the senators, whom I'll use as horses,
I will be drawn in a chariot...
Our enemy, led like a dog in chain,
As I descend or reascend in state,
Shall serve for my footstool.[24]

John Ford in *Love's Sacrifice* (1633) recalls Tamburlaine's triumphant
march in a comical context:

Thus do we march to honour's haven of bliss,
To ride in triumph through *Persepolis*.[25]

William Rowley in *A New Wonder* (1632) colours his scene with the
familiar imagery:

A noyse above at Cards
How now, how now, my roaring *Tamberlaine*,
Take heede, the Soldan comes.[26]

And John Cooke's play *Greene's Tu Quoque* (1614) has the telling comment –

'S foot, she plays the terrible, tyrannising *Tamburlaine* over him.[27]

In Prynne's *Histriomastix* (1632) this Puritan writer attacks stage plays in a scene in which the soldiers capture a player and he is commanded:

Look up, and play the *Tamburlaine*, you rogue you.[28]

Ford and Dekker in *The Sun's Darling*, which was certainly written before 1630 but printed as late as 1657, hark back to *Tamburlaine* with –

I sweat like a pamper'd jade of Asia,
and drop like a Cob-nut of *Africa*.[29]

In his *Maid of Honour* (1627) Massinger parodies prettily in a scene featuring a boy playing a page –

Page   Do it, and neatly,
Or, having first tripped up thy heels, I'll make
Thy back my footstool.
Sylli. Tamburlaine in little!
Am I turned Turk? What an office am I put to![30]

Habington's *Queen of Aragon* (1640) is evidently assured of a response in his audience when his queen recalls:

An emperor did serve
As footstool to the conqueror, and are we
Better assur'd of destiny?[31]

Marlowe had no idea what a gift he was giving to his successors in the drama. These constant allusions to his works, which did not stop at *Tamburlaine* but also apply to *Faustus* and *The Jew of Malta*, testify to his enormous influence.

Cowley's play *The Guardian* which was acted before Prince Charles at Cambridge in 1641 makes use of the perennial allusion –

Blade. First, leave your raging, Sir: for though you should roar like *Tamerlin* at the Bull, 'twould do no good with me.

Truman. I *Tamerlin?* I scorn him, as much as you do,
for your ears. I have an action of slander against you,
Captain; you shall not miscal me at your pleasure...
.....
Truman. Well, Sir! I'm not angry; but I'll not be call'd
      Tamerlin by any man.[32]

In 1648, the year of the outbreak of the civil war, appeared Sir John
Suckling's *The Goblins* in which he brings the author of *Tamburlaine* on
the stage:

      Enter Poet and Theeves
Devil. O, they have fetcht him off.
Poet. Carer er so lo carer,
Or he that made the fairie Queene.
1 Thief. No, none of these:
They are by themselves in some other place;
But here's he that writ *Tamberlane.*
Poet. I beseech you bring me to him,
There's something in his Scene
Betwixt the Empresses a little high and clowdie,
I would resolve my selfe.
1 Thief. You shall Sir.
Let me see – the Author of the *bold Beauchams,*
And *Englands Joy.*
Poet. The last was a well writ piece, I assure you,
A Brittane I take it; and Shakespeares very way;
I desire to see the man.[33]

In the comedy written by the first Duke of Newcastle, *The Variety*
(1649) the theatrical allusion is still going strong:

the horses will runne as the devill were in the poope,
for he drives like a *Tamberlaine.*[34]

Outside the theatres writers also resorted to *Tamburlaine.* Both Nashe
and Greene used allusions to Marlowe's play apart from their jibes at him
or Alleyn, as did Gabriel Harvey. Sir William Alexander, Lord Stirling,
the Scottish poet, in his long poem *Doomsday* (1637) introduces the
famous theme –

And *Tamberlaine*, the terrour of that age,
On lightning *Baiazet* did thundering light,
Tam'd for a foot-stoole in an iron cage.[35]

The Water Poet, John Taylor, fulminated against the London coaches drawn by Belgian horses which offered competition to his transport by water: 'I was but little inferiour to *Tamburlaine*, being iolted thus in state by those pampred Iades of *Belgia*',[36] and expresses his disapproval in rhyme:

And fulsome Madams, and new scuruy Squires,
Should iolt the streets in pomp, at their desires,
Like great triumphant *Tamburlaines*, each day
Drawn with the pamper'd Iades of *Belgia*.[37]

Even this does not exhaust the recollections in the literature of the time which drew inspiration in one way or another from Marlowe's *Tamburlaine*.

Marlowe's Contemporary Critics

Brilliance, alas, all too often excites envy. Among the University Wits was one who harboured virulent envy towards all who succeeded better than he himself in the literary arena – Robert Greene, who was also an unabashed plagiarist of any successful work that appeared. Several plays written in direct imitation of *Tamburlaine* followed hard upon the first performances by Alleyn and the Lord Admiral's Men, for the writers of the time were quick to learn. But the closest imitation came from the pen of Robert Greene, whose *Alphonsus, King of Aragon* must have been written hot upon the appearance of *The First Part of Tamburlaine the Great*. Greene never believed in letting any grass grow under his feet where there was an opportunity to score in literary one-up-manship. By 1587 he was already a well established writer of romantic fiction, but was a newcomer to dramatic writing when Marlowe came to London, and he was therefore especially keen to make his mark as a dramatist, equal to Marlowe if not beyond him.

Storojenko and Bakeless have done impressive work in demonstrating the extent and almost identical approximation of Greene's script and story-line, scene by scene, with Marlowe's play.[38] In addition the number of outright plagiaristic passages in a near-Marlovian blank verse contained in *Alphonsus* when compared with *Tamburlaine* leaves no doubt that Greene was modelling his play consciously on Marlowe's work, hoping to reap a similar success. Lodge, who later collaborated with Greene in writing *A Looking-Glass for London* before setting off on his island voyages, was doing the same. Everyone was at it. But it was the obvious identification of Greene's *Alphonsus* with *Tamburlaine* in almost every particular that made him a ready target for criticism, for there existed a lively critical theatre audience with newly sharpened tastes. Inevitably odious comparisons were drawn.

Despite his strenuous attempt to emulate Marlowe's martial vein, Greene's *Alphonsus, King of Aragon*, proved – oh chagrin! – not a 'hit' but a 'flop'. Neither the subject nor the style of dramatic composition featuring one dominating heroic character was suited to Greene's lighter talents. He was a clever writer of light romances and pastorals, but he had chosen the wrong model for his individual talents. It was a lesson he was never to learn, for whenever a great success was scored by one of his rival dramatists (and Greene was no born dramatist), whether the theme was suited to his pen or not, he could never resist rushing into the field with his imitation of the same model.

He took his failure over *Alphonsus* hard, with petulant moans in print in his frame-work tales, *Perimedes the Blacksmith*, published in 1588, which he prefaced with an expression of his sour grapes over Marlowe's success in his Letter to the Gentlemen Readers.

[Greene's *Alphonsus* lampooned in a play comparing his failure with the great success of *Tamburlaine*.]

'I keepe my old course, to palter vp something in Prose, vsing mine old poesie still, *Omne tulet punctum*,* although latelye two Gentlemen Poets, made too mad men of Rome beate it out of their paper bucklers: & had it in derision, for that I could not make my verses iet vpon the stage in tragicall buskins, eurie word filling the mouth like the faburden of Bo-Bell, daring God out of heauen with that Atheist *Tamburlan*, or blaspheming with the mad preest of the sonne: but let me rather openly pocket vp the Asse at *Diogenes* hand, then wantonlye set out such impious instances of intollerable poetrie, such mad and scoffing poets, that haue propheticall spirits, as bred of *Merlins* race, if there be anye in England that set the end of scollarisme in an English

---

* *Omne tulit punctum* – He has won every point (From Horace's *Ars Poetica*)

blanck verse, thinke either it is the humor of a nouice that tickles them with self-loue, or to much frequenting the hot-house..If I speake darkely Gentlemen, and offend with this digression, I craue pardon, in that I but answere in print, what they haue offered on the Stage: but leauing these phantasticall schollers..at last to *Perymedes the Black Smith*, who sitting in his holi-dai-sute,to enter parlee with his wif, smugd vp in her best apparrell, I present to your fauors.'[39]

Greene is at his best as a story-teller. He gives his *Preface to the Gentlemen Readers* a sweet beginning and ending, a dainty sandwich with a dash of what Nashe would call 'mustard-pot paper' in the middle, to open his newest novel whereby he aims to recoup his blemished reputation after the failure of *Alphonsus*, which had evidently been lampooned in a play (probably at Cambridge where both he and Marlowe were known). Not content to leave it at that, he next engaged the helping hand of his young friend, that 'byting Satirist' Tom Nashe, when he shortly arrived to take up a literary career in London. Nashe was nothing loathe to accept the task to write a prefatory letter for Greene's next novel *Menaphon, Camillas Alarum to slumbering Euphues in his melancholie Cell at Silexedra* which appeared in 1589, in which Nashe had evidently been commissioned to attack Marlowe in his best satirical style. Nashe rose to his assignment with typical gusto, lashing out in a spirited double-barrelled attack against both the actor and the author of *Tamburlaine*, whose joint success had so bested Greene.

'I am not ignorant how eloquent our gowned age is growen of late; so that euerie mœchanicall mate abhorres the english he was borne too, and plucks, with a solemne periphrasis, his *ut vales** from the inkhorne; which I impute not so much to the perfection of arts, as to the seruile imitation of [Edward vainglorious tragœdians, who contend not so seriouslie to Alleyn] excell in action, as to embowell the clowdes in a speach of comparison; thinking themselues more than initiated in Poets immortalitie, if they but once get *Boreas* by the beard, and the heauenlie bull by the deaw-lap. But herein I cannot so fully bequeath them to follie, as their idiote art-masters, that [Marlowe] intrude thēselues to our eares as the alcumists of eloquence;

---

* *Ut vales* – How are you? (Colloquial)

who (moūted on the stage of arrogance) think to outbraue better pens with the swelling bumbast of a bragging blanke verse. Indeed it may be the ingrafted ouerflow of some kilcow conceipt, that ouerclo̅ieth their imagination with a more than drunken resolution, beeing not extemporall in the inuention of anie other meanes to vent their manhood, commits the digestion of their cholerick incumbrances, to the spacious volubilitie of a drumming decasillabon. Mongst this kinde of men that repose eternitie in the mouth of a player, I can but ingrosse some deepe read Grammarians, who, hauing no more learning in their scull, than will serue to take vp a commoditie; nor Arte in their brain, than was nourished in a seruing mans idlenesse, will take vpon them to be the ironicall censors of all, when God and Poetrie doth know, they are the simplest of all. To leaue these to the mercie of their mother tongue, that feed on nought but the crummes that fal from the translators trencher, I come (sweet friend) to thy *Arcadian Menaphon;*'[40]

[Cambridge scholars who wrote satirizing Greene's *Alphonsus*]

No one (to my knowledge) has ever read this passage as referring to *both* Edward Alleyn (the vainglorious tragedian) who played Tamburlaine and was catapulted to fame in the role, and Marlowe (the idiot art-master) who wrote the play. Having dealt with them, Nashe turns to jeer at some university men who have written a college play making fun of Greene for his inability to make his 'verses iet vpon the stage in tragicall buskins, euerie word filling the mouth like the faburden of Bo-bell; daring God out of heauen with that Atheist *Tamburlan*', as he had protested in *Perimedes the Black Smith*. There can be no doubt that Nashe's brief had been to use his gift of satire to spike Greene's rivals and critics. That Greene hated Alleyn is clear from his many attacks on this great 'Roscius' of the Elizabethan stage, and he would certainly not have wished Nashe to leave him out!

Some critics profess that Nashe's satirically witty passage is too obscure to be understood by us latter-day speakers of the English language, but in this instance he is surely unambiguous. Greene later referred to Marlowe as 'thou famous gracer of Tragedians' (in his *Groatsworth of Wit* Letter), the 'Tragedians' being the actors for whom he wrote his tragic roles, while he, Marlowe, is their 'gracer'. In the above, Nashe's reference to 'vainglorious tragoedians' who 'excell in action' (i.e. acting) and 'embowell the clowdes in a speach of comparison' thereby partaking of the immortality of the poets whose works they perform, makes it clear that a great actor is thus described. Greene's constant criticism of Alleyn was that he was too proud (vainglorious) and assumed fine airs, whereas he owed all his fame to the playwrights who provided him with superb dramatic texts, and these were poorly paid for their artistic works. It was a sore point with Greene to the end of his life, and he never missed an opportunity to berate Alleyn for his conceit and pride.

It is plain that Nashe, having dealt with the 'vainglorious tragoedians', is then turning his barbed pen in another direction: 'But herein I cannot so fully bequeath them to follie, as their idiote art-masters' (i.e. Christopher Marlowe, M.A.) who wrote this play full of 'the bumbast of a bragging blanke verse'. Putting 'tragoedians' and 'art-masters' into the plural is merely a convention. There can be no doubt that Nashe is directing his satire at one particular person in each of these categories, and that his readers would know perfectly well to whom he was referring.

In delegating to Nashe the task of lambasting Alleyn and Marlowe in print, Greene had engaged a sparkling young satirist, who makes an equally scathing demolition of Kyd for his popular *Spanish Tragedy* and for his early play on *Hamlet* featuring a ghost. His employment in this assignment is to give a puff to his friend's new romance *Menaphon*, and he does this in an incisive critique of contemporary authors ending with his commendation of Greene's prose as a perfect model of good style. In truth, much of *Menaphon* was culled from Lyly's *Euphues*, which had set a high fashion at Court; but no matter, for in this instance Greene had chosen a suitable model which he emulated successfully adding much charm of his own.

Today Greene's *Menaphon* holds little interest, and its sole claim to fame is for Nashe's preface in which this 'brave Columbus of tearmes' (as Gabriel Harvey called him for his invention of words ending in -ize with which he enriched the language)[41] sounds off against both the famous author and actor of *Tamburlaine*. Nashe is often brilliantly inventive and highly diverting in his satirical quips and cranks, but he is so enamoured of his own cleverness that he loses control and becomes wearisome in his endless play on variations on the same theme, and in his juggling with words he does sometimes become obscure. These are typical Elizabethan failings.

In this exuberant literary age, when the exciting opportunities opened up by the printed word with its enticement to achieve immortal posterity in print dazzled men, they all aspired to become poets and writers, tumbling words onto the page in prose and poetry – admiring, criticising, improving, discussing and eagerly reading each other's efforts, and so carried away that they were reluctant to expunge a word. Kipling's blessed Blue Pencil was unknown and would have been unwelcome, for they were in-love with words and wallowed in their own prolixity.

By comparison with most Elizabethan writers Marlowe is superb in his clarity and precision of expression, and his economy of writing. His high astounding terms and soaring flights of poetry are disciplined by a mind that is discerning and essentially rational. Underlying all the virtuosity of his dramatic writing is a refinement and a discriminating restraint in the use of learned allusions that is rare for the Elizabethan age – especially in a university man. For Marlowe, although highly educated, was himself of common stock and he wanted to be understood by common men and women, as well as by those blessed with education from whom he could expect a finer appreciation. Compared with Nashe, or Greene or Gabriel Harvey, who love to parade their classical learning, and are all notable critics of Marlowe for his 'pride' and for the extravagance of his bombastic verse, it is Marlowe who is the least conceited. Paradoxically, it is Marlowe who shows the true humility of the artist in his dedication to perfection to the point of restraint. Compared to these and most of his contemporary writers, Marlowe's clarity and self-discipline in his writing show his innate sensitivity to the reaction of his listeners. He did not deluge his audiences with the self-indulgence of wordy, over-long speeches requiring severe pruning, because his instinct was to write in order to create *drama* and dramatic impact; his purpose, not to show off his cleverness and learning, but to entertain and to move his audiences emotionally. This he has achieved even in presenting to us such an unlikely character with whom to identify as Tamburlaine.

Greene, who was Marlowe's severest and most persistent critic, yet hastened to imitate him, doubtless sensing his quality. Algernon Charles Swinburne, that ardent Victorian protagonist of Marlowe's genius, in assessing Greene's *Alphonsus* called it a 'feeble and futile essay in hopeless and heartless imitation... bloody, very wordy, very vehement', but 'spiritless and passionless'.[42] He was even more scathing about Lodge's strenuous, imitative effort in *The Wounds of Civil War*, describing it as 'lamentable...its dulness is dense and malarious'.[43] Comparing Marlowe with his contemporary dramatists, Greene, Lodge and Peele, he declares: 'Marlowe differs from such people, not in degree, but in kind; not as an eagle differs from wrens and titmice, but as an eagle differs from frogs and tadpoles.' And he adds the percipient observation: 'Among all English poets he was the first full-grown man.'[44]

This despite his immaturity. For in all his dramatic works, this yet unfinished genius, whose plays have come down to us for the most part mutilated, truncated or altered by other hands, has unfailingly given us drama full of vitality and human passion, clothed in a divinely musical poetic form. *Tamburlaine* is conceived in beautiful poetry, even if much of it is what the critics are pleased to call 'rant', it is magnificent rant. If the play is blood-thirsty and full of cruelty, so was its original, Timurlane, and Marlowe is seeking to give us a portrait of that extraordinary character. He succeeded with universal acclaim. His characterization and the style he consciously created to express this more than life-size personality is, in fact, dramatically nothing less than brilliant, and shows what an innate dramatist Marlowe was from the first. *Tamburlaine the Great* is a truly remarkable and unique masterpiece. A young man's creation for all time.

Greene's and Nashe's jeers and jibes at the 'famous gracer of Tragedians' who had risen in their midst, were but signs of their own impotence to match him. Undeterred by these flea bites, Marlowe and Alleyn continued their joint success. Alleyn adding further Marlovian roles to become identified with his name, notably the title roles of two plays of utterly different theme and style which shortly came from Marlowe's pen, *The Jew of Malta* and *Doctor Faustus*, which each augmented the triumph of 'Tamburlaine', dramatist and actor.

III *An 'Armada' English History Play*

FOLLOWING HIS OUTSTANDING success with his two plays on Turkish history, the Two Parts of *Tamburlaine the Great*, Marlowe turned to the dramatization of English history. The very next play that he probably wrote after *Tamburlaine*, as is deduceable from its certain date of composition, was his first English history play *Edward the Third*, which I have critically examined in depth in my *Christopher Marlowe and the Armada*. There is the strongest evidence that it is from Marlowe's hand and his alone.

To date there has never been agreement about its authorial attribution among those who purport to have studied this play, which has mainly been somewhat superficial; nor have any of these scholars noticed that the play is the unnamed author's celebration of the victory over the Armada – a fact which is undeniably established by the text, most particularly by the speeches of the French Mariner, beginning with his announcement of the sighting of –

> The proud Armado of King Edward's ships
> . . . .
> Majestical the order of their course,
> Figuring the hornéd circle of the moon:
>> Act II, Sc.3. 11.64–72

This would immediately have alerted his Elizabethan audiences to what was in store, though it seems unaccountably to have passed his modern critics by unremarked. Unremarked also is the Mariner's long speech describing the battle of Sluys, which is deliberately couched entirely in terms of the Armada campaign, fought with cannon and gunfire and describing actual incidents that occurred during the naval campaign of 1588 in which Christopher Marlowe himself had participated.

My research establishing this, presented in my Armada study referred to above, I repeat here because this play is of enormous significance in Marlowe's early development as a dramatist. This, his first English history play, was enthusiastically acclaimed by Elizabethan audiences and especially drew the envious taunts of Greene and Nashe, which reflect the enduring success of the Marlowe-Alleyn theatrical partnership, for the young Alleyn's performance as the Black Prince – a tremendously popular, historical, hero-figure in Elizabethan times – won the hearts of his audiences and riled Greene to renew his attack on him, and fortuitously thereby to cast light on the authorship of the play.

Although not the greatest of Marlowe's plays, it is not surprising that *Edward the Third* was tremendously popular in his day; written in celebration of the momentous victory over the Spanish Armada it seized the popular imagination and proved to be another trend-setter even out-doing *Tamburlaine* in its far-reaching influence on English dramatic writing, for it launched the prolific spate of English history plays that flowed from the pens of his contemporary dramatists from 1588 onwards. The prefatory essay, 'Mirror of Kingship' in the Folger Library's edition of *Henry the Fifth*, which is the Shakespearean companion piece to Marlowe's *Edward the Third* just as *Richard II* is the companion piece to *Edward the Second*, presents the impressive data relevant to this striking development in English drama:

'The reign of Elizabeth, especially the last two decades, saw an enormous interest in history and in historical plays. Felix Schelling, in his history of Elizabethan drama, has estimated that something like 220 plays during the Elizabethan period were drawn from the chronicles of British history, and that approximately half of these plays have survived. From 1588 to 1606, "more than a fifth of all contemporary plays" had for their themes some episode of British history. King John appeared in at least six plays, Henry V and Edward III in seven, Richard III in eight, and Henry VI was a character in at least ten. Of Shakespeare's plays, thirteen, or about one-third, used British history, or legend that passed for history, as their theme. The appetite for historical reading matter was enormous and the greatest poets and writers set out to satisfy this interest.'[1]

Note the delimiting dates that Schelling gives – 1588 to 1606! As I shall show, the stimulus for this tremendous production of historical dramatic writing came once again from the rare, innovative genius of Christopher Marlowe whose pen set the fashion for dramatic writing. Not for nothing has he been named the 'Morning Star' of the greatest period of dramatic writing this country has ever known. His personal commemo-ration of the victorious naval campaign of 1588 fired the imagination of his audiences and engendered ambition in his contemporary dramatists to emulate him in the dramatization of their history, for with this play he showed them the way by turning to Holinshed's *Chronicles* for his source. His inspiration was doubtless also his own love of history nurtured in him by his Canterbury upbringing and his education under the *aegis* of the great Cathedral in an environment steeped in history where, as a boy, he would daily have seen the tomb of the Black Prince, his armoured figure lying under the magnificent canopy near the choir where the choristers sang.

It is of unusual fascination that this play was born out of the author's personal experience of a great event in English history to which the young Marlowe, aged twenty-four, responded with patriotic ardour that found expression in writing this historical drama. Following the defeat of the Spanish Armada in the late summer of 1588, which was sealed by the last battle fought off Gravelines on Monday 29th July (Old Style) or 8th August (New Style calendar as used by Spain and the Continent) when the 'Invincible Armada' took its final pounding from the English guns and fled into the inhospitable waters of the North Sea, the mood in London, indeed in all England and the Protestant world, must have been one of euphoria and tremendous relief.

Lord Admiral Howard, conscious that the dreadful weather and the hand of a merciful Deity had aided their own gallant efforts against so formidable a foe, added a plea in his last letter to Walsingham written aboard the *Ark* as they were pursuing the fleeing Spanish fleet through appalling storms: 'Sir, I pray to God that we may be all thankful to God for it; and that it may be done by some order, that the world may know we are thankful to him for it.'[2]

The Queen would not have needed prompting. She ordered that 19th November be kept as a day of national prayer throughout the kingdom in thanksgiving to God for their deliverance from the Spaniards, and in London there was held a special royal thanksgiving service in St Paul's Cathedral on 24th November attended by the Queen and all her Court. Doubtless Marlowe would have been there too if he had been in London. It is even more likely that he would have been present at the great thanksgiving service in Canterbury Cathedral on the day of national prayer, 19th November, for it would have been the natural thing for him to have gone home to the bosom of his family for a spell of recuperation and his mother's good home-cooking following the severe privations of the Armada campaign, when finally food became pitifully short in supply and the beer turned sour, and many who had survived the dangers of battle succumbed to the dreaded ship's fever.

During that autumn of 1588, in the atmosphere of national thanksgiving for dangers overpassed, combined with exuberant rejoicing in taverns and on the streets with bonfires and fireworks, Christopher Marlowe was writing a play which was his personal tribute in celebration of this great victory over King Philip of Spain's 'felicissima armada'. His patriotic thoughts were drawn to the familiar and revered figure of that famous English prince named 'the soul of chivalry', Edward the Black Prince, whose magnificent tomb graces the South aisle of Canterbury Cathedral's choir, which would have been a favourite spot attracting the boy Christopher's steps in his daily passage through the Cathedral to the King's School, perhaps pausing there to dream, his imagination stirred by the gilded effigy lying cross-legged in his armour, above which were displayed his 'achievements' – the tabard, helmet and gauntlets he wore in battle, and his armorial shield. The boy's education at King's under such an ardent historian and bibliophile as Dr John Gresshop, the headmaster, would have taught him the historic exploits of the heroic Black Prince, which were stirring features of the reign of his father, King Edward III, the accredited chief founder of the English navy, whose memorable military campaign in France was preceded by the total destruction of the French navy at the great naval victory of Sluys in 1340.

This naval victory presented a marvellously apt analogy with the victory over the Spanish Armada. The reign of Edward III was an inspired choice for his play. These two, the warlike and romantic Edward III and his heroic and popular son, the Black Prince, he would make joint heroes of his drama. After the important initial naval victory over the French, the invasion of France by King Edward to claim the French throne by descent through his mother developed into one of the most brilliant military campaigns of English history, famous for the battles of Crecy and Poitiers, in which the heroic exploits of the Black Prince contributed to the snatching of amazing victories against tremendous odds. This presented aspects of warfare that provided inherent dramatic possibilities for his pupil pen.

Thus the first English history play was conceived – a deliberate choice by the dramatist – as his patriotic celebration of the great English victory over the Spanish navy. He would make use of the historic parallel by cleverly transforming the speeches ostensibly describing the decisive naval battle of Sluys in 1340 to reflect the recent great naval battles of 1588, bringing in details from his *own* experience during the campaign against the Armada which were yet fresh in his recollection.

My research has revealed that whoever wrote this apocryphal play wrote it out of his personal experience having taken part in that momentous naval campaign. For instance, the only ship named in the play is the

The Tomb of the Black Prince.
Photograph by Tony Whitcomb
Courtesy of the Dean and Chapter of Canturbury Cathedral.

Nonpareille which was the flagship of Drake's second-in-command, Thomas Fenner, whose letters prove that he had been engaged in gathering intelligence at sea in the period prior to the arrival of the Armada in English waters. Only two days before the sighting of the Spanish fleet Fenner had been instructed 'upon the sudden' to repair to the coast of Brittany. This last minute assignation could only have been to pick up espionage agents, or a special agent who was returning bearing intelligence from France. The evidence all points to this having been Marlowe, who was one of Sir Francis Walsingham's and Lord Burghley's most trusted agents, who had been operating in France there to ascertain whether the French supporters of the Holy League were organizing military assistance for King Philip's 'Great Enterprise'. Fortunately, the French were too embroiled in their internal troubles to be able to offer such help.

The research for this, which can only be briefly reviewed here, concerns the twelve-folio manuscript in the British Museum's Cotton MSS Julius F.X. ff. 95–101, which is a first-hand report on the entire Armada campaign, written by someone who was an observer and participant with the English navy, as is made clear by the reporter's use of the personal pronouns 'we' and 'us' when reporting 'accidents' of the naval war in the campaign, in which are included details found nowhere else in the documents, letters and 'able minutes' despatched to Walsingham from aboard the ships of Her Majesty's navy, or subsequently written. We now know that this report was commissioned by Lord Admiral Howard for presentation to Sir Francis Walsingham, who was Marlowe's boss to whom Marlowe regularly reported as an agent. The voluminous State Papers on the defeat of the Spanish Armada are all preserved in the archives of the Public Records Office, with the exception of this important report which is found in the Manuscript Department of the British Museum, and this segregation reflects the document's curious history, which is a fascinating story in itself.

For some reason, at which we can only guess, this report, the *only original* report in English that was ever made on the entire Armada campaign, based on first-hand reportage, was left unfinished, unsigned and unauthorized, for several blanks remain in the manuscript where names were to have been filled in after checking – an indication that it was probably written at sea while possibilities of communication were difficult. There are also occasional blots as though of sea-water. In my study, referred to above, I have made an exhaustive calligraphic comparison with the extant 'Collier Leaf' from *The Massacre at Paris*, now in the Folger Library, and Marlowe's signature and the manuscript of the Armada report entitled 'A Relation of Proceedings', and there can be no doubt that these are all in the same hand. The correlation is striking, and the hypothesis is supported by other evidence to suggest beyond reasonable doubt that this Armada report was written by Marlowe. The responsibility for preparing such a report for Lord Admiral Howard would have fallen naturally to his hand as Walsingham's agent, who was present on board with the English navy after being picked up by Captain Fenner in the *Nonpareille* just before the commencement of the naval battles. His employment in this task by the Lord Admiral would probably have been at Walsingham's suggestion.

Howard had promised Walsingham to send him 'at better leisure' an expansion of 'A Brief Abstract of Accidents', which he had earlier enclosed with his letter from aboard the *Ark* in the final days of the fighting. This promise was fulfilled in this comprehensive report, as was suggested by Professor J.K. Laughton, who transcribed the entire *State Papers on the Defeat of the Spanish Armada* for the Naval Records Society. Evidently, the report in its unfinished state remained in the possession of Howard, and for some reason was not delivered as promised to Walsingham. Instead Howard gave it to Petruccio Ubaldino, the Florentine historian resident in London, to be translated into Italian for dissemination abroad to give the correct version of the great sea-battles to those on the Continent where false rumours were rife. But this Italian version was also withheld, as we learn from Ubaldino's sad, disgruntled reference to the Queen's decision to disallow the publication of his Italian version. Consequently, this, too, remained in manuscript until it was finally given to Augustine Ryther for re-translation *back* into English. This was accomplished by Ryther's friend 'J.L.' and printed in 1590 entitled '*A Discourse concerninge the Spanishe fleete inuading Englande in 1588*' as the accompanying text for Ryther's engravings of Robert Adams' famous charts depicting the whole Armada campaign. A curious history indeed!

Thus, delayed by two years, the English reading public received the only contemporary report on the great naval victory of 1588. Ryther's book apologizes for the long lapse but offers no reasons for it. His book was sold in conjunction with Adams' charts so that Englishmen might relive the campaign, the text now however in transmogrified form having gone through the vicissitudes of translation firstly into Ubaldino's ornate Italian with his 'embellishments' freely added, and then re-translated into English, in which much of the vivid impression of the first-hand reportage of the original is lost.

Professor Laughton's perceptive comment on the possible authorship of this original report is interesting:

'The identity of the author it is impossible to guess. It is more literary in style than any of the letters written by Howard, or his secretary or his secretary's clerk.'[3]

The comparison of calligraphy made has revealed that here we have, I believe, a unique and historically important document in Marlowe's hand, demonstrating his prose style, which shows him in his capacity as a most able and trusted government agent. His reportage is couched in the language of an authoritative intelligence agent who is accustomed to writing not only to give information, but also to advise, and it has a remarkable modernity in its style. He could well pass for a competent journalist of the present day. Ubaldino criticized the report for being 'written plainly' and proceeded to 'adorn' his translation with his Italianate ornamentation, utterly spoiling its freshness and immediacy.

The extraordinary history of this report has in all probability to do with a simmering rivalry between Lord Admiral Howard and his Vice-Admiral Drake, who also commissioned his own report on the Armada campaign from Ubaldino – in Italian. This likewise remained in manuscript and never saw the light of day so far as the reading public were concerned, until a recent translation.[4]

It is one of the most intriguing aspects of the aftermath of the great Armada victory, in which Marlowe had played a part. The final testimony of his personal involvement in this chapter of the naval history of his time is confirmed by the play here under consideration, the apocryphal *Edward the Third*, into which by a comparison with the Armada report it is demonstrated that he incorporated a dramatization of his own recent naval experience.

'Edward the Third' and the Armada

A play specially written to celebrate this great victory could hardly fail to make a stirring impact on its audiences – the more so when it came from the pen of London's most popular playwright, Christopher Marlowe, with Edward Alleyn playing the part of one of England's best-loved heroes, the Black Prince. And so it did. For this is the play that is referred to again and again by that invaluable pair of literary commentators of the contemporary theatrical scene, Greene and Nashe.

It is from the satirical allusions of Greene and Nashe that we learn that the Marlowe-Alleyn theatrical partnership had achieved another significant stage 'hit' in 1588/89, which their readers would readily have recognized from the thinly-veiled, cryptic comments couched in their typical canting terminology, wherein they point to the author, and the actor, and identify the play for us.

The printer Cuthbert Burby published this play in 1596 under the title *The Raigne of King Edward the third: As it hath bin sundrie times plaied about the Citie of London*, but without naming the author or the company who had played it. It was entered in the Stationers' Register on 1st December 1595:

Cutbert Burby: Entred for his copie vnder the handes of wardens A book Intitled EDWARD the THIRD and the Blacke Prince their warres with kinge JOHN of Fraunce.
vjd.[5]

Burby's publication in 1596 was followed by further editions in 1599, 1609, 1617 and 1625, testifying to its popularity.

Edward the Third is included in the Shakespeare apocryphal works and has been edited by Tucker Brooke and G.C. Moore Smith, among others, and is rated at some importance in the selective editions of collected plays of the period. Its disputed authorship revolves mainly around the argument as to whether Shakespeare had a hand in the love-episode in the play, but both cogent internal and external evidence reveals that this is unquestionably Marlowe's work throughout.

It is a remarkable fact that of the eminent scholars who have studied this play and pronounced opinions on its authorship, even including its editors, not one has commented on its Armada connection which is clearly and undeniably presented in the text – a blind spot that can only be attributed to a lack of historical perspective on the part of the English literary scholars concerned, for whom the date of the play's publication, 1596, at a time when the Armada had receded into history, has obscured this association. There has been no agreement on its possible authorship, and much confusion exists in the assessments of the play made to date, most of which exhibit only superficial study.

However, to his contemporaries, there was no confusion, nor any doubts as to its obvious Armada connection. They would have received his message loud and clear. There can be no doubt that Marlowe's 'Armada' play would have been chosen for performance at Court that Christmas, when on 29th December 1588 the Lord Admiral's Men were playing,[6] the Court being then at Richmond.

The Queen and her Lord Admiral would have delighted to see this play with its patriotic theme, incorporating a vivid description of a sixteenth-century-style 'Armada' battle of Sluys – which was actually fought in 1340 – in which Lord Howard would certainly have recognized the 'accidents' related in the French Mariner's speech – for it was by a subtle bending of history that our dramatist achieved his aim. The bending of history for dramatic purposes is a technique that Marlowe had already used in *Tamburlaine the Great*, and it was a trick that Shakespeare was also to resort to on occasion.

The starting point for our investigation to establish the authorship of *Edward the Third* is with the topical allusions in the prose works of Greene and Nashe. The most important of these are Greene's satirical comments in his romantic novel *Francescos Fortunes Or the Second Part of Never Too Late,* published in 1590, which precisely pinpoint the author, the actor, and the play.

Typically, Greene is on his old hobby-horse, and is once again satirizing the great actor who is his *bête noire*, Edward Alleyn, *alias 'Roscius'*, harping on his favourite theme, the pride and self-aggrandisement of an actor who is in reality no more than the mouth-piece of the dramatic-poet who supplies his text.

> 'Why *Roscius*, art thou proud with *Esops* Crow, being pranct with the glorie of others feathers? of thy selfe thou canst say nothing, and if the Cobler hath taught thee to say *Aue Caesar*, disdain not thy tutor because thou pratest in a Kings Chamber:'[7]

Marlowe, who supplied the actor *'Roscius'* with his script in which he utters the cry *'Ave Caesar!'* is here designated as 'the Cobbler' identifying him by reference to his father's trade, just as Greene and Nashe constantly twitted poor Gabriel Harvey as the son of a rope-maker. In this text we are given all the canting allusions needed to identify the actor, the author and the play, as will be established in due course. The actor is Alleyn, whose canting name was *'Roscius'* just as the canting name for London was ancient *Rome*; the play in which he appeared is identified by a quotation from a speech containing the words 'Ave Caesar' which were spoken in a scene taking place in the 'Kings Chamber'; and the playwright who taught him to say these words was 'the Cobbler' *alias* Marlowe. This reading alone makes sense!

As early as 1588 in his *Perimedes the Blacke-Smith*, Greene had launched his attack on Marlowe describing his style as 'filling the mouth like the faburden of Bo-Bell' and had identified him by reference to 'mad and scoffing poets, that haue propheticall spirits, as bred of *Merlins* race' in the Preface of that work.[8] These satirical allusions are reflected also in the text of his *Menaphon*, published in 1589 in which he referred to Marlowe as 'a Cobblers eldest sonne', establishing this clearly as a synonym for Marlowe interchangeable with 'Tamburlaine' by echoing criticism of Marlowe's versification expressed by Nashe in his Preface to this same work (See quotations on pages 59–61) in which he scathingly describes Marlowe's high astounding terms as 'the swelling bumbast of a bragging blanke verse' and 'the spacious volubilitie of a drumming decasillabon'; while Alleyn is criticized as a vainglorious tragedian. Greene added his jibe in the text:

'Whosoeuer *Samela* descanted of that loue, told you a *Canterbury* tale; some propheticall full mouth that as he were a Coblers eldest sonne, would by the laste tell where anothers shooe wrings."[9]

Here 'a Coblers eldest sonne' is unmistakably Marlowe – all the connotations are there, and Greene wrote for his readers to understand and enjoy his lampoons, not to obfuscate them. Again he is petulantly referring to the disparaging comparisons made between his play *Alphonsus* with Marlowe's *Tamburlaine*.

In his long Preface to *Menaphon* Nashe had further referred to Alleyn making the association between him as '*Roscius*' and '*Caesar*' clear to his readers:

'...when as the deserued reputation of one *Roscius*, is of force to inrich a rabble of counterfets; yet let subiects for all their insolence, dedicate a *De profundis* euerie morning to the preseruation of their *Caesar*...'[10]

Nashe is not so much lampooning Alleyn here, whose reputation as '*Roscius*', the famous actor of ancient Rome *alias* London, is 'deserued', as warning the 'rabble' of actors never to forget their dependence on their great leading actor, (*Roscius-alias-Caesar*) whose reputation has brought them good box-office takings by attracting large audiences to 'inrich' them, hence they should devoutly pray for the 'preseruation of their *Caesar*'. Nashe was, in fact, a sincere admirer of Alleyn, as is apparent once he is no longer under the baleful influence of Greene, who hated the great actor. What is significant in the above allusion is that Nashe links the well-known synonym for Alleyn as *'Roscius'* here with *'Caesar'* which in 1589 is topically relevant to the play *Edward the Third*, to which these satirical references are leading us.

The dates and the historical background to these canting references are extremely important for their elucidation. In the late 1580s and early 1590s Edward Alleyn was without rival, and no one else but he is eligible for the accolade of *'Roscius'*. This period is also the hey-day of Marlowe's supremacy as London's premier dramatist.

Again in 1592, in his *Piers Penniless*, Nashe associates the words 'Ave Caesar' with a speech from a play that was written by 'the Cobbler' which was spoken by the actor who is identified as 'the Cobbler's Crow'. 'Crow' is another well-known Elizabethanism for an actor. By 1592 Marlowe had supplied his actor, Edward Alleyn, with a galaxy of star roles as Tamburlaine, Barabas in *The Jew of Malta*, Doctor Faustus, and the Black Prince in *Edward the Third*, so that to call Alleyn 'the Cobbler's Crow' is an apt description for he was indeed repeatedly seen as Marlowe's actor. These two stood in a special relationship to each other from the moment of Marlowe's first success with *Tamburlaine* – a fact that has been missed by the paucity of research that has been devoted to Edward Alleyn, a remarkable man who emerges as a far more important figure in the Elizabethan theatrical scene than has so far been suspected.

In the following passage Nashe is clearly pointing to the unique partnership that had been established between Marlowe (the Cobbler) and Alleyn (his Crow) by 1592, when it would have been readily understood by his readers among London's theatre-loving public:

'The Cobler's crowe, for crying *Aue Caesar* bee more esteemed than rarer birds that haue warbled sweeter notes vnrewarded.'[11]

It is the old song again, Nashe here voicing his friend Greene's complaint that the actor Alleyn, because he speaks lines written for him by the famous dramatist Christopher Marlowe, is more 'esteemed' than is Greene whose works are sold cheap – hence 'unrewarded' – with the implication that 'The Cobbler' has gained acclaim once more with the play in which his 'Crow' cries 'Aue Caesar'.

These canting allusions were a language devised by Greene and Nashe to make satirical sallies on the reputations of Alleyn and Marlowe in such a way that their readers would immediately recognise the persons referred to, and enjoy the lampoon. It is nonsense to imply, as many critics have, that this canting language is no longer easily discernible to us today. It is as clear as daylight once we have taken the trouble to elucidate the cross-references. In every instance the clues are precise and unambiguous, for they are so devised as to fit *exactly* the play, the circumstances and the persons alluded to, the whole object being that there shall be no possibility of missing the target of their satire with their carefully loaded lampoon-gun.

If we now gather together all these canting allusions, we shall see clearly that our satirists are aiming at another joint success of Marlowe (the Cobbler) and Alleyn (Roscius-Caesar) – namely the historical drama, *Edward the Third*, in which Alleyn played the Black Prince whose rousing curtain speech at the end of the first scene announces the martial theme of the play with his exultant cry: 'Ave Caesar!'

> *Prince*: As cheerful sounding to my youthful spleen
> This tumult is, of war's increasing broils,
> As, at the coronation of a king,
> The joyful clamours of the people are,
> When 'Ave Caesar!' they pronounce aloud.
> *Edward the Third* Act I, Scene 1. 11.160–4

One can imagine that the young Edward Alleyn would have given the words full value, with lusty voice and throwing his cap in the air for joy at the thought of donning armour and seeing action in battle at last to win his spurs. All this promise the play fulfills. This rousing war-cry from the throat of Alleyn at the end of the first scene is made in the 'Kings Chamber', or King Edward's royal council chamber, as Greene precisely identifies for us:-

'if the Cobler hath taught thee to say *Aue Caesar*, disdain not thy tutor because thou pratest in a Kings Chamber:'[12]

There is no other play in 1589 to which these allusions can possibly apply, and here they fit the scene, the circumstances, the actor Alleyn and the author Marlowe, in every punctilio in the Elizabethan canting tradition. When we come to examine in detail and in depth the text of *Edward the Third* it becomes absolutely clear that the target has been hit with a resounding clang – for this is Marlowe's play, and could be from no other pen. It is his very first essay at an English history play and is also of particular interest because, for once, it is not a tragedy, and it contains the only scenes of romantic comedy we have from his pupil pen.

The opening scene of the play immediately reveals the Marlovian touch. King Edward is in his council chamber listening to the recital of his lineal descent from the French King Philip, named le Beau, through his mother Isabel, by which the exiled nobleman Robert of Artois is persuading him that he is the rightful heir to the French throne, and that the present Valois occupant is but a usurper. Fired with ambition by this seductive information King Edward determines to claim what is rightfully his, when the French King's envoy, Lorraine, is announced. He has come to remind Edward that he owes fealty to the French King John for the Dukedom of Guyenne, and must pay him 'lowly homage' for the same within forty days or forfeit the dukedom. This sparks a dramatically effective rejoinder:

> *King Edward.* See how occasion laughs me in the face!
> No sooner minded to prepare for France,
> But straight, I am invited – nay, with threats,
> Upon a penalty, enjoined to come:
> 'Twere but a childish part to say him nay.
> Lorraine, return this answer to thy lord:
> I mean to visit him as he requests –
> But how? Not servilely disposed to bend,
> But like a conqueror to make him bow.
> His lame, unpolished shifts are come to light;
> And truth hath pulled the visard from his face,
> That set a gloss upon his arrogance.
> Dare he command a fealty in me?
> Tell him, the crown that he usurps is mine;
> And where he sets his foot, he ought to kneel.
> 'Tis not a petty dukedom that I claim,
> But all the whole dominions of the realm;
> Which, if with grudging he refuse to yield,
> I'll take away those borrowed plumes of his
> And send him naked to the wilderness.
>
> Act I, Scene 1, 11.67–86

Lorraine, on behalf of his lord, King John, answers defiantly, and in the hot repartee that follows Prince Edward takes a lively part. Finally King Edward brings it to a dramatic climax by drawing his sword in a symbolic gesture that is reminiscent of Tamburlaine's famous presentation of his sword to the Virgins of Damascus, who are to suffer death in accordance with his edict of revenge on the inhabitants for failing to submit their beseiged city to him before the third day.

Tamburlaine. (drawing his sword)
Behold my sword; what see you at the point?
First Virgin. Nothing but fear and fatal steel, my lord.
Tamb. Your fearful minds are thick and misty then,
For there sits Death; there sits imperious Death,
Keeping his circuit by the slicing edge.
Tamburlaine the Great, Part One. Act V, Scene 1. 11.108–112

King Edward. (drawing his sword)
Lorraine, behold the sharpness of this steel;
Fervent desire, that sits against my heart,
Is far more thorny-pricking than this blade;
Edward the Third, Act I, Scene 1. 11.108–110

Marlowe's imaginative use of stage properties to lift his drama to achieve a heightened emotional response is a favourite trick that Shakespeare also uses.

The Modern Critics

G.C. Moore Smith has pointed out the similarities in the stage property tricks in *Edward the Third* and *Henry V* – a dramatic historical masterpiece written in Shakespeare's brilliant maturity, which nevertheless owes much of its stage-craft to this first English history play from Marlowe's 'prentice hand. The parallels, first noted by Miss Emily Phipson, are numerous, running right through the two plays:

> 'The opening scene, in which the King is satisfied of his title to the French crown, closely corresponds to *Henry V*, Act I, Scene ii; the general contrast in the war between French arrogance and cowardice, and English duty and valour, is the same in the two plays; Prince Edward's rebuke to Audley for dreading the odds (IV.iv) has its analogue in Henry V's rebuke to Westmorland (IV.iii); the taunting gifts of the jennet and the prayer-book to the Black Prince (IV.iv) correspond to the gift of the tennis-balls to Henry V (I.ii); in both plays we have French sneers at the appetites of the English; and in both a roll-call of the dead after victory.'[13]

Thus again we have parallel dramatic treatment in Shakespeare's *Henry V* and Marlowe's *Edward the Third* – partly derived from the similarities in the histories of these two reigns, but this does not explain all, and since it has been claimed by some that these things indicate the hand of Shakespeare in *Edward the Third*, it is relevant to remember that similar and even closer parallels exist between Marlowe's *Edward the Second* and Shakespeare's *Richard II*, as Bakeless has strikingly demonstrated. (See Bakeless's comparison of these two plays quoted on page 125).

The widely held assumptions that Marlowe was only capable of writing one type of play, employing a sufficient injection of rant and bombast, with one larger-than-life dominant character, and that he wrote only tragedies since no known comedy has been identified from his pen seem to have blinded almost all who purport to have studied *Edward the Third* to the probability that here we have a play that is from Marlowe's hand, even Warnke and Proescholdt, who made a fairly thorough study of the play. However, F.G. Fleay does definitely attribute *Edward the Third* to Marlowe on the basis of Greene's and Nashe's canting allusions which other scholars have discounted, most of these critics having made their assessments on seemingly brief study, but in common with several others Fleay believes that Shakespeare's hand is to be detected in the love episode, making this a hybrid play.[14]

A.F. Hopkinson is the only English critic to give the entire play to Shakespeare,[15] joining the enthusiastic German scholars who see nothing but Shakespeare in this work. Hopkinson rejects any possibility of Marlowe's authorship on the grounds that he finds no rant or bombast in the play, and he claims that the characterization, dramatic treatment and versification are unlike Marlowe's known plays, none of which contains the proportion of rhyming lines that are a feature of *Edward the Third*. This last is as much as to say that Marlowe, who is a great poet whose influence can be detected in Shakespeare, Milton and Keats, could not have written a play entirely in rhyme had he been so minded. Equally Shakespeare varied the proportion of rhyming lines from many to none at all, and even chose to use prose predominantly on occasion – so that this is not a valid argument. Of bombast and rant there is none in *Edward the Second*, a late play, nor in *Dido*, an early play, and little enough in any other work apart from his *Tamburlaine* where it has its proper place. Hopkinson's findings *against* the hand of Marlowe in versification are cancelled out by Fleay's *for* his authorship based on his analysis of the prosody of *Edward the Third*. Thus two critics of its versification reach *completely opposite conclusions*. The contradictory commentaries of the critics are a notable aspect of the critical studies made of this play, most of which are disappointingly superficial while readily offering subjective judgements. Bakeless, usually such a perceptive critic of Marlowe, opines on a slight study of the work: 'There is no valid reason for assigning *Edward the Third* to Marlowe'.[16] He dismisses Greene's allusion as too obscure but misquotes it by *omitting the vital clue* which is –

'because thou pratest in a Kings Chamber'.

He gives only the preceding quotation, concluding with '..and if the *Cobler* hath taught thee to say *Aue Caesar*, disdain not thy tutor'. Here he cuts it short with a full stop, where there is none! This enables him to comment that whereas the words 'Ave Caesar' do occur in *Edward III* they might equally belong to a play now no longer extant. It is of course highly unlikely that any other play, extant or not, would *also* have these very words uttered in a 'Kings Chamber'. Unaccountably Bakeless also casts doubt on the allusion to Marlowe as 'the *Cobbler*', which he says 'may be a taunt against Marlowe's parentage, but it may merely allude to a fable'.[17]

If so, what relevant fable does he have in mind? This is totally to misunderstand Greene's satire, and it is poor detective work that leads nowhere. And he has, in common with the other erudite critics, failed to notice *the striking Armada connection in the play*.

A.W. Ward finds some affinity to Marlowe's writing in *Edward the Third* but ascribes this to an early play by Marlowe which was rewritten by some unknown hand to form the present work.[18] Ward also fails to note the Armada connection, but he draws attention to the development of the character of Edward III in the final scene of *Edward the Second* as he reaches his majority and assumes the mantle of kingship and avenges his father's murder with the execution of the traitor, Mortimer. The two reigns are closely intertwined, and Bakeless agrees that this is a valid argument although remaining unconvinced that Marlowe could have written both plays.

Tucker Brooke also passed superficial judgement unconvincingly proposing Peele as the possible author, presumably swayed by the proportion of rhymed lines in the play, yet admitting: 'It must be conceded that *Edward III* is a finer production than any with which Peele is at present accredited.' He adds in a flash of genuine perception that the dramatist, whoever he may have been, was 'one of the truest poets and most ardent patriots, certainly, of his generation.'[19] Swinburne, expressing admiration, nevertheless falls back on evoking a phantom playwright who was 'a devout student and humble follower of Christopher Marlowe'.[20] And Moore Smith goes one better by claiming that this unknown dramatist wrote 'in the manner of Shakespeare' – at least in the love episode in the play, which some believe may be Shakespeare's interpolation, although these romantic scenes, in fact, demonstrably reveal Marlowe's hand.

Karl Warnke and Ludwig Proescholdt, whose opinions carry weight by the objectivity of this partnership and their more thorough study of the whole play, point out that the love episode cannot be seen as an interpolation or later addition since it is *integral* to the play's structure.[21] While denying that any part of the play is, in their view, attributable to Shakespeare, they do not propose an alternative author. Their rejection of Shakespeare's authorship is mainly on the grounds that it is neither mentioned by Meres as Shakespeare's play, nor is it included in the Folios, and Heminge and Condell would certainly have known its authorship. The general failure to recognize Marlowe's style, versification and his idiosyncratic tricks of composition with which the play literally abounds, is only matched by the failure of all the critics, not excepting its editors, to note its Armada connection – which is surely the most remarkable aspect of this play!

It is certain that *Edward the Third* was conceived and written as a celebration of the victory over the Spanish Armada as a timely offering for the Christmas season of 1588. The internal evidence proves this. The choice of the reign of Edward III was deliberate, for he was the founder of our navy and wrested the supremacy of the seas from the French and Spanish; and after the battle of Sluys in 1340, in which the English navy totally destroyed the French navy, Parliament awarded King Edward III the title of 'Sovereign of the Sea', in commemoration of which he had a gold coin cast bearing the emblem of a ship. In my study *Christopher Marlowe and the Armada* I have shown that the speeches of the French Mariner are a deliberate and moving dramatization of his own recent experience of the Armada campaign and represent a fascinating autobiographical touch. The French Mariner's first sighting of King

Edward's approaching fleet gives the audience a foretaste of what is to come by significantly recalling the Spanish Armada 'figuring the hornéd circle of the moon', whose black-painted ships are here transformed into the colourful assembly of the English navy which is advancing as an invasion fleet (as was the Spanish Armada) sailing in the famous battle formation of the Spaniards in the configuration of the crescent moon: (the relevant passages are italicised)

> *Mariner.* Near to the coast I have descried, my Lord,
> As I was busy in my watchful charge,
> *The proud Armado of King Edward's ships:*
> Which, at the first, far off when I did ken,
> *Seem'd as it were a grove of withered pines;*
> But, drawing near, their glorious bright aspect,
> Their streaming ensigns, wrought of coloured silks
> Like to a meadow full of sundry flowers,
> Adorns the naked bosom of the earth:
> Majestical the order of their course,
> *Figuring the hornéd circle of the moon:*
> And on the top gallant of the Admiral
> And likewise of the handmaids of his train,
> The Arms of England and of France unite
> Are quarter'd equally by heralds' art:
> Thus, tightly carried with a merry gale,
> They plough the ocean hitherward amain.
>
> Act III Sc.1. 11.62–78

[This is just how the Armada appeared to those who first saw it in the distance, like a black forest of masts.]

King John, alarmed at this news, asks:

> But where's our Navy? How are they prepared
> To wing themselves *against this flight of ravens?*
>
> Act III Sc.1, 11.83–84

We pause to ask, Why should the French King refer to King Edward's fleet as a 'flight of ravens' when the Mariner has just described the English navy to him as of 'glorious bright aspect' and 'Like to a meadow full of sundry flowers'? Clearly the dramatist, here reliving his own recent, vivid experience of those black-painted ships of the Armada which they had fought and pursued throughout the naval campaign, has momentarily slipped into his personal recollection of what he saw then,

It is such subconscious errors that provide tellingly revealing touches confirming the authorship of Marlowe, whose participation in the Armada campaign is documented,[22] and he is here recalling his own Armada experience.

King John bids the Mariner return, if he 'survive the conflict', to report the outcome to him, which he anxiously awaits.

> *King John.* Retreat is sounded; one side hath the worse:
> O, if it be the French, sweet fortune, turn;
> And, in thy turning, change the forward winds,
> That, with advantage of a favouring sky,
> Our men may vanquish, and the other fly!
> *Enter Mariner*
> My heart misgives: – say, mirror of pale death,
> To whom belongs the honour of this day?
> Relate, I pray thee, if thy breath will serve,
> The sad discourse of this discomfiture.
>
> Act III, Scene 1, 11.132–140

In 'pale death' we immediately encounter a favourite word-image of Marlowe's which he uses in *Dido Queen of Carthage*, in *Tamburlaine* and in *The Massacre at Paris*. The reader wishing to pursue these stylistic similarities further is recommended to the detailed stylistic examination made in the above mentioned work, where it will be found that the stylistic evidence for Marlowe is overwhelming.

The Mariner's description of the battle which now follows is extraordinary, for it is a telescoped account of the main battles of the Armada campaign which the manuscript 'A Relation of Proceedings' reports. Every incident or 'accident' in the Mariner's speech can be found in the report written for Lord Admiral Howard and intended, as Howard's own letter states, for presentation to Sir Francis Walsingham, who was Marlowe's boss in the espionage service for whom Marlowe would have been accustomed to write his intelligence reports, and it is likely that research may yet discover more intelligence reports that are attributable to Marlowe, who was, I believe, an agent of considerable importance. The Mariner's entire speech is couched in the terms of *a sixteenth century naval battle using cannon and gun-shot*, whereas the Battle of Sluys in 1340 was fought with bows and arrows! Holinshed's detailed account of this battle is abandoned and the dramatist becomes totally immersed in his poetic rendering of the fierce Armada battles of

84

his recollection. It is the bending of history to a purpose in celebration of contemporary history – a rare piece of artistic licence(see following pages).

In the close correspondence between the naval battle described in this speech and Marlowe's 'A Relation of Proceedings', the Mariner seems to fuse with the dramatist in reliving his Armada experiences. He recalls the thunder of the cannon that was like the continuous roll of musketry, and the heavy pall of smoke that blotted out the sun's light making a seeming night of day; the deafening roar above which no human voice could be heard, so that in this 'hideous noise...each to other seemed deaf and dumb'; and the poignant recollection in the line 'No leisure serv'd for friends to bid farewell:' – these are memories of personal experience with which this whole passage vibrates.

In this wonderfully evocative speech we find also several examples of Marlowe's stylistic idiosyncracies. His distinctive use of double-barrelled adjectives, first developed in his translation of Lucan and Ovid, are here superbly represented in the 'iron-hearted navies' and the 'through-shot planks', and King John's dramatic 'mirror of pale death', an association of imagery that is typical of Marlowe. Garrett Mattingly, whose marvellous account in his book *The Defeat of the Spanish Armada* draws on a thirty-years study of Spanish documents as well as Dutch and English accounts to complement the picture of this great naval campaign and its historical context, informs us that in the final battle:

'The tough layers of Spanish oak guarding the lower hulls of the galleons were not smashed, but they were pierced repeatedly...Their upper works were only musket-proof at best, and by evening they had been beaten to bloody flinders. The slaughter on the upper decks must have been terrible.'[23]

And again: 'The crew of one of the *urcas* saw Bertendona's great carrack drive past, her decks a shambles, her battery guns silent and blood spilling out of her scuppers as she heeled to the wind...' Marlowe's Mariner paraphrases this vividly:

Purple the sea, whose channel fill'd as fast
With streaming gore, that from the maimed fell,
As did her gushing moisture break into
The crannied cleftures of the through-shot planks.

In the *Mariner's speech* (opposite) the italicized lines are commented on below comparing them with the "accidents" reported in "A Relation of Proceedings" and other relevant sources on the Armada campaign.

1. Iron cannon balls and iron cannon were used in the sixteenth century navies. The Queen's navy still possessed many of these although Wynter had replaced as many as he could with brass culverins. The Spanish navy had predominantly iron cannon.

2. Admiral meeting Admiral was the opening gambit of the Armada campaign – or so it was intended, when the Lord Admiral's *Ark* challenged de Leiva's *capitana* of the Levant squadron, *La Rata Coronada* riding in the port wing facing the enemy in the position of honour and danger, believing that this was the Admiral's ship. "A Relation of Proceedings" tells us, "the *Ark* bare up with the admiral of the Spaniards wherein the Duke was supposed to be and fought with her."[24]

3. This recollects the fierce battle of Tuesday 23rd July when, as Garrett Mattingly puts it, "the roar of the cannon...was like the continuous roll of musketry, and the smoke was blinding."[25] In this pall of smoke daylight penetrated only intermittently and the noise must have been deafening. "A Relation" tells us "there was neuer seene a more terrible valew of greate shott."[26]

4. In the final battle off Gravelines, the punishment the Armada took resulted in decks strewn with dead and wounded and running blood. The upper works of these galleons "were only musket-proof at best, and by evening they had been beaten to bloody flinders."[27] The "through-shot planks" is an apt description.

5. "A Brief Abstract of Accidents" enclosed with Howard's letter of 7th August reports: "The 30th, one of the enemy's great ships was espied to be in great distress by the captain of her Majesty's ship called the Hope; who being in speech of yielding unto the said captain, before they could agree on certain conditions, sank presently before their eyes."[28] On the same day a great armed merchantman of the Spanish fleet went down within sight of both navies.

6. The *Nonpareille* was Captain Fenner's ship (vice-admiral of Drake's squadron). This is the ship on which I believe Marlowe served for she was reconnoitring the French coast for intelligence just prior to the outbreak of hostilities. Her appearance here in *Edward the Third* underlines this hypothesis. The "black snake of Boulogne" is probably a descriptive identification of a black-painted sleek, low-slung ship built as a galleas, of which there were four in the Spanish navy; "black snake" does not seem to be the actual name of the ship as *Nonpareille* obviously is, and she features frequently in "A Relation of Proceedings".

7. These two lines describing the weather and tide are authentic Holinshed, and prove that he had the text before him. To have ignored all the rest of Holinshed's data is therefore quite deliberate on the part of the dramatist. This confirms his intention to make this play his Armada victory celebration.

The Mariner's Tale

Mariner

My gracious sovereign, France hath ta'en the foil,
And boasting Edward triumphs with success.

1.   These *iron-hearted navies*,
When last I was reporter to your grace,
Both full of angry spleen, of hope, and fear,
Hasting to meet each other in the face,
At last conjoined; and *by their Admiral*

2.   *Our Admiral encounter'd many shot:*
By this, the other, that beheld these twain
Give earnest penny for a further wrack,
Like fiery dragons took their haughty flight;
And, likewise meeting, *from their smoky wombs*
Sent many grim ambassadors of death.

3.   Then gan the day to turn to gloomy night,
And darkness did as well enclose the quick
As those that were but newly reft of life,
No leisure serv'd for friends to bid farewell;
And, if it had, the hideous noise was such
As each to other seemed deaf and dumb.
Purple the sea, whose channel fill'd as fast

4.   *With streaming gore, that from the maimed fell,*
As did her gushing moisture break into
The crannied cleftures of the through-shot planks.
Here flew a head, dissevered from the trunk,
There mangled arms and legs were toss'd aloft,
As when a whirlwind takes the summer dust
And scatters it in middle of the air.

5.   *Then might ye see the reeling vessels split,*
And tottering sink into the ruthless flood,
Until their lofty tops were seen no more.
All shifts were tried, both for defence and hurt:
And now the effect of valour and of force,
Of resolution and of cowardice,
We lively pictured; how the one for fame,
The other by compulsion laid about:

6.   Much did the *Nonpareille,** that brave ship;
So did the black snake of Boulogne, than which
A bonnier vessel never yet spread sail.

7.   But all in vain; *both sun, the wind and tide,*
Revolted all unto our foemen's side,
That we perforce were fain to give them way,
And they are landed. – Thus, my tale is done:
We have untimely lost, and they have won.

[* It is spelt in the Quarto dated 1596 as *Non per illa*]

Act III Sc.1, 11.141–184.

87

Then comes a remarkable description of the effects of cannonades.

> Here flew a head, dissevered from the trunk,
> There mangled arms and legs were toss'd aloft,
> As when a whirlwind takes the summer dust
> And scatters it in middle of the air.

This is reminiscent of Tamburlaine who in teaching his sons physical courage asks his war-hating son, Calyphas, whom he despises as a coward:

> Hast thou beheld a peal of ordnance strike
> A ring of pikes, mingled with shot and horse,
> Whose shattered limbs, being tossed as high as Heaven,
> Hang in the air as thick as sunny motes,
> And canst thou, coward, stand in fear of death?
>
> *The Second Part of Tamburlaine* Act III Sc.2, 11.96–102

And describing the art of war to his sons he explains the means by which to

> Besiege a fort, to undermine a town,
> And make whole cities caper in the air.
>
> Act III Sc.2, 11.60–61

Tamburlaine is indeed full of 'mangled' carcasses for Marlowe leaves us in no doubt as to the horrors of war, man's oldest and most constant occupation.

It is interesting to compare Marlowe's poetic dramatization with the excerpt below from his manuscript report of one of the fiercest fights fought against the Armada.

> 'This fighte was very nobly contynewed from mornynge vntill the eavenynge the Lo: Admyrall beinge allways [in] the hottest of the encounter. And it may well be sayed that for the tyme there was neuer seene a more terrible valew of greate shott nor a more hott fighte then this was for [A harquebus was a heavy hand gun supported on a crock or rest.] althoughe the musketteres and harquebysers of crocke were then infynyte yet colde they not be decearned nor hard for the great ordnaunce came soe thicke that a man woulde haue iudged it to haue ben a hot skirmishe of small shotte beinge all the fighte longe wthin halfe muskett shott of the enemye.'[29]

This is graphic reporting by Marlowe in his capacity as an Elizabethan journalist, one might say. He doubtless joined the English navy in the first instance as a secret agent when Walsingham's espionage service carried the heavy responsibility for spying out the Spanish stratagems and activities. Drake's old companion-at-arms, the experienced sea-dog Thomas Fenner, captain of the *Nonpareille*, was patrolling the seas, gathering intelligence up till the last moment when the Armada was finally sighted assembling off the coast of the Isles of Scilly on 19th July (Old Style) and reported to Drake at Plymouth by one of the scouting barks. Evidence suggests that it was in Fenner's ship the *Nonpareille*[29] that Marlowe sailed and took part in the battles that ensued – for no one in the Elizabethan navy was a mere passenger, from the commanders of the fleet downwards. All were active.

Significantly, there is only one ship named in the Mariner's account – the *Nonpareille*. Certainly that is a French name, but the author did not invent or add any other names for these French ships, the 'black snake of Boulogne' being a descriptive epithet for a low-slung galleas, of which there were four, each painted black, in the Spanish navy, useful ships being powered both by sail and oars with three hundred galley slaves per ship. Naming one ship only was surely deliberate, because the dramatist wanted only *his* ship to sail in this, his dramatized account of what had been for him a great and memorable experience.

In the same way he did not invent a name for a ship to place in the argosy of *The Jew of Malta*, but chose to put *The Flying Dragon*, which rode in Dover harbour in his childhood, into his play.[30] There he must have seen her when he visited his maternal grandparents and watched the ships with eager curiosity. He chose this name not because he lacked imagination to create names for his ships, or because he was too lazy to think of any. It was, one senses, because he wanted to introduce these personal hallmarks into his dramas. Such autobiographical touches are a typical trait of Marlowe's works, but of all these the Mariner's speech is the strongest and longest, testifying to the powerful impact this experience had made on him. At the end of the speech, having had his 'Armada fling', he returns to Holinshed to include the natural forces – the weather and tide – that gave King Edward his victory, for he had delayed his attack purposely until the sun had moved behind his ships and his longbowmen were able to shoot with devastating accuracy, causing great slaughter on the crowded decks of the French ships, before closing in to grapple and fight hand-to-hand on deck as was the order of the day. The weapons used were what H.J. Hewitt in *The Organisation of War under Edward III* describes as 'competent arms' – bows and arrows, both longbow and crossbow, lances, pikes, swords and knives.[31] Holinshed does not mention cannon, although they were just being introduced and Edward III transported a few of these novel engines of war for use in sieges. He placed some cannon forward with his front-line archers at Crecy, but they were certainly not used at sea.

Yet what we are deliberately presented with in the Mariner's speech is an *account of the gunfight against the Armada* in Marlowe's recent experience. Deliberately, because it cannot be other than a conscious decision on the part of the dramatist. He was not such a fool as to mistake what he read in the *Chronicles* of Holinshed, yet the sea-battle of Sluys is served up to his audience entirely in terms of the gun-battle against the Spanish Armada – which Elizabethan theatre-goers would have relished!

We know the author consulted Holinshed, for the last lines of the Mariner's speech are a paraphrase of Holinshed's very words concluding his account:

> '...at length the Englishe men hauing the aduantage, not onely of the Sunne, but also of the wynde and tyde, so fortunately, that the Frenche Fleete was dryuen into the streyghts of the Hauen, in such wyse that neyther the Souldiours, nor Mariners coulde helpe themselues, insomuche that bothe Heauen, the Sea, and Winde, seemed all to haue conspyred agaynst the Frenche menne.'[32]

In *Edward the Third* this is rendered:

> ... both sun, the wind and tide
> Revolted all unto our foemen's side.

These two lines alone are authentic Holinshed. Had our dramatist wished to make a dramatic speech based on history he would have found a wealth of detail in Holinshed's lengthy account of this great naval battle, for he names the commanders who, on the French side, included 'a Geneweis named Barbe Noir' who was a notable seaman and the only one who managed to extricate his ship from the danger of being grounded in the haven. Holinshed describes various incidents of the capture of ships, and tells of the slaughter on the decks, mentioning the numbers slain and naming those of nobility who fell. None of this information is used because the dramatist clearly had another purpose in mind.

After his great naval victory, King Edward's army being landed, the play continues with the equally brilliant and victorious campaign on

French soil, and now the Black Prince takes the stage for he shares the honour of the leading roles in the play with King Edward. This is a far cry from the one-character dominant role of Marlowe's most famous works, and this aspect may also have weighed with those who failed to recognize a new development of his genius in this singular play.

The Love Episode

Marlowe's innate versatility and originality have been sufficiently remarked on, hence it is to be expected that he would not always be doing what he had done before, but new departures are to be constantly looked for. Thus *Edward the Third* breaks new ground for Marlowe in several ways. It was his first attempt at an English history play using Holinshed's *Chronicle* as his main source. It is the only play in his canon which is not a tragedy. It is the only example we have of his writing a romantic comedy, for such is the delightful love episode which is the prelude to Edward's military campaign in France. Assuming by hypothesis that this is indeed Marlowe's play, there is ample evidence that the love episode is from his pen as much as the rest of the play; in fact, the stylistic affinity is *especially* strong in the expressions of romantic love in *Edward the Third* compared with the same in *Tamburlaine*; there is undeniably the closest correspondence in style, versification, mood and passion in these passages. Tamburlaine's ardent love for Zenocrate is such that she is like a priceless jewel to him – beyond compare! His language to her is full of superlatives.

> Ah, fair Zenocrate! – divine Zenocrate!
> Fair is too foul an epithet for thee.

This is in *precisely* the same mood and style that King Edward uses when he eulogizes the Countess, ordering his courtier-poet to describe her in hyperbolic language that knows no limits!

> Better than beautiful, thou must begin;
> Devise for fair a fairer word than fair.

Compare Tamburlaine's entire speech (quoted on pages 10-12) with King Edward's love speeches below in which the resemblances are numerous and striking. Edward begins by invoking 'some golden Muse' to bring his poet 'an enchanted pen' thus recalling memories for his audience of his famous panegyric on 'Beauty, mother of the Muses' in his recently written *Tamburlaine* in which he developed this theme,

> If all the pens that poets ever held
> Had fed the feelings of their masters' thoughts,

which is arguably the most famous in the whole of Marlowe, and would certainly have evoked immediate recognition in his Elizabethan audiences. Edward's speech of passionate adoration for the Countess echoes Tamburlaine's familiar lyrical outpouring on Zenocrate, inviting his audiences to associate Tamburlaine's grand passion with the King's by referring directly to raising 'drops in a Tartar's eye' and making 'a flintheart Scythian pitiful'. Both Edward's and Tamburlaine's love-speeches are such unabashed transcendent panegyrics as proclaim them to be from the pen of Marlowe, the poet of passion and beauty. Here Edward instructs his courtier to compose a poem to move the Countess to respond to his passionate love for her.

> *King*. Now, Lodowick, invocate some golden Muse,
> To bring thee hither an enchanted pen,
> That may for sighs set down true sighs indeed,
> Talking of grief, to make thee ready groan;
> And when thou writest of tears, encouch the word
> Before and after with such sweet laments
> That it may raise drops in a Tartar's eye
> And make a flintheart Scythian pitiful;
> For so much moving hath a poet's pen;
> Then, if thou be a poet, move thou so,
> And be enrichéd by thy sovereign's love.
> For, if the touch of sweet concordant strings
> Could enforce attendance in the ears of hell,
> How much more shall the strains of poets' wit
> Beguile and ravish soft and human minds?
> *Lodowick*. To whom, my Lord, shall I direct my style?
> *King*. To one that shames the fair and sots the wise;
> Whose body is an abstract or a brief,
> Contains such general virtue in the world.
> Better than beautiful, thou must begin;
> Devise for fair a fairer word than fair,

And every ornament that thou wouldst praise,
Fly it a pitch above the soar of praise.
For flattery fear thou not to be convicted;
For, were thy admiration ten times more,
Ten times ten thousand more the worth exceeds
Of that thou art to praise, thy praises worth.
Begin; I will to contemplate the while:
Forget not to set down, how passionate,
How heart-sick, and how full of languishment,
Her beauty makes me.
Lodowick.   Write I to a woman?
King. What beauty else could triumph over me,
Or who but women do our love lays greet?
What, thinkest thou I did bid thee praise a horse?

Ac II Sc.1, 11.65–98

With this parting shot of ironic wit, the King retires to nurse his passion. The resemblance of the above speech to Marlowe's *Tamburlaine* – *sans* rant and bombast, for here it would be completely inappropriate dramatically – shows how Marlowe is now developing his powers as a dramatist. It is so striking it requires no emphasis. Marlowe is wont to quote himself, as his other works sufficiently testify, so that the claim of some critics that this is some other dramatist plagiarizing Marlowe's *Tamburlaine* is but specious hypothesizing, unsubstantiated unless this phantom playwright can be named. Such subjective criticism casts doubts on his ability, serving to rob Marlowe of the credit due to his developing genius for the general consensus is that the love episode represents the finest part of the play. These scenes are certainly the most entertaining! And they present an excellent foil, as romantic interlude, to the scenes of the military exploits that follow, in which Marlowe is employing the dramatic concept and technique that proved so effective in making a balanced theatrical entertainment of *Tamburlaine* by introducing the love story of Tamburlaine and Zenocrate.

His purpose is also to show the self-indulgent, womanizing side of Edward's nature, that led in later life to his domination by an evil mistress, Alice Perrers. Edward's characterization in the play is the more rounded, being flawed by his very human failings. The scene between the love-sick King and his courtier-poet Lodowick is especially delightful and shows what we could have expected in romantic comedies from Marlowe's pen as he developed to maturity.

After musing aloud for a while King Edward returns to see how Lodowick has been faring in the composition of his love-poem, and finds he has to give his poet a lesson in how to write poetry, for in the King's opinion the poor fellow has not acquitted himself at all well.

> *King Edward.* Read, Lord, read;
> Fill thou the empty hollows of mine ears
> With the sweet hearing of thy poetry.
> *Lodowick.* I have not to a period brought her praise.
> *King.* Her praise is as my love, both infinite,
> Which apprehend such violent extremes,
> That they disdain an ending period.
> Her beauty hath no match but my affection;
> Hers more than most, mine most and more than more:
> Hers more to praise than tell the sea by drops,
> Nay, more than drop the massy earth by sands,
> And sand by sand print them in memory:
> Then wherefore talkest thou of a period
> To that which craves unended admiration?
> Read, let us hear.
> *Lodowick.* 'More fair and chaste than is the queen of shades' –
> *King.* That line hath two faults, gross and palpable:
> Comparest thou her to the pale queen of night,
> Who, being set in dark, seems therefore light?
> What is she, when the sun lifts up his head,
> But like a fading taper, dim and dead?
> My love shall brave the eye of heaven at noon,
> And, being unmask'd, outshine the golden sun.
> *Lodowick.* What is the other fault, my sovereign Lord?
> *King.* Read o'er the line again.
> *Lodowick.* 'More fair and chaste' –
> *King.* I did not bid thee talk of chastity,
> To ransack so the treasure of her mind:
> For I had rather have her chased than chaste.
> Out with the moon line, I will none of it;
> And let me have her likened to the sun:
> Say she hath thrice more splendour than the sun,
> That her perfections emulate the sun,
> That she breed sweets as plenteous as the sun,
> That she doth thaw cold winter like the sun,

That she doth thaw cold winter like the sun,
That she doth cheer fresh summer like the sun,
That she doth dazzle gazers like the sun;
And, in this application to the sun,
Bid her be free and general as the sun,
Who smiles upon the basest weed that grows
As lovingly as on the fragrant rose.

Act II Scene 1, 11.140–165

In this we have Marlowe's iterative use of words and imagery in building up a climax, so effectively used in *Tamburlaine* which was on the boards in the previous year. It is a trick he learned from Ovid, and is one of his most characteristic traits. In translating Ovid's *Amores* at Cambridge he had repeatedly written such lines as:

Accept him that will serve thee all his youth,
Accept him that will love with spotless truth,
.....
And she to whom in shape of swan *Jove* came,
And she that on a feign'd bull swam to land.

Elegy III

These are love poems, and in *Edward the Third* he is writing love scenes, so that the memory of Ovid is strongly evoked and the style subconsciously pervades his writing. Marlowe in romantic mood echoes himself, and this is a cogent argument, for dramatic parallelism revealing the same mind at work is perhaps even more indicative of authorship than reliance on an analysis of prosody, which is subject to the mood and emotion of a poet of such sensitivity as Marlowe, who varies his style and metrics according to the character and situation he is portraying, as Dr Bakeless has shown.[33] Marlowe is always the dramatist as well as the poet, and his writing mirrors the character who is speaking.

His portrait of the Countess shows Marlowe's technique in creating a character, for here he ranges widely in his research to find attributes that will enhance this portrayal of 'a true English lady'. He found his heroine in William Painter's story, taken from Bandello, in his *Palace of Pleasure*, a collection of pseudo-historical tales from classical and European writers, to which Marlowe turned for a suitable episode to provide the romantic element for his play. Painter's book was a favourite source of inspiration to the Elizabethan dramatists who followed in Marlowe's wake. Marlowe took Painter's story of King Edward III's attempted seduction of the Countess of Salisbury, which is fictional with a possible basis of historical gossip, but altered it to give it far more dramatic power. He transformed the virtuous and beautiful but insipid heroine by adding the attributes of the quick-witted and high-spirited Countess Agnes of Dunbar, whose saucy taunting of her enemies is described in Holinshed, to enliven the character of his Countess of Salisbury; thus he created a delightful creature who is not just beautiful and virtuous, but courageous, sprightly and intelligent with a flashing wit, and a strong and noble character. A *real* lady who proves more than a match for the handsome, lascivious King.

This Countess is proof against all King Edward's passionate wooing, so that, baulked in his illicit desires, he then tricks her father, the Earl of Warwick, by obtaining his promise on oath to aid the King in a project dear to his heart, only to find he has bound himself to importune his daughter to accede to the King's lustful longing. Miserably the Earl discharges his loathsome task, which, to his great relief, is hotly flung back at him by his daughter in utter horror. Warwick then launches on the long speech containing the well-known line in Shakespeare's Sonnet 94 – 'Lilies that fester smell far worse than weeds' – which fits its context here perfectly.

> *Warwick.* Why, now thou speak'st as I would
>   have thee speak:
> And mark how I unsay my words again.
> An honourable grave is more esteem'd
> Than the polluted closet of a king:
> The greater man, the greater is the thing,
> Be it good or bad, that he shall undertake:
> An unreputed mote, flying in the sun,
> Presents a greater substance than it is:
> The freshest summer's day doth soonest taint
> The loathed carrion that it seems to kiss:
> Deep are the blows made with a mighty axe:
> That sin doth ten times aggravate itself,
> That is committed in a holy place:
> An evil deed, done by authority,
> Is sin and subbornation: deck an ape
> In tissue, and the beauty of the robe
> Adds but the greater scorn unto the beast.
> A spacious field of reasons could I urge
> Between his glory, daughter, and thy shame:
> That poison shows worst in a golden cup;

Dark night seems darker by the lightning flash;
*Lilies that fester smell far worse than weeds;
And every glory that inclines to sin,
The shame is treble by the opposite.
So leave I with my blessing in thy bosom,
Which I then convert to a most heavy curse,
When thou convertest from honours golden name
To the black faction of bed blotting shame.

Act II Sc.1, 11.430-457

The love-sick King meanwhile talks like a man distracted, amazing his courtiers with his moodiness. Irritably he calls for the soldier's drum to be silenced – his thoughts are all of love, not war, and his mind is filled with nothing but the Countess's beauty. But when Prince Edward arrives to speak with his father, Edward is reminded by the boy's resemblance to his mother of Queen Phillippa, and, pulling himself together, he resolves to leave for France, when he is brought the news that the Countess wishes to see him – and he is at once enthralled again. This vacillation is closely reminiscent of Dido in the thrall of her love for Aeneas. Marlowe sees people in love as swayed by their passions in this manner, typically beyond rhyme or reason.

The Countess arrives escorted by Lodowick, whom the King sends packing so that he may be alone with his heart's desire, and the Countess informs him she will give herself to him – but on one condition: that he has both her husband, Salisbury, and his Queen murdered. To which, after slight demur, he agrees. Thus she has exposed the depth to which he is prepared to sink to gratify his desire.

It is at this point that Marlowe lifts the play to high drama. The Countess, pretending she is about to yield herself to the King, turns suddenly holding two daggers – her 'wedding knives' she calls them – one for Edward to kill the Queen, the other for herself which she will plunge into her heart unless Edward promises that he will never again solicit her. Shocked into shame at this spirited defence of her chastity, the King is restored to his better self and straightway giving his promise goes towards her in admiration of a nobler kind, with a passing mention of Lucrece:

Arise, true English Lady, whom our Isle
May better boast of than ever Roman might

---

*This line is quoted by Shakespeare in Sonnet 94 which has a similar theme extolling the beauty of the youth whose fair exterior does not match his character as shown in his deeds

Of her, whose ransack'd treasury hath task'd
The vain endeavour of so many pens:
Arise; and be my fault thy honours fame,
Which after ages shall enrich thee with.
I am awaked from this idle dream.

Act II Sc.2, 11.194–200

Calling his 'brave warriors' together the King vigorously issues orders for their imminent departure for France; the love-sick swain is transformed into the man of action in the twinkling of an eye. It is a nice touch of character observation.

King Edward kept a gay court; he loved music and singing, dancing and feasting, and jousting. In 1349, nine years after the battle of Sluys, he celebrated Saint George's day, 23rd April, with the founding of the Order of the Garter. Holinshed tells this story and in his marginal note names the Countess of Salisbury as the lady whose garter was the origin of this witty and thoroughly English chivalric institution:

'It chanced that Kynge Edwarde finding eyther the garter of the Queene or of some Lady with whome hee was in loue, beeing fallen from hir legge, stouped downe, and tooke it vp, whereat, diuerse of the nobles founde matter to jest, and to talke their fancies merily, touching the Kyngs affection towards the woman, vnto whome hee said, that if hee liued, it shoulde come to passe, that most high honor should be giuen vnto them for the garters sake: and there vpon shortly after, he deuised and ordeyned this order of the garter, with such a posey, whereby he signified, that hys Nobles iudged otherwise of him than the trouth was.'[34]

The countes of Salisbury

Perhaps there was a basis of truth then in the story romantically linking Edward with the Countess, and King Edward's order of chivalry was in reality inspired by the lady's noble defence of her chastity – a chivalrous commemoration of a beautiful woman's exalted nature? At any rate Marlowe divined this to be the truth for his line 'Which after ages shall enrich thee with' indicates that he took Holinshed's marginal note seriously. Marlowe's version of the story is nearer to the truth in spirit than Bandello's tale *via* Painter, in which the unhistorical ending has Edward marrying the (widowed) Countess instead of forcing her to be his mistress – an ending which is both completely fictional as well as undramatic. Marlowe's twist to the story could have been historical, and it strikingly contrasts the two characters of the Countess and King Edward, making a high point in the drama.

This dramatic ending to the romantic episode gives a marvellous impetus to the play as it launches into the dramatization of one of the most brilliant periods of victorious English naval and military history which the following scenes unfold to the audience. Warnke and Proescholdt, whose far more thorough study of this play has convincingly demonstrated that the love-episode cannot be an interpolation, but is integral to the whole dramatic concept; and, being placed at the beginning of the play directly after its opening scene announcing King Edward's intention to claim the crown of France, it has a deeper significance than merely to entertain with a romantic interlude. While satisfying the need to balance the play with feminine and romantic interest and providing an opportunity to present the amorous side of King Edward's nature, it also introduces powerfully the underlying theme of the play, which permeates the drama at a deeper level with moral, philosophical content, and is the unifying theme that runs right through the play.

William Armstrong in his Introduction to *Elizabethan History Plays* sums up the view put forward by Warnke and Proescholdt, pointing out the importance of this second, parallel theme, which presages 'Shakespeare's portrayal of the education of Prince Hal in the two parts of *Henry IV* and his ideal kingship in *Henry V.*' [35]

'Once it is appreciated that the basic themes of the play are the education of princes and the illustration of king-becoming virtues, its various episodes assume a meaningful relationship. The education comes especially through learning to respect those covenants on which honour and civilization depend. The eloquent Countess of Salisbury convinces Edward that his passions have put him in danger of committing "high treason against the King of Heaven", who instituted the marriage bond before He appointed kings. Similarly, Villiers convinces Charles of Normandy that princes cannot countermand the parole given by a soldier. Later, when King John of France would revoke the safe-conduct which Charles has given to Salisbury, he, too, is taught that kings must not abuse their powers. The kingly virtues are illustrated by Edward's care in ensuring that war against France would be just, by the fortitude displayed by the Black Prince at Crecy and Poitiers, and by Edward's clemency towards the six burghers of Calais. Contrasts are used to throw these themes into relief; David of Scotland is a breaker of covenants, and when John uses Frenchmen to fight for his usurped crown, he is represented as a tyrant, a 'thirsty tiger' tearing the entrails of the realm.'[36]

This unifying theme also establishes the irrationality of the arguments put forward claiming that the love-episode represents an interpolation or later addition by Shakespeare. Such a suggestion can now be seen to be untenable for it would destroy the very fabric of the play, not merely unbalance it. *Edward the Third* is, in fact, a finely crafted play, and a recent production by Toby Robertson has testified to its exciting theatrical viability in performance.[37] The love-episode is a delight when experienced on the stage, but the whole play is effective theatre as proved by this modern revival which had many fine moments and some excellent character portrayals. King John is cast as the villain of the piece, and the juxtaposition of the two sides, the Frenchmen versus the English, is presented with nicely pointed contrast in witty repartee and sardonic humour. The battle scenes are drawn with lively interest that maintains the dramatic tension. Marlowe is never a bore!

Conclusions on the Whole Play as from the Hand of Marlowe

Edward the Third must have been written the year after *Tamburlaine*, and as 1588 was a busy year with the threat of the Armada hanging over England it was probably the very next play he wrote. Having stomached criticism of his bombastic style in *Tamburlaine* he may have wanted to show his critics that he could also write in another vein, and he seems to be seeking a lower key for this English history play, although there are echoes of *Tamburlaine* still discernible. In the ritual donning of the young Prince Edward's armour before the battle of Crecy, which was to prove his baptism of fire and win him his spurs, Marlowe employs his favourite device of a refrain to impart a ritualistic effect as he had done in *Tamburlaine*, first in Zenocrate's lament over the tragic death of Zabina and Bajazeth in Part One, and again, most memorably in Tamburlaine's great mourning elegy at the death of Zenocrate.[38] These are both funeral dirges. In *Edward the Third* the occasion for his use of this device is at an important occasion which also has a religious significance, but of an inaugural not a terminal kind, like the christening of a child or a confirmation – here to bring especial blessing on the young Prince who was destined to become famous as 'the soul of chivalry' and to attain great victory in arms.*

> *Enter four Heralds, bringing in a coat of armour, a*
> *helmet, a lance and a shield.*
>
> *King.* Edward Plantagenet, in the name of God,
> As with this armour I impall thy breast,
> So be thy noble unrelenting heart
> Wall'd in with flint of matchless fortitude,
> That never base affections enter there:
> Fight and be valiant, conquer where thou com'st!
> Now follow, Lords, and do him honour too.
> *Derby.* Edward Plantagenet, Prince of Wales,
> As I do set this helmet on thy head,
> Wherewith the chamber of thy brains is fenc'd,
> So may thy temples, with Bellona's hand,
> Be still adorn'd with laurel victory:
> Fight and be valiant, conquer where thou com'st!
> *Audley.* Edward Plantagenet, Prince of Wales,
> Receive this lance into thy manly hand;
> Use it in fashion of a brazen pen,
> To draw forth bloody stratagems in France,
> And print thy valiant deeds in honour's book:
> Fight and be valiant, vanquish where thou com'st!
> *Artois.* Edward Plantagenet, Prince of Wales,
> Hold, take this target, wear it on thy arm;
> And may the view thereof, like Perseus shield,
> Astonish and transform thy gazing foes
> To senseless images of meagre death:
> Fight and be valiant, conquer where thou com'st!
> *King.* Now wants there nought but knighthood, which
>   deferr'd
> We leave, till thou hast won it in the field.
>
> Act III, Sc.3, 11.179–205

It is not a great poetic passage, for the lyricism and passion that inform Tamburlaine's splendid dirge are absent, but the mind that fashioned both is cast in the same poetic mould. A much finer example of Marlowe's

---

*Is there a recollection of his armoured figure with his helmet and shield in Canterbury Cathedral in this ritualistic arming of the Black Prince?

powers developing in this, his lower-key style *sans* bombast, is found in the speech of the old campaigner, Audley, brilliantly depicting the massed army of the French assembled before the battle of Poitiers which he reports to Prince Edward.

> *Audley.* This sudden, mighty, and expedient head
> That they have made, fair Prince, is wonderful.
> Before us in the valley lies the king,
> Vantaged with all that heaven and earth can yield;
> His party stronger battled than our whole:
> His son, the braving Duke of Normandy,
> Hath trimm'd the mountain on our right hand up
> In shining plate, that now the aspiring hill
> Shows like a silver quarry or an orb,
> Aloft of which the banners, bannerets,
> And new replenish'd pendants cuff the air
> And beat the winds, that for their gaudiness
> Struggles to kiss them: on our left hand lies
> Philip, the younger issue of the king,
> Coating the other hill in such array,
> That all his gilded upright pikes do seem
> Straight trees of gold, the pendants leaves;
> And their device of antique heraldry,
> Quarter'd in colours, seeming sundry fruits,
> Makes it the Orchard of th'Hesperides:
> Behind us too the hill doth bear his height,
> For like a half moon, opening but one way,
> It rounds us in; there at our backs are lodg'd
> The fatal crossbows, and the battle there
> Is govern'd by the rough Chatillion.

Act IV, Sc.4, 11.10–34

The reference to the 'half moon' is significant, bringing us back again to the Armada whose crescent moon battle formation had posed such a dire threat to the English navy. The Black Prince and his valiant few were here environed with threat – the huge army of the French far outnumbering the English force, massed in glittering array on the surrounding hills. This speech sets the scene for us vividly with its taut, allusive imagery that imparts a sense of expectancy and the thrill of danger challenging the courage of the English to the uttermost point, in which, weighing the tremendous odds, the Prince philosophizes on death and welcomes the challenge. In the event, it was not the size of the enemy army but the valour of the few that won the day.

The battle that ensues is dramatically effective with the strange occurence of the flight of ravens that hovers over the French army, darkening the sky, (echoing the Mariner's sighting of King Edward's gaily bedight 'armado' of ships which King John mis-describes as a 'flight of ravens' – was our dramatist anticipating these dire ravens?) which struck terror in the superstitious French who had heard a prophecy that flights of birds and flint stones rising from the earth would spell disaster to them. The English attacking with great ferocity drive the fearful French to flight. When their supplies of arrows fail they seize flint stones from the field and stone them to death. So this ancient prophecy is fulfilled, making an unusual and dramatic event of this battle.

There is more subtlety in this play than at first seems apparent, in its apt touches that add just the colour or the historical verisimilitude that the dramatist wanted. This is particularly evident in his choice and presentation of material drawn from this exceptionally long and brilliant reign. Marlowe proves once again what a careful craftsman he is, for a great deal of thought has gone into the selection of historical events; these he has perforce had to telescope in time in order to encompass them within one dramatic presentation, which he achieves by having only one King of France, John, and eliminating King Philip, for two kings of France would have been an unnecessary complication to his plot, and he naturally wanted to include both the famous battles of Crecy and Poitiers, which took place in successive reigns.

In a small deft touch he points the audacity of Edward in quartering the arms of France with those of England which are born on the standards of his ships advancing on Sluys[39] – by which he symbolically throws down the gauntlet to King John. The verbal slanging match that precedes the first encounter in the field with the French is used to display the opposing sides, King John taunting Edward with treasure of gold and pearls to win in fair fight, if he can do so – reminiscent of *Tamburlaine* again, which Edward scornfully rejects with telling sarcasm –

> If gall or wormwood have a pleasant taste,
> Then is thy salutation honey sweet,
>
> Act III Sc.3, 11.72–73

informing him he is come 'To skirmish, not for pillage, but for the crown'. This scene is well used to develop the characters of the protagonists.

Prince Edward joins in hotly; the old campaigner Audley is insulted by Charles, Duke of Normandy, (King John's son) who calls him an 'aged impotent'. The French are presented as uncouth and unchivalrous, the English more dignified in their replies. This is typical of Marlowe's witty use of invective between opposing sides to heighten the drama as in *Tamburlaine, The Jew of Malta, The Contention, True Tragedy* and *harey the vj,* Edward the Second* and *The Massacre at Paris.*

Edward emerges from this word battle as a man of human frailty who is yet truly a man of dauntless courage. King John's final taunt doubtless went home wherein he refers sneeringly to Edward's love affair:

> For what's this Edward but a belly god,
> A tender and lascivious wantonness,
> That th'other day was almost dead for love?
> And what, I pray you, is his goodly guard?
> Such as, but scant them of their chines of beef
> And take away their downy feather-beds,
> And presently they are as rusty stiff,
> As 'twere a many over ridden jades,
> Then Frenchmen, scorn that such should be your lords,
> And rather bind ye them in captive bands.
> *All French.* Vive le Roi! God save King John of France!
> *John.* Now on this plain of Crecy spread yourselves, –
> And, Edward, when thou darest, begin the fight.

11.155–167

This much discussed love episode should now be seen in the context of the play's entire dramatic structure. It is dramatically and thematically basic to the concept of the play, and it is vital to the presentation of the character of Edward, warts and all, as a real human being. The Countess of Salisbury, on the other hand, is Marlowe's own creation. The amalgamation of the character of the witty Agnes of Dunbar, 'Black Agnes' as she was called, with the Countess of his story was a stroke of inspiration. Our introduction to her is in a scene when she mercilessly taunts the Scottish King and the Earl of Douglas, her captors, whom she overhears bargaining over possession of her person and her jewels, when in the nick of time she is saved by the arrival of King Edward and his

---

*harey the vj is Henslowe's name for what later became *I Henry VI*, which is discussed in Chapter VIII 'A New Play at the Rose with its New Look'.

army, and the Scotsmen flee. We know immediately what sort of lady this is, and why her charms exert such a powerful attraction on Edward for she has both wit and beauty, a double enchantment.

It is of interest that it is when King Edward falls in love that rhyme makes its appearance. It is as though Marlowe is using rhyme as a symbolic device to suggest the dart of Cupid entering the King's heart, for from the moment that he sets eyes on her he begins to speak in rhyme! As the Countess greets him at her Castle gate and begs him to enter and partake of her hospitality, Edward becomes enamoured of her. Knowing his weakness for women, and fearing the power of her fatal attraction for him, he at first claims he cannot stay but must pursue the Scots. When the Countess pleads with him to remain at least a little while to acᶜ ⸱ of her hospitality, he makes further excuse:

> *King Edward.* Pardon me, Countess, I will come no near;
> I dream'd tonight of treason, and I fear.
> *Countess.* Far from this place let ugly treason lie!
> *King.* No farther off, than her conspiring eye, (*Aside*)
> Which shoots infected poison in my heart,
> Beyond repulse of wit or cure of art.
> Now, in the sun alone it doth not lie,
> With light to take light from a mortal eye;
> For here two day stars that mine eyes would see
> More than the sun steals mine own light from me.
> Contemplative desire, desire to be
> In contemplation, that may master thee!
> Warwick, Artois, to horse and let's away!
>
> Act II, Sc.1. 11.125–137

Apart from the love episode, where rhyme is used in the first encounter of the King and the Countess, rhyming couplets are only used to end some of the scenes; as they are used also occasionally in *Tamburlaine* to end a scene and at the end of both Parts of *Tamburlaine*. *Faustus* and *The Jew of Malta* end with a rhyming couplet, and the latter play has a few rhyming passages ending a scene, but most notably Ithamore breaks into verse when in the arms of the courtezan Bellamira:

> *Ithamore.* Content: but we will leave this paltry land,
> And sail from hence to Greece, to lovely Greece;
> I'll be thy Jason, thou my golden fleece;

105

Where painted carpets o'er the meads are hurl'd,
And Bacchus' vineyards o'erspread the world;
Where woods and forests go in goodly green,
I'll be Adonis, thou shalt be Love's Queen.
The meads, the orchards, and the primrose-lanes,
Instead of sedge and reed, bear sugar-canes:
Thou in those groves, by Dis above,
Shalt live with me, and be my love.

The Jew of Malta, Act IV, 11.314–324

Thus we see Marlowe's use of rhyme as an inspirational device associated with romance. It is interesting to note that Shakespeare's most romantic play, *Romeo the Juliet*, is intermittently in rhyme which is given to Romeo when conversing with Benvolio, and the balcony scene ends in rhyme; and Friar Lawrence and Lord and Lady Capulet speak largely in rhyme. There is also a great deal of rhyme in *Love's Labour's Lost* and in *A Midsummer Night's Dream*.

Edward the Third with its romantic episode depicting the amorous King in the toils of his passion, represents a new departure for Marlowe which he has so delightfully realized as dramatic entertainment, and at the same time he establishes the underlying theme of his play in Edward's inner struggle to master his illicit desire. Prince Edward's presence reminds him of his Queen, and he soliloquyses:

King Edward. Still do I see in him delineate
His mother's visage; those his eyes are hers,
Who, looking whistly on me, make me blush:
For faults against themselves give evidence;
Lust is a fire, and men like lanthorns show
Light lust within themselves, even through themselves.
Away, loose silks of wavering vanity!
Shall the large limit of fair Brittany
By me be overthrown, and shall I not
Master this little mansion of myself?
Give me an armour of eternal steel!
I go to conquer kings; and shall I not then
Subdue myself? and be my enemies' friend?
It must not be. – Come, boy, forward, advance!
Let's with our colours sweet the air of France.

Act II, Sc.2, 11.88–100

The Countess 'with a smiling cheer' has thereupon requested an audience with King Edward and he is immediately hooked once more, but the statement of his intent has been made and with it the tenor of the play is set.

At the end of the play this theme is brought full circle when Queen Philippa begs the lives of the six burghers of Calais to be spared. Edward had begun by playing a heavy hand of retribution, like a Tamburlaine refusing mercy because he had decreed that these six men were to be the sacrifice his conquering pride and authority demanded. But the Queen pleads eloquently:

> Ah, be more mild unto these yielding men!
> It is a glorious thing to stablish peace,
> And kings approach the nearest unto God
> By giving life and safety unto men:
> As thou intendest to be king of France,
> So let her people live to call thee king;
> For what the sword cuts down or fire hath spoil'd,
> Is held in reputation none of ours.

And Edward listens and relents:

> *Edward.* Although experience teach us this is true,
> That peaceful quietness brings most delight,
> When most of all abuses are controll'd;
> Yet, insomuch it shall be known that we
> As well can master our affections
> As conquer other by the dint of sword,
> Phillip, prevail; we yield to thy request:
> These men shall live to boast of clemency,
> And, tyranny, strike terror to thyself.

> Act V, 11.39–55

So the lesson of self-mastery is once more brought before his attentive audience. It is Marlowe proselytising through the medium of his dramatic work – a characteristic trait that has hardly been remarked by his critics. In *Edward the Third* it is again the influence of a woman at the end which brings the King to his more civilized self, and this famous incident of clemency all but closes the play. There remains the delivery of the captured Scottish King David by his captor John Copland to the King's hand; followed by the arrival of Salisbury to report the tragic news that Prince Edward has been slain at Poitiers, which is then dramatically changed from grief to joy when the young Prince arrives on the scene, victorious, hale and hearty, bringing the French King John with him as his baleful prisoner. The English royal family thus joyfully re-united prepare to sail back to England with their royal prisoners. So ends the play on a high note of victorious achievement.

The selectiveness with which Marlowe used his source material underlines his intent to write a commemorative play for the Armada victory. This play presents the happiest years of the reign of King Edward, making a unique feature of its conclusive naval victory at Sluys. It speaks well for the historical sense of Elizabethan audiences that the playwright could rely on their keen appreciation of his analogous presentation of this historical event. The play was hugely popular, and Edward Alleyn's association with it fully justifies its inclusion here.

The extraordinary history of the manuscript 'A Relation of Proceedings' has only been touched upon here, but its unique importance will be apparent. It adds significantly to our knowledge of Marlowe, whose career in intelligence has been insufficiently researched. This report highlights the high standing he enjoyed as a government agent in a position of trust and prestige with Walsingham and Burghley, while its relationship to *Edward the Third* is of a special nature unparalleled in any play of the period. This play can now be seen to hold a unique place in Marlowe's canon: it was a 'first' in almost every respect. His first attempt at an English history play; his first play that was not a tragedy; his first play to contain scenes of delightful romantic comedy revealing a new facet of his protean genius; his only play to reflect personal experience in such a striking manner. And it is of particular interest that it was with this play that the great cycle of English historical dramas was launched, the crowning glory of which are the Shakespearean histories, born out of the experience of Elizabethan England's victorious naval campaign against Philip of Spain's 'Invincible Armada', which brought England that peace so necessary for the development of her greatest period of drama in which, from 1588 onwards, the Muse of history exerts such a powerful inspirational influence.

IV *Three Plays of the Pembroke Players*

THE CANON of dramatic works accredited to Marlowe's name numbers only seven over the period of his creative activity which most critics judge to be from about 1586 to the winter of 1592–3, for *The Massacre at Paris* was on the boards as a new play in January 1593 and was probably his last dramatic work.

His accepted canon comprises:

The Tragedie of Dido Queene of Carthage	printed 1594
Tamburlaine the Great, Devided into two *Tragicall Discourses*	Parts 1 and 2 printed 1590
The Famous Tragedy of the Rich Jew *of Malta*	printed 1633 (extant edition)
The Tragicall History of D. Faustus	printed 1604
The troublesome raigne and lamentable *death of Edward the second, King of England*	printed 1594
The Massacre at Paris	printed undated

For a writer of his genius barely one play per year is a meagre achievement. The Shakespearean canon of thirty-six plays over a span of eighteen years from, say, 1593 to 1611, gives a steady production of two plays a year, and most Elizabethan dramatists matched or exceeded this output. John Bakeless comments:

'Presumably.....some of Marlowe's plays have been lost, especially if we accept Fleay's assertion that "Marlowe probably wrote two plays a year from 1587 – 1593" though we now have but seven "acknowledged as his".'[1]

In the hot-bed of London's theatrical world at this time one would expect at least two plays a year from the fecund, creative powers of the vigorous, young Marlowe. Even if we accept the inclusion of *Edward III*, as his first essay in English historical drama, and the lost *Scanderbeg*, and the Kentish domestic tragi-comedy *Arden of Faversham*, we are still short of four plays to fill the period of his apparently dormant creativity; and this at a time when the evidence of his established works reveals the wide range of his quest for ever new fields in which to diversify and develop his great dramatic and poetic gifts which were rapidly maturing and gaining in power.

Especially relevant to this problem is the disputed authorship of the two related history plays on the Wars of the Roses, which were first published in two 'bad' quartos under the titles, *The First Part of the Contention betwixt the two famous Houses of Yorke and Lancaster*, in 1594, and *The True Tragedy of Richard Duke of Yorke*, in 1595, by the printer Edward Millington, who states that the *True Tragedy* was acted by the Earl of Pembroke's Men, and hence doubtless was also its companion piece *The Contention*, although, as so often, he annoyingly omits to name the author. Both plays have a distinctly Marlovian ring, but almost thirty years later they take their place in the First Folio as *The Second Part* and *The third Part of Henry the Sixt* respectively, each play bearing considerable additional material and signs of internal revision of the text. This is seen as the contribution made by William Shakespeare, thus providing justification for Heminge's and Condell's claim that they were plays from Shakespeare's hand. These two 'bad' quartos comprise approximately one half and two-thirds of the text in the Folio version of *Henry VI 2* and *3* respectively.

These two plays on the Wars of the Roses have been the battleground of Shakespearean scholars for the last two hundred years. The authorship of these anonymous works has been seen as crucial to the problem of Shakespeare's 'lost years', from the last documentary evidence of his marriage to Anne Hathaway, and the christening of their children, a daughter Susanna, followed by the twins, Hamnet and Judith, the latter two on 2nd February 1584/5. Thereafter history draws a blank, until the record of the Christmas performances given by the Lord Chamberlain's Men at the Court at Greenwich for which payment was received on the following 15th March 1594/5, when the payees on behalf of the company were Kempe, Shakespeare and Richard Burbage. It is the only occasion when Shakespeare's name appears in this particular capacity during the reign of Queen Elizabeth, and is the only evidence that is wholly reliable. History is not always as liberal with its evidence as we would wish, and it is this blank that Shakespearean scholars, whose discipline tends to be that of English literature rather than history, seem to find so insupportably disturbing that they are tempted to elaborate all kinds of fancies to fill it. Consequently these two history plays of the Pembroke's Men have been seized upon as neatly filling the gap of Shakespeare's hypothetical activity as a dramatist in London prior to 1594. For this reason alone has their authorship been so hotly contested in an atmosphere emotionally charged with the commitment to Shakespeare at all costs, without regard for the claims of Marlowe, who is quite unfairly denigrated in the process, as is clearly demonstrated in the quotations from the writings of Peter Alexander and Dover Wilson in the ensuing review of this controversy. Fortunately, Marlowe has found formidable champions in Tucker Brooke and Bakeless and Allison Gaw, and, the battle being joined, presents an interesting intellectual exercise.

I make no apology for reopening the issue and challenging the 'new orthodoxy' to answer the evidence here put forward afresh. For too long has the self-imposed necessity of providing evidence of Shakespeare's earlier emergence as a practising playwright clouded the issue, and the attribution of these plays to Shakespeare has been allowed to override the validity of both the external and the strong internal evidence identifying these plays as of Marlowe's authorship.

In 1921 Dr C.F. Tucker Brooke undertook a detailed textual analysis of these two plays, because he found that no adequate textual examination had been conducted, although argument and counter-argument concerning the authorship of the plays continually exercised the minds of scholars. The result of his objective, critical and, indeed, exhaustive investigation of their authorial problems was to ascribe both plays without any doubt to Marlowe's hand in his thesis *The Authorship of the Second and Third Parts of 'King Henry VI'*, published in Transactions of the Connecticut Academy of Arts and Sciences, 1921. He has been supported by Dr Allison Gaw in his masterly exposé of the vexed question of the authorship of the companion work in the trilogy, the Folio's *The first Part of Henry the Sixt* in *The Origin and Development of 1 Henry VI* published in 1926, in which he has brilliantly demonstrated that this is clearly a collaborative play, which is mainly, but not all Marlowe's work, with a remarkable theatrical history that is the subject of Chapter VIII.

Today the orthodox school adopts a diametrically opposite view attributing the authorship of the entire *Henry VI* trilogy to Shakespeare's hand alone, despite the fact that it has been impossible to refute Tucker Brooke's or Dr Gaw's finely argued theses. The orthodox position has been achieved by the expedient, not of refuting Tucker Brooke's irrefutable arguments, but by misrepresenting them and by-passing them; and in the

111

case of Dr Gaw's great thesis, by simply ignoring its existence, apart from a mere passing reference to it – a courtesy nod as from one scholar to another. This nod comes from Peter Alexander, who is the man responsible for having staged a feigned refutation of Tucker Brooke's findings concerning Marlowe's authorship of *The Contention* and *True Tragedy* as will be established in the following examination of the argument. The present firmly entrenched orthodox view of the authorship of the *Henry VI* trilogy as by Shakespeare's hand alone exists, therefore, on unsound and contentious foundations.

Significantly, the only scholar of stature who has in more recent years re-examined Tucker Brooke's evidence in the detail it deserves has endorsed his findings as conclusive. This is John Bakeless in his monumental two-volume biography, *The Tragicall History of Christopher Marlowe*, published in 1942, in which he has added yet further confirmatory evidence to support Dr Brooke's thesis.

Marlowe's other important biographer, Frederick S. Boas, in his *Christopher Marlowe*, 1940, gives an overall brief review of the opposing arguments concerning the authorship of these plays, but remains cautious about taking any side in this contentious contention; but, for our purposes, his concise resumé of Tucker Brooke's thesis will suffice as introduction to the problems.

'The literary quality of *The Contention* and *The True Tragedy*, in Brooke's view, points to Marlowe as being their author. They exhibit "a brilliant synthesis of plot and emotion", and "the whole tangled story is resolutely pitched in a single key". Moreover, the respective relations of Henry VI, Queen Margaret, Suffolk, and Prince Edward in these two plays are closely akin to those of Edward II, Queen Isabel, Mortimer, and Prince Edward in *Edward II*. The versification, with its predominant number of end stopped lines, and its absence of double endings, is characteristic of Marlowe. But the most concrete support for Marlowe's claim is found by Brooke in the remarkable number of passages in *The Contention* and *The True Tragedy* which have parallels in Marlowe's accepted plays or which are repeated in the quartos themselves. Such parallelism and repetition are both characteristic of Marlowe's technique. Brooke gives a list of twenty-eight parallels with plays in the recognized Marlovian canon, fourteen of which are with *Edward II* and nine with *The Massacre at Paris*. He gives also fifteen examples of repetition within *The Contention* and *The True Tragedy*.'[2]

Dr Gaw gives acknowledgement to Tucker Brooke's work and amplifies Boas's statement:

'In 1912 Dr C.F. Tucker Brooke, through a careful examination of the external and internal evidence relating to *The Contention* and *The True Tragedy*, and especially of a series of forty-three groups of parallel passages strongly typical of Marlowe and interweaving those plays with the entire list of Marlowe's undoubted dramas, proved conclusively, to my mind, his thesis that both of these plays were originally the sole work of Marlowe.'[3]

Surprisingly, in view of the intense interest in this problem, there has been no commensurate in-depth study of the texts of these two plays since Tucker Brooke, apart from Peter Alexander's treatment in 1929, which has again been refuted by Bakeless. Nevertheless, modern scholarship has elected to follow Alexander in uncritical obedience and has contrived to steer a devious course which avoids actual confrontation with this mass of carefully collated evidence by substituting subjective opinion and hypothesis for objective research.

The 'new orthodoxy' that has become established claiming these plays as solely the work of Shakespeare is based on the not-so-new theory first put forward by J.S. Smart in 1928 and developed by Peter Alexander in his *Shakespeare's Henry VI and Richard III*, published 1929. Alexander is clearly interested, not so much in objectively examining the textual evidence of *The Contention* and *The True Tragedy* in relation to Marlowe's works, but in finding a plausible explanation for the beginning of Shakespeare's career in the absence of anything linking him with any of the acting companies before Christmas 1594.

The texts of the quartos of *The Contention* and *The True Tragedy* constitute one half and two-thirds respectively of *2* and *3 Henry VI* in the First Folio, showing the typical abbreviated version of texts printed in so-called 'bad' quartos of the period, and both plays were performed by the Earl of Pembroke's Men, as also was Marlowe's *Edward II*. This association of all three plays with Pembroke's Men gives Alexander his starting point. To summarize, his hypothesis is as follows:

1.   The two curtailed versions of *2* and *3 Henry VI* published in 'bad' quartos as *The Contention* and *The True Tragedy* represent surreptitious copies of Shakespeare's plays furnished by the actors of Pembroke's company to the printer, Thomas Millington.

2.   Shakespeare had already written the complete *Henry VI, Part 2 and 3* for the Pembroke company in or about 1590, or the actors could not have obtained the text for their surreptitious copy to sell to the printer.

3.   Since Shakespeare had written these plays in about 1590 for the Pembroke Men he must already have been installed as a member of that company as actor or resident playwright *before* Marlowe arrived on the scene to write his *Edward II* for them.

4.   Marlowe, therefore, wrote his *Edward II* after Shakespeare's two history plays and *in imitation* of them. Marlowe is thereby revealed as the follower of Shakespeare and not the innovator of the English history play, as had always hitherto been accredited to him. He was only Shakespeare's imitator and it was Shakespeare who was the true innovator of this popular genre of drama.

This neatly turns the tables in favour of Shakespeare's authorship of *The Contention* and *True Tragedy* and additionally gives him the credit as the originator of great English historical drama. Nothing so mundane as 'evidence' is produced to support any of these bold assertions, and not the slightest evidence of Shakespeare's connections with the Earl of Pembroke's Men in 1589/90 exists. All this is pure guess work on the part of Alexander; nevertheless, he is adamant on the matter, citing the First Folio, published 33 years later, as his 'Bible':

'Marlowe, when he came to write for Pembroke's men, found Shakespeare one of the company, and his *2 and 3 Henry VI* in their repertoire: that these pieces were by Shakespeare is attested by Heminge and Condell, Shakespeare's editors.'[4]

And he confidently asserts when repeating this argument in his more recent work, *Shakespeare*, published in 1964:

'Marlowe, finding these plays popular, set himself to write something on the same lines. The notion that Marlowe was the originator of the English history play, and that Shakespeare was, in Mr Bakeless's words, beginning slowly and clumsily to follow in the way Marlowe had marked out for him, is an assumption that rests on the assumption that Shakespeare could not yet write for himself and completely

114

misrepresents the relationship between *Edward II* and *2* and *3 Henry VI*.[5]

Leaving aside the quite unjustified accusation against Bakeless (who uses *no* such words as 'slowly and clumsily' to describe Shakespeare at any point in his comparative study of Marlowe and Shakespeare), it is clear from the start that it is Alexander who is basing his entire hypothesis on assumption based on assumption. He cites the First Folio, printed thirty-three years later if we date these plays to 1590 (and Heminge and Condell were not associated with the Pembroke Players), as his sole 'evidence' that these plays were in origin and throughout their development entirely Shakespeare's work: a claim that anyone knowing anything about the vagaries of the Elizabethan theatrical world in relation to the dramatic works it handled must realise is not, and cannot be cited as, conclusive evidence. A great deal of rewriting and revision of old plays went on at this time, and Bakeless is not disputing that Shakespeare later revised and added to the *Henry VI* plays to present them in the form in which they appear in the Folios, neither is Tucker Brooke. They are, after all, both great Shakespearean scholars, though not blind to Marlowe's genius. Fortunately for Marlowe his *Edward II* was printed in a what we may take to be a reasonably fair copy by William Jones in 1594 and bears on its title-page the rare authorial ascription 'Written by Chri. Marloe, Gent.' But the two other Pembroke history plays bear no such ascription and they are clearly representativeof the many 'bad' quartos surreptitiously published during Elizabethan times by actors seeking a little extra cash, or by the literary pirates who took down plays in short-hand during performances and sold their texts to the eager printers. Play texts were difficult to come by, since the acting companies owned the scripts and guarded them jealously against publication, for their repertoire of play scripts was their stock-in-trade investment for which the exploited playwright was but meagrely paid when he parted with the creation of his Muse for a few pounds to the actors' company, probably after a first reading of his manuscript in some tavern. Thereafter the dramatist had no further rights, no copyright, or claim on his work: the actors' company owning it could revise it, interpolate scenes, or adapt it by cutting and so on to suit their theatrical purposes, and they alone could sanction its publication, which often bore testimony to the company or companies who had performed the play, but omitted any mention of the author.

It was just such a publication of playscripts which evidently brought the Pembroke plays onto the printers' market in 1594 and 1595, as a result of the dire straits in which the Pembroke Men found themselves from the long closure of the theatres during the severe plague year of 1593, which extended well into 1594 before all restraint on theatrical performances was lifted. The Pembroke company had not gone on tour into the provinces, or abroad, as had most of the other players, and we know that they were reduced to selling off their stage properties, apparel and play scripts in order to keep the wolf from the door. Philip Henslowe's letter to Edward Alleyn (quoted on page 345) confirms this.

It is in these circumstances that Alexander seizes on a convenient explanation for the great number of parallels noted by Tucker Brooke and Bakeless in the three Pembroke plays – *The Contention, The True Tragedy* and *Edward II*. Alexander claims that all these parallels are due to the poor memories of the actors who were putting together the scripts from their recollection of their parts in *The Contention* and *The True Tragedy* to sell them surreptitiously to the printer, and, as they had all also acted in *Edward II*, they muddled up some of the lines from that play with their parts in the other two somewhat similar history plays. So it was, that the actors produced a garbled version of the texts of *The Contention* and *The True Tragedy* for the printer, and what emerged was a kind of hybrid between what Shakespeare had written in his two history plays, and what Marlowe wrote in his *Edward II*.

This blatantly sophistical argument falls apart at first glance for if this is *really* the explanation of the many parallels in these plays – that they derive from the actors' faulty memories of their parts – why is it that they are still there in the Folio versions *after* Shakespeare had revised the plays? This point does not seem to have occurred to Alexander.

Dr Alexander first expounded his argument at some length in 1929 when he made a strenuous attempt to demolish Dr Tucker Brooke's thesis, not by refuting it, but by substituting his own assumptions for Tucker Brooke's meticulously assembled evidence. He reiterates his arguments in his *Shakespeare* in 1964, but this time making *no reference whatsoever* to Tucker Brooke's great work, but harking back instead to the long outdated work of Edmund Malone, who was writing two centuries ago, between 1778 and 1790, on the same theme *without*, however, having made any thorough textual examination on which to base his opinions as Tucker Brooke had done.

'In his dissertation on the *Henry VI* plays, Malone had attributed the quartos, *The Contention* and *The True Tragedy* to Greene and Peele. At the further prompting of Farmer, his evil genius in this affair,

116

Malone changed his mind and decided they were the work of Marlowe. It is true the quartos contain many passages and lines identical with or similar to lines and passages in Marlowe's *Edward II*. These passages, however, were not inserted by Marlowe but by the actors who put together these quartos from memory; and they inserted the passages from Marlowe because, having played in 2 and 3 *Henry VI* as well as in *Edward II*, they failed to keep clear and distinct the differences between many situations in Shakespeare's pieces and Marlowe's history that might very easily be confused. That the same company of actors played in these pieces is clear from the title-pages of *The True Tragedy* and *Edward II* where they are described as having been acted by Pembroke's company, *The Contention* clearly belonged to the same company.'6

This explanation conveniently begs the question of the parallels with Marlowe's other dramas, *The Massacre at Paris* (nine in number), *Dido* (one) and *Tamburlaine* (three parallels). However, this does not give Alexander a moment's pause. He curtly dismisses the first two mentioned plays on the grounds that the parallels are only a few in number (they total ten in all). He states categorically:

'These groups may therefore be ignored. The recollections from *Tamburlaine*, though few, are more convincing.' [He feels he can allow himself this show of impartiality because he has the answer already up his sleeve.] 'As *Tamburlaine* was a widely known play by 1594 there is nothing surprising in these interpolations. That the echoes from *Edward II* are *The Contention's* largest debt to Marlowe is also what the date and circumstances of its production would lead us to expect.'7

This is strange because Alexander maintains that *The Contention* had already been written *before Edward II*, so how could it owe that play any 'debt'? Alexander's facile answer to Dr Tucker Brooke's thoroughly researched textual evidence, then, is that the parallels between what he considers to be Shakespeare's plays and Marlowe's *Edward II* are not true parallels at all but merely actors' 'interpolations', and as such cannot be taken as evidence of authorship; while those from *Tamburlaine* represent 'recollections' (it is not clear whether he means Shakespeare's or the actors' 'recollections' here), and the rest of the parallels can be ignored because they are so few in number. As we shall see, Alexander is not consistent about this last point either. He uses an argument when it suits him, and when it does not he discards it.

In the main, Alexander's hypothesis rests on his claim that the 'bad' quartos of the two *Henry VI* plays represent the product of the actors' faulty memories, who, while reconstructing these plays surreptitiously for the printer without resort to a script, muddled up their lines from the three disparate but rather similar history plays that were in their repertoire, with a result that is unique even in the extensive genre of 'bad' quartos that have come down to us!

In support of this argument, Alexander goes to considerable length to present examples of how actors in the eighteenth century constructed pirated versions of Sheridan's popular theatrical works. Sheridan's *School for Scandal* was for some time only available to theatrical managers under constraint that it was not released to other theatres. The theatre manager of the Exeter theatre at this time, being unable to obtain a script and desperately wanting to put on this play, persuaded an actor, John Bernard, to produce a piratical script for him, and this is how he did it. (Bernard left an account of how he worked at reconstructing his play script which Alexander quotes in full.)[8] Bernard had himself played three main characters in the successful run of *The School for Scandal* at Bath, while his wife had played two of the principal female roles (at alternate times in each case) and from recollection of their parts, and the additional help of three other actors who had been in the company, Bernard produced a fair script for the theatre manager at Exeter, Hughes, who put on this version of the play as an undetected piracy at his theatre where it played to full houses until the end of the season.

The above 'proof' of his arguments, however, has no bearing on his hypothesis in fact since only *one* play, *The School for Scandal*, is involved, and not *three* plays as required to substantiate his claim that actors muddle up their parts from *different* plays.

As further evidence Alexander gives a second example of a theatre manager who himself, without the help of any actors, having seen a performance of Sheridan's operatic work, *The Duenna*, managed to construct a piratical version using a book of the songs, which he had obtained; relying on his own memory of certain jokes in the work; and cobbling up the rest of the dialogue by cribbing from a collection of old plays on Spanish themes. Thus he put together a production that somewhat resembled Sheridan's popular musical play.

These examples Alexander triumphantly presents to us as *proof* to substantiate his hypothesis that the Pembroke Men reconstructed a somewhat confused version of the plays in which they had performed, in which they muddled up the lines from one play, *Edward II*, with the other two. His second example of *The Duenna* has no relevance whatsoever as it is not a parallel situation, the manager working from song sheets and play scripts on Spanish themes and some recollection of jokes.

The first example of *The School for Scandal* is, of course, exactly what we all accept as the way in which actors compiled their surreptitious copies, usually with a fair degree of success, and *without confusing two or three plays together* as Alexander maintains the Pembroke Men did. So this, again, is not proof of his theory at all. On the contrary, *The School for Scandal* is an example of what actors generally would be well capable of doing, the Pembroke Men included. Namely, that actors collaborating to reproduce a play script can provide a fair approximation of the text for the printers from their recollection of the parts they had played. This represents no great feat for an actor. I well recall that, having had the good fortune to go to a school where Shakespeare's plays were performed as a regular end of term event, we readily absorbed everyone else's part. I found I knew the whole plays by the end of the performances. Once my two friends and I gave a 'send-up' performance of the entire *Tempest* after the show to the delectation of a hilarious circle of our peers – though I hardly remember a word of it now. This kind of nonsense is fairly common in amateur dramatic clubs. Actors who are trained to perform in repertory acquire prodigious memories, and are able to take over another actor's part at split second notice. But as for confusing two play scripts, let alone three plays with each other – impossible for an actor! Such a muddle-head would not survive long in a repertory company. An actor trained to perform alternating plays in repertory has no problem in keeping the scripts of his plays discrete for the text is linked in his mind with the character he is portraying, which is of the essence of the art of acting – even at its most superficial level – and such confusion as Alexander suggests is unheard of.

Peter Alexander shows that he is out of his depth in this context, and his whole hypothesis is based on a fallacy about how an actor's memory works. The actor has quite a different problem relating to faulty memory, that which is known as 'drying' on stage, either in performance or rehearsal. This it is which is clearly demonstrated in the many 'bad' quartos which show how the actors' faulty memories work, for when an actor's recollection fails and he 'dries' his mind will characteristically leap forward to pick up the same speech some lines further along, thus omitting several lines and curtailing the text to produce a shortened version. Here we have the origin of the abbreviated speeches in *The Contention*, for instance, which is half the full length version of *2 Henry VI* and *The True Tragedy* which is two-thirds of *3 Henry VI*. But since we cannot now tell for sure whether the longer version of a given speech is that which resulted from later revision, which is what we have in the First Folio, I give an example of such an abbreviated speech from a scene in Marlowe's *The Massacre at Paris*, an obviously truncated piratical text which only runs for barely one and a half hours in performance, compared with the extant manuscript from this scene believed to be in Marlowe's hand, which reveals a text double the length of the printed edition.[9]

In this scene a soldier has been told off by the Duke of Guise to kill his rival in love, the courtier Mugeroun, one of King Henry's favourites, who is having an affair with the Guise's Duchess. A comparison of corrupt printed and manuscript versions shows that the soldier's bawdy prose speech is well recalled, if not word perfect, but a fair rendering, given here in the curtailed printed text.

> *Soldier:* Sir, to you, sir, that dares make the duke a cuckold, and use a counterfeit key to his privy-chamber door; and although you take out nothing but your own, yet you put in that which displeaseth him, and so forestall his market, and set up your standing where you should not [*omission*] and whereas he is your landlord, you will take upon you to be his, and till the ground that he himself should occupy, which is his own free land; if it be not too free – there's the question; [*omission*] and though I come not to take possession (as I would I might!) yet I mean to keep you out; which I will, if this gear hold.   (11.813–824)

The first omission is: '*But you will saye you leave him rome enoughe besides: thats no answere hes to have the choyse of his owne freeland*'. The second is a reference to legal terms: '*and will needs enter by defaulte, whatt thoughe you were once in possession yett Comminge vpon you once vnawares he frayde you out againe. Therefore your entrye is mere Intrusione this is againste the lawe ser:*'[10]

Mugeroun's death cry, 'Trayterous guise ah thou has murthered me', is also omitted. But the biggest cut is in the Guise's speech over the dead body of his victim, of which only four lines are given in the printed text out of fifteen in the manuscript. I have italicised the printed text lines in the speech below; these provide the sense to carry on the play's momentum, but no more. This is typically how a corrupt text makes its cuts, leaving the bare bones of a play. The Guise enters and pays off the soldier before soliloquizing:

> Guise: *Hold thee tale soldier take the this and flye (Exit.)*
> thus fall Imperfett exhalatione
> W^ch our great sonn of fraunce Cold not effecte
> a fyery meteor in the fermament
> *Lye there the kinges delyght and guises scorne*
> *revenge it henry yf thow liste or darst*
> *I did it onely in dispyght of thee*
> fondlie hast thow in Censd the guises sowle
> y^t of it self was hote enoughe to worke
> thy Iust degestione wth extreamest shame
> the armye I have gathered now shall ayme
> more at thie end then exterpatione
> and when thou thinkst I have forgotten this
> and y^t thou most reposest one my faythe
> then will I wake thee from thie folishe dreame
> and lett thee see thie self my prysoner.
>
> *Exeunt.*[11]

The above is a typical instance of how a piratical text appears in usually somewhat abbreviated form, occasionally with words altered but keeping the sense of what is being said, whilst in blank verse the lines may be shortened losing their metrical quality. Actors were used to having speeches cut, for when the Elizabethan companies went on tour they often gave abbreviated versions of the plays in their repertoire for country audiences. Another characteristic ploy is paraphrasing the content of a speech, of which the actual words are only half remembered but the gist of the text is clear. Of all these typical memory failings there is plenty of evidence in the 'bad' quartos. But there is not one jot of evidence to substantiate Peter Alexander's claim that the parallels in *The True Tragedy* and *The Contention* could be construed as actors' interpolations from another play by faulty memory, or that actors are inclined to make this kind of confusion of texts between different plays in their repertoire. The only instance Alexander himself is able to offer of anything remotely resembling something like it is the following:

'Such transferences are found in the later piracies from Shakespeare: the Bad Quarto of *Hamlet* incorporates in its text a line from *Twelfth Night* and *The Merry Wives of Windsor* (1602) borrows a line from *Hamlet*.'[12]

This is hardly convincing evidence. Firstly, these are only *single* lines in each case, and since he himself has dismissed ten lines in Tucker Brooke's parallels as being too insignificant so that they can be 'ignored', the same standard, by his own dictum, must apply. Secondly, these parallels or 'interpolations', transferences or borrowings, according to how you view them, are both from the *same* author's works, and not from author to author, so that they fall into the category of self-repetitions of which Tucker Brooke has given copious examples within Marlowe's own works. Alexander omits to give either line references or the quotations themselves, which supposes that the examples are not particularly convincing as evidence or he would surely be less casual about demonstrating them to us. Presumably these errors are present in the Folio?

Writers, it is generally recognized, have a tendency to repeat themselves, just as Tucker Brooke has shown that Marlowe does – the same phrases, imagery, vocabulary, and modes of expression come out again and again, sometimes with disturbing frequency that has to be guarded against, as anyone re-reading a type-script or manuscript must know. A totally different mental activity is involved in creative writing to that of memorizing a play script by heart, and the revealing verbal parallelisms which bestrew a writer's work unconsciously are the basis of the identification of authorship by means of parallelisms. Although Alexander does not go so far as to disclaim the validity in general of the parallelism as the yardstick by which authorship may be assessed, he rejects it in this particular case because it does not suit his purpose!

One is bound to acknowledge the subtlety with which Alexander has contrived to bedevil the argument surrounding the attribution of these plays to the authorship of Shakespeare *versus* Marlowe by a devious evasion of the issue. If he insists – as he does – that the two 'bad' quartos under discussion are the 'muddled scripts' of plays by two different authors, while Tucker Brooke identifies them on the basis of internal evidence as being solely the work of Marlowe, even though in corrupt texts, there is no common ground for criticism as each is arguing from a totally different standpoint. By this means Alexander has skilfully altered the ground of this particular contention and has avoided the necessity of meeting Tucker Brooke on his ground, which Alexander must know is unassailable. Having thus shifted the interpretation to that of 'interpolations', which concept is foreign to Tucker Brooke's thesis, he yet implies that he is concerned with this idea by asking:

'How does he [Tucker Brooke] distinguish between the repetitions of Marlowe and the repetitions of the actors, and how can he decide whether an echo from *Edward II* or *The Massacre at Paris* is original to the text, or an interpolation?'[13]

Alexander should ask this question of himself, for the confusion is in his own mind, not in Tucker Brooke's. He is not in the least concerned with notions of actors' memory failings, which I have shown are fallacious, nor is he concerned to hypothesize to seek to superimpose explanations on his findings so that by 'interpretation' they will yield evidence that is otherwise entirely lacking of Shakespeare's activity and presence in London. Tucker Brooke's whole concern is with the text he has undertaken to study to which he applies all the scholarly techniques available to us to elucidate identification of authorship, and in which he has performed a task of masterly clarification and exhaustive detail to present his objectively reasoned and scholarly conclusions. By comparison Alexander's hypothesis, based on fallacy, which he presents as his challenge to the redoubtable Professor Tucker Brooke, emerges as mere feigned fencing, fighting the shadow and evading the substance of Tucker Brooke's thesis.

The Contention Continues

Having shifted the ground from parallels to interpolations by the actors, Peter Alexander then proceeds to use similar tactics to disparage Tucker Brooke's assessment of the metric and verse characteristics of these plays which further confirm Marlowe's hand. Alexander therefore casts serious doubt on the value of versification tests as having validity in such authorial investigations. He turns his attention next to two putative scripts, which he calls X and Y texts, which may have been available to the printer Pavier to supply a small number of extra lines. Tucker Brooke considers these of slight importance, but Alexander elevates them to a place of paramount importance, imputing arguments to Tucker Brooke which he never made! This part of Alexander's contorted contention is found in Appendix A, 'The X and Y Texts', in which his arguments are sufficiently exposed to discredit him.

There is, however, another aspect of this scholarly battle of the texts that requires an airing here, for it concerns the dramatic technique of Marlowe's works.

Alexander, having had his feigned fencing bout with Tucker Brooke in his 1929 criticism, and evidently feeling he has satisfactorily disintegrated his thesis, encouraged by the approving support he had received from his scholarly orthodox colleagues, subsequently drops Tucker Brooke's name from all further reference, perhaps fearful lest this ghost has not really been laid. In writing his popular *Shakespeare* in 1964 he reverts instead to attacking the antiquated Malone as though this protagonist for Marlowe's authorship of these Pembroke plays had been the only one over the last two hundred years, and, having dealt with Malone's long out-dated case, he asserts with superb confidence:

> 'It is now possible to reconstruct the evidence of Shakespeare's connexion with Pembroke's company, the errors of Malone and those who have been misdirected by him put aside.'[14]

Alexander's use of the words 'evidence' and 'hypothesis' might also be queried. In the above statement he speaks of reconstructing evidence, whereas since it is non-existent in the first place it cannot be 'reconstructed', and he should properly speak of 'constructing a theory' about Shakespeare's connections with Pembroke's company. In presenting his case Dr Alexander consistently refers to Tucker Brooke's carefully amassed internal evidence as a 'hypothesis', whereas he insists on calling his own hypothesis 'evidence'. However, it seems that his bold assertions and forcible championship of Shakespeare have won him the following of the majority of orthodox Shakespeareans for the last sixty years, including many eminent names, and he gains strong support from Dover Wilson in the recapitulation of his argument in his (Alexander's) *Shakespeare* (1964):

> 'Now that *The Contention* and *The True Tragedy* can be dismissed as unauthorized versions put together after the failure of Pembroke's company in 1593, and that the suggestion that the recollections from *Edward II* that these pieces contain are evidence of Marlowe's authorship is seen to be baseless, it is possible to compare *2* and *3 Henry VI* directly with *Edward II*. This comparison reveals a number of parallels between them; but as Professor Dover Wilson in his Introduction to *2 Henry VI* has summed up the matter:
>> Once the parallels are studied in relation to the sources of *Henry VI* Marlowe is revealed as unquestionably the borrower, since, in three cases, the passages in *Edward II* are neither guaranteed by history *nor required by the dramatic context*, [my italics, A.D.W.] while those in *Henry VI* are obviously taken from the chronicles."[15]

This objection is so extraordinary and so transparently aberrant as to require an answer. In the first place, it was Tucker Brooke who first pointed out the three examples in *Edward II* in which historically inaccurate transferences are made, but to suggest, as Dover Wilson does, that they are not so used for dramatic relevance is patently absurd as I shall show by quotation. But even more important is to demonstrate that Shakespeare's plays provide numerous examples of exactly the same kind of wresting of historical facts for dramatic purposes when it suits the context of his play to do so. The comparison below shows identical examples of unhistoricity on the part of Shakespeare in his *Richard II* in which he borrows very significantly from Marlowe's *Edward II*. Shakespeare's debt to Marlowe is far greater. Dr Bakeless has well demonstrated the close similarities in the two plays:

'Each king makes a levy upon his subjects' property, and each dramatist uses this fact to help on the catastrophe. Each king is caught unprepared by the return of an absent enemy. Each is forced, after a hesitation of which each author makes full dramatic use, to abdicate. Each, in his anger, destroys a physical object: Edward a letter, Richard a mirror. Each is eventually murdered, and the coffin of each is brought on the stage in the final scene.

Granting that most of this is history, that each play contains other elements not used in its companion-piece, and that the emphasis – especially on the exact roles of the two sets of favorites – is different, it is nevertheless hard to believe that Shakespeare's choice and his structural combination of historical incidents were uninfluenced by Marlowe's".[16]

And next we come to the crux of the accusations levelled – the borrowings of historical elements transferred from one play to another *without historical validity*, for which Messrs Wilson and Alexander so severely criticise Marlowe.

'The favourites are put to death on much the same grounds in each play. In *Edward the Second* Mortimer says
    The proud corrupters of the light-brainde king
    Haue done their homage to the loftie gallowes.
In *Richard II* Busby and Green are executed after Bolingbroke's accusation,
    You have misled a prince, a royal king.

This is especially striking because Shakespeare's version *does not accord with history*. [My italics, A.D.W.] The Busby, Bagot, and Green of actual fact were not responsible for the real king's misdeeds. Gaveston and the Spensers were. Shakespeare found the accusation dramatically effective and took it over from Marlowe in blithe indifference to fact.

Again, in *Richard II*, Bolingbroke condemns Busby and Green because

> You have in manner with your sinful hours
> Made a divorce betwixt his queen and him,
> Broke the possession of his royal bed,

which is true enough of Edward's favorites but not of Richard's. Shakespeare's king and queen were actually in entire harmony. In both these cases Shakespeare kept Marlowe's play a little too closely in mind.'[17]

These examples do not exhaust the incidence of such misuse of historical facts in Shakespeare's plays, as I would have thought Alexander and Wilson would be aware. In the case of Marlowe's borrowings from his own but recently written history play, *The Contention*, he re-used selected historical facts in the context of the play he had in hand *in order to enhance the dramatic situation* and this is certainly done intentionally for this is precisely and superbly what his 'borrowings' achieved, as demonstrated below.

1. The first two historical inaccuracies in Marlowe's *Edward II* are directly lifted from *The Contention* verbatim and appear closely together in a scene in which Marlowe uses them to paint a picture of a kingdom threatened and in chaos in the crumbling reign of the weakly Edward II. They are dramatically valid here for he is carefully building up the mounting tension between the incompetent, effeminate and increasingly despised Edward and his nobles, which shortly leads to his deposition.

> *Lancaster:* Look for rebellion, look to be depos'd
> Thy garrisons are beaten out of France,
> And, lame and poor, lie groaning at the gates;
> *The wild Oneil, with swarms of Irish kerns,*
> *Lives uncontroll'd within the English pale;*
> *Young Mortimer: The haughty Dane commands the narrow seas,*
> While in the harbour ride thy ships unrigg'd.

Lancaster: What foreign prince sends thee ambassadors?
Young Mortimer: Who loves thee, but a sort of flatterers?

Edward II 11.964–974

Although no O'neill was rampaging in Ireland during the reign of Edward II, and the Danes were not threatening invasion either, the references to Ireland would immediately have awoken a response in his Elizabethan audiences for there Raleigh and Gray had fought the wild Irish kerns, and there was unceasing resurgence of rebellion; while the threat of invasion, not by the Danes, but by Spaniards, created dramatic tension by the re-awakening of recent memories in the hearts of Londoners when the Armada threatened. Marlowe, the dramatist, knew exactly how to play on topicalities to evoke the responses from his audiences that he desired. He was not the favourite dramatist of the theatre-goers without good reason.

Far from weakening his claim to authorship of these plays, these examples underline the correctness of Tucker Brooke's findings. Only a man who knew his chronicles almost by heart for this period, having recently based two plays on them, would so confidently wrest the information he needed to spice his drama so pointedly.

2. Yet another example, which is not a direct quotation but exemplifies the use of historical facts relating to one historical character as applied to another (as has also been done regarding Talbot, the hero of *1 Henry VI*, quoted in Chapter VIII page 244) is the reference, *historically inapplicable to Edward II*, though dramatically and poetically justified, to King Edward's jousting exploits in France when he was wooing his queen, Isabel, which Marlowe uses to add poignancy to the portrayal of the king's sufferings in his dreadful final imprisonment.[18]

Edward: And there, in mire and puddle, have I stood
This ten days' space; and, lest that I should sleep,
One plays continually upon a drum;
They give me bread and water, being a king;
So that, for want of sleep and sustenance,
My mind's distemper'd, and my body's numb'd,
And whether I have limbs or no I know not.
O, would my blood dropp'd out from every vein
As doth this water from my tatter'd robes.
Tell Isabel the queen, I look'd not thus,

When for her sake, I ran at tilt in France,
And there unhors'd the Duke of Cleremont.
Lightborn: O, speak no more, my lord! this breaks my heart.

11.2511–2523

To pathos is added irony, for Lightborn has come to murder Edward. It is a powerful scene which moves its audiences as few other can do to the same intense degree of pity and horror. The sharp contrast Marlowe introduces with the picture of the jousting, victorious, young king and the pathetic figure in dripping, filthy rags, adds to the pity evoked. This aspect seems to be unaccountably lost on Dover Wilson who pronounces the verdict that these parallels are *not* 'required by the dramatic context'. Neither Wilson nor Alexander appears to have much interest in Marlowe as a dramatist.

Tucker Brooke has demonstrated that Marlowe typically borrows from his own works. Such self-quotations occur in almost all creative artists; Beethoven quotes Beethoven, Bruckner echoes Bruckner, and Berlioz repeats himself. There are other examples of Marlowe quoting Marlowe verbatim, so that these verbatim parallels in *The Contention* and *Edward II* argue strongly for the same authorship.*

In conclusion, it will be clear from the foregoing exposition that the irrefutable case presented by Dr Tucker Brooke stands essentially unaffected by Dr Alexander's battery of assault, which turns out to have been misdirected and fuelled by some rather suspect gunpowder that has backfired on him.

Finally, when Alexander turns to comparing the texts of the two 'bad' quartos of *The Contention* and *The True Tragedy* with the First Folio texts he is able to cease hypothesizing and emerges as the scholar he is when his judgement is not bedevilled with pro-Shakespearean bias. His final dismissal of Tucker Brooke's argument is unconsciously revealing:

'When, however, the Quartos are more closely examined Professor Tucker Brooke's concession shrinks into nothing at all; there is no evidence for assuming the existence of the Marlowe originals for these defective Quartos other than 2 and *3 Henry VI*; and if the Marlowe parallels prove anything about authorship it is that 2 and *3 Henry VI* are by Marlowe.'[19]

---

* Examples of parallelisms culled from Tucker Brooke's thesis and Bakeless' work on these *Henry VI* plays are given in Appendix B.

Alexander is thereby admitting that the parallels in *Henry VI* are strongly present and strongly redolent of Marlowe. They are no figment of the imagination, no mere hypothesis. One cannot escape them. He has attempted to explain them with the assumption of Shakespeare's presence in London as a member of the Pembroke players. This assumption is given credence by the assumption that Greene is referring to Shakespeare as 'Shake-scene' in his *Groatsworth of Wit* in September 1592. This is the second misconception which has so misled scholars which needs to be objectively and thoroughly re-examined.

V   *Greene's **Groatsworth** of Wit:*
The Whole Story

IN HIS DEATH-BED DIATRIBE, which he entitled *Greenes Groats-Worth of witte*, published posthumously in September 1592, Robert Greene singled out for particularly virulent satirical criticism a great actor whom he described as being 'in his owne conceit the onely Shake-scene in a countrey'. Scholars have long cherished the tenacious belief that Greene was thereby referring to Shakespeare. An examination of Greene's life and writings here sheds new light on this assumption.

On 3 September, 1592, Robert Greene, Master of Arts of two Universities, as he liked to style himself, had died utterly destitute and in pitiful circumstances for which he heaped blame and opprobrium on one whom orthodox scholars claim he named 'Shake-scene'; he was by Greene's description clearly identified as an actor, and Greene had long harboured resentment against the whole tribe of the acting profession because it was they who waxed rich on the proceeds of the theatres, while the dramatists who supplied them with the plays which provided these riches, all of them men who were their betters in education, and generally in class also, were frequently 'driven to extreme shifts' to make ends meet. The arrangement that prevailed in Elizabethan times, whereby the dramatist sold his work to the actors and lost all rights in it by this one transaction, was certainly a very unjust one, but no one smarted so much under it as Greene, who had an inflated estimation of his own value as a writer.

By 1592, when he fell terminally ill, he had been writing prolifically for the theatre for five years and, to keep his cash flow at the level of his inordinate appetite for drinking and wenching, from his pen there also flowed a copious literary output of romantic novels, frame-work tales for light reading, prodigal son stories, social pamphlets, repentances, treatises and tracts – anything that could be sold to furnish him with money, he wrote, and preferably for a quick return. This is perhaps what kept him writing plays; it was a cash down transaction and one against which loans were freely available from the actor-manager-cum-banker for whom he wrote. Of his dramatic works probably not all have survived, or been identified, but we can with certainty attribute to him:

> *Alphonsus King of Arragon*
> *Looking-Glass for London and England*
>   (in collaboration with Thomas Lodge)
> *Orlando Furioso*
> *Friar Bacon and Friar Bungay*
> *James IV*

and attributed to him but not confirmed:

> *The Pinner of Wakefield*
> *Selimus*
> *Locrine*
> *George-a-Greene*
> *A Knack to Know a Knave*

His known and apocryphal dramatic works total only ten, but this is probably not all he had produced, for he claims that the actors depended on his busy pen more than on anyone else to supply them. He was noted for being a very rapid writer, and an excess of two plays a year would have been well within his reach.

It was to 'those Gentlemen his Quondam acquaintance, that spend their wits in making plaies' that Greene addressed himself in the last words that he penned as he lay sick unto death in the house of a shoemaker in Dowgate, which is located between London Bridge and Mansion House, not far from the river. The kindly cobbler and his good wife had taken him in out of pity, else he would have 'perished in the streetes' he wrote in the letter he sent to the wife he had abandoned for his London trulls, begging her to forgive him and pay his debt to his host, Isam the shoemaker, a sum of ten pounds.[1]

We know a great deal about Robert Greene's life and death thanks to his passionate self-interest in advertising his woes and grievances, his life and his sins, his desire to reform his wicked ways, from his death-bed confessionals of which he managed to write two, despite being 'deeplyer searched with sicknesse than ever heretofore', or even three if we are to include the undated and improbably titled, *Greenes Vision: written at the instant of his death*. The two we are here concerned with are:

Greenes Groats-Worth of witte: bought with a million of Repentance

The Repentance of Robert Greene, Maister of Artes

Both were published before the end of 1592. In addition we have further detailed information on the circumstances of Greene's last days from the pen of Gabriel Harvey, Greene's implacable enemy, who was seeking to retaliate for the unwarranted and scurrilous attacks being made in recent publications by Greene on the reputations of the Harvey family, the father, a rope-maker of Saffron Walden, Harvey himself and his two brothers.[2]

Finding that Greene was dead and beyond the law of libel, Harvey contented himself with nosing out the sordid details of the poor man's miserable end, and publishing these – a piece of reportage which unfortunately redounded on the head of the hapless Harvey, and has effectively turned the tables to so besmirch his own reputation for his uncharitable act, that posterity has (unfairly) tended to side with Nashe and Greene. We may, however, be grateful to Harvey for uncovering so much to our eyes, which will to some degree assist us in our search for the elusive figure of the man whom orthodox scholars believe represents William Shakespeare in Greene's famous Letter of advice to his 'Quondam acquaintance', in which he rages against one described by him with heartfelt bitterness in a passage of mounting opprobrium that has brought Robert Greene more fame in posterity than all the rest of his voluminous writings put together. After a general invective against Actors, he launches his attack against one individual of this troupe who has offended him:

'Yes trust them not: for there is an vpstart Crow, beautified with our feathers, that with his *Tygers hart wrapt in a Players hyde*, supposes he is as well able to bombast out a blanke verse as the best of you: and beeing an absolute *Iohannes fac totum*, is in his owne conceit the onely Shake-scene in a countrey.'[3]

Note that in this passage the words 'Crow' and 'Shake-scene' (both of which are well known colloquial terms that were generally understood as referring in a derogatory manner to Actors) have been capitalized by the printer as common nouns, which was almost standard practice in the printing of the period. Thus, in this text we find the following common nouns are all capitalized: Father, Maister, Teacher, Sonne, Seruant, Schollers, Cittie, Tragedians, Tyrants, Death, Diabolicall Atheisme, Satyrist, Comedie, Puppets, Anticks, Apes, Vsurer, Gentlemen, Maisters, Temple, Tapers, and so on. All the *Proper Names*, on the other hand, are not merely capitalized, but are printed in *italics*: *Greene, Caine, Iudas, Iulian*, yong *Iuuenall*, and *Iohannes fac totum*, and *Robert Greene*.

Sweet boy, might I aduise thee, be aduisde, and get not many enemies by bitter wordes: inueigh against vaine men, for thou canst do it, no man better, no man so well: thou hast a libertie to reprooue all, and name none; for one being spoken to, all are offended; none being blamed no man is iniuried. Stop shallow water still running, it will rage, or treade on a worme and it will turne: then blame not Schollers vexde with sharpe lines, if they re-proue thy too much liberty of reproofe.

And thou no lesse deseruing than the other two, in some things rarer, in nothing inferiour; driuen (as my selfe) to extreme shifts, a litle haue I to say to thee: and were it not an idolatrous oth, I would sweare by sweet S. George, thou art vnworthy better hap, sith thou de-pendest on so meane a stay. Base minded men all three of you, if by my miserie you be not warnd: for vnto none of you (like mee) sought those burres to cleaue: those Puppets (I meane) that spake from our mouths, those Anticks garnisht in our colours. Is it not strange, that I, to whom they all haue beene beholding: is it not like that you, to whome they all haue beene beholding, shall (were yee in that case as I am now) bee both at once of them forsaken? Yes trust them not: for there is an vp-start Crow, beautified with our feathers, that with his Tygers hart wrapt in a Players hyde, supposes he is as well able to bombast out a blanke verse as the best of you: and beeing an absolute Iohannes fac totum, is in his owne conceit the onely Shake-scene in a countrey. O that I might intreat your rare wits to be imploied in more profitable courses: & let those Apes imitate your past excellence, and neuer more acquaint them with your admired inuentions. I knowe the best husband of

glorie vnto his greatnes: for penetrating is his power, his hand lyes heauie vpon me, hee hath spoken vnto mee with a voice of thunder, and I haue felt he is a God that can punish enemies. Why should thy excellent wit, his gift, bee so blinde, that thou shouldst giue no glorie to the giuer? Is it pestilent Machiuilian pollicy that thou hast studied? O peeuish follie! What are his rules but meere confused mockeries, able to extirpate in small time the generation of mankinde. For if Sic volo, sic iu-beo, holde in those that are able to commaund: and if it be lawfull Fas & nefas to do any thing that is beneficiall, onely Tyrants should possesse the earth, and they striuing to exceed in tyrannie, should each to other be a slaughter man; till the mightiest outliuing all, one stroke were lefte for Death, that in one age mans life should end. The brocher of this Diabolicall Atheisme is dead, and in his life had neuer the felicitie hee aymed at: but as he began in craft, liued in feare, and ended in despaire. Quam inscrutabilia sunt Dei iudicia? This murderer of many brethren, had his conscience feared like Caine: this betrayer of him that gaue his life for him, inherited the portion of Iudas: this Apostata peri-shed as ill as Iulian: and wilt thou my friend be his dis-ciple? Looke but to me, by him perswaded to that liber-tie, and thou shalt finde it an infernall bondage. I knowe the least of my demerits merit this miserable death, but wilfull striuing against knowne truth, exceedeth all the terrors of my soule. Defer not (with me) till this last point of extremitie, for litle knowst thou how in the end thou shalt be visited.

With thee I ioyne yong Iuuenall, that byting Sa-tyrist, that lastlye with mee together writ a Comedie. Sweet

The text of Greene's *Groatsworth of Wit* Letter.

From this examination of the printed text it is clear that we are not seeking for a man *named* by Greene as 'Shake-scene' homophonously intended to identify a man with a name such as Shakespeare, or Shakeshaft, or Shake-anything, any more than we should be looking for a man named 'Crow' (which is quite a common surname). No. We ought to be looking for an actor whom Greene identifies for us clearly by *naming* him *Iohannes fac totum* because he was a man of large energy with many strings to his bow, including the writing of mediocre blank verse plays. This immediately removes from our search the pre-occupation with William Shakespeare which has so bedevilled the identification of the correct character to whom Greene is pointing us, for he had no intention whatsoever of directing our attention to a man with a name in any way homophonous with 'Shake-scene', which may be compared with Greene's description of Marlowe as 'thou famous gracer of Tragedians' which is similarly not italicized. The capitalization of common nouns was random, as here in lower case 'g' but capitalized 'T'. Compare this with Greene's actual naming of Marlowe as that 'Atheist *Tamburlan*' and as one of *'Merlins* race' (see page 59–60).

In 1592 nothing is known of Shakespeare, so that Greene's quotation of a line from *The True Tragedy of Richard Duke of York* which appears unchanged in the First Folio's *Part three of Henry the Sixt,* quoted by Greene with one word altered to make it fit a Player whom he is denouncing for his hard-heartedness, has made the connection all too readily for minds eager to be alerted to the strong suspicion that here was the much sought-after clue to Shakespeare's presence in London. That there has been endless trouble in connecting the character of this 'Shake-scene', as depicted by Greene in his bitter attack against the Actor, with what we know of Shakespeare, might have indicated that we were on the wrong scent; but in order to be a successful Sherlock Holmes in the labyrinth of Elizabethan literary allusions, one has to have objectivity, and this quality is in somewhat short supply in Shakespearean studies.

As discussed in the previous chapter, the authorship of *The True Tragedy,* and hence of the line, *Oh Tygres Heart, wrapt in a Womans Hide* in that play is attributable to Marlowe, which removes any connection of this quotation with Shakespeare in 1592. The well-known connotation of extreme cruelty and deceitfulness which the image of the tiger held for the Elizabethan mind is further explored at the end of this chapter. For the present we are more concerned with the term 'Shake-scene'.

To shake a stage was a commonly used term descriptive of a great Elizabethan actor's performance. Elizabethan theatrical performances were vigorous and often included dancing and tumbling interludes. An actor was required to be versatile and active, and voice technique and gesture were traditionally larger than life. The famous comic actor, Will Kempe, in his account of the achievement of his challenge to dance from London to Norwich – an extraordinary feat! – described by him in *Kemps Nine Daies Wonder*, addresses his fellows as 'My notable Shake-rags'. Ben Jonson uses *shake* as a term well-known as referring to the art of acting in his day, and not having any punning reference to the name Shakespeare in his encomium prefacing the First Folio:

> 'to heare thy Buskin tread
> And shake a Stage;'

Both 'Stage' and 'Buskin' are capitalized as common nouns. Ben Jonson knew exactly what he was doing when he used the term to 'shake a Stage', and to him and the Elizabethan/Jacobean readers there was no connection with the actor's *name* which Jonson does not mention anywhere near this line, as he would have done if he wished to bring the words into association; but such homophonous usage was not intended by Jonson, nor yet by Greene. Here is the passage from the Folio.

> 'I would not seeke
> For names, but call forth thund'ring *Æschilus*.
> *Euripides*, and *Sophocles* to vs,
> *Paccuuius*, *Accius*, him of *Cordoua* dead,
> To life againe to heare thy Buskin tread,
> And shake a Stage: Or, when they Sockes were on,
> Leaue thee alone, for the comparison
> Of all, that insolent *Greece*, or haughty *Rome*
> sent forth, or since did from their ashes come.
> Triumph, my *Britaine*, thou hast one to showe,
> To whom all scenes of *Europe* homage owe.'[4]

It was Thomas Tyrwhitt who first 'discovered' Shakespeare under the guise of 'Shake-scene' in 1778, and ever since the identification has become increasingly accepted as unquestionably correct, although intense debate has raged over the whole two hundred years around Greene's meaning and reason for his virulent attack on William Shakespeare, as there is no other evidence that they even knew each other. A few eminent Shakespeareans such as Dr Allison Gaw have repudiated this identification as untenable and even ridiculous, but his is a lone voice of reason drowned by the clamour of confused argument, which is myopically concentrated on the few words in Greene's Letter which refer to the Actor in question, as quoted on page 163.

However, if we really set out to discover the origin of Greene's attack, we must cast our net wide to reveal all we can about the interesting and controversial Bohemian author of this famous Letter – which orthodox criticism has singularly failed to do. Robert Greene's life and death have had such ample coverage from his own and his contemporaries' writings, that there is little excuse for misinterpreting his printed words. In casting the net wide to catch the big fish, who was the target of his bitter accusations in his *Groatsworth* Letter, it is relevant to review and compare all Greene's autobiographical writings.

Of Greene's two interesting death-bed confessionals, the *Repentance* is a straightforward autobiography, which tells us briefly that he was born in the city of Norwich, of honest parents who were solicitous for his education and sent him to school in Norwich, where the bright boy distinguished himself sufficiently to enable him to progress to the University of Cambridge. Modern research has established that he matriculated at St John's College as a sizar (which is the poorest category of student) on 26th November 1575, when he would have been aged seventeen. His baptismal entry in the church of St George in the parish of Tombland in Norwich gives us the date 11th July 1558, and we learn that his father was a saddler.[5] Research has further established that he received his B.A. in 1578 at Cambridge, and his M.A. on 7th July 1583 when he returned to Cambridge and entered Clare Hall.[6] He was then twenty-five years old. As a mature man of thirty years he obtained a second degree as Master of Arts at Oxford, in July 1588. He was therefore something of a permanent student and proud of it. It was the redeeming feature of his dissolute character that he loved learning, and in this he was truly a child of the English Renaissance.

He apparently learned easily without undue necessity for hard work, for at Cambridge he misspent his time in his youth. He must have been a great disappointment to his father who had hoped to make him 'a profitable member of the Common-welth, and a comfort to him in his age', perhaps following him in his trade of saddlery. Greene confesses that he did not listen 'to the wholesome advertisements' of his parents, and once away from home the rot quickly set in.

'..being at the Vniuersity of Cambridge I light amongst wags as lewd as my selfe, with whome I consumed the flower of my youth,

136

who drew mee to trauell into Italy, and Spaine, in which places I sawe and practizde such villainie as is abhominable to declare. Thus by their counsaile I sought to furnish my selfe with coine; which I procured by cunning sleights from my Father and my friends, and my Mother pampered me so long, and secretly helped mee to the oyle of Angels, that I grewe thereby prone to all mischiefe: so that beeing then conuersant with notable Braggarts, boon companions and ordinary spendthrifts, that practized sundry superficiall studies, I became as a Sien grafted into the same stocke, whereby I did absolutely participate of their nature and qualities. At my return into England, I ruffeled out in my silks, in the habit of a *Malcontent*, and seemed so discontent, that no place would please me to abide in, nor no vocation cause mee to stay my selfe in: but after I had by degrees proceeded to Maister of Arts, I left the Vniuersitie and away to London, where (after I had continued some short time, & driuen my selfe out of credit of my frends) I became Author of Playes, and a penner of Loue Pamphlets, so that I soone grewe famous in that qualitie, that who for that trade growne so ordinary about London as *Robin Greene*.'[7]

This is only a brief resumé of his life leading up to his achievement of fame as a London literary figure. Then he goes back into his history to fill out some details.

Seemingly after a brief spell in London, where he launched his career as a writer of romantic fiction, he returned to Norwich and heard a sermon preached in the church of St Andrew's which so moved him that he fell into terror of hell-fire and resolved to reform his life. 'But this good motion lasted not long in mee', he confesses. But it is probable that it may have encouraged him to marry and break his liaisons with loose women, doubtless being urged to do so by his concerned parents, for the girl who became his wife was a virtuous piece who did her best to reclaim him, as he tells us:

'.....soone after I married a Gentlemans daughter of good account, with whom I liued for a while: but forasmuch as she would perswade me from my wilfull wickednes, after I had a child by her, I cast her off, hauing spent vp the mariage money which I obtained by her.'[8]

This short-lived marriage must have taken place in late 1585 or early 1586, for by the following June, he was back in London to register his latest literary offering to the public, his *Farewell to Folly*, another collection of edifying tales written for 'the Gentlemen Students of both Vniuersities', some of whom he says 'haue bene wantons with me' and have 'spent their wits in courting of their sweetehearts and emptied their purses by being too prodigall'[9] This was registered at the Stationers' Hall on 11 June, 1587. At this time he had begun writing for the theatre for in 1587 his first play, *Alphonsus King of Arragon,* appeared. The chronology of this period in Greene's life is important in our search for our missing man, 'Shake-scene', or rather *Iohannes fac totum.*

Greene continues:

'After I had wholy betaken me to the penning of plaies (which was my continual exercise) I was so far from calling vpon God, that I seldome thought on God.'

In Greene's case Atheism seems to have been the real thing – an utter denial of God.

'I seemed as one of no religion, but rather as a meere Atheist, contemning the holy precepts vttered by any learned preacher; I would smile at such as would frequent the Church, or such place of godly exercise, & would scoffe at any that would checke mee with any wholesome or good admonition: so that here in I seemed a meere reprobate, the child of *Sathan*, one wipt out of the booke of life, and as an outcast from the face and fauor of God, I was giuen ouer to drunkennes, so that I lightly accounted of that company that would not intertaine my inordinate quaffing. And to this beastly sinne of gluttonie, I added that detestable vice of swearing, taking a felicitie in blaspheming & prophaning the name of God, confirming nothing idlely but with such solemne oths, that it amazed euen my companions to heare mee. And that I might seeme to heape one sinne vpon another, I was so rooted there in, that whatsoeuer I got, I stil consumed the same in drunkennes.'[10]

Greene tells us self-pityingly that 'though I knew how to get a friend, yet I had not the gift or reason how to keepe a friend: for hee that was my dearest friend, I would bee sure so to behaue my selfe towards him, that he shoulde euer after professe to bee my vtter enemie, or else vowe neuer to come in my company.'

I feel that this may be slight exaggeration on the part of the self-deprecating Greene, here in his most extravagant *mia culpa* mood, for

Nashe had certainly not abandoned him (though he denies Gabriel Harvey's allegation that he was Greene's 'inwardest companion') having been present at 'that fatal banquet of Rhenish wine and pickled hearing' which was the onset of Greene's illness, and he doughtily took up the cudgels on Greene's behalf to belabour Harvey for posthumously maligning Greene's reputation. The extra relish to his self-denigration may have been spurred by Nashe's absence in the country at the time of his illness, of which they were probably mutually unaware; and alone at his end he certainly was, but for his faithful mistress, that 'sorry ragged quean, of whom he had his base son, INFORTUNATUS GREENE',[11] as Harvey tells us, who was sister to a rogue called Cutting Ball, whom Greene is said to have employed (perhaps as a body-guard?) until he was hanged at Tyburn.

Next, Greene tells of some good friends in Aldersgate who tried to strengthen his will to reform, for they evidently feared for his health:

'For coming one day in to Aldersgate street to a welwillers house of mine, hee with other of his friendes perswaded mee to leaue my bad course of life, which at length would bring mee to vtter destruction, wherevpon I scoffingly made them this answer. Tush, what better is he that dies in his bed than he that endes his life at Tyburne, all owe God a death: if I may haue my desire while I liue, I am satisfied, let me shift after death as I may.'

As for Hell –

'Hell (quoth I) what talke you of hell to me? I know if I once come there, I shall haue the company of better men than my selfe. I shal also meete with some madde knaues in that place, & so long as I shall not sit there alone, my care is lesse."[12]

Here follows a marvellous passage of self recrimination and fear of hell fire as he now in his extremity perceives it. Five pages of it! Faustus's last anguished cry echoes in this, but with Greene, an essentially superficial man, though talented, it sounds typically insincere, as Marlowe's Faustus does not. One senses with Robin Greene that only his dire condition induces his present fear, and that, once recovered, as so often before, he would revert as on many previous occasions after a bout of illness.

'I did with the Dog, *Redire in vomitum*, I went again with the Sow to wallow in the mire, and fell to my former follies as frankly, as if I had not tasted any iot of want, or neuer been scourged for them; my daily custome in sinne had cleane taken away the feeling of my sinne: for I was so giuen to these vices aforesaid, that I counted them rather veniall scapes & faults of nature, than any great and greeuous offences..'13

Greene's *Repentance* and his Letter appended to his *Groatsworth of Wit* provided a terrible salvoe of ammunition for the Puritan critics of the theatres and the evils of plays. They must have lapped it up as proof positive of the godlessness of playwrights and the ghastly nemesis that would be visited on all those who indulged in such pursuits. Even in the shadow of death Greene was foolish and blind to the consequences of his actions. Never had there been such a soul-baring in print! He made sure that his last utterances would be widely read, for he knew well the taste of his readers for scandal.

Along with his continual exercise in writing plays, he continued with his other popular literary works.

'These vanities and other trifling Pamphlets I penned of Loue, and vaine fantasies, was my chiefest stay of liuing, and for those my vaine discourses, I was beloued of the more vainer sort of people, who beeing my continuall companions, came still to my lodging, surfeiting with me all the day long.'14

God then put it in his head, 'to lay open the most horrible Coosenages of the Conny-catchers, Cooseners, and Crosse-biters' which he hopes will do some good and be 'beneficiall to the Common-wealth of England'. Delving into the secrets of the Elizabethan underworld was doubtless also done to bring some benefit to Robert Greene, for he wrote for money. And so he ends, appending a Letter to his 'deare Wife', hoping she will forgive him. It was five years since he last saw her, and they were his playwriting years.

His dissolute and drunken manner of life took their toll in his early death, and his claim to inordinate drinking was no exaggerated boast, for Nashe told Gabriel Harvey that he could never have matched Greene's expenditure on drink: 'in one yeare hee pist as much against the walls as thou and thy two brothers spent in three.'15 However, his voluminous writings tell another tale: thirty-one prose works, containing a fair amount of poetry, for Greene interspersed and embellished his romances with many delightful poems, and at least a dozen plays, written at great speed.

140

As Sir E. Brydges, an ardent apologist for Greene, has remarked, 'haste could not destroy...dissolute habits could not extinguish, and...the prejudices of an immoral and degraded name could not withdraw from the public favour'[16] his literary achievement, much of it in the genre of what one might loosely term story telling, which he did with great charm and delicacy.

We turn now from his autobiography to an example of such story telling, which is in this case also autobiographical, in order to compare the two for the purpose of our man-hunt. There is, indeed, much scattering of autobiographia in Greene's writing for he was a self-conscious artist, intensely interested in Robert Greene; but whereas the reflections of Greene's own life that appear in his *Francescos Fortunes: Or the Second Part of Greenes Never Too Late* (published 1590) are an idealized picture of himself as he probably would have liked to be, and are but superficially and partly autobiographical, his *Groatsworth of Wit* is *intentionally and consciously an autobiographical tale* which is written and conceived to match and to mirror his appended Letter to the 'Gentlemen of his Quondam acquaintance'. It is a point that has been missed by the myopic searchers for Greene's much reviled Actor, the 'Shake-scene' who treated him so meanly that he died utterly destitute.

However, at the risk of being tedious, since Shakespearean critics frequently tend to refer to *Francescos Fortunes* as an autobiographical piece, and in their minds equate it with his, to our purpose, much more relevant and important *Groatsworth of Wit* story, it is necessary to demonstrate from this work by quotation that they are not the same at all.

That all writers sometimes reflect their own experiences in their fictional writings is, I believe, a truism, and certainly when we have Greene's work before us his obsessive, introverted interest in himself, sins and all, is clearly evident. He seems frequently to be peeping at us from the eyes of his characters, even when in idealized form as in *Francescos Fortunes*. This romance is one of Greene's frame-work tales in which the story is told by a story-teller, in this case a Palmer. Francesco's tale begins as a true love story such as ladies like to read, about a lover, the virtuous young Francesco, who woos a maiden, and wins her, much against her father's wishes, so that dowryless they have to begin their life together in poverty. But they are idyllically happy and survive by their industry, she working with her needle, and he tutoring, until the father finally relents. All is bliss until now, but then Francesco has to leave his beloved Isabella to go on a business journey. Whilst absent Francesco falls prey to the wicked wiles of a courtezan named Infida, and being entrapped by this ravishing piece of treachery is robbed of all his money.

'Thus euerie way destitute of meanes to liue...he calde to minde that he was a scholler, and that although in these daies Arte wanted honor, and learning lackt his due, yet good letters were not brought to so lowe an ebbe, but that there might some profite arise by them to procure his maintenance. In this humour he fell in amongst a companie of Players, who perswaded him to trie his wit in writing of Comedies, Tragedies, or Pastorals, and if he could performe anything worth the stage, then they would largelie reward him for his paines...[Francesco] getting him home to his chamber writ a Comedie, which so generally pleased all the audience, that happie were those Actors in short time that could get any of his workes, he grewe so exquisite in that facultie.'[17]

Here, with a pat on the back for himself, we reach the autobiographical reflections in this tale, and what is interesting is that Francesco's encounter with the players occurs *after he has left his wife*, which is, I believe, when Greene also met the Player who similarly offered him employment as his 'plaimaking poet' as told in his autobiographical *Groatsworth* story where he is married to 'a proper Gentlewoman'.

The Palmer takes up the story-telling in a discourse in defence of plays and playwrights, which is clearly Greene's own opinion put into the mouth of his character who is thus drawn onto the subject:

'Now gentle Palmer, seeing we are fallen by course of prattle to parlie of Playes...shewe me your iudgement of Playes, Playmakers and Players.' Whereupon he expounds: 'It chanced that *Roscius* & he met at a dinner, both guests vnto *Archias* the Poet, where the prowd Comedian dared to make comparison with *Tully*: which insolencie made the learned Orator to growe into these termes: why *Roscius*, art thou proud with *Esops* Crow, being pranct with the glorie of others feathers? of thy selfe thou canst say nothing, and if the Cobler hath taught thee to say *Aue Caesar*, disdain not thy tutor because thou pratest in a Kings Chamber: what sentence or conceipte of the inuention the people applaud for excellent, that comes from the secrets of our knowledge. I graunt your action, though it be a kind of mechanical labour, yet wel done tis worthie of praise: but you worthlesse, if for so small a toy you waxe proud.

At this *Roscius* waxt red, and bewraied his imperfection with silence: but this check of *Tully* could not keepe others from the blemish of that fault, for it grew to a generall vice amongst the Actors, to excell in pride as they did exceede in excellence, and to braue it in the streets, as they bragge it on the stage: so that they reueld it in *Rome* in such costly roabes, that they seemed rather men of great patrimonie, than such as liued by the fauour of the people.

..... 'Thus sir, haue you heard my opinion briefly of plaies, that Menander deuised them for the suppressing of vanities, necessarie in a common wealth, as long as they are vsed in their right kind: the play makers worthy of honour for their Arte: & players, men deseruing both prayse and profits, as long as they wax niether couetous nor insolent.'[18]

Such utterances as these would not have endeared Robert Greene to the actors! Rome was the canting name for London, and the actors would be in no doubt as to who was intended. *We note here the seeds of mutual dislike and that antagonism between himself and one great leading actor* whose name had become a synonym for *Roscius*, which finally bursts forth on the pages of his whimsically entitled autobiographical tale: *Greenes Groats-Worth of witte, bought with a million of Repentance.*

Our author is at pains to bring in the groat whereby to hang his moralizing tale, hence the father of *Roberto* (*alias* Robert Greene) is a character of Greene's fancy, an old usurer, greedy and miserly, 'golds bondman'; one of Greene's most amusing and sharply observed character portraits. The younger brother of the tale, *Lucanio*, is likewise fictional, for he does not figure in Greene's straight autobiography, nor has research so far discovered a Luke or Lucas Greene as younger son of the family. The beginning of the tale, then, shows Greene in his popular and entertaining, romancing vein with some deft touches of autobiographical detail to the character of *Roberto*, who, Greene expressly tells us at the end, *is a representation of himself.*

For anyone wishing to discover who 'Shake-scene' really was this story is essential reading.

GREENES GROATS-WORTH OF WITTE,
BOUGHT WITH A MILLION OF REPENTANCE

'In an Iland bounded with the Ocean there was somtime a Cittie situated, made riche by Marchandize, and populous by long peace....An old new made Gentleman herein dwelt, of no small credit, exceeding wealth, and large conscience: hee had gathered from many to bestow vpon one, for though he had two sonnes he esteemed but one, that being as himselfe, brought vp to be golds bondman, was therefore held heire apparent of his il gathered goods.

The other was a Scholler, and maried to a proper Gentlewoman, and therfore least regarded, for tis an old sayd saw: To learning & law, thers no greater foe than they that nothing know: yet was not the father altogether vnlettered, for he had good experience in a *Nouerint*, and by the vniuersall tearmes therein contained, had driuen many a yoong Gentleman to seeke vnknowen countries, wise he was, for he boare office in his parish and sat as formally in his foxfurd gowne as if he had been a very vpright dealing Burges: he was religious too, neuer without a booke at his belt, and a bolt in his mouthe, readye to shoote through his sinfull neighbor.

And Latin hee had some where learned, which though it were but little, yet was it profitable, for he had this Philosophye written in a ring, *Tu tibi cura* [take care for yourself], which precept he curiously obserued, being in selfe loue so religious, as he held it no poynt of charitie to part with anything, of which hee liuing might make vse.

But as all mortall thinges are momentarie, and no certaintie can bee found in this vncertaine world: so *Gorinius*, (for that shall bee this vsurers name) after manye a gowtie pang that had pincht his exterior partes,...was at last with his last summons, by a deadly disease arrested, wheragainst when hee had long contended, and was by Phisitions given ouer, he cald his two sonnes before him: and willing to performe the old prouerbe *Qualis vita finis Ita* [of what kind the life is, so the end], he thus prepard himselfe, and admonished them. My sonnes (for your mother sayd ye were) and so I assure my selfe one of you is, and of the other I will make no doubt.

You se the time is com, which I thought would neuer have aproched and we must now be seperated, I feare neuer to meete againe. This sixteene yeares dayly haue I liude vexed with disease: and might I liue sixteene more, howe euer miserably, I should thinke it happye. But death is relentlesse, and will not be intreated witles:

and knowes not what good gold might doo him: senseles, & hath no pleasure in the delightfull places I would offer him. In briefe,I thinke he hath with this foole my eldest sonne beene brought vp in the vniuersitie, and there fore accounts that in riches is no vertue. But thou my son, (laying then his hand on the yongers head) haue thou another spirit: for without wealth, life is a death: what is gentry if welth be wanting, but bace seruile beggerie. Some comfort yet it is vnto me, to thinke how many Gallants sprunge of noble parents, haue croucht to *Gorinius* to haue sight of his gold: O gold, desired gold, admired gold: and haue lost their patrimonies to *Gorinius*, because they haue not returned by their day that adored creature? How many Schollers haue written rymes in *Gorinius* praise, and receiued (after long capping and reuerence) a sixpenny reward in signe of my superficial liberality. Breefly my yong *Lucanio* how I haue beene reurenst thou seest, when honester men I confesse have been sett farre off: for to bee rich is to bee any thing, wise, honest, worshipful, or what not. I tel thee my sonne: when I came first to this Citie my whole wardrop was onely a sute of white sheepe skins, my wealth an old groat, my woonning, the wide world. At this instant (o greefe to part with it) I haue in ready coine threescore thousand pound, in plate and Iewels xv. thousand; in Bondes and specialties as much, in land nine hundred pound by the yeere: all which, *Lucanio*, I bequeath to thee, only I reserue for *Roberto* thy wel red brother an old groat, (being ye stocke I first began with) wherewith I wish him to buy a groats-worth of wit: for he in my life hath reprooud my manner of life, and therefore at my death, shall not be contaminated with corrupt gaine. Here by the way Gentlemen must I digresse to shewe the reason of *Gorinius* present speach: *Roberto* being come from the Academie, to visit his father, there was a great feast prouided: where for table talke, *Roberto* knowing his father and most of the company to be execrable vsurers, inuayed mightely against that abhorred vice, insomuch that he vrged teares from diuers of their eyes, and compunction in some of their harts. Dinner being past, he comes to his father, requesting him to take no offence at his liberall speach, seeing what he had vttred was truth. Angry sonne (said he) no by my honestie (and that is som what I may say to you) but vse it still, and if thou canst perswade any of my neighbours from lending uppon vsurie I shold haue the more customers: to which when *Roberto* would haue replyde hee shut himselfe into his studdy and fell to tell over his mony.

This was *Robertos* offence: now returne, wee to sicke *Gorinius*, who after he had thus vnequally distributed his goods and possessions, began to aske his sonnes how they liked his bequestes, either seemed agreed, and *Roberto* vrged him with nothing more than repentance of his sinnloke: to thine owne said he, fonde boy, & come *Lucanio*, let me give thee good counsell before my death: as for you sir, your bookes are your counsellors, and therefore to them I bequeathe you. Ah *Lucanio*, my onely comfort, because I hope thou wilt as thy father be a gatherer, let me blesse thee before I dye. Multiply in welth my sonne by any meanes thou maist, onely flye Alcyhmie, for therein are more deceites than her beggerlye Artistes haue words, and yet are the wretches more talkative than women. But my meaning is, thou shouldest not stand on conscience in causes of profit, but heap treasure upon treasure, for the time of neede: yet seem to be deuout, els shalt thou be held vyle, frequent holy exercises, graue companie, and aboue al vse the conuersation of yoong Gentlemen, who are so wedded to prodigalitie, that once in a quarter necissitie knocks at their chamber doores: profer them kindnesse to relieue their wants, but be sure of good assurance: giue faire wordes till dayes of paiment come, & then vse my course, spare none: what though they tell of conscience (as a number will talke) looke but into the dealinges of the world, and thou shalt see it is but idle words. Seest thou not many perish in the streetes, and fall to theft for neede: whom small succor woulde releeue, then where is conscience, and why art thou bound to vse it more than other men? Seest thou not daylie forgeries, periuries, oppressions, rackinges of the poore, raisinges of rents, inhauncing of duties even by them that should be al conscience, if they ment as they speake: but *Lucanio* if thou read well this booke (and with that hee reacht him *Machiauels* workes at large) thou shalt se, what tis to be so foole-holy as to make scruple of conscience where profit presents it selfe.

Besides, thou hast an instance by thy threed bare brother here, who willing to do no wrong, both lost his childes right: for who woulde wish any thinge to him, that knowes not how to use it.

So much *Lucanio* for conscience: & yet I know not whats the reason, but some-what stinges mee inwardly when I speake of it. I father said *Roberto*, it is the worme of conscience, that vrges you at the last houre to remember your life, that eternall life may followe your repentance. Oute foole (sayd this miserable father) I feele it now, it was onelye a stitch. I will forwarde with my exhortation to

Lucanio. As I said my sonne, make spoyle of yoong Gallants, by insinuating thy selfe amongst them, & be not mooued to thinke their Auncestors were famous, but consider thine were obscure, and that thy father was the first Gentleman of the Name: *Lucanio,* thou art yet a Bachelor, and soe keepe thee till thou meete with one that is thy equal, I meane in wealth: regarde not beautie, it is but a bayte to entice thine neighbors eye: and the most faire are commonlye most fond, vse not too many familiars, for few prooue frendes, and as easie it is to weigh the wind, as to diue into the thoughtes of worldlye glosers. I tell thee *Lucanio,* I have seene four-scoore winters besides the od seuen, yet saw I neuer him, that I esteemed as my friend but gold, that desired creature, whom I have so deerly loued, and found so firme a frind, as nothing to me hauing it hath beene wanting. No man but may thinke deerly of a true frend, & so do I of it hauing it vnder sure locks, and lodging my heart there-with.

But now (Ah my *Lucanio*) now must I leaue it, and to thee I leaue it with this lessen, loue none but thy selfe, if thou wilt liue esteemd."[19]

So the father dies, and is interred 'with some solemnitie'.

'But leauing him that hath left the world....passe wee to his sonnes: and se how his long laid vp store is by *Lucanio* lookyd into. The youth was of condition simple, shamfast, & flexible to any counsaile, which *Roberto* perceiuing, and pondering howe little was lefte to him, grew into an inward contempt of his fathers vnequall legacie, and determinate resolution to work *Lucanio* al possible iniurie, hereupon thus conuerting the sweetnes of his studdye to the sharpe thirst of reuenge, he (as Enuie is seldome idle) sought out fit companions to effect his vnbrotherly resolution.'[20]

He finds his means ready to hand among the 'deceiuing Syrens' of the town, one of whom he approaches with a plan to seduce his simple 'shamfast', but lusty, young brother, who had up till now led a sheltered life under the strict controlling hand of his old father, whom he had docilely obeyed in all things, and was now at a loose end not knowing what to do with himself. Nothing loathe to listen to *Roberto's* urging that what he needs to complete his happiness is the love of a pretty wife, he agrees to accompany him to see if such a pleasing creature can be found. *Roberto* had meanwhile plotted with the courtezan *Lamilia* to introduce his innocent, young brother to her so that she could work her charms on him, and marry him. Once the bird was ensnared *Roberto's* reward would be a half share in the fortune which *Lamilia* would easily get her hands on. Cunningly leading his brother past *Lamilia's* house, where she is sitting at the open window playing her lute and singing 'with a delicious voyce', they are invited in, and the young man is hooked in no time by this beautiful and experienced young woman, 'her selfe like a seconde Helen', who flatters him with a pretence of having fallen in love with him at first sight. No sooner are they wedded, however, than *Lamilia* gives *Roberto* his marching orders and completes his betrayal by telling *Lucanio* how his brother had meant to trick him out of half his fortune. *Lucanio* then throws him out of the house, and his rejection by his family and loss of hopes of restitution are total. Utterly disconsolate, *Roberto* vents his sorrows in singing a song against the falseness of the *Lamilias* of this world:

> *'What meant the Poets in inuectiue verse,*
> *To sing Medeas shame, and Scillas pride,*
> *Calipsoes charmes, by which so many dyde?*
> *Onely for this their vices they rehearse,*
> *That curious wits which in this world conuerse,*
> *May shun the dangers and enticing shoes,*
> *Of such false Syrens, those home-breeding foes,*
> *That from their eyes their venim do disperse.*
> *So soone kils not the Basiliske with sight,*
> *The Vipers tooth is not so venemous,*
> *The Adders tung not halfe so dangerous,*
> *As they that beare the shadow of delight,*
> *Who chaine blind youths in tramels of their haire,*
> *Till wast bring woe, and sorrow hast despaire.*

'With this he laid his head on his hand, and leant his elbow on the earth, sighing out sadly,

> *Heu patior telis vulnera facta meis!*
> [Oh how I suffer wounds made by my own darts!]

On the other side of the hedge sate one that heard his sorrow: who getting ouer, came towards him, and brake off his passion. When hee approached, hee saluted *Roberto* in this sort.

Gentleman quoth hee (for so you seeme) I haue by chaunce heard you discourse some part of your greefe; which appeareth to be more

148

than you will discouer, or I can conceipt. But if you vouchsafe such simple comforte as my abilitie may yeeld, assure your selfe, that I wil indeuour to doe the best, that either may procure you profite, or bring you pleasure: the rather, for that I suppose you are a scholler, and pittie it is men of learning should liue in lacke.

Roberto wondring to heare such good wordes, for that this iron age affoordes few that esteeme of vertue; returnd him thankfull gratulations, and (vrgde by necessitie) vttered his present griefe, beseeching his aduise how he might be imployed. Why, easily quoth hee, and greatly to your benefite: for men of my profession gette by schollers their whole liuing. What is your profession, said *Roberto*? Truly sir, saide hee, I am a player. A player, quoth *Roberto*, I tooke you rather for a Gentleman of great liuing, for if by outward habit men should be censured, I tell you, you would bee taken for a substantiall man. So am I where I dwell (quoth the player) reputed able at my proper cost to build a Windmill. What though the world once went hard with me, when I was faine to carry my playing Fardle a foote-backe; *Tempora mutantur*, [*Times change*] I know you know the meaning of it better than I, but I thus conster it, its otherwise now; for my very share in playing apparell will not be sold for two hundred pounds. Truly (said *Roberto*) tis straunge, that you should so prosper in that vayne practise, for that it seemes to mee your voice is nothing gratious. Nay then, saide the Player. I mislike your iudgement: why I am as famous for *Delphrigus*, & the King of the *Fairies*, as euer was any of my time. The twelue Labors of *Hercules* haue I terribly thundred on the Stage, and plaied three Scenes of the Deuill in the Highway to heauen. Haue ye so (saide *Roberto*?) then I pray you pardon me. Nay more (quoth the Player) I can serue to make a pretie speech, for I was a countrey Author, passing at a Morrall, for twas I that pende the Morrall of mans witte, the Dialogue of Diues, and for seuen yeers space was absolute Interpreter to the puppets. But now my Almanacke is out of date:

> The people make no estimation,
> Of Morrals teaching education.

Was not this prettie for a plaine rime extempore? if you will ye shall haue more. Nay its enough, said *Roberto*, but how meane you to vse mee? Why sir, in making Playes, said the other, for which you shall be well paid, if you will take the paines.

Roberto perceiuing no remedie, thought best in respect of his present necessitie to try his wit, & went with him willingly: who lodged him at the Townes end in a house of retayle.'[21]

Lucanio meanwhile was being fleeced of his wealth by *Lamilia* who, 'hauing bewitched him with her enticing wiles, caused him to consume in lesse than two yeeres that infinite treasure gathered by his father'. But it is *Roberto* with whom we are concerned, whose rise and fall mirrors the life of Robert Greene. 'But *Roberto* now famosed for an Arch-plaimaking poet, his purse like the sea somtime sweld, anon like the same sea fell to a low ebbe; yet seldom he wanted, his labors were so well esteemed.'[22]
However, he became dishonest and fell into evil practices.

'He had shift of lodgings, where in euery place his Hostesse writ vp the wofull remembrance of him, his laundresse, and his boy; for they were euer in his household, beside retainers in sundry places.'[23]

He boasts that his companions were drawn from London's low life. Greene's biographer, J.C. Jordan and other commentators have questioned whether his experience of the Elizabethan underworld was really first hand, for he could have drawn his information from other men's books on the subject. However, we have the testimony of Nashe, who informs Gabriel Harvey in the great battle in print following Greene's death: 'I and one of my fellowes, *Will Monox*, (hast thou neuer heard of him and his great dagger?) were in company with him a month before he died, at that fatal banquet of Rhenish wine and pickled hearing (if thou wilt haue it so).'[24] We learn also of Greene's association with Cutting Ball. These are not fictional. The young, literary Bohemians seem to have been on good terms with underworld characters. Robert Greene certainly associated with riff-raff, and Nashe, and Peele also, if we are to credit any of the stories told of him, though Marlowe we know moved in higher circles. Greene had a dishonest streak in him; likewise *Roberto* in this story:

'His companie were lightly the lewdest persons in the land, apt for pilferie, perjurie, forgerie, or any villainy. Of these hee knew the casts to cog at cards, coossen at Dice, by these he learned the legerdemaines of nips, foystes, conny catchers, crosbyters, lifts, high Lawyers, and all the rabble of that vncleene generation of vipers: and pithily could he paint out their whole courses of crafts.'[25]

150

Which exactly describes what Robert Greene did in his social pamphlets on the nefarious skills practised by the rogues of London who lived by their wits, a cunning, parasitic strata of Elizabethan society, made ruthless by the will to survive at all costs. But beneath the sordid exterior there was sometimes a heart of gold, for Greene's 'sorry quean', a girl from a criminal background, stayed with him in his dire sickness, the poor comforting the poor. Like this girl's brother, Cutting Ball, some of *Roberto's* companions came to a sticky end, but he refused to be forewarned, and:

> 'nothing bettered, but rather hardened in wickednesse [became] ...hatefull almost to all men, his immeasurable drinking had made him the perfect Image of the dropsie, and the loathsome scourge of Lust tyrannized in his bones: lying in extreame pouerty and hauing nothing to pay but chalke, which now his Host accepted not for currant, this miserable man lay comfortlesly languishing, hauing but one groat left (the iust proportion of his Fathers Legecie) which looking on, he cryed: O now it is too late, too late to buy witte with thee: and therefore will I see if I can sell to carelesse youth what I negligently forgot to buy.
>
> Heere (Gentlemen) breake I off *Robertoes* speach; whose life in most parts agreeing with mine, found one selfe punishment as I haue doone.
>
> Heereafter suppose me the saide *Roberto*, and I will goe on with that hee promised: *Greene* will send you now his groats-worth of wit, that neuer shewed a mites-worth in his life: & though no man now bee by to doo mee good: yet ere I die I will by my repentaunce indeuour to doo all men good.'[26]

Then follow some charming verses of authentic Elizabethan melancholia, and a list of ten golden rules for a virtuous life, before Greene finally comes to his famous Letter. Before considering this much-quoted missive, we pause to take stock of what we have learned about Greene from his autobiographical and other writings.

Firstly, he was a well educated man, Master of Arts of two universities, and very proud of his learning. He had considerable talent, charm and facility as a writer. On the debit side, he was of weak moral fibre; self-indulgent, selfish, of dubious honesty, a self-confessed malcontent, spoiled by his mother; drink and loose women were his undoing, and extravagant living made him unscrupulous; superficial repentance inspired his campaign against the evils of the criminal class; but his innate vanity made him impatient that the world had not accorded him the honour, the acclaim and the secure living he craved. He was consumed with envy of the success of others, and, in particular, resentful of the actors whom he accused of unfairly profiteering from his writings. This resentment was of long standing. He seems to have exerted some influence over the much younger Nashe, who joined with Greene in envious attacks on the reputations of their contemporaries, although some of this, as on Marlowe and Alleyn, seems to have been a mischievous reflection of his friend Greene's views, rather than his own, especially since Nashe himself had hardly any business dealings with the actors. Nashe's views must now be considered, however, as they have a bearing on our eventual findings.

In his first literary offering, the letter 'To the Gentlemen Students of both Universities' prefacing Greene's *Menaphon* in 1589, Nashe also attacked the players, although he himself was not then a playwright and had no reason for a personal grudge against them. Nevertheless, he uses words very similar to Greene's, and identical epithets presaging Greene's description of the Player in the *Groatsworth of Wit* story. He expresses the same scornful attitude towards actors, which Greene had also repeated in his criticism of *Roscius* in *Francescos Fortunes*. Here is the passage from Nashe:

'Sundrie other sweete Gentlemen I know, that haue vaunted their pens in priuate deuices, and trickt vp a companie of taffeta fooles with their feathers, whose beautie if our Poets had not peecte with the supply of their periwigs, they might haue antickt it vntill this time vp and downe the countrey with the King of the *Fairies*, and dinde euery daie at the pease porredge ordinarie with *Delphrigus*. But *Tolossa* hath forgot that it was sometime sackt, and beggers that euer they caried their fardles on footback: and in truth no meruaile, when as the deserued reputation of one *Roscius*, is of force to inrich a rabble of counterfets; yet let subiects for all their insolence, dedicate a *De profundis* euerie morning to the preseruation of their *Cesar*, least their encreasing indignities returne them ere long to their iuggling to mediocrity, and they bewaile in weeping blankes the wane of their Monarchie.'[27]

Nashe lacks Greene's blissful lucidity (for I protest Greene is never obscure), and our young satirist is too obsessed with being as clever and witty and as topical as he knows how, but we get the gist – just. To paraphrase in modern English:

He knows some Gentlemen (University types, no doubt) who have written plays for private performances (most noblemen's houses regularly held such entertainments, as did the universities) and have with their dramatic poetry (their 'feathers') and wit (the 'periwigs'?) embellished the actors' performances (tricked up a company of taffeta fools with their feathers), and but for this the players might have been left to make their livings trudging up and down the country carrying their properties (their 'fardles') pick-a-back (like hikers) to perform their old stock of plays at country towns under their leader (the King of the Fairies or Delphrigus) who dined them regularly on humble fare at the local tavern (the ordinary, which served peas porridge). Like Tolossa (he must bring in his erudition, this being modern Toulouse, which was sacked and plundered by the Roman consul Caepio, but later restored and became famous as a centre of literary culture) they quickly forget what their beggarly lives were before their great leading actor, Roscius (the most famous actor of ancient Rome) enriched them by means of performances at his higher level, and they should pray every morning (dedicate a De profundis to the Lord) that their Caesar (alias Roscius) may continue to lead them in this exalted style or they may have to return to juggling for a living, and they should therefore beware of being too proud, or they might lose their supremacy and mourn its loss in blank verse as the playwrights have taught them.

As has been previously stated, by 1589 Edward Alleyn's pre-eminence as an actor was so well-established that *Roscius* had become a synonym for him. The association implied in Nashe's passage is that in his country days (Alleyn had spent his youth in provincial touring companies) he had played the leading roles of *King of the Fairies* and *Delphrigus* in the old morality plays, just as the Player in Greene's *Groatsworth of Wit* tells Roberto he had done. Thanks to the new dramatists who excel in blank verse drama he has now attained the crown of *Roscius, alias Caesar.*

At the risk of tedious repetition – for this has already been mentioned in connection with the authorship of *Edward the Third* – because these synonymous identifications have often been superficially and dismissively treated by scholarly commentators, I draw attention to the significant linking of *Roscius* (Alleyn) with *Caesar* (referring to the Black Prince?)

Next Greene in his *Francescos Fortunes* (1590) alludes also to 'the Cobbler' (Marlowe) while echoing Nashe's passage from his Preface to Greene's romance *Menaphon* (quoted above – the 'taffeta fooles' led by the *King of the Fairies-Delphrigus* who is also *Roscius-Caesar*). What is important for the present investigation is that *Roscius* (Alleyn) and *Caesar* (Alleyn) are repeatedly linked in a manner that obviously suggests that contemporary readers would readily understand the connotations. These synonyms are all clearly identifiable and were repeatedly used in print, and their purpose is to point, not to obscure. There is no other interpretation possible which make sense of these highly revealing texts than that given above. It is thus clear that Edward Alleyn featured importantly in Greene's life, and that his attitude towards him is tinged with envy and resentment as far back as 1588. Greene finds Alleyn to be too proud – too big for his boots – and this attitude is reflected in Nashe's statements. I say reflected, for whereas young Nashe's references to the great actor in the passage quoted from his Preface to Greene's *Menaphon* have been interpreted by most scholars as being original to Nashe, whom Greene later merely imitated in his *Groatsworth* description of the Player, this cannot be so. The scholars have got it the wrong way round. Nashe himself tells us he had been abroad and came 'from the other side the Seas' landing at '*Grauesende* Barge, the eight of *August*, [in] the first and last yeere of *Martinisme*'[28] – that year being 1589. Richard Simpson has pointed out the correct conclusion which other scholars have missed.

> 'After so long an absence,' he writes, 'it is not likely that he could have been an original authority for literary affairs which had occurred while he was away...Hence his publications of 1589 must be supposed to represent, not the fruits of his own experience, but the ideas decanted into him. Greene may be assumed to have crammed him with what had to be said as introduction to *Menaphon*; and the identity of idea, as well as of phrase, between Nashe's epistle and things which Greene subsequently wrote will prove this assumption to be correct.'[29]

Undoubtedly, Greene would have delighted to relate to his friend, newcome to join him in London, the highly entertaining anecdote of his encounter with the Player, who had popped up from behind the hedge and offered him employment as a playwright, having introduced himself as *King of the Fairies*, no less! and their joint use of this appellation suggests that it had become a standing joke with them. If Nashe, to whose satirical humour this would have had enormous appeal, incorporated it into his Preface to *Menaphon*, where it had no personal significance for him for he is there merely reporting what he had heard from Greene, it is clearly in its *correct* context in Greene's autobiographical *Groatsworth of Wit* tale. Why should Greene, a man not lacking in fertile imagination or humorous invention, lamely copy Nashe's epithets to describe his Player? Such a view is not reasonable. If Greene used the identical epithets, it was surely because they were *true to the incident he describes from his personal experience* in his autobiographical tale. It is Nashe who is quoting Greene, not the other way round.

In late 1585, or early 1586, Greene had married, and, having spent the marriage dowry and abandoned his wife, had reached a low point in his profligate life when he met the Player, whom we may assume he then accompanied to London, reaching the metropolis some time in May 1587 to commence his career as dramatist for Alleyn's company. Meanwhile the *King of the Fairies* was metamorphosed into the highly successful *Roscius*, *alias* Edward Alleyn, leading player of the Lord Admiral's Men, whose performance in the title role of *Tamburlaine the Great* made theatrical history that same year. Thus Greene met competition from Marlowe from the very beginning.

Without question, *Roscius*, who figured so largely in Greene's life, was Alleyn who employed him, hence he was the Player whom Greene met. Alleyn was undoubtedly the very epitome of a great 'Shake-scene', and in Greene's eyes he *was* an upstart, and too authoritative, for he was a far younger man than Greene, and not of a university education, yet he had risen within a few months of arriving in London to a position of theatrical pre-eminence and affluence – an 'vpstart Crow' indeed!

But we are not looking merely for an 'vpstart Crow' who fits the description 'Shake-scene' for his acting prowess. We are looking for an actor who also turned his hand to playwriting in blank verse in imitation of Greene and his fellow dramatists. The Player who is *King of the Fairies* wrote country Morrals for the Puppets, but there is more required to qualify him for the part of *Iohannes fac totum*. Our investigation is not yet ended.

We look now at Greene's Letter, which is charged with bitterness against one who is an actor-cum-writer for the stage, to whom Greene has rendered services which he feels have been miserably rewarded. This is the burden of his Letter in which the figure of one particularly well-known exploiter of playwrights, a man of some importance in the theatrical scene, is dominant.

GREENE'S GROATSWORTH OF WIT LETTER

To those Gentlemen his Quondam acquaintance,
that spend their wits in making plaies, R.G.
wisheth a better exercise, and wisdome
to preuent his extremities.

If wofull experience may moue you (Gentlemen) to beware, or
vnheard of wretchednes intreate you to take heed: I doubt not but you
wil looke backe with sorrow on your time past, and indeuour with
repentance to spend that which is to come. Wonder not, (for with thee
wil I first begin) thou famous gracer of Tragedians, [here he is addressing
Marlowe] that *Greene*, who hath said with thee (like the foole in his
heart) There is no God, shoulde now giue glorie vnto his greatnes:
for penetrating is his power, his hand lyes heauie vpon me, hee hath
spoken vnto mee with a voice of thunder, and I haue felt he is a God
that can punish enemies. Why should thy excellent wit, his gift, bee
so blinded, that thou shouldst giue no glorie to the giuer? Is it pestilent
Machiuilian pollicy that thou hast studied? O peeuish follie! What are
his rules but meere confused mockeries, able to extirpate in small time
the generation of mankind. For if *Sic volo, sic iubeo* [*So I will, so
I order*], hold in those that are able to commaund: and it it be lawfull
Fas & nefas (Lawful & unlawful) to do any thing that is beneficiall:
only Tyrants should possesse the earth, and they striuing to exceed
in tyrannie, should each to other be a slaughter man; till the mightiest
outliuing all, one stroke were lefte for Death, that in one age mans
life should end. *The brocher of this Diabolicall Atheisme is dead,
and in his life had neuer the felicitie hee aymed at: but as he began
in craft; liued in feare, and ended in despaire. *Quam inscrutabilia sunt
Dei iudicia?* [*How inscrutable are God's judgements*] This murder of
many brethren, had his conscience seared like *Caine*: this betrayer of
him that gaue his life for him, inherited the portion of *Iudas*: this
Apostata perished as ill as *Iulian*: and wilt thou my friend be his
disciple? Looke but to me, by him perswaded to that libertie, and thou
shalt find it an infernall bondage. I knowe the least of my demerits
merit this miserable death, but wilfull striuing against knowne truth,
exceedeth all the terrors of my soule. Defer not (with me) till this last
point of extremitie; for little knowst thou how in the end thou shalt
be visited.

---

*Greene is referring to Pietro Aretino, an evil follower of Machiavelli who gained
an odious reputation.

With thee I ioyne yong *Iuuenall*, that byting Satyrist, [here he is addressing Nashe] that lastly with mee together writ a Comedie. Sweet boy, might I aduise thee, be aduisde, and get not many enemies by bitter wordes: inueigh against vaine men, for thou canst do it, no man better, no man so well: thou hast a libertie to reprooue all, and name none; for one being spoken to, all are offended; none being blamed no man is iniured. Stop shallow water still running, it will rage, or tread on a worme and it will turne: then blame not Schollers vexed with sharpe lines, if they reproue thy too much liberty of reproofe.

And thou no lesse deseruing than the oher two, in some things rarer, in nothing inferiour; [George Peele is the poet-dramatist here addressed] driuen (as my selfe) to extreme shiftes, a litle haue I to say to thee: and were it not an idolatrous oth, I would sweare by sweet S. George, thou art vnworthy better hap, sith thou dependest on so meane a stay. Base minded men all three of you, if by my miserie you be not warnd: for vnto none of you (like mee) sought those burres to cleaue: those Puppets (I meane) that spake from our mouths, those Anticks garnisht in our colours. Is it not strange, that I, to whom they all haue beene beholding: is it not like that you, to whome they all haue beene beholding, shall (were yee in that case as I am now) bee both at once of them forsaken? Yes trust them not: for there is an vpstart Crow, beautified with our feathers, that with his *Tygers hart wrapt in a Players hyde*, supposes he is as well able to bombast out a blanke verse as the best of you: and beeing an absolute *Iohannes fac totum*, is in his owne conceit the onely Shake-scene in a countrey. O that I might intreat your rare wits to be imploied in more profitable courses: & let those Apes imitate your past excellence, and neuer more acquaint them with your admired inuentions. I knowe the best husband of you all will neuer proue an Vsurer, and the kindest of them all will neuer proue a kind nurse: yet whilest you may, seeke you better Maisters; for it is pittie men of such rare wits, should be subiect to the pleasure of such rude groomes.

In this I might insert two more, that both haue writ against these buckram Gentlemen: but lette their owne workes serue to witnesse against their owne wickednesse, it they perseuere to maintaine any more such peasants. For other new-commers, I leaue them to the mercie of these painted monsters, who (I doubt not) will driue the best minded to despise them: for the rest, it skils not though they make a ieast at them.

But now returne I againe to you three, knowing my miserie is to you no newes: and let mee hartily intreat you to be warned by my harms. Delight not (as I haue done) in irreligious oathes; for from the blasphemers house, a curse shall not depart. Despise drunkennes, which wasteth the wit, and maketh men all equall vnto beasts. Flie lust, as the deathsman of the soule, and defile not the Temple of the holy Ghost. Abhorre those Epicures, whose loose life hath made religion lothsome to your eares: and when they sooth you with tearms of Maistership, remember *Robert Greene*, whome they haue often so flattered, perishes now for want of comfort. Remember Gentlemen, your liues are like so many lighted Tapers, that are with care deliuered to all of you to maintaine: these with wind-puft wrath may be extinguisht, which drunkennes put out, which negligence let fall: for mans time is not of it selfe so short, but it is more shortened by sinne. The fire of my light is now at the last snuffe, and for want of wherewith to sustaine it, there is no substance lefte for life to feede on. Trust not then (I beseech ye) to such weake staies: for they are as changeable in minde, as in many attyres. Wel, my hand is tyrde, and I am forst to leaue where I would begin: for a whole booke cannot containe their wrongs, which I am forst to knit vp in some few lines of words.

Desirous that you should liue, though himselfe be dying:
Robert Greene.[30]

Some touching concern for his fellow-writers is here (to my mind) movingly expressed if also inadvisedly, for Greene was ever rash in misjudging the effects of his actions. Nashe in the following year did indeed have a severe attack of 'Repentance' and from his contrite pen flowed his *Christs Teares ouer Ierusalem*, possibly engendered by Greene's remonstrance in this Letter; but he soon got over it and reverted to attacking Gabriel Harvey with renewed venom and vigour in his wittiest and most scurrilous, satirical vein. Never was there such a 'flyting' seen in print as this ding-dong battle between Nashe and Harvey. Marlowe for his part had probably already written his *Doctor Faustus*, in which echoes of repentance akin to Greene's soulful cries for forgiveness for his sins and the thundering voice of God are heard. But I believe he now revised this play (perhaps for a timely new production by Alleyn) which would explain the maturity of the verse, which does not consort with the early date of its composition indicated by other textual/external evidence.

158

For George Peele it was perhaps already too late, for he died (according to Francis Meres) of the pox four years later.[31] Nevertheless one is aware that underlying or overlaying all Greene's penitent protestations and virtuous admonitions is his obsession with the merciless and extortionate treatment he has received at the hands of those Puppets, the actors, and especially one leading actor for whom he has conceived a personal hatred. Self-pity rises to a fine climax as he writes of the hard-hearted bargain-driver, whose *Tygers hart wrapt in a Players hyde* paints him forth in words as bitter as he could conceive. To Greene and the Elizabethan readers the imagery of the tiger symbolized a creature of both extremest cruelty and deceitfulness; anyone so described was merciless and devious. Thus Dido, in Marlowe's *Dido Queen of Carthage*, when she is being forsaken by her lover, Aeneas, who has set his mind on sailing away to Italy where the gods have destined him to found the great Roman Empire, accuses him in words that every Elizabethan audience would have understood as signifying that Aeneas was killing her with his heartlessness.

> And wilt thou not be mov'd with Dido's words?
> Thy mother was no goddess, perjur'd man,
> Nor Dardanus the author of thy stock,
> But thou art sprung from Scythian Cuacasus,
> *And tigers of Hyrcania gave thee suck.*
> Ah, foolish Dido, to forbear so long!
> Go, go, and spare not: seek out Italy:
> I hope that that which love forbids me do,
> The rocks and sea-gulfs will perform at large,
> And thou shalt perish in the billows' ways,
> To whom poor Dido doth bequeath revenge:
>
> Act V, Sc.1, 11.155–173

It is a great speech of womanly rage and rant, at the end of which Aeneas marches off and sails for Italy, while Dido, mad with grief, prepares to kill herself in a sacrificial death to love and all faithless lovers.

In his desperate plight Greene uses the pitiless tiger image for a similar purpose. Absolutely penniless, he had presumably appealed to the Player-manager, Alleyn, for a loan, or payment in advance upon the promise of a new play – and was refused. Left to die in an abject state of homelessness and want, and unable to buy the medicines he needed for his sickness, it is no wonder he took his revenge by likening this Actor-manager to the cruellest creature he could conjure up. He knew that he was making an accusation that would strike home in the theatrical world by parodying a line from a scene which presented a picture of utter heartlessness. Dr Allison Gaw, who accepts Tucker Brooke's ascription of the play from which this line was taken, *The True Tragedy of Richard Duke of York*, to Marlowe, has interpreted the authentic Elizabethan conception of this theatrically powerful scene for us eloquently:

> 'The 'tiger's heart' line from *The True Tragedy* was parodied by Greene evidently as well-known, just before September 3, 1592. It is usually taken for granted that Greene, in quoting it, is referring to Shakespeare's "plagiarism" of it in *3 Henry VI*. But the whole theory of such an accusation is, as Dr Brooke has well shown, baseless. Further, the line is almost always referred to by critics as simply "a line that occurs in *The True Tragedy*" or "in *3 Henry VI*". But this is an understatement, born of our habit of considering plays from the standpoint of the study rather than the theatre. It is really the opening line of the climactic accusation in perhaps the most powerful speech of invective that had, up to that time, ever been heard upon the English stage – a speech for which Shakespeare, in revision, could do little more than slightly amend the metre. In it the captured York, surrounded by his triumphant foes and confronting the bitterest of them, Queen Margaret, scathingly answers her heartless mockery, his passion mounting step by step until, holding out to her the napkin soaked with the blood of his little son, Rutland, he comes to the crowning instance of her unwomanliness.

> > Oh Tygers hart, wrapt in a womans hide!
> > How couldst thou draine the life bloud of the childe,
> > To bid the father wipe his eies withall,
> > And yet be seene to beare a womans face?

> And in the next four lines his self-control breaks, and the rest of the fifty-four lines is given in tears. The speech on the stage must have been memorable, and the quoted line, the chilled steel point to the anger as it bores down in the recollection, unforgettable.'[32]

All this, as Greene well knew, would not have been lost on the Actor for whom he intended it. Ivor Brown in his *Shakespeare* (1949) has also appreciated this point.

> 'The passage must have been powerfully delivered in the theatre and left its mark on the memory of the audiences, otherwise there would

have been no point in pulling out the first line quoted, altering one word, and so talking of "Shake-scene's" possession of a "Tyger's hart wrapt in a Players hyde". Nor would there have been any point in the taunt if Shakespeare had not been known as an actor.'[33]

Shakespeare was not known as an actor is 1592; but Edward Alleyn most certainly was. For *Shakespeare*, read *Alleyn*, and we begin to have a really relevant interpretation of this evidence; one which makes sense at every point that is touched.

In his relations with Greene and the playwrights Alleyn is identified as a man who was in a position of exploiter of their admired inventions, a grudge of long standing with Greene, which boiled to a head because of a recently sustained injury just prior to his death in September of 1592. This particular incident is also identifiable, and a very curious and revealing piece of theatrical history it proves to be, which is the subject of Chapter VIII, 'A New Play at the Rose With Its New Look'.

We have evidence of Alleyn's personal business association with Greene; and we know that the penurious dramatists were often dependent on advance payments on plays in the process of writing, so that by the time the piece was completed they had already consumed most of the price of their dramatic effort. Such an impecunious individual as Greene would doubtless be continuously in this state, and was very likely thus embroiled from the start of his association with Alleyn, which dates from his inception as a dramatist, and in all probability began with a loan to the down-and-out *Roberto* whom the Player met by the hedge in 'Groatsworth' country.

Henslowe's theatrical records provide ample evidence of his loans of money paid on account for plays that were in process of writing, as in the instance below to Drayton and Dekker:

Lent vnto m^r [willso] drayton & m^r dickers the
27 of July 1598 in pt of a Boocke called Haneballe   } xxx^s
& Hermes the some of. . . . .

pd vnto m^r drayton & m^r deckers the 28 of July
1598 in full payment of a boocke called haneball   } x^s
& hermes other wisse called worsse feared then hurte

lent vnto m^r deckers the same time vpon the
next boock called perce of winschester   } x^s
[34]

So we see Thomas Dekker is already committed to write his next play for Henslowe's company and the loan account is an on-going transaction.

There is no evidence of actual interest charged in these financial dealings over playscripts, but we may assume this was taken into account in the price which was paid for the script, which would doubtless be lower than if these dramatists had been free to sell and bargain for their plays on the open market.

However, we do have actual documentary evidence proving that Alleyn did charge interest on private loans which he floated. This is in a letter written many years later to Alleyn, who had long retired from acting and was living in affluence at Dulwich, from his old acting colleague, Charles Massey, who had fallen on hard times and is suing to Alleyn for a loan.

> Ser, diverse ocasions .... a[n]d ma[nye] crosses sense hath brovght me in tow det .... Ser fifte povnds wovld pay my detes, wch for on hole twelve month I would take vp and pay the intreste, and that I myght the better pay it in at the yeares ende, I wovld get m^r Jvbe to reseve my gallery mony, and my qua[r]ter of the hovse mony for a yeare to pay it in wth all, and if in [six] monthes I sawe the gallerye mony wovld not dow [then in] the other six monthes he shovld reseve [my whole] share, only reservinge a marke a wek[e to furnish] my hovse with all .... ther is one mr mathvs at the bell in newgat market, that six wekes agoe did offer me fifte povnds for a twelfmonth gratis, bvt he desird good secvrete ....[35]

The brackets indicate much worn paper with almost illegible words. The letter is tentatively dated by W.W. Greg to 1613 when Alleyn, by then a very wealthy man, was just beginning to build his charitable institution at Dulwich. The inference is that Alleyn was well known as a *moneylender on interest*, and Massey's careful assurance of repayment shows that he understood that Alleyn was not a man to be trifled with in these matters. Massey had no 'good secvrete' to offer to the other would-be lender, so he turned to Alleyn who evidently loaned only on interest. He does not mention the rate of interest charged, but we may be sure it would not have been usurious.

Both Alleyn and Henslowe were acting as small-time bankers in an age when banking facilities were not available to the ordinary citizen, rendering a service that kept many an unfortunate man out of debtors' prison. Henslowe's pawnbroking business is also to be seen in this light, and not as a reprehensible activity making capital out of the misfortunes of others.

Alleyn was, in fact, an extraordinarily kind-hearted and charitable man, ever ready to help those who were deserving of help, but he drew the line at giving charitable assistance to wastrels and profligates – like Greene, and he had moreover had experience of Greene's dishonesty.[36] It would have been entirely in character for him to have shown no mercy towards Greene when he came begging to him for a loan, and to have sternly shown him the door. Alleyn never confused business with charity, and in his eyes his relationship with Greene was strictly one of business. Greene's attitude, as may be clearly seen from his Letter, was that the actors *owed* him support when he was in his penniless state because, in his view, they had grown rich on his dramatic works for which they had never properly remunerated him.

There is evidence among the valuable manuscripts preserved at Dulwich College to suggest that Alleyn bought Greene's plays direct from him[37] – possibly for himself, as he evidently did Marlowe's, or on behalf of the company – so that it would have been to Alleyn rather than to Henslowe that Greene would have turned. Hence the accusation of heartlessness in Greene's Letter is precisely applicable to Alleyn, whom he by implication is also accusing of usurious practice in his dealings. There is no obscurity in Greene's words when seen in this, the correct historical setting of his business association with Alleyn, against whom he is fulminating:

> Is it not strange, that I, to whom they all haue beene beholding: is it not like that you, to whome they all haue beene beholding, shall (were yee in that case as I am now) bee both at once of them forsaken? Yes trust them not: for there is an vpstart Crow, beautified with our feathers, that with his *Tygers hart wrapt in a Players hyde*, supposes he is as well able to bombast out a blanke verse as the best of you: and beeing an absolute *Iohannes fac totum*, is in his owne conceit the onely Shake-scene in a countrey.

Note that Greene alters 'womans hide' to 'Players hyde' denoting the Player of his *Groatsworth* story. This is pointed and deliberate, for his Letter is placed as a pendant to his autobiographical tale. He wants his readers to know that this same Player is the very man!

Clearly this actor who is 'in his owne conceit the onely Shake-scene in a countrey' is that proud actor whom Greene has repeatedly attacked in his satirical jibes since 1588—the *'Roscius'* of Rome/London who was also termed a 'vainglorious tragedian' by Nashe (at Greene's instigation). They are not talking about a proliferation of great actors as *'Roscius'*, but only of one, for at this period Alleyn had no rival.

Typically, Greene has been careful to provide his readers with a recognisable thumbnail sketch of this hated actor, in his satirical portrait of the Player who employs *Roberto* (clearly identified as Greene himself) as his 'Arch-plaimaking poet' who boasts that he had been a successful 'countrey Author', naming two of his works, 'the Morrall of mans witte' and 'the Dialogue of Diues'. But this Player also has the critical acumen to realise that the university gentleman, *Roberto*, could do more for the players than he can, for his style is now out of date, as he readily admits. This betokens a man of judgement. Alleyn was such a man; astute in business, enterprising, immensely talented as an actor, intelligent, literate, and energetic.

Assuming that Alleyn is the Player – for he alone fits this part in Greene's life – who is a self-confessed author of country-style plays for his company, thereby earning himself extra money as well as status with the players, is there any reason to suppose that on returning to London, there finding fame and being exposed to the stimulating experience of performing leading roles in Marlowe's splendid blank verse dramas and the plays of Greene, Peele and others writing in this medium, he should have *ceased* his play-writing activities and not also tried his hand at writing in blank verse? Rather the contrary. After all, he had learnt great speeches in blank verse by heart, so that the metre must have become second nature to him. For this ambitious and resourceful young man of the theatre it would be entirely in character for him to emulate his 'betters' in this field.

Several of the best actors of Alleyn's day wrote plays as well as acting in them. Robert Wilson, a much older man, had for years supplied London with his morality-type plays written in verse. Richard Tarlton wrote at least one play. Samuel Rowley and his friend and fellow actor, Charles Massey, and the actors William Borne, John Singer and Robert Shaa (or Shawe) all wrote plays, the acquittances for which are recorded in Henslowe's *Diary* which he kept for the Rose Theatre.[38] These five men were members of Alleyn's company. If these actors could write plays, then why not the most talented actor of them all, Edward Alleyn? He had a superb sense of stage-craft, and a long experience in interpreting character. My research on his career shows him to be a man of discriminating taste, highly intelligent, imaginative, enterprising, creative and ambitious to advance himself. Alleyn even aspired to a knighthood towards the end of his life, which however eluded him. In the context of the theatrical scene of so many playwriting actors it would be surprising if he had *not* written any plays. Henslowe records ten unidentified plays which were sold by Alleyn to the company, which W.W. Greg suggests Alleyn was merely acting as broker for, whilst admitting he can find no other authors on whom to father these works and there is *every reason* to believe they were written by Alleyn himself. That the actor accused by Greene was also a playwright is confirmed by Henry Chettle who published *Greenes Groats-Worth of witte: bought with a million of Repentance* in September 1592. No sooner was it available at the bookshop than the furore began. Just as Greene had intended, his death-bed accusations against *Iohannes fac totum* struck home and created a stir in London's theatrical circles. Alleyn could hardly fail to recognise himself as the subject of this libellous attack, and with him Marlowe was stung by the dangerous imputations of 'Atheism'. Evidently they both paid Chettle a visit to complain about the publication. This was that same successful duo whom Greene had sniped at all his literary life, and at his death he aimed the *coup de grace*. But it is Alleyn we are concerned with here.

He was obviously particularly concerned to disclaim the unflattering picture of himself as an extortionate usurer and an incompetent playwright. Chettle mollified him by promising to make amends by printing a denial of Greene's allegations, which he did presently in his prefatory Letter to a pamphlet of his own, his *Kind-Harts Dreame*, in which he meets Greene's ghost in company with Tarlton and other deceased well-known characters. He described Greene as 'a man of indifferent yeares, of face amible, of body, well proportioned, his attire after the habite of a schollerlike Gentleman, onely his haire was somewhat long, whome I supposed to be Robert Greene, maister of Artes:'[39]

His prefatory Letter to this tale, which is known as Chettle's 'Reply' or 'Apology', is equally famous as being allegedly the first reference to Shakespeare-'Shake-scene', testifying to his personal qualities and his growing fame in London, which is merely argument *in circulo* and a tissue of wishful thinking. Once again the identification with Edward Alleyn is singularly apt on all counts. Chettle testifies that he has himself –

'seene his demeanor no lesse ciuill than he exclent in the qualitie he professes: Besides, diuers of worship haue reported, his vprightnes in dealing, which argues his honesty, and his facetious grace in writting that approues his Art.'[40]

All are agreed that 'the qualitie he professes' refers to his acting, in which Alleyn was indeed most 'exclent', whereas in 1592 we have no documentary evidence at all of William Shakespeare's association with any acting company in London or elsewhere, for these are his 'lost years' for which all is conjecture.

Chettle's testimony concerning the offended party's 'vprightnes in dealing, which argues his honesty' has been twisted this way and that in an effort to make it fit William Shakespeare somehow, leaving scholars after two hundred years of arguing still puzzled as to what Chettle is referring to concerning his 'honesty'. Had Shakespeare been plagiarizing Greene's plays? they ask, And is that why Greene was so incensed with him? They feel sure it must have been some *literary* transgression that had caused this bitter *contre temps* between the dying Greene and the man they see as Shakespeare-'Shake-scene'. But none of their conjectures fits the bill.

On the other hand, without any whisper of doubt, Chettle's reference to 'his vprightnes in dealing' applies precisely to Edward Alleyn in his business transactions with Greene and the other dramatists as theatre-manager-cum-banker. Alleyn's many business transactions preserved in the Alleyn Papers at Dulwich show him to be principled, efficient, shrewd and scrupulously honest in his financial dealings. Greene was deliberately libelling Alleyn in an attempt to wreak his revenge, implying that he underpaid him for his dramatic works, and was moreover usurious in his money-lending. In this business relationship with Alleyn we find the motive for Greene's vengeful action clearly indicated. It is traceable right back to the beginning of their association as described in the whole story of the *Groatsworth of Wit*, wherein Greene encountered the Player who engaged him as his 'plaimaking poet' and who also describes himself as 'a countrey Author'.

Alleyn's entitlement to be accepted not only as a sometime country playwright writing 'morrals' for his 'Puppets', but as a considerable minor dramatist of blank verse plays, which his own company performed in their repertoire with ongoing box office success, is fully discussed in Chapter VII, 'Johannes Factotum and His Works'. The evidence presented establishes beyond any doubt that Chettle would have seen some of Alleyn's plays and is speaking from personal experience in referring to 'his facetious grace in writting that approues his Art'.

Finally, Chettle's testimonial of his *civil demeanour* is particularly apt, for Alleyn was noted for his affability. At this time he was about to marry Joan Woodward, Henslowe's step-daughter, and ally himself with a family of some substance and respectability. She brought him a very handsome dowry of lands and property, and there would be no dearth of persons 'of worship' (meaning gentlemen of some standing and property), for Henslowe and the wealthy widow whom he had married had a wide circle of friends, many also at Court where Henslowe held a minor office, who would readily have come to speak on behalf of his future son-in-law. Alleyn himself was also on the best of terms with his patron, Lord Admiral Howard.

Alleyn and Joan Woodward were married in October 1592, so that Greene's bitter pamphlet was almost a wedding present!

Before investigating further the evidence for Alleyn as a minor dramatist in addition to his outstanding career as an actor, we shall linger somewhat longer with Greene's *Groatsworth of Wit* to make a full examination of the orthodox Shakespeareans' contention that this pamphlet was aimed at William Shakespeare as 'Shake-scene'. This view has now held sway for two hundred years and is consequently well entrenched, so that it is both appropriate and necessary to restate the arguments for this case in order that the reader can then make up his or her own mind.

VI *The Case for 'Shake-scene' presented by the New Orthodoxy*

THE IDENTIFICATION of Robert Greene's 'Shake-scene' as Shakespeare has been argued by the orthodox Shakespeareans on minute points of interpretation and re-interpretation of the text of Greene's Letter in its narrowest terms. The passage on which their intense concentration is focussed comprises only this:

'Base minded men all three of you, if by my miserie you be not warnd: for vnto none of you (like mee) sought those burres to cleaue: those Puppets (I meane) that spake from our mouths, those Anticks garnisht in our colours. Is it not strange, that I, to whom they all haue been beholding: is it not like that you, to whome they all haue beene beholding, shall (were yee in that case as I am now) bee both at once of them forsaken? Yes trust them not: for there is an vpstart Crow, beautified with our feathers, that with his *Tygers hart wrapt in a Players hyde*, supposes he is as well able to bombast out a blanke verse as the best of you: and beeing an absolute *Iohannes fac totum*, is in his owne conceit the onely Shake-scene in a countrey'.[1]

These words have been gone over again and again like a steam roller flattening the road – the road to lead them to 'Shake-scene'-Shakespeare in London in 1592. This is the sole goal of the orthodox approach, which pays no attention to the other passages in this Letter which are relevant to the identification of the Actor in question. For instance the following:

'Let those Apes imitate your past excellence, and *neuer more acquaint them with your admired inuentions. I know the best husband of you all will neuer proue an Vsurer, and the kindest of them all will neuer proue a kind nurse.'*[2] [My italics]

The italicised lines are totally ignored, for in them Greene implies that these 'Apes' are affluent men who use their wealth garnered from the profits of performing the plays to act as usurers to the (impecunious) dramatists, like himself, from whose 'admired inuentions' their wealth

168

stems; while his acquaintances, his fellow dramatists – even those careful at husbanding their money – would never dream of lending to others on terms of usury as the actors do. Greene's words imply that he had been unfairly dealt with in a *financial* sense, therefore he strongly advises his fellow playwrights to cease writing plays for such unfair and meagre returns which serve to enrich the actors who will show no gratitude to the poor dramatist when he is (as Greene now is) in desperate need. Again, at the very end of his Letter he reverts to the reason for his plight.

'The fire of my light is now at the last snuffe, and for want of wherewith to sustaine it, there is no substance lefte for life to feede on. Trust not then (I beseech ye) to such weake staies: for they are as changeable in minde, as in many attyres. Wel, my hand is tyrde, and I am forst to leaue where I would begin: for a whole booke cannot containe their wrongs, which I am forst to knit vp in some fewe lines of words.'[3]

Greene is dying for want of sustenance: he has no food to feed his line of life, and no money (as we learn from Gabriel Harvey) even to buy medicines for his illness, and this he lays at the door of the Actors, those 'weake staies', and especially one Actor, who refused to support him in his desperate need. These many clues scattered throughout Greene's Letter and his *Groatsworth of Wit* story are not pursued by the orthodox scholars, for their interest lies elsewhere. It is essential to their argument that the evidence of Greene's Letter testifying to his *financial* predicament be ignored – consistently by all – for this points all too clearly in the wrong direction to serve their purpose. It was the actor-manager of the Elizabethan theatrical world who purchased the plays, and hence would authorize advance payments for work in process of writing as loans to the down-and-out dramatist; and there is ample documentary evidence of this for the Alleyn-Henslowe partnership, then just begun in early 1592, who acted as bankers to the dramatists – but none at all for William Shakespeare.

For the orthodox scholar the entire gist of Greene's complaint against the great Actor, whom they insist on naming 'Shake-scene', is seen solely in terms of a *literary* offence concerned with his dramatic works. As previously pointed out, this Actor was not named 'Shake-scene' (Shakespeare or Shake-shaft or Shakerley) any more than he was named 'Crow', but thus *accurately described* by Greene for Alleyn was indeed 'the onely Shake-scene' of his day, of whom Ben Jonson wrote 'others speake but onely thou dost act' – and this was long after the younger Burbage had become Alleyn's heir to the Thespian crown! The name Greene chose for his man was '*Iohannes fac totum*', just as he named Thomas Nashe 'yong *Iuuenall*' but described him as 'that byting Satyrist', and he *accurately described* Marlowe as 'thou famous gracer of Tragedians' but did not consider it necessary to name him, knowing that his contemporary readers would have no difficulty in recognizing precisely to whom he was referring in every instance. Why cannot we do the same? The identification of the great Actor is made easy for us by Greene's autobiographical story and is borne out by research into the theatrical scene of the period. Once this is perceived, everything hangs together. However, we will now present the case for 'Shake-scene' from the point of view of orthodox scholarship, both old and new, and see what they make of it.

A recent comprehensive review by D. Allen Carroll entitled, *Greene's 'Vpstart Crow' Passage: A Survey of Commentary* (1985) has provided just what is required in a clear and concise form. Carroll begins by reminding us of the prime importance of the above quoted passage in Greene's Letter.

'It is the first text after the plays themselves to command our attention. And yet its special kind of vitality is so unsettled and complicated that we have not been able to agree as to its meaning or meanings. We turn to it again and again, and consequently have produced a small literature on the subject.'[4]

Scholars have been so puzzled by Greene's outburst against one 'Shake-scene', as they see him, who is without doubt in their minds none other than Shakespeare, that argument has necessarily concentrated around the matter of how to make his image fit the context of Greene's words. The more they argue, the more they remain bewildered. As Carroll explains:

'Something ambiguous hovers at the center of Greene's expression just at the point where we might hope, in this the first certain allusion to Shakespeare in London, for a reliable clue to Shakespeare's early practice as a dramatist. It was largely on a particular reading of Greene's outburst that for years we assumed that Shakespeare began his career by revising the plays of others.'[5]

This was Edmund Malone's view based on the belief that *The True Tragedy* with its 'Tygers hart' line was written by Greene (later Malone changed his mind and said it was written by Marlowe) and had been revised by Shakespeare who was thus appropriating and re-writing Greene's work, and hence guilty of plagiarism.

'The word *bombast*, meaning to "amplify and swell out", described exactly what Greene was suggesting Shakespeare did to the work of others.' (i.e. in revising their plays).[6]

However, others did not agree. Carroll proceeds to review the dissenters.

' "This passage from Greene", J.S. Smart complained in 1928, 'has had such a devastating effect on Shakespearean study that we cannot but wish it had never been written or never discovered'.'[7]

And Smart proceeded to do something about this state of affairs. (In the following quotation the 'borrowing' he refers to is literary borrowing or plagiarism – not financial borrowing which poor Greene had much more in mind.) Carroll explains:

'That Greene had borrowing of some kind in mind was, however, generally taken for granted until the third decade of our century when books by J.S. Smart (1928) and Peter Alexander (1929) changed our minds about Greene's meaning and thereby started a new orthodoxy about Shakespeare's beginnings.'[8]

In a previous chapter we have seen how Alexander did doughty battle with Tucker Brooke to wrest from him the authorship of *The Contention* and *True Tragedy* as Marlowe's and claim it for Shakespeare. Since Shakespeare was (according to Alexander) already a fully fledged dramatist prior to Greene's death-bed Letter in 1592, and was not merely employed in revising old plays, it followed that –

'the phrase "upstart Crow, beautified with our feathers" does not mean, as Malone supposed, that Shakespeare had stolen from the plays of others. It means no more than that he is an actor and thus relies for profit and applause on the lines of writers such as Greene and his friends...It was a grievance long standing with Greene, and he had clearly used the same image with exactly this meaning in 1590 in *Francescos Fortunes: Or The Second Part of Greenes Neuer too Late* –

why *Roscius* art thou proud with *Esops* Crow, being pranct with the glorie of others feathers? of thy selfe thou canst say nothing, and if the Cobler hath taught thee to say, *Ave Caesar*, disdain not thy tutor, because thou pratest in a Kings chamber.

It is in this sense alone that Greene and his fellows used the crow image.'[9]

(Alexander, here 'interpreting' Greene, carefully omitted to mention that *Roscius* is a synonym for Edward Alleyn and 'the Cobler' for Marlowe, which rather weakens the relevance to Shakespeare).

Alexander, establishing the prevailing 'new orthodox' view, scrutinizes Greene's reference to 'his *Tygers hart wrapt in a Players hyde*' and he points out:

' "the force which attaches in English to the use of *his* before such a deprecatory quotation ..... indicates that the victim is being condemned out of his own mouth". Greene in fact provides an example of the sort of rubbish, in his judgement, which Shakespeare writes, and which we are expected to condemn; and he deliberately misquotes it to get in another hit at the rival's profession as a player.'[10]

There is no appreciation here of the connotation of the 'Tygers hart' as representing a symbol in Elizabethan eyes of extreme cruelty and heartlessness, as also of deceit. To an Elizabethan audience it is inconceivable that the 'Tygers hart' speech would be seen as 'rubbish'. They would have applauded it to the skies as the height of great drama! They adored that sort of thing. In my humble opinion the very essence of Greene's bitter attack is completely misunderstood by these wranglers over words.

However, to continue Carroll's interesting commentary. Next Smart attacks the word 'factotum', which he claims –

'did not then mean what it does now: "a man-of-all-work, a servant who does odd jobs about the place" (OED.1.c)...a meaning that might well suggest that Shakespeare, among other tasks, fixed up old plays. It meant instead "a person of boundless conceit, who thinks himself able to do anything, however much beyond the reach of his abilities", or, as defined by the Oxford English Dictionary, which quotes Greene's words, "a would-be universal genius" (1.-b).'[11]

Carroll explains: 'Malone's interpretation completely reversed the original meaning'. (Now corrected for us by Smart above with resort to O.E.D.).

In case we have not quite understood the drift of Greene's diatribe against 'Shake-scene', Alexander has kindly paraphrased it for us:

'If these puppets have forsaken me with whom they once so closely associated for their own profit, they will be much readier to forsake you to whom they never sought to cleave. Just as it is strange that I to whom they owe so much, so it is likely that you to whom they owe so much, should, both of us, be forsaken by them. "Both" in Greene's sentence does not refer to two persons, as some have supposed, but to the two subjects of the verb forsaken – Greene on the one hand and his three friends on the other. And the actors have this further inducement for dispensing with their services: there is an actor, one like Roscius proud with AEsop's crow being prankt with the glory of others feathers...who, not content to masquerade in the borrowed plumage which all his kind enjoy, ventures to imitate the very voice of his betters; he "supposes he is as well able to bombast out a blanke verse as the best". The players Greene implies will naturally prefer the work of one of their own tribe.'[12]

If I may interpolate in Mr Carroll's exposition of Alexander here, (who is wide of the mark of Greene's sense!) far from fearing that the actors will forsake Peele and the strikingly successful Marlowe who was at the height of his powers in 1592, Greene is advising his friends to abandon the actors – *'neuer more acquaint them with your admired inuentions'*. These are Greene's own words, not Alexander's 'interpretation'. He cannot be beseeching his friends with dire warnings to *cease* writing for the actors, and at the same time claim that the actors will turn to some new playwright of their own profession, no longer caring for the works of Peele and Marlowe who were their box-office-hit men of the moment. That is nonsense. Greene has indeed been forsaken by the actors, and by one hard-hearted great actor in particular, but it was *not* by a rejection of his dramatic work, but by a refusal to lend him money when he was in need and dying in penury. Perhaps someone will kindly paraphrase this passage for us:

'I knowe the best husband of you all will neuer proue an Vsurer, and the kindest of them all will neuer proue a kind nurse.'

This encapsulates the kernel of the sense in which Greene is 'forsaken'. He was left penniless! And since he did not have a play to offer, he could get no more credit. Far from 'dispensing with their services' the actors were anxious to keep any successful dramatist working exclusively for their own company, as Henslowe's *Diary* amply evidences. Henslowe himself confesses that the running of a loan account for his dramatists, by which they drew money in advance on the plays they were currently writing for the resident company, was expressly to his own advantage for this kept the dramatists *tied to his* theatre – they couldn't afford to go anywhere else! Which practice sufficiently proves how totally mistaken Alexander's facile 'interpretation' of Greene's Letter is, when he asserts that Greene is complaining that the actors were forsaking him (and Marlowe *et al*) because they now had their own man, Shakespeare!

Mr Carroll continues with what I take to be unconscious humour:*

> 'Most scholars quickly accepted the Smart-Alexander understanding of the thrust and detail of Greene's attack.'[13]

All was well in the camp of the New Orthodoxy until J. Dover Wilson upset the applecart by resuscitating Malone's argument that Greene must have been referring to Shakespeare's *plagiarism* of his (Greene's) and others' work. He claimed that the 'upstart Crow, beautified with our feathers' was, of course, Horace's Crow (i.e. the crow who steals others' literary works and passes them off as his own), not Aesop's Crow (who is a counterfeit puppet or actor spouting the words supplied to him by the dramatists). Carroll comments:

> 'While Wilson has reconverted few to Malone's reading of Greene, he has turned many back to their texts, and the ensuing consideration has not cleared the Smart-Alexander reading of doubts raised. Most of the effort has sought an accommodation which allows for the presence of the Horatian allusion but not for a charge of plagiarism in Wilson's or the modern sense of the word.'[14]

Wilson had cited Henry Chettle's famous Reply in support of his reading of Greene's attack as a charge of plagiarism against 'Shake-scene'-Shakespeare.

We also need to look at this interesting piece of contemporary evidence of the furore raised in Elizabethan literary-theatrical circles by Greene's virulent outburst, amounting to a libel, against the man whom he named *Iohannes fac totum*, and whom he had clearly described for all to recognize

---

* A "Smart-Alec" is one who is too clever by half and thinks he knows it all!

him as 'the onely Shake-scene in a countrey' – an actor of considerable fame and standing – no one to touch him. So far as we can judge of William Shakespeare's record through his life he never made the grade as any notable actor, his value to the players being as their resident dramatist. And at the time of this public commotion in London's theatre-land, raised by the posthumous publication of *Greenes Groatsworth of Wit* in September 1592 – to which Tom Nashe testified 'what a coyle there is with pamphleting on him after his death',[15] – our William Shakespeare, wherever he then was, was certainly not known as a great actor by London audiences.

Henry Chettle was a printer and man of letters who later was to join Philip Henslowe's stable of dramatists and to write for him, mainly in collaboration with his friend Anthony Munday and others, writing and collaborating in no less than forty-nine plays in the space of five years.[16] In 1592 he was still in the printing business and it had fallen to his hand to publish *Greenes Groatsworth of Wit* in the September of 1592. This had brought, as repercussion hot-foot upon its publication, the visits to his shop of certain worried parties who recognized themselves therein maligned or damagingly misrepresented. 'The famous gracer of Tragedians', Marlowe, one assumes was annoyed about the dangerous imputations of Atheism, and '*Iohannes fac totum*' about the bitter accusations of his dishonest dealings with his playwrights, with the imputation that he had turned a heart as pitiless as a 'Tygers' to the dead man's pleas for financial succour with the implication of usury, and, moreover, the slur on his ability to write blank verse dramas. Chettle hastened to make amends in his carefully worded preface to his own pamphlet *Kind-Harts Dreame* published in the winter of 1592-3:

To the Gentleman Readers

About three moneths since died M. *Robert Greene*, leauing many papers in sundry Booke sellers hands, among other his Groatsworth of wit, in which a letter written to diuers play-makers, is offensiuely by one or two of them taken, and because on the dead they cannot be auenged, they wilfully forge in their concietes a liuing Author: and after tossing it two and fro, no remedy, but it must light on me. How I haue all the time of my conuersing in printing hindred the bitter inueying against schollers, it hath been very well knowne, and how in that I dealt I can sufficiently prooue. With neither of them that take offence was I acquainted, and with one of them I care not

175

if I neuer be: The other, whome at that time I did not so much spare, as since I wish I had, for that as I haue moderated the heate of liuing writers, and might haue vsde my owne discretion, (especially in such a case) the Author beeing dead, that I did not, I am as sory, as if the originall fault had beene my fault, because my selfe haue seene his demeanor no lesse ciuill than he exclent in the qualitie he professes: Besides, diuers of worship haue reported, his vprightnes of dealing, which argues his honesty, and his facetious grace in writting, that aprooues his Art. For the first, whose learning I reuerence, and at the perusing of *Greenes* Booke stroke out what then in conscience I thought he in some displeasure writ; or had it beene true, yet to publish it, was intollerable: him I would wish to vse me no worse than I deserue. I had onely in the copy this share, it was il written, as sometime *Greenes* hand was none of the best, licensd it must be, ere it could bee printed which could neuer be if it might not be read. To be breife I writ it ouer, and as neare as I could, followed the copy, onely in that letter I put something out, but in the whole booke not a worde in, for I protest it was all *Greenes*, not mine nor Master Nashes, as some uniustly haue affirmed.[17]

The incriminating words in Greene's Letter which Chettle said he 'stroke out' because 'to publish it, was intollerable', would doubtless have been a gratuitous reference by Greene in his ultra-religious mood of death-bed recrimination and piety to allegations concerning Marlowe's 'Atheism' – that he disputed the theological concept of the Holy Trinity – which would certainly have brought Hell Fire onto his head! Even to publish it would have proved dangerous, as Chettle recognized. He wanted nothing to do with heresy.

Henrie Chettle, as he signs himself, had obviously scented the deadly taint of Atheism which Greene had fastened on Marlowe, and scuttled to safety by disclaiming his acquaintance, or desire for acquaintance with one so dangerous to know. Six months later Thomas Kyd would suffer on the rack for this same taint caught from his association with Marlowe.

Carroll summarizes the orthodox reading of Chettle's Reply, which tantalizingly again mentions no names. The identifications are all based on Greene's Letter.

'To the one, Marlowe, Chettle offers no apology, but to the other, Shakespeare, he offers the sincerest of apologies through handsome compliments. For Wilson, the response had been directly to Chettle, an obscure printer, possibly by Shakespeare himself, either in person or else in some form by some of his supporters, by "diuers of worship", that is, by "several noblemen interested in defending the slandered poet".'[18]

Regarding the last piece of hyperbole, Samuel Schoenbaum puts this quietly into perspective for us: 'The Elizabethans made careful distinctions in their forms of address. Noblemen they would refer to as divers of honour; *worship* applied to gentlemen.'[19] So the imaginary picture of 'several noblemen' springing to our slandered poet's defence is, as so much else with Shakespeare, unsubstantiated; moreover, at this time he was not yet acknowledged as a 'poet' for *Venus and Adonis* would not appear for a twelve-month.

Carroll continues:

'Chettle himself has observed Shakespeare's "demeanour" to be as "ciuil" as he "exclent in the qualitie he professes" (acting) – thus answering the charge of pride and, perhaps, the implication ("Anticks") of buffoonery. And others of worth have "praised his facetious grace in writting, that aproues his Art" – answering the attack on Shakespeare's style (facetious meaning polished and witty).'[20]

So far, so good. But now Dover Wilson comes up again with an awkward question:

'But why drag in that pointed reference to "honesty" and "uprightness of dealing"?'

Carroll augments this:

'The charge had to have been sufficient to provoke a response at all and clear enough as dishonesty to provoke this particular one. The specific charge, Wilson notes, is not denied. Shakespeare just may have been uncomfortable from the sense that, even if he and his company were well within their rights, 'the rewriting of large portions of plays purchased from others was scarcely a "normal practice".'[21]

Here I regret it is necessary to intervene again to put Professor Wilson right on this last point. It was indeed a 'normal practice' to alter and rewrite plays. The often drastic cutting of scripts was essential to adapt them for provincial performance when the company went on tour with a much smaller troupe of actors. Chettle himself when he went to work for Henslowe was often engaged in altering and rewriting, as his biographer Harold Jenkins tells us:

> 'He [Chettle] alters and adapts other men's work according to the needs of the moment – the Company seem to have found him particularly useful in this respect; he collaborates with other dramatists to piece together a play with the speed which the Admiral's men required; usually he is dependent on Henslowe for his very means of subsistence. He procures money in advance on plays that the Company commission him to write, and to keep the wolf from the door he obtains private loans from Henslowe, often of pitifully small sums. The Diary shows that a greater number of small borrowings were made by Chettle than by any other writer. It is extraordinary that the mercenary Henslowe gave way so regularly to his appeals. Perhaps he realised Chettle's value in the rapid creation of dramatic material and the rehandling of old plays; perhaps the stern business-man had some special regard for the distressed hard-worked dramatist....Whatever his motive, he was a good friend to Chettle in times of need, and the only friend who was likely to afford him any material assistance; for Chettle's other friends, his brother playwrights, were almost as impecunious as he was himself.'[22]

It seems a pity for poor Chettle that he did not himself heed the advice of Robert Greene in his *Groatsworth of Wit*, but subsequently abandoned printing for the precarious and penurious livelihood of a dramatist. Henslowe was frequently baling him out with numerous small advance loans on the plays he was altering or writing for the company, as Jenkins has remarked, although there is nothing particularly 'extraordinary' about this for Henslowe did so regularly for those who requested loans as we have seen. Jenkins is here under the spell of the legend that Henslowe was nothing but a mercenary exploiter of the dramatists and actors because he acted as their banker and so kept them out of the debtors' prisons of the day.

Chettle's employment as dramatist exemplifies the true situation with regard to the rewriting of other men's work. Where, then, does this leave the charge of 'plagiarism' against Shakespeare which has been made the subject of so much heart searching? According to Dover Wilson, Shakespeare may have felt 'uncomfortable' at the charge of plagiarism, and he feels that the concomitant charge of cruelty (the 'Tygers hart' taunt) and the pathos of Greene's death would have 'touched Shakespeare much nearer in September 1592 than any talk of an Upstart Crow'.[23] We are not told by Professor Wilson what special *cruelty* Shakespeare is supposed to have inflicted on poor Greene. Can plagiarism, which was so commonly practised, have been this extreme cruelty? We are frankly puzzled. Perhaps Carroll will enlighten us if we read on.

> 'Even Alexander, though he seemed to question Wilson's interpretation of the *Myrrour* passage' [this being taken from *The Myrrour of Modestie* of 1584 in which "Esops Crowe, ... deckt hir selfe with others feathers, or like the proud Poet *Batyllus*, which subscribed his name to *Virgils* verses and ..... presented them to Augustus" as his own] – 'and continued to defend his own reading, was willing to admit that "Greene's manner of expressing himself is not without a certain ambiguity or confusion, and [that] what may have been obvious at sight to his fellow playwrights is still puzzling to the modern reader"; so that the letter taken by itself does not enable us to determine exactly what Greene meant.'[24]

The puzzlement continues:

> 'Some who accept that theft is the charge restrict the sense in which Greene could have meant that such a charge was applicable to Shakespeare. Thus for E.A.J. Honigman .... "Greene's crow was not meant to suggest that Shakespeare had revised plays by one or two other writers, but that he had pilfered *sententiae* and examples," selected feathers, that is, not the whole cloak.'[25]

For others, however:

> 'The specific charge against Shakespeare, many feel, ought to be seen as part of a general attack in the passage against players and playwrights. This attack, properly understood, in turn belongs to an ongoing conflict at the time, first between the University Wits (Greene, Nashe, Peele, and others) and the actors, and, second, between the wits and the uneducated, professional playwrights, (Shakespeare, Munday, Kyd, and others).'[26]

Still floundering and groping for something tangible:

> 'We cannot know whether some specific injustice, real or imagined, directed Greene's wrath against Shakespeare, something said or done. Greene seems not to have been very scrupulous in his dealings with the players.'[27]

He then quotes the instance of Greene having sold *Orlando Furioso* twice over. But what this has to do with Shakespeare is not clear. It certainly had to do with Alleyn, for Greene sold it both to the Lord Admiral's and the Queen's Men.

'Nor do we know precisely what theatrical arrangements obtained during that summer to make Shakespeare's ascendancy so manifest and threatening to Greene. Before the theaters were closed on 23 June for the plague, the leading company was the Strange-Admiral combination playing for Henslowe at the Rose. A number of Greene's plays from the old Queen's Men had passed on to Edward Alleyn and thus to this group. Some hold that Shakespeare began his career with Queen's and replaced Greene as its leading playwright, which might explain Greene's hostility.'[28]*

And so the guesswork goes on, often taking refuge in a minute discussion of the exact meaning of a phrase or word in these much-disputed texts. Janet Spens, questioning Dover Wilson's reading of Chettle's Apology when he queries why Shakespeare's 'honesty' should be in question, comes up with: ' "his uprightness of dealing, which argues his honesty" means no more than "his conduct shows him to be a gentleman", with *honesty* meaning *honour* and carrying the connotation of "gentle birth and breeding".'[29]

Whereas:

'For Andrew S. Cairncross the Horatian *honestus* is intended, meaning "decent, gentlemanly": and "vprightnes of dealing" lacked then the business flavour it has now.'[30]

In his *Survey of Commentary* on Greene's Letter and Chettle's Reply, Mr Carroll here seems to have strayed into his famous namesake's delightful land of Looking-Glass.[31]

Humpty Dumpty took the book, and looked at it very carefully. "That *seems* to be done right – " he began.
"You're holding it upside down!" Alice interrupted.
"To be sure I was!" Humpty Dumpty said gaily, as she turned it round for him. "I thought it looked a little queer. As I was saying, that *seems* to be done right – though I haven't time to look it over

---

* That Greene was the leading playwright of the Queen's Men is not proven, and Shakespeare's connection with them is pure conjecture.

thoroughly just now – and that shows that there are three hundred and sixty-four days when you might get un-birthday presents – "

"Certainly," said Alice.

"And only *one* for birthday presents, you know. There's glory for you!"

"I don't know what you mean by 'glory'," Alice said.

Humpty Dumpty smiled contemptuously. "Of course you don't – till I tell you. I meant 'there's a nice knock-down argument for you!'"

"But 'glory' doesn't mean 'a nice knock-down argument!'" Alice objected.

"When *I* use a word," Humpty Dumpty said in a rather scornful tone, "it means just what I choose it to mean – neither more nor less."

"The question is," said Alice, "whether you *can* make words mean different things."

"The question is," said Humpty Dumpty, "which is to be master – that's all."

Alice was too much puzzled to say anything, so after a minute Humpty Dumpty began again. "They've a temper, some of them – particularly verbs, they're the proudest – adjectives you can do anything with, but not verbs – however, *I* can manage the whole lot! Impenetrability! That's what *I* say!"

"Would you tell me, please," said Alice, "what that means?"

"Now you talk like a reasonable child," said Humpty Dumpty, looking very much pleased. "I meant by 'impenetrability' that we've had enough of that subject, and it would be just as well if you'd mention what you mean to do next, as I suppose you don't intend to stop here all the rest of your life."

"That's a great deal to make one word mean," Alice said in a thoughtful tone.

"When I make a word do a lot of work like that," said Humpty Dumpty, "I always pay it extra."

"Oh!" said Alice. She was too much puzzled to make any other remark.

It may well be that with Humpty Dumpty, 'we've had enough of that subject', but at the risk of over-stating the argument, I shall conclude with a quotation from Dr Gaw, whose incisive mind is here directed to the question of Greene's *Groatsworth of Wit* accusation, and in presenting his view it is to be remarked that here speaks a great Shakespearean scholar who can nevertheless see clearly what is presented to his discriminating gaze without being misled by preconceived opinions concerning Shakespeare.

'Even at the cost of repetition the reasons must be here summarized why it is impossible to consider the passage in *Groatsworth of Wit* as accusing Shakespeare of plagiarism in connection with *3 Henry VI*. (1) The very conditions of Elizabethan play ownership make any such allegation meaningless. If a company that owned a play employed a second writer to adapt it to their later needs, they were in the position of a house owner who has certain additions built to his residence by another than the original architect. Under such conditions the original architect has no ground for claiming that the second builder has appropriated his work. Nor is there, to my knowledge, any parallel case of such resentment on the part of any other Elizabethan dramatist toward another playwright for a similar reason. This case would be unique.

(2) But Greene says concerning 'Shake-scene' merely that he thinks he can write high-sounding blank verse as well as the best of his competitors and that he is egotistical.'[32]

I have already quoted Dr Gaw's assessment of Greene's use of the *Tygers hart* allusion. (See page 160). His appreciation of the historical facts is the basis which makes the logic of his arguments clear and unassailable.

'That there is any accusation of plagiarism in it has always been a pure assumption', he declares, and then summarizes the reasons why such assumptions are inconclusive, being arguments *in circulo* so that they can never, in fact, be substantiated.[33] This is not in accord with orthodox opinion which accepts the "Shake-scene"-Shakespeare *alias* as established beyond a shadow of doubt. Samuel Schoenbaum, the acknowledged greatest living Shakespearean authority, claims: 'the *Groatsworth of Wit* contains – no question – a desperate shaft directed at Shakespeare.'[34]

Dr Gaw begs to differ. He soberly concludes his finely reasoned critique of the orthodox acceptance of the 'Shake-scene' reference: 'It would seem that the assumed accusation may well be dismissed from further consideration in connection with discussions of Shakespeare's life and work.'[35] Gaw's argument dating from 1926 has never been refuted because it is irrefutable. It has simply been passed over in silence.

The knotty problem that faces the orthodox school is that there is a total lack of evidence connecting Shakespeare with any acting company prior to December 1594. F.E. Halliday comments:

'The first official notice of Shakespeare as a player occurs in the Chamber Accounts for performances at Court on 26th, 27th December, 1594, for which he was one of the payees on 15th March, 1595: "William Kempe William Shakespeare & Richard Burbage seruants to the Lord Chamberleyne". If he were with Strange's before this, as he may have been, it is odd that he should not have been mentioned in the cast of *The Deadly Sins*, in the Licence of 1593, or by Alleyn in his correspondence, for after all Strange's had acted one of his plays, and perhaps more, while Greene's oblique attack and Chettle's apology of 1592 testify to his importance.'[36]*

Without Greene's *Groatsworth* reference as meaning 'Shake-scene'-Shakespeare, there is nothing to provide even a hypothetical basis for a hypothetical reconstruction of his early career. D. Allen Carroll ends his paper with a statement which puts in a nutshell the reason why Greene's death-bed utterance is seen as of such vital importance:

'From Greene's attack and the response it started, we learn that by the summer of 1592 Shakespeare was a successful dramatist and accomplished actor, was possessed of influential friends ready to testify to his good character and graceful style and was recognized by a hostile eye as being on the verge of becoming London's leading dramatist.'[37]

This is the perfect example of argument *in circulo*, as Dr Gaw has pointed out, because we must first accept *without question* that 'Shake-scene' is Shakespeare and no one else. Which is tenuous, as Carroll's paper has unintentionally demonstrated for there is little consensus of opinion even on the meaning of some of Greene's words. There is a desperate illogicality in their reasoning. The Smart-Alexander argument sees the accusation of plagiarism as irrelevant, substituting the claim of the 'new orthodoxy' that Greene's bitterness against 'Shake-scene' is mainly because he fears that his rise as a dramatist threatens him and his fellow playwrights' livelihood. Since this 'threat' was then still largely in the future, and could not affect the dying Greene anyway, nor could it have caused much loss of sleep to the highly successful Marlowe, or even to Peele, it is not explained how this could have evoked such a virulent attack from Greene,

* Halliday is referring to *harey the vj* of *I Henry VI*, the subject of Chapter VIII.

implying *extreme cruelty* – an attack far in excess of the sarcastic jibes he threw at Marlowe when *his* rising star appeared as a threatening rival indeed. Alexander's bogus 'threat' is negated by the historical fact that long after Shakespeare had reached the peak of his success, other dramatists still thrived, many of them new on the scene – Ben Jonson, Heywood, Marston, Beaumont and Fletcher. To suggest that Shakespeare was about to eclipse Greene, Marlowe, Peele if they had lived, and that it was the *fear of being ousted* by this newcomer that drove Greene into such a frenzy of bitter invective and self-pity is, frankly, ridiculous! It is only in posterity that Shakespeare has eclipsed all.

Greene, moreover, prophesies that newer dramatists will be left 'to the mercie of these painted monsters', who will exploit them, as they have him, for they are usurious, merciless, tiger-hearted. What any of this has to do either with plagiarism, or envy of an actor-playwright's success as a threat to established playwrights, I am at a loss to see. For Greene is, in fact, urging his friends to *cease* writing to supply the players with their 'admired inventions' so that the actors will then feel the pinch as he himself, owing to their miserliness towards him, is now feeling it, and is dying in desperate poverty.

To recapitulate. We know that Henslowe acted as banker to his dramatists, and we know that this was also Alleyn's role as head of his company, buying scripts for the company or as a private purchase for his own investment. Advances were made on plays in process of writing, but this time the request had been refused. The heartless exploiter of his talents had shut the door on Greene's plea for a further loan. *This* is the explanation of Greene's pathetic complaint about 'an Vsurer' and those hard-hearted 'painted monsters' who 'will neuer proue a kind nurse'. The interpretation of this passage is equally important as that referring to the 'vpstart Crow' or 'Shake-scene', but it has been deliberately ignored because it could not be made to apply to Shakespeare. It certainly applies to Alleyn in his business relations with the dramatists, and it is doubtful that he would have felt charitably inclined to Greene, a notorious profligate. In that case the charge of hard-heartedness would have fitted.

The correct interpretation of Greene's Letter is equally clearly supported by Chettle's Apology. Chettle tells us he was not acquainted with Alleyn personally before this encounter, but had 'seene his demeanor no lesse ciuill than he exclent in the qualitie he professes', which is generally agreed as a reference to the actor having been seen in a performance; which would have been surprising had he not seen the famous Alleyn on the boards for Chettle was keenly interested in the drama and later allied himself to Alleyn's step-father-in-law, Henslowe, as one of his most prolific playwrights. He was evidently eager to ingratiate himself with Alleyn, who was a gentleman although an actor, a man of property and held in high esteem for his theatrical success, and already, I believe, in a business alliance with Philip Henslowe, and if not yet married to Joan Woodward at the time of his visit to Chettle, then the union was about to take place – the date of their marriage was 22nd October 1592. Alleyn was on the best of terms with his patron, the Lord Admiral Howard, and both he and Henslowe had friends in the gentrified class and were well known at Court where Henslowe held a minor office. The 'diuers of worship' who came forward to speak on his behalf would have presented no problem to Alleyn.

Of his plays we shall treat in the next chapter. *Faire Em* had been performed 'sundrie times' in the City of London by 1592, so that Chettle as a man interested in the theatre would probably have seen it, or heard talk of it.*

This is not mere hypothesis. There is evidence and reason to support it, and every particular fits with Greene's and Chettle's words without any straining to make it fit. Alleyn as Greene's 'Player' emerges without ambiguity as the 'vpstart Crow', whose great success had so riled the envious Master of Arts, whose earnings in his literary career did not keep pace with his pecuniary needs so that he was dependent on Alleyn's on-going loans. Greene's vindictive Letter was the final outburst against the unfair and usurious business relations that existed between himself and the successful actor-manager Alleyn.

Doubtless both Alleyn and Marlowe would have averred that Greene was making false accusations against them, being sick in body and mind, poor man. As he himself confessed, his groatsworth of wit had eluded him to the end, and he had been foolhardy; even when he was trying to make amends by doing some good, he only caused harm. His admonitions to Marlowe proved the kiss of death. Only seven months later the hunt for this 'Atheist' was up in earnest. Nashe rallied by calling the *Groatsworth of Wit* 'a scald triuial, lying pamphlet', and he piously hastened to write his *Christs Teares ouer Ierusalem*.[38]

Four hundred years later Greene's pamphlet is still causing contention, but of a different kind. What we are seeking to establish here is the historical truth as to against whom *precisely* his dire accusations were directed.

---

* See the critical analysis of *Faire Em*, pages 194 ff attributing this play to Edward Alleyn's authorship.

VII *Johannes Factotum and his Works*

IT HAS BEEN NOTED that Robert Greene came late onto the theatrical scene as a dramatist. By 1587 he was already aged twenty-nine and an established writer of romantic fiction, a Master of Arts of Cambridge, and about to receive a second degree from Oxford; married, but separated, and confirmed in a dissolute way of life. Arriving back in the metropolis he now settled to a new career as a dramatist in addition to his other writings, pouring forth words by the yard to maintain his profligate life-style.

With Edward Alleyn it was quite the opposite. In almost every way these two were a complete contrast to each other. Alleyn was eight years younger than Greene, and his theatrical career was marked with precocity bringing him to a position of success, affluence, fame and authority at the age of twenty-one. After a youth spent touring the provinces, he returned to London – probably sometime during 1585 – and in 1587, when already at the head of the Lord Admiral's Men, he joined forces with that new-come genius, Christopher Marlowe, and together they rode the crest of the wave of fame as 'Tamburlaine the Great' – actor and dramatist *par excellence* of the London stage. The brilliant success of this duo sparked off deeply ingrained envy in the breast of Robert Greene. Greene even more than Nashe may be aptly described as a man who was 'tormented with other mens felicitie.'[1] In his moment of self-knowledge as he surveyed the sorry scenes of his past life in his *Repentance*, he himself recognized that envy was the sin that tainted his nature and had warped his life with discontentment.

Thus it is psychologically all of a piece with Greene's personality that he should have conceived a resentment against Alleyn from the start, when he was obliged to accept charitable assistance from the young, upstart player who at nineteen was already at the head of his troupe of 'puppets' and took Greene under his wing, as he tells us, and 'lodged him at the Townes end in a house of retayle'. Doubtless he also lent the penniless *Roberto* money in earnest of the first play he would write for the company. If this was a comedy, as indicated in the semi-autobiographical *Francescos Fortunes*, and on a romantic, pastoral theme, it would doubtless have been well received, for this was the genre in which Greene was most at home.

Had he only had the sense to stick to it and develop his talents in that field his contribution to our dramatic literature might well have ranked far higher. But, with the tremendous success of *Tamburlaine*, he felt his nose put out of joint, and his envious nature impelled him to emulate Marlowe in his *Alphonsus King of Arragon* with the resulting belly-flop which only redoubled his envy and resentment against the Alleyn-Marlowe team, whose continued rise to fame and acclaim he found himself powerless to match.

The chronology of Greene's encounter with Alleyn is important in order to establish that this hypothesis is correct. Robert Greene's meeting with Edward Alleyn, according to his account in the *Groatsworth of Wit*, took place somewhere in the country, and not in London. We do not know exactly when Alleyn left the Earl of Worcester's Men to join the Lord Admiral's which became his permanent company. They were formerly Lord Howard's Men and emerged as the Lord Admiral's servants when Charles Howard of Effingham was made Lord High Admiral of the Fleet in 1585, at which time a reorganisation seemingly took place. Edward Alleyn, together with several of the Worcester's Men, joined them, and Alleyn became the company's head and leading actor although in 1585 still only aged nineteen. This company always went on tour in the summer months, so that Alleyn was probably touring with the Lord Admiral's Men when he encountered Greene, for at the time of their meeting he was evidently at the head of his company of actors. The date of this fortuitous meeting would most likely have been in the late summer of 1586.

This dating would coincide with the breakdown of Greene's short-lived marriage to the 'proper Gentlewoman' whom he wedded in Norwich[2] and, having squandered the marriage allowance, had forsaken for the harlots he preferred. He was subsequently wending his way disconsolately towards London in hope of making a living by his writings. Although the 'shamfast' younger brother, like the usurer presented as his father (in place of the honest saddler who was Greene's real parent) of the *Groatsworth* story are fictional characters, one feels that the cunning courtezan *Lamilia* was real enough, and it was probably due to her 'Calypso charms' that he now found himself with an empty purse. At the very latest Greene must have arrived in London by the early summer of 1587 for his *Farewell to Folly* was entered at the Stationers' Register on 11th June 1587. Thus the approximate dating of their meeting in late 1586 falls into place without any straining to meet the circumstances. This reconstruction fits Greene's autobiographical story perfectly.

Edward Alleyn was then already an affluent young man, not yet turned twenty, owning some property inherited from his father in London, and the leading actor of his company when he met up with the penniless

Greene in that country lane. His boast of having been 'a countrey Author, passing at a Morrall', for the space of the past seven years may be thought to represent an exaggeration, but to have begun his playwriting activities at the age of thirteen is by no means beyond the capabilities of a bright, ambitious lad with an inbred sense of theatre, and early experience of acting and memorizing parts, for whom writing could have begun with altering and improving existing plays. He had been brought up on a diet of traditional, country, morality-type plays and allegorical dramatic works, and was obviously aspiring to something better. Alleyn would have been largely self-taught, and there is evidence of a quality of mind and character well above that of an average actor. Such a young man would very naturally have turned his energies early in life to writing and devising country entertainments for the players to perform. And he had the intelligence to be self-critical, for the Player tells *Roberto*, 'my Almanacke is out of date', and he recognizes that the University Wit he discovers by the hedgerow could infuse new life into their dramatic repertoire. Here speaks Alleyn, the practical man of the theatre, who was so well suited to leading an acting company to success, which is undoubtedly why he was invariably chosen for this position. This also indicates that Alleyn was by now leading a London company of players, and no longer with a provincial troupe, for whom the more sophisticated dramatic works would not have been of such vital importance. Alleyn was actively seeking to improve his company's repertoire, and his sponsorship of first, Greene, and then Marlowe, shows his discriminating taste.

In Greene's satirical sketch Edward Alleyn's known interest in education – to the furthering of which he devoted his fortune and the last years of his life – is also cleverly characterized in the wryly humorous couplet the Player tosses off to impress *Roberto*:

> *The people make no estimation*
> *Of Morrals teaching education.*

'Was not this prettie for a plaine rime extempore?' he asks, pleased with himself. *Roberto* dismisses this with a tinge of contempt. It is the sort of thing that would have irritated Greene, for here was a supremely self-confident, very successful young fellow dressed in fine clothes with plenty of money. He must have secretly disliked Alleyn at sight.

Muriel Bradbrook has suggested that the Player is merely a caricature of a stock figure representing 'a successful Actor' – not a real-live individual, but a composite portrait embodying all those traits in actors in general which Greene derided. However, then she back-tracks to propose the notion that Greene is pointing to the country-born William Shakespeare in the Player's country association.[3] This would be a very weak hint since there were many actors of country origin in London, and Greene is far too concerned to pin-point his man to have resorted to anything so feeble and ambiguous. It would apply equally to Edward Alleyn who had spent a country-bred youth. There is no validity in the argument that since the usurer, old *Gorinius*, is not a portrait of Greene's real father, the respectable saddler, therefore it follows that the Player is also not a real character from Greene's life. This is to mistake Greene's art as a writer. He deliberately set out to open his story in this way so that he could introduce the bequest of the *groat* whereby hangs his tale and *the moral he wishes to point*. He also had in mind to attack usury, which the impecunious Greene hated above all sins of mankind; hence making old *Gorinius* an Usurer had special significance for him. The beginning of his tale is fancy, with some touches of self-portraiture to *Roberto*, but as his story unfolds it slips into pure autobiography, as Greene himself tells us.

The invitation to his readers to suppose him the said *Roberto* 'whose life in most parts agreeing with mine' would clearly indicate to those who knew Robin Greene that the 'Player' with whom he had dealings throughout his career as a 'plaimaking poet' was one Edward Alleyn of the Lord Admiral's Men. Tom Nashe had earlier referred to the provincial actor as 'King of the Fairies' and 'Delphrigus' *alias Roscius-Caesar* whom everyone knew as Alleyn, so that the identification can hardly be more obvious. This is not just a stock caricature of an actor: it is clearly and precisely Edward Alleyn, and the actors would know what parts he had played when touring the provinces for he tells *Roberto* that he was 'famous' in these parts. 'The twelue Labors of Hercules haue I terribly thundred on the Stage' is a boast that proclaims the young Alleyn!

Richard Simpson has pointed out that Nashe had been abroad in Ireland and Italy when he was summoned by Archbishop Whitgift 'to oppose Martin Marprelate with his weapons of scurrility and lampoon'.[4] Nashe's reputation for satire earned at Cambridge had at last done him good. He entered the lists on 8th August 1589 with his cock-a-hoop *Countercuffe giuen to Martin Junior by...Pasquil of England*, and once in London he joined Greene to satirize the successful Marlowe-Alleyn team hoping to sting Marlowe to inaugurate a famous battle in print in emulation of that which was waged in ancient Rome between rival writers. But his lampoons were totally ignored by Marlowe, so Nashe had no joy there.

Simpson, in rightly claiming that Nashe's references to the 'Player-King-of-the-Fairies' are those epithets 'decanted into him' by Greene, believed that these were pointing at Shakespeare, and he claims that Nashe in 1589 was attacking him as an 'actor-author'.[5] But this is error. It was only Greene who, three years later in his *Groatsworth of Wit*, attacked this hated actor as an *actor-author*, by which time Alleyn had launched on a career as a London dramatist in addition to acting and managing his company, and engaging in financial dealing. The whole point of Greene's final virulent attack on this particular 'vpstart Crow' is to barb it with recognition!

Casting around in his mind for a suitable name to identify his enemy Greene chose *Iohannes fac totum*: a would-be universal genius; a man with many strings to his bow. We shall see in following his life in subsequent chapters that this sums up Edward Alleyn to a tee! He continued to add strings to his bow all his life, and by 1592, from having been a youthful deviser of 'Morrals' and simple country plays for the 'puppets' he had progressed to writing blank verse plays for London audiences. And so that we should see him all the more clearly in this portrait, Greene provides his readers with a clue. The Player boasts to *Roberto* that 'I am reputed able at my proper cost to build a Windmill'. Why a Windmill? one is prompted to ask. This is subtle and intentional, for nothing is irrelevant in this clever story.

The play which has been identified for us by Greene's sarcastic remarks about the author as being from the pen of Edward Alleyn-*alias*-the Player in the *Groatsworth of Wit* (for one of the identification marks of this character in Greene's life is that he *wrote blank verse plays which Greene held to scorn*!) is the play he had lampooned the previous year in his preface to *Farewell to Folly* (1591 edition) which is undoubtedly *Faire Em, the Miller's Daughter of Manchester*. The Windmill features in this play, making this an unmistakable identification tag for his contemporary readers, who would in all probability have seen Faire Em 'sundrie times publiquely acted in the honourable citie of London', as the title page tells us.

Faire Em

Faire Em, or rather its author, has been generally accepted by critics as the target of the lampoon that Greene inserted into his preface written for the 1591 edition of his *Farewell to Folly*, which W.W. Greg[6] has credibly argued was the first edition of this work although it was registered for publication as long ago as 11th June 1587, but no edition of that date is known. In any event Greene's preface is dated to this 1591 edition by his use of the term 'Martinize' culled from the currently raging Martin Marprelate controversy, in which Greene was one of the anonymous writers together with his friend Nashe. A preface was usually considered the suitable place in which to let off a few satirical squibs, and this one of Greene's begins enticingly addressed:

To the Gentlemen students of both Vniuersities health.
Such wags as haue bene wantons with me, and haue marched in the Mercers booke to please their Mistris eye with their brauerie, that as the frolike phrase is haue made the tauerne to sweat with riotous expences, that haue spent their wits in courting of their sweetehearts, and emptied their purses by being too prodigall...[7]

So, warming to his subject, he comes to his satirical exposure of the author of a certain play well-known currently to his readers, whom he sets out to ridicule for his lack of scholarly expertise in his biblical sources, presenting him as an ignoramus who is cast in exactly the same mould as the *Iohannes fac totum* of his *Groatsworth of Wit* whom he stigmatizes as one who 'supposes he is as well able to bombast out a blanke verse as the best of you'. Greene is of course here addressing fellow university students, educated men like himself. His pen gleefully barbed he launches into his attack:

And he that can not write true Englishe without the helpe of Clearkes of parish Churches, will needes make him selfe the father of interludes. O tis a iollie matter when a man hath a familiar stile and can endite a whole yeare and neuer be beholding to art? but to bring Scripture to proue any thing he sayes, and kill it dead with the text in a trifling subiect of loue, I tell you is no small peece of cunning. As for example two louers on the stage arguing one an other of vnkindnesse, his Mistris runnes ouer to him with this canonicall sentence, *A mans conscience is a thousande witnesses,* and hir knight againe excuseth him selfe with that saying of the Apostle, *Loue couereth the multitude of sinnes,* I thinke this was but simple abusing of the Scripture. In charitie be it spoken I am perswaded the sexten of Saint Giles without Creeple gate, would haue beene ashamed of such blasphemous Rhetoricke.[8] [My italics]

Godless and blasphemous Greene may have been in real life, but he knew his biblical texts as an university educated man, and he knew how to appear virtuous in spotting when these were misapplied in print. Such knowledge has no relevance to religiosity, for Greene was not religious, whereas Alleyn was – but the loose application of biblical texts is merely Greene's convenient stick with which he can belabour Alleyn. The two relevant speeches which Greene was lampooning are readily identifiable in *Faire Em*, when the heroine berates her lover, Manville, in a lovers' quarrel:

> *Em*: Thy conscience Manuile [is] a hundred witnesses
>
> 1.1424

and earlier in the same scene the Danish King Zweno says to his daughter Blanche:

> *Zweno*: Yet that loue that couers multitudes of sinns
> Makes loue in parents wink at childrens faults.
>
> 11.1385-6

Having identified the play as *Faire Em* scholars have searched assiduously for an author who might fit Greene's attack, and one remotely possible candidate, has been found in Robert Wilson, also a leading actor some sixteen years senior to Edward Alleyn, who turned his hand to writing plays of the morallistic, allegorical type in which stock characters representing the vices and virtues appear. These enjoyed a long popularity, and Wilson is a skilful playwright. It has been suggested that he was the 'R.W.' who was author of the Marprelate pamphlet, *Martin Mar-sixtus*, entered in the Stationers' Register on 8th November 1591, and published that year. This pamphleteering, puritanical 'R.W.' attacked Greene as one of those lascivious authors who 'put on a mourning garment, and crie, Farwell,'[9] which clearly identified Greene whose two repentant works, *Greenes Mourning Garment: Given him by Repentance at the Funeral of his Love*, and his *Farewell to Folly* appeared in 1590 and 1591 respectively. Greene's satirical pen was actively involved on the counter-side in the Marprelate pamphleteering war in opposition to the Puritans, which drew 'R.W.'s' counter-blast.

This identification of an 'R.W.' who was attacking Greene as a lascivious playwright, has sent scholars searching through the texts of plays credited to the actor-playwright Robert Wilson, and sure enough two similar quotations from the scriptures have been turned up, although they are in two different plays by Wilson which were at least a decade old by 1591. One is in *The Three Ladies of London*, published in 1584 so obviously a very old play, in which the character Conscience has the line:

Conscience: What need further triall, sith I Conscience am a thousand witnesses.

Sig. F2ᵛ

and in *The Three Lords of London*, published in 1590, hence an old play by then:

Pomp: And love doth couer heaps of combrous euils.
Pleasure: And doth forget the faults that were before.

Sig. C4

These two examples of similar expressions dredged up from two very old plays by Wilson have provided critics with a weak handle to argue that *Faire Em* was also from Wilson's pen. However, if this is so then further parallels and stylistic identification marks would be required to substantiate it, and these are conspicuously non-existent. Such proverbial sayings were a common currency and not too much should be argued from their existence in Wilson's morality plays and their use in *Faire Em*, which is a totally *different* type of play from Wilson's known works. There is absolutely no stylistic similarity to support the theory of his authorship of this play, and the association of Wilson with the 'R.W.' of the Marprelate controversy is tenuous, indeed, it is quite illogical. The Marprelate pamphleteers were antagonists by virtue of the nature of this pro- and anti-ecclesiastical establishment controversy, inspired by the Puritans, and this in itself is enough to explain 'R.W.'s' attack on Greene. Wilson was himself both an actor and a playwright so is hardly likely to have been engaged on the side of the Puritans! nor is there the slightest evidence that he was the Puritan writer of *Martin-Mar-sixtus*, this suggestion stemming entirely from Shakespearean scholars' baffled search for the author of *Faire Em* whom Greene was criticising. Moreover, Robert Wilson was a well-educated man, who was noted for his learning and 'extemporall witte',[10] so that he does not fit the picture of the ignoramus lampooned by Greene. 'R.W.' are not such very unusual initials, so that the identification is weak, if not ridiculous.

We must look elsewhere for our author of *Faire Em*, and an obvious hint is presented in Greene's scathing *Groatsworth* clue of the 'Windmill' which his 'Player' boasts he can build! And a windmill is featured in *Faire Em*. The identification of Edward Alleyn as author of this play holds up flawlessly. Alwin Thaler, Greg, Simpson and Fleay have all placed this play in the category described as a 'country play' written originally for provincial performance, and in this instance hailing from Lancashire. Edward Alleyn's mother came from Lancashire, being born Margaret Towneley. She has doubtful claim to being of the famous Lancashire family of that name, though possibly of its fringes. If Edward Alleyn had Lancashire grandparents still living whom he visited during his provincial touring years when his company would certainly have played at Chester and Manchester, he could have heard from them, and from his mother, the legend that is the basis of the play. Its Lancashire origin would have had appeal.

Among Alleyn's Papers is a copy of a Lancashire ballad about a bonny wench of Adlington in Lancashire, the last verse of which is:

> Farye well the streates about *Adlingtunn*,
>   That be so many and steppe;
> Full often times hav I gonne thereby
>   In dry wether and wett;
> And all was for that bon[n]y wenches sake,
>   Which now is dead allake;
> For allake shall I neuer se hir no more.[11]

Lancashire ballads were evidently, therefore, of interest to Edward Alleyn. Perhaps he was even in love with a Lancashire lass in his adolescence?

Faire Em was evidently written for Lord Strange's Men, with whom Edward Alleyn had close connections from about 1589/90, and the title page informs us of this company:

Faire Em, the Millers daughter of Manchester: With the loue of William the Conqueror. As it was sundrie times publiquely acted in the honourable citie of London, by the right honourable the Lord Strange his seruants.

This is an apparently corrupt quarto, undated and giving only the printers' initials T.N. and I.W. The text is just over 1500 lines. It is written in passable, workmanlike blank verse with particularly copious alliteration; it has a well-constructed dramatic framework and is clearly the work of someone who understands theatre, but is no poetic genius. The story is based on a popular Lancashire historical character, a heroic Saxon at the time of the Norman Conquest, the love affairs of whose beautiful daughter, Faire Em, became the subject of a ballad that was known in London ten years before the play appeared, and may have added to its popular reception by London audiences.[12]

Alwin Thaler has suggested that *Faire Em* was originally written for performance either at one of the lavish civic ceremonies at Manchester, or at functions in Chester or Liverpool, or, as is more likely, for private performance at one of the Lancashire stately homes of the Earl of Derby.[13] Ferdinando Stanley, Lord Strange, who was heir to the earldom, maintained his own troupe of players, Lord Strange's Men, who played regularly at the family mansions, particularly at Christmas as is revealed in the records of the Earl of Derby's household. The Derby Household Accounts for the relevant years 1586 to 1590 are fortunately extant, and were regularly if laconically kept by the Steward of the Household, William Ffarington, who records frequent appearances of players, both visiting troupes and Lord Strange's own company.[14] The palatial residences of the Earls of Derby were comparable in splendour to the royal court on a diminished scale. Ffarington presided over a household of one hundred and fifty servants, all male apart from the laundresses and the nurses in attendance on Lord Strange's little daughters. These 'servants' included Grooms of the Bedchamber, Gentlemen-in-Waiting, and Clerks of the Kitchen, offices held by the well-born sons of Lancashire's great families and wealthy gentry, just as men of nobility vied for such offices at the Queen's court. Ffarington himself was a well-to-do man of considerable property, who served three Earls of Derby in succession and was accounted a valued friend of the family. Whether Ffarington approved of players is perhaps in doubt as he permitted 'noe vagrant p^{r}sons...be kept aboute the house',[15] and his cherished ideal of a well-ordered household perhaps inclined him to class actors in this undesirable category, but he had to put up with them several times a year, for both Henry, Fourth Earl of Derby, and his son Lord Strange, dearly loved to see a play. It was for this noble family that *Faire Em* was written as is borne out by the naming of the company who played it, and by textual evidence.

Although the play was acted in London by Lord Strange's Men, probably in 1590 and 1591, Alwin Thaler suggests that it had received its première in a private performance before Lord Strange and his father, the Earl of

Derby, when the Earl's good friend Sir Edmund Trafford was present as their guest, for the play twice mentions Sir Edmund by name, and the hero of the drama is his Saxon ancestor, the famous subject of the Lancashire historical legend of the time of the Norman Conquest.

The Traffords were an old established Lancashire family tracing their lineage back to the days of Canute, and having their seat at Trafford Park in the parish of Manchester. Ralph or Randolphus Trafford, ancestor of Sir Edmund Trafford, was reputed to have disguised himself as a miller at the time of the Norman Conquest to evade capture, but he was evidently later reconciled to the Conqueror and allowed to retain his lands, and in honour of this historical episode the Trafford's crest was a flail or threshing whip, the tool used by the millers in removing the husk from the wheat before grinding the flour. In the play *Faire Em* the story is fictionalized and the heroine's father who personifies Ralph Trafford is named Sir Thomas Goddard, but in two important speeches, one at the beginning and one at the end, pointed reference is made to Sir Edmund Trafford by name in such a way as though he might be expected to be present in the audience, indicating his family connections with this historic incident and his family crest, the flail, which would not have had significance unless intended as a direct compliment to this locally important and puissant member of the Lancashire gentry. If he was personally present to enjoy the play's first performance, the players would doubtless have expected a generous monetary reward from him for their presentation of the play thus honouring him.

Assuming by hypothesis that we have the right author in our sights, it would be very much in character for the ambitious, young Edward Alleyn to seize such an advantage, and Strange's Men would have been delighted to receive such a play from his hands. It evidently carried its popular success back to London, where audiences equally enjoyed this romance of pseudo-history, somewhat simple and ingenuous, but appealing to the tastes of a theatre-going public only recently exposed to blank verse drama. The play's premiere, as Thaler suggests, would most likely have had its setting in one of the three palatial mansions owned by the Earl of Derby, Knowsley in Lancashire being his chief seat, but practically comparable great houses were Lathom and New Park to which the family rotated with their 'court'. The Derby Household Books reveal that Sir Edmund Trafford was several times a resident guest at Knowsley and Lathom during the years 1587 and 1589 (in Armada year the Earl was absent) and the presence of his son, the 'yong Mr Trafforth' is frequently recorded together with Lord Strange and his family at Knowsley, Lathom and New Park.[16]

Sir Edmund Trafford had an illustrious name and was a powerful influence in the North of England, as has been established by Alwin Thaler's researches.[17] He was one of the ecclesiastical commissioners for the North and was especially noted for his uncompromising attitude in religious matters and his patriotism and diligence in seeking out such dedicated Jesuits as Father Campion, whose avowed aim was the re-Catholicizing of England. Campion named him a 'bitter enemy' of the Jesuits, and his staunch prosecution of the campaign against recusancy and Jesuit intrigue among the pro-Catholic Northerners won him warm praise from the Privy Council expressed in their grateful letters.[18] As a magistrate and Sheriff of the County of Lancashire he worked closely in an official capacity with the Earl of Derby, the Lord Lieutenantof the County, whose Catholicism was combined with total loyalty to Elizabeth's government. Together with William Chaderton, Bishop of Chester, and Sir John Biron they were the chief ecclesiastical commissioners for the County of Lancashire primarily responsible for recusancy in their district. In a time of recurrent Catholic intrigue Sir Edmund Trafford played a stabilizing part as the trusted servant of the Protestant government and was seen in the North as a man to be reckoned with. His considerable wealth and influence combined with his position as Sheriff of Lancaster, and his personal reputation as a notable soldier, made him important in the County – an importance which was doubtless enhanced by his close friendship with the blue-blooded family of the Earl of Derby, whose peerage was impeccable. Such a man would be well worth honouring with a play.

The historic tale of the Trafford's stand against William the Conqueror was a popular local legend which evidently inspired the ballad entitled 'The Miller's daughter of Manchester' printed in 1581, which was probably the basis of the play *Faire Em*. That this was so is hinted at by Greene who makes the sarcastic jibe a few lines before his overt attack on the author of the mediocre play identified as *Faire Em* in his Preface to *Farewell to Folly* when he refers pointedly to authors who 'if they come to write or publish in print, it is either distilled out of ballets, or borrowed of Theological poets'.[19] This is clearly a clue indicating the play Greene has under fire, which in its full title quotes the ballad sheet: *Faire Em, the Miller's Daughter of Manchester* – another identification tag!

Bethinking himself of the connections of Sir Edmund Trafford with the noble family of the patron of the players, Lord Strange, it occurred to our playwright to try his hand at making a play of this old story as a suitable entertainment to offer to their Lord. The specific reference to Sir Edmund Trafford in the text is indication that such an intention was in the mind of the author of *Faire Em*, who must have been aware that Sir Edmund Trafford, named by the Earl as among his 'very loving ffrends'[20] would be invited to be present as his honoured guest on such an occasion.

Evidence that the playwright was setting out deliberately to pay a compliment to Sir Edmund Trafford is also seen in his reference to his family crest, 'the flail', and the crest was of fairly recent addition to his coat of arms; according to Flower's *Visitation of Lancashire*, 1567, it had been granted by Lawrence Dalton, Norroy, at this time when 'several Chester and Lancashire families made additions of crests to their plain prescriptive coat-armour which they had previously borne.'[21]

The traditional story of Sir Edmund Trafford's ancestor, Randolphus Trafford, from which the family crest derives, is told by the antiquary Thomas Hearne in his *Discourses of English Antiquaries*, 1771. Researching the armorial devices of English families he writes: 'The ancientest I know or have read is that of Traford or Trafard in Lancashire, whose arms [crest] are a labouring man with a flayle in his hand threshinge, and the written mott: *Now Thus*, which they say came by this occasion: that he, and other gentlemen opposing themselves against some Normans, who came to invade them; this Traford dyd them much hurte, and kepte the passages against them; but that at length the Normans having passed the ryver, came sodenlye upon him, and then he, disguising himselfe went into his barne and was threshing when they entered, yet beinge knowen by some of them, and demanded why he so abased himself, answered, *Now thus.*'[22]

In the play the emphasis of the main plot is shifted to the romance of the heroic Saxon's beautiful daughter, Em, and her three lovers, who are tested as to their genuine love for her by her dissimulation of deafness and blindness. Mandeville, who was her first love to whom she had given her heart, deserted her and proved false, while the faithful and noble Valingford wins her.

Richard Simpson has done some valuable early research on the play in relation to its Lancashire connections, but he stretches the point in trying to relate the main plot to the episode of Alexis and Rosamund in Greene's *Mourning Garment*, to which it frankly bears no similarity. The subplot has some affinity with Greene's *Ciceronis Tamor or Tullies Love*, which he dedicated to Lord Strange, so his derogatory criticism of *Faire Em* may have been aggravated by jealousy of patronage. The supposed similarity between the love plot and Greene's *Friar Bacon and Friar Bungay* is very tenuous, although probably anything Alleyn wrote was a red rag to the bull for Greene. It is probable that this play was Alleyn's first composition in blank verse.

Simpson's reading of far-fetched fustian associations in the plot of *Faire Em* – in which Fleay joins him – is, frankly, silly, and is not supported by other critics. But he is one of the few students of Greene's *Groatsworth of Wit* who has paid some attention to the autobiographical story of the bequest of the 'groatsworth of wit' to *Roberto* (of which he gives a poor synopsis) and he sees the 'Windmill' which the Player claims he can build, as pointing to him as author of *Faire Em, the Millers daughter*; but he then argues backwards from the *a priori* assumption that Greene is referring to Shakespeare under the name 'Shake-scene' to saddle Shakespeare with the authorship of *Faire Em*. Thus, what Thaler calls 'the devoted but perverse pro-Shakespearean enthusiasm of Simpson' has landed Shakespeare with the authorship of this undistinguished dramatic work.[23] Although the Windmill connotation to *Faire Em* is valid, it does not point to Shakespeare. True, that the old plays *Mucedorus*, *Faire Em* and *The Merry Devil of Edmonton* were all bound together for the library of King Charles II under the label *Shakespeare Volume I* [24], but not one of these plays can today be ascribed to his hand. As Tucker Brooke has rather unflatteringly commented: '*Faire Em* is a thoroughly childish and inartistic production. Its only charm rests on the fact that it exhibits, with much of the crudity, also something of the heartiness and freshness of childish performances.'[25] This play merits Greene's sarcastic censure! Simpson's approving assessment is unwittingly particularly pertinent to all we know of Edward Alleyn's character and attitude of mind: he finds the play 'full of moral uprightness, common sense, rectitude of judgment, and soundness of feeling.'[26] These qualities are the characteristic qualities of Edward Alleyn himself.

As Alwin Thaler has summed it up, for the purposes of our investigation: 'The basic fact...is that *Faire Em* at the outset and again at the end pays tribute to one Sir Edmund Trafford, a mighty man of Lancashire...at the time the play was written, and head of a family dating back to the time of Canute.'[27] Here is the passage containing the first reference:

> *Enter the* Miller *and* Em *his daughter*
> *Miller*: Come daughter we must learne to shake of pomp,
> To leaue the state that earst beseemd a Knight
> And gentleman of no meane discent,
> To vndertake this homelie millers trade:
> Thus must we maske to saue our wretched liues,
> Threatned by Conquest of this haplesse Yle:
> Whose sad inuasions by the Conqueror,

Haue made a number such as we subiect
Their gentle neckes vnto their stubborne yoke,
Of drudging labour and base pedantrie.

The Miller then introduces himself as Sir Thomas Goddard, this name
possibly deriving from the ballad version of the story, but then proceeds
to make the connection with Sir Edmund Trafford, whose ancestor had
been Randolphus Trafford, here represented as Goddard.

> *Sir Thomas Godard* now old *Goddard* is
> *Goddard* the miller of faire Manchester.
> Why should not I content me with this state?
> As good Sir Edmund *Trofferd* did the flaile.
> And thou sweete *Em* must stoope to high estate,
> To ioyne with mine that thus we may protect
> Our harmles liues, which ledd in greater port
> Would be an enuious obiect to our foes,
> That seeke to roote all Britaines Gentrie
> From bearing countenance against their tyrannie.
>
> Act I sc 2, 11.88-107

This assuredly is not the language of Shakespeare, even though it is
blank verse! The complimentary reference to Sir Edmund Trafford and
his crest, with a passing glance at his ancestral history when a noble
Trafford similarly demeaned himself in fleeing the vengeance of the
Normans, comes at the beginning of the play. At the end, when William
the Norman has been chastened by thwarted love and is reconciled to the
honourable Saxon nobleman, Goddard, another complimentary reference
is put into the mouth of the Conqueror.

> *William*: Sir Thomas *Goddard* welcome to thy Prince
> And fair *Em*, frolike with thy good father,
> As glad am I to finde Sir *Thomas Goddard*
> As good Sir *Edmund Treford* on the plaines;
> He like a sheepheard and thou a countrie Miller.
>
> Act II, 11.1526-1530

What we may call the sub-plot featuring William the Conqueror,
concerns the violent passion the king conceives for the lady whose portrait
he sees painted on the shield of a Danish nobleman at his court, the

Marquess Lubeck. With this scene the play opens. Here William confesses his passion:

> *Exit all but* William *and the* Marques.
> *William*: Now *Marques* must a Conqueror at armes
> Disclose himselfe thrald to vnarmed thoughts,
> And threatened of a shaddowe, yeeld to lust;
> No sooner had my sparkeling eyes beheld
> The flames of beautie blasing on this peece,
> But sodenly a sense of myracle
> Imagined on thy louely Maistres face,
> Made me abandon bodily regarde,
> And cast all pleasures on my woonded soule:
> Then gentle *Marques* tell me what she is,
> That thus thou honourest on thy warlike shield.
> And if thy loue and interest be such,
> As iustly may giue place to myne,
> That if it be: my soule with honors wings
> May fly into the bosome of my deere.
> Yf not, close them and stoope into my graue.
> *Marques*: Yf this be all renowned Conqueror:
> Aduance your drooping spirites, and reuiue
> The wonted courage of your Conquering minde,
> For this faire picture painted on my shield
> Is the true counterfeit of loueli[e] *Blaunch*
> Princes and daughter to the King of *Danes*:
> Whose beautie and excesse of ornamentes
> Deserues another manner of defence,
> Pompe and high person to attend her state,
> Then *Marques Lubeck* any way presents.
> Therefore her vertues I resigne to thee,
> Alreadie shrinde in thy religious brest,
> To be aduaunced and honoured to the full.
> Nor beare I this an argument of loue:
> But to renowne faire *Blaunch* my Soueraignes child,
> In euerie place where I by armes may do it.
> *Will*: Ah *Marques*, thy wordes bring heauen vnto my soule,
> And had I heauen to giue for thy reward
> Thou shouldst be thronde in no vnworthie place.
> But let my vttermost wealth suffice thy worth,

Which here I vowe, and to aspire the blisse
That hangs on quicke atchieuement of my loue,
Thy selfe and I will traueile in disguise,
To bring this Ladie to our Brittaine Court.
Marques: Let *William* but bethinke what may auayle,
And let me die if I denie my ayde.
Will: Then thus the Duke *Dirot* and Therle *Dimach*
Will I leaue substitutes to rule my Realme,
While mightie loue forbids my being here,
And in the name of Sir *Robert* of *Windsor*
Will I goe with thee vnto the Danish Court.
Keepe *Williams* secretes *Marques* if thou loue him.
Bright *Blaunch* I come sweete fortune fauour me,
And I will laud thy name eternally.

Exeunt.

Act I sc 1, 11.36-85

In this passage all the faults – one might call them gross and palpable – of the self-taught, but highly imaginative and theatrical, but mainly untutored young Edward Alleyn are apparent. He confidently dashes in with his flamboyant, but somewhat inaccurate use of language, so long as it 'sounds' right to his ears, by which any disciplined scholar can see why Greene makes such sport with him, claiming that he 'cannot write true English' – for the author of *Faire Em* is at times even a bit of a 'Dogberry' with words. Consider his 'base pedantrie' in Goddard's first speech, which is inappropriately slipped in to finish off the line. This seems to be a reflection of Marlowe's opinion of pedantic scholars, who were held in scorn by Giordano Bruno and the free thinkers of Marlowe's circle. Alleyn obviously greatly admired Marlowe. And what are we to make of this curious alternative effort?

No sooner had my sparkeling eyes beheld
The flames of beautie blasing on this peece,
But sodenly a sense of myracle
Imagined on thy louely Maistres face,
Made me abandon bodily regarde,
And cast all pleasures on my woonded soule:

11.39-44

Doubtless the groundlings would accept it as 'poetical' – and imbued with an actor's tones of passion it would come across with a strong sense of theatrical emotion, but the lines do not bear close literary analysis. This would hardly matter as these plays were rarely printed, and existed on the living stage for their effect, so that scores, if not hundreds of such minor plays have never been subjected to the scrutiny of scholars for they have perished in manuscript. *Faire Em* was probably no worse and no better than most of these which were well liked in their day. What remains a matter of amazement is that anyone could have ascribed this play to Shakespeare's hand! It is a well-crafted stage production, and tells a good story with popular romantic appeal, and its stylistic oddities would have largely escaped notice in a lively performance – but it is no masterpiece of literature.

I particularly like his closing couplet to the scene –

> Bright *Blaunch* I come sweete fortune fauour me,
> And I will laud thy name eternally.
>
> 11. 84-5

This is typically Edward Alleyn, and we shall find the characteristics of his style in other works – crude, theatrical, ingenuously noble in sentiment; his good and evil tend to be black and white; vigorously expressed with a marked tendency to alliteration, and now and then a quaintness of expression and exaggerated imagery. Here is another example of the author's absurdities of style in a speech by Em's third lover, the well-born Mountney:

> *L. Mountney*: Although a millers daughter by her birth
> Yet her beautie and her vertues may suffice
> To hyde the blemish of her birth in hell,
> Where neither enuious eyes nor thought can perce,
> But endlesse darknesse euer smother it.
>
> Act II. 11.306-310

Simpson comments: 'violent contrast and far-fetched imagery which makes a girl's beauty hide her low birth in hell is almost too much, even for Greene.'[28]

There are some comic scenes with the miller's man, Trotter, in which the Windmill is prominently featured with mention of corn being ground, and customers waiting for their flour. These scenes are crude, low comedy. Trotter is also in love with the Miller's beautiful daughter.

Enter Em, *and* Trotter *the Millers man, with a kerchife*
on his head, and an Vrinall in his hand

Em: *Trotter*, where haue you beene?

Trott: Where haue I bene? why, what signifies this?

Em: A kerchiefe, doth it not?

Trott: What call you this, I praye?

Em: I saie it is an Vrinall.

Trott: Then this is mystically to giue you to vnderstand
I haue bene at the Phismicaries house.

Em: How long hast thou beene sicke?

Trott: Yfaith, euen as long as I haue not beene halfe well
and that hath beene a long time.

Em: A loytering time I rather imagine.

Trott: It may be so: but the Phismicary tels me that you can help me.

Em: Why, any thing I can do for recouerie of thy health
Be right well assured of.

Trott: Then giue me your hand.

Em: To what end.

Trott: That the ending of an old indenture
Is the beginning of a new bargaine.

Em: What bargaine?

Trott: That you promised to do any thing to recouer my helth.

Em: On that condition I giue thee my hand.

Trott: Ah, sweete Em!   *Here he offers to kisse her*

Em: How now, Trotter? your maisters daughter?

Trott: Yfaith, I aim at the fairest.

Act II. Sc.1. 11.352-375

This is homely humour. The complications of the two romantic plots interweave to maintain interest: they involve disguise and dissimulation, crossed love, and the eventual exposure of insincerity and the triumph of virtue in a rather artificial story-line in the convention that suited Elizabethan tastes.

Faire Em is an unsophisticated dramatic entertainment, but its appeal in its day to the people of 'faire Manchester', recurrently referred to thus in the text, and the provincials of Lancashire, whether important officials or commoners, was assured by its element of folk tale and local history, seasoned with a dash of patriotic heroism and romantic intrigue with a moral message. Such a play, it is reasonable to suggest, is most likely to have been written by someone with local connections and sentimental attachment to Lancashire rather than by a complete outsider, and someone who had an association with Lord Strange's company. Such a man was Edward Alleyn.

It is now necessary to attempt to put a date to the play. Greg thinks that it was 'on stage between 1589 and 1591', but he has in mind its London performances.[29] Lord Strange's Men were playing at the Cross Keys in Gracechurch Street, in the City of London, in November 1589, and probably again in the City during 1591-2, before taking up residence at the Rose early in 1592 when Alleyn became head of a company mainly of Strange's Men. *Faire Em* was 'sundrie times publiquely acted' in London probably in 1589 and 1591, but its premier performance would logically have been in Lancashire by Lord Strange's Men in one of their patron's mansions. This hypothesis is strongly favoured by Alwin Thaler, with supportive evidence, to show that it was designed for some special performance at one of the Earl of Derby's stately homes in the presence of his friend, Sir Edmund Trafford. Sir Edmund Trafford died in May 1590, so that this predates the play to somewhere between 1587 and 1589, in which years he was in close association in an official capacity with the Earl of Derby, who 'named him, as early as 1578, first among his "very loving ffrends", the knights and squires of Lancashire's Salford Hundred.'[30]

The Derby Household Books, meticulously kept by Ffarington, record the daily comings and goings of the ceaseless stream of visitors to the great house in which the Earl and his family were then residing, for they alternated between Knowsley, Lathom and New Park – all in Lancashire – of which Knowsley was the Earl's chief residence, but the others must also have been very grand. The number of visitors who 'came & wente', or stayed as guests for several days, represent a tremendous flow of social intercourse. Ffarington records by name all important visitors and family friends, relatives, and who had 'pretched' the sermon on Sunday. He invariably notes the arrivals and departures of his master, the Earl, and Lord Strange and Lady Strange and their children.

Among these named guests we find Sir Edmund Trafford and his son several times during the years relevant to our investigation.

The week ending 29th July 1587 Ffarington records:*

'on Monday the xxiiii[th] my L. rode to S[r] Ryc. Mollynewx & the howsehold removed from Lathom to Konwsley; on Frydaye S[r] Ryc. Shirborne and M[r] Awdytours came & made declaration of my L.

---

* My italics throughout these excerpts from the Derby Household Books.

Awdaite, wch daye my L. Bushoppe & his wiffe...& many others came; on Satturdaye Sr Edmund Trayfforth & his Sone.'[31]

The Bishop of Chester and his wife together with Sir Edmund Trafford apparently stayed the weekend, perhaps also to conduct official business for both were ecclesiastical commissioners for Lancashire with the Earl, for Ffarington records for the week ending 5th August 1587 at Knowsley:

'On Mondaye my L. Bushoppe of Chester & his wiffe & also Sr Edmunde Traifforth did all dep^rte awaie.'[32]

In the week ending 12th August 1587 at Knowsley, he records 'yong Mr Trayfforth' as a visitor, and again at the beginning of September.

Ffarington's entry for the week ending 2nd September is of particular interest:

'On Sonday my L. came to Knowsley his standing house, where mett him...dyvers gent. of fflinteshire, who tarryed there untill Mondaye...on Thursday Mr Comptrowller, Mr Rec^r, Mr Traifforth...on Friday my L. begane his jorney towards the Cowrte, & from thence as Ambassado^r into the Lowe Countryes.'[33]

The Earl's journey was, of course, in connection with the peace negotiations he was to conduct with the Duke of Parma on the eve of the launching of the Spanish Armada, when in all probability Marlowe accompanied him being sent as Lord Burghley's agent to attend the early stages of this protracted game of chess.[34]

Upon the Earl's departure Knowsley's staff were reduced from one hundred and forty to thirty-four, and Lord Strange remained there doing much hunting 'to kill Venyson', and there were 'many Huntesmen & Howndes' at Knowsley the week ending 17th November.[35]

Lord Strange celebrated Christmas there and his company of players came to present plays. We know this because at the week ending 30th December 1587 the Earl paid a visit home from the Court where he had been all this while, for the commission was not due to set forth until January 1587/8, and Ffarington – who also seems to have been away, for entries had been sparse – now records:

'on Frydaye my L. the Earle came home from the Cowrte, & the same nighte came my L. Bushoppe, Mr Stewarde, Mr Receyver, M^r ffoxe; on Saturday Sr Tho. Hesketh. *Players went awaie*, & the same day...many strandgers came to Knowsley.'[36]

Whenever a company of players who are not Lord Strange's arrive to perform, Ffarington always notes these by name – Leicester's, Queen's and Essex's are all mentioned, so that when he writes merely 'Players' we may assume it must be Lord Strange's company, for they are never mentioned *by name* once, and certainly they must have played before their Lord. Thaler comments: 'My notes show...that Lord Strange was present at all the performances of the unnamed company; [it is] noteworthy that all but one of these performances came during the Christmas holiday season, exactly when the Stanleys would, presumably, have been most likely to see plays by their own company.'[37] In 1588/89 they also played just before Lent.

How many times the Players had been playing over Christmas we do not know, nor to whom, except that obviously it would be to their Lord and his family and friends. Whether this was the occasion when *Faire Em* was played is doubtful, for we have no confirmation of the Traffords being present.

The Earl stayed at Knowsley for the christening of his latest grandchild – the third daughter of Lord and Lady Strange – when 'many gentle women came to the Crystenyng', in the first week of the new year; and then departed again for the Court and thence abroad.[38]

On the 17th February the household at Knowsley 'brake uppe & my L. s^rvantes went to borde wadges' (that is, they were paid to board out) for this was to be an exceptionally long closure during Armada year, when presumably Lord and Lady Strange and their children were otherwise engaged, he with mustering at Liverpool and she probably living with friends. However, there was to be a grand re-opening of the Derby establishment after the Armada was defeated, and the Earl returned 'from his Jorneye & Imbassadge from fflanders', this time at New Park.

Ffarington entered for the week ending 28th September 1588:

'On Thursdaye the xxvi^th of this September my L. began his howseholde, and then came him selfe; on Fryday my La. Strandge & the little children of hers came...'[39]

Next we have many entries of visits by 'Mr Trafforth' at New Park, on 5th and 12th October, and 2nd and 30th November. On 12th October also 'the Quenes Players' had come to play.

Christmas of 1588/9 was spent at Lathom, and here during the Twelfth Night festivities we have what *may possibly have been the première* of *Faire Em*, for it is Lord Strange's Men who are playing, and although Sir Edmund Trafford is not mentioned by name the play was given before my Lord's Council, which would have included Sir Edmund, and there was a large gathering present of 'dyvers strandgers' as though this was some important occasion. Following the prolonged absence of the Earl on his embassage this would have been a very suitable celebration for his return to his stately homes in Lancashire with a patriotic Lancashire play. Ffarington records for the week ending 4th January 1588/9 at Lathom:

'Sondaye Mr Carter pretched, at wch was dyvers strandgers; on Monday Mr Stewarde; on Tvesdaye the rest of *my L. Cownsill*, & also Sr Jhon Savadge, & *at nyght a Playe was had in the Halle*, & the same nyghte *my L. Strandge came home...*'[40]

And on the eve of Twelfth Night Lord Strange's Men (always the unnamed Players) played again – as seen in the entry for the week ending 11th January 1588/9:

'Sondaye Mr Caldewall pretched, & *that nyght the Plaiers plaied*';[41]

On Monday we are told that 'Mr Trafforth', who is Sir Edmund's son, arrived with a few more gentlemen guests, and Ffarington's entries at this time indicate that the Earl's Council had stayed as guests from the Tuesday before, which would have been 31st December, for they are not mentioned as having either departed or arrived again in the interim, and Ffarington is punctilious about these comings and goings, so they could have seen both play performances, and the week ending 25th January records their departure and the closing up of the house after all the festivities:

'..my L. Strandge's children went awayes, & also Mr Receyver, Mr Stewarde, M^r ffoxe, & the reste of *my L. Cownsell*; on Tvesdaye my L. & my L. Strandge went all towards London: and the same daye his Lordshippes howse brake uppe at Lathom.'[42]

The eminent gentlemen of the Earl's Council therefore stayed for two and a half weeks, probably combining the conviviality of the end of the Christmas season with some catching up on government affairs after the long interruption caused by the Armada and the Earl's absence at the abortive peace negotiations. These entries in Ffarington's diary appear to be the only possible time when *Faire Em* could have received a private performance in honour of Sir Edmund Trafford at one of the Earl's houses, for although during 1589 frequent performances by acting companies are recorded none co-incides with a visit by Sir Edmund, or by 'my L. Cownsell'.

The Queen's Players seem to have been favourites, for they came to Knowsley in the week ending 12th July and 'plaied ii severall nyghtes',[43] and again in September the Queen's Players alternated with the Earl of Essex's Players in two successive weeks, even giving two performances in one day, one company in the afternoon and the other performing 'at nyght'.[44] The Earl's and his family's appetite for drama was keen! Unfortunately Ffarington never mentions what plays are performed.

Sir Edmund's last visit was in the week ending 9th August when he was at Knowsley at dinner on the Tuesday, and on 'Wednesday Sʳ Edmond wente'.[45] In May 1590 Sir Edmund Trafford died.

Whilst the evidence presented has not established Alwin Thaler's interesting hypothesis with satisfying certainty that the première of *Faire Em* was given by Lord Strange's Men at one of the Stanley's stately homes in the presence of the Earl and Sir Edmund Trafford, the likelihood remains feasible. It may, of course, have been first played in 'faire Manchester' itself, which this flattering reference may be suggesting, and where both the Stanleys and the Traffords had splendid town residences – perhaps privately at Sir Edmund's house, Trafford Park.

The Earl as Lieutenant of the County Palatine of Lancashire and Sir Edmund as Sheriff had much official business to do with the dignitaries of Manchester and Chester. At New Park on 4th October 1589 Ffarington records that 'Mʳ Maire of Chester & some of his brethrē came & went'.[46] Lord Strange was invested as alderman of Chester in 1586 & gave a 'rich banquet' on that occasion.[47] He also became Mayor of Liverpool in 1588.[48] Such aldermanic festivals tended to be extremely lavish occasions when banquets were sometimes followed by the performance of a play, and Lord Strange's Men would certainly have tried to present this play in Manchester and the surrounding Lancashire district as often as possible for there their audiences would have been most appreciative of its local flavour. It is tempting, however, to see the pre-Twelfth Night festivities at Lathom in January 1588/9 as this special occasion of *Faire Em's* première.

What has been confirmed is that this play has indisputable Lancashire connections, as already well demonstrated and researched by Simpson and Thaler; and that this, and its performance by Lord Strange's Men are both consistent with its authorship by Edward Alleyn, an ambitious young actor-playwright of part Lancashire blood.

Further, that it was this play at which Greene aimed his sarcastic criticism, which the play's stylistic and literary peculiarities amply merit, and which he linked with the 'Player' in his *Groatsworth* story with the image of the Windmill. This would otherwise be totally fanciful and meaningless if not seen as another of his clever identification tags, with which Greene and Nashe delighted to amuse their readers, all of them obvious enough to their contemporaries. These two had developed a language of synonyms to disport themselves at Alleyn's (and Marlowe's) expense, in mockery. Greene was the leader in this, driven by his own envious nature, but followed by Nashe to whom satire was meat and drink, although by 1592 Nashe withdrew from attacking Alleyn, whom he evidently greatly admired as a superb actor.

Further, that the stylistic characteristics of this play, as well as its subject matter and philosophy of life expressed in the text are all consistent with what we would expect to find in a play written by Edward Alleyn. In due course the internal characteristics of *Faire Em* will be compared with another extant play which I believe is from Edward Alleyn's hand, and it will be seen that the similarities are striking.

Further, that it was in the tradition of Elizabethan actors of the more intelligent sort, even those who had slight gifts for such exercises, to set their hands to writing plays – as Henslowe's records testify. Clearly it would have been both unusual and out of character for the enterprising, literate and intelligent young Edward Alleyn to have desisted from making the attempt to write plays with the best of them. And, moreover, this is precisely what the Player in the *Groatsworth* story affirms is his bent. Edward Alleyn, who kept a fascinating *Diary* for five years in his retirement, was obviously a man who enjoyed putting pen to paper, and some of his letters, particularly the long and mortified letter he wrote to John Donne, the poet and Dean of St Paul's, whose daughter Constance became his second wife, leave us in no doubt as to his ability to express himself with clarity and considerable eloquence when writing prose, and not emulating 'his betters' in blank verse. Alleyn was probably largely self-educated, but he was a man of parts, and he aspired to improve himself continually, hence learnt rapidly. If he wrote at all he would not have stopped at one play, and we shall now investigate the evidence for a body of works from his pen.

The Lord Admiral's Company's Playwrights

In Henslowe's theatrical accounts are acquittances for play-scripts sold to the company by Edward Alleyn, which are couched in exactly the same words as those paid to other playwrights mentioning them by name as the payees for the 'play boocke' they are selling. The assumption made by Greg and others, is that when Edward Alleyn is the payee and no other name of any author is mentioned, this is to be interpreted that Alleyn has *not* written the play himself, but is merely reselling the work of some other (unnamed) dramatist whose play he had bought expecting to make his own profit in the transaction. This assumption is totally unwarranted. Alleyn was not a man who would have invested his money in plays by nameless authors who have disappeared into limbo. When he bought a play-script himself as an investment, it was a great dramatic work from Marlowe, not from some nameless nobody. Edward Alleyn was a man of discriminating taste, and he was a good judge of genius in dramatic writing. He seems to have had a select stable of the more brilliant, well-educated 'plaimaking poets' of the University Wits, and it is possible that, in addition to Marlowe, he may occasionally have bought a play direct from Greene, or Peele, but Marlowe's works were what he was most interested in, and I imagine he paid a good price for the privilege of possessing these masterpieces.

We know that he owned Marlowe's *The Massacre at Paris* for he sold it to the company of his own theatre, the Fortune, in 1601 together with two other plays presumably by Alleyn himself since no author for these has been found, in a package for £6, these being all old plays 'wch wer played' and had had a season or two on the boards and hence were no longer top rating as box office draws – rather like selling a second-hand car which had done some mileage. All Alleyn's sales of his play-scripts are of this kind, old plays of his which he no longer found profitable to keep, and was selling before their value had completely expired. In the sale of *The Massacre at Paris* we have the sole extant documentary evidence of Alleyn's personal ownership of a play by Marlowe, although I suspect he also owned *Dr Faustus* and *The Jew of Malta*. Apart from Marlowe's work, all the plays sold by Alleyn here listed are lost since they were presumably never published.

pd at the Apoyntment of the companye the
18 of Janewary 1601 vnto E Alleyn for iij boockes } vj^li 49
wch wer played called the french docter the
massaker of france & the nvtte the some of...........

211

The French Doctor has not been identified. Greg offers endless conjecture concerning its possible identification, none of which is conclusive, but prefers to ignore the only real piece of *documentary evidence* – that Edward Alleyn was *paid* for the play, so why should he not have written it? The other play is identified as *Crack Me This Nut*, which was performed by the Lord Admiral's Men as new on 5th September 1595, and thereafter sixteen times until 23rd June 1596. Nothing is known of this play, but Greg suggests the title is a proverbial phrase.[50] That sounds very like Alleyn! Again, the one *fact* we have as incontestable documentary evidence is that Alleyn was paid for it, so why should he not have written it? Both these plays were in the repertoire of the Lord Admiral's Men and were never performed by any other company.

The earliest record of a sale by Alleyn of a play to the company is in January 1598, following his first retirement in late 1597.

> pd vnto my sonne Edward alleyn the 21 of
> Janewary for the playe of vayvod for the company } xxxx^s [51]
> the some of xxxx^s I saye pd.........1598

Having sold this old play to the company, they staged a revival, and Henry Chettle, then just commencing as a playwright, was apparently asked to do some revision on it, for which he was paid £1 'at the apoyntment of thomas dowton',[52] who was head of the Lord Admiral's Men after Alleyn's first retirement, when he went with his wife, Joan, to live in Sussex. But this cannot be interpreted as meaning that Chettle was the original author. He was used extensively by Henslowe for revising old plays and such hack work for small sums of money, and he wrote prolifically, mostly in collaboration with others, after abandoning his printing business for the theatre.

There are a great number of such sales of plays made by Alleyn dating from 1601, when he had built his own theatre, the Fortune, and was evidently willing to allow his plays to become the property of the actors who were by then virtually his own company, to whom he eventually leased his theatre on most generous terms. Doubtless the reason his play-scripts were lost and are not found among the Alleyn Papers at Dulwich is because they perished in the fire that destroyed the entire stock of the company when the Fortune was burned down in the middle of the night, when no one was there to salvage anything, on 9th December 1621. And doubtless Marlowe's plays if there in manuscript also perished.

212

With only one exception these are all straightforward cash payments to Alleyn for old plays, and not advances of money 'in earnest' of a play in process of being written, as he did not sell his work until it had already been played for a season. But in the following we seem to have evidence of a play that was only partly finished when payment was advanced.

pd at the apoyntment of E Alleyn the 6 of
Janewary 1601 in pte of payment of A
Boocke called the spaneshe fygge the   } iij li 53
some of..

Greg has various theories concerning this play. Firstly he thinks that Henslowe made an error in writing 'at the apoyntment of E Alleyn' as the person authorizing the payment (to himself), but it was normal to make these transactions either 'at the appointment of the company' – presumably after a play reading had been held to assess the play as worth purchasing for their repertoire – or on the authority of one of their leading actors, who might have recommended the play having read it himself. Edward Alleyn as actor-manager was certainly qualified to give such authority, even if it was for a play of his own. Probably he was in need of some cash just then, so drew it on the play he was writing. Nothing dishonest about that, and it is written in Henslowe's hand, so was a business deal. Greg suggests that this play is the same as Dekker's *The Noble Spanish Soldier*,54 entered in the Stationer's Register on 16th May 1631. Can this be a play written thirty years earlier? And why did Henslowe fail to mention Dekker? This is wild conjecture.

pd vnto edward alleyn at the a poyntment
of the company the 22 of aguste 1601 for the   } xxxxs 55
Boocke of mahemett the some of....................

Fleay had tentatively identified this play as Peele's *Turkish Mahomet and Hiren the Fair Greek*, but as this was never performed by the Lord Admiral's Men that suggestion is ruled out. Greg believes it is an old play *Mahomet's Pow* mentioned by Peele in 1589, which play Fleay in turn identifies as Greene's *Alphonsus King of Arragon*.56 All this is nothing more than conjecture. Neither Fleay nor Greg give even a passing thought to the only documentary evidence we have, which is that Alleyn *was paid for it in exactly the same terms as other playwrights are paid for their work*, therefore why is he not eligible to be its author?

pd at the Apoyntment of the 19 of septemb₃
1601 for the playe of the wysman of weschester } xxxxˢ [57]
vnto my sonne E Alleyn the some of...................

This was performed by the Lord Admiral's Men as 'ne' on 2nd December 1594. Although Greg says 'Fleay is almost certainly right in identifying this with *John a Kent and John a Cumber*, a manuscript of which, signed by Munday and dated December 1595 is extant', this, of course, cannot be so if the play was already performed as *new* on 2nd December 1594. Greg, however, suggests it may 'possibly represent a revision'.[58] But revising a play which is still so new seems illogical. It was also very popular, being in constant repertory performance – played thirty-two times between December 1594 and 18th July 1597, which makes the supposition of a revision even more unreasonable. Greg further comments: 'This supposition [i.e. that Munday revised it] is borne out by the mention in the Admiral's inventories of Kent's wooden leg, which, if it belonged to this play, *appeared in some episode not found in the extant version.*'[59] [My italics]

This, to my simple mind, suggests that it is *not* the play in manuscript by Munday. Again, the only *fact* we have to go on is that Edward Alleyn was paid for it, a sum which identifies it as an old play, not a new one, which had been performed in the Admiral's repertoire. Its very title, *The Wise Man of Weschester* is curiously suggestive of Alleyn's taste and sound moral attitude. It was another Lancashire play, perhaps written during Alleyn's extended tour of the long plague, when his letter to his wife dated August 1593 asks her to forward post to 'shrowsbery or to west chester or to york to be keptt till my lord stranges players com'.[60]

Next a play called 'vortiger':

pd at the Apoyntment of the company vnto
my sonne E Alleyn for A Boocke called [m]vorti[m]ger } xxxxˢ [61]
the 20 of novemb₃ 1[5]601 the some of........................

In Henslowe's theatrical records he entered a play he calls 'valteger' as new on 4th December 1596, for which properties had been bought for its production on 28th November.[62] This play Greg claims is the same as 'vortiger', which in turn 'is almost certainly the same as "henges", i.e. *Hengist* acted as an old play 22 June 1597. *Hengist King of Kent* is the title of a manuscript of Middleton's *Mayor of Queenborough* ... a play in which the characters Vortigern, Vortimer, and Hengist all appear. There is nothing in Middleton's play, as printed (1661) to suggest early work, but the combined looseness and complexity of the plot may be due to the author having worked over old materials.'[63] It is true that Henslowe tended to name plays by their leading characters, and his 'henges' may be the same as 'valteger' if this is indeed also 'vortiger' which Alleyn sold to the company in November 1601, which may be Henslowe's spelling of it, for of 'valteger' we have no other record. It is very likely that Alleyn's 'vortiger' and 'henges' – given one performance on 22nd June 1597 – are the same play, but Middleton did not begin to write for Henslowe until 1603. Perhaps he eventually reworked Alleyn's old play, but this does not argue against the evidence that Alleyn wrote a play on Hengist featuring Vortiger, which he sold to the company in 1601. This evidence Greg does not even glance at, as though not worthy of consideration.

Greg, while having done valuable spade work in attempting to identify these old plays in Henslowe's lists of the Admiral's repertoire, is remarkably loathe to concede that the actors of the Admiral's company were enthusiastically given to playwriting – Samuel Rowley, Charles Massey, William Borne (or Bird) John Singer, Robert Shaa (or Shawe) were all actors of this company who wrote plays. Of some there is evidence which is so explicit that even Greg cannot deny it.

pd vnto w^m Borne at the apoyntment of
[A Boocke] company the 20 of desemb$_3$ 1601
In earnest of A Boocke called Judas w^{ch} $\left.\begin{array}{l}\\\\\\\end{array}\right\}$ xx^s [64]
samewell Rowly & he is a writtinge some of
some .... vij^{li} xix^s vj^d

This is the first time we have any evidence of Borne attempting to write a play, which he is doing here in collaboration with Rowley, so Henslowe makes note of the fact, whereas with those who were old hands at playwriting he does not bother to state what is obvious, namely that the payee is also the author. The play Borne and Rowley were writing was completed 24th December 1601 when they received 'fulle payment for a Boocke called Judas' of £5 [65]. The play was performed early in January 1601/2, for Anthony Jeffes was lent xxx^s to 'bye cloth for the playe Judas' on 3rd January.[66]

Charles Massey also wrote plays, although Greg is very doubtful about accepting this.

pd at the apoyntment of the companye
the 18 of ap^{r}ell 1602 vnto charles massey
for a playe Boocke called malcolm Kynge
of scotts the some of.. } v^{li}

Lent vnto Edward Jube the 7 of marche 1602
to geue vnto Charlles masseye in earneste of
A playe called the sedge of doncerke wth
alleyn the pyrete the some of............................ ^{67} } xxxx^s

Greg reluctantly concedes: 'There seems no reason to question his authorship of these pieces, though as we have no other evidence of his literary activity, it is impossible to speak confidently on the point. Certainly neither was an old play.'[68] Massey dined with Edward Alleyn on 18th March, 15th April 1621, and 21st July 1622 at the latter's house in Dulwich, as noted by Alleyn in his *Diary*, and on 19th November 1621 Alleyn gave him 5s 'att His playe'. Greg comments: 'a slight confirmation of his literary ventures'.[69] But surely if Massey was paid £2 'in earnest of a play' there is no clearer evidence possible that he is the author of that work! Greg's quibbling is unreasonable and unjustified.

The case of Robert Shaa's only play (so far as we have evidence) is relevant, as here Henslowe, who has never had a play from Shaa's pen before, enters into a cautious agreement with Shaa in case the play proves disappointing.

Layd owt for the companye the 10 of desemb₃ 1602
vnto Robarte shawe for A boocke of the 4 sonnes
of amon the some of.. } xl^s [70]

Memorandum that I Robert Shaa
haue receaued of m^r Phillip Henslowe
the some of forty shilling vpon a booke
Called the fower sones of Aymon wch booke
if it be not playd by the company of the
fortune nor no[r]e other company by my [copy] ⟨lea..⟩
I doe then bynd my selfe by theis p^{r}sents to
repay the sayd some of forty shillings
vpon the delivery of my booke att Cristmas
next wch shall be in the yeare of our Lord
god 1603 & in the xlvjth yeare of the

216

Raigne of the queene
      p̱ me Robt Shaa [71]

Despite the double evidence of payment to Shaa for a play-script, called 'my booke', and Henslowe's elaborate insurance policy against the failure of the play to meet with the approval of the company – Shaa being evidently a novice – Greg remains obstinately sceptical about crediting Shaa with the authorship, even though he can propose no other author for the piece. Robert Shaa's elegant signature betokens a literate man of an artistic nature, and a dramatist must be allowed to make a beginning somewhere – so why not here? Unfortunately no theatrical records were kept at this period to show whether the play was ever performed, but neither is there an acquittance for the return of this advance payment, so we may assume it was played. In the absence of any other author, the conclusion must be that Shaa wrote the play he was selling. The same goes for Alleyn. Of plays for which no other author than Alleyn is known we have so far noted: *The French Doctor, Crack Me this Nut, Vayvode, The Spanish Fig, Mahomet, The Wise Man of Weschester*, and *Vortiger*. There are yet three more.

pd vnto my sone EA for ij bocke called ⎫
phillipe of spayne & Longshanckes the 8 ⎬ iiij^{li} [72]
of aguste 1602 the some of.............. ⎭

Longshanks was performed by the Admiral's Men as a new play on 29th August 1595, and given fourteen performances until 9th July 1596. Greg comments: 'The only known play on the subject is Peele's *Edward I*, surnamed Longshanks, entered at the Stationers' Register on 8th October 1593 and printed the same year'.[73] This effectively rules it out as a new play in 1595; so the above *Longshanks* is evidently a different play from *Edward I* which was already old in 1593.

Philip of Spain is 'clearly an old piece belonging to Alleyn', is all Greg has to say on this, and no satisfactory authorial identification is offered.[74]

The one record made by Henslowe which surely seals the case beyond possible doubt for Alleyn as author of the play-scripts he is selling to the company, and definitely not as a dealer in the works of other nameless authors, is that for the play *Tambercam*, in which Henslowe refers to the play as 'his Boocke'.

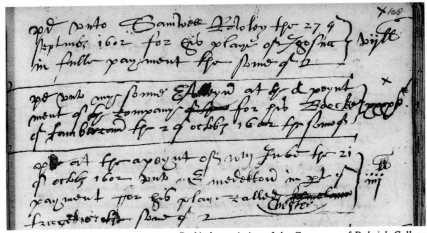

> pd vnto my sonne E Alleyn at the A poynt
> ment of the company [of the] for his Boocke   } xxxxs[75]
> of tambercam the 2 of octob₃ 1602 the some of

The same entry is duplicated by Henslowe on folio 116 verso, and there crossed out, presumably because he found that he had repeated it.

> pd vnto my sonne E Alleyn at the A
> poyntment of the company for his
> Boocke of tambercame the 2 of octob₃   } xxxxs
> 1602 the some of.....................

At the top of this page is an entry to Thomas Heywood using the identical term 'his Boocke'.

> pd vnto Thomas hewode the 30 of septemb₃
> 1602 in fulle payment for his Boocke of   } iij^li
> oserecke the some of...................................   [76]

If Henslowe's 'his Boocke' means that Heywood wrote it, then it means equally that Alleyn wrote 'his Boocke', and even the sober Dictionary of National Biography[77] concedes this regarding the play *Tambercam*. The form of words obviously indicates authorship. Henslowe often writes casually in an acquittance for a play from Chettle 'A Boocke', from Dekker 'A comody', from Heywood 'A Boocke', from Haughton 'A playe', or from Rowley 'the boock', but he is not inferring that these dramatists are dealing in someone else's manuscript, nor can this be assumed for Alleyn just because Henslowe entered the sale as 'A Boocke' and not as 'his Boocke'. He knew Chettle, Dekker, Heywood, Haughton, Rowley as playwrights, and there can be no doubt that he knew his 'sonne' Edward Alleyn also as a playwright therefore he did not need to specify.

There is only one instance of a sale of a work by Alleyn which was not his own play, to our definite knowledge, and this was of Marlowe's *The Massacre at Paris*, which was one of several plays by Marlowe which it is believed Alleyn owned.

This was the calibre of play in which Alleyn would have invested. But those who claim the other ten plays recorded in the *Diary* are not by Alleyn, must then explain who these nameless authors are whom Alleyn so favoured with his patronage, purchasing their scripts direct rather than allowing the company to acquire them.

Both Greg and Fleay have attempted to identify the plays and to apportion them to other known dramatists, with total lack of success. I suggest therefore that the name of Edward Alleyn can be confidently added to the list of minor dramatists of the period, several of whom were also members of the Lord Admiral's Men, who seem to have been a company of scribbling actors emulating their actor-manager, Edward Alleyn.

The multiple evidence of acquittances for playscripts to Edward Alleyn in his 'father's' *Diary* supports Greene's satirical ascription of *Faire Em* to the Player who built a Windmill featured in his *Groatsworth* tale, who on all other counts has been unassailably indentified as Edward Alleyn, who employed Greene as his 'Arch-plaimaking poet' and loaned him money. Alleyn's entry into the lists as a playwright drew Greene's ire and scorn, and the stylistic characteristics of the author of *Faire Em* all support the conclusion that he was Edward Alleyn. These are:

1. The play's strongest feature is its well constructed dramatic framework showing the experience of stagecraft one would associate with a professional actor-manager.
2. The sometimes strange usage of English (lampooned by Greene) suggests a self-educated man.
3. The author's penchant for alliteration suggests a man bred in the old dramatic traditions of the country.
4. His imitation of Marlowe's high flown language, sometimes with ludicrous results, and even of his opinions (e.g. pouring scorn on 'base pedantrie') reveals his intimate knowledge of Marlowe's plays.

5. The author's moralizing stance accords with Alleyn's religious attitude as evinced in his life and letters.

6. The play's simple honesty, lack of sophistication and rather naive humour in a folk history of Lancashire would appeal to Alleyn's personal taste on which his *Diary*, preserved among the Alleyn Papers at Dulwich, throws revealing light. As we come to know Alleyn more intimately it becomes plain that this is just the kind of play he would have written, and the well-developed dramatic sense of what will be effective in the theatre is just what one would expect of him. He knows how to tell a tale.

These characteristics accord with all we can discover about Alleyn as we follow his life, and in *Faire Em* they are combined to produce a popular play for Elizabethan audiences. In performance the literary weaknesses were easily glossed over, and these self-same qualities are to be seen in one other extant play of the Lord Admiral's Men which there is good reason to believe was also from the pen of Edward Alleyn.

A KNACK TO KNOW AN HONEST MAN was written, to judge by its title, as a riposte to Greene's satirical comedy *A Knack to Know a Knave*, which was, I believe, the last play Greene wrote before his death, in collaboration with Nashe, as referred to in his *Groatsworth of Wit* Letter addressing Nashe as 'yong *Iuuenall*, that byting Satyrist, that lastly with mee together writ a Comedie'.* Both plays were in the Lord Admiral's repertoire.

A marked idiosyncracy of Edward Alleyn's psychological make-up was his love of ceremony that contributed to his self-esteem by being special to himself. Alleyn especially loved making a large gesture to mark the days of personal significance in his calendar: these were for the anniversaries of his birthday, 1st September 1566, and his wedding day, 22nd October 1592. He contrived by careful planning to celebrate the consecration of the chapel of his College of God's Gift in Dulwich on his fiftieth birthday, on 1st September 1616, when the Archbishop of Canterbury presided over the ceremony.

---

* This play is discussed in depth in Chapter IX, "Greene's Last Comedy".

All his life he celebrated his wedding anniversary with a special mark of recognition, and when living in his mansion at Dulwich it was always kept on the nearest Sunday to the 22nd as 'our wedding daye' with a lavish Sunday dinner party of invited guests.[78] Having in mind his predilection for a special way to honour his wedding day, it is perhaps significant that a new play, called *A Knack to Know an Honest Man*, was presented at the Rose on Alleyn's second wedding anniversary, 22nd October, apparently intended as a riposte to Greene's play – and we have to remember that Greene's vicious libel on Alleyn in his *Groatsworth* came out just before Alleyn's wedding! On examination this second 'Knack' play has all the stylistic characteristics noted in *Faire Em*.

It is extant in an evidently unauthorized printed edition by Cuthbert Burby to whose hand it is entered in the Stationers' Register on 26th November 1595, in which the title page states merely that it had been 'sundrie times plaied about the Citie of London' without naming its company, the Lord Admiral's Men who played it at the Rose. Like *Faire Em*, the play was also known in ballad form, but in this case the ballad came out *after* the play and was presumably inspired by its success in the theatre, for only two weeks after its first performance as a 'ne' play recorded by Henslowe, John Danter entered his copyright in the Stationers' Register for 'a ballad wherein is shewed a Knacke howe to knowe an honest man from a knaue.'[79]

As the ballad entry indicates, the title of the play was a deliberate crib of Greene's play of 1592, *A Knack to Know a Knave*, but apart from this there is no resemblance to Greene's social satire in plot, or style or genre of drama.

A Knack to Know an Honest Man is a better play than *Faire Em*, chiefly because it has a much superior plot, which is fast moving, interesting and credible, whereas the plot of *Faire Em* is really rather silly. The new play proved to be one of the most successful plays in the Lord Admiral's repertoire, being performed twenty-three times between 22nd October 1594 and its last recorded performance on 3rd November 1596.[80] Its long run and popularity are testified by an allusion to the play discovered by Greg in *The Roaring Girl*, accredited to Middleton and Dekker, and acted by Prince Henry's Men, formerly the Lord Admiral's Men, which was printed in 1611:

Maister Gallipot: I pray who playes a Knacke to Know an honest man in this company?

Act IV, Scene 2

The source of the play's Italian plot is not known. Quite possibly it was original to the author, a highly moral tale of virtue rewarded, typical of Alleyn. The play opens dramatically with a duel between Sempronio and Lelio, two young gentlemen of Venice who had been bosom friends until Lelio discovered that Sempronio had attempted to seduce his lovely wife Annetta, who, however, did not succumb to his amorous advances but told her husband of his friend's perfidy. This is the cause of the duel, for which they have chosen a field in the country outside Venice, where they fight unaware that a shepherd is by to observe them. Lelio in his rage slays Sempronio, and then flees. The shepherd hies himself to Venice to report the deed to the Venetian authorities and Sempronio's family, who set up a hue and cry for Lelio, who has taken a swift farewell from his wife, Annetta and their daughter Lucida, explaining how he has slain Sempronio and must now flee for his life. But Sempronio, left for dead in the field, is found by a hermit, who carries him to his cave and resuscitates him with tender nursing, the Venetians meanwhile imagining that some wild beast had carried off the carcass. Restored to life and given spiritual guidance by Philip, the hermit, Sempronio returns to observe his fellow Venetians under the guise of a stranger who calls himself 'Penitent experience'. The style imitates Marlowe's trick of repetition.

Enter Sempronio *disguised with* Phillip

Sempronio: Here leaue me father, walke no further forth,
Leaue me supposed dead, reuiu'd by thee,
Hide thou my name, and couer from the world,
My fortunes and my birth, and all misdeeds,
Here is that Venice that beheld me fond,
Here is that Venice that shall beholde me wise,
Looke how thy science hath disguisde these lookes,
So hath thy councell reconcilde my heart,
I hate all worldly pompe, I scorne lewd lust,
This tongue from tempting in dishonest loue
Shall labour to releeue the innocent,
Farewell, thou knowest my vow,
Which I haue sworne to keepe irreuocable,
Neuer to disclose my name,
Vntill such time as thou releasest me.

11.292-307

222

So the story marches on with the disguised Sempronio ever present to point the moral of man's evil ways as he observes Fortunio attempting to seduce Lelio's beautiful daughter Lucida; Annetta being importuned and threatened with the confiscation of the little wealth remaining to her. Lelio has fled to his noble-minded father-in-law Brishio, who helps him to escape in one of his ships, knowing that he is risking his own life in succouring his son-in-law, now condemned as a murderer. A faithless servant betrays his master's good deed to the elders of Venice, and Brishio is exiled, never to return on pain of death. Brishio is presented as the exemplar of purest, noblest, truest manhood. In exile he obtains honourable service in the army of the City State of Milan, which is at war with its neighbour, Florence, only to discover to his horror that Lelio has obtained like service with the Medicis of Florence, the enemy he is committed to fight; so the two, father-in-law and son-in-law, face each other on opposing sides on the battlefield. Meanwhile Sempronio (Penitent experience) is given ample opportunity to deliver many a wise homily and make moral reflections on the sinful state of men as observed in the base actions of Venetian gentlemen who should know better. Fortunio and Marchetto are two such, intent on plundering Lelio's vulnerable family and property – Fortunio lusting after the lovely, young Lucida, and Marchetto after his money though also nothing loathe to make a pass at Annetta. The women, as in *Faire Em*, remain virtuous and incorruptible.

In the following passage with its abundant alliteration, we readily discern the stylistic traits of the hand that wrote *Faire Em*. Although the language is simple enough, it will be noticed that at times it does not bear analysis and hardly makes proper sense. There is also an effort to appear 'deeply read' in the allusion to 'Dania' and 'Dalia' – the former evidently Danae, but the latter some pseudo-classical character introduced for 'effect'.

> *Fortunio*: Tell me Marchetto ere thou go
> What precious thing is hid in Lelios house,
> That likes thee best.
> *Marchetto*: I long to be the Lord of all his coine.
> *For*: And I long and labour for his daughters loue.
> *Mar*: But by your patience, worthie Lord,
> I deeme my choice is best,
> For who so gaineth wealth,
> Hath beautie tide as captiue to his coine,
> And worldly pleasure tendeth on his traine.
> *For*: But in respect of beautie, it is vaine,

Riches are baites to teach vs nigardines,
But beautie to be bountie teacheth meanest men.
Mar: Ioue first wonne Dania in a golden shower.
For: But Dalia's ouerprest with power,
Wealth is the bodies slaue, but beauty guids the mind
And feeds the sense, and animates the wit.
Mar: But wealth by golden gifts commandeth it,
The fairest Ladies for a little bribe,
Will let Diogenes disport awhile,
Gold is a God in this desired age.

11.326-346

The adjective 'desired' in the last line is not quite right, and what are we to understand by 'But beautie to be bountie teacheth meanest men'? or by 'But Dalia's ouerprest with power'? Nor is it clear what Diogenes is doing in this context. There is a distinct tendency to use language quaintly, as in the following random examples taken from the text:

Lelio: Ah looke on these you care desiring eies.

1.126

Fortunio: Hie thee from Venice speedily, for if thou stay
But two houres space, thou art adindged death.

11.607-8

Senator: Our senators in Venice are well schoold in such haps,
And can doome of things, not by thy teares,
Or sorrow working wordes

11.162-164

Sempronio: What doo these flatterers where free men walke?
Hearke my Fortunio, I will tell a tale,
An oxe in Memphes with his poaring tongue,
Licking in doctious weeds did so foretell
His following death: a wretch like to my selfe,
Beating Marchettos cloake, doth prophesie
His following shame, vnles he mend his life.

11.481-487

The author of both *Faire Em* and *A Knacke to Know an Honest Man* has no inhibitions about making up adjectives to suit his 'poetic' line. In the above passage we have 'poaring tongue' and 'doctious weeds' which appear to be of his own invention.

The author of both *Faire Em* and *A Knacke to Know an Honest Man* has conversation and repartee well mastered, but is out of his depth in using unusual words and his longer speeches become involved and knotted, sometimes ridiculously so. He tends to adopt a curious word order in an attempt to achieve blank verse, and his alliteration is a constant characteristic throughout. Here are some more choice examples culled from *Faire Em* for comparison.

William the Conqueror, having fallen suddenly in love, is here excusing his sad looks to his courtiers:

> Ah, good my Lords, misconster not the cause;
> At least, suspect not my displeased brows:
> I amorously do bear to your intent,
> For thanks, and all that you can wish, I yeeld.
> But that which makes me blush and shame to tell
> Is cause why thus I turn my conquering eyes
> To cowards looks and beaten fantasies.
>
> 11.9-15

> . . . .
> . . . .
> *Valingford*: We go, and wish thee priuate conference
> Public affects, in this accustomed peace.
>
> Act I Sc.1 11.30-31

Even if we take it that 'affects' should read 'effects' the syntax is very strange. The use of the adverb 'amorously' in 'I amorously do bear to your intent' is another oddity; as also is 'Only revengement of a priuate grudge'. (1.1044). The following speeches by Em's lover Manvile also exhibit syntaxical curiosities. Em pretended deafness to be her affliction which her lover here bewails.

> *Manuile*: Ah Maistres, somtime I might haue said my loue
> But time and fortune hath bereued me of that,
> And I am abiect in those gratious eyes
> That with remorse earst sawe into my griefe,
> May sit and sigh the sorowes of my heart.
>
> 11.403-407

And, again –

> *Manuile*: Ah impudent and shamelesse in thy ill,

That with thy cunning and defraudfull toung,
Seekest to delude the honest meaning minde:

11.418-420

The last three lines of the first speech above do not really make sense, although we do have to remember that this is a corrupt text. In the last quotation we have the characteristic use of adjectives which are quaintly invented in 'defraudfull toung' and 'honest meaning minde' – but very Elizabethan.

Returning to *A Knacke* again, here is a purple passage which epitomizes all the author's idiosyncrasies. Sempronio is reporting to Fortunio upon his return from his embassage to Lucida and Annetta with rich gifts from Fortunio to seduce the former, and to win Annetta for Marchetto also, which both ladies have rejected in disgust.

> *Enter* Fortunio *and* Marchetto.
> *Fortunio*: Here comes my cynicall attendance
> Wee shall haue newes what Lucyda intendes.
> *Sempronio*: Goe cast thee headlong from a mounttaine top,
> Or in the deepest seas goe drowne thy selfe,
> Goe liue thou wretch among the barbarous beasts,
> Where Italy may neuer heare thy name.
> For vertue vowes to laugh in looking on,
> To see you perish in your peeuishnes.
> *For*: A dreadfull enterance to a dolfull tale,
> Speake man, what newes from Lucyda?
> *Sem*: Shee spyes thy poyssoned message in thy face,
> Shee scornes thy gyftes, and vowes to hate thee euer,
> To thee lewd lossell fayre Annetta sends,
> A troope of curses chayned with bitter sighes,
> Come Lordes lets lyghten vs of heauie things,
> There lies my cloake & cap, now throw your swoordes aside,
> And let vs three lyke fleeting vnycornes,
> Runne blushing through the streets in to the wood,
> There let Fortunio cut Marchettos throat,
> That councelled him to rauish chastytie,
> There penitent experience with his bat,
> Shall beate Fortunios tender wanton sides,
> That sought to spoyle holy virginitie,
> Lastly my selfe will syt and teare my haire,

And weepe vntil I choake my selfe with wet,
To see nobilytie so much disguisd.
For: Hence sorrow boding messenger be gone,
Rage now shall ouer rule discretion,
Gather thy frends Marchetto follow mee,
This nyght wee will surprise them in their beds,
And teach them kyndnes who will learne no loue.

11.760-791

Sempronio's impassioned speeches abound in what might be called malapropisms of imagery:

To see you perish in your peeuishnes	1.767
Shee spyes thy poyssoned message in thy face	1.770
And let us three lyke fleeting vnicornes	
Runne blushing through the streets in to the wood	11.776-7
And weepe vntil I choake my selfe with wet	1.785

Sometimes such inappropriate language seems to be directly inspired by a striving after alliteration as in 'perish in your peeuishnes'.

And what shall we make of Fortunio's –

This nyght wee will surprise them in their beds,
And teach them kyndnes who will learne no loue.

11.790-1

Ravishing these virtuous and unwilling ladies seems a strange way to 'teach them kyndnes'! And how does one *learn love*? What does it really *mean*? This matter of conveying a clearly expressed meaning is secondary to the author of both the plays at certain moments, for to him of primary importance is to give an impression of poetic declamatory style in his speeches when strong emotion is being expressed by the character, and at such times he fills out a blank verse line with nonsense quite happily when rising to this challenge. It is chiefly in his moments of 'high-flown' style that he tends to some very strange usage of English, for then he is obviously out of his depth, but quite unaware of the fact for he has no inhibitions about misusing words. Is not this the man whom Greene lampooned as an ignoramus, pointing him out as 'he that cannot write true English'? And does not this aptly sum up the author of both *Faire Em* and *A Knack to Know an Honest Man*? – particularly in his most poetically aspiring blank verse moments?

In both plays the author has mastered repartee and dialogue well, and there are some good scenes, many telling dramatic moments, and there is a sound sense of stage-craft and dramatic structure. These are all aspects of the undoubted expertise of a great actor-manager such as Alleyn, and he also has a vivid imagination and considerable inventiveness to contribute, without which no dramatist could succeed. But he betrays his lack of education when he attempts to soar into poetry in emulation of Marlowe, who clearly seems to be his most admired model, but all he achieves is a kind of ridiculous parody of 'poetic' blank verse.

The main examples of his ridiculous high-flown style come in the speeches given to the Conqueror in *Faire Em* when expressing his ardent love, and when elevated persons such as the King and his Courtiers are speaking; with homely characters and more commonplace dialogue he deals effectively. In *A Knack* his failings are most noticeable in impassioned speeches, but this is a later work than *Faire Em* and there is evidence of more assurance in handling the drama. I believe that *Faire Em* may have been his first venture into blank verse, and this gives it even more point as the target for Greene's spiteful attack. Alleyn was a man who had missed out in his education and he longed and aspired to be well educated. He bought himself a Latin dictionary and founded a college to give to poor boys what had been denied him. The classically educated and learned Greene despised him for his lack of learning and derided his ambitions using them as sticks to beat him.

The marked stylistic similarities as well as choice of theme, which may be equated with the *Groatsworth* Player's interest in 'Morrals teaching education' suggest that both these plays are the work of Alleyn. A very strong case supports his authorship of *Faire Em* with its 'Windmill' setting pointed at by Greene, and its Lancashire origin and connection with Strange's Men. The internal echoes of an identical turn of mind and style in the author of *A Knack to Know an Honest Man* argue that this play is from the same hand, and that the hand was Alleyn's. Its presentation as a new play on his *second wedding anniversary* – Alleyn and Joan Woodward were getting married just about the time that Greene's *Groatsworth of Wit* appeared in the bookshop – as his reply to Greene's malicious libel of him, also makes its point. With this neat riposte to Greene's play *A Knack to Know a Knave* he was getting his own back, showing that this 'vpstart Crow' was 'as well able to bombast out a blanke verse as the best' of them!

The foregoing arguments and evidence have presented a case for Edward Alleyn as a minor dramatist, successful at his own level, having his own company and theatre in which to ensure that his plays were performed. In subsequent chapters, as his career and life are investigated, the more we know about this actor, the more certain it becomes that this ambitious young man would have aspired to writing plays as well as acting in them, and since it is indisputable that other members of his own company were busily writing plays, then why not he? Indeed, especially why not Alleyn?

Orlando Furioso: An Extant Actor's Script

The only other dramatist from whom Alleyn seems to have purchased for himself was Greene, and the fact that, on his own testimony, he began his playwriting career indebted to Alleyn argues that he was, in a sense, tied to his apron strings, which must have riled him. Fortunately, we possess authentic evidence of Greene's business connections with Alleyn. It is a piece of fascinating documentation in the form of a unique, annotated playscript of part of Greene's *Orlando Furioso*, which is among Alleyn's personal papers at Dulwich College, and the inference is that he owned this play.

The manuscript is a transcript of the actor's part of Orlando with its cues, this role being obviously played by Alleyn himself. Such actors' parts would be prepared by the theatre scribe. The conclusion that Alleyn himself played the part of Orlando is inescapable when we see that the annotations on the manuscript are, where sufficiently clear, all identifiable as being in Alleyn's hand; often minutely written between the lines, these additions consist of interlineated corrections, and added words or instructions. They have been closely studied by Greg, who has carefully corroborated the statements made by J.P. Collier into whose hands this curious and invaluable manuscript first came, and whose regrettable reputation for forgery later in his life means that everything that has passed through his is suspect until re-examined by a reputable scholar. Greg has confirmed that the identifiable annotations (some being too cramped to make certainty possible) are all in Alleyn's hand. This wonderful find is, to date, the only known manuscript of an actor's part that has come down to us from the 16th or early 17th century. Fifteen separate annotations are recognizably in the hand of Edward Alleyn. Greg comments:

'This fact lends such a rare interest to the manuscript that it is desirable to go into the matter rather fully. In spite of the admitted difficulty of identifying with certainty the hand of small insertions – the most extensive in the part consisting of a single line (208) –

I have no doubt that Collier was at least right in supposing that the majority of those we here find were written by Alleyn himself.'[81]

Originally the manuscript had been in the form of a scroll, and when Collier first obtained the roll it was in three pieces of varying lengths, which together would have measured about 18 feet by 6 inches in width. This has now long since been divided into leaves and bound, placed at the end of a volume of Alleyn's collected papers in the Dulwich manuscripts (M.S. I, 138. folios 261-71). The beginning is missing, and the condition is somewhat spoiled with gaps and mutilations due to bookworm depredation and age, with some fragments misplaced during the process of binding. Nevertheless, it remains an invaluable and remarkable document that takes one back into Elizabethan theatrical life and time with a recollection that is vividly alive. The writing of the copy appears to be that of a professional scribe, and is quite different from that of the annotator, who uses several different inks as though the alterations were made at different times when he was studying his part, probably speaking it aloud. What a pity we cannot also hear the great actor's voice!
Greg concludes:

'On consideration, therefore, I incline to believe that all the alterations and corrections in the part which are clearly not by the original scribe are by Alleyn...From the fact that Alleyn corrected the part, the inference that he studied it and therefore, since his company is known to have performed a play of the name, that he actually acted Orlando, is irresistible.'[82]

In the following selection from the manuscript, all the corrections and additions in the corrector's hand are printed in heavy black type *when identified as representing Alleyn's autograph*. The rest is written in what we may assume to be the hand of the playhouse scribe, and represents the part of Orlando with its cues. In the first example a whole line has been inserted by Alleyn between the lines written by the scribe:[83]

whers medor, say me for truth wher medor is	**Strip 8**
yf Iupiter hath shutt him wth young Ganymede	
by heauen Ile fetch him, from y[e] heles of Ioue	
inconstant base iniurius & vntrue	line 208
such strupetts shall not scape away wth life	

Alleyn may have dictated some of the insertions to the scribe to write in. In the following one word has been added, the adjective 'crimson', to make the line scan.

Argalio these be the lockes Apollo turnd to bowes   **Strip 9**
when **crimson** Daphne ran away for loue   line 239

In the next, the name 'Galaxsia' is inserted –

Clyme vp the clowdes to **Galaxsia** straight   line 243
and tell Apollo, that orlando sitts
making of verses for Angelica

There is no mention of Galaxsia in the text of the Quarto, so that this seems to be an original piece of invention by Alleyn. The Quarto line reads –

Then goe thy waies and clime vp to the Clowds

In the next example there are two interlineations written in by the scribe later, having omitted them in error it seems; then in a blank he left is added a single word by Alleyn: 'poel' (pole). This passage criticises poetry.

[scribe] **as how fellow/**
wher is the Artick bear late baighted   line 265

[scribe]   **/scurvy poetry a litell to long**
    from his **poel**....   by force [his cue]
Oh my sweet Angelica, braue^r than Iuno was
but vilayne she conuerst wth Medor

In the next 'away w^t thes rages' (rags) is interlineated by Alleyn

Argalio why sufferest   **Strip 10**
this olde trott, to come so nere me
away w^t thes rages   line 295
fetch me the Robe, that prowd Apollo wea^{r}s
that I may Iett it in the capytoll

The scribe left blanks occasionally, probably having difficulty in deciphering Greene's handwriting which Chettle informs us was sometimes 'none of the best', trusting to Alleyn to fill them in. In the following the printed Quarto text is identical except for the spelling of 'Nymosene', and it has 'Cynthia tunes conceites'. Here Alleyn filled in blanks –

> **neymoseney** hath kist the kingly Ioue   line 315
> and entertāȳd a feast wth in my braynes
> making her daughters solace on my browes.
> methinks I feel how Cinthias **Tyms** conceipts
> of sad repent, & **meloweth** those desires
> that frenzy scarse had ripened in my braynes

In the following the brackets indicate much worn paper or scarcely legible letters: 'wrasteld' is inserted by Alleyn in a blank.

> Hath then the fr⟨n⟩zy of Alcumenes ch⟨ild⟩   **Strip 11**
> ledd fourth ⟨my⟩ th⟨oug⟩ghts, wth far mo^re ega^r rage
> then **wraste⟨ld⟩** in the brayne of phillips sonne   line 351
> when madd wth wyne, he practised Clytus fall

In the next passage Alleyn had added 'proud' in the margin.

> Then mayst thou deme, some second mars frō heauē
> is sent, as was Amphitrios foster sonne
>   /crowne [scribe]
> to vale thy plumes, and heaue the frō a
> **proud** what thou art, I wreke not of thy gree   line 394
> as Lampethusas brother frō his coach
> praucing, & ⟨se⟩ one went his course
> and tombled from Ap⟨o⟩llos chariott
> so shall thy fort⟨u⟩nes, and thy honor fall

Two further insertions are made in this passage in blanks left by the scribe

>   /pride [scribe]   **Strip 13**
> faire nimphe, about whose browes, sitts cloras
> **& Clisias** bewty trippes about thy looks   line 480
> ꝑdon thy Lord, who perst wth Ielowsie
> darkned thy vertues, wth a great ecclipse

<blockquote>
pardon thy Lord faire saynt Angelica
whose loue stealing by steppes into extremes
grew by suspition to causlesse Lunacye   line 485
</blockquote>

The last word inserted, 'causlesse', is of a kind favoured by the author of *Faire Em*, who writes, for instance, 'staylesse of the world'. These insertions and corrections are not made by a hand that is unused to writing and touching up dramatic works, or by one who is uninformed regarding the scanning of a blank verse line, or who lacks imagination, but show rather that the corrector, who was undoubtedly Alleyn, possessed some expertise in dealing with poetic scripts. Such a man could doubtless also write a blank verse play himself if he had a mind to do so. In one instance of these corrections in particular, we find that the printed text of the Quarto is quite different. This is the manuscript version:

<blockquote>
Kinde Clora make her couch, fair cristall springs   line 10
washe you her Roses, yf she long to drinck
</blockquote>

The Quarto has –

<blockquote>
Faire Flora make her couch amidst thy flowres,
Sweet Christall springs, wash ye with roses,
When she longs to drinke.
</blockquote>

Alleyn's hand wrote in 'Clora'. Greene identified Ovid's Chloris with Ariosto's Cloride, which is perhaps where Clora came from to add her alliteration to 'Kinde' and 'couch' and 'cristall' which the scribe had already written.

All writers, of course, used alliteration more or less markedly at times, including Marlowe, but with Alleyn, in those plays which I have suggested were from his hand, the alliteration is often crudely obvious. Clearly he was a great admirer of Marlowe and the other educated men who wrote plays which he acted, and when he came to write himself he was consciously modelling himself on them and was trying hard to emulate 'his betters', and he managed it with sufficient success to pass muster with the groundlings and the general theatre-goers. Even in the above samplings of Alleyn's additions to Greene's script we see his innate sense of theatre, as in 'away with these rags' which adds a dramatic flourish to the otherwise tame request 'fetch me the Robe that prowd Apollo weare'. As already remarked, it would indeed be surprising if Alleyn had not written any plays; and here he is shown making dramatic improvements to Greene's text.

How *Orlando Furioso* came into the possession of Edward Alleyn and the Lord Admiral's Men throws a sharp light on Greene's sometimes unscrupulous dealings with the actors. In the anonymous pamphlet, *The Defence of Conny catching: by Cuthbert Cunny-catcher, Licenciate in Whittington Colledge*, published in 1592 in reply to Greene's social pamphlets exposing the trickery of the various categories of rogues, thieves and con-men whose criminal activities he had familiar knowledge of, there is this interesting revelation:

'Aske the Queens Players, if you sold them not *Orlando Furioso* for twenty Nobles, and when they were in the country, sold the same Play to the Lord Admirals men for as much more. Was not this plaine *Conny-Catching* Maister R.G.?' [84]

The Queen's Men went on an extended tour in 1589 when they even travelled as far as Scotland, and I suggest this is when Greene contrived this piece of double dealing. Greg and most others favour a later date for the play; Jordan, however, gives good reason for dating it to 1588 for *Orlando Furioso* is another attempt on Greene's part to emulate a recent highly successful play, this time Thomas Kyd's *The Spanish Tragedy* written in 1587, for it was Greene's way to follow a new fashion before allowing any time for it to grow cold. Kyd's revenge tragedy with its raging mad scenes was received with tremendous acclaim, and rivalled *Tamburlaine* in giving theatre audiences a popular catch-phrase – 'Hieronimo, beware! go by, go by.'

In emulating Kyd with a play in which its hero, Orlando, also goes mad, Greene fell again into the pitfall of choosing an unsuitable model for his light-weight talent, which excelled in pastoral romance, not heavy tragedy, and even Alleyn's histrionic prowess was unable to raise *Orlando Furioso* in the public's estimation as a great dramatic success.

If Alleyn knew about Greene's double dealing over *Orlando*, he probably shrugged the matter off, seeing to it that he came out best in the deal. Having bought the script in good faith, he played the part, and no other company could have hoped to rival him with a greater Orlando! It was the Queen's Men who would have been the losers in Greene's double dealing. Greg suggests, giving cogent reasons, that '*Orlando* was purchased in the second instance, not by the Admiral's men as such, but by Alleyn personally',[85] and this view supports all that the present findings indicate as the historic circumstances of their relationship.

How the Queen's Men and the Lord Admiral's sorted out the matter of shared rights in the play one can only guess. That Alleyn played the title role at the Rose on 21st February 1591/2 is a certainty, but by then it was no longer a new play. This was when Alleyn was heading Lord Strange's Men, and Greg suggests that we have evidence here that *Orlando Furioso* was a play script that Alleyn owned personally since it came with him to the Rose, and was not retained by the Lord Admiral's as one of their stock of plays, for at this time they departed to make a tour of the Continent whilst Alleyn opted to remain in London.

There is also internal evidence of a date of composition not long after the defeat of the Spanish Armada to which the following is surely a reference:

> And what I dare, let say, the Portingale,
> And Spaniard tell, who mann'd with mighty fleets,
> Came to subdue my islands to their kings,
> Filling our seas with stately argosies.
>
> Act II, Sc.1. 11.82-85

It is a pale hint compared with *Edward the Third*, but the eager ears of audiences would have picked it up. On 29th December and 11th February the Lord Admiral's Men played at the Court,[86] and it is possible that Alleyn may have forestalled the Queen's Men by performing *Orlando* at one of these 'command performances' before the Queen, for there is a curious ambiguity about the claims made on the title page of the quarto. This states merely that the play was performed 'before the Queenes Maiestie' *without naming any company*. With the death of Tarlton, Queen Elizabeth's favourite clown, in September 1588, the Queen's Men declined in popularity. They played only once in the Christmas season of 1591, whereas the combined company of Strange's headed by Edward Alleyn played six times, and his star was obviously in the ascendant with the Queen.

It has been generally assumed that Greene wrote primarily for the Queen's Men, and is even stated as a fact that he was their leading playwright. But this is certainly not borne out by the evidence. Of all Greene's canonical plays *only* the quarto of *Frier Bacon and Frier Bongay* (1594) claims 'As it was plaid by her Maiesties seruants', and the first evidence of this play is of its performance at the Rose by Strange's Men under Alleyn on 19th February 1591/2. Hence Alleyn had obviously acquired it – perhaps as part of the settlement with Queen's over *Orlando Furioso*? Both these plays, together with *Looking Glasse* remained with

Alleyn when the Lord Admiral's Men departed abroad (presumably taking the company's stock of plays with them) so that we may assume that Alleyn personally owned these three plays by Greene or they would surely have gone with the company. All the rest of Greene's canonical works were published without naming any company.

Of *Looking Glasse*, written with Lodge, published in 1598, Greg comments: 'There is no indication of the company to which it originally belonged', [87] but he then assumes it belonged to the same company that owned *James IV* who were 'probably the Queen's Men', because the clown is referred to as Adam –

Wife to Clown: Oh but Adam, I am afraid to walke so late because of the spirits that appeare in the Citie.

(*Looking-Glass 1.1594*)

He claims that Adam ('evidently an actor') is named in *James IV*, which he thinks belonged 'probably' to the Queen's Men. But the reference he gives for *James IV* (ed. Collins, 1. 2268 s.d.) has the stage direction: 'Enter [Oberon] and Antiques, and carrie away the Clowne', with no mention of Adam at all. The preceding scene features the comic characters Slipper and Andrew. So that this is guesswork on Greg's part. All we know for certain is that all Greene's canonical plays with the exception of *Alphonsus* and *James IV* were in the season at the Rose under Alleyn's management in 1591/2. We have firm evidence of Greene's association with Alleyn in a business relationship to bear out the conclusion that Greene was far more closely involved with him and the Lord Admiral's Men than with the Queen's Men.

Orlando Furioso is significant as being a unique strand in the cumulative evidence which links Robert Greene with Edward Alleyn in a peculiarly personal professional relationship. The extant playscript of the part of Orlando shows Alleyn as a critic deftly touching up and improving a play-script for performance, adding a line or word discriminatingly. From this long experience in handling play-scripts of all kinds, it is but a short step to actually writing a scene for a play which was about to go into rehearsal and lacked something which Alleyn deemed important for its maximum success at the Rose theatre, where he had just joined Philip Henslowe in the winter of 1591/2. Here he is shown engaged in close collaboration with his special dramatist, Marlowe, to ensure the success of their new play at the Rose, and, in this instance, not merely as the actor-manager who had commissioned it, and who was directing the play on the boards,

236

but also as one who in an emergency turned his hand to writing a couple of brief scenes for this urgently needed production.

The fascinating evidence next presented is a development based on some remarkable textual research by Dr Allison Gaw, which reveals Edward Alleyn in his working relationship with Christopher Marlowe, together with the other two leading playwrights of his stable, Robert Greene and George Peele, in a way that highlights the flexible manner of Elizabethan play-production. We are afforded a unique insight into a rare piece of theatrical history.

VIII   *A New Play at The Rose with its New Look*

IN THE EARLY MONTHS of 1592 circumstances gave rise to an unusually close collaboration between Edward Alleyn and Christopher Marlowe, together with two of his fellow dramatists, Robert Greene and George Peele; both of them well known to Alleyn, for their works were being performed by his company.

Alleyn had just formed his alliance with Strange's Men and together this syndicate formed the strongest acting troupe then in existence. They included many experienced actors, among the principals being Augustine Phillips, Thomas Pope, John Hemminge, George Bryan, William Sly, and probably William Kempe and Richard Burbage. The latter's name appears in a leading role in the 'Platt' or plot of *The Seven Deadly Sins*, a play by the famous comedian Richard Tarlton who had died in 1588, and which must have been the play performed under the name *Four Plays in One* given at the Rose this season. If the 'Platt', which is among Allyen's possessions at Dulwich, dates from 1592 (and why else should it have been among Alleyn's personal papers if this were not the case?) then Burbage was certainly with them at the Rose. Alleyn had quarrelled with the elder Burbage the previous May, but presumably the prospect of staying with the best actors of the company, and maybe inducement to play leading roles instead of the minor parts he had hitherto played, would have won Richard Burbage over. At any rate, there is no evidence of his presence with any other company than Strange's Men.

Henslowe had just spent a goodly sum on his renovations, and was doubtless anxious to recoup this. The Rose, in its spanking new paintwork, stood ready inviting theatre-goers to cross the river to see what was on offer, and it was probably with some sense of occasion that he took a new page in his *Diary* and inscribed it with an opening flourish for what he hoped would be a profitable season.

> In the name of god Amen 1591
> beginge the 19 of febreary my
> lord stranges mene A ffoloweth
> 1591
> Rd at fryer bacvne the 19 of febreary....satterdaye....xvij^s iij^d

238

Rd at mvlomvrco the 20 febreary........................xxix^s
Rd at orlando the 21 of febreary.....................xvjs vj^d [1]

Two plays by Greene, his *Friar Bacon* and *Orlando Furioso*, and one by Peele, for Henslowe's 'mvlomvrco' must be his *Battle of Alcazar*. Between them Alleyn and Strange's Men possessed a repertoire of proven old favourites with which to begin their season, but if they hoped for a good box office they were disappointed. They had opened on a Saturday and played on Sunday (which was strictly against the law, but it was often bent), and through a seven-day week with only moderate success. Alleyn was ambitious to impress in his alliance with Henslowe, and he realised that what was urgently needed was a new play with some startling attraction that would make theatrical news. The matter was urgent and called for speed and ingenuity to attract audiences to the Bankside as the fashionable theatrical resort of the future. These, then, are the circumstances which gave birth to the play that boosted box office records and fully vindicated Alleyn's choice of author, subject and style of production, for it remained a winner. It was a new history play named *harey the vj*.

With great satisfaction Henslowe noted in his *Diary* the takings of the new play:

ne — Rd at harey the vj the 3 of marche 1591 ... iij^{li} xvj^s 8^d [2]

£3 16s 8d! The play was performed no less than fourteen times during the season, more than any of the other plays in their repertoire, and once having taken to the ferries to cross to the smartly refurbished Rose, the audiences were happy to come again and again to see their old favourites. Box office takings remained high for the entire season. Edward Alleyn and Christopher Marlowe had woven their magic once again, for as we shall see, it was this winning combination in another variant which achieved this breakthrough for Henslowe.

The play which Henslowe recorded in his *Diary* as *harey the vj* has been identified for us by a contemporary reference to it by Tom Nashe in his *Pierce Penilesse: His Supplication to the Diuell*, (entered in the Stationers' Register on August 8, 1592 and published that year) in which next to his marginal note, 'in defence of playes' he describes the ecstatically emotional reaction of the audience at the death of the hero, Talbot. He is evidently writing particularly with history plays in mind.

'First, for the subiect of them (for the most part) it is borrowed out
of our English Chronicles, wherein our forefathers valiant acts (that
haue line long buried in rustie brasse and worme-eaten bookes) are

reuiued, and they themselues raised from the Graue of Obliuion, and brought to pleade their aged Honours in open presence: than which, what can be a sharper reproofe to these degenerate effeminate dayes of ours?

'How would it haue ioyed braue *Talbot* (the terror of the French) to thinke that after he had lyne two hundred yeares in his Tombe, hee should triumphe againe on the Stage, and haue his bones newe embalmed with the teares of ten thousand spectators at least, (at seuerall times) who, in the Tragedian that represents his person, imagine they behold him fresh bleeding?'[3]

Nashe is not exaggerating, for the total of the fourteen performances it received in 1592 came to considerably more than ten thousand spectators.

The play in which brave Talbot, 'the Frenchmens only scourge' dominates as a hero figure until he nobly and movingly expires at the end of Act IV, can be none other than the opening play of the trilogy on the Wars of the Roses which appears in the First Folio as *The first Part of Henry the Sixt,* taking its place there before the Second and Third Parts which were *The Contention* and *The True Tragedy* discussed in an earlier chapter, which Marlowe had but recently written for the Pembroke Men. The additional scenes which were later written to marry (literally) the First and Second Parts to form a consecutive trilogy by introducing the marriage of the young Henry VI to Margaret of Anjou, and which bear clear evidence of later interpolation, did not yet exist.

The first Part of Henry the Sixt, as the play is printed in the First Folio, is the subject of our study, and we shall find it a most revealing text. The play shows every sign of hasty composition, and it is certainly the worst and most unevenly written of the *Henry VI* plays. Indeed it is unique among the dramatic works attributed to Shakespeare in its descent at times to literary mediocrity and even banality, but – caviare to the general it proved. The Elizabethan audiences loved it, and probably not least because of the spectacular production which the ingenious Alleyn devised for it, which must have made theatrical history at the time. He had in mind to make striking theatrical use of a new feature with which the renovation of the Rose had adorned this theatre. It now sported a turret from which the flagpole with its flying pennant rose into the air. And this little superstructure was, as we shall see, very much in Alleyn's mind when he commissioned the new play.

Alleyn's career, hitherto an unalloyed success story, was at a crucial point. In May of the previous year, 1591, he had fallen out with the elder

240

Burbage, at whose theatres in Shoreditch he had been playing as leading actor with the Strange's Men; and the upshot was he completely broke with James Burbage and taking the better part of Strange's Men with him had allied himself with Henslowe on Bankside. Having burned his boats he simply could not afford to have a failure in their new season at the Rose. The success of the new play was to be his saving, and he evidently bent all his energies to meeting the need of the moment. Above all, he urgently required a new play that would be a sure-fire 'hit'. And the dramatist to whom Alleyn would naturally turn would have been Christopher Marlowe, who had written his greatest roles for him and whose plays had never failed as box office triumphs. No other dramatist could claim such a record of unfailing successes. It is inconceivable that Alleyn, in this moment of urgent need, should have turned to any one other than Marlowe – and assuredly not to the unknown William Shakespeare even if he had been around in London, for which we do not have any valid evidence.

The hypothetical reconstruction is as follows. Speed in putting the new play on the boards was vital, and it was therefore agreed to call in two or three more dramatists to write the scenes simultaneously once the plotting and division of the parts had been determined. Collaboration was a common enough practice, though Marlowe always preferred to work alone, but in the exceptional circumstances pertaining he agreed. As we shall see, the men called in to assist on this urgent project were well known to both Marlowe and to Alleyn, all having plays currently in the Strange's repertoire. We can visualize the four of them – for there were four in this little consortium – sitting around a table together having a pre-production conference; Marlowe outlining the plot of the play and deciding, agreeing, how best to allocate the scenes to suit the talents and inclinations of his co-dramatists, with Alleyn explaining his ideas as to how the Rose's new turret would be featured in the staging. The subject of the play was evidently carefully chosen to provide opportunities for Alleyn to use this novel structural addition in a theatrically striking way.

For his inspiration Marlowe had turned to history once more, to a period he was already steeped in, having but recently written two plays for Pembroke's Men on the Wars of the Roses, so that he would have been well primed for writing a play at such short notice on the earlier part of the reign of the young Henry VI, then still a minor, which part would certainly have been played by a boy in the original production of *harey the vj*. There was an additional reason for choosing this part of his turbulent reign as the subject for the new play, as its history is set in the wars in France, and this held great topical interest for Englishmen at this time. News of the siege of Rouen, where the Earl of Essex was prosecuting the war on behalf of Queen Elizabeth's ally, Henry IV, formerly Henry of Navarre, the champion of the Huguenots, had been reaching Londoners all through that December, and by February news was received that the Duke of Parma was marching to the relief of Rouen. The Earl of Essex had arrived back in London on 19th January 1591/2 hoping to persuade Elizabeth to sanction desperately needed additional support for the French King, which, with her usual parsimony in such matters, she at first flatly refused. However, by late February she relented and signed an order for the levying of 1600 men, to be raised partly in Kent, Sussex and London, where masterless men might expect to find themselves taken up. This was the background then, which doubtless influenced the choice made by Marlowe to write a play about a war in France more than two hundred years ago, between the English and French led by Joan of Arc, *in which Rouen is largely featured*, the city being taken in the play first by the French led by Joan of Arc, and then re-taken by the English led by the valiant Talbot. What could be better suited to tickle the taste for topicality in their theatrical entertainment which the Elizabethans relished?

It is significant that this topicality of the historic background relating to Rouen has, in part, been superficially imposed, for the exaggerated importance given to Rouen in the action of the play was, in fact, historically inaccurate. The military incidents depicted occurred to *other* French towns, but were transferred to Rouen in the play. This underlines the correctness of the identification of the new play at the Rose, *harey the vj*, with *1 Henry VI* (on which doubt has sometimes been expressed), for such topicality written into the play at the expense of historicity would *only* have been done for a purpose. Rouen was being especially 'featured' to give the added spice of topicality, and the historical inaccuracies were quite deliberate.

Against this background we now consider the evidence presented by Dr Allison Gaw, whose meticulous research has vividly reconstructed for us the production of *harey the vj* as it was first presented at the Rose on 3rd March 1591/2 in his delightful book, *The Origin and Development of 1 Henry VI*.

Retracing Dr Gaw's detailed investigation of the collaborative authorship of *harey the vj* assumes special importance for the present thesis because it reveals Christopher Marlowe and Edward Alleyn in an actual working relationship in the theatre. The making of this hybrid play also sheds a sharp light on the relationship between Alleyn and Greene in the last months of Greene's life. Apparently these two almost came to blows during this production – or so the evidence suggests. This play was, I believe, the genesis of Greene's vitriolic attack on 'Shake-scene'. Gaw's study has therefore unique value for all students of Shakespeare and the Elizabethan theatre.

Dr Gaw's entire thesis is based on the First Folio text of *The first Part of Henry the Sixt* which has preserved for us unusually precise stage-directions relating to what must have been the original production of *harey the vj*, deriving from the playscript written in the divers hands of the playwrights who were working collaboratively on the piece in order to complete it in some haste. The scenes allocated to them were probably being written simultaneously by the four playwrights in the consortium to meet the time-scale required by Alleyn and Henslowe who had commissioned it. From this point on we follow Dr Gaw's thesis.

Noticing the unusual detail of the stage instructions in the First Folio text of this play, Dr Gaw comments:

'That the manuscript was...the work of men not in the habit themselves of conducting the rehearsals of their work [is] indicated by the fact that stage-directions concerning details of acting, costume, and stage-management, comparatively rare in the typical Shakespearean text, here occur frequently, and usually phrased without the crisp curtness of the practised actor-playwright.'[4]

For example:

Stage	*The French leape ore the walles in their shirts.*
Direction	*Enter severall wayes,* Bastard, Alenson, Reignier,
in II, i.	*halfe ready, and halfe unready.*

First Folio, *Histories*, p.101, l.720

This seems to suggest the presence of Alleyn, hovering anxiously to precipitate the work, already thinking ahead how the action of the play was to be presented. The most interesting of these stage-directions refer to the new superstructure, the turret. In renovating his Rose theatre, Henslowe spared no expense. His long list of the charges and materials purchased rarely specifies the work carried out, but Dr Gaw has deduced from the stage-directions in *1 Henry VI* that he added a wooden superstructure carrying the mast or flagpole, which was the first example of a turret topping the theatre which became a standard feature of all Elizabethan theatres. Dr Gaw suggests that it may have been the inspiration of Edward Alleyn, who conceived that this additional level could be used in a spectacular way in a play production especially written to feature it. As Gaw amusingly suggests:

'the first new play presented in the rebuilt house...seems especially and uniquely to "feature" the turret, as the New York Hippodrome might 'feature' a new artificial lake.'[5]

Evidence of the existence of this novel turret and the specially devised theatrical 'featuring' of it in the new play is substantiated by the First Folio text of *The first Part of Henry the Sixt*, which shows that Alleyn must have worked out in detail how best he could exploit this theatrically exciting level to the full, and he undoubtedly had an eye to this in the writing of the play. Dr Gaw comments:

'The early Elizabethan audience loved scenes of extreme physical danger, torture and the like. In *2 Tamburlaine,* V,i, Marlowe had already hung a living man in chains upon the stage and directed volleys of musketry against him. In Holinshed's *Chronicles*, one of the principal sources of *1 Henry VI* ..... was described a scene employing a cannon – a scene into which it was possible for the author, or authors of the play to introduce the chief hero, giving him a sensational first entrance and at the same time, perhaps, featuring the new superstructure.'[6]

This is exploited to the full in the play (I,iv) under what must have been the close instruction and guidance of Edward Alleyn who knew exactly what he wanted in the scene, in which he contrived, with a stroke of theatrical wizardry, to introduce both the play's hero, Talbot, and the new turret simultaneously high-lighted, so to speak, early in the drama.

'After a fifty-line description in I,i, of his almost superhuman exploits and his capture by the French, he [Talbot] enters in person in a scene (I,iv) the details of which are borrowed from Holinshed *but with which historically Talbot had no connection*'.[7]*

*(My italics. We seem to have encountered something like this before – when Dover Wilson and Peter Alexander accused Marlowe of introducing historically transferred data into *Edward II* – done, as here, for dramatic purposes. Yet according to their view that Shakespeare wrote all the *Henry VI* plays, here *he* would be doing this same unforgivable thing.) But now

to demonstrate the matter to our eyes, is the scene in question as it appears in the First Folio.

> *Enter the* Master Gunner *of Orleance, and his Boy*
> *M. Gunner.* Sirrha, thou know'st how Orleance is besieg'd,
> And how the English haue the Suburbs wonne.
> *Boy.* Father I know, and oft haue shot at them,
> How e're vnfortunate, I miss'd my ayme.
> *M. Gunner.* But now thou shalt not. Be thou rul'd by me:
> Chiefe Master Gunner am I of this Towne,
> Something I must doe to procure me grace:
> The Princes espyals haue informed me,
> How the English, in the Suburbs close entrencht,
> Went through a secret Grate of Iron Barres,
> In yonder Tower, to ouer-peere the Citie,
> And thence discouer, how with most aduantage
> They may vex vs with Shot or with Assault.
> To intercept this inconuenience,
> A Peece of Ordnance 'gainst it haue I plac'd,
>
> First Folio, *Histories* p.99, 11.463-79

Having given instructions to his son to keep watch so that they can shoot any Englishmen who appear, he exits. In this dramatically tense situation with a 'Peece of Ordnance' trained onto it, Talbot and other of the English leaders make their entrance 'on the Turrets', as the stage direction tells us.

> *Enter* Salisbury *and* Talbot *on the Turrets with others*
> *Salisb. Talbot,* my life, my ioy, againe return'd?
> How wert thou handled, being Prisoner?
> Or by what meanes got's thou to be releas'd?
> Discourse I prethee on this Turrets top.
> *Talbot.* The Earle of Bedford had a Prisoner,
> Call'd the braue Lord *Ponton de Santrayle,*
> For him was I exchang'd, and ransom'd.
> But with a baser man of Armes by farre,
> Once in contempt they would haue barter'd me:
> Which I disdaining, scorn'd, and craued death,
> Rather then I would be so pil'd esteem'd:
> In fine, redeem'd I was as I desir'd.

But O, the trecherous *Falstaffe* wounds my heart,
Whom with my bare fists I would execute,
If I now had him brought into my power.
    Salisb. Yet tell'st thou not, how thou wert entertain'd.
Tal. With scoffes and scornes, and contumelious taunts,
In open Market-place produc't they me,
To be a publique spectacle to all:
Here, sayd they, is the Terror of the French,
The Scar-Crow that affrights our Children so.
Then broke I from the Officers that led me,
And with my nayles digg'd stones out of the ground,
To hurle at the beholders of my shame.
My grisly countenance made others flye,
None durst come neere, for feare of suddaine death.
In Iron Walls they deem'd me not secure:
So great feare of my Name 'mongst them were spread,
That they suppos'd I could rend Barres of Steele,
And spurne in pieces Posts of Adamant.
Wherefore a guard of chosen Shot I had,
That walkt about me euery Minute while:
And if I did but stirre out of my Bed,
Ready they were to shoot me to the heart.
        Enter the Boy with a Linstock
    Salisb. I grieue to heare what torments you endur'd,
But we will be reueng'd sufficiently.
Now it is Supper time in Orleance:
Here, through this Grate, I count each one,
And view the Frenchmen how they fortifie:
Let vs looke in, the sight will much delight thee:
Sir *Thomas Gargraue*, and Sir *William Glansdale*,
Let me haue your expresse opinions,
Where is best place to make our Batt'ry next?
    Gargraue. I thinke at the North Gate, for there stands Lords.
    Glansdale. And I heere, at the Bulwarke of the Bridge.
    Talb. For ought I see, this Citie must be famisht,
Or with light Skirmishes enfeebled.
        Here they sho[o]t and Salisbury *falls downe.*
    Salisb. O Lord haue mercy on vs, wretched sinners.
    Gargraue. O Lord haue mercy on me, wofull man.
    Talb. What chance is this, that suddenly hath crost vs?

246

Speake *Salisbury*; at least, if thou canst, speake:
How far'st thou, Mirror of all Martiall men?
One of thy Eyes, and thy Cheekes side struck off?
Accursed Tower, accursed fatall Hand,
That hath contriu'd this wofull Tragedie.
In thirteene Battailes, *Salisbury* o'recame:
Henry the Fift he first trayn'd to the Warres,
Whil'st any Trumpe did sound, or Drum struck vp,
His Sword did ne're leaue striking in the field.
Yet liu'st thou *Salisbury*? though thy speech doth fayle,
One Eye thou hast to looke to Heauen for grace.
The Sunne with one Eye vieweth all the World.
Heauen be thou gracious to none aliue,
If *Salisbury* wants mercy at thy hands.
Beare hence his Body, I will helpe to bury it.
Sir *Thomas Gargraue*, hast thou any life?
Speake vnto *Talbot*, nay, looke vp to him.
Salisbury cheare thy Spirit with this comfort,
Thou shalt not dye whiles –
He beckens with his hand, and smiles on me:
As who would say, When I am dead and gone,
Remember to auenge me on the French.
Plantaginet I will, and like thee, [Nero]
Play on the Lute, beholding the Townes burne:
Wretched shall France be onely in my Name.
            Here an Alarum, and it Thunders and Lightens.
What stirre is this? what tumult's in the Heauens?
Whence cometh this Alarum, and the noyse?
            Enter a Messenger
    Mess. My Lord, my Lord, the French haue gather'd head.
The Dolphin, with one *Ioane de Puzel* ioyn'd,
A holy Prophetesse, new risen vp,
Is come with a great Power, to rayse the Siege.
            Here Salisbury *lifteth himselfe vp and groanes*
    Talb. Heare, heare, how dying *Salisbury* doth groane
It irkes his heart he cannot be reueng'd.
Frenchmen, Ile be a *Salisbury* to you.
Puzel or *Pussel*, Dolphin or Dog-fish,
Your hearts Ile stampe out with my Horses heeles,
And make a Quagmire of your mingled braines.

Conuey me *Salisbury* into his Tent,
And then wee'le try what these dastard Frenchmen dare.
Alarum. Exeunt.

The first Part of Henry the Sixt, I, iv. 11.489-585
First Folio. Histories pp.99-100

Note that there was a blank left in the Folio text where editors have inserted [Nero] as though whoever was writing this scene could not recall the name of – ? who was it? – some Roman emperor or other, and intended to ask one of the other dramatists to fill it in later. This lacuna in the text is surely a significant pointer to the author of this crude scene. It seems highly doubtful that it could have been written by a university educated man, though certainly by one who knew a great deal about the theatrical tricks that go to achieving dramatic impact, as demonstrated by Dr Gaw in his reconstruction of the scene in performance which is quoted below.

This then is the first scene that 'features' the new turret simultaneously with the first entrance of the hero, Talbot. The novelty of all this no doubt obscured the banality of the writing in this scene from its fascinated Elizabethan audience, but seen on the printed page we cannot fail to be struck by the exaggerated histrionics it exhibits. Only expert production can present this to a modern audience without raising a guffaw.* Surely Marlowe (or Shakespeare) never wrote anything as bad as this! The authorial responsibility for this scene is discussed later, but here we first examine Dr Gaw's suggestion that this play was *especially commissioned to feature the Rose's new turret*. This is how he interprets the staging of this scene.

'In the scene as written, I. iv, the Master Gunner and the Boy first place the piece of ordnance on the extreme front of the stage and explain its purpose, thus creating dramatic tension. Salisbury, Talbot, Gargrave, and Glansdale then appear, probably on the turret platform in the DeWitt sketch. For the benefit of the audience Salisbury immediately identifies Talbot, inquires concerning his release from captivity, and calls attention to their (theatrically) novel position: *Discourse I prethee on this Turrets [not Towers] top*. Through eighteen lines Talbot complies, the tension of the audience increasing in the presence of the loaded cannon and the unsuspecting victims. On Talbot's line, *Ready they were to shoot me to the heart*, the Boy

*This scene is heavily cut in modern productions.

enters below with the lighted fuse. The actors above probably here enter the turret itself and appear at the window, looking through this narrow *secret Grate*. They are then facing generally east from the westerly located stage. They briefly consult as to the best method of attack on the city. From the stage level the fatal shot is fired, being probably aimed somewhat high. The hero is spared, but Salisbury and Gargrave fall below the level of the turret window. Talbot describes in some detail their wounds and actions, which are invisible to the audience; refers in his promise of revenge, to the one-eyed sun, then prominent in the southern heavens; and likens himself to Nero, who from a similar height had *Play[ed] on the Lute, beholding the Townes burne.* At the entering Messenger's tale of French success Salisbury, who while hidden has roughly changed his make-up, *lifteth himselfe up* to the window again, *and groanes*: and Talbot, for the benefit of the pit below, identifies the now blood-bespattered face fleetingly seen at the aperture: *Heare, heare, how dying Salisbury doth groane,* and with a climactic threat closes the scene.'[8]

Gaw adds:

'There is no possibility that this is an interpolation. It is the carefully prepared entrance of the hero. In literary style it is among the crudest scenes in the play, and it utterly lacks any trace of revision. It is certainly of the original stuff of *harey the vj*.'[9]

A further interesting observation merits quotation:

'In reply to Salisbury's question, *Where is best place to make our Batt'ry next?* Gargrave answers, *I thinke at the North Gate, for there stands Lords,* i.e. 'Lord's' the headquarters of the Lord General, the citadel; and Glansford, *And I heere, at the Bulwarke of the Bridge.....*Now it certainly seems to be too striking to be a mere coincidence that as the actors stood in the turret of the Rose theatre in the Bankside suburb and looked out of the east window of the turret over the pit and over the theatre wall toward the eastern section of the city, the two most prominent structures before them were the Tower of London and London Bridge, the former, the citadel of London, *there* and the latter *here* just as described in the scene. When we remember the instinctive bent of the Elizabethan theatre toward realism and the delight of the Elizabethan audience in seeing London described under a foreign guise (a delight that Ben Jonson later brilliantly ministered to)....it seems highly probable that, on the mention of the citadel and the bridge, the actors in the turret pointed out over the theatre wall toward the Tower and the Bridge, while the audience, with the sudden thrill of pleasure that always comes in the theatre when more is meant than meets the ear, recognized that their own London was being made to serve as the imagined Orleans of the play. Here again would be an opportunity for an added element of novelty in the use of the turret: and it is certainly worthy of note that *the Rose is the only theatre of London before 1599 that fits the indicated topography.*'[10]

Alleyn's mind as director and planner of both the production and the devising of the play in a way that is tailor-made to suit the renovated theatre is clearly evident in the above reconstruction of the first turret scene, which is set at Orleans, and his hand is equally evident in the second turret scene presenting the taking of Rouen. The sense of his energetic promotion of this theatrical project to achieve this successful coup for the Rose must have endeared him in the eyes of that careful businessman, Henslowe, to whom Alleyn was to ally himself by marriage before the year was out.

In *harey the vj*, in which Marlowe was again turning his hand to the imaginative recreation of history using characters culled from the pages of the *Chronicles*, the part of the hero, Talbot, calls for an energetic, agile actor to represent a valiant soldierly type, but the physical description of him given in the play accords not at all with the physique of the gigantic Alleyn. It would have presented a great opportunity for young Richard Burbage if he were with the company. I suspect that the part Alleyn would have chosen for himself would be that of the proud Cardinal Winchester, whose beard is mentioned pointedly in the text by Gloucester in their quarrel in I, iii:

> Priest, beware your beard,
> I meane to tugge it, and cuffe you soundly.
> First Folio, *Histories*, p.99 11.414-5

Winchester is an important, but not a large part in this play, which would have suited him admirably. Alleyn must have been a very busy man working closely with the dramatists, for the conception of the turret

250

scenes with their complementary text and precise stage-directions, mutually confirming each other, are intrinsic to the Folio play as printed. These were not superimposed. Even the little that has so far been presented of this play has, I suggest, pointed to the inescapable conclusion that it was of multiple authorship. The story of the creation, or perhaps one should rather say of the concoction, and bringing to birth of this curious hybrid piece, as reconstructed by Dr Gaw by his interpretation of the internal evidence of the Folio text is admirably thorough and convincing. The belief that *1 Henry VI* is a composite work written by several playwrights is subscribed to by a galaxy of orthodox scholars:

Sir Sidney Lee, F.G. Fleay, A.W. Ward, Grant White, F.E. Schelling, Barrett Wendell are eminent critics who all place Marlowe's name high among the proposed authors, some favouring also Peele, Lodge, Kyd and especially Greene whose name features prominently though with little consensus on how much of the play could be attributed to him. Dr. A.W. Ward thinks he was mainly responsible, although 'it can hardly be doubted that Marlowe – and perhaps Peele and Lodge – were prominently concerned in this strange, but by no means intrinsically improbable, partnership.'[11] Tucker Brooke and J.Q. Adams head a body of opinion favouring Shakespeare's hand in the play only as the ultimate reviser whose work welded it into the trilogy as the First Part of the *Henry VI* plays.[12] But it was F.G. Fleay alone [13] who undertook the task of a comprehensive study in depth of the text as printed in the First Folio. This proved very revealing, providing a unique basis on which to detect the different hands in the play which has formed the springboard for Dr Gaw's thesis.

It was Fleay's inspired notion to seize upon the curious variations of the spellings of the proper nouns naming the main characters and places in this history which are a peculiarity of the Folio's text.[14] Since the variant of a particular spelling *was adhered to throughout a scene in which the name appeared* he concluded that that scene had been the work of a particular author who favoured this spelling; consequently, he divided the play according to these spelling idiosyncracies which must have been present in the manuscript delivered to the printer of the Folio text, and this represented the *original* manuscript version put together at the time of the first production, to which later interpolations (in revision) had been added without rewriting the whole. Now it may be objected that Elizabethan spelling, even of proper names, was far from consistent, and this is true. Yet if we study the Folio text of this play it is a fact that *scene by scene* there is amazing consistency in the variant spellings used within the play. Printers, used to dealing with a weird and wonderful range of spellings in the manuscripts provided for them to print, were already exhibiting a trend towards a definite form of standardized spelling for many English words in general use, as can be seen in comparing extant manuscripts with printed texts of the period. However, in the case of proper nouns, the printer would accept the author's version of the spelling as being correct and would not alter or 'standardize' it. In this instance, it is an interesting corollary of Fleay's spelling-test-division of the play that it has led to the identification of four distinct authors on the *basis of the stylistic differences* within the scenes thus apportioned.

The division Fleay made on the basis of the Folio's spelling idiosyncracies revealed groupings of scenes which were eminently sensible and coherent if one dramatist were to work on them simultaneously whilst others were writing the rest of the play. For instance, the scenes allocated on the spelling test formula to Author A. proved to include *all* those scenes which deal with the great Gloucester-Winchester rivalry which runs like a thread through the play. And this kind of coherence emerged with all the other spelling-test-divisions. This gave confidence that there was validity in pursuing this approach. Here are the divisions for the four groupings as made on this basis:

Spelling idiosyncracies

Author A. uses: *Gloster* (Gloucester by others: (and always dissyllabic, never trisyllabic) *Reynold* (Reignier or Reigneir by others) *Roan* (dissyllabic, whereas monosyllabic by others)

Author B. uses: *Gloucester* (once as Glocester which may be a misprint) *Reignier* (occasionally Reigneir) *Joane de Puzel* (Pucell by others)

Author C. uses: *Burgonie* (Burgundy or Burgundie by others) *Pucelle* (Puzel in Author B) *Joane* (Jone in Author D) *Roan* (as a monosyllable)

Author D. uses: *Gloucester* (invariably) *Reignier* (never Reigneir as in B) *Jone* (Joane in B. and C.)

Dr Gaw comments:

'One of the chief bases for this division, that of the spelling of certain proper names, is, as here employed, more or less mechanical; but for that reason it is all the more valuable, both as in general the result of the automatic operation of fixed spelling habits in the writer, and as not so liable to subjective errors of interpretation due

SUMMARY OF THE AUTHORSHIP OF
THE SCENES OF 1 HENRY VI

Folio Scene Division	Modern Scene Division	Contents of Scenes	Author in harey the vj	Shakespeare's participation
ACT I				
Sc. i (a)	I, i	Funeral of Henry V at London; Gloucester and Winchester quarrel; news of French revolt; news of capture of Talbot	Marlowe	
(b)	I, ii	Joan of Arc meets the Dauphin near Orleans	B	Slight additions
(c)	I, iii	Gloucester and Winchester quarrel before the Tower of London	Marlowe & B	
(d)	I, iv	Talbot and Salisbury on Orleans turret; Talbot swears to avenge Salisbury	B*	
(e, f)	I, v-vi	Joan and the French take Orleans	B*	
ACT II				
Sc. i (a, b)	II, i-ii	The English recapture Orleans	B	
(c)	II, iii	Talbot foils the Countess of Auvergne	B	
(d)	II, iv	York and Somerset quarrel in Rose Garden		Entirely new
(e)	II, v	Mortimer death scene	Marlowe	
ACT III				
Sc i (a)	III, i	Gloucester accuses Winchester before King	Marlowe	Ll. 1-40
(b)		York is restored to his rank	Marlowe	
(c)		Exeter's first soliloquy	Marlowe	
Sc. ii	III, ii	Joan's strategem and the torch in the turret; the French take Rouen; the English recapture it; Bedford dies	C	Ll. 50-56?
Sc. iii	III, iii	Joan wins Duke of Burgundy back to France	C	
Sc. iv (a)	III, iv	Talbot is made Earl by the King in Paris	B	
(b)		Vernon and Basset quarrel in behalf of York and Somerset	Marlowe	
ACT IV				
Sc. i (a)	IV, i	The King is crowned at Paris; Talbot tears the garter from the knee of Fastolfe	B	
(b)		York and Somerset resume quarrel of Vernon and Bassett; King reproves them	Marlowe	Largely rewritten
(c)		Exeter's second soliloquy	Marlowe	
(d)	IV, ii	Talbot's army trapped near Bordeaux	Peele	Largely rewritten
(e)	IV, iii	Messenger appeals to York to aid Talbot	Peele	Interpolations
(f)	IV, iv	Lucy and Captain appeal to Somerset	Peele	Rewritten
(g,h)	IV, v-vi	Talbot and his son in battle	Peele	
(i)	IV, vii (1 - 50)	Talbot and his son slain	Peele	Rewritten
(j)	IV, vii (51 - 96)	Lucy recovers Talbot's body; he eulogizes Talbot to the French	Peele	Interpolations
Sc. ii	V, i	Gloucester gains King's consent to peace and betrothal to daughter of Earl of Armagnac; Exeter's third soliloquy; Winchester pays Pope for Cardinalship	Marlowe	
Sc. iii (a)	V, ii	French army intercepted by English	Peele	
(b)	V, iii (1 - 44)	Joan conjures; is captured by enemy	Peele	
(c)	V, iii (45 - 195)	Suffolk woos Margaret of Anjou for the King		Entirely new
(d)	V, iv	Joan condemned to the stake	Peele	Ll 36 - 54
(e)		Winchester for England concludes peace	Peele	
ACT V				
	V, v	Suffolk induces King to wed Margaret		Added. Not by Shakespeare

* B's part taken over by C responsible for second Turret scene (My suggestion).

to the personal equation of the investigator. Although largely ignored by commentators since Fleay's discovery of them, these points must be accorded the consideration they deserve.'[15]

Dr Gaw took Fleay's spelling formula as his own basis of investigation and developed his thesis from this stand-point, Fleay having left the work incompleted. After checking Fleay's original approach he found that:

'. . . differences of spelling in the cases of certain proper names are so distributed and vary so consistently in accord with the content and literary traits of the passages in which the variants occur as to make it impossible that they should originate either with play-house transcribers or with printing-house compositors, but are explicable only on a basis of differences in authorial manuscript.'[16]

As we shall see it was remarkable to find how closely the authorial styles on investigation bore out the correctness of this division. Here reprinted is Dr Gaw's table analysing the scene divisions, the authorial ascriptions, and the eventual revisions in the First Folio text which were additional to the original *harey the vj* and must have been carried out at some time after the other two history plays on Henry VI (*The Contention* and *The True Tragedy*) had been acquired from the Pembroke company to whom they originally belonged.

Authorship and Scene Division

As will be seen in the Table of Authorship and Scene-Division, the part allocated to Author A. starts with its powerful opening scene, which marks A. as the main plotter of the whole play. Dr Gaw comments:

'The opening scene of *1 Henry VI* is a studied preparation for the various elements in the ensuing play, combining with the outbreak of the Gloucester-Winchester dispute a vivid relation of the capture by the French of the heroic Talbot, together with an adroit hint foreshadowing the sorcery of Joan of Arc. It shows a realization of the power of detailed climax found, I believe, nowhere as in Marlowe among the pre-Shakespeareans.'[17]

Thus Marlowe's hand is immediately detectable in A. as the chief dramatist.

254

The play opens with the Funeral of Henry V, and the first speech from Bedford confirms our suspicion that this must indeed be from Marlowe's pen.

> *Bedford.*
> Hung be ye heauens with black, yield day to night;
> Comets importing change of Times and States,
> Brandish your crystall Tresses in the Skie,
> And with them scourge the bad reuolting Stars,
> That haue consented vnto *Henries* death:
> King *Henry* the Fift, too famous to liue long,
> England ne're lost a King of so much worth.
>
> *First Folio, Histories*, p.96 11.9-15

Echoes of Tamburlaine's magnificent elegy on the death of Zenocrate immediately sound in our ears:

> Black is the beauty of the brightest day;
> The golden ball of heaven's eternal fire,
> That danc'd with glory on the silver waves,
> Now wants the fuel that inflam'd his beams;
> And all with faintness, and for foul disgrace,
> He binds his temples with a frowning cloud
> Ready to darken earth with endless night.
>
> *The Second Part of Tamburlaine the Great*, II, iv 11.1-7

Dr Gaw comments:

'In this brief scene of 137 lines we have ten echoes from Marlowe's *Tamburlaine, Contention, True Tragedy, Edward II, Jew of Malta*, and *Lucan* – five dramatic works and one non-dramatic, the last not intended for oral delivery and not even registered for printing until September 28, 1593. The mind of the man who wrote the scene was permeated with the style, thought, and tricks of phraseology of Marlowe. Its metrics, too, are his: 2.1 per cent of feminine endings, and 13.2 per cent of pyrrhic final feet.'[18]

Marlowe as Author A. is further supported by the choice of themes in the play allocated to him.

'The Gloucester-Winchester passages immediately suggest Marlowe, all of whose greatest works emphasize a central study of some form of ambitious egotism. Conquest, magic, wealth, royal flattery, wholesale murder, are simply means by which Tamburlaine, Faustus, Barabas, Gaveston, and the Duke of Guise respectively satisfy their craving for dominance. Winchester is but another of their tribe. Further, Marlowe's mature dramas except *Edward II* tend to inveigh against, not Christianity, but the non-Christian conduct of its professors. Here the spirit of passages in *2 Tamburlaine*, *The Jew of Malta*, and *The Massacre at Paris*, again flames out in Gloucester's attack on the Cardinal.'[19]

Worldly ambition is the motivating force of Winchester's character as A. portrays him. It is his hypocrisy that Gloucester detests and the play has barely begun when the first taunt is flung:

> *Gloster.*
> Name not Religion, for thou lou'st the Flesh,
> And ne're throughout the yeere to Church thou go'st,
> Except it be to pray against thy foes.
>
> 11. 50-2

and a little later in a dramatic confrontation –

> Thou that giu'st Whores Indulgences to sinne,
>
> 1. 401

and again –

> Presumptuous Priest . . . .
> No Prelate, such is thy audacious wickednesse,
> Thy lewd, pestiferous, and dissentious prancks,
> As very infants prattle of thy pride.
> Thou art a most pernitious Vsurer,
> Froward by nature, Enemie to Peace,
> Lasciuious, wanton, more then well beseemes
> A man of thy Profession, and Degree.
>
> First Folio, *Histories*, p.105, 11.1212-24

These views are essentially Marlowe's, which he expresses again and again through the mouths of the characters in his plays. For him ignorance and hypocrisy were the two deadliest sins, and his iconoclasm was the expression of his revolt against them. As Dr Gaw has commented, the appeal of the theme offered by the historical characters and events of the early part of this reign made it a natural choice:

'And to what material would Marlowe most naturally turn but to a period of English history in which he had recently in imagination been living, and in which some of his most recent successes had been made? And in the course of the collaboration what characters and scenes would he most naturally choose to develop as his part of the work but those of the "Proud Cardinall of Winchester", whose "Tragicall end" is featured on the title-page of the *Contention*, and the dominant Duke of York, the advertising power of whose name was so great that it gave the title to the *True Tragedy*, although the Duke himself dies before the play is one-quarter finished?'[20]

Dr Gaw remarks on a typically Marlowan touch in A.'s dramatic technique which is found in five of the scenes allocated to his hand. These scenes all end with –

'the emptying of the stage of all the characters but one, who then utters a significant soliloquy. This technique is employed in the play *1 Henry VI* only in the A. scenes.'[21]

He examines in great detail the scene depicting the death of Mortimer, which previous scholars had assigned to Shakespeare's hand as an interpolation in what they have otherwise accepted as a collaborative play. Analysing the versification Dr Gaw found that 'the metrical peculiarities incline heavily on the side of Marlowe...Highly significant, too, is the use in the scene of the verbal ending *-ed* abnormally pronounced as a separate syllable for the sake of the metre', which is more common in Marlowe than in Shakespeare; 'the characteristic echoes of idea and phrase', and 'the dramatic technique strongly confirms all this evidence assigning it to Marlowe.'[22]

> *Enter* Mortimer, *brought in a Chayre, and Iaylors*
> *Mort.* Kind Keepers of my weake decaying Age,
> Let dying *Mortimer* here rest himselfe.
> Euen like a man new haled from the Wrack,
> So fare my Limbes with long Imprisonment;
> And these gray Locks, the Pursuiuants of death
> *Nestor*-like aged, in an Age of Care,

Argue the end of *Edmund Mortimer.*
These Eyes, like Lampes, whose wasting Oyle is spent,
Waxe dimme, as drawing to their Exigent.
Weake Shoulders, ouer-borne with burthening Griefe,
And pyth-lesse Armes, like to a withered Vine,
That droupes his sappe-lesse Branches to the ground.
Yet are these Feet, whose strength-lesse stay is numme,
(Vnable to support this Lumpe of Clay)
Swift-winged with desire to get a Graue,
As witting I no other comfort haue.
But tell me, Keeper, will my Nephew come?
　　　　Keeper. Richard Plantagenet, my Lord, will come:
We sent vnto the Temple, vnto his Chamber,
And answer was return'd, that he will come.
　　　　Mort. Enough: my Soule shall then be satisfied.
Poore Gentleman, his wrong doth equall mine.
Since *Henry Monmouth* first began to reigne,
Before whose Glory I was great in Armes,
This loathsome sequestration haue I had;
And euen since then, hath *Richard* beene obscur'd,
Depriu'd of Honor and Inheritance,
But now, the Arbitrator of Despaires,
Iust Death, kinde Vmpire of mens miserie,
With sweet enlargement doth dismisse me hence:
　　　　　　11. 1071-1100

Richard comes and receives long conference and advice, in which the
dying Mortimer recounts the history of former reigns and reminds Richard
of his royal lineage, concluding –

　　　　　　Thus the *Mortimers*
In whom the Title rested, were supprest.
　　　　Rich. Of which, my Lord, your Honor is the last.
　　　　Mort. True; and thou seest, that I no Issue haue,
And that my fainting words doe warrant death:
Thou art my Heire; the rest, I wish thee gather:
But yet be wary in thy studious care.
　　　　Rich. Thy graue admonishments preuayle with me:
But yet me thinkes, my Fathers execution
Was nothing lesse then bloody Tyranny.

Mort. With silence, Nephew, be thou pollitick,
Strong fixed is the House of *Lancaster,*
And like a Mountaine, not to be remou'd.
But now thy Vnckle is remouing hence,
As Princes doe their Courts, when they are cloy'd
With long continuance in a settled place.

11. 1162-77

With few more words Mortimer dies, and Richard ends the scene with a soliloquy, a kind of obsequy spoken over the dead body of his Uncle.

Rich. And Peace, no Warre, befall thy parting Soule.
In Prison hast thou spent a Pilgrimage,
And like a Hermite ouer-past thy dayes.
Well, I will locke his Councell in my Brest,
And what I doe imagine, let that rest.
Keepers conuey him hence, and I my selfe
Will see his Buryall better than his Life.
Here dyes the duskie Torch of *Mortimer,*
Choakt with Ambition of the meaner sort.
And for those Wrongs, those bitter Iniuries,
Which *Somerset* hath offer'd to my House
I doubt not, but with Honor to redresse.
And therefore haste I to the Parliament,
Eyther to be restored to my Blood,
Or make my will th'aduantage of my good. *Exit.*

The first Part of Henry the Sixt, V,v. 11.1186-1200
First Folio, *Histories,* pp. 104-5

Many of the stylistic traits referred to can be seen in this excerpt. These mark it clearly as part of the original work of Marlowe. Dr Gaw claims that none of this represents later revision by Shakespeare, the entire scene being strongly characteristic of Marlowe. He sums up:

'In view, therefore, of the dramaturgic necessity for such a scene in the original version; the adequacy of the dramatic technique of V, v, old-fashioned as it is, for the purpose; the lack of any indication that this is a rewriting of an earlier form or that it contains interpolated material; the facts that it is echoed in the succeeding original scene, and that it contains irremovably embedded within itself the kernel

259

of later expansion into II, iv;...and its strongly Marlowan and absolutely un-Shakespearean metrics; – it seems to be impossible to avoid the conclusion that the scene is a part of Marlowe's original contribution to the play, written on a somewhat higher poetic level than the subject matter of *1 Henry VI* in general inspired in him.'[23]

In more ways than one *harey the vj* bears out the evidence of its circumstantial birth – in haste to meet a present urgent need.

'...the play bears many evidences of haste. In the first place it is without doubt the work of many hands, and a man like Marlowe, who...had a prominent part in it, and whose great works are strictly individual compositions, does not turn over a large part of a play to several collaborators unless pressed for time...There are, too, a number of irreconcilable inconsistencies in the play, betraying work delivered before it had been matured.'[24]

The 'irreconcilable inconsistencies' will be more in evidence when we examine the work of the other collaborators than in Marlowe's, for he was ever the professional. In this play there is no doubt that his was the guiding hand. But the haste and fragmentation of the play must have affected him, for Dr Gaw remarks that the scenes in his part 'are by no means wholly typical of Marlowe at his best. They lack the poetic élan that we usually expect to find in him – he probably viewed the drama in general as a hurried hack order and could not fully rise to it.'[25]

I have not dealt with the analysis of versification in presenting the case of Author A. to which Dr Gaw pays meticulous attention in making his authorial identification, because I have felt that matters of prosody can be misleading when presented in brief, as here when condensing the findings of another's major work. Nevertheless, to conclude the case for Marlowe, Dr Gaw has established that for those scenes given to Author A. 'in 452 lines out of the total of 939, the metrical criteria ... are wholly harmonious with the theory of Marlowe's authorship'.[26]

Such brief cullings as I have given do not do justice to Dr Gaw's detailed scene-by-scene examination of the text ascribed to the hand of Author A. but it is neither possible nor appropriate to give a fuller review here for Dr Gaw's book is the source to which the interested reader should turn.

Who then were the other men to whom Marlowe and Alleyn turned for help on this urgent task? We examine next the case for *Author D*, as his is a relatively uncomplicated matter involving the tying up of all the ends in the play. He has the end of the Talbot story, the end of the Joan story, and the end of the play as it was originally written concluding with the declaration of 'a solemne peace' between England and France (Henry's marriage to Margaret of Anjou being added in revision).

D.'s part includes the famous Talbot death scene, so praised by Nashe. In this he dies together with his young son, who had joined him in France merely to receive a training in arms, but valiantly insists on fighting in the war by his father's side. D. writes in rhyming couplets, instead of blank verse, which adds to the mawkishness of this passage. Gaw finds the couplets with their 'stichomythic lachrymose whine'[27] to be absolutely unlike the style of Shakespeare, or of Marlowe for that matter, but the audiences loved this weepy scene and it was left untouched by the revisionist, having proved its popular appeal – as testified by Nashe.

> *Alarums. Excursions. Enter old* Talbot *led.*
> *Talb.* Where is my other Life? mine owne is gone.
> O, where's young *Talbot*? where is valiant *Iohn*?
> Triumphant Death, smear'd with Captiuitie,
> Young *Talbots* Valour makes me smile at thee.
> When he perceiu'd me shrinke, and on my Knee,
> His bloodie Sword he brandisht over mee,
> And like a hungry Lyon did commence
> Rough deeds of Rage, and sterne Impatience:
> But when my angry Guardant stood alone,
> Tendring my ruine, and assayl'd of none,
> Dizzie-ey'd Furie, and great rage of Heart,
> Suddenly made him from my side to start
> Into the clustring Battaile of the French:
> And in that Sea of Blood, my Boy did drench
> His over-mounting Spirit; and there di'de
> My *Icarus*, my Blossome, in his pride.
> > *Enter with* Iohn Talbot, *borne.*
> > *Serv.* O my deare Lord, loe where your Sonne is borne.
> > *Tal.* Thou antique Death, which laugh'st vs here to scorn,
> Anon from thy insulting Tyrannie,
> Coupled in bonds of perpetuitie,
> Two *Talbots* winged through the lither Skie,
> In thy despight shall scape Mortalitie.
> O thou whose wounds become hard fauoured death,

Speake to thy father, ere thou yeeld thy breath,
Braue death by speaking, whither he will or no:
Imagine him a Frenchman, and thy Foe.
Poore Boy, he smiles, me thinkes, as who should say,
Had Death bene French, then Death had dyed to day.
Come, come, and lay him in his Fathers armes,
My spirit can no longer beare these harmes.
Souldiers adieu: I haue what I would haue,
Now my old armes are yong *Iohn Talbots* graue."   *Dyes*

First Folio, *Histories*, pp.113-4, 11.2230-63

Apart from his favoured adoption of couplets D is differentiated in that he uses not Holinshed's *Chronicles*, but Halle as his historical source. He over-emphasises Talbot's age, though this is perhaps dramatically valid here as contrast to his son's youth – whereas elsewhere Talbot is presented as the virile, energetic leader and daring hero-soldier. But his treatment of Joan presents the most extraordinary contradiction of characterization in the play, and is inexplicable *unless this is assessed as the work of different hands*. D's part has the responsibility for dealing with Joan's capture and death.

'It is here that the unforgivable insult (far in excess of any foundation in their sources in the Chronicles) is offered to the memory of the Maid of France. She is shown actually begging aid of invisible Fiends whom, according to her statement she "had been wont to feed...with [her] blood" and she mingles her pleas with offers of unchastity:

My body shall
Pay recompense, if you will graunt my suite

while in V,iv, she repeatedly denies her father, mendaciously vaunts noble birth, lies concerning her sorcery, claims exemption from the stake on the grounds of pregnancy with the assignment successively to Charles, Alencon, and Reignier of the illicit fatherhood of her unborn child, and finally passes to her doom cursing her captors and cursed by them. *Except for a moment of elevation in Joan's defence* these scenes, like all of the D passages, are, from a literary point of view, at best mediocre."[28] [My italics]

Significantly, Gaw points out – regarding the above italicized passage –

'The one touch of elevation given to Joan, lines 32-35, contradicts the other parts of the scene.......in putting into her mouth a defence in exalted language of her chastity and her heaven-sent power, and a scathing rebuke of her persecutors as

> polluted with your lustes,
> Stain'd with the guiltless blood of Innocents,
> Corrupt and tainted with a thousand Vices,

the whole in such elevated mood and with such dramatic power (both far above D's level elsewhere) as curiously to defeat the obvious dramatic intention of the scene by rewinning our admiration for the character whom D intended to make repulsive. An examination of the metrics of the passage unmistakably confirms the suspicion aroused by its superiority and by its incongruity with its surroundings. The 22.2 per cent of feminine endings in these lines, as compared with 5.5 per cent in the remainder of the scene, marks this as an interpolation by Shakespeare."[29]

This is clear evidence of the hybrid nature of the play.

Who was D.? Dr Gaw finds no difficulty in identifying him. After having meticulously examined the style, the versification, the use of classical allusion (marking him as a university educated man), and a certain tendency to the use of archaisms such as *wot* (*God wot*; *We English warriors wot*) which he states is 'a favorite with Peele',[30] he comes down firmly in favour of George Peele, an older member of the University Wits who was more especially a friend of Marlowe's than he was of Greene or Nashe. Dr Gaw concludes his assessment of D thus:

'After a careful comparison of D.'s work with that of Peele most closely analogous to it, I have not a shadow of doubt that D. was Peele.'[31]

Peele would doubtless have been glad to participate in this rush assignment for he was chronically short of money, and he was well known to Alleyn for his *Battle of Alcazar* was already in Alleyn's repertoire at the Rose.

Author B. His part of the play consists of the Talbot scenes dealing with the siege, relief and final capture of Orleans; his visit to the Countess of Auvergne; his elevation to the rank of Earl; and his denunciation of Falstaffe at the coronation of the King: all these forming a 'homogeneous

263

series of 508 lines, with no indication of rewriting or interpolation'[32] – that is, by Shakespeare. Author B. uses Holinshed as his source, and although he invents freely 'when necessary', he follows his historic source more closely than A. or C. or D. sometimes even borrowing Holinshed's phraseology; but his research was limited, not wide like Marlowe's, who had already written *The True Tragedy* and knew that Henry was only a babe in arms of nine months when his father died and he inherited the crown, of which fact B. is unaware when he gives Henry the lines in greeting Talbot, for here he makes a historical gaff which it is quite unnecessary to slip into the speech:

> When I was young, (as yet I am not old)
> I doe remember how my Father said
> A stouter Champion never handled Sword.
>
> First Folio, *Histories*, p.109, III, iv. 11.1709-11

Dr Gaw makes the point that young King Henry in this play must originally have been played by a boy, which later caused some difficulty when his marriage to Margaret was interpolated into the play in revision, in order to link it with *The first Part of the Contention*, which is another story.

Author B. remarks Dr Gaw, is notable for his 'love of learned allusions' which is a characteristic of that 'Maister of Arts of two Universities', Robert Greene, who loved to make a show of his erudition. He mentions:

> ' "Astraea's Daughter", "Adonis' garden", "Rhodope", and the "rich jewell'd coffer of Darius",... "Mars in his true moving",... "the nine Sibyls", "Debora", "Caesar" in a reference to a story from Plutarch, "Mahomet", "Helen, the mother of Constantine", and "St. Philip's daughters", as well as a quotation (in *oratio obliqua*) from Froissart, associated with mention of "Samsons and Goliasses" ' [33].

Many of these classical allusions appear in the speeches in praise of Joan of Arc, B.'s *Puzel*, which Gaw has pointed out are in his most elevated style.'

Greene's biographer, J.C. Jordan, remarks of Greene's variably successful dramatic works that his finest moments are always in the handling of women, his most credible and charming creations being such characters as Margaret in *Friar Bacon*, and contributing not a little to that play's success. Jordan comments on another characteristic of Greene's works, that he has the ability to blow the fresh air of the countryside through his pages;[34] pastorals not tragedies were his scene, and this, too, is apparent in B's introduction of Joan at the court of the Dauphin, here called the Dolphin.

264

Puzel. Dolphin, I am by birth a Shepheards Daughter,
My wit untrayn'd in any kind of Art:
Heauen and our Lady gracious hath it pleas'd
To shine on my contemptible estate,
Loe, whilest I wayted on my tender Lambes,
And to Sunnes parching heat display'd my cheekes,
Gods Mother deigned to appeare to me,
And in a Vision full of Maiestie,
Will'd me to leaue my base Vocation,
And free my Countrey from Calamitie:
Her Ayde she promis'd, and assur'd successe.
In compleat Glory shee reveal'd her selfe:
And whereas I was black and swart before,
With those cleare Rayes, which shee infus'd on me,
That beautie am I blest with, which you may see.
Aske me what question thou canst possible,
And I will answer vnpremeditated:
My Courage trie by Combat, if thou dar'st,
And thou shalt finde that I exceed my Sex.
Resolue on this, thou shalt be fortunate,
If thou receiue me for thy Warlike Mate.

First Folio, *Histories*, p.98, I.ii. 11.274-94

Greene was too vain, self-indulgent and selfish to be capable of deep emotional attachment, but women were indispensable to him in real life and his interest in them is reflected in his literary and dramatic works. Drunkenness and lack of money made his own life sordid, but he compensated by idealizing and romancing, yearning for repentance and better things; imagining himself capable of the true love and loyalty he lacked, he lifts himself to higher levels when his dramatic subject is female. B's treatment of Joan of Arc is similar to that by A. (Marlowe) and in direct contrast to that given her by D. (Peele). Dr Gaw remarks:

'B. rises into really musical eloquence in her praise in the 31 lines of I, vi.'[35]

Like A. the speeches B. puts into the mouth of the Maid of Orleans are 'pure and elevated as to Joan's own language, but eliciting an immediate declaration of love from Charles and sneers from the nobles as to the sexual situation.'[36]

Dr Gaw further notes that 'the dialogue after the entrance of Joan is of higher quality than B. shows himself capable of elsewhere save in I, vi; there is a real elevation of character in the speeches of Joan that is superior to B.'s characterization in other scenes;'[37]

Dr H.D. Gray has remarked that the episode in which Talbot meets the Countess of Auvergne 'has his [Greene's] characteristic "smartiness" in the turning of the tables'.[38]

Greene's male characters are usually less successful. J.C. Jordan comments that they tend to be representations of types rather than fully realized people, and the portrayal of a forceful male personality to dominate a play was beyond him, as shown in his failure with *Alphonsus King of Arragon* and *Orlando Furioso*, both very weak in the dramatization of the characters of the male title roles. The same criticism applies to B. whose male characters Gaw finds 'show no subtlety of characterization, apparently not comprehending conflict of character in distinction from conflict of action.' Dr Gaw also finds B.'s dramatic technique weak a weakness he shares with Greene, with one exception.

'At only one place does B. show any real knowledge of how to create suspense, namely where in I, iv, at the ominous line

Ready they were to shoot me to the heart

the boy enters with the linstock to the cannon below the turret, and after a pause of thirteen lines fires the shot that kills two of the four English above.'[39]

This, I suggest, is more than mere co-incidence. In this scene Dr Gaw has pinpointed a significant fact, that we have here the *single* instance of a *successfully realized moment of dramatic suspense in B.'s part*, and it is found in the first turret scene which also is the worst written so far as literary merit goes ('among the crudest scenes in the play') and in contrast to the other scenes allocated to B.'s hand exhibits 0.0 per centage of feminine endings compared to B.'s average of 9.1 per cent, which surely suggests that another hand wrote this scene. Whoever wrote the scene was obviously primarily concerned with the *staging of the business* which is carefully thought out to the last detail: how the wounded Gargrave will change his make-up while hidden from view and then rise up again to look through the *secret Grate* to show his blood-bespattered face to the audience, groaning in agony. The writing of the scene is essentially designed to complement this theatrical 'business'. Moreover, the

266

versification is a radical departure from B.'s usual style in being uncharacteristically alliterative *and* repetitive. As we shall see later, it has marked similarity to the writing of Author C. who had responsibility for the second turret scene.

The inference from the timing of this production in the Rose's history, as well as from the internal evidence of the play is that it was designed to feature the theatre's new turret as a 'draw' to bring in the audiences who had so far shown no great interest in crossing over to Bankside for their theatrical entertainment. That it would have been Edward Alleyn who was vitally interested in making striking theatrical use of the turret in the new play is obvious. In comparing the hand of Author C., with the writing of this turret scene in B.'s part we shall see that the similarities in the writing of B.'s turret scene, and Author C.'s turret scene bear out strongly the probability that these two turret scenes are by the same hand, and, as I suggest, that hand was none other's than Edward Alleyn's. The probability is that he interfered in B.'s part to rewrite the turret scene and in doing so he did not trouble to alter B.'s idiosyncratic spelling of *Joane de Puzel* which Dr Gaw has followed as the identification mark of Author B. and has, therefore, in this instance been misled.

Our first consideration is, however, to identify Author B. with as much certainty as possible. Dr Gaw has already extracted many similarities favouring his identification with Robert Greene, and he is supported by F.G. Fleay, the only other commentator to have contributed really significant work on the authorial question to establish this as undoubtedly a collaborative play; and they are by no means alone in rating the name of Greene high among suspected authors, some critics even having attributed the authorship of the whole play to him, though without having studied it in depth. Gaw summarizes his conclusions, adding the following to the points already made:

'The treatment of history by B. is about what might be expected of the author of Greene's pseudo-historical plays if somewhat restrained by collaboration with one used to treating his English sources with some seriousness; and Greene's stage technique is about on a level with that of B. except where he has some special inspiration in romantic atmosphere or essentially feminine interest, neither of which appear in B.'s section of *1 Henry VI* except in the first appearance of Joan of Arc at the French court, where B. likewise rises distinctly above his general level. B.'s rise into a higher poetic atmosphere in I, vi, to end the act, is also very much like Greene's occasional upward vault, and requires something of Greene's power; and the resemblance between Greene and B. in the use of classic allusion is striking. B.'s peculiar sing-song balance with its pivoting of passages on *and*, *or*, and the like, appears strongly at times in Greene, though at other times in the same play it will be entirely absent (as also in B.'s *1 Henry VI*, I, ii); the balanced line of the type, "The fainting army of that foolish king," the percentage of which is 0.5 in the total 703 lines assignable to B. occurs with a percentage of 0.5 in *James IV* and 0.4 in *Friar Bacon*; and B.'s use of the odd phrase and of various then obsolescent compound conjunctions are among Greene's most distinctive traits.'[40]

'All these points argue strongly that B. is Greene,' concludes Gaw. Nevertheless he finds one, to his mind, insuperable difficulty, which prevents him from accepting this identification without reservation, namely, the variation in the percentage of feminine endings, which fluctuates from 0.0 per cent in 27 lines of I, iv, through 12.0, 13.3, 0.8, 9.1 (his average) to 16.6. These are too high for Greene whose average percentages in *Friar Bacon* and *James IV* are only 3.5 and 3.2 respectively. However, I do not find that Dr Gaw has sufficiently taken into account the brevity of the scenes, which always artificially exaggerate the result. Wide fluctuations are shown in his table for Marlowe's part in the play also because the text submitted to the test is of insufficient length. Additionally, in the case of B. no account has been taken – for the reason that Dr Gaw did not consider this possibility – of another hand in the writing of the first turret scene, I, iv. which occurs in B.'s part of the play, and numbers 111 lines. This, together with the brief scene following immediately upon the turret scene, which numbers 39 lines, are, as I hope to show, by another hand than B.'s so that Dr Gaw's claim that B.'s 508 lines are without 'indication of rewriting or interpolation' requires modification. He was rigorously adhering to the spelling test division in making this claim for all the scenes he and Fleay allocate to Author B. and he had only Shakespeare's revision in mind, not the intrusion of another hand.

'In I, iv, v, vi, and II, i, ii, they contain six cases each of the spellings *Ioane* (differentiating B. from D., who spells the name *Ione*) and *Puzel*, (differentiating B. from C. and D., both of whom spell it *Pucell*.) In III, iva, and IV, ia, are three cases of *Glo(u)cester*, the one in dialogue being clearly trisyllabic in scansion (differentiating B. from A. who has only disyllabic *Gloster*) ..... and four cases of *Burgundy* (differentiating B. from C., whose form is *Burgonie*).'[41]

268

As already mentioned briefly, there is evidence for a strong suspicion that the writer of the *two turret scenes* in the play was the fourth man, C. whose style and versification are in marked contrast to all the other three – one cannot place him in the ranks of the University Wits! Allowing for this interpolation, we find that the similarities with Greene's style are *all in those scenes which are unaffected by this removal of part of B.'s supposed contribution*, and his case is immediately strengthened thereby.

Dr Gaw does not mention that Greene's long association with both Alleyn and Marlowe's circle lends added credibility to his involvement in this rush job, though he considers Nashe (tentatively) as a possibility for Author B. on the very grounds of his known association with Marlowe, although in his case this is not supported by long connection with Alleyn as one of the dramatists working for him as Greene was regularly. No other candidate for the identity of B. has any of the necessary characteristics assembled by Dr Gaw in what is an impressive list of concurrences with all we know about Robert Greene, and I have no doubt myself that this collaborator with Marlowe and Peele in the hastily written *harey the vj* was none other than Greene.

Turning now to *Author C.* Dr Gaw remarks:

'*Apparently his first interest was in the second turret scene.*'[42]
[My emphasis].

Only two scenes are allocated to this fourth writer; they are the consecutive III, ii and iii, forming a compact contribution to the play which impinges little on what has gone before or after, but slips neatly into the whole. The character given prominence in these two scenes is Burgundy (whom C. spells *Burgonie*), who had previously played only a very subordinate role in scenes by B. and D.

What is of significance in the history of this play, giving it the format of a collaborative work that makes it unique in the Shakespearean and Marlovian canon, is that it was intimately linked with the re-opening of the Rose, sporting its novel turret, and that the play was required especially to feature this.

Dr Gaw comments regarding Author C.:

'...the exact identity of the author is of little consequence.' [He was no literary genius]. 'The important point is, the facts suggest that after Act IV had been assigned to D., a fourth writer discovered another method of utilizing the turret, and was therefore asked to work it out and to write the following scene, and that he made the most of the scanty material left him. It is a striking fact that as the turret was employed to give a spectacular introduction to B.'s hero, Talbot, so a similar spectacular use was made of it to open the contribution of C.'[43]

Now, who this fourth writer would be, it is almost unnecessary to ask at this point in our investigations. Alleyn, I suggest, took over the writing of B.'s turret scene, when Greene, who was noted for being an extremely rapid writer, completed his part early but had not featured the turret as Alleyn wanted. Alleyn then rewrote this scene, but without altering Greene's spelling of the names. This would explain why there is no trace of Greene's hand in B.'s part relating to the use of the turret. It is entirely plausible to associate Alleyn with the writer who 'discovered another method of utilizing the turret' and 'made the most of the scanty material left to him'. Here is a sample of his writing:

> *Enter* Pucell *disguised, with foure Souldiers with*
> *Sacks vpon their backs.*
> *Pucell.* These are the Citie Gates, the Gates of Roan,
> Through which our Pollicy must make a breach.
> Take heed, be wary how you place your words,
> Talke like the vulgar sort of Market men,
> That come to gather Money for their Corne.
> If we haue entrance, as I hope we shall,
> And that we finde the slouthfull Watch but weake,
> Ile by a signe giue notice to our friends,
> That *Charles* the Dolphin may encounter them.
> *Souldier.* Our Sacks shall be a meane to sack the City,
> And we be Lords and Rulers ouer Roan,
> Therefore wee'le knock.
> > *Knock.*
> *Watch.* Che la.
> *Pucell. Peasauns la pauure gens de France,* *
> Poore Market folkes that come to sell their Corne.
> *Watch.* Enter, goe in, the Market bell is rung.
> *Pucell.* Now Roan, Ile shake thy Bulwarkes to the ground.
> > *Exeunt.*

---

* Marlowe, who grew up in Canterbury where there was a large community of French-speaking Huguenots, would have been able to help Alleyn with this smattering of French.

270

Enter Charles, Bastard, Alanson.

Charles. Saint *Dennis* blesse this happy Stratageme,
And once againe wee'le sleepe secure in Roan.

Bastard. Here entred *Pucell*, and her Practisants:
Now she is there, how will she specifie
Here is the best and safest passage in.

Reig. By thrusting out a Torch from yonder Tower,
Which once discern'd, shewes that her meaning is,
No way to that (for weaknesse) which she entred.

      Enter Pucell *on the top, thrusting out a Torch burning.*

Pucell. Behold, this is the happy Wedding Torch,
That ioyneth Roan vnto her Countreymen,
But burning fatall to the *Talbonites.*

III, ii. 11.1424-1455

Dr Gaw comments: 'his versification is markedly alliterative'.[44] Of alliteration one can find frequent examples elsewhere in the text, for it was widely present in the Elizabethan poetic idiom, but what is singular in C's work is that it is too contrived, forced, even clumsy. C. is no poet. To quote from his two short scenes, III, ii, and iii.

France, thou shalt rue this Treason with thy tears, If *Talbot* but suruiue this Trecherie.	11.1464-5
God morrow Gallants, want ye Corn for Bread?	1. 1471
Foule Fiend of France, and Hag of all despight	1. 1487
Now where's the Bastards braues, and *Charles* his glikes?	1. 1569
Care is no cure, but rather corrosive,	1. 1588
Besides, all French and France exclaims on thee,	1. 1652

But what I have found even more striking is his penchant for repetition of the same word for emphasis, often combined with alliteration, as follows:

These are the Citie Gates, the Gates of Roan,	1. 1424
Looke on thy Country, look on fertile France	1. 1636
See, see the pining Maladie of France; Behold the Wounds, the most unnaturall Wounds, Which thou thy selfe has giuen her wofull Brest.	11. 1641-3

Now these same stylistic traits are markedly present in the first turret scene, also, and in the brief scene immediately following it, which (on the basis of Fleay's spelling test, which Gaw adopts) both come into B.'s part, and which Gaw consequently accepts as being from B.'s hand, for he had no reason to suspect that there had been any interference in his part. The following are taken from I, iv, which is B.'s turret scene.

How far'st thou, Mirror of all Martiall Men?	l. 545
Accursed Tower, accursed fatall Hand,	l. 547
Salisb. O Lord haue mercy on us, wretched sinners.	
Gargraue. O Lord haue mercy on me, wofull man.	ll. 541-2
Speake *Salisbury*: at least, if thou canst speake:	l. 544
Heare, heare, how dying *Salisbury* doth groane.	l. 578

And from the brief scene that follows (of only 39 lines) presenting the skirmish between *Talbot* and the French led by *Ioane* de Puzel, we have:

Here, here shee comes. Ile haue a bowt with thee:	
Deuill, or Deuils Dam, Ile coniure thee.	ll. 594-5
Goe, goe, cheare vp thy hungry-starued men,	l. 611
A Witch by feare, not force, like *Hannibal*,	l. 616
Are from their Hyues and Houses driuen away.	l. 629
For none would strike a stroake in his reuenge.	l. 632

One has the feeling that C. was an admirer of Marlowe's early work, where, as in *Tamburlaine*, alliteration is used poetically, often to beautiful effect. C.'s is but lame imitation, but it seems obvious that it is Marlowe whom he is making a vain effort to emulate. All this is in marked contrast to the next scene which falls into B.'s part by the spelling test division, and to those other scenes in B.'s part from here on. The difference is well demonstrated in this excerpt from I, vi. which is genuine B. *alias* Greene waxing lyrical in praise of a woman, the divinely inspired Joan.

> *Puzel.* Aduance our wauing Colours on the Walls,
> Rescu'd is Orleance from the English.
> Thus *Ioane de Puzel* hath perform'd her word.
> *Dolph.* Diuinest creature, *Astrea's* Daughter,
> How shall I honour thee for this successe?

Thy promises are like *Adonis* Garden,
That one day bloom'd, and fruitfull were the next.
France, triumph in thy glorious Prophetesse,
Recouer'd is the Towne of Orleance,
More blessed hap did ne're befall our State.
    Reigneir. Why ring not out the Bells alowd,
Throughout the Towne?
Dolphin command the Citizens make Bonfires,
And feast and banquet in the open streets,
To celebrate the ioy that God hath giuen vs.
    Alans. All France will be repleat with mirth and ioy,
When they shall heare how we haue play'd the men.
    Dolph. 'Tis *Ioane*, not we, by whom the day is wonne:
For which, I will diuide my Crowne with her,
And all the Priests and Fryers in my Realme,
Shall in procession sing her endlesse prayse.
A statelyer Pyramis to her Ile rear,
Then *Rhodope's* or *Memphis* euer was.
In memorie of her, when she is dead,
Her Ashes, in an Vrne more precious
Then the rich-iewel'd Coffer of *Darius*,
Transported, shall be at high Festiuals
Before the Kings and Queenes of France.
No longer on Saint *Dennis* will we cry,
But *Ioane de Puzel* shall be France's Saint.
Come in, and let vs Banquet Royally,
After this Golden Day of Victorie.
       Flourish   *Exeunt.*
        I, vi, 11. 641-72.

It is a splendid passage which takes its place worthily in a First Folio play, and shows Greene at his best. The contrast between this and what has just preceded is, to my mind, conclusive evidence of the hybrid nature of this play, and of the interference in the part originally allocated to B. in that scene designed to 'feature' the turret, and its pursuivant skirmish. The fact that Dr Gaw has adhered rigorously to the spelling test divisions throughout in his investigation, meant that he necessarily lumped all these scenes together as being from the same pen. It is not surprising, therefore, that whilst he noted marked similarities linking B. with Greene, he also found dissimilarities, and being unable to account for these he finally pronounced his verdict as 'Not proven', albeit suspected.

The dissimilarities in B.'s part to Greene's style, which I have isolated in the turret and skirmish scene following it, are matched by the marked similarities in the second turret scene and its follow-on scene constituting C.'s contribution to this play. The conclusion that C. was therefore responsible for both these turret scenes is not only entirely probable, it seems to be the only conclusion possible; and that he was a man who was particularly interested in making theatrically effective use of the Rose's new turret is self-evident. All this points directly to Alleyn as Author C, – a proper '*Iohannes fac totum*'!

Author C. is in many other ways singular. Dr Gaw summarizes his work as follows:

'C.'s treatment of his sources, too, is distinctive. While none of the other collaborators hesitates to adapt and add to the historical facts freely in order to obtain dramatic effects, no one so extravagantly wrests history as C. Apparently his first interest was in the second turret scene. In order to obtain the effect of the appearance of Joan in the turret with the flaming signal (III, ii, 1-32) he combines details from the English capture of Evreux by stratagem, transferred from the English to the French credit, with the story of the cresset of light at the time of the French capture of Le Mans (in Holinshed twenty-one pages distant), and applies both to a wholly fictitious capture and recapture of Rouen. Again, in order to achieve the pathos of the aged and dying man sitting on a chair on the battlefield to encourage the English troops, he greatly exaggerates the age of Bedford and predates his death by four years, thereby....possibly forcing a later substitution of York for Bedford in the work of D. at V, iv. The change of date, by which the Duke of Burgundy's defection from the English cause in 1435 is made to precede the capture and burning of Joan in 1431, must have been arranged in the original plotting of the play in order to prepare for IV, i, the work of B.; but C. is responsible for the fact that Joan's argument to Burgundy in regard to the capture and release of the Duke of Orleans by the English is the exact reverse of the truth as the Chroniclers give it, although C. was in personal touch with the account, as is evident by his alone using the spelling *Burgo(g)nie* and by his following Halle's chronicle verbally in III, iii, 23-25. It is significant, too, that C. alone seems, in a search for additional material, to have resorted to Fabian and, either directly or indirectly, to Geoffrey of Monmouth. Stylistically, also, C. stands somewhat apart: he makes Joan speak of "*the* Talbot", address the French King and nobles as 'your honors', and use the odd phrase "unto Parisward"; he employs the Latinisms "Talbonites", "extirped", and "expulsed", and "prejudice [i.e. injure] the foe";...and his versification is markedly alliterative.'[45]

The word 'expulsed' is a favourite of Alleyn's which he uses frequently with reference to those of his aged pensioners who misbehaved and forfeited a place in his charitable institution by becoming drunk or fornicating with the aged sisters; and we have already noted that two plays suggested as being from his hand share the stylistic characteristic of being 'markedly alliterative'. All Gaw's findings point us in the same direction, that it is Alleyn's hand that he has here detected.

One may pause here to ask, can there be a reason for the author ransacking for his source material the chronicles of Holinshed, Halle, Fabian and even Geoffrey of Monmouth? Whilst not unique, for Marlowe sometimes ranged widely in his searches, such a method is ideally suited to the collaboration of several writers on the play; but in no other work has his wide reading resulted in discrepancies and inconsistencies of interpretation of his material as here. These inconsistencies do not derive from a wide use of sources, but from the haste with which a collaborative work from several minds was put together.

Dr Gaw sees slight indications of retouching and interpolation in C.'s scenes, but in essence he feels these stand as written by C. Having no comparison to make with a known author's work he is cautious. He asks, 'Who was C? It is difficult to say'. His final comment on Author C. touches the very point of my thesis concerning Edward Alleyn as a minor playwright of his day.

'At the time there were undoubtedly writing for the theatre men whose very names have vanished, as witness many of the plays entered in the early records in Henslowe's *Diary*.'[46]

And so in Dr Gaw's thesis C. fades from our view into the limbo of the forgotten men of the theatre.

That Dr Gaw did not identify C.'s hand in B.'s part is not surprising for he had, so to speak, tied his hands in setting himself a task of identification based on the mechanical, and hence commendably objective, criteria supplied by the variant spellings of names dividing the play. As we saw, this arbitrary division was corroborated in examining the stylistic differences; only in B.'s case was uncertainty cast in Dr Gaw's mind because of what one could call a stylistic wobble, or hiccup, arising from the discrepancies caused by C.'s intrusion into B.'s part, which was masked by the spelling division still adhering to the scene. It is therefore gratifying to find that Dr Gaw's well-tuned ear and sharp mind detected something of this, although he was unable to account for it. He nevertheless associated it with the Talbot scenes.

> 'Even the central thread of the play, the Talbot story, is certainly by more than one writer, as if the original author had discovered that he could not complete his section within the necessary time and had found it necessary to obtain assistance..'[47]

Unwittingly he has hit the nail on the head. This is significant confirmation. Today the Fourth Man, who was collaborator C. on *harey the vj*, has, I suggest, been credibly resurrected in the towering figure of Edward Alleyn, that great actor and theatrical practitioner, who, being a most versatile, enterprising character also turned his hand to playwriting in blank verse.

If this conclusion is correct, it provides us with a tantalizing scenario which exactly mirrors the situation underlying the bitter antagonism, laced with smouldering hatred and a deep sense of injustice, that bursts forth from Greene in his death-bed accusation against the 'vpstart Crow, beautified with our feathers, that with his *Tygers hart wrapt in a Players hyde*, supposes he is as well able to bombast out a blanke verse as the best of you: and beeing an absolute *Iohannes fac totum*, is in his owne conceit the onely Shake-scene in a countrey.'

Can one conceive anything more galling to the vainglorious Greene, who had a high estimation of his own talents as a writer, than to have the upstart actor, Edward Alleyn, step into *his* shoes to take over the writing of a scene in his part of the play? The implication of the *Groatsworth* Letter is moreover that Marlowe and Peele *would know exactly to what circumstance Greene is referring* for they were all writing in collaboration on *harey the vj*. Greene was doubtless working under pressure to get the play finished, with Alleyn urging him on while explaining how he wanted the stage 'business' written into B.'s turret scene so that the audience would understand what was going on, and possibly 'talking down' to the dramatist, – in such a situation one can imagine Greene's resentment and imagine Greene's resentment and irritation boiling up. Matters which Alleyn, as a practising actor, would understand so well are the very things that Greene, essentially a literary man, a writer of fanciful romantic novels for cultured Elizabethan ladies to read rather than by natural inclination a dramatist, would have had little understanding or flair for. Perhaps Alleyn showed impatience with the dramatist, who could not have been in the best of health, for six months later Greene was dead. The red-bearded *Roberto*, one imagines, would not have been slow to anger, but with temper flaring would have exploded, uttering a string of shocking oaths, and perhaps flounced out, leaving Alleyn to write the scene – or, more probably, he rewrote it, without altering the spelling of proper names, putting in all the theatrical business for which the scene is so remarkable, and which Gaw has so perceptively detected and demonstrated in his reconstruction of I, vi. (see pp, 245–249).

The situation would have been ripe for such an outcome. Greene and Alleyn had ever been on a collision course. Alleyn's character was in every way the opposite of Greene's for he was essentially practical, industrious, orthodox, religious and clean living; a man whose fastidiousness in matters of personal and domestic hygiene is reflected in his careful instructions to his wife, his 'good sweett mouse', when they were first married and he was on tour while she was still in plague-infested London, and in his regulations for his College on health, diet and cleanliness. Such a man could but have viewed Robert Greene's profligate life-style and drunken habits with distaste, probably with disgust. Towards the end of his life, at any rate, Greene may not have been clean and neat in his person – Gabriel Harvey tells us that in his last illness he harboured lice, and he disapprovingly mentions Greene's 'ruffianly haire' and his 'vnseemely apparell'.[48] Sympathy for Greene's pleas of poverty would, one feels, have been scant on Alleyn's part. Theirs was a business relationship, and it may be doubted if any love was lost on either side. Loans would have been strictly on a basis of advances on payment for work in progress and not as charitable hand-outs, with penalties for default in repayments. If this were not so, the charge of usury made in the *Groatsworth of Wit* Letter would have been pointless. It is a reasonable assumption, knowing the state of Greene's finances at the end of his life, that he was already in debt to Alleyn, and hence his remuneration for the last work he did for him had probably already been consumed. Such is the implication in the *Groatsworth* accusation.

In the writing of *harey the vj*, if my reading of the evidence is correct, we have the very situation from which that bitter Letter written from the gall of his heart on his death-bed was engendered. If Alleyn took over the writing of his turret scene from Greene, this situation is *precisely* reflected in his most bitter fulminations against the 'vpstart Crow', in which he is giving vent to deeply felt emotions of humiliation, frustration, anger and injustice. His words are a heart-cry! –

> 'Yes trust them not: for there is an vpstart Crow, beautified with our feathers, that with his *Tygers hart wrapt in a Players hyde*, supposes he is as well able to bombast out a blanke verse as the best of you: and beeing an absolute *Iohannes fac totum*, is in his owne conceit the onely Shake-scene in a countrey.'

How deeply mortified Greene would have been at being displaced by this upstart actor who contributed his blank verse to their play on a par with Marlowe and Peele! – this mere Player, who 'supposes he is as well able to bombast out a blank verse as the best of you'!

All that had transpired between Alleyn and Greene over the writing of the turret scene for *harey the vj* he evidently told to Nashe, and it was 'no newes' to the two who were involved with Greene and Alleyn in this drama, and this fact is glanced at in Greene's line: '*now returne I againe to you three, knowing my miserie is to you no newes*'. He is not referring to his illness, – for of that they probably had no knowledge – but to his miserable treatment by Alleyn in this recent collaboration. The insufferable arrogance of this 'vpstart Crow' in taking over Greene's scene! If authors B. and C. had fallen out over the turret scene, then their quarrel would not have been a quiet affair. We know that Alleyn, when roused, had a temper for he had but recently stormed off to join Henslowe after an almighty quarrel with Burbage. Greene was an intemperate man, given to swearing as he himself confesses. It would have been quite a resounding tempest of words that rang through the Rose theatre when these two disagreed!

Is it not echoes of this that are still to be heard in Greene's bitter Letter?

These scenes of personal interplay are conjectural, but then so are the *supposed* contacts between Greene and Shakespeare, and between Shakespeare and the Earl of Pembroke's Men put forward so confidently by Peter Alexander on no shred of evidence to support them. Whereas the relationship between Greene and Alleyn is securely based on the *consistent evidence* of Greene's attitude towards the 'Roscius' of the day in his writings, and on what has been established concerning the personalities, the predilections and the business dealings of Edward Alleyn and Robin Greene. To this is added the evidence of Author C.'s involvement in *harey the vj*, whose prime interest in the turret scenes, and whose style of writing both fit Alleyn exactly. This identification is not wild surmise. It is built on the foundation of literary detection of F.G. Fleay and Allison Gaw; and it brings us full circle to the reason for Greene's anguished Letter, shedding a new light on the circumstances and making that famous epistle fully understandable at last.

As I surmise, the final humiliation for Greene came when he swallowed his pride and turned in his desperate plight to Alleyn for another loan – and was refused. His promises that the cash loan requested would be 'in earnest' of yet another new dramatic work from his pen would have been received with scepticism by Alleyn, for it must have been obvious that Greene was now a sick man, and probably dying. The door was shut in his face in his hour of pitiful need. And the destitute and ailing dramatist paid this tiger-hearted 'vpstart Crow' back in the only coin he had – bitter words in black ink.

That, I suggest, is the real story behind *Roberto* Greene's agonized and envenomed *Groatsworth* Letter, which has for two hundred years been misread and misunderstood. This unfortunate misreading has been the result of treating Greene's famous Letter with blind disregard for its genetic link with the dying author's moralizing, autobiographical tale, so cleverly devised by him to present to his readers the 'Player' who *employs* the university-educated *Roberto* Greene to exploit his talents as his 'Arch-plaimaking poet' and who, moreover, *dared* to presume to 'bombast out a blanke verse as the best of you' – *you* being his 'Quondam acquiantance' so recently engaged in writing *harey the vj* with him, in which the 'Player' rewrote Greene's part to meet his theatrical requirement for featuring the turret. Greene himself leads us by the hand to his goal, carefully identifying for his readers the persons – on the one hand, the hated actor, *Iohannes fac totum*, he is bent on wreaking his revenge upon before he dies; and on the other, his legitimate collaborators in recent dramatic writings, thereby also shedding light on the play, *harey the vj*.

The vital importance of properly understanding Greene's deathbed testimony cannot be overestimated. In taking Greene at his word and following his deliberately pinpointed signposts, it is a matter for rejoicing to find that every aspect of this theatrical history has been illuminated. Gaw's thesis, begun by Fleay and so perceptively concluded by Gaw, falls perfectly into place, finally validated as the historical truth concerning the collaborative authorship of the curiously uneven text of *1 Henry VI*. This has never been explained satisfactorily except by Dr Gaw.

In the light of Gaw's thesis we now know why Greene was *specifically* addressing Marlowe and Peele. To tie up the last piece of evidence that the *Groatsworth* gives us, it is also necessary to identify the collaborative play that Greene tells us he wrote, shortly before his death, with his young friend, Nashe,

'yong Iuuenall, that byting Satyrist, that lastly with mee together writ a Comedie?'

We are seeking a play that must be identifiable with Greene's style, but must at the same time reflect the influence and style of Nashe. Again, it is the admirable work of previous scholars in the field that has effectively prepared the path leading to the identification of the topical, satirical comedy that neatly fits the bill.

A most pleasant and
merie nevv Comedie,

Intituled,

A Knacke to knowe a Knaue.

Newlie set foorth, as it hath sundrie
tymes bene played by ED. ALLEN
and his Companie.

VVith K E M P S applauded Merrimentes
of the men of Goteham, in receiuing
the King into Goteham.

Imprinted at London by Richard Iones, dwelling
at the signe of the Rose and Crowne, nere
Holborne bridge. 1594.

IX *Greene's Last Comedy*

THE PLAY we are now considering has survived only in four copies of a somewhat corrupt text acquired by the printer Richard Jones, who entered it in the Stationers' Register on 7th January 1593/4, and printed it that year. The title page is of particular interest. It is unique in the annals of play publication of the period in dispensing with the patronage of a nobleman and naming 'ED. ALLEN and his Companie' as having performed the play, thus accrediting Edward Alleyn with the possession of his own company of players. This testifies to the extraordinary standing Alleyn had achieved in the theatrical world by 1594, when the printer of a playscript advertised it as performed by Alleyn's company, using his name as a selling point.

> A most pleasant and / merie new Comedie / Intituled, /
> *A Knacke to knowe a Knaue* / Newlie set foorth, as it
> hath sundrie / tymes bene played by ED. ALLEN / and his Companie./
> *With KEMPS applauded Merrimentes* / of the men of Goteham,
> in receiuing / the King into Goteham.

The play's first performance was recorded by Henslowe in his *Diary* as a 'ne' play on 10th June 1592, when the takings were appropriately high at '111^{li} xijs'.[1] It was performed seven times between 10th June and 24th January 1592/3, the receipts varying from 52 shillings on its second performance, but never dropping below 23 shilling, which rates as a very satisfactory box office return. The question we have to address, is whether this 'merie new Comedie' was the last play that Greene wrote, as he informs us, in collaboration with Nashe.

Before considering the internal evidence this play presents, there are certain external practicalities to be born in mind that relate to the situation depicted in Greene's *Groatsworth* Letter. Greene chooses his words very carefully, and when he informs us that he wrote a comedy 'lastly' with his friend Nashe, that must mean it was the latest piece he wrote for the stage. In that case, it would necessarily have been written just after *harey the vj* and before Nashe departed for the country to evade the escalating plague in London. This timing, as well as the description of it as a 'merie new Comedie' and the date of its first performance at the Rose, all fit *A Knack*. Before pursuing this investigation, we ask the question: If this play is that very comedy we are seeking from Greene's and Nashe's hand, how did it come to be sold to Alleyn? The bad blood engendered suggests that it was Nashe who would have negotiated its sale; and the fact that it was sold to Alleyn's company would have had to do with Greene's perennial indebtedness. He probably owed Alleyn money and had committed the play on advance payments 'in earnest' of its completion before it was ever begun. Nashe's reformed attitude towards Alleyn dates from just this time, when he probably became acquainted with him personally. He had previously had no direct dealings with Alleyn, but he now praised him warmly in his *Pierce Penilesse*.[2] A complete *volte-face* which otherwise has no explanation. Whatever Greene may have felt about him, Nashe obviously came to like and admire the actor. Alleyn was an astute judge of dramatic talent, and he may well have recognized that Nashe's contribution to *A Knack* had signally helped to lift that play into the popular category it enjoyed. The analysis of the text will substantiate that Nashe's contribution was not negligible, and he possessed a natural dramatic flair such as Greene never developed. Yet he wrote little for the stage, and what he did has perished, with the exception of his *Summer's Last Will and Testament*, a delightful entertainment of words, songs and music, which is not a play and does not show his dramatic powers. Satire was his real love, and of this he wrote prolifically. The play here under consideration is a satirical comedy.

In determining whether *A Knack to Know a Knave* is correctly identifiable as Greene's last comedy, the timing is all important. A very thorough and detailed critical study by Hanspeter Born, curiously titled *The Rare Wit and the Rude Groom: The Authorship of A KNACK TO KNOW A KNAVE in Relation to Greene, Nashe & Shakespeare* (1971) is very much to the point of the present thesis since Born aims to bring Shakespeare into the picture as Greene's 'Shake-scene'. Born cites P.E. Bennett's investigation of the sources used for *A Knack* which revealed that Ubaldino's *Le Vite delle Donne Illustri*, printed in London in 1591, alone of the possible sources presents Ethelword (Ethenwald in *A Knack*) as marrying Alfrida *before* he obtains the King's permission, and also omits all reference to hunting as the King's reason for his visit to Ethenwald, making this a deliberate visit to spy out what Ethenwald is up to.[3] *A Knack* follows this closely. Born therefore concludes that the dependence of the play on a source not available before 1591, together with its abundance of topical allusions dating the text make it all but certain that the play was written in the months immediately preceding Henslowe's entry of its first performance on 10th June 1592.

This is confirmed by Arthur Freeman in his paper, 'Two Notes on '*A Knack to Know a Knave*'' in 1962:

'The constellation of allusions to and by *A Knack* is, in its dates, curiously compact. The play may with some safety be dated very shortly before its first recorded performance, and has all the earmarks of a hastily constructed pot-boiler.'[4]

This last comment reflects the striking unevenness of the text, which is probably due less to hastiness in writing, implying carelessness, than to the fact that we have here a surreptitiously printed play. This suspicion is confirmed by the peculiarities of the title page ascription to 'ED. ALLEN and his Companie', which could not have been authorized by the Lord Admiral's Men or their actor-manager Alleyn, who was all his life a loyal servant of his patron.

It has been implausibly suggested that Greene's 'Comedie' written together with Nashe was a prose work, his *Quip for a Courtier*, entered in the Stationers' Register on 21st July 1592, but, as Born has pointed out, the whole gist of the *Groatsworth* is concerned with actors, hence this must have reference to a stage work, not a prose piece which Greene had registered in his own name with no mention of Nashe. The play that meets the criterions in all essentials is *A Knack to Know a Knave*. It is the sole feasible candidate for the clue in Greene's Letter that this was his *last* comedy, and it again links Greene with Alleyn, whose company at the Rose were already playing no less than three of Greene's other plays in their repertoire – *Orlando Furioso* (the title role being played by Alleyn), *Friar Bacon*, with which their new season had opened, and his *Looking-Glass for London and England*. This gives point to Greene's moan in his Letter that no other playwright had so much benefitted the players as himself.

The plot of *A Knack* is strongly reminiscent of Greene's other plays in many details. *Firstly*, it is a pseudo-history in which sixteenth century characters are superimposed on a tenth century legend, that is itself treated very freely, which is typical of Greene. He specialized in the writing of pseudo-history – *Alphonsus*, *James IV*, and *John of Bordeaux* are all in this category, and the same element enters into *Friar Bacon*, although Greene affects to grace his dramatic works with the title of a 'history'. *A Knack* is just another such a semi-historical hotch-potch.

Secondly, the play consists of a double plot that is skilfully integrated, which is a distinctive characteristic of Greene's late plays. His handling of a two-plot structure is one of Greene's strengths as a dramatist. Indeed, he made a definite contribution to the Elizabethan drama by his development of the well-crafted interweaving of two plots into an effective dramatic narrative, the first instance of this being in his *Friar Bacon* in 1589. He adapted this technique from his experience as a story-teller of framework tales in his more complex use of a main plot with an elaborate framework in *James IV*. These two, his most successful dramas, are both characterized by a skilful manipulation of the plots. Neither of the two rival candidates who have been proposed by critics for the authorship of *A Knack*, Peele and Robert Wilson, is known to have used a similar construction in their dramas.

Thirdly, parallels with Greene's prose style abound in *A Knack*. Typically he makes transpositions and repetition of characters from play to play, who are first presented stating their personal characteristics, followed by action or events in which they are shown behaving true to type. Such established features of Greene's style permeate *A Knack*.

Fourthly, Greene's dramatic works have affinity with the old morality plays, and his prose works similarly bear testimony to his essentially didactic nature. Born sees strong parallels between *A Knack* and Greene's moralizing prose work *A Quip for an Upstart Courtier*, which was probably written at the same time as *A Knack*. He points out that the preface to *A Quip* 'could almost serve as a prologue to *A Knack*.'[5]

Greene's didactic moralizing is characteristic of all his works, but it increasingly took over in the last years of his life when, with the writing of his social pamphlets, he even adopted a new motto – *Pro Patria Nascimur* – to signify to his readers the new purpose of his writings, posing as a patriotic crusader against moral corruption and social evils. Greene was an inveterate poseur!

The reforming Greene took up his pen in 1590 with *Greenes Vision* and his *Farewell to Folly*, promising his readers in his reformed zeal that 'as you had the blossomes of my wanton fancies, so you shall haue the fruites of my better laboures'.[6]

Thereafter the didactic moralizing strain is strongly represented. His social pamphlets, proving highly successful financially, encouraged him in his newly turned over leaf. This development towards didactic moralizing is increasingly characteristic of his late plays, and we would therefore expect to find it strongly present in his last comedy, if this is indeed the anonymous *A Knacke to knowe a Knaue* printed in 1594 following its successful performances at the Rose. The play's run in the Rose's summer season of 1592 was rudely interrupted, firstly by the disturbances in

Southwark caused by the riots of the apprentices on Sunday 11th June, the day after the first performance of *A Knack*; (this incident is dealt with in some detail in Chapter XI, 'The Rose') and, secondly, by the closure of the theatres owing to the plague that followed immediately thereafter. The play was presented again at the Rose during the brief allowed resumption of playing at Christmas 1592/3 when the plague ban was lifted for the festive season, its topicality still popular with London audiences.

We can trace the progress of Greene's moralizing vein as an ever greater obsession – one might rather call it an indulgence – in his dramatic works through *Alphonsus, Friar Bacon*, the *Looking-Glass* (where it emerges strongly) and *James IV*; the latter his best play, acknowledged by John Churton Collins as his masterpiece, but having nevertheless passages in which the moralizing tendency becomes at times 'excessive' in Born's opinion.[7] This natural progression may be seen to culminate in *A Knack to Know a Knave* which can more accurately be described as a secularized morality play, than as a satirical comedy, though it partakes of both. Born comments: 'A strong moralizing strain runs through *A Knack* from the opening scene to the final speech. Time and again sententious moral homilies form static islands in a play otherwise crowded with action.'[8] It fits perfectly into Greene's development.

The *Looking-glasse for London and England*, in which Lodge collaborated with Greene, has been described as a 'belated morality' that 'is steeped in moral pessimism and attacks such evils as the arrogance of power, the oppression of the poor, godlessness, usury, corruption of lawyers and judges, sexual looseness, etc. The spirit of moral denunciation that pervades the *Looking Glass* is very much present in *A Knack*, where however the passages of moralizing comment are better integrated into the plot. Whilst in *Looking Glass*, Oseas functions as a passive chorus of condemnation, the main homilists in *A Knack*, Honesty and Dunstan, also take part in the action'.[9] Thus Born; who draws the conclusion that this later play shows 'progress in dramatic efficiency',[10] which is what one would naturally expect if this is Greene's last work.

The art of writing is self-revealing, and the perceptive critic who is attuned to the character and personality, opinions and attitudes of the writer whose work he is studying cannot fail to note the personal characteristics exhibited in his works. Fortunately Greene is one of the easiest to recognize, because amazingly consistent in his characteristic attitudes, despite being an inveterate imitator of others.

No writer was more acutely sensitive to the dictates of fashion in the literature of his time than Robert Greene. He leapt to the challenge to cut a dashing figure in every new literary form as it emerged, never innovating but swift to imitate, and that, alas, often slavishly, thereby doing his own considerable talents a disservice. This was, I believe, because his was essentially a weak nature, given to self-indulgence, and desiring always a quick return in ready cash and easy fame, and he was incapable of judging himself or others wisely and accurately. His public moralizing stance was a compensation for his own moral inadequacy. He was forever going to reform himself, but never had the strength of will to do so.

Yet, strangely, there is no doubt he ran considerable personal risk in exposing the malpractices of the Elizabethan underworld in his social pamphlets, and showed real personal courage in doing so. The villains he studied at close quarters in order to write about their nefarious practices felt threatened by his exposures and in turn threatened him with vengeance. These were the 'conny-catchers', whose victims were fleeced of their money and possessions by artful dissimulation of friendship, in which a group of scoundrels worked in consort using a skilfully devised psychological approach; the 'cross-biters', who incited sexual jealousy and practised blackmail; the 'priggars' or horse thieves, and 'nips' and 'foists' who worked as cut-purses and thieves. Every type of cheating at cards, the wiles of harlots, and the 'Black Art' of lock-picking were discovered in all their subtlety and detail in Greene's series of five pamphlets, revealing the methods of skulduggery of each criminal art and craft that was assiduously studied and mastered and successfully employed by this criminal community. It was a school for scoundrels that Greene described in vivid, pithy language cleverly suited to this exercise in criminology. Sometimes blanks are left in his text where Greene threatened to disclose the names of those villains who were personally known to him. The harlot who is the subject of his *Disputation between a Hee and a Shee Conny-Catcher* swore that she would stab him with the knife she always carried about her as soon as she could find the opportunity. As J.C. Collins comments: 'Greene certainly went in danger of his life'.[11] But he stoutly claimed: 'Let them do what they dare with their bilbowe blades, I feare them not.'[12] He seems to have relished the risks he took, and, had he not been prevented by his death, he planned indeed to publish a 'Catalogue of all the names of the Foysts, Nyps, Lifts, and Priggars in and about London'.[13] And, being Greene, doubtless he relished even more the fame that his one-man campaign against this evil strata of society brought him.

Yet Greene was no puritan. He hated the Puritans and was firmly on the side of the Anglican bishops in the Marprelate controversy to which he claims to have contributed. However, we need not take Greene's moralizing in his writings for the stage too seriously despite his remarkable achievement in his social pamphlets, for he had a sneaking sympathy with sinners (so long as they were not of the most evil kind in his estimation) and probably his success in infiltrating their ranks to gain his first-hand knowledge of their devious methods of operation owed something to this basic affinity in sinfulness. Like the rascals he studied, he, too, set out to make money out of sin; in his case, out of reporting sin, writing about sin, and himself confessing to sin to make a sensational impact on his readers. We know Greene rather too well from his soul-baring confessional writings to be completely taken in by him.

Typically, in his *James IV* his 'tiresome moralizing'[14] is superimposed on a play in which the plot is, in contrast, distinctly lacking in any ethics or moral standards! Greene's own superficial and facile acceptance decrees that wrongs may be lightly forgiven without any real change of heart – the slate wiped clean with a little breast-beating, after which, as he himself did, the return to pleasurable sinning may recommence. The utterance of repentance is enough. All this is a-piece with Greene's own life and philosophy. The writer and the man are separate entities. An inveterate profligate himself to the end, he was always on the verge of reformation; his message: Do not do as I do, but as I say.

This attitude is reflected in all his plays in the mitigation of severe punishment of the wrongdoers after dire threats, which are then turned aside at the last moment. Their sinfulness, having provided him with the material for his moralizing, may then be liberally pardoned. In *A Knack* the sympathetic treatment of Philarchus, who had beaten his old father, is typically Greene's philosophy; Ethenwald is likewise reprieved and his betrayal of the King's trust is called 'a merry jest' by Bishop Dunstan. It is interesting that Greene's condoning of sin is in a subtly different category from the mercy shown by Shakespeare, for whom genuine repentance is the liberating force in the reformation of the forgiven character. With Greene this is not assured. However, the hardened criminals, the usurers, oppressors of the poor, and upstart court flatterers whom Greene detested, are punished with unusual severity in *A Knack* reflecting Nashe's sadistic streak. The punishment of sinners also provides opportunities for the Devil to make his appearance and hale them off to Hell. Magic and the introduction of the supernatural are indispensable devices in all Greene's known dramatic works.

Waldo F. McNeir has observed of Greene that although the use of magic was a popular convention in many Elizabethan plays, both tragedies and comedies, 'Yet it cannot be said of any other known dramatist of the period of Greene's activity that his use of the supernatural makes it his unfailing stock in trade.'[15] We find it used twice in *A Knack*.

Greene – a rapid writer as has been noted – was addicted to self-repetition more than most, sometimes making wholesale transpositions from his prose works to his plays, re-using the same situations, the same characters, and even the same names in his haste to turn out saleable works. Born points out further close parallels between *A Quip* and *A Knack* in the character of the Knight in *A Quip* and the Knight in *A Knack*. They are practically identical: both exhibit the same benevolent attitude, are equally hospitable to the poor and those in need, both are just and kind, both models of honour and selflessness. In his moralizing vein depicting the miscreants in (a) *A Quip* and (b) *A Knack* we are presented with (a) Envy at court, and (b) the Courtier Perin; with (a) Covetousness in the city, and (b) Cutbert Conycatcher; with (a) Contempt and Disdain in the country, and (b) Walter the Farmer. These are the three main heads under which Greene's social criticism falls in *A Quip*. They are also three of the four main themes of the satire in *A Knack*, in which the fourth is represented by the hypocritical Priest.[16] This, as Born points out, is the only example of a Puritan in a play attributable to Greene, and this is doubtless an indication of Nashe's influence, whose anti-Puritan work *Pierce Penilesse* was then in course of writing.

The strong moralizing strain running through *A Knack* from start to finish exhibits all of Greene's typical attitudes and prejudices, most of which he shared with Nashe, as McKerrow has noted in drawing parallels between Greene's *A Quippe for an Vpstart Courtier* and Nashe's *Pierce Penilesse*[17], making them ideal partners in a collaboration which had begun with Nashe's Preface to Greene's *Menaphon*. The two were of like mind. Both were anti-Puritan and participated in the Marprelate pamphlet war, Nashe firing off his devastating satirical squibs at the behest of Archbishop Whitgift, who was his patron in 1592, the year of the present investigation. Whitgift was interested in the drama and enjoyed private performances at his court in Croydon. He would have approved of *A Knack*, which attacks social evils that were currently in the news at this time – a factor of importance in accurately dating the play.

Born has researched the news-worthy topical scandals which are reflected in the play.

'The allusions to contemporary events with which the satirical part of the play is larded, are also in line with the proposed date of 1592.

If it is true to say that much of the satire in the play is of a general nature and that the accusations against usury, corn-engrossing and other economic evils could have emanated from the pen of almost any Tudor writer at almost any time, it is no less evident that a number of allusions must have dealt specifically with matters that were very much in the public eye at the time of the play's composition.'[18]

Born then reveals the relevance of the play's scenes to current events with particular reference to (a) the crimes of Walter the Farmer, and (b) John the Priest.

Clark reads the Inditement: [accusing the Farmer]
First, he hath conueyed corne out of the land to feede the Enemie.
(11.1263-4)

John's crime is the obtaining of –

'the Kings seale
To carie Tin, Lead, Wool and broad Clothes beyond seas"
(11.1784-5)

This, put into the contemporary scene, reflects the political condition in which England was newly engaged in war with the Catholic faction in France where Essex was heading the English expeditionary force in August 1591.[19] Accordingly, from August 1591 on through 1592 the Privy Council suspended all trading with the enemy overseas. Their Letter dated 15th August 1591 refers to breaches of these sanctions:

'we are enformed...that there are divers persons who contrary to her Maiesty's lawes and the alleadgence haue transported and conueied ouer the seas into such partes as are not in league and amitie with her Maiestie great store of victual and other prohibited merchandizes and munition (as wheat, beef, tallow, hides, and lead) to the great preiudice of the realm and strengthening of the enemie.'[20]

For this crime Honesty suggests that hanging is appropriate – but the sentence is commuted to being shot 'as a dissembling Hypocrit.'
Born reveals a precedent for John's case in a scandal that occurred in April 1592, two months before the play was performed. Two merchants

had obtained a licence 'under fraudulent pretences' to export 'twentie packes of Kersyes, fower packes of broad clothes, three packes of bayes and three packes of course clothe stockinges.'[21] Subsequently the Privy Council discovered their real intent and the customs officers were ordered to 'cause staie to be made of the bark with the merchandizes.'[22] Broad cloth is specifically mentioned in *A Knack* as the item that John wishes to transport overseas. Making John a puritanical priest who engages in these activities was very topical in 1592 for the Martin Marprelate controversy was in full swing.

Greene's social pamphlets were also enjoying a vogue, and Born, citing P.E. Bennett, points out that the author of *A Knack* trades on the currency of the word 'cony-catcher', which occurs 33 times in the text, 'a term made popular by the appearance of Greene's first cony-catching pamphlets at the end of 1591.'[23] He further notes that *A Knack* contains references to two plays that were recently performed, one marked 'ne' by Henslowe on 11th April 1592, *Titus and Vespasian*, and the other, *Locrine*, which has been attributed to Greene by several critics and is among his accepted apocryphal works. It would be typical of Greene to draw attention to one of his own plays.

All Greene's favourite targets in social evils are attacked in *A Knack*, and, as well, its 'veiled political barbs' spiked with social satire suit nicely with the influence of Nashe whose element was satire. The material on which they drew, and which probably inspired their collaboration in this satirical comedy, was currently in the news in the months when it is all but certain that it was being composed as a timely dramatic commentary to set the tongues of the gossiping groundlings wagging. It was just this effect that Greene and Nashe sought with all their writings.

Born's detailed critical assessment of this play is masterly throughout in his understanding of Greene's character as a dramatist and writer.

'The play is extremely variegated, blending into one dramatic concoction elements of romance, satire, melodrama, court comedy, low farce and morality. It features high-flown rhetoric with a generous ration of classical references, down-to-earth slapstick comedy, moral lessons and homilies. The very diversity of *A Knack* places the play firmly within the range of Greene's temperament.'[24]

Both Greene's faults and virtues are well represented in the play, and Born is able to demonstrate with ease that *A Knack* is the product of essentially the same ingredients mixed according to the same recipe as his canonical plays.

Further telling evidence of Greene's responsibility in the composition of *A Knack* is seen in the repetition of narrative situations in his prose romances and in his plays. Comparing *A Knack* with *Friar Bacon*, we find in the romantic sub-plot in each play that there are identical situations in which Ethenwald and Lacy respectively are commanded to woo beautiful, humbly born young women, Alfrida and Margaret, the former for the King, the latter for the Prince of Wales. Each proxy wooer falls in love with the lady himself and breaks his troth with his royal overlord, and has to face the dire consequences.

> Lacie shall die as traitor to his Lord   *Bacon*, 1.1012

> For I haue sworne as trulie as I liue,
> That I will neuer pardon Ethenwald.   *A Knack*, 11.1706-7

Then follows a sudden change of heart to clemency couched *in similar phrases and words*, in both *Bacon* and *A Knack*.

> Lacie, *rise vp*. Faire Peggie, *heeres my hand*,
> The Prince of Wales, hath conquered all his thoughts,
> And all his loues he yeelds vnto the Earle.
> Lacie, *enioy the maid* of Fresingfield;
>
> . . .
>
> Once, Lacie, *friendes againe*, come, we will post.
>   *Bacon*, 11.1045-8, 1068

> Ethenwald, *stand vp*, and *rise vp* Alfrida,
> For Edgar now giues pardon to you both.
>
> . . .
>
> Ethenwald, *giue me thy hande* and *we are friends*,
> And *loue thy wife* and liue together long.
>   *A Knack*, 1722-3, 1748-9

These obvious parallels could be explained either by outright plagiarism or, as is argued by the circumstances of 1592, by the working of the same mind of a dramatist who is characterised by his tendency to frequent self-repetition, which is typical of Greene.[25] Born further observes: 'The denouement of the romantic intrigue in *A Knack* also shares one important plot element with the scenes that unravel the complications in *Alphonsus*, *Looking Glass*, *John of Bordeaux* and *James IV.* In all these plays impending catastrophe is at the last moment averted by the sudden intervention of a wise (presumably old) man who brings a misguided prince to his senses.'[26]

In the early plays, 'The sudden changes of mind that make Alphonsus (in *Alphonsus*), Rasni (in *Looking Glass*), Prince Edward (in *Friar Bacon*) turn away from their disastrous course seem psychologically unconvincing and dramatically ineffective.'[27] But in his later plays he improves on this by providing additional forces to persuade the sudden change of heart – and this is also the case in *A Knack* where the magical powers of Dunstan evoke Asmoroth to his aid, a spirit who obeys him. (The corrupt and abbreviated text of the Quarto does not help here.) The problem is resolved by a combination of Dunstan's moral persuasion and Asmoroth's supernatural intervention.

Another stylistic similarity is found in *James IV* and *A Knack* when the agent who is to effect the King's aims appears out of nowhere, so to speak, and interrupts the King's speech, which evokes an angry response and astonishment at the intruder's impudence. Yet another similarity between the known plays of Greene and *A Knack* is in the introduction of unrelated scenes, which are independent interpolations, but which serve to comment on or highlight an attribute of the events or of a character in the play. This technique, typical of Greene's dramas, appears in *A Knack* (i) in the scene with the unfilial Philarchus, who cruelly beat his old father, where its function is moral comment; and (ii) in the scene with the men of Goteham, where it provides comic relief. These also help the illusion of the passing of time, and present Edgar as a wise and popular monarch whose reign was noted for its benign reformation of evil practices, and a blessing to his subjects.[28]

Disguise is a device beloved of the Elizabethan dramatists, not least Shakespeare, but in Greene it is another fixed and indispensable ingredient of his dramatic practice. Like his use of magic, disguise is a device he copiously puts to use. In *Alphonsus*, the King is disguised as a pilgrim; in *Orlando*, the hero as a common mercenary soldier, Angelica as a shepherdess, Marsilius and Mandricand as palmers; in *Friar Bacon*, Lacy as a country swain, Prince Edward as the fool; in *James IV*, Queen Dorothea as a man; in *A Knack*, Alfrida as the kitchen maid, and Kate, the kitchen maid as Alfrida, and King Edgar appears disguised, first, as a farmer with Dunston likewise as a farmer, and then with his courtiers as a judge with his court of law. Disguise as it is used by Greene typically tends to be overdone.

Among Greene's strongest stylistic traits is his love of classical allusion. Born has shown that the concordance of classical and biblical names in *A Knack* with Greene's known works is very high. It includes fifteen favourites which 'appear in more than half of the thirteen volumes of Grosart's edition' (of Greene's *Poems and Plays*).[29]

Like Marlowe, Greene also had a taste for exotic splendour, (possibly in direct imitation of *Tamburlaine* and *The Jew of Malta*) and he loves to dwell on 'orient pearl' and 'precious stones', 'bright topaz' and the rich silks of Tyre, costly furnishings, luxurious perfumes. A peculiarity of Greene's is that he specialized not only in pseudo-history, but pseudo-mineralogy, pseudo-botany and pseudo-zoology, inventing strange creatures that never existed, and 'fantasticall plants and stones'.[30] In *A Knack* we encounter such a fantastical creature, the Ianamyst, attributing it to Pliny, who was wholly innocent of this exotic invention, in order to give it an air of classical verisimilitude.

> For *Pliny* writes, women are made lyke waxe,
> Apt to receue any impression:
> Whose mindes are lyke the Ianamyst
> That eates, yet cries, and neuer is satisfied:
>> *A Knack*, 11.1425-8

Dunston astonishes the audience with the following imaginary flora and fauna:

> Or lyke the Violets in *America*, that in sommer yeeld odifferous smell,
> And in winter a most infectious sauour:
> For at euery ful sea they flourish, or at euery dead ope they vade:
> The fish *Palerna* being white in the calme,
> Yet turneth black with euery storme:
> Or lyke the trees in the deserts of *Africa*,
> That flourish but while the southwest wind bloweth.
>> *A Knack* 11.1186-1192

This is a very corrupt text, but the pseudo embellishments are typically Greene.

Having invented some new denizens of his world of nature, Greene not only re-uses his self-created herbs and precious stones in his works, but, being an 'inveterate self-plagiarizer' – as an essential part of his rapid-writing economy – he constantly revamps his plots and also repeats the names of his characters. Thus in *A Knack* Philarchus is another version of Philarkes (another ungrateful son) in *Penelope's Web*; Kate, the kitchen maid in *A Knack*, is twin to Kate, the dairy maid, in *Greenes Vision*. In *A Knack* the Priest, the Farmer and the Knight have all stepped out of the pages of *A Quip*. In the following scene the Bailiff of Hexham addresses his four sons on his deathbed in the very tones of old Gorinius in Greene's *Groatsworth of Wit*.

Enter Baylief of Hexam, and his foure sonnes, to wit,
a Courtier, a Priest, a Conicatcher, and a Farmer.
    Bayly. My sonnes you see how age decaies my state,
And that my lyfe lyke snow before the sun,
Gins to dissolue into that substance nowe,
From whose inclosure grew my fyre of lyfe;
Yet ere I yeeld my selfe to death, my sonnes,
Giue eare, and hear what rules I set you downe.
And first to thee my sonne, that liuest by wit:
I know thou hast so many honest sleights,
To shift and cosen smoothly on thy wit,
To cog and lie, and braue it with the best,
That twere but labour lost to counsell thee,
And therfore to the next, *Walter*, that seemes to shew a
                               husband man:
My sonne, when that thy master trusts thee most,
And thinks thou dealest as truelie as himselfe,
Be thou the first to worke deceit to him;
So by that means thou maist inrich thy selfe,
And liue at pleasure when thy maister's dead:
And when to market thou art sent with woll,
Put sand amongst it, and twill make it weigh,
The weight twise double that it did before,
The ouerplus is thine into thy purse.
But now my sonne, that keeps the Court,
Be thou a means to set the Peeres at strife,
And currifauour for the commons loue.
If any but in conference name the King,
Informe his Maiestie they enuie him;
And if the King but moue or speake to thee,
Kneele on both knees, and say, God saue your Maiestie.
If any man be fauoured by the King,
Speake thou him faire, although in heart thou enuie him.
                                 11.242-277

Corrupt though the text is, we get the flavour of Greene's *Groatsworth* tale. (See pp.144–146)

Like Gorinius, the dying Baylief of Hexham dispenses with giving his counsel to his eldest son, but for a different reason: this young man is already a past master of sin and needs no lessons in the art. This play antedates the writing of Greene's *Groatsworth* so that plagiarism is ruled out. If both are from his hand then this is Greene's typical self-repetition, and the dying, sinful, old father must have been fresh in his mind at the time of penning his *Groatsworth*. Much of the language is almost identical.

Turning next to the Priest, his second son, the old man advises him:

> Giue eare, my sonne,
> I haue a lesson yet in store for thee:
> Thou must (my son) make shew of holinesse,
> And blinde the world with thy hipocrisie:
> And sometime giue a pennie to the poore,
> But let it be in the Church or market place,
> That men may praise thy liberalitie.
> Speak against usurie, yet forsake noe pawnes,
> So thou may'st gaine three shillings in the pound:
>
> 11.281-289

The brothers respond, telling how they have absorbed this philosophy, for which the father commends them, saying 'your liues bewray whose sonnes ye are!' and exhorts them to follow in his footsteps paying no heed to those that 'feare the fearfull Iudgment day'.

> Liue to your selues while you haue tyme to liue,
> Get what you can, but see ye nothing giue:
> But hearke my sonnes, me thinks I heare a noyse,
> And gastlie visions make me timorous,
> Ah see my sonnes, where death, pall Death appeares,
> To summon mee before a fearfull Iudge:
> Me thinks reuenge stands with an yron whip,
> And cries repent, or I will punish thee:
> My heart is hardened, I cannot repent.
>
> 11.361-369

So the Devil comes and carries him away. The contrasting scene in *A Knack* is that in which an aged Father complains to King Edgar that his son Philarchus (a favourite courtier of the King) has spurned his own father now he is old and poor, and insulted him by striking the old man when he upbraided his son for his wanton faithlessness to the man who

296

raised him. He asks the King to arbitrate. Philarchus declares his sorrow and penitence for his past behaviour. The King lends his robes and sceptre to the Father to judge in the case himself. Ample opportunity for moralizing is thus provided, and when the Father pronounces the penalty as exile, the King steps in to mitigate this with a pension to live abroad in the country of his choice until such time as he be recalled to the King's court, extending at the same time protection and freedom from want to the old man. Honesty comments on the nefarious activities of 'the Bailief's sonne of Hexham, Cutbert Conicatcher and a Broker', and he then brings the King in disguise to observe for himself, together with his deceitful Courtier Perin (another of the brothers, who acts as Judge!) and Bishop Dunstan (posing as a Farmer). The matter is so contrived that Perin is trapped into pronouncing sentence upon himself. By various means all four evil brothers are exposed and, in this case, all are cruelly punished. Born suggests that Nashe's influence is evident in the harsh sentences meted out, for his sadistic streak is evident in the glee with which he recounts the terrible tortures of Jack Wilton in *The Unfortunate Traveller*,[31] and this is not typical of Greene, where so much else in the play is patently reminiscent of his works.

A *Knack* is too corrupt a text to provide reliable metrical and verse tests, although those made by Born do agree well, on the whole, with the hypothesis that this is Greene's play and certainly do not contradict it. However, he comments, 'construction is a useful test for the determination of authorship [for] even if a play exists only in a corrupt version, we can still detect the author's method of organising his material.'[32] This has been shown to accord in all important details with Greene's method of play-construction, a skill which he had mastered particularly well, and which is also the most effective element in *A Knack* contributing greatly to the success the play enjoyed. Construction is also 'less prone to imitation than the more superficial elements of style' which could be suspected as plagiarism.[33]

In considering the strongly didactic moralizing content of *A Knack* we have to remember that the play dates from the period at the end of Greene's life, and is a candidate for his missing 'Comedie', when he had avowedly dedicated himself to his crusade against social evils. Born observes that: 'It would be surprising if Greene had *failed* to take advantage of the success of his prose pamphlets and had not turned their subject matter into a play. Greene must have realised that the stage presented an excellent platform for the dissemination of his ideas and for the denouncement of social evils.'[34]

This was the traditional role of the drama since its inception in the morality play, and Greene's playwriting, which retained this affinity from the first, had through the impetus of his didactic spirit progressed almost full circle back to the morality in his last play, if this is identified as *A Knack*.

The concoction of the mix in *A Knack* has been shown to be most typically Greene's. He was first and foremost a good story-teller and proud of it, and Born's summing up acknowledges this.

> 'What good qualities the play possesses – liveliness, variety, competent plotting, brisk pace – are qualities that can be observed in most of Greene's plays and stories. On the other hand, the defects of *A Knack* – lack of substance, unconvincing characterization, failure to achieve organic unity, long patches of tedious and shallow moralizing – are equally typical of Greene.'[35]

Apart from Born's thesis, the only full-length study of this play available to date is P.E. Bennett's monograph *A Critical Edition of A Knack to Know a Knave* (1952, issued on University Microfilms: Ann Arbor, Michigan) and Born gives him full and appreciative acknowledgement: 'Bennett's evaluation of the evidence led him – against his will as it were – to adopt the hypothesis that Robert Greene was the author of the original version of *A Knack to Know a Knave*.'[36] Born's own summation of the impressive case for Greene's authorship which he has put together is a confirmation of Bennett's conclusion.

> 'There can be few anonymous plays, for which the internal evidence with regard to the authorship question is as massive. If the attribution of a play on internal evidence alone can ever be justified, then surely it must be in the case of *A Knack*. Not only does the analysis of different aspects of the play point unmistakably to Robert Greene as its author, but an evaluation of the play as a whole leads to the same conclusion.'[37]

If, by hypothesis, we accept Greene's as the main hand responsible for *A Knack* in its pseudo-historical theme cast in a morality-type play, with its individual quirks strongly reminiscent of Greene and its many parallelisms with his works, held in a well-constructed two-plot dramatic concept, we need also to find evidence of Nashe's contribution if this play is to meet the description of a collaborative work. This also is not far to seek, and is mainly provided by the two-plot structure.

1. The main plot presents Honesty's campaign to expose corruption by his discovery of the criminal practices of the four detestable brothers who each personify a different social evil.

2. The sub-plot is a love-intrigue in which Ethenwald, Earl of Cornwall, steals a march on King Edgar in the pursuit of Alfrida's love, and finally, with the help of Bishop Dunstan's magic, succeeds in keeping his bride and subduing Edgar's wrath to the point of a total reconciliation.

These two plots, while independent, are smoothly joined and developed in alternation, a structure that lends itself ideally to collaborative composition. While Honesty acts as the central pivot of the exposure of the social evils plot, Ethenwald features as the centre of the love-intrigue, and King Edgar functions as the unifying chief character in both the love-intrigue and as arbitrator in the exposure of the knaves. As Born has noted, 'The author strengthens this link by placing Edgar between two councillors, one good [Dunston], one evil [Perin], in the tradition of the morality play, and these also appear in both plots. The smooth integration of the King and Perin into two totally different plots implies considerable organising skill on the part of the dramatist who plotted the play.'[38]

The dramatic construction would naturally have been Greene's area of responsibility as the senior, more experienced partner, and we have Nashe's own warrant that he deferred to Greene in the matter of plotting a play: 'hee subscribing to me any thing but plotting Plaies, wherein he was his crafts master.' On the other hand, in most things Nashe claims they were equals: 'none that euer had but one eye, with a pearle in it, but could discern the difference twixt him [Greene] & me; while he liu'd (as some Stationers can witnes with me).'[39]

G.R. Proudfoot has detected indications of Nashe's hand in *A Knack* in some individual predilections reflected in the play, for instance, such as –

(a) Nashe's aversion to palmistry and physiognomy (McKerrow I, p.370) comparable with *A Knack*, (1.74.)

(b) The character personifying Christmas, satirically describing him as a miser in *Summer's Last Will* (McKerrow III, p.280) may be compared with similar expressions in *A Knack*, (11.961-5.)[40]

The theme of social evils is the main subject of Nashe's satire in *Pierce Penilesse, His Supplication to the Diuell*, also published in 1592, in which he complains with satirical humour to the Devil about the evil customs of his day, and launches biting barbs against the 'Martinists', concluding with a debate about Hell. Nashe was busy upholding his reputation as a 'Martin-queller'. The minor character of Piers Plowman in *A Knack* as well as the Puritan, John the Priest, are likely to have been suggested by Nashe. But his main contribution was the development of the sub-plot of the love-intrigue with the character of Ethenwald, who is unlike any creation from Greene's pen.

'Whatever qualities Greene possessed as a playwright,' comments Born, 'the art of drawing convincing life-like characters was not one of them.'[41] He sees Ethenwald as a 'many-faceted, almost protean character'[42] in contrast to the 'stereotyped figures' of other characters in *A Knack*. Born's tendency here to hyperbolic praise of Ethenwald is influenced by the aim of his thesis, which is to detect the hand of Shakespeare in the writing of this character, for which there is neither warrant in the circumstances surrounding this play, nor in the text sufficient to support this hypothesis. It is another case of wishful thinking. Suffice it to say, that the character of Ethenwald stands out as the best rounded and most lively that this corrupt text has to offer, and this assessment is entirely consonant with the capabilities of Nashe as I shall show by comparison with the semi-dramatization of his satirical prose works.

Unfortunately, there is no known extant dramatic work of Nashe's with which we can compare *A Knack*, excepting his *Summer's Last Will and Testament*, which resembles a masque with music rather than a play. It was probably written during the summer of 1592. The lyrical quality of Nashe's writing is demonstrated in the following excerpt. The character *Sol* enters 'verie richly attir'de, with a noyse of Musicians before him,' and answers the criticisms of *Winter*, *Autumn*, and *Summer* (who has raised him up to his height of temporary glory.)

> *Sol.* Musique and poetrie, my last two crimes,
> Are those two exercises of delight,
> Wherewith long labours I doe weary out.
> The dying Swanne is not forbid to sing.
> The waues of *Heber* playd on *Orpheus* strings,
> When he (sweete musiques *Trophe*) was destroyd.
> And as for Poetry, woods eloquence,
> (Dead *Phaetons* three sisters funerall teares
> That by the gods were to *Electrum* turnd,)
> Not flint, or rockes of Icy cynders fram'd,
> Deny the sourse of siluer-falling streames.
> Enuy enuieth not outcryes vnrest:

In vaine I pleade; well is to me a fault,
And these my words seeme the slyght webbe of arte,
And not to haue the taste of sounder truth.

11.524-538

Summer's final speech in reply is not without a touch of satire in his bequests to the various categories of humanity of long days, short nights and drought to those who would least appreciate these, bequeathing –

My long dayes to bondmen and prisoners,
My short nights to young married soules,
My drought and thirst to drunkards quenchless throates,

11.1832-34

— so that even in the lyrical enchantment of this musical entertainment Nashe cannot resist introducing satire. His last line, 'Weepe, heauens, mourne, earth, here Summer ends' is in the beloved minor key we associate with Elizabethan music. Here we have Nashe in the vein, I suggest, we can detect in *A Knack* – lyrical with an irrepressible touch of satire – which is in contrast to his scurrilous, satirical writings, but in them all his utterances are marked with scintillating wit, comic word-pictures provoking laughter in his reader, delighting to shock, and always highly original. No one expresses *Schadenfreude* with greater glee than Nashe!

Disappointingly, Born's otherwise impressive thesis shows only scant study of Nashe, and he attributes to Shakespeare's hand aspects of the 'many-faceted' Ethenwald that clearly reveal Nashe: 'Other attributes that make Ethenwald a sophisticated character are his keen interest in language and his talent as an actor.'[43] Both attributes are strongly present in Nashe. His avid interest in language is a striking feature of his satirical writings, and his Preface to Greene's *Menaphon* is an impressive critique of contemporary literary style. Words were Nashe's weapons in satire. He studied style, and was no 'shallow-brain'd censurer' of other men's literary work. Not for nothing was he hailed by his enemy Gabriel Harvey as a 'braue Columbus of tearmes',[44] who was himself an adept judge of language. Nashe's writings are a rich mine of imaginative and original language. He also enjoyed inventing characters to enliven his lampoons with a little drama assigning himself a part in the play-acting. At Cambridge he took part in student plays, acting in them and doubtless also writing them – activities that landed him in hot water with the authorities. He was reputedly sent down 'before his time' because of the scurrilous part he played as the 'Varlet' in one of these student dramas, and left behind

301

him a reputation as a young scamp who became the terror of the dons. After his departure from the university under a cloud of disgrace, the authorities, we are told, were wont to dub any young trouble-maker 'a verie Nashe'.[45]

It can hardly be disputed that Nashe would have been capable of, and personally suited to the creation of such a character as Ethenwald, who stands out as of a calibre of dramatic invention different from and superior to Greene's. Ethenwald is just such a witty, bright, young spark as Nashe would readily have identified with. There is, I suggest, much of Nashe himself in this impish young nobleman, who accepts the King's commission to woo Alfrida on his behalf with a jaunty air in a flowery speech showing how he plans to win her with flattering words, which is really a sly parody of courtly wooing:

> I will, my Lord, woo her in your behalfe,
> Plead loue for you, and straine a sigh to show your passions,
> I will say she is fayrer than the Dolphins eie,
> At whome amazde, the night stars stand and gaze,
> Then will I praise her chin, and cheeke, and prety hand,
> Long made lyke *Venus*, when she usde the harp,
> When *Mars* was reueling in *Ioues* high house.
> Besides, my Lord, I will say she hath a pace,
> Much like to *Iuno* in *Idea* vale,
> When *Argus* watcht the Heifer on the mount:
> These words, my Lord, will make her loue, I am sure,
> If these will not my Lord, I haue better far.
>
> ll. 215-216

The last line just hints at the idea he has immediately conceived, of stealing the beauteous lady for himself. Born comments: 'Ethenwald's satire is twofold. It mocks Petrarchan love conventions and it satirizes the stylistic habit of indiscriminately accumulating classical figures, a practice much favoured by Greene. But how are we to explain the presence of a parody on Greene in a play written by Greene?'[46]

The answer appears obvious to Born. He sees this as evidence of Shakespeare's 'revising' hand on which he then builds a tenuous hypothesis. But the true answer is, I suggest, that we have here Nashe's contribution adding his spark of fun in his typically satirical vein, in which he is not just satirising Greene, but the whole convention of hyperbole in the use of high-flown classical allusions in the praise of a lovely woman who is

302

being courted. Greene was but one of many who followed a well established fashion. Nashe, the sprightly satirist, here turns the convention into a butt for his satire. Nashe had a lively sense of the absurd. It would be typical of him to concoct 'the grotesque reference to the dolphin's eye and the absurdly conflated mythological similes [that] have been introduced advisedly',[47] as Born remarks. And satire, of course, *is* Nashe's province which he could never leave for long.

This is not Shakespeare, who was not a satirist, though he made ebullient fun of the sonneteering vogue in *Love's Labour's Lost* to which he himself was a contributor. It is typically Nashe who, with Greene's concurrence, is gleefully satirizing this very convention of hyperbolic wooing with the piling on of classical allusion, neatly done so that King Edgar does not suspect that fun is being made of his serious intent. In the same way Cuthbert Conycatcher is a satire on Greene's cony-catching social pamphleteering, and his appearance in *A Knack* would seem to confirm the suspicions expressed by E.H. Miller and H.C. Hart that the anonymous pamphlet, *A Defence of Conny-Catching* was a 'literary hoax' written by Greene and Nashe[48] – or by Nashe with Greene's approval. Here we have exactly the same satirically mischievous touch which is Nashe's chief characteristic. Obviously in apportioning the writing of *A Knack* the character of Ethenwald was given to Nashe to develop, and he showed himself capable of creating this lively, rounded character who bears many of his own personal traits.

Later, in his actual wooing of Alfrida for himself, Ethenwald uses not a single mythological allusion or hyperbolic compliment. His wooing is passionate and sincere, moving and effective, and he uses a witty ploy, pretending that his eyes are affected and he cannot see properly – the same device used by Webster in *The Duchess of Malfi* which may perhaps have been suggested to him by *A Knack* if he ever saw the play.

Alfrida: Why let me see your eies (my Lord) looke vpon me.
Ethen: Then twil be worse.
Alfrida: What, if you looke on me? then Ile be gone.
Ethen: Nay stay, sweet loue, stay beauteous *Alfrida,*
And giue the Earle of *Cornwel* leaue to speake:
Know *Alfrida*, thy beautie hath subdued,
And captiuate the Earle of *Cornwels* heart.
Briefly, I loue thee...

11. 1152-1159

303

It is a very effective and natural piece of wooing. He then asks Osrick for Alfrida's hand, and the match is made. On the other hand, the King in this morality-type play is typical of Greene's creations in *Friar Bacon* and *James IV* featuring royal lechers, and his intentions towards Alfrida are frankly stated to Bishop Dunstan at the outset:

> *King:* Beleeue me, *Dunston*, if she be so faire,
> She will serue our turne to make a Concubine,
> Me thinks tis good some tyme to haue a loue,
> To sport withall, and passe away the tyme.
> *Dunston:* I, my good Lord, *Dunston* could wel allow of it,
> If so your Grace would marrie *Alfrida*.
> *King:* What, wouldst thou haue me marie her I neuer saw?
> Then men would say I doted on a wench:
> But *Dunston*, I haue found a policie,
> Which must indeed be followed to the full:
>
> 11. 184-193

Ethenwald is then called to carry out the wooing for the King who instructs him:

> Tell her, she shall be honoured in my Loue,
> And beare a childe that one day may be King:
>
> 11. 201-2

As Born has noted, the King, Dunstan, the Knaves, Philarchus, the Knight, Piers Ploughman, and the minor characters are all 'type figures' readily identifiable with Greene's work and style. Ethenwald is the exception. His part is 'totally free from moralizing' and from Greene's favourite 'decorative digressions'; his speeches are more striking in their imagery, which is often drawn from nature, and when he uses classical allusions they are often used ironically as deliberate parody.[49]

In his attempt to associate Shakespeare with this play Born returns again and again to Ethenwald's soliloquies, of which there are three in *A Knack*, as significantly different from Greene's use of the soliloquy, and as containing examples of imagery which Born compares with Shakespeare, in particular the 'spider-image' and the 'billows-image' in Ethenwald's second soliloquy. A characteristic of Greene's dramatic technique is that his genuine soliloquies showing mental conflict are spoken while other characters are on stage. For each of his soliloquies Ethenwald is alone.

This is similar to Marlowe's soliloquizing technique, and there is more affinity between Nashe's and Marlowe's style than anyone else's, so far as we may judge from the little we have of Nashe's dramatic work. He is supposed to have collaborated with Marlowe on *Dido Queen of Carthage* – although when, (Nashe was only fifteen when Marlowe was probably writing this early work at Cambridge) or how much of his hand is in the play, if any, is a problem I have addressed in my *Scanderbeg, the Young Marlowe*.[50] It is a grave omission in Born's otherwise thoroughly researched thesis, that he has not made any textual comparisons with Nashe's works with regard to those noticeable differences he finds in the language, imagery and characterisation of Ethenwald, but straightway assumes that these are attributable to the hypothetical 'reviser' of *A Knack* whom he has introduced in order to bring Shakespeare into his thesis. In fact, all those tell-tale discrepancies that Born attributes to Shakespeare's hand are logically, regarding the historical context of this play, as well as stylistically readily attributable to Nashe, whom Born has somewhat cursorily dismissed as having made only a minor contribution to *A Knack*. This is to ignore Greene's own testimony regarding his last play which tells us that 'yong *Iuuenall*, that byting Satyrist,...lastly with mee together writ a Comedie'. This does not imply that Nashe's part in the enterprise was negligible – it was written *together*.

However, largely ignoring Nashe's claim and plumping directly for Shakespeare, Born writes: 'Further light on the revision theory may come from examining the soliloquies in *A Knack*. The soliloquy is a dramatic convention which is handled differently by different playwrights.'[51] He is in agreement with Kenneth Muir's criticism that Greene's soliloquies are 'crudely done' when they are expressing inner conflict in the character's mind. Serious characters speaking in self-examination are given to 'tedious rhetorical debate' and their soliloquies tend to be larded with 'historical and classical allusions or moralizing maxims', and suffer from 'academic pedantry'.[52] Greene's most effective use of the soliloquy is in comic monologues as in *Friar Bacon*. A peculiarity of some of Greene's soliloquies is that they are directly addressed to the audience, in which case they fall into a different category from the true soliloquies when the character (always one of his main *dramatis personae*) is thinking aloud to himself, but in the presence of other actors on the stage. These idiosyncracies of Greene are present in *A Knack*, but are mainly absent in Ethenwald's soliloquies.

Ethenwald's first soliloquy sets the scene for the love intrigue. He enters alone.

Ethenwald: The night drawes on, & *Phoebus* is declining towards
the West.
Now shepheards bear their flocks vnto the folds,
And wintred Oxen fodered in their stalles
Now leaue to feede, and gin to take their rest,
Black duskie cloudes inuyron round the globe,
And heauen is couered with a Sable robe,
Now am I come to doe the kings command.
To court a Wench & win her for the King.
But if I lyke her well, I say no more,
Tis good to haue a hatch before the dore:
But first I will moue her Father to prefer
The earnest suit I haue in canuasing,
So may I see the Maid, woo, wed, I and bed her to:

ll. 721-733

This has the lyricism of Nashe of which there is ample evidence in his
Summer's Last Will and Testament. His second soliloquy contains the
imagery Born associates with Shakespeare.

My fancies thoughts, lyke the labouring Spyder,
That spreads her nets, to entrap the sillie Flie:
Or lyke the restlesse billowes of the seas,
That euer alter by the fleeting ayre,
Still houering past their woonted passions,
Makes me amazed in these extremities,
The King commands me on his embassage,
To *Osricks* daughter, beauteous *Alfrida*,
The height and pride of all this bounding ill,
To poste amaine, plead loue in his behalfe,
To court for him, and woo, and wed the mayd,
But haue you neuer heard that theame,
Deceit in loue is but a merriment,
To such as seeke a riuall to preuent,
Whether (distraught) comes my vnruly thoughts,
It is the King I cosen of his choise,
And he nil brook Earl *Ethenwald* should prooue
False to his Prince, especially in loue.
Then thus it shal be, Ile tel the king the maid is fair,
Of nut browne cullour, comelie and fair spoken,

306

Worthie companion to an Earle or so:
But not a Bride for *Edgar*, *Englands* King,
This will alay the strong effects in loue,
Fame wrought in *Edgars* mind of *Alfrida*.
Well, Ile to court, and dallie with the King,
And worke some means to draw his mynde from loue.

ll. 901-926

Middleton associates spiders with Nashe in *The Black Book* where he finds Pierce (Nashe) lying asleep in his bed with 'the spindle-shank spiders...stalking over his head as if they had been conning of *Tamburlaine.*'[53] Born makes much of the imagery of the spider with which the speech opens, which he claims may 'be counted among Shakespeare's stock images. It appears as early as *2H6.*'[54] (Here, however, it should rightly be attributed to Marlowe, if this is his play as testified by Tucker Brooke, Bakeless, and Gaw, debated in Chapter IV.) Born concedes that the spider-image was so generally used by Elizabethan writers that 'the value of the spider-image as evidence for our hypothesis diminishes.'[55] (i.e. as evidence for Shakespeare). Greene used it only once when he lifted it direct from Lyly. So that Born finds he is reduced to the second image of the billows as 'typically Shakespearean'.

Or lyke the restless billowes of the seas,
That euer alter by the fleeting ayre,
Still houering past their woonted passions. ll. 903-5

Shakespeare certainly uses sea imagery constantly and in a great variety of ways, as impressively demonstrated by Professor A.F. Falconer, RN., in *Shakespeare at Sea* (1964) and its sequel *A Glossary of Shakespeare's Sea and Naval Terms including Gunnery* (1965). Here Born himself plays the 'labouring Spyder' in weaving his web to present what he sees as Shakespeare's hand in the speech with numerous examples of billows-imagery from his works. Born asks: 'Why should billows hover? And why should they hover past wonted passions? I think the image becomes intelligible if we compare it with Shakespeare's sea-, wind- and wave-images. It has been observed that Shakespeare was interested in nature mainly as a mirror of human life. For instance, he invests animals with human qualities and defects. In the same way he often personalizes the sea.'[56] He then quotes from Falconer's book explaining a somewhat similar 'billows-image in *2H6.*'

'The wind has its greatest effect on the crest of waves, tending to
drive them faster than the mainbody and thus causing them to break.
In a virulent wind, "spindrift", a sort of driving spray, is swept from
their tops and is carried along the surface of the water, flying like
a vapour or rising in clouds:

> the winds
> Who take the ruffian billows by the top
> Curling their monstrous heads and hanging them
> With deaf'ning clamour in the slippery clouds.'

Born compares this with the 'restless billows' in *A Knack* which he
thinks 'very possibly describe the same natural phenomenon ... The
billows-image in Ethenwald's speech is far from obvious, and rather
intricate. It takes imagination (coupled with keen observation) to describe
the phenomenon of "spindrift" as

> ..... restlesse billows of the seas,
> That euer alter by the fleeting ayre,
> Still houering past their woonted passions.'[57]

He qualifies this further: 'As, in the participial clause, the billows are
even given their own *passions*, there can be no doubt that they are
invested with human qualities', and in Shakespeare billows are 'almost
invariably personalized and described in terms of human emotions and
actions. The billows are *ruffian* (*2H6*, III, i, 22), *inconstant* (*H8*, Prol.,
1.15), *they hang their heads* (*H8*, III, i, 1.10), the *chidden* billows *pelt*
the clouds (*Oth.*, II, i, 1.12). They *speak* (*Tmp.*, III, iii, 1.96), *kiss* the
moon (*Per.*, III, ii, 1.58).'[58]

The personalization of nature is, of course, nothing new. Marlowe had
done it in the earliest work we have from him, his *Dido*: '*Disquiet* seas,
lay down your swelling looks' (I, i, 1.122); and in Dido's anguished
speech of invective (IV, iv, 11.126-160) everything is personalized, the
sails, the tackling, the wood of the ship that 'would be *toiling* in the
wat'ry billows/ To *rob* their mistress of her Trojan guest'; the water is
scolded, 'Why did it *suffer* thee [the ship's wood] to *touch* her breast,/
And *shrunk* not back, *knowing* my love was there?' and the '*base*
tackling...*dares* to heap up sorrow to my heart'.

In *Tamburlaine* the imagery concentrates on the sun, the sky and
celestial objects, all personalized: 'The sun, *unable to sustain* the sight,/
Shall *hide* his head' (*Tamb.2*, I, iv, 11.168-9); 'The golden ball of heaven's

eternal fire,/ That *danc'd* with glory on the silver waves,/ Now *wants* the fuel that inflam'd his beams,/ He *binds* his temples with a *frowning* cloud' (*Tamb.2*, II, iv, 11.2-7); the sea '*washeth* Cyprus with his brinish waves' (*Tamb.2*, III, v, 1.12). The sky is exhorted: '*Weep*, heavens, and *vanish* into liquid tears!' (*Tamb.2*. V, iii, 1.1), '*Blush*, heaven' (Tamb.2, V, iii, 1.28) and – 'Earth, *droops*' (Tamb.2, V, iii, 1.16). At his end Faustus is drawn up 'like a foggy mist,/ Into the entrails of yon *labouring* cloud', and the clouds '*vomit* forth into the air', and have 'smoky mouths'. (*Faustus*, 11.1475-1480). Compare this with the personalization in a line from Nashe cited on page 301. The trait is traceable to Marlowe. In *Edward the Third*, which I attribute to Marlowe, the 'new-replenish'd pendants *cuff* the air/ And *beat* the winds, that for their gaudiness/ *Struggles to kiss* them;' (*Ed.III*, IV, iv, 11.20-22) and, 'Poor sheepskin! how it *brawls* with him that beateth it!' (II, ii, 1,48).

The personalized imagery of nature is the language of poets, hence it was Marlowe and Shakespeare, who developed it to its finest limit, as one would expect. But Nashe, too, was no mean poet. His *Summer's Last Will* is a dainty, poetic piece. Ver's song, 'Spring, the sweete Spring, is the yeres pleasant King', shows our satirist in happy contrast to his scurrilous satirical vein, descanting on nature: 'The fields *breathe* sweete, the dayzies *kisse* our feete', and 'the pretty birds doe sing,/ Cuckow, iugge, iugge, pu we, to witta woo.' (11. 161-172; McKerrow III pp. 23-29). Might one not say, This is 'Shakespearean'?

It has been noted that the most telling comparison that Born offers is taken from *2H6*, which on the evidence of Tucker Brooke's meticulous scholarly study (never yet satisfactorily dismissed) is Marlowe's play. The case for Shakespeare that Born tries to argue is weakened from the onset.

If we return to Nashe for evidence that he is the co-author of *A Knack*, whose particular contribution is in the creation of Ethenwald, we find that even his non-poetical, satirical writings yield something that is relevant to the case. Taking up his 'ink-squittering' pen to belabour Harvey again after a two-year interim of truce, Nashe opens his *Haue with you to Saffron-walden or Gabriell Harueys Hunt is vp* (1596) with the promise that, having heretofore only 'marcht faire and softly, like a man that rides vpon his owne horse, and like the *Caspian* sea seeme neither to ebbe nor flow, but keep a smooth plain forme in my eloquence', he will now 'powre hot boyling inke on this contemptible Heggledepegs barrain scalp.'[59] (Harvey having gone bald by this time).

Nashe's plan of campaign in this publication, he announces, is that his 'whole Booke' will be cast 'in the nature of a Dialogue' in which the 'interlocutors' are to be '*Senior Importuno,* the Oppenent', '*Grand Consiliadore,* chiefe Censor or Moderator', '*Domino Bentiuole,* one that stands, as it were, at the line in a Tennis-court, and takes euerie ball at the volly', and '*Don Carneadas de boone Compagniola,* who, like a busie Countrey Iustice, sits on the Bench, and preacheth to theeues out of their own confessions', (this character is in a sense a parody of his late friend Greene); and with these, '*Piers Pennilesse* Respondent',[60] who is Nashe himself. He naturally allocates himself a leading part in this play-acting, and enjoys himself hugely. The case being opened (which already assuredly had his readers chuckling), we give a sampling of Nashe's 'Dialogue':

Benti:	From sharpe to come to the poynt: as farre as I can learne, thou hast all the aduantage of the quarrell, since both the first and last fire-brand of dissention betwixt you was tost by the Doctour.
Respond: (Nashe)	Tossing (by your fauour) is proper to the sea; and so (like the sea) doth hee tosse water, and not fire.
Benti:	That is tost or cast water on fire: if hee did so, he is the wiser.
Respon:	On a fire of sea-cole, you meane, to make it burne brighter.
Benti:	A fire that the sea will coole, or *Haruey* find water inough to quench, if you looke not too it the better.
Respon:	I warrant, take you no care, Ile looke to his water well inough.
Imp:	But me thought euen now thou contemndst him, because he tost water and not fire; whereas, in my iudgement, there is not a hairs difference betwixt being burnd and being drownd, since death is the best of either, and the paine of dying is not more tedious of the one than the other.
Respon:	O, you must not conclude so desperate, for euerie billow *brings* not death in the mouth of it... [My italics]

[The Argument is protracted]

Consil:	In anie case leaue this big thunder of words, wherein thou vainly spendst thy spirits before the push of the battaile; and if thou hast anie such exhaled heat of reuenge in the vpper region of thy braine, let it lighten and flash presently

in thy aduersaries face, and not a farre off threaten thus idely.

Respon: Threaten idely, said you? Nay, sure, Ile performe as much as hee that went about to make the dyuing boate twixt *Douer* and *Callis*, and as lightning and thunder neuer lightly goe asunder, so in my stile will I temper them both togither, mixing thunder with lightning, and lightning with thunder, that is, in dreadfull terror with stripes, & sound thrusts with lowd threats. Tell mee, haue you a minde to anie thing in the Doctors Booke? speake the word, and I will helpe you to it vpon the naile; whether it bee his words, his metaphors, his methode, his matter, his meeters. Make your choyce, for I meane to vse you most stately.

Cam: Then, good gentle Frend, (if you will) let's haue halfe a dozen spare-ribs of his rhetorique, with tart sauce of taunts correspondent, a mightie chyne of his magnificentest elocution, and a whole surloyne of his substantiallest sentences and similes.

Respon: And shall; I am for you; Ile serue you of the best, you may assure yourselfe: with a continuat *Tropologicall* speach I will astonish you, all to bee spiced & dredged with sentences and allegories, not hauing a crum of any cost bestowed vpon it more than the Doctors owne cooquerie.

Import: *Tropologicall*! O embotched and truculent....

Consi: It sounds like the ten-fold ecchoing rebound of a dubble Cannon in the aire, and is able to spoyle anie little mouth that offers to pronounce it.

Respon: Gentlemen, take God in your minde, & nere feare you this word *Tropologicall*, for it is one of *Dick Harueys* sheepes trattels in his *Lamb of God*. [This is the book written by Gabriel's younger brother Richard who was rector of Chislehurst]

Import: I, *Dick Harueys*, that may wel be;....but for the Doctor, trie it who will, his stile is not easie to be macht, beeing commended by diuers (of good iudgement) for the best that ere they read.[61]

This appears to be generous praise by Nashe for his Opponent Harvey, but now *Piers Pennilesse* Respondent (Nashe himself) declares he will take on this 'contriued pile of pure English', obviously with the intention of making mincemeat of it. He proceeds to prepare his readers for the entertainment as though they were an audience at a theatre:

> *Respon*: Hem, cleare your throates, and spit soundly; for now the pageant begins and the stuffe by whole Cart-loads comes in.[62]

I have indulged in over-quoting, but this is irresistible stuff, even if it does tend to come in by the cart-load, for Nashe, once in full spate, cannot stop himself and he covered page after page scratching with his goose-quill. Our young satirist had stamina! And his eager readers apparently lapped it up. In the foregoing we get the flavour of Nashe's art, and I suggest that it shows that he would have been fully capable of writing the part of Ethenwald (without any help from Shakespeare), and was in every way suited to the role of Greene's co-author in *A Knack*, a satirical social comedy of distinct topicality in 1592. We have Nashe's testimony in addition to Greene's that they were collaborators in plays, and according to Nashe the printers could not differentiate between their styles of writing. It is our task here to try to separate and identify their hands.

Probably the two friends collaborated closely even when the allocation of parts was made by the division of the main and sub-plot, as suggested. The most striking scenes of Ethenwald's part displaying those characteristics noted by Born of the 'many-faceted' type are in the early part of the play which contains Ethenwald's first two soliloquies. When we come to the scene in which news is received that the King is about to visit Ethenwald and his bride Alfrida, newly-wed, to see for himself how beautiful this lady is (and, as Ethenwald fears, to try to cuckold him), there is indication of a close collaboration by both dramatists writing one scene. It opens with Ethenwald's third soliloquy in which the fantastic pseudo-creature, the Ianamyst, makes its appearance, suggestive of Greene's hand. But the soliloquy effectively builds suspense and dramatic tension as to what will happen (untypical of Greene) and Ethenwald enters alone to soliloquize (untypical of Greene), and throughout the scene that follows we sense the presence of both Greene and Nashe working *together.*

Enter Ethenwald *alone*
Ethenwald, be aduised, the King hath sent to thee,

Nay, more, he means to come and visite thee,
But why, I theres the question?
Why tis for this, to see if he can fynd,
A front whereon to graft a paire of hornes:
But in plain tearms, he comes to Cuckold me,
And for he means to doe it without suspect,
He sends me word he means to visite me:
The King is amorous, and my wyfe is kinde,
So kind (I feare) that she wil quickly yeeld
To any motion that the king shal make:
Especially if the motion be of loue:
For *Pliny* writes, women are made lyke waxe,
Apt to receiue any impression:
Whose mindes are like the Ianamyst,
That eates, yet cries, and neuer is satisfied:
Well, be as it is, for Ile be sure of this,
It shall be no waies preiudice to me:
For I will set a skreene before the fyre,
And so preuent what otherwyse would ensue:

ll. 1412-1433

The level of writing accords with Greene's throughout the rather silly scene in which Kate, the kitchen maid, appears disguised as Alfrida in order to prevent the King from gaining sight of Alfrida in all her beauty. Greene enjoyed writing women's parts, which were his most successful dramatic characters, and it is in Alfrida's speech describing how she will receive the King that further evidence of Greene's hand is detectable, typical of his style and repeating details of dress and ornament from two descriptions in his known works.

Ethenwald: .... but heare you wyfe, what do you think
in this, that *Edgar* means to come and be your guest?
Alfrida: I thinke my Lord he shall be welcom then,
And I hope that you will entertaine him so:
That he may know how *Osrick* honours him:
And I will be attyred in cloth of Bis,
Beset with Orient pearle, fetcht from rich Indian
And all my chamber shall be richly, [sic]
With Aras hanging, fetcht from *Alexandria*,
Then will I haue rich Counterpoints and muske,

Calamon, and Casia, sweet smelling Amber Greece,
That he may say, *Venus* is come from heauen,
And left the Gods to marie *Ethenwald*.

ll. 1446-1458

Born compares this with the following description taken from *Greenes Vision*:

His Roabes of Bisse, were crimsen hew,
Bordred round with twines of blew;
In *Tyre* no richer silke solde,
Ouer braided all with golde:
Costly set with pretious stone,
Such before I neere saw none.
A massie Crowne vpon his head,
Chequerd through with Rubies red.
Orient Pearl and bright Topace,
Did burnish out each valiant place.

(Grosart, XII, p.275)

And this is further supported by Rasni's speech from *Looking Glass*:

That for this deed ile decke my *Aluida*
In Sendall and in costly Sussapine,
Bordred with Pearle and India Diamond,
Ile cause great *Eol* perfume all his Windes
With richest myrre and curious Amber greece.
Come, louely minion, paragon of faire,
Come, follow me, sweet goddesse of mine eye,
And taste the pleasures *Rasni* will prouide.

ll. 885-92

It can hardly be doubted that Alfrida's speech above came from Greene's pen. Ethenwald's alarmed response to his wife foresees the amorous King and his alluringly dressed and perfumed Alfrida committing adultery. Aside he exclaims:

Zwouns, they are both agreed to cuckold me.
But heare you wyfe, while I am master of the Barke,
I meane to keepe the helmster in my hand.   ll. 1459-61

He then insists that Alfrida is banished to the kitchen, and the servant Kate be dressed up to represent Alfrida before the King. The altercation

314

between Ethenwald and Alfrida suggests that here we have an example of truly collaborative writing in which each dramatist severally takes his part in the dialogue – Nashe for Ethenwald, Greene for Alfrida – in the quarrel scene, giving Greene the opportunity he doubtless would have relished of writing Alfrida's speech cited above. The King, who seems to have been Greene's part, now enters into the love-intrigue. The scene following, in which all the characters are stereotypes who behave unconvincingly – apart from Ethenwald, whose lines are limited to protestations concerning Alfrida – seems to be mainly written by Greene.

It is feasible that the play was largely written in this kind of close collaboration, each dramatist writing the parts for certain characters allocated to him, and perhaps making suggestions here and there to each other. A less satisfactory alternative where this particular scene is concerned, is that Greene for some reason wrote the whole scene himself, beginning with Ethenwald's opening soliloquy including the Ianamyst. Born, however, purports to see Shakespeare's hand in this unremarkable piece of blank verse. He makes much of the element of suspense created by Ethenwald's soliloquy. He comments:

'The net of hints and intimations that sustains suspense through the whole romantic plot of the play and which is essential for the proper development of this plot is bound to remind us of Shakespeare'.[63]

This he sees exemplified in the soliloquy under discussion. He continues:

'Greene never acquired the knack of preparing his audience properly, nor did he generally succeed in creating tension. Either he predicted exactly what was going to happen and thus turned the subsequent scene into an anticlimax, or he left his audience in the dark.'[64]

In other words, Greene was not a born dramatist, for this innate sense of what will 'work' dramatically was not in him. Whereas, as Harry Levin has remarked, 'Marlowe was a born playwright',[65] and Shakespeare, of course, understood the value of 'holding something in reserve up his sleeve' to create dramatic tension and keep the audience guessing. But Nashe also had dramatic flair as is obvious from his satirical writings, which are essentially 'dramatic'. He skilfully and teasingly prepares his readers, building the anticipation of his mischievous 'flyting' of Harvey in which he scores from one point to the next. This is brilliantly conducted, and makes one regret the more that no play of Nashe's survives. The fact that his *Isle of Dogs* was banned is proof that it was effective drama!

Ethenwald's third soliloquy is necessarily determined as to its content by the plot at this stage, so that it can hardly be seen as an interpolation by the hypothetical 'reviser' Shakespeare. Nevertheless, pursuing his hypothesis, Born explains the appearance of the Ianamyst as Shakespeare's parody of Greene by 'a deliberate *reductio ad absurdum* of certain idiosyncracies of Greene's prose. In view of Shakespeare's known aversion to certain aspects of Greene's style he may well have been the creator of the Ianamyst.'[66] This, I suggest, is *hypothesis ad absurdum*. To the best of my knowledge there is no shred of evidence of 'Shakespeare's known aversion' to Greene's style, and there is also no cogent reason for introducing Shakespeare into the debate concerning *A Knack*. Born achieves his platform for this simply by ousting Nashe as Greene's sole co-author for which we have Greene's testimony.

Born also ignores Marlowe. He quotes from Shakespeare's then unwritten plays to supply references to 'Scythia' and the 'barbarous Scythian',[67] but omits to mention Marlowe's 'Scythian *Tamburlaine*' who was well known to audiences in 1592. He also seems unaware that Marlowe first significantly developed the *caesura* for dramatic effect in a blank verse line, and quotes only Shakespeare's later use of this. Born sees only a Shakespearean reflection in its use in Ethenwald's four-foot line in the soliloquy – 'But why, theres the question?' He concludes erroneously:

> '*Unlike any other Elizabethan playwright*, Shakespeare tailored his verse for delivery on the stage. Broken lines and short lines create pauses in the metrical flow and give the actor the opportunity to fill them with complimentary gestures. Often a metrical irregularity – a pause or an extra-metrical exclamation – helps to place a dramatic stress or to enliven the rhythm of the verse.'[68] [My italics]

As Bakeless has sufficiently demonstrated, Marlowe was writing just such short lines for *dramatic* purposes before Shakespeare: 'The brutal scenes in which the captives are ill-treated in *Tamburlaine* contain many abrupt verses of this sort, as do other passages intended to suggest the bluntness of the soldier.'[69] Typical examples are:

Come, bring in the Turke.	(I *Tamb*. 1.1570)
My Lord, how can you suffer these?	(*Ibid*. 1.1664)
What now? In love?	(*Ibid*. 1.302)

| News, news. | (*Ibid.* 1.305) |
| How now, what's the matter? | (*Ibid.* 1.306) |

Skating on thin ice, Born makes much of the extrametrical end to the first soliloquy, 'Who is here? what ho.' (1. 734) and the similar ending to the third soliloquy:

> Twere good I questioned with my father first,
> To heare how he affected towards the King
> What ho.   11. 1434-36

Born makes his point: 'While Greene, in his canonical plays ends all his soliloquies on mannerly ten-syllable lines, Shakespeare often indicated the end of a soliloquy by a short exclamation, a command, a question, or a call for a servant.'[70] He then cites examples from Shakespeare to support his 'revisionist' hypothesis; but, alas, in Born's closed academic world it seems that Marlowe is no longer studied, for he is unaware that Marlowe *also* ends his famous soliloquy in *Tamburlaine* declaring –

> That virtue solely is the sum of glory,
> And fashions men with true nobility.
> Who's within there?
>
> *I Tamb.* V, ii. 11.188-191

So what does this prove? *Not* that Marlowe had any hand in *A Knack*, but neither did Shakespeare. One wonders why such a hypothesis could have seemed feasible? Born's study of *A Knack to Know a Knave*, which began so convincingly, disintegrates from the point at which he becomes obsessed with bringing Shakespeare into the picture on a basis of unreasonable, dubiously arguable theorizing. Born's attitude exemplifies the disturbing trend in today's Shakespearean scholars to pretend that Marlowe never existed! He has thus misled himself into working on an untenable hypothesis. This distorted view derives from Peter Alexander's denegration of Marlowe, to which Born pays tribute claiming its academic respectability:

'As it is generally agreed, that Marlowe, in *Edward II* borrowed from *2* and *3 H6*, Alexander concludes that these plays must have been in existence and with Pembroke's men early in 1591.'[71]

That is true, but as I have demonstrated by reference to Tucker Brooke's and Bakeless' work Marlowe was borrowing from his *own* works, not from Shakespeare. Labouring under the false assumption that 'Shake-scene' was Shakespeare and that the *Henry VI* trilogy was written by Shakespeare in 1590 to 1591/2, Born concludes his book with an extraordinarily complicated theory to explain how these three plays came to be written, which is pure hypothesis. Dover Wilson has stated the problem:

'Yet if Shakespeare wrote *1 Henry VI*, which first appeared on 3 March 1592, he could hardly have completed its sequels, *2* and *3 Henry VI*, in time for them to be acted, and become sufficiently famous with the London public before 3 September, the date of Greene's death.'[72]

This demonstrates, once again, the insuperable difficulties inherent in the orthodox concept concerning the authorship of *Henry VI*, which is bolstered by the misunderstanding of the identity of 'Shake-scene' that has bedevilled Shakespearean scholarship and misled much potentially valuable research into a blind alley. Born is not alone in having suffered from the effects of this delusion, which has encouraged his misguided and gratuitous introduction of Shakespeare as a hypothetical 'reviser' of *A Knack* to the neglect of Nashe's claim. It is not for us to invent history, but to interpret it.

On firm ground Born has made a valuable contribution in providing convincing evidence for Greene's authorship of *A Knack*, which it is impossible to dismiss. As a by-product of his arguments for Shakespeare he has effectively also made a strong case for Nashe's co-authorship by revealing the difference in the characterization of Ethenwald, who is untypical of Greene – a rounded, credible human being, imbued with Nashe's own brand of 'cheeky panache' and 'nonchalant impudence'.[73] Born's description of the personality traits he detects in this character are those very qualities that clearly portray his creator, Nashe. Ethenwald as the hero of the sub-plot reflects Nashe's main contribution in the love-intrigue which conveys 'a realistic presentation of the relationship between the sexes',[74] in contrast to 'the pretty romanticism' typical of Greene's love scenes which reflect the superficiality of Greene's nature. Born finds that 'the wooing scene in *A Knack* is in tone half-playful, half-serious, with a strong satirical undercurrent.' He comments that this 'does remind us of Shakespeare'.[75] One can equally say that it accords perfectly in mood with Nashe's touch, who was an inveterate satirist even when writing in his most lyrical, poetic style. Both in his lyricism and in his expression of genuine passion Ethenwald (Nashe) has more affinity with Marlowe's than with Greene's lovers.

Albeit a bad quarto, the text furnishes ample evidence of Greene's and Nashe's collaboration. Emphasis at the end of the play in Honesty's address to the audience is again centred on the current social evils in Greene's didactic manner:

Honesty....You that wil damne your selues for lucres sake,
And make no conscience to deceiue the poore:
You that be enemies of the common wealth:
To send corne ouer to inrich the enemie:
And you that doe abuse the word of God,
And send ouer woolle and Tin, broadcloth and lead,
And you that counterfeyt Kings priuie seales,
And thereby rob the willing minded Communaltie,
I warne you all that vse such subtill villanie,
Beware least you lyke these be found by *Honestie*,
Take heed I say, for if I catch you once,
Your bodies shall be meat for Crowes,
And the Deuill shall have your Bones.

This speech concludes the scene in which Honesty asks the King –

Honesty: But will your Grace grant me one boone?
King: Whats that *Honesty*?
Honesty: That I may haue the punishing of them.
Whom I haue laboured so to fynde.

11. 1837-1840

Judgement of Nashian ferocity is then passed. Thus Greene and Nashe sign their joint authorship of the play.

Independently Born and Bennett have, I suggest, correctly identified *A Knack to Know a Knave* as Greene's last comedy for which they have presented an undeniably strong case. Nashe's part in it, which Born underrated in order to supplant him with Shakespeare in his 'revisionist' theory, fits both the textual and external evidence in every detail, and reveals a close and harmonious collaboration. As reflected in Greene's address to 'yong Iuuenall' in his Letter, this appears to have been a happy partnership which he remembers with affection. Greene and Nashe had enjoyed a long and compatible relationship as writers commenting satirically on the London literary scene, and this play was a fitting conclusion. It seals Nashe's part as a playwright in the trio of dramatists whom Greene addresses as his 'Quondam acquaintance', all of whom had been associated with him in recent dramatic work for the hated '*Iohannes fac totum*' whom he is lambasting in his Letter. These revelations give valid meaning and point to his *Groatsworth* missive as never before perceived.

Greene's importance in shedding light on the contemporary drama that was being played out in London during 1592 as he was ending his life, assures his place in history. His *Groatsworth of Wit* has dramatically highlighted the true situation of this bitter quarrel that caused a storm in London's theatrical circle that had long-lasting repercussions for its two dominant figures. I believe that Edward Alleyn was secretly smitten with remorse, which he finally expiated in his early retirement from the stage to devote his wealth to the foundation of his College of God's Gift for the poor; while for the 'famous gracer of Tragedians', Marlowe, the knell of his doom was sounded by the accusation of Atheism, publicly and in print. Greene's envy of these two had its revenge in full measure. Nashe, perhaps seeking to make amends, wrote his lost 'Elegy' on Marlowe[76] prefacing his posthumous publication of *Dido Queen of Carthage* in 1594, which remains for us the saddest loss of all. What it might have told us we can only speculate.

Portrait of Edward Alleyn

(Courtesy of Dulwich Picture Gallery, Alleyn's College of God's Gift)

X   *The Great 'Shake-scene'*

IT WAS NO EXAGGERATION to describe him as 'the only Shake-scene in a countrey', for Edward Alleyn was certainly that, and a man of many parts – literally – and in every sense of the term, a *Johannes factotum*. These descriptions epitomize the man who is revealed in the documentation of the Alleyn Papers, which he left to be preserved under the careful protection of his charitable foundation at Dulwich. We lack a definitive biography of Alleyn. Despite the existence of this comprehensive store of information on him, most books on him treat him in relation to his famous foundation rather than as the man himself, who was in many ways an outstanding character. He was a man of prodigious energy, motivated by goodwill and inspired by noble ambitions; ceaselessly busy, planning, organising, building, creating, advising, socializing, always on the move, always involved and committed to the task in hand, and ever ready to entertain and amuse himself and others. His conviviality had a serious incentive. He was constantly seeking to improve himself, and his personal library testifies to his interests. The books it contained have disappeared, but we have the record of twenty-six of the more substantial volumes he bequeathed to his College in 'A note of those Bookes wch ye w^orp Edward Alleyn founder of this College left after his death'. These included eight books on history, among them 'Liuies Historyes, Plinyes Historyes, Stowes Chroni.' and 'A History of ye Roman Emperors'; ten religious and theological works, some in Latin; a 'Virgill in English', and a 'Dictionarium Poeticum'.[1] Elsewhere in this documentation we find that he owned medical books, and collected medical and herbal recipes, many in manuscript written in his own hand.

He was also a collector of verses in manuscript, which are still among his Papers, most of these written in another hand than his own, suggesting that they may have been presented to him by his friends. Two are written in Ben Jonson's hand; one a copy of Martial's epigram 'Vitam quae faciunt beatiorem' in an English translation: 'The things that make life happier'; and the other, Sir Henry Wotton's poem beginning 'How happy is he born and taught'. The single reference he made to Shakespeare was jotted on the back of a letter dated 19th June 1609, from Thomas Bowker concerning a mastiff whelp, noting Alleyn's purchase of 'a book Shaksper Sonetts – 5^d'.[2]

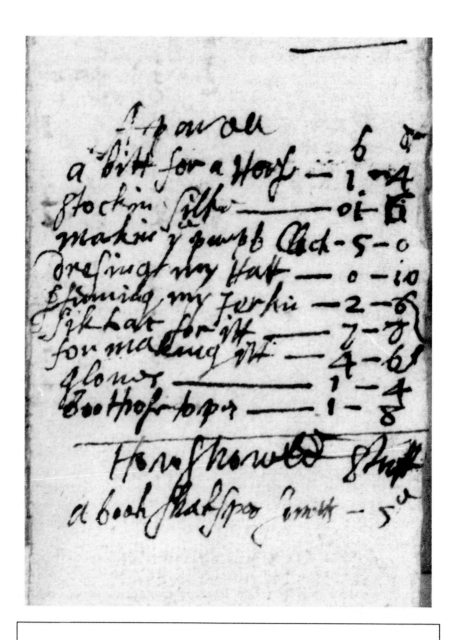

Edward Alleyn's note on the back of a letter dated 19th June 1609 recording his purchase of 'a book Shaksper Sonnetts - - 5ᵈ'.

By kind permission of the Governors of Dulwich College.

This precious copy has since disappeared. Clearly Alleyn was a man with some taste for literature and an avid reader of historical and theological books.

His long reign of supremacy in the theatrical world was only one part of his life; we might call it the First Act, as Bacon so aptly described his foundation at Dulwich 'the Last Act'. After he retired finally from acting, he continued his friendships and close business interests with his professional colleagues, entertaining them to dinner at his home. On one such occasion his guest was John Heminge. But of William Shakespeare, apart from the one tantalizing snippet of information regarding Alleyn's purchase of the Sonnets, there is no hint anywhere in all these voluminous Papers, which has surprised and dismayed Shakespearean scholars and, perhaps, accounts for the regrettable neglect of research on Alleyn, whose importance has been underestimated.

Edward Alleyn was, to judge by the accolades given him by his contemporaries, undoubtedly the greatest actor of his day, even when compared with his nearest rival, Richard Burbage, who began to emerge five years later than Alleyn, but whose career was continuous for thirty years, and extended fifteen years beyond the time of Alleyn's final retirement from the stage leaving the limelight to Burbage, who had by this time become identified with the great Shakespearean roles which were created exclusively for his company. Even this did not dim the lustre of Alleyn's name. Acting is an art that is, as much as any other art, only brought to its highest expression when it stems from creative and imaginative powers allied to intelligence. With these qualities Edward Alleyn was endowed. In him we sense the inner frustration (whether conscious or sub-conscious) arising from the lost opportunities of his itinerant acting youth in which he was denied the advantages of a higher education that would have given scope to his intellectual development; and which his innate intelligence, and his middle class standing as the son of a propertied innkeeper, might well have yielded him had he received regular schooling in settled circumstances with proper encouragement for his youthful studies; as, for instance, had been Robert Greene's good fortune and which gained him a place at Cambridge university. Alleyn might then have proceeded to a distinguished career as a divine instead of triumphing in the ephemeral productions of the stage, for there is a close correlation between the church and the stage, priest and player; and Alleyn was genuinely devout; a much more conventional, straightforward, uncomplicated nature than Marlowe, who was destined to turn his back on divinity to serve his diviner Muse.

324

All his life Alleyn was to remain deeply interested in education. He swiftly reached the peak of his acting profession, but became disenchanted with the theatrical life, opting to retire early from the stage when aged only thirty-one and at the pinnacle of his fame, although he later resumed acting in response to Queen Elizabeth's request. Before he was turned forty he began to plan the founding of his college of education at Dulwich, where he used his theatrical and bear-garden profits to invest in land to provide for his grand design. He rose to considerable eminence as a man of wealth and outstanding charity. By the time he was fifty he had disbursed the then enormous sum of ten thousand pounds towards founding his College of God's Gift at Dulwich, which his shrewd investments and genius for organisation enabled him to do without curtailing his liberal hospitality and constant generosity to his many dependants, and the poor and needy to whom he was a veritable father-figure. He never turned away empty-handed those who, in his eyes, were the deserving poor or friends in need, but his charity did not extend to wastrels or dishonest or immoral folk. He summarily 'exspulsed' drunkards or fornicators from his charitable institutions. Doubtless Robert Greene, a habitual drunkard, spendthrift and licentious womanizer, would have been placed in the 'undeserving' category and sent packing when he came begging for a loan, and for this Greene stigmatized Alleyn as heartless. The very opposite was the truth. Alleyn's whole life testifies to his compassionate nature and immense kindliness – though his typically Elizabethan attitude to blood sports might seem to belie this.

The unique personal memorabilia of the Alleyn Papers has most fortunately survived the centuries despite periods of incredible neglect and cavalier treatment, some of it at the hands of those eminent scholars who freely borrowed them and carelessly mislaid, lost or even added deliberate forgeries to these manuscripts, and can be studied in the archives of Dulwich College Library. They include the muniments relating to Alleyn's charitable foundation, as well as miscellaneous legal documents, financial accounts, intimate letters, and some rare theatrical manuscripts; and his remarkable personal *Diary*, written in his fluent Elizabethan Secretary hand in his idiosyncratic spelling, which he kept meticulously for fully five years from Michaelmas 1617 (the year after his College Chapel had been consecrated) until Michaelmas 1622. We shall be dipping into this treasure store to establish the kind of man Edward Alleyn was. He emerges as a human being of real stature.

Edward Alleyn was indeed built on a large scale. As a young man he was destined to greatness in his sphere by his physique and his inborn talent, for he was strikingly tall, long-limbed and of imposing presence. He had an air of authority about him even when young and looked maturer than his years: a commanding figure, and a face with equally strong features, piercing dark eyes, a somewhat long and prominent nose, and a firm chin covered by a square-trimmed beard in his portrait, which he would have shaved off for some of his roles. He had the look of a man not to be trifled with, and doubtless he possessed a deep and booming voice (such a one as *Roberto* might well find 'nothing gratious') which could be heard throughout the auditorium of an Elizabethan theatre with its open roof. He was a born tragedian.

We have only Fuller's authority for the information that Edward Alleyn was 'bred a Stage-player' as he never refers to it himself.[3] We know he spent much of his youth touring with a provincial company and that he returned to London probably in 1585-6, a fully fledged actor ripe for great things. The London theatre-goers at once recognized his outstanding talent, and they took him to their hearts in his first great role as 'Tamburlaine the Great'. The following year, 1588, the supreme comic actor, the celebrated Richard Tarlton, died, and his mantle of pre-eminence on the stage fell onto the broad shoulders of young Alleyn.

There are more references in print to Tarlton and Alleyn than to any other actors of the time. It was to be another five years before Richard Burbage presented any challenge, and his reputation was undoubtedly enhanced by the superlative Shakespearean roles it was his good fortune to play. The same can be said for Alleyn in that he had Marlowe's leading parts to launch him on the road to fame, but for sheer histrionic power there seems to have been no one to match him. He made advances in the technique of the actor's art which, in his own day, make him comparable with Stanislavsky, for he set a standard in the interpretation of character in the roles he played which made the performance unforgettable, and other aspiring actors took him as their model. Here an appraising critic remembers the distinctive gait that Alleyn developed in his interpretation of the hero *Cutlack* in the play of that name:

> Clodius, methinkes, lookes passing big of late,
> With Dunstan's browes, and Alleyn's Cutlack's gate.
> What humours possess'd him so I wonder:
> His eyes are lightning and his words are thunder.[4]

This epigram from the anonymous collection *Skialetheia, or the Shadow of Truth*, 1598, attributed to Edward Guilpin, refers to a performance by

326

an actor who is evidently aping Alleyn's style of acting: not only his 'Cutlack's gate' but also his flashing eyes and thunderous speech would have been modelled on the great '*Roscius*' of the English stage, for the name of the famous Roman actor soon became a synonym for Edward Alleyn. By 1592 his reputation was at its height, and Nashe, now no longer dependent on Greene's patronage to launch him on a literary career, instead of reflecting Greene's prejudiced opinions speaks with his own appraising voice in his *Pierce Penilesse*, published that year:

'Not Roscius nor Æsope, those admyred tragedians that haue liued euer since before Christ was borne, could euer performe more in action than famous *Ned Allen*.'[5]

Ben Jonson's praise of Alleyn in his *Epigrams* (1616) represents the opinion of a connoisseur well qualified to pass judgement.

> If *Rome* so great, and in her wisest age,
> Fear'd not to boast the glories of her stage,
> As skilfull *ROSCIUS* and graue *ÆSOPE*, men,
> Yet crown'd with honors as with riches, then;
> Who had no lesse a trumpet of their name
> Then *CICERO*, whose euery breath was fame;
> How can so great example dye in mee,
> That, *ALLEN*, I should pause to publish thee?
> Who both their graces in thy selfe hast more
> Out-stript, then they did all that went before:
> And present worth in all dost so contract,
> As others speake, but onely thou dost act.
> Weare this renowne: 'Tis just, that who did giue
> So many *Poets* life, by one should liue.[6]

Alleyn's fame lingered long after his death despite an acting career punctuated by retirement. Thirty years after his second and final retirement (which he outlived by another twenty-two years pursuing a second career as Master of the Royal Game and founder of a charity) Thomas Heywood recalled his great triumphs on the stage in his edition of *The Famous Tragedy of the Rich Jew of Malta*, which he published in 1633. It is the only extant edition of Marlowe's play, and contains this accolade to Edward Alleyn in 'The Prologue to the Stage at the Cocke-pit' written by Heywood for his revival of this old play.

	We know not how our Play may passe this Stage,
* Marlo	But by the best of Poets in that age*
	The *Malta Jew* had being, and was made;
*Allin	And He, then by the best of Actors play'd:*
	In *Hero* and *Leander*, one did gaine
	A lasting memorie: in *Tamberlaine*,
	This *Jew*, with others many: th' other wan
	The Attribute of peerlesse, being a man
	Whom we may ranke with (doing no one wrong)
	Proteus for shapes, and *Roscius* for a tongue,
	So could he speake, so vary;

Edward Alleyn was born in the parish of St Botolph's, Bishopsgate, London on 1st September, 1566. His father, also named Edward Alleyn, purchased an inn in Bishopsgate in the year of Edward's birth and is thereafter styled 'innholder'.[7] He hailed from Buckinghamshire, being the second son of Thomas Alleyn of Willin in county Buckingham and Mersham in county Bedford, and had married Margaret Townley, daughter of John Towneley of county Lancaster.[8] Five sons were born, John, (c.1556) Oliver (who died 1563), Edward, William and Percival, of whom only John, the eldest, and Edward survived to manhood. His father died when Edward was only four years old, but he left his widow endowed with lands and tenements and 'good leases and redy mony' by his will eventually to pass to his sons and be equally divided among them.[9] Edward's inheritance features later in his bequests for the foundation of his College of God's Gift at Dulwich, wherein he adds 'all those messuages, lands, tēnts and hereditaments with the apptenances in the pish of Saincte Butolphes without, Bishoppsgate, London which descended and came to the said Edward Alleyne by and from his said father Edward Alleyne, Gent, deceassed'.[10]

Thus he commemorated the father whose name he bore, and whom he lost at such a tender age, in the great charitable, educational foundation he bequeathed to posterity and which meant immeasurably more to him than all his theatrical success and fame.

We do not know exactly when Margaret Alleyn remarried taking John Browne, haberdasher, as her second husband. The first reference to her as the wife of John Browne is in a deed dated 1580,[11] but it would be surprising if she had remained a widow for as long as ten years in an age when well-endowed widows tended to remarry quickly, and having been left with a family of boys to bring up she would probably have felt the

328

need for a husband the more. Fuller states that their step-father had some connection with the acting profession as a side-line to his haberdashery, and certainly the two surviving brothers, John and Edward Alleyn, were both launched early in life on an acting career. G.L. Hosking suggests that John Browne was more interested in turning Edward's histrionic talent to account than in the boy's education.[12] A lad with a natural flair for acting would have been a lucrative asset to a company of actors, being cast to fill the female parts until his voice broke, and he would be especially valuable if able to sing well. Edward Alleyn was undoubtedly musically gifted, for the first reference to his profession describes him not as a player, but as a 'Musicion'.[13]

His step-father's presumed connection with theatrical affairs probably derives from the two actors named Browne, Edward and Robert, who were members of the same company as the Alleyn brothers over the years spanning their careers. Robert Browne is also associated with Edward and John Alleyn in a deed of sale dated 3 January 1588/9 in which their fellow actor, Richard Jones, disposes to them all his share of 'playinge apparells, playe Bookes, Instruments, and other comodities' held by him 'Ioyntelye with the same Edwarde Alleyn John Allen Citizen and Inholder of London and Roberte Browne yoman' for the sum of £37.10s.[14]

This seemingly brotherly association of Robert Browne with the two Alleyns prompts the conclusion that there may have been a relationship with John Browne. Perhaps both the Brownes were his sons, but no evidence confirming this has been found. It is an interesting indication of the sensitivity to subtle class distinctions of the time that Jones and Browne are both designated 'yoman', while Edward Alleyn in the preamble is described as 'of London, gentleman', indicating that he owned property. He was already on the upward climb. His brother John, ten years his senior, was following in his father's footsteps as an innkeeper. He left acting after 1591 and in 1594 became a 'distiller', but he died in 1596.

John Alleyn is first referred to as an actor with the Earl of Sheffield's players, a provincial company, in 1580. It is a reasonable deduction that his younger brother Edward, then only a lad of thirteen, would have been in the same company with him as a boy player and trainee, but as such he would not have been listed.

The first record we have of Edward Alleyn as a player is at the age of seventeen in March 1583/4 with the Earl of Worcester's Men, together with the two Brownes and the above-mentioned Richard Jones. These players were the servants of William Somerset, 3rd Earl of Worcester, and were essentially a provincial company with a long history of touring the traceable as far back as 1555, but with no record of any performance in London. On this occasion they were visiting Leicester. Arriving in the city on Friday, 6th March 1583/4, or possibly a day or two before the date of this report, they found that the Queen's Men had been there before them on 'Tuesdaie the third daie of mc̄he 1583' and had obtained from the Mayor a 'lycence to play & for aucthorytye showd fōth an Indenture of Lycense from on Mr Edmonde Tylneye Esquier Mr of her Mats Revells'.[15]

The Worcester's Men were highly incensed about this for it seems that, having inadvertently left their 'box' (containing papers?) at the inn in Leicester, the Queen's Men had stolen their commission. The gist of their complaint is not very clear.

Friday the 6 of mc̄he

Certen players cam before Mr Mayor at the Hall .... who sayed they were the Earle of Woster's men: who sayd the forsyd playr̄s were not lawfully aucthorysed, & yt they had taken from them there cōmys̄s, [commission] but it is untrue for they forgat there box at the Iñ in Leic̄. & so these men gat yt & they sed the syd Haysell was not here hymself... [16]

This last mentioned was George Haysell, their chief actor, cited in their Indenture, whom the Worcester's Men claimed was not in fact present in Leicester. The record is obscure, but evidently there was a sense of grievance against the Queen's Men which rankled, and when the Mayor refused permission for further performance in the city on that day at three o'clock as the Worcester's Men requested, trouble ensued.

In the memorandum dealing with the resultant contretemps, the players are named, being:

Robt Browne, James Tunstall, Edward Allen,
Wm. Harryson, Thos. Cooke, Ryc. Johnes,
Edward Browne, Ryc. Andrewse.[17]

These apparently were in the deputation from the Worcester's Men facing the Mayor and his corporation about the matter in hand.

Memorandum, that Mr Mayor did geve the aforesaid playours an angelle towardes theyre dynner, and wild them not to playe at this present, being Frydaye the vi[th] of Marche for that the tyme was not conuenyent. The foresaid playours met M[r] Mayor in the strete near M[r] Newcombe's house, after the angelle was given aboute a ii howers, who then craued lycence agayne to play at thre, and he told them they should not: then they went away and sed they wold play, whether he wold or not, and in dispyte of him, with dyuers other euyl and contemptuous wordes...these men contrarye to M[r] Mayor's commaundement, went with ther drummes and trumppytes thorowe the towne in contempt of M[r] Mayour, neither wold come at his commandment by his officers vse [sic] worship.[18]

However, this little drama was soon happily ended with the tendering of earnest apologies, so that Mr Mayor seems (inexplicably) to have relented completely and the Worcester's Men were allowed to play that very afternoon after all!

Nota. These seyd playours haue submitted themselues, and are sorrye for there wordes past, and craued pardon, desyeringe his worship not to wryte to there master agayne them, and so vppon there submyssion they are licensed to play this instant at thre p.m. and also they haue promysed that vpon the stage in the begynyng of there play to shoe vnto the herers that they are lycensed to playe by M[r] Mayor, and with his good will and that they are sorye for the wordes past.[19]

One wonders what part young Edward Alleyn played in all this, for only three years later he was heading his company, and at seventeen he was probably already as tall as a man. He possessed great powers of persuasion, and perhaps he exercised them on this occasion to win over the Mayor of Leicester. This rather curious incident gives us an insight into the kind of life he led touring the provinces during his youth. We do not know if he ever attended a regular school, but literacy was an essential requirement for an actor. The skills of reading and writing and of calculation of figures are well attested in Edward Alleyn's extant letters, accounts and papers. A youngster of Edward Alleyn's energy, intelligence and enterprising spirit would be largely self taught, and we have evidence of his love of books. Alleyn was a man of sensibility, and perhaps even as a youngster he made an impression on the Mayor of Leicester for he was obviously born to rise.

There is a break in the records of the Earl of Worcester's Men from 1585 for four years, until after the death of the old Earl in 1589 when the company was revived by his successor, Edward Lord Herbert. In the interim Edward Alleyn and his brother John had joined the Lord Admiral's Men in London, bringing with them several of the former Worcester's players – Robert Browne, Edward Browne, Richard Jones, and James Tunstall (or Dunstan). This transfer suggests the dissolution of the old Worcester's Men whereby the Lord Admiral, Charles Howard, 2nd Baron of Effingham, who had been created Lord High Admiral of the Fleet in 1585 when his players are first known as the Lord Admiral's Men, gained a strong company of experienced actors who were now headed by their most brilliant member, the young Edward Alleyn. It seems likely that the reconstitution of this company took place in 1585-86 for it was in the following year, 1587, that the Lord Admiral's emerged as one of the most important theatrical companies in London owing its strength and success in great part to 'famous Ned Allen'.

Despite their success, conditions during the late 1580s for maintaining a thriving company of players were difficult. Puritan opposition was mounting, and whilst noble patronage was the actors' sheet anchor, the Queen herself had in 1583 formed her own company of players, the Queen's Men, whose twelve members were drawn from the choicest actors of the existing companies. The most renowned of these was the superlative comic actor Tarlton. Competition between the leading rival companies was hot. It was probably to meet this that Edward Alleyn formed a joint company in late 1590 or early 1591 amalgamating players of the Lord Admiral's and Lord Strange's Men, an association of the best of both that was for a time unrivalled even by the Queen's Men. In the winter of 1591 they played six times at the Court, a record number of performances for any one company.

By 1592 this association had resolved itself into a company entirely of Strange's Men under Edward Alleyn, a unique arrangement. In all his peregrinations in combination with other acting companies, Alleyn remained faithful to the great nobleman who was his patron, Lord Charles Howard of Effingham, who was created first Earl of Nottingham in 1596, and was Lord High Admiral of the Fleet for thirty-four years. He belonged to that branch of the family of the Dukes of Norfolk who were always loyal to Queen Elizabeth. He was a great favourite of the Queen who knew well how to value a courtier of such exemplary character, probity and wisdom. Alleyn seems to have had an excellent relationship with him over the years, and he continued to be known as Servant of the Lord Admiral whatever his activities. His friendly relations seem to have extended to his patron's family for in his *Diary* many years later he notes that on Sunday 7th July 1622 he had dinner with the Countess of Kildare. This was Frances Howard, the Earl of Nottingham's daughter, then a widow. As is his wont he carefully records his daily expenses:

	1^i	s	d
I dind att Detford w^t ye Countes off Kildare giuen in ye morning to a pore woman y^t brought a letter from Lo: Carry 1^s giuen att ye Chirch 6^d to ye coachman & gardyner 1^s so	0	2	6 [20]

The issuing of passports for travel abroad was over the signature of the Lord Admiral, Charles Howard, and in 1592 several actors of the Admiral's company decided to go on tour to Leyden and Germany and probably elsewhere on the Continent, whilst Alleyn, who opted to remain in London, continued as head of Lord Strange's Men. The passport, signed by Lord Howard, names Robert Browne, John Bradstreit, Thomas Saxfield (Sackville) and Richard Jones, authorizing them to leave England to tour on the Continent:

avec intention .... d'exerciser leurs qualitez en faict de musique agilitez et jouez de commedies, tragedies et histoires."[21]

It is dated 10th February 1591/2. The decision to go abroad may have been as a result of what had happened in the latter end of 1591. The combined companies of Lord Admiral's and Strange's had been playing at Burbage's Theatre in Shoreditch, and perhaps also at his subsidiary theatre, the Curtain nearby, when a quarrel flared up between Edward Alleyn and the proprietor, James Burbage. The cause is not known, but the upshot was that Alleyn stormed off the premises with his men. Taking what was probably the entire company with him, minus the four Admiral's men who went abroad, he crossed the river and entered into an agreement with Burbage's rival, Philip Henslowe, to perform for the forthcoming season at his theatre, the Rose, on Bankside in the Liberty of Southwark south of the Thames.

It was an important move which opened a new chapter in Alleyn's fortunes, leading to a happy and life-long association with the Southwark businessman, Philip Henslowe. This shrewd theatrical investor had married Agnes Woodward, the well-endowed widow of his former employer, bailiff to Viscount Montague, and used his acquired wealth to start him on the road to theatrical management. Having no experience of stage craft

Portrait of Joan Woodward after she became Mrs Edward Alleyn.

In his *Diary* Philip Henslowe noted the union of two young people which must have given him great satisfaction and joy. Joan Woodward, his step-daughter, was about twenty years old and Edward Alleyn just twenty-six:

> Edward alen wasse maryed vnto Jone Woodward the 22 daye of octob₃ 1592 In the iiij & thirtie yeare of the Quene Matie Rayne elyzabeth by the grace of god of Ingland france & Iarland defender of the fayth. [22]

(Courtesy of Dulwich Picture Gallery, Alleyn's College of God's Gift)

himself, an alliance with the immensely talented and practical man of the theatre, young Edward Alleyn, must have held great attraction. The result of Alleyn's first season at the Rose was that in October 1592 he married Henslowe's step-daughter, Joan Woodward, thus sealing his business partnership and joining a highly respectable London household. So step-son-in-law and step-father-in-law together mounted the ladder of affluence through marriage, though in both cases genuine affection sweetened the union.

Henslowe had no children of his own and to him Edward Alleyn became his 'wellbeloved sonne', while Alleyn found in Henslowe the father he had lost so early in life. A close bond developed between them and they formed a united, industrious, well regulated and loving theatrical family, respectable despite this association with a much criticised profession. Edward Alleyn was fond of children and his one regret must have been that their marriage remained childless, for which he eventually compensated by taking under his wing the orphans of his College of God's Gift at Dulwich. There were also the boys in the players' company, from one of whom a delightful letter survives among Alleyn's papers, evidently written while the company was on tour, to Alleyn's wife Joan. Written as from the boy John Pyk (Pyg) it is in Alleyn's handwriting, and was evidently intended as a joke, for although the marginal inscription pretends it was written by 'mr doutone' (Thomas Downton, who was one of the leading actors with the company) without Alleyn's knowledge, it was obviously concocted by Alleyn and Pyk, perhaps with Downton's help. It is undated.

> mysteris yor honest ancyent and
> Loving servant pige hath his
> humbell comendā to you and to my
> goode master hinsley & mystiris and to
> my m^{rs} sister bess for all her harde
> delying w^t me I send her harty
> Comendā hoping to [p]be behowlding
> to her agayne for the opinyng of
> the coberde: and to my neyghbore
> doll for calynge me vp in a mornyng
> and to my wyf sara for making clean
> my showes & to that ould Jentillman
> mounsir pearle y^t ever fought
> w^t me for the blok in the chemeney

corner & though yo^u all Look for
the redy retorne of my proper person
yett I swear to you by the fayth of a
fustyan kinge never to retorne till
fortune vs bryng w^t a Joyfull
metyng to lovly london I sesse

yor petty prety pratlyng parlying pyg
by me John pyk

[*vertically in the left hand margin*]

mystiris I praye yo^u kepe this that
my mayster may se it for I gott on to
wright it m^r doutone & my m^r knowes nott of it

[*addressed:*] To his loving m^{rs} mysteris Alline
on the banck syd over agaynst the clynk [23]

It was customary for an actor who was married and possessed a settled
home to take into his household a boy, who was apprenticed to him as
a fledgling actor, to whom he would teach his art. This was doubtless the
position of young Pyk in the Alleyn home at this time, and happy the
boy whose good fortune it was to be placed under Alleyn's protecting
wings, as this letter testifies. Pyk remembers everyone at home with
obvious affection and pokes endearing boyish fun at them. Beginning,
very properly, with his 'good master' Henslowe and his wife, and his
'mrs' Joan Alleyn's sister Bess, despite her apparent strictness with him
(her hard dealing), for which she compensates by opening the cupboard
(containing cakes or sweets, perhaps?) for which he sends her his hearty
commendations and hopes 'to be behowlding to her agayne'; and his
'neyghbore doll', presumably a servant who sleeps in the adjacent room
and calls him every morning; and 'my wyf sara', another servant (?)
whom he pretends to fancy as his 'wife', who cleans his shoes for him;
and the old gentleman playfully named 'Monsieur' as though he were a
Frenchman, who is his rival for the corner seat in the inglenook fireplace.
And all this is addressed to his 'loving Mrs. Mistress Alleyn on the
Bankside over against the Clink'.

He longs to be back in 'lovly london' and this has an especially poignant
ring to it if this letter (without date) was written during the extended tour
which was forced on the players by the severe plague of 1593 when all
the theatres in London were closed for the year – indeed restraint of plays

was effectively from June 1592 to May 1594, although with lessening of the spread of infection during the colder winter months the theatres were traditionally allowed to resume playing for the Christmas season.

The five months interim from June to December of 1592 had probably been partly taken up with a tour of country playing by most of the London companies, although even fear of the plague did not invariably drive them out of the capital as one might expect. The chief actors were not always willing to face the hardships of provincial touring and sometimes left the company to foot it from town to town on their own, as George Haysell had left his men to proceed without him to Leicester in March 1583/4, and as Alleyn did in 1603 when he went to Sussex to enjoy some hawking and fishing while his players departed on tour.

The long plague had gathered momentum throughout 1592, worsening with the warm weather. The Rose closed on 22nd June with a performance of *A Knack to Know a Knave*, identified here as Greene's and Nashe's collaborative moral satire. Nashe had left London to seek the purer air and sea-breezes of the Isle of Wight to stay with his patron, and Greene was in London sickening, not from the plague, but from dropsy and probably a dose of the pox, his restless pen still writing, writing to the end. We know that Strange's Men had left London to go on tour, but their company was large and it is likely that Alleyn did not accompany them for he had a special interest in remaining at the Bankside. He was courting Joan Woodward. Simultaneously he was cementing his relationship with Philip Henslowe. Robert Greene's vitriolic attack on him carries the obvious implication that he had seen Alleyn in person about a loan when the crisis of bankruptcy and the onset of his fatal illness struck him down. This was probably in late July or the beginning of August for on 3rd September he was dead, and within a few weeks London would have been buzzing with gossip about Greene's scandalous allegations.

Greenes Groats-worth of Witte bought with a million of Repentance was entered at Stationers' Hall on 20th September 1592 to William Wright 'vpon perill of Henrye Chettle' with 6d paid for the dubious privilege to that gentleman, and *The Repentance of Robert Greene Maister of Artes* followed not long after on 6th October to John Danter for Cuthbert Burbie. The printers and publishers would have been eager to cash in on the newsworthiness of these scandalous pamphlets so it may be expected that speedy publication followed.

The Strange's Men who were on tour, would have returned home by 22nd October for on that day Alleyn was married to Joan Woodward, Henslowe's step-daughter. It was an important event in the theatrical world, and throughout his life Alleyn continued to celebrate his wedding anniversary as a day of rejoicing and hospitable feasting.

The slanderous gossip engendered by Greene's deathbed diatribe is unlikely to have dampened the guests' spirits at his nuptials for the players well knew Greene's embittered disposition towards their profession and probably this only added spice to the quips and jokes on that happy occasion. We may be sure that John Pyk, the 'fustian king', enjoyed himself at the wedding festivities which were traditionally lavish and hearty to judge by the warm hospitality for which Alleyn became noted, and naturally music and dancing would form a lively part of the celebration.

The Elizabethans knew well how to enjoy themselves. People needed light relief in the gathering gloom of the city in which never a day passed but the tolling death knell was heard. The plague concentrated the mind wonderfully on living: and on dying. The sharpened sense of human mortality found expression in the poetry and music of the age. Out of this atmosphere of encroaching doom Thomas Nashe created a charming, elegiac little poem as part of his *Summer's Last Will and Testament*, a witty and intelligent entertainment of semi-dramatic interludes and songs, as light as gossamer, tinged with gentle melancholy, to while away the tedium of a winter day at Court. The following is one of the songs sung by the Children of St Paul's when they performed this entertainment before the Archbishop of Canterbury at his Palace at Croydon in the winter of 1592.

> *Adieu, farewell earths bliss,*
> *This world vncertaine is,*
> *Fond are lifes lustfull ioyes,*
> *Death proues them all but toyes:*
> *None from his darts can flye,*
> *I am sick, I must dye:*
> > *Lord haue mercy on vs!*
>
> *Rich men, trust not in wealth,*
> *Gold cannot buy you health;*
> *Phisick himselfe must fade,*
> *All things to end are made,*
> *The plague full swift goes bye:*
> *I am sick, I must dye:*
> > *Lord haue mercy on vs!*

Beautie is but a flowre,
Which wrinckles will deuoure;
Brightnesse falls from the ayre
Queenes haue died yong and faire,
Dust hath closde Helens *eye:*
I am sick, I must dye.
   Lord haue mercy on vs!

Strength stoopes vnto the graue,
Wormes feed on Hector *braue,*
Swords may not fight with fate,
Earth still holds ope her gate.
Come, come, the bells do crye,
I am sick, I must dye.
   Lord haue mercy on vs!

Wit with his wantonnesse,
Tasteth deaths bitternesse:
Hels executioner,
Hath no eares for to hear
What vaine art can reply.
I am sick, I must dye.
   Lord haue mercy on vs.

Haste therefore eche degree
To welcome destiny:
Heauen is our heritage,
Earth but a players stage,
Mount wee vnto the sky:
I am sick, I must dye.
   Lord haue mercy on vs! [24]

The reality was more grim. The relaxation of playing over Christmas proved an illusory relief for by 21st January 1592/3 the death toll was mounting again, and all restraints were reimposed. Strange's Men gave their last performance of the winter on 1st February with Alleyn playing *The Jew of Malta*, and the theatres closed not to reopen for eleven months. There was nothing for it but to take his company on an extended tour in which they visited Bath, Bristol, Shrewsbury, Chester, York and Canterbury. Alleyn must have been deeply worried about the young wife he left behind, his 'sweett mouse' as he called her. One of his company lost his entire family – his wife and all his children who were living in Shoreditch. This may be the Robert Browne, who had been with Alleyn throughout their early acting career, but who was at this time probably touring with the rest of the Lord Admiral's company on the Continent, and not with Alleyn and Strange's Men. Such tragedies hovered always around the people, for ignorance and disease marched hand in hand to make the expectation of life short. Edward Alleyn was one of the most enlightened of his contemporaries on matters of health and hygiene, and the Henslowe household living at Bankside near the Clink prison – not a salubrious district by any standard – may have owed their immunity from infection in some measure to the good advice he wrote to his young wife in August 1593 when the plague was at its height, urging her to maintain strict hygiene in their home. She was evidently still living with the Henslowes for the letter is addressed to 'mr hinslo on of the gromes of hir maist chamber dwelling on the bank sid right over against the clink'.

Emanell

My good sweett mouse I comend me hartely
to you And to my father my mother & my
sister bess hoping in god thought the siknes [sic. thought = though]
beround about you yett by his mercy itt may
escape yor house wch by ye grace of god it
shall therfor vse this corse kepe yor house
fayr and clean wch I knowe you will
and every evening throwe water before yor dore
and in yor bakcsid and haue in yor windowes
good store of rwe and herbe of grace and
wt all the grace of god wch must be obtaynd
by prayers and so doinge no dout but ye lord
will mercyfully defend you: now good mouse
I haue no newse to send you but this thatt
we haue all our helth for wch the lord be praysed
I reseved yor letter att bristo by richard couley
for the wich I thank you I haue sent you by this
berer Thomas popes kinsman my whit
wascote because it is a trobell to me to cary it
reseave it wt this letter And lay it vp for
me till I com if you send any mor letters

340

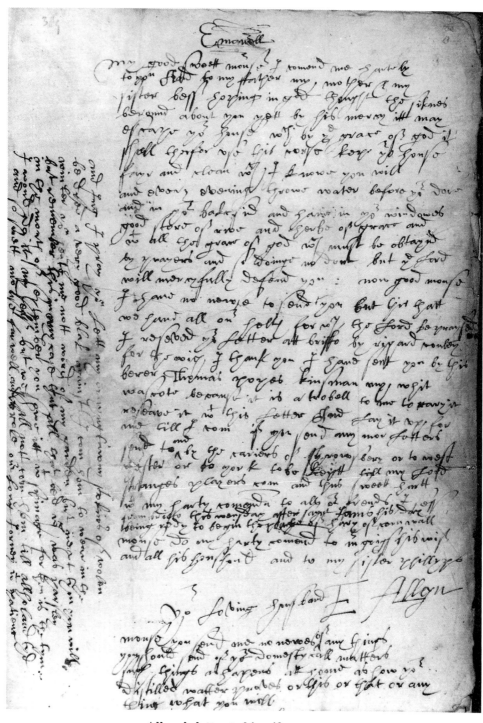

Alleyn's letter to his wife

By kind permission of the Governors of Dulwich College

send to me by the cariers of shrowsbery or to west
chester or to york to be keptt till my lord
stranges players com and thus sweett hartt
w^t my harty comendā to all o^r frends I sess
from bristo this wensday after saynt Jams his day
being redy to begin the playe of hary of cornwall
mouse do my harty comend to m^r grigs his wif
and all his houshould and to my sister phillyps

Yo^r Loving housband E Alleyn [25]

He adds a postscript:

> mouse you send me no newes of any things
> you should send of yor domestycall matters
> such things as hapens at home as how yor
> distilled watter proves or this or that or any
> thing what you will

Further in the left hand margin written vertically he adds:

and Jug I pray yo^u lett my orayng tawny stokins of wolen
be dyed a very good blak against I com hom to wear in the
winter   yo^u sente me nott word of my garden but next tym you will
but remember this in any case that all that bed wch was parsley
in the month of september you sowe itt w^t spinage for then is the tym:
I would do it my self but we shall nott com hom till allholand tyd
and so swett mouse farwell and broke ou^r long Jorney w^t patienc

There is a note of yearning for his home and 'domestycall' comforts
as the actor travels the road from town to town with his fardle on his back.
Meanwhile in London the plague had sharply increased from mid-July,
reaching its peak in August. In the week of 14th August the authorities
no longer published the figures of the death rate for fear of spreading
despondency. Henslowe's letters are a poignant record of a brave family.
The following letter from Philip Henslowe paints a grim picture. It has
been dated tentatively to August 1593 and must have been written later
than Alleyn's of 1st August from Bristol.

Wellbeloved Sonne edward allen. After owr hartie Comendationes bothe
I & you^r mother & syster bease all in generall dothe hartieley comende
vs vnto you & as for you^r mowse her comendationes comes by yt seallfe
wch as she sayes comes from her harte & her sowle prainge to god day
daye & nyghte for you^r good heallth wch trewley to be playne we doe soe

342

alle hoopinge in the lorde Jesus that we shall haue agayne a mery meting
for I thancke god we haue be flytted wth ffeare of the sycknes but thanckes
be vnto god we are all at this time in good healthe in owr howsse but
Rownd a bowte vs yt hathe bene all moste in every howsse abowt vs
& wholle howsholdes deyed & yt my frend the baylle doth scape but he
smealles monstrusly for feare & dares staye no wheare for ther hathe deyed
this laste weacke in generall 1603 of the wch nomber ther hathe died of
them of the plage 113[5]-0-5 wch hause bene the greatest that came yet
& as for other newes of this & that I cane tealle youe none but that
Robart brownes wife in shordech & all her chelldren & howshowld be
dead & heare dores sheat vpe....[26]

This may be the family of Robert Browne who was a member of the
Earl of Worcester's Men and who joined the Lord Admiral's with Alleyn.
There were, however, three Robert Browns known to Alleyn. During the
plague the parishes were required to give weekly returns of all deaths for
the week on Tuesdays, and the old crones whose office it was to view
each corpse and determine the cause of death had to deliver their reports
to the parish clerk, so that on Wednesdays he could give an account of
how many of the dead were victims of the plague. These figures were
published. Henslowe is quoting the total of all deaths before deductions
were made and then the total for plague deaths. His letter continues with
news of the joiner who is making a 'coat cupboard' (Henslowe wrote
'corte coberd') and a bedstead for the newly married couple on whose
house considerable improvements were in progress. He has evidently
received Alleyn's letter, for he makes reply:

> ...& as for you^r garden yt is
> weall & you^r spenege bead not forgoten you^r orenge colerd stockenes
> died but no market in smythfylld nether to bye you^r cloth nor yet
> to sealle yor horsse for no mane wold ofer me a bove fower pownd
> for hime therfor I wold not sealle hime but haue seante hime in
> to the contrey tylle youe Retorne backe agayene..[27]

And so with many kind commendations to and from friends, and
prayers for all their continued good health, he concludes

> ...& thankes be to god you^r poore
> mowsse hath not ben seack seance you weant.

| You^r lovinge wiffe tylle | You^r poore & a sured frend |
| death Jone allen | tell death Phillippe Hensley |

His next extant letter is dated 14th August, which was the week of peak figures for plague deaths when these were withheld from the public, but Henslowe has a shrewd idea of what they must have approximated.

Jesus

wellbeloued Sonne edward allen I and you[r] mother & you[r] sister Beasse haue all in generalle ou[r] hartie commendations vnto you & verey glad to heare of you[r] good healthe w[ch] we praye god to cone tenew longe to his will & pleassur for we hard that you weare very sycke at bathe & that one of you[r] felowes weare fayne to playe you[r] parte for you w[ch] wasse no lytell greafe vnto vs to heare but thanckes be to god for a mendmente for we feared yt mvche because we had no leatter frome you when the other wifes had leatters sente w[ch] mad you[r] mowse not to weape a lyttell but tocke yt very greauesly thinckinge y[t] you had conseved some vnkindenes of her be cause you weare ever wont to write w[t] the firste & I praye ye do so stylle for we wold all be sorey but to heare as often frome you as others do frome ther frendes for we wold write oftener to you then we doo but we knowe not whether to sende to you therfore I praye you for geat not you[r] mowsse & vs for you seant in one leatter that we Rettorned not answeare wheather we Receued y[m] or no for we Receued one w[ch] you made at seant James tide wher in mackes mensyon of you[r] whitte wascote and your lvte bockes & other thinges w[ch] we haue Receued...

Here follow messages of a 'hundered comendations from you[r] mowsse' and prayers for his health wishing he may soon be able to come home and

..... be eased of this heavey labowre & toylle & you sayd in you[r] leater that she seant you not worde how you[r] garden & all you[r] things dothe prosper very well thanckes be to god for you[r] beanes are growen to hey headge & well coded & all other thinges doth very well but your tenantes weax very power for they cane paye no Reant nor will paye no Rent whill myhellmas next & then we shall haue yt yf we cane geat yt...[28]

Both Henslowe and Alleyn owned houses from which they drew rent, but the plague had serious consequences for the livelihoods of a great many people. Henslowe also misses the actors for he remarks ruefully,

'I growe poore for lack of them' – the playhouses being now closed. The sickness brought poverty in its wake. He repeats thanks for Alleyn's good counsel on taking precautions against the infection, which he promises they follow to the letter. And after more of 'this and that', he gives the latest news about the plague:

..... and as for newes of the sycknes
I cane not seand you no Juste note of yt be cause ther is command
ment to the contrary but as I thincke doth die wthin the sitteye
and wthout of all syckneses to the nomber of seventen or eyghten
hundreth in one weacke & this praynge to god for you^r health
I ende frome london the 14 of aguste 1593

you^r lovinge wiffe to   you^r lovinge ffather & mother
comande tell death   to owr powers P.H.   A [29]
Johne Allen

This letter like the previous one is addressed to him as one of my Lord Strange's players but vouchsafes no place where it may have reached him.

Too my wealbeloued
husband m^r Edwarde
Allen on of my lorde
stranges players
this be delyuered
wth speade.

Probably the letters from all the wives and friends were sent together in one package, as seems to have been the case with those received from the itinerant players, as is implied in the next letter dated 28th September when the plague had begun to decline and exact figures were once again available. After beginning 'Right wealbeloved Sonne edward allen' with the usual commendations, Henslowe chides him for not writing more often:

now sonne leate vs growe to alyttell vnkindnes wth you becausse we cane
not heare from you as we wold do that is when others do & if we cold as sartenly
send to you as you maye to vs we wold not leat to vesete you often
ffor we beinge wthin the cross of the lorde you littell knowe howe we do
but by sendinge for yt hath pleassed the lorde to vesette me Rownd a
bowte & almoste all my nebores dead of the plage & not my howsse ffree
for my two weanches haue hade the plage & yet thankes be to god leveth
& ar welle & I my wiffe & my two dawghters I thancke god ar very well
& in good heallth now to caste a waye vnkindnes & to come to owr newes [30]

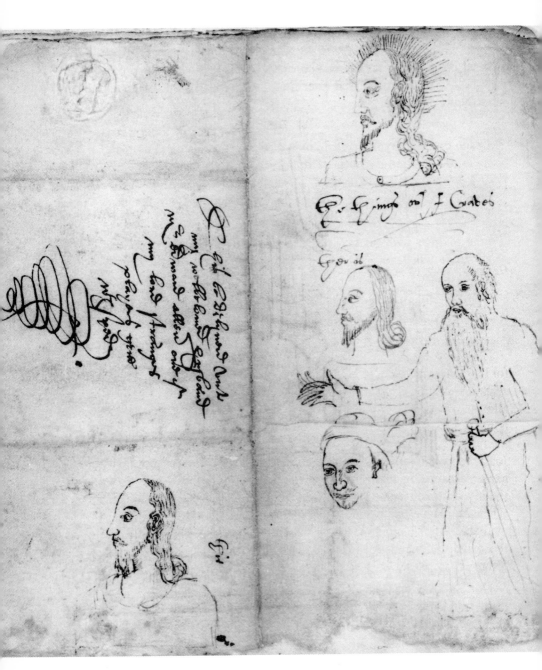

Heslowe's sketches drawn on the back of his gently chiding letter to his "sonne" for failing to write home. It was addressed by his wife, "This be deliured vnto / my welbeloued husband / Mr Edward allen now of / my lord stranges / players giue / with speed" / ending with a decorative flourish.

By kind permission of the Governors of Dulwich College

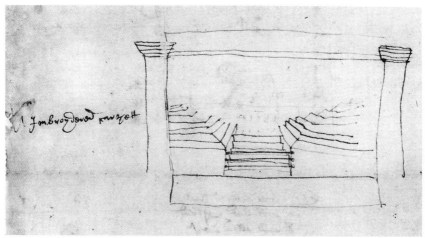

Heslowe's sketches (reverse side)

Henslowe repeats himself about the market at Smithfield and no sale for his horse, and there was no cloth available for retail. The fair had been curtailed to three days with restriction to wholesale dealing, but had been allowed on account of its vital importance to the cloth trade. His 'newes' is mostly repetition of domestic matters about Alleyn's dyed stockings, the progress of the joiner's work on his house (presumably where he and Joan are going to live when he returns), and the 'spenege bead' in the garden now sown. Finally he comes to the interesting information which sheds light for us on the theatrical scene –

> ..... & as for my lorde a
> penbrockes wch you desier to knowe wheare they be they ar all at home
> and hauffe ben t⟨his⟩ v or sixe weackes for they cane not saue ther carges
> ⟨w⟩^th trauell as I heare & weare fayne to pane the⟨r⟩ parell...

Not only did they pawn their apparel, but they sold three playscripts to the publisher, the subject of hotly disputed authorship in a previous chapter.

Henslowe continues:

> ..... & this I eand praysinge god that it doth
> pleass hime of his mersey to slacke his hand frome visietinge vs
> & the sittie of london for ther hath abated this last two weacke
> of the sycknes iiij hundreth thurtie and five & hath died in all

betwexte a leven and twealle hundred this laste weack wch I hoop
Jn the lord yt will contenew in seasynge euery weack that we
may Reioysse agayne at owr meatinge...

Thus gradually the long plague was abating and the longed for return
to London and the reopening of the theatres drew nearer. The household
of the Henslowes had mercifully escaped, although two of the servants
contracted the disease but had survived. Probably they had been well
nursed, for among Edward Alleyn's papers are notes on physick and
medicinal recipes written in his hand. These are for infusions of herbs
combined with ingredients mainly of vegetable origin, such as olive oil,
vinegar, cloves, lemons and wormwood, and show considerable
understanding of their healing properties. He also made poultices for
external application, and his circle of friends, relatives and neighbours
often resorted to him for advice and a little effective doctoring, whilst his
'pretious balms' were in wide demand. Alleyn was keenly interested in
health and medicine and in the *Diary* he kept at Dulwich he noted his
purchase of 'a book of ye generall pracktis off phisick' for 6s. 8d. (quite
a large sum in those days) on 29th November 1617.[31] In later life he
numbered many doctors amongst his friends, including the famous
physician, William Harvey, discoverer of the circulation of the blood,
whom he entertained among the guests at his hospitable table at his manor
house in Dulwich. Alleyn's enlightened approach to medicine is in striking
contrast to that of Sir Francis Bacon – a bit of a hypochondriac – whose
belief in outrageous concoctions appears rather bizarre, by comparison.
For instance, he recommends the drinking of an infusion of 'sealed earth,
snake's blood, coral, pearls, the shell of the fish dactylus' as a remedy
for closing the bowels.[32] Sir Francis was one of the eminent guests whom
Edward Alleyn feasted at the banquet he gave to celebrate the founding
of his College of God's Gift in Dulwich on 13th September 1619. But
I don't imagine they exchanged recipes for medical treatments on that
occasion.

Of special interest among Alleyn's manuscripts at Dulwich are the
inventories of theatrical costumes in his hand. The actors' playing apparel
was immensely lavish, being the most costly part of their equipment, far
in excess of what was paid out for playscripts for their repertoire. The
Player whom Greene meets in his *Groatsworth* story is hardly exaggerating
when he claims that 'my very share in playing apparell will not be sold
for two hundred pounds', at which *Roberto* is duly impressed. Alleyn's
inventory comprises upwards of 82 items of clothing, mainly in velvet

348

and satin and taffeta, richly ornamented with gold lace and gold and silver trimmings. His itemized wardrobe includes 16 gowns, 16 antick suits, 17 jerkins and doublets, 11 French hose, 8 Venetians, and 14 cloaks, all the garments being listed according to type. The following is his inventory of cloaks, many of them quite magnificent, to which have been written some spurious additions made in a forger's hand, to wit, that of the Shakespearean scholar John Payne Collier, who had free access to these papers at Dulwich College during the 1840s and was unable to resist the temptation to 'improve' their value by appending the forged names of characters from plays by Shakespeare in an attempt to introduce 'evidence' of a theatrical association between Shakespeare and Alleyn.

Clokes

1. A scarlett cloke wth ij brode guould Laces: w^t gould buttens of the sam downe the sids **for Leir**
2. A black velvett cloke
   A scarlett cloke Layd [the] downe w^t silver Lace and silver buttens
4. A short velvett cap clok embroydered w^t gould and gould spangles
5. A watshod sattins clok w^t v gould laces
6. A pur[l]pell sattin w^{t}elted w^t velvett and silver twist **Romeos**
7. A black tufted cloke cloke
8. A damask cloke garded cloke garded w^t velvett
   A longe blak tafata cloke
   A colored bugell for aboye
   A scarlett w^t buttens of gould fact w^t blew velvett
12. A scarlett fact w^t blak velvett
13. A stamell cloke w^t [b]gould lace
14. blak bugell cloke [33]

These lists written in Edward Alleyn's hand presumably comprise his personal theatrical wardrobe or stock. Elizabethan plays were always performed in the dress and fashion of the time, so that actors sometimes bought costumes from the company's theatrical wardrobe for themselves, though whether they intended to wear them as their own daily wardrobe, or were building up a personal theatrical wardrobe as Alleyn had evidently done, we cannot tell. Henslowe includes numerous notes in his theatrical *Diary* of accounts for the sale of costumes to the actors.

Sowld m^r Richard Jones player A manes gowne of
Pechecoler In grayne the 2 of septmb₃ 1594 to be payd
by fyveshellenges a wecke Imedyatly folowinge &
beginynge as ffowloweth [34]

Sowld vnto Jeames donstall player the 27
of aguste 1595 a manes gowne of purpell coller
cloth faced wth conney & layd on the sleues wth
buttenes for xxxxiijs iiijd to be payd xx^s in
hand & xxiij^s iiijd at mychellmase next cominge
after the datte a boue written I saye for.....[35]

} xxxxiijs iiijd

Sowld vnto steuen magett the 20 of Jenewary
1595 A dublet of fuschen playne & a payer of venesyones
of brade cloth wth ij laces of belement for xvjs to
be payd by xij^d a wecke begenynge the 23 of Jeneway
1595 beinge saterdaye & so forth Receued as
foloweth [36]

The actors apparently paid no regard to the Elizabethan prohibition
whereby the common people were not allowed to wear the fashions and
materials reserved for those who, in this class conscious society, were able
to claim that they were gentlemen, as prescribed by the Statute of Apparel
introduced by Mary Tudor and still in force throughout Elizabeth's reign.
The players flaunted themselves in fine clothing off stage as much as on.
It was yet another source of envy to Robert Greene who at first mistook
the 'Player' for a 'Gentleman of great living'.

Edmund Malone, who had been privileged to use, and even borrow the
Alleyn Papers from the Library of Dulwich College in the 1780s, had also
published other similar inventories of theatrical costumes and properties
and play-books of which we now have only his printed text for he
carelessly lost the originals. These very much longer inventories would
appear to have been in Henslowe's hand to judge by the spelling
peculiarities. They comprise almost two hundred items, mainly theatrical
costumes, but also musical instruments (timbrels, trumpets, drums, chimes
and bells, treble and bass viols, a scittern and a 'bandore'); an armoury
of swords, lances, bucklers and shields, helmets, a suit of armour; theatrical
properties ranging from Neptune's fork and garland, Cupid's bow and
quiver, a hobby horse, a bay tree, golden apples, a cauldron, a cage, a
rock, and so on to old Mahomet's head, and Tasso's picture. The boy actor
Pyk is several times mentioned for he evidently played leading female

350

roles, and so is Will Somers, the clown, in connection with particular costumes, and occasional characters in the plays are named. Twenty-nine play-books belonging to the company, the Lord Admiral's, are listed, but they contain no famous works of known literary value, many of them being otherwise unknown. No titles of plays sold by Alleyn to the company feature in the list.[37]

Referring to the lost inventories from which Malone had printed his text, J.P. Collier pompously compares his own publication of the extant inventories from Alleyn's Papers in his *Memoirs of Edward Alleyn,* 1841, and has the effrontery to claim specifically that his forged additions are all in the hand of Edward Alleyn.

> 'Inventories, not dissimilar, were printed by Malone, but they were taken from Henslowe's Diary (though not now remaining in it) and consisted of properties and dresses belonging either to the company at large, to himself alone, or to himself and Alleyn in partnership. Neither do they present any such curious points of speculation, as the preceding list, which, as has been stated, *is entirely in the hand-writing of the subject of the present memoir.*'[38] [My italics]

Collier's 'curious points of speculation' are, of course, his own forged additions of the names of characters from Shakespeare's plays, as in the inventory of cloaks above, and such fanciful embellishments as 'for the Moore in Venis' and 'in Pericles'. Collier had constant free access over a period of ten years to the manuscripts in the Dulwich College archives with the total trust of the College librarian, when he was able to tamper unsuspected and managed to interpolate no less than eighteen separate forged entries. Some of these forgeries he blatantly published in his *Memoirs of Edward Alleyn* and in his further selection *The Alleyn Papers.* It is as though he intentionally or subconsciously undervalued this unique MSS collection because it had failed to reveal new information concerning Shakespeare with which he hoped to startle the world and gain an immortal name for himself as the discoverer of new documentary evidence on the Bard. Collier exemplifies an extreme case of what could be diagnosed as severe Shakespeareaphobia which was further complicated by symptoms of envy of the pre-eminence of his predecessor as *the* great Shakespearean scholar, the revered Edmund Malone, who had enjoyed total free access to the Alleyn Papers, having been allowed to borrow them, literally taking possession of the archives for he kept them at his home for fourteen years, during which time he made only superficial use of them. They were not returned until after his death by his literary executor, the younger James

Boswell. By then, with astonishing and reprehensible carelessness he had managed to lose several theatrical inventories of costumes and properties, and mss play-books and plots, which have never been recovered. We know of their existence because they had been referred to in print. So that between them, these two famous Shakespearean scholars, eminent in their day, have done lamentable damage to these precious documents. The detection of six of Collier's most palpable forgeries gave rise to a furore that shook the world of Shakespearean scholarship for twenty years, involving scrutiny of every document and antiquarian book that had passed through his hands, and is summed up in C.M. Ingleby's *Complete View of the Shakespere Controversy*, published in 1861.

It was not until C.F. Warner undertook the immense task of cataloguing all the Dulwich College manuscripts and muniments, which he completed in 1881, that the rest of Collier's forgeries were finally discovered and exposed. The invaluable work done by Warner in bringing order into these papers with the most meticulous care and study, adding accompanying illuminating and erudite commentaries, has saved these archives containing Alleyn's unique personal records from further deterioration and loss. He has been followed by William Young's completion of his excellent two-volume *History of Dulwich College* in 1889. These two dedicated scholars, quietly and unsung, have brought their integrity and outstanding academic skill to bear on the task and have accomplished an inestimable service in bringing these manuscripts into focus for future students. Young's second volume presents the first authoritative life of the Founder, Edward Alleyn, together with a complete and accurate transcript of his *Diary*, in which many of G.F. Warner's illuminating notes are incorporated, thus giving us a source book on Alleyn which is invaluable.

The Diary of a Jacobean Gentleman

Edward Alleyn's *Diary*, although recording his minutest daily expenditures, is also a vivid human document of a Jacobean gentleman's life which reveals to us the man and his wide interests, and is sprinkled with fascinating titbits of information which we glean incidentally, for this is essentially his personal accounts book, in which he jotted down the cost of his journeyings, mostly to and from London, and his many miscellaneous purchases and transactions, and totted up each month's total expenditures with satisfying regularity and detail. It is a social history, not written for publication. It will not be irrelevant to take an anticipatory peep into it so that we may know him better, for although he was fifty-one when he began writing his journal, a man maturing from his twenties to late thirties, whom we are considering in this thesis, does not appreciably alter his character and tastes although his occupation and life-style have changed.

We know where during these five recorded years he went almost daily, and what was his mode of travel; we know what he did and whom he met; who were the people with whom he transacted business, and in which inns or eating houses known as 'ordinaries' he took his meals and drank on his frequent jaunts into town; and which theatres he visited, though regrettably he fails to note the names of the plays seen; what friends or strangers from diverse walks of life, from the great to the humble, he dined with as guest, or entertained at his own hospitable table at Dulwich where, on Sundays in particular, he seems to have kept open house.

He farmed his lands, taking a personal interest in the running of his farms, and we know when his wheat was reaped, or his sheep sheared, or his cattle drenched; or when his mare foaled; and what purchases he made at the cattle fair at Croydon, where he dined at the Archbishop of Canterbury's Palace with Archbishop Abbot, and the Dean of St Paul's, John Donne the poet, whose daughter Constance became his second wife, and Sir Edward Sackville, later 4th Earl of Dorset, for Alleyn was accepted into the society of the noblemen of the realm as a much respected gentleman. The Earl of Arundel invited Alleyn over to show him his collection of pictures and statuary, evidently valuing his opinion of works of art as a cultured man. Alleyn himself also expended money on collecting paintings, which he later donated to his college, but they are not accounted among works of artistic value being mainly portraits of the kings and queens of England done by very minor artists.

Alleyn had an easy relationship with people of all classes. Among his friends were knights and ladies, doctors of medicine, gentlemen of the inns of court, writers and actors, tradesmen and craftsmen, people of the small business community of Southwark, ministers of religion, as well as his neighbours, his tenants and farmworkers whom he treated as friends and not mere employees. He had an extraordinarily wide circle of friends and acquaintances.

A closer acquaintance of Edward Alleyn increases our respect for him. William Young, who has lovingly transcribed Alleyn's *Diary* in the second volume of his great *History of Dulwich College*, in summarizing Alleyn's life and achievements is moved to comment on his remarkably wide range of activities, interests and talents. He was in truth a man with many strings to his bow. This is how William Young sees him:

'It is true that, in addition to founding the College of God's Gift, he had in his life played many parts –

    Musician
    Actor
    Manager and Owner of Theatres
    Master of the Royal Game
    Animal Breeder
   *Sportsman
    Money-lender
    Church warden
    Land Jobber and Agent
    Landowner
    Patron of and Dealer in Livings"[39]

To these I would add –

    Dramatist
    Builder of his College, his Theatre and his Almshouses
    Philanthropist
    Farmer and Gardener
    Herbalist and amateur physician

Such a man would certainly answer to the description of a 'Johannes Factotum', which is exactly as Greene pictured him even at the age of twenty-six, for his wide-ranging talents and activities must already have been apparent, when his great energy and organising ability were directed to both creative and practical ends in his theatrical career, his writing, his financial and property interests.

---

*Alleyn's favourite sports were hawking and fishing.

354

In his fascinating *Diary* Alleyn appears an active and very busy man, almost daily on horseback, usually riding the five or six miles to Southwark where he leaves his horse, paying 2d for his keeping – a kind of parking ticket – and taking thence a boat across the river to London. His most frequent entry is 'water...4d'. The days of the week he records with little drawings of the zodiacal signs, as here for Tuesday, 8th June 1619 –

| 8 ♂ I went to London to yᵉ temple water | 0.0.4 |
| bought a book of witches | 0.0.3 [40] |

Often it is legal business that engages him in connection with his College or other properties, but he combines it with a shopping expedition, every item purchased carefully noted. As – 'Lute strings' (8d); and books, both for himself and his scholars, 'a Dictionarie for yᵉ boys' (10d) and '2 gramars for yᵉ chilldren' (1s. 10d.); 'a bottle of clarett wine' (1s. 5d.); 'a yelow sadle' (9s); 'a sattin embroydered Hat band' (3s); 'seed pease & beans' (£1. 2s. 9d.); 'Shooes att sᵗ Luks fayer' (10s. 6d.); 'a bitt for my Horss' (1s.); to such small necessities as 'an iron chafingdish' (7d); '2 urinalls' (4d); and 'a little brasse Ladle' (4d).

He seems to have been responsible for all the miscellaneous shopping for the household. As well as clothing, shoe mending is a constantly recurring item for all of Alleyn's extended family, as everyone walked for miles in those days.

Alleyn regularly employed a tailor who was a kinsman, Mathias Alleyn. Every month he enters long itemized lists of clothing made by Mathias for himself, his wife, her sister Bess, their servants, and the orphan children and pensioners. The items listed of materials bought give an interesting insight into the costumes of the time. The following is a typical account, here for the month of March 1618, which is preceded by Alleyn's order for the weaving and dyeing of woollen broad cloth for Mathias to make up. The columns show the old currency of 12d. (denarius) to 1 shilling, and 20 shillings to the pound.

March 1618

a trwe some of yᵉ charge my broad clothe being 31 yʳds

inpimis 99ˡ of wool 12ᵈ yᵉ 1	4	19	0
spining 59ˡ of wool 2ᵈ yᵉ 1	0	10	0
spining 40ˡ for warpe 2ᵈ yᵉ 1	0	08	4
weaving and fulling itt	2	03	0
for dieing itt 9ˢ for dressing 9ˢ			[41]

	s	d	
for sleeving a chamlett dublett	2	6	⎫
buttons & buttone Hole silke	1	2	⎬ 0 4 0
fustian for ye Coller & wast band	0	4	⎭
my night gowne making	5	6	⎫
2 yards off whight cotten	3	0	⎬ 0 10 10
1½ yards off Jeane fustian	1	4	⎭
canvas for yᵉ coller & sewing silk	1	0	
a p off black Hose making	1	8	⎫
fustian for yᵉ pocketts	0	5	⎬ 0 02 9
canvas & wight Lining for yᵉ waste & can	0	4	⎭
mending a p off Cloth Hose	0	4	⁴²

Then follows the account 'for my wife', including a 'taffata wastcot'
and 'altering yᵉ skertts', and 'for bess' for a 'peticoat' and 'making Her
gowne' with 'whale boanes for itt'.

The month's account ends with one –

for the Children

3 Ells & a ½ off canvas for ther coate strait lining	4	0	⎫
pd for 18 dosen off brass buttons for ther coates	2	3	⎬
whipcord to set on yᵉ buttons	0	3	⎬ 1 0 0
Incle for yᵉ slitte off ther coate to binde them	0	2	⎭
for making 12 coates	13	4	⁴³

The entry for 16th December reads:

water att London	0	0	4	
bought 5 songe books for yᵉ boyes	0	4	0	
a quier of pap wᵗ 5 rules for songes	0	0	6	⁴⁴

Legal fees feature largely, and he had a regular account with a scrivener
named Lionel Tuchborne. His chief farmhand was the wheelwright Raph
Canterbury, who also mowed the grass and did repairs. Repairs and
improvements to the buildings, both his own and his college occur fairly
frequently.

The first page of Alleyn's Diary, beginning September 1617

(By kind permission of the Governors of Dulwich College)

Payment of his 'Servaunts wagis' is a regular entry, and we learn their names and rates of pay; the men receive more than the women; at first there are four, then six, then eight with his wife's new lady's maid. Once he dismissed a servant whom he found making merry with his food and drink, carousing with a lot of his pals at his master's expense. Alleyn was not inclined to be soft with people who were dishonest or delinquent, though he was sometimes remarkably patient, and both tolerant and forgiving over the misdemeanours of his schoolmasters whom he engaged to teach his orphans. These men were unreliable, absented themselves without leave and caused him worry. He himself was punctilious about his commitments and his calendar notes his regular disbursement to his charities. On 18th October 1617 he enters:

'pd ye pore theyr pencion 8. 8. 0.'[45]

This sum of £8. 8s. 0d. is the standard monthly payment, but in August 1621 it was only £7. 14s. 0d. because he had 'expulsed' one of his male pensioners, presumably for getting drunk, or being lecherous and fornicating with the poor sisters – misdemeanours which were not tolerated. Occasionally a death or burial, a christening or marriage, or the sickness of a friend or acquaintance is recorded, giving us a glimpse of 17th century society, with many references to contemporary trades and crafts and commodities then in use. Like a true Englishman he notes what the weather is doing. His entry for 'februarie 2' 1617/18 reads simply:

☾ 'a boysterus daye off wind from ye East'[46]

Alleyn lived on Bankside in Southwark, where the scent of the sea is sometimes in the wind, for more than twenty years from the day he united his fortunes with Philip Henslowe and became his son-in-law. It seems to have been a harmonious relationship, although the two men were very different – and this difference is reflected in the *Diary* each of them kept, which are both extant and are unique records of the period.

Edward Alleyn's *Diary* records his cost of living and daily disbursements while pursuing his many interests and activities – his outgoings. Philip Henslowe's *Diary*, on the other hand, is mainly the record of moneys coming in to him – his incomings. It is primarily an accounts book, reflecting this gentleman's interest in business and money making.

Henslowe's Theatrical Diary

The famous theatrical *Diary* of Philip Henslowe appears to have been begun by his brother John as an accounts book for their iron mining interests in Ashdown Forest. Philip took over the old book and used the remaining blank pages to add the records of his London theatrical business, his pawnbroking and banking transactions of small loans to the playwrights and actors, who always seemed to be on the verge of bankruptcy, as well as needy tradesmen, housewives and neighbours urgently requiring cash. The main exception to these are the records of his building expenditures for renovating his theatre, which was a recurring outgoing to service and keep its wooden structure intact.

Philip Henslowe was of Sussex stock, but came to settle in London's environs, in Southwark on the south bank of the Thames, some time before 1584, leaving his brother John and brother-in-law Ralph Hogg to manage the Ashdown estate, where, in addition to the mining and smelting of iron ore, charcoal burning and tree-felling and the cutting of timber for various trade outlets were carried on. The erroneous belief that Henslowe had been living in Southwark before 1577 has now been corrected by R.A. Foakes and R.T. Rickert in their edition of *Henslowe's Diary* (1961)[47] But by 1584 Henslowe had certainly settled down on the Bankside having married Agnes Woodward, the widow of his former employer, the Bailiff of the Viscount Montague who owned property in Southwark. By his marriage to this lady he acquired considerable wealth and two step-daughters, one of whom Edward Alleyn married.

Henslowe practised to augment his acquired wealth by shrewdly diversifying his business activities, for he was no slug. He became a dyer, which was a thriving Bankside industry on account of the easy access to the river water. Perhaps it was he who dyed his 'sonne' Edward Alleyn's orange tawny stockings a good black, as requested. Henslowe also bought and sold goat skins, and manufactured starch. He engaged in pawnbroking and money lending, and invested in property in Southwark and elsewhere, owning several inns and lodging houses, as well as brothels – although Henslowe, like the Bishop of Winchester who owned most of the Southwark stews, was a very respectable personage. He was a Groom of the Chamber to Queen Elizabeth, and became a Gentleman of the Sewer of the Chamber to King James, which were coveted Court offices bringing a certain kudos to the holder. He was a vestryman, and then a church warden of St Saviour's in Southwark, and was a governor of the local grammar school. Henslowe valued respectability.

But it is for his least respectable connection (in Elizabethan eyes), namely the theatrical profession, that he holds interest for us today. His invaluable theatrical records relating to his Bankside theatre, the Rose, have been preserved through his fortuitous, close relationship with the great actor who became the founder of Dulwich College, where these papers were deposited for safe-keeping. But for this, they would most likely have perished with so much else which is now lost to us.

In contrast to Edward Alleyn's orderly, well organised *Diary* with its meticulously kept monthly and quarterly accounts, Henslowe's is a haphazard affair, not presented in chronological order for he seems to have commenced his entries at any page at which the book opened to his hand so that the years veer from 1595 back to 1592, and jump forward to 1598 or the early 1600s. Some records are even entered with the book reversed, his main object seemingly being to use up all available space. Fortunately Henslowe is punctilious about always entering the date, including the year, with each record, so that we can find our way through the maze; and within the limits of the page space he has left himself, he does try to group his entries, like with like, such as loan accounts to the company for play-books and costumes all together in one part, a season of theatrical performances and so on. There is a kind of method in his madness that emerges with some fascination as one becomes more familiar with this extraordinary volume. His apparently random method doubtless originates from the fact that he was using one book for several different kinds of records simultaneously; and so he began keeping his daily theatrical performances and box office receipts in one place, his building work and repairs to the theatre in another, his pawn accounts in another, and so on. But as the pages filled up he no longer had space for all he needed under one particular heading, and so the groups converged and then became split up as he had to take a fresh page elsewhere in the book. Edward Alleyn must sometimes have smiled quietly to himself at his 'father's' method of book-keeping for he must have wasted a lot of time trying to find his place, unless he kept the book bristling with markers.

The diversity of entries in the *Diary* is also remarkable, for these range from the all-important theatrical records of entire seasons and years of performances at the Rose; purchases of play-scripts identifying their authorship; theatrical finance in the form of loan accounts to the company and to individual actors and dramatists; payments to the Master of the Revels, Edmund Tylney; purchase and sale of costumes, often with a description of the items, and payments to the tailor and lace-maker employed; legal business, property deals and rent collections; itemized building accounts for the theatre's repairs, as also for his wharves; illuminating memoranda about his own affairs and his family, such as his expenses for his orphaned niece and nephew who became his charges; his maintenance of a private soldier named Peter for whom he buys his livery and weapons; to his very personal 'doodlings', and a collection of recipes for 'simples' and poultices for aches and ailments – some rather revolting, such as one that uses fried earthworms for curing an earache! while others smack of witchcraft; and he includes instructions for card games and a kind of clock patience. Business and pleasure, communal and private matters intermingle and incidentally reveal something of the man himself.

If Henslowe's inconsequential presentation appears a muddle to us, he evidently knew what he was about, and we may be grateful that he recorded so constantly and informatively, scratching away with his quill pen to give us this amazing book, which is a mine of detailed information that proves almost inexhaustible the more one delves into it.

Henslowe's *Diary* also throws a light on the career and personality of Edward Alleyn which has not heretofore been perceived.

Sit-in threat by actors to save historic Rose Theatre

By Nigel Reynolds
Arts Correspondent

HUNDREDS OF actors and other protesters last night threatened to prevent developers starting building work today on the site of the historic Rose Theatre in Southwark, south London. They said they would not leave unless forced to by a court order.

The Democrat MP, Mr Simon Hughes, who is leading the fight to preserve the remains of the Rose — the only Elizabethan theatre ever uncovered —said: "There will be no violence, but we plan to link arms and block the gates when the developers arrive. They will have to get court orders to get us off the site."

The Rose took on a carnival air earlier yesterday as about 3,000 people went to the site, where work is due to start at 6 am, for what may be their last glimpse of the theatre where William Shakespeare performed, and where several of his plays were staged.

Leading figures in the theatre world, including Sir Peter Hall, Dame Peggy Ashcroft, Dame Judi Dench, Ian McKellan and the casts from several West End shows, took to a makeshift stage to deliver performances and readings.

Archaeologists said they

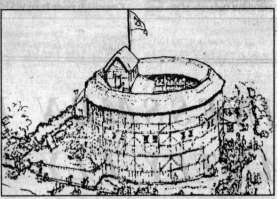

An historian's impression of the Rose Theatre

believed they may have found part of a stage that pre-dated the Rose, built in 1587, showing that the site had been used as a theatre even earlier than first believed.

Although the site's owners, Imry Merchant Developments, have promised to rebury the site carefully in sand and gravel to preserve the remains for later re-excavation, the campaigners claim that more than a dozen 55ft piles will be driven through the remains unless the company re-designs its office block

Sir Peter Hall, former director of the National Theatre, told the rally that damaging the Rose

was "like the Greeks knocking down the Parthenon to make a car park".

Mr Hughes, MP for Southwark and Bermondsey, said that re-designing the block to put the remains on public view would cost Imry no more than £2 million.

Mr Hughes, who read out messages of support for the campaign from Lord Olivier — "it would be sweeping our heritage under concrete" — and Sir John Gielgud, also said that the Prince of Wales and Prince Edward had written to Mr Ridley, Environment Secretary, urging him to save the Rose.

Extract from The Daily Telegraph, *Monday May 15 1989*
Reproduced by permission.

362

XI *The Rose*

PHILIP HENSLOWE'S EYE for business had early seen that investment in London's entertainment industry held promise of tidy profits. On March 24th 1584/5 he purchased the lease of a plot of ground lying between Bankside's river walk and Maiden Lane, with easy access to the river stairs. It is described as a messuage, that is a dwelling house with its adjoining land, 'then Called the little rose with Twoe gardens', which may mean a front garden and a back garden, or, more likely, it was divided, perhaps by a hedge, into a flower garden and a vegetable plot. It had passed from Thomasyn, widow of Ralph Symonds, fishmonger of London of the parish of St Mildred, Bread Street, who leased it to William Gryffyn of London, vintner, for 31 years, who in turn assigned it to Robert Withens, of London, vintner, from whom Philip Henslowe acquired it.[1] The plot was almost 100 foot square and on it stood a small tenement or dwelling house, which he planned to convert to the use of 'victualinge', which we may interpret to mean a refreshment room, and to this end he brought in as a partner in his venture, a grocer, named John Cholmley, who was to have the monopoly of providing the victuals to be sold there. Henslowe had already begun to build a 'play howse' on the ground next to the tenement when he entered into his partnership with John Cholmley, for this Indenture, dated 29th January 1586, tells us that the 'play howse' is 'now in framinge and shortly to be ereckted and sett vppe vpone the same grounde or garden plotte'. Perhaps it had been a rose garden, as it was named the Little Rose. According to their agreement, Henslowe was to have responsibility for completing the playhouse, for which the building contract had been assigned to John Griggs, Carpenter. It seems that Henslowe was seeking capital to complete the project he had begun, for Cholmley's part in this was to provide certain sums of money in quarterly instalments to be paid to Henslowe to the total of £816, in return for which he would receive a half share of the profits from the theatre once it was functioning, this to be binding for a period of eight years and three months, after which the partnership would be dissolved.

As Greg established, there is no truth in the oft repeated statement that there was already 'a playhouse called the Little Rose' on this land.[2] So much inaccuracy about the building and origin of the Rose, the first theatre on Bankside, has been current (see Sir Sidney Lee in DNB among others) that it is worthwhile giving this interesting document at length here, omitting only the repetitious legal jargon where it adds nothing to our understanding of the facts. It was first printed, in somewhat abbreviated form, by Greg, and is available in an excellent transcript almost complete by R.A. Foakes and R.T. Rickert in their up-to-date and valuable edition of *Henslowe's Diary*, 1961.

THIS INDENTURE made the Tenthe day of Januarye Anno 29 Eliz. dñi 1586....betwene Phillippe Hinshley Cittizen and Dyer of London one thonne pty and John Cholmley Cittizen and grocer of London one thother ptye Witneseth that the said partyes...are entrid into partnershippe in the ...posessinge...of all that pcell of grownde or garden plotte Contayninge in lenghe and bredthe sqare every waye ffoorescore and fourteene foote of assize little more or lesse As also...in the...benifytts somes of moneye proffitte and Advauntage of a playe howse now in framinge and shortly to be ereckted and sett vppe vpone the same grounde or garden plotte from the Daye of the Date of these p^rsents for and duringe and vntill the ende and terme of Eighte yeares And three monethes from thence nexte ensuinge...yt is...agreed...That yt shall and maye be lawfull to and for the said John Cholmley...To have...The moytie or one halfe of All suche some and somes of money gaynes profytt and Comodytye wch shall...become due for the saide pcall of grounde and playe howse when and after yt shalbe ereckted and sett vpe by reasonne of any playe or playes that shalbe showen or played there or otherwysse howsoever...And...the saide Phillippe Hinshley...To have...The other moytie...That he the saide John Cholmley shall...have...All that small tēnte or dwellinge howse scittuate and standinge at the sowthe ende or syde of the saide pcell of grownde or garden plotte to keep victualinge in or to putt to any other vse or vsses whatsoever...the same howse neare adioyninge vnto a lane there Comonly Called mayden Lane now in the tenure of the saide John Cholmley o^r assignes wth free...passage...as well by and through the Alleye there called Rosse Alleye leadinge from the Ryver of thames into the saide pcell of grownde As allso in and by and throughe the waye leadinge into the saide mayden Lane....And....That the saide Phyllipe...shall [at his] owne pper Coste and Chargis wth as muche expedicōn as may be ereckte fynishe and sett vpp or cause to be erected finished and sett vpe by John Gryggs Carpenter his servants or assignes the saide playhouse wth all furniture thervnto belonginge...All wch premisses...ar scittuate...on the bancke syde in the pyshe of St Savoyes in Sovthworke in the County of Surr In consideracõn wherof the saide John Cholmley...dothe...graunte to...Phillipe Hinshley...well and truly to paie for a yerlye anuytie the some of Eighte hundreth and Sixteene Pounds of lawfull moneye of Englande in mann^r and forme followinge that is to saye One the feaste Daye of the Nativitie of St John Baptiste...Twentie five Pounds and Tenne shillings...And so further after that from feaste daye to feaste daye quarter to quarter and yeare vnto yeare....quarterly one every of the like feaste dayes....Twentie five Pounds and Tenne shillings vntill all the saide somme of Eighte hundreth and Sixteene Pounds be so truly Contented and payde....And yf yt shall happen the saide...quarterly paymẽts...to be behinde and vnpayde...by the space of twentye and one dayes...after any feaste daye...then and from thencforthe the said Copartnershippe...shalbe voyde...And that yt shall and maye be lawfull to and for the saide Phillipe Hinshley...to renter And the saide John Cholmley...vtterly to expell...And further the saide ptyes...doe graunte eyther wth other by these p^rsents that yt shall and may be lawfull to and for the saide Phillype Hinshleye and John Cholmley...ioyntly to appoynte and pmitte suche psonne and psonnes players to vse exersyse & playe in the saide playe howse...And...that the saide Phillype Hinshley and John Cholmley shall and wilbe there p^rsent them selves or appoynte theire sufficiente debutyes or assignes wth them selves or otherwysse at their Choyse to Coleckte gather and receave all such some and somes of moneye of every psonne & psonnes resortinge and Cominge to the saide playe howse to vew see and heare any playe o^r enterlude at any tyme or tymes to be showed and playde duringe the saide terme of Eighte yeares and three monethes excepte yt please any of the saide ptyes to suffer theire frends to go in for nothinge. And that all suche some and somes be equally devided...whereof the said Phillipe Hinshleye...to have the one halfe...And...John Cholmley...to have the other And further the said Phillipe Hinshleye...shall...paye...All and all mann^r of quitte rents and other rente Chargis due and payable to the Lorde or Lords of the pmisses...belonginge to the saide pcall of grounde...at or before the xxix^th daye of September nexte cominge...And likewayes the saide John Cholmley and Phillipe Hinshleye...doe...graunte eyther wth other...That they...shall after the saide xxix^th daye of September nexte Cominge at their equalle Costs and Chargis repare amende sustayne mantayne and vpholde the saide playehowse [.....] brigges wharffs and all other the wayes and brygges now leadinge...into onto and from the saide pcell of grownde and other the p^rmisses wth thapp^rteññces therevnto belonginge al [sic] all tymes hereafter when and as often as neede shall require duringe the saide terme of Eighte yeares & three monethes...And further the saide Phillipe Hinshley...dothe...graunte to and wth the saide John Cholmeleye...That he...will not pmitte or suffer any psonne o^r psonnes other than the saide John Cholmley...to vtter sell o^r vtter sell o^r putt to sale in or aboute the saide pcell of grownde...any breade o^r drinke other then suche as shalbe solde to and for the vse...of the saide John Cholmley....In witnes whereof the saide ptyes to theis p^rsente Indentures Interchaungeably haue sett their Seales the day and yeres firste aboue written/

By me John Cholmley grocer"[3]

One amusing piece of evidence emerges. Even an Elizabethan impresario, it seems, gave complimentary theatre tickets away to his friends, a custom also practised by the Burbages. Henslowe was not altogether the tight-fisted financier he has been painted. However, in the above legal document his shrewd and cautious business mind is clearly discernible. He makes a binding agreement with Cholmley in which not the slightest loophole exists; Cholmley has to pay up his £25. 10s. quarterly on time, or he forfeits everything to Henslowe. How this worked out in practice, we do not know. Foakes and Rickert suggest that Cholmley may at some time have dropped out from the partnership, because Henslowe always refers to his theatre as simply 'my play howse'. It is always his presence at the theatre of which we are very much aware; he is there daily, taking the box office money and calculating his gallery share, though it is not clear to whom the other share(s) must be paid. Henslowe's detailed accounts of the gallery takings invite close scrutiny, for from them we can still glean much information to clarify our understanding of how an Elizabethan theatre operated. Nor is the view propagated by Fleay and Greg necessarily correct – though generally accepted – that the Rose under Henslowe's management represents an a-typical Elizabethan theatre. This has been questioned by Foakes and Rickert, whose careful re-transcript of Henslowe's *Diary* and theatrical papers has once again made his records readily available. Further study of these unique documents is likely to confirm this judgement.

Five years after the Rose was built, it seems that the flimsy wooden structure that Griggs had erected was in need of renovation, and in the winter of 1591/2, in accordance with the obligation to maintain their theatre in good order, Henslowe launched on a fairly extensive rebuilding programme to smarten up and improve his theatre. It was at the time when this work on the Rose was receiving its finishing touches that Edward Alleyn and Lord Strange's Men arrived to become the resident company at its reopening in February 1591/2. It is from the date of the beginning of the partnership between Alleyn and Henslowe onwards, that we have the invaluable record of theatrical performances, listing the plays by name, their dates of performance, Henslowe's share of the gallery box office, what plays were new, or 'ne' as Henslowe records in the margins, which company was performing them; all with reference to his theatre, the Rose, with the exception of a brief ten-day season at the theatre at Newington Butts in June 1594. This makes the Rose *by far the most important theatre of the period*, for of no other do we have comparable precise detailed day-to-day information covering a period of five years, from 1592 to 1597. Thereafter there is still periodic coverage, sometimes puzzling as to what it exactly signifies, but always fascinating historically, with much other valuable theatrical data. Henslowe's theatrical *Diary*, like Edward Alleyn's more intimate journal, was his personal record and not kept for our enlightenment, and his method of keeping his accounts presents some problems and discrepancies worthy of further comment, especially regarding the dates and his accounting methods.

Earlier critics have tended to misjudge Henslowe as an ill-educated, 'illiterate' man because of the whimsicallity of his spelling, and as ignorant because he makes frequent errors in writing the dates in his *Diary*, often switching casually from one year to the next. Familiarity with Elizabethan manuscripts soon dispels the validity of allegations of illiteracy on account of strange and inconsistent spelling. Elizabethan schoolmasters did not teach spelling for it was not then standardized; they taught writing meticulously, and encouraged their pupils to acquire the art of writing beautifully and stylishly. Henslowe scratched away quite adeptly with his quill, and he spelt as he spoke, which was probably with a Sussex accent. He was certainly careless when writing the names of plays being performed, which involves us in a bit of guesswork, but carelessness is not a sign of illiteracy. He similarly took little trouble about writing the date correctly according to Elizabethan practice, but this I put down to his rather endearing absent-mindedness. His errors did not bother him at all, for he knew perfectly well what his writings and his dates meant. The trouble was that the Elizabethan New Year began on Lady Day, 25th March or the spring quarter day, which Henslowe tended to ignore as being illogical (which it is) and he was still writing 'ap^rell 1593' when he should have changed to 'ap^rell 1594'. At other times his memory went into reverse, and he wrote 1593 when he should still have been writing 1592 for the January, February and March months when he had privately decided that the proper time for the new year to begin *was* on 1st January. When we bethink ourselves of the mental effort we have to make when we first date a cheque of letter in our New Year, which begins with great celebration to mark the event on 1st January, and yet we often write the old year's date from sheer habit before recollecting ourselves, Henslowe's absent-minded errors appear very understandable. The change-over in mid-month must have been the very devil to remember. Henslowe thought so too, and he did not care too much which year he wrote in these, his personal, private accounts, so long as the cash was correct, and he had remembered to enlist the blessing of God for his financial transactions, for he religiously began each new theatrical season with his dedication to the Almighty. Thus he heads his record for the winter season in 1592 after the theatres had been closed by the first onset of the plague that summer

> In the Name of god Amen 159[2]3
> beginnge the 29 or desemb₃ 4

He wrote 1592, which was correct, but altered it to 1593, which is wrong, and then proceeded to enter eight plays correctly dated as 'desemb₃ 1592' and 'Janewary 1592'; but on 8th January he suddenly switches to 1593, and then remains in that year although according to the Elizabethan calendar it was still 1592 until 25th March, and we have to resist the temptation to think he means our 1594. No matter. So long as Henslowe's absent-mindedness is recognized, this need not confuse us. But when we come to the end of this winter season, there seems at first sight to be genuine error, for we find duplicated entries for the self-same date in two consecutive lists. The only explanation for this must be that he is now managing two separate theatres, for two plays could not possibly be performed on the same stage on the same day, all performances being matinées. His first list is on folio 8 of his *Diary* and records twenty-six performances by Strange's Men from 29th December until 31st January, which we may take to refer to the winter season at the Rose. The entries for duplicated dates appear as follows, at what I shall call *Theatre A* and *Theatre B*. Last three performances at *Theatre A* (on folio 8):-

Rd at titus the 25 Jenewaye 1593 .... xxxs

ne – Rd at the tragedey of the gyves 30 ....iijli xiiijs

Rd at mandevell the 31 or Jenewarye ⟨. . .⟩ .... xijs 5

(The brackets indicate much rotted and frayed paper making this illegible). Henslowe's 'tragedey of the gyves' is the first performance of Marlowe's *The Massacre at Paris*, which took place on 30th January 1593 (or 1592 in the Elizabethan calendar – we must beware of being confused by Henslowe's whimsical date switches.) His 'titus' is not *Titus Andronicus* but another play altogether. With 'mandevell' on 31st January the season ends at *Theatre A*, assumed to be the Rose.

Henslowe then turns to a new page and at the top of folio 8 verso he *repeats* the last two dates, 30th and 31st January, giving the year 1593 as before, and this is definitely the same year, 1592/3 or 1593, and the *same two dates in January*, which I believe to be recordings of performances at *Theatre B*. Three performances only are recorded at *Theatre B*, after which all playing ceased on account of the plague.

Three performances at *Theatre B*. (on folio 8 verso) [brackets round July indicate error].

Rd at frier bacon on the 30 of [July] Jenewarye 1593 .... xijs

Rd at harey the vj the 31 of Jenewarye 1593 .... xxvjs

Rd at the Jewe of malta the j of febreary 1593 .... xxxvs 6

End of this brief season. That these performances are duplicates on the same days as the foregoing that the year is 1593 (or 1592/3) is established by the fact that Henslowe's next entry on the same page is for the opening of the winter season on 27th December 1593 *after* an eleven months' closure owing to the plague of that year. The puzzle of these three performances at *Theatre B* may have its solution in the warrant issued by the Privy Council enjoyning Lord Strange's Men 'to plaie three daies at newington Butts', which has never been satisfactorily explained as it is undated, though it obviously has some bearing on the closure of the theatres owing to the plague.

Whereas not longe since vpon some Consideraĉons we did restraine the Lorde Straunge his sᵉrvauntes from playinge at the rose on the banckside, and enioyned them to plaie three daies at newington Butts, Now forasmuch as wee are satisfied that by reason of the tediousnes of the waie and y^t of longe tyme plaies haue not there been vsed on working daies, And for that a nomber of poore watermen are therby releeved, Yo^u shall pmitt and suffer them or any other there to exercise y^{em} selues in suche sorte as they haue don heretofore, And that the Rose maie be at libertie wthout any restrainte so longe as y^t shalbe free from infection of sicknes, Any Comaundem^t from vs heretofore to the Contrye notwthstandinge:[7]

This warrant is undated and hence has inspired considerable conjecture as to the circumstances to which it applies. Dr G.F. Warner has suggested that it refers to the resumption of playing in the summer of 1594 after the plague had abated, but, as Greg points out, the company was no longer Lord Strange's, having become in quick succession, the Earl of Derby's as from 25th September 1593 when Ferdinando Lord Strange succeeded to the Earldom, and following his untimely and tragic death on 16th April 1594, were taken over by the Lord Chamberlain, Henry Lord Hunsdon.

Greg has put forward an interesting theory linking the warrant with the events surrounding the riots in Southwark that broke out on Sunday 11th June 1592 when the tempers of the apprentices ran high 'by occasion & pretence of their meeting at a play' which had constituted a 'breach of ye Sabboth'. The apprentices were expressing their historic resentment against the Kings Marshal who had sought to 'intermeddle in the part which was Guildable'.[8] This is obscure, but it may perhaps be a reference to a Guild play that the apprentices were performing on the Sabbath – for there was *no* performance at the Rose on that Sunday, being the only theatre on Bankside in 1592. The Marshall had attempted to suppress the apprentices, thus arousing youthful anger. The Lord Mayor, William Webb, was then called in to restore order which he finally managed about 8 p.m. pacifying the rioters with whom he expressed some sympathy when writing to Lord Burghley next day, for he was of the opinion that the Kings Marshal men were to blame for exciting the disturbance.[9] However, the Privy Council received complaints of other disorderly incidents from the Earl of Derby in his Lieutenancy of Lancashire, and in considering these various civil disturbances they were in a punitive mood and decided to order a restraint of all playing to quell civil disobedience, as expressed in the following letter addressed to the Justices of Middlesex from their Lordships' sitting on 23rd June 1592.

Moreover for avoiding of theis unlawfull assemblies in those quarters yt is meete you shall take order that there be noe playes used in anye place neere thereaboutes, as the theator, curtayne or other usuall places there where the same are comonly used, nor no other sorte of unlawful or forbidden pastymes that drawe togeather the baser sorte of people from hence forth untill the feast of St Michaell.[10]

Other similar injunctions were sent to a number of 'precincts' including Newington, and the Liberties of the Clink, Paris Garden and the Bankside south of the river. Their Lordships were evidently Puritanically inclined at this time, and the result was a general closure which seems to have been unconnected with the threat of the plague which did not reach serious proportions until the beginning of August, 1592. Taking into account all these factors, my reconstruction of the events is as follows.

The authorities acted very promptly upon their Lordships' letter, for the Rose's performance on 22nd June proved to be their last, probably their rehearsals on 23rd June having been interrupted with the distressing news that all playing was prohibited until Michaelmas. On receipt of the order of restraint, it would seem, the summer being come, that the Lord Strange's Men immediately packed their fardles on their backs and set off on tour, leaving Henslowe and, I believe, also Alleyn to try to obtain the lifting of this unlooked for restraint. Their company being large, however, could not survive intact on tour (a point made in their petition below), and the actors were smarting under the injustice of the order, for the rioting had had nothing to do with them. Alleyn was a man of too much resource tamely to buckle under these (unfair) restrictions without seeking a possible way out. He and Henslowe resolved, therefore, to see what could be achieved by petitioning the Lords to lift the restraint, using every argument they could tactfully muster. The sad plight of the Thames watermen, who were impoverished by their loss of custom from ferrying the play-goers across the river, was their strongest suit for moving their Lordships to sympathy for their request.

Accordingly, two petitions were got up, one from the Lord Strange's Players, and one supporting their case with more moving pleas and the signatures and marks of many local watermen was organised by Philip Henslowe, who as a long-term resident and local businessman was a well-known neighbour of the Bankside watermen many of whom he must have known personally. Neither of these petitions is dated, but Greg is surely correct in associating both of them with the closure of the Rose following the Southwark riots in June 1592, when the plague had not yet risen to the level at which public playing was affected; so that it would be erroneous to assume that the Rose was closed *in the first instance* on account of the plague – though as it transpired, the plague's escalation during the hot summer days ensured that it remained closed until December.

Both these interesting petitions are extant among the Alleyn Papers at Dulwich. First, the Petition of Strange's Men to the Privy Council, which Greg gives the conjectural date July – August 1592 (?), but which I suggest must have been either June or, at latest, beginning of July for by early August the plague's spread would have made any such appeal null and void.

To the right honorable o^r verie good Lords, the Lords of her ma^ts. moste honorable privie Councell
Our dueties in all humblenes remembred to yor hono^rs. fforasmuche (righte honorable) oure Companie is greate and thearbie o^r chardge intollerable, in travellinge the Countrie, and the Contynuaunce thereof, wilbe a meane to bringe vs to division and seperac͡on, whearebie wee shall not onelie be vndone, but alsoe vnreadie to serve her ma^tie, when it shall please her highenes to commaund vs, And for that the vse of o^r plaiehowse on the Banckside, by reason of the passage to and frome the same by water, is a greate releif to the poore watermen theare, And o^r dismission thence, nowe in this long vacation, is to those poore men a great hindraunce, and in manner an vndoeinge, as they gen^rallie complaine, Both o^r, and theire humble petic͡o and suite thearefore to yor good honno^rs is, That yo^u wilbe pleased of yor speciall favo^r, to recall this o^r restrainte, And pmitt vs the vse of the said Plaiehowse againe/And not onelie o^r selues But alsoe a greate nomber of poore men shalbe especiallie bounden to praie for yor Hono^rs
Your hono^rs humble supp^ts
The righte honorable the Lord Straunge
his servants and Plaiers [11]

That there was co-ordination in preparing the two petitions is evident from the above reference to one from the watermen, which is addressed to the Lord Admiral, Charles Howard, who was Edward Alleyn's patron with whom he enjoyed a cordial relationship. Greg suggests that Howard may have been patron of the watermen. Watermen traditionally served in the navy. Their signatures and 'marks' are appended.

To the right honorable my Lorde Haywarde Lord high Admirall of Englande and one of her ma^ties moste honnorable previe Counsayle

In a most hvmble manner Complayneth and sheweth vnto your good Lordeshippe, your poore suppliants and dayly Orato^rs Phillipp Henslo, and others the poore watermen on the bancke side/ whereas yor good L. hath derected your warrant vnto hir ma^ties Justices, for the restraynte of a playe howse belonginge vnto the saide Phillipp henslo one of the groomes of her ma^ties Chamber So it is if it please your good Lordshipp, that wee yor saide poore watermen have had muche helpe and reliefe for vs our poore wives and Children by meanes of the resorte of suche people as come vnto the said playe howse, It maye therefore please your good L. for godes sake and in the waye of Charetie to respecte vs your poore water[e]men, and to give leave vnto the said Phillipp Henslo. to have playinge in his saide howse duringe suche tyme as others have according as it hathe byne accustomed/ And in yor honnors so doinge yo^u shall not onely doe a good and a Charitable dede but also bynde vs all according to oure dewties, wth oure poore wives and Children dayly to praye for your honnor in mvche happynes longe to lyve

    Isack Towelle   William dorret m^r of her maie[g]stes barge

    Gylbart ⊢ Rockett marke on   wyllm̄ hodgy[s] quens man
    of her m^ties wattermen

    Edward ⚲ Robartes mark on of   Thomas + Jarmonger on of
    her m^ties wattermen   her m^ties wattermen

        thomes toy   William M Tuchenner on of
                           her m^ties mean

    Thomas + Edmanson marke

    Edwarde + Adysson on of   James Russell
    her m^ties wattermen   Henry Draper
                       fardinandoo Black
    W T Jeames + Granger   Parker Playne

    xpoffer ⌁ topen marke 12

The implication of the wording 'during such tyme as others have according as it hathe byne accustomed' is that the Rose was especially affected by this restraint because the Southwark riots had been local, whereas the other theatres had been only temporarily closed or perhaps not at all. The plea for their Lordships' 'speciall favo^r, to recall this o^r restrainte, and pmitt vs the vse of the said Plaiehowse again' clearly refers to some other cause than the inexorable plague against which there could be no redress. Greg has further pointed out that the first indication of serious concern about the infection is in the Privy Council's reference of 13th August 1592 to 'the contagion of the plaige dailie increasing in London'.[13] The petition from Lord Strange's Men mentioning 'this long vacation' and their 'travellinge the Countrie' leaves no room for doubt that this belongs to the summer months. However, whereas the wording of these petitions is strongly suggestive of their connection with the closure of the Rose following the Southwark riots of June 1592, as Greg has impressively argued, I do not believe that he is correct in linking these petitions with the warrant for Newington Butts which is a response to a similar plea from the watermen to allow resumption of playing at the Rose. The fact that the two petitions are preserved among the Alleyn Papers may mean that they were, in fact, never delivered owing to the inevitable playhouse closures resulting from the escalation of the plague in August 1592. On studying the text of the warrant (see pp. 369–370) it is seen that it does not fit the circumstances rehearsed in the two petitions.

In the first place, the warrant, which is similarly undated, is evidently a sequel to an earlier warrant which had enjoined the Lord Strange's Men 'to plaie three daies at newington Butts' which would have been a strange way to respond to the urgent pleas of the petitioners begging their Lordships to succour the poor watermen by allowing the Bankside theatre, the Rose, to re-open. At the time of their petition the company of Lord Strange had been 'travellinge the Country' so that there would have been little time for them to return and take up residence at Newington first even if the illogicality of sending them thither did not apply. This warrant seems to have been a response to another, later petition pleading the poor watermen's plight, which was probably based on the petitions Alleyn had carefully preserved to provide blue-prints for similar occasions, with slight alterations of wording to suit the circumstances. The warrant, moreover, refers to the 'tediousnes of the waie' to Newington Butts as having been a source of complaint by the players, and this is far more applicable to the winter months than to the summery days suggested by Greg in his linking of this warrant with the two petitions, which make no mention whatsoever of Newington. I therefore suggest that this warrant refers to the period of the brief reopening of the theatres in the winter of 1592–3 when the colder weather brought its temporary decrease in the spread of the infection, and the theatres were allowed to resume playing for the Christmas season. It is precisely here that we find the curious record in Henslowe's *Diary* of an overlap of the last two performances at the Rose with the first two of *exactly three performances* at another theatre, which he omits to name. This surely must be the three performances at Newington Butts referred to in the warrant.

We know that during the plague many actors were unemployed and eager for any work. Why Strange's Men had been enjoined to play at Newington, rather than at the Rose for three days (the *Diary* dates are 30th January to 1st February inclusive), we do not know, but my guess is that it was something to do with the plague in London, for Newington lies further out in what was then the open country, and the warrant rescinding this order specifically states that 'the Rose maie be at libertie w^{th}out any restrainte so long as yt shalbe free from infection of sicknes'. There is nothing in the warrant to suggest that the injunction to play at Newington had been a result of any irregularity or misdemeanour at the Rose. Its text merely states that 'vpon some Consideracons we did restraine the Lord Strange his s^{r}vaunts from playinge at the rose on the banckside'. Had there perhaps been a higher number of deaths from the plague in Southwark, which was a very populous place in those days? And had it then been thought it was after all safe to return to the Bankside, so that both theatres were mounting performances?

Newington was a small village just beyond the Elephant and Castle situated a mile south of the Thames. The archery butts were located there, which drew sportsmen to the place, and a theatre existed about which, unfortunately, very little is known and which seems to have been used only intermittently. Since two days' performances appear to be running concurrently at the Rose, and at 'the other place', which I suggest must be Newington Butts, Edward Alleyn would have had to split his company, augmenting it with several hired actors, possibly from Pembroke's Men who were desperate to earn a few shillings during the plague restraint and, as we learn from Henslowe's letter, they were soon pawning their theatrical stock of apparel and selling their playscripts. It may be assumed that Alleyn and Henslowe were able to get up a petition at short notice with the support of the watermen, their neighbours on Bankside, probably using their earlier petitions for copy, in order to obtain this favourable about-turn for the reopening of the Rose. Probably they hoped to be able to play at *both* Newington and the Rose having evidently assembled sufficient forces to play at both theatres simultaneously. But it so happened that the plague was again seriously on the increase and pre-empted the implementation of the favour granted.

All the circumstantial evidence relating to the warrant places it in this winter context and is reflected in Henslowe's *Diary* of the end of January, beginning of February 1592/3. And it would seem that we have here evidence of Henslowe's first association with Newington Butts as a theatrical venue, which it is believed he subsequently developed, though the theatre is only once mentioned by name in his *Diary*.[14] Whatever records he kept for it otherwise have not survived.

There followed the eleven-months-long closure while the plague raged in London. Henslowe's records of the eventual resumption of playing in the winter of 1593–4 give interesting indications of Alleyn's return after his prolonged tour and reveal his various alliances with different companies at this time when great disorganisation among the theatrical groupings prevailed. Alleyn surmounted these problems because his talents gave him a peculiarly strong position. When the Rose reopened on 27th December 1593 'In the name of god Amen', it is apparent that Edward Alleyn had now severed his association with Strange's, who had become the Earl of Derby's Men in September 1593 and were probably recalled to play before the Earl for the Christmas season at his stately home. It is 'the earle of susex his men' who are ensconced at the Rose from December to February presenting their own repertoire which is totally different from Strange's and Alleyn's. That is until their penultimate performance on 4th February when they present *The Jew of Malta*, which can only mean that Edward Alleyn was playing the title role he had made singularly his own and which play was his own property. In that last week of their residence at the Rose the Sussex Men also gave a new play – as indicated by Henslowe's 'ne'

'ne – Rd at titus & ondronicus the 23 of Jenewary....iij^{li} viijs'[15]

This is January 1593/4, and it is the Earl of Sussex his men with the shadowy presence of Alleyn who are responsible for putting it on. *Titus Andronicus* might therefore suggest the emergence of William Shakespeare as a dramatist attached to the company of the Earl of Sussex and not to the Lord Chamberlain's Men. My conviction, however, is that this lurid Senecan tragedy was the joint work of Marlowe and Kyd, whose patron and patroness were the Earl and Countess of Sussex. Thomas Kyd's last work *Cornélie*, translated from the French of Robert Garnier, was dedicated to the Countess, published in 1594. The identification of the Earl of

Sussex as Kyd's 'Lord' is consistent with the plaintive allegations which Kyd made in his letter to Lord Puckering concerning his affronted Lord's repudiation of Marlowe's reputed 'atheism'. This fits Sussex, but it does not fit Derby, for Ferdinando Lord Strange (whom some critics maintain must have been Kyd's 'Lord') was himself sympathetic to the courageous, broad-minded intelligentsia of the circle of brilliant men with whom Marlowe associated, and he would have been aware that the charge of atheism was the weapon used by the authorities to instil fear into the ignorant, the superstitious and the bigotted to retain power over those who dared to swim against the tide of reactionary authority. George Chapman, chief poet of the circle known as 'The School of Night', in dedicating his poem *The Shadow of Night* to Matthew Royden, who was both his own and Marlowe's close friend, wrote of the Earl of Derby:

'When I remember my good *Mat* how ioyfully oftentimes you haue reported vnto me that most ingenious *Darby*, deepe searching *Northumberland* and skill-embracing heir of *Hunsdon* had most profitably entertained learning in themselues to the vital warmth of freezing science and to the admirable lustre of their true nobility...'[16]

Compare this with Kyd's avowal to Lord Puckering regarding his Lord's opinions as expressed in his letter after he had been arrested and racked on suspicion that the 'atheist' document found in his room had been his.

'When I was first suspected for that Libell that concern'd the state, amongst those waste and idle papers (wch I carde not for) & wch vnaskt I did deliuer vp, were founde some fragments of a disputation toching that opinion, affirmd by Marlowe to be his, and shufled wth some of myne vnknown to me by some occasion of o^{r} wrytinge in one chamber twoe years synce.
My first acquaintance wth this Marlowe, rose vpon his bearing name to serve my Lo: although his Lp never knew his service but in writing for his plaiers, ffor never cold my L. endure his name, or sight, when he had heard of his conditions, nor wold in deed the forme of devyne praiers vsed in his Lps house haue quadred wth such reprobates."[17]

This quite obviously cannot be the Earl of Derby, the friend of the free-thinking Earl of Northumberland and Lord Hunsdon, admired by Roydon and Chapman who were among Marlowe's best friend. It does, however, square with the Earl of Sussex, whether we are talking about the father or the son who acceded to the title in December 1593.

The Earl of Sussex has been suggested as having been Kyd's Lord by both Greg[18] and Chambers[19], and this is supported by Dr F.S. Boas,[20] the biographer of Marlowe and of Kyd, and certainly his dedication to the Countess is a strong argument. But Tucker Brooke queries this on the grounds that it was not until December 1593 that her husband became fifth Earl of Sussex. However, this is not to say that he had not been Kyd's patron before this. All he can argue is that the young Lord Robert prior to becoming Earl of Sussex 'does not seem to have maintained players', and that the company of his father, the fourth Earl, 'were at the time mentioned by Kyd a provincial troupe that could not have engaged Marlowe's service.'[21]

It is, however, not possible to be absolutely certain of these facts, for a lack of evidence cannot be confidently construed to mean that the answer is negative. We have seen how false assumptions concerning Marlowe have become accepted as the truth in the case of his relations with his family and Canterbury, simply because evidence to confirm his filial association with his parents and native city was lacking. Recent research has brought to light fascinating new evidence illuminating his Canterbury associations and information on his family to show that these assumptions were quite wrong. A great deal of documentation on the theatrical companies has been lost, and we cannot make such absolute assumptions. Lord Strange before he became Earl of Derby maintained his own company of players, and since Robert, fifth Earl of Sussex, certainly was patron of a company of Sussex Men who were playing at the Rose in January 1593/4 for thirty performances with a wide repertoire of thirteen different plays, it is questionable as to how 'provincial' they actually were before this time.

The one fact we have to go on, is that among their plays they possessed *Titus Andronicus*, which was performed as a new play on 23rd January 1593/4 and the box office takings are commensurate with a new play – £3. 8s.

Dr Bakeless, while acknowledging the strongly stylistic affinity of this play with Marlowe's known plays, feels obliged to accept that this cannot be Marlowe's work because it was marked 'ne' by Henslowe fully eight months after Marlowe's tragedy on 30th May 1593.[22] But this takes no cognizance of the disruption caused by the long plague of 1593. The play may well have been left in the Sussex Men's hands many months prior

378

to this but was not performed in London with the large cast it required until the reassembly of the players for their winter season at the Rose in 1593/4. The speedy appearance of the quarto published by John Danter in February 1593/4 probably reflects the dire need of the players for ready cash. Kyd, when he was arrested, imprisoned and racked would obviously have been at great pains, literally, to distance himself from a close association with Marlowe to nullify the implication of the inescapable fact that an incriminating paper belonging (as he maintained) not to him but to this undesirable 'atheist' had been found in his possession, and the most natural course would be to distance the time between their last being together. Two years was in all probability an exaggeration reflecting the painful stretching poor Kyd was undergoing. It is likely to have been much less. And what *did* they write in one room together? No satisfactory answer has been given, but the most obvious one is *Titus Andronicus*, which was in the Sussex Men's repertoire in January 1593/4 when it was offered to London audiences as a new work. This gory play is as near a companion piece to Kyd's *Spanish Tragedy* as it is possible to conceive, with the added touch of Marlowe's genius which lifted it with only a passing question mark into its place in the First Folio.

That is surely the true explanation of the Kyd-Marlowe association, and it also clarifies the inescapable problem of the significant affinity of this play with Marlowe, over which scholarly battles have been fought which it is no need to repeat here.

Marlowe could not have seen *Titus Andronicus* making its debut at the Rose in January 1593/4, although he might have attended the first performance of his *Massacre at Paris* in the previous January, for on 30th May 1593 he had 'gon to liue with beautie in Elyzium', as Henry Petowe so charmingly put it. Kyd also was dead before the end of the year after having seen his *Cornélie* to the press. Its dedication to the Countess of Sussex had probably been conceived as a peace offering in the hope that his Lady would be able to prevail upon the Earl to take him back into his service, from which his involvement with Marlowe's disgrace had debarred him.

How then did *Titus Andronicus* find its way from the Sussex Men's to the Lord Chamberlain's Men with whom Shakespeare was playing the following Christmas? This company was originally Lord Strange's, became briefly Lord Derby's until his tragic murder on 16th April 1594, and then passed to the patronage of his friend, George Carey's father, the first Lord Hunsdon, who was Lord Chamberlain. Alleyn in his association with Sussex's Men had, I suggest, acquired the play, for he next made an alliance with the joint companies of the Sussex's Men and the Queen's Men, who played for eight performances only at the Rose, from 1st April to the 8th.[23] From the rapid regroupings of the companies it is clear that this is a period of flux, and from the repertoires presented we can identify the presence of Edward Alleyn with them. Henslowe's records are our guide.

> In the name of God Amen begininge at easter 1593
> the Quenes men & my lord of Susexe to geather [24]

The plays they offer are:

2 performances of *Friar Bacon* (Alleyn's in repertoire of Admiral's)
1 performance of *The Ranger's Comedy* ("   "   "   )
2 performances of *The Jew of Malta*   ("   "   "   )
1 performance of *The Fair Maid of Italy* (Sussex's)
2 performances of *King Lear** (Queen's)

By the beginning of May the Lord Admiral's Men have returned home, and Alleyn rejoins his own company. They give three plays at the Rose (*The Jew of Malta*, *The Ranger's Comedy*, and *Cutlack*), and they then join with the Lord Chamberlain's Men for a brief joint season at Newington Butts; it is not clear why, unless the Rose is temporarily closed for repairs. Henslowe records nothing for the Rose, but he identifies the theatre for this season of ten performances:

> In the name of god Amen begininge at newing
> ton my Lord Admeralle men & my Lorde chamberlen
> men As ffolowethe 1594 [25]

Again they give *The Jew*, *Cutlack*, and *Bellendon* – which all remain with the Lord Admiral's in their regular repertoire, but here *Titus Andronicus* is played again twice, its first reappearance since it was performed by the Sussex's Men. But after this it disappears from Alleyn's and the Admiral's repertoire, and this must mean that it *passed at this time* into the possession of the Lord Chamberlain's and became eventually associated with Shakespeare's plays of which they had the monopoly. It had, surprisingly, only a poor box office rating at Newington Butts, of only 'vj^s' and 'xij^s' at these two performances, so that maybe Alleyn felt he had misjudged the play and was not reluctant to part with it. He also seems to have discarded Kyd's still popular *Spanish Tragedy* at this time, for it disappears from the repertoire, although it had been performed thirteen times during

---

* This is an old play, not Shakespeare's.

the first season at the Rose, being often in the top bracket of Henslowe's gallery records. This is puzzling. Was Alleyn upset by rumours that Kyd was maligning Marlowe's reputation after the tragedy perhaps? Alleyn appears to have been a loyal admirer of Kit Marlowe always, and it would have been in character for him to have rejected the work of one whom he saw as his traducer. Not until 7th January 1597 does a play called 'Joronymo' make its reappearance in Henslowe's records, and then it is marked 'ne', which may indicate that it had been revised. In 1601 and 1602 Ben Jonson is paid for writing additional scenes to 'Jeronymo' and 'geronymo' if this indeed refers to Kyd's old *Spanish Tragedy*, which was presumably played at the Fortune, and would later have perished in the flames when the theatre burnt.

Alleyn seems to have had his favourite roles, and throughout his career he retained Marlowe's plays in his repertoire, being probably owned by him personally: *The Jew of Malta, Doctor Faustus, Tamburlaine the Great, Parts 1 and 2*, and *The Massacre at Paris*. We know that the latter was in Alleyn's possession for on 18th January 1601 he sold to the company (who were now the sharers in the Lord Admiral's at the Fortune) three plays which were then no longer new works, for the sum of £6, being 'the massaker of france', 'the french docter', and 'nvtte',[26] the latter two being, as I have suggested, Alleyn's own works. Alleyn had resumed playing when his own theatre, the Fortune, opened in 1600, and it would have been natural casting for him to have played Marlowe's anti-hero, the Guise, in *The Massacre*, whose great opening monologue is the most authentic sample of Marlowe's genius that has survived in the corrupt text we now have.

Marlowe's *Massacre at Paris* is unique among his works in several respects. Firstly, it dramatizes a piece of contemporary 16th century history which must have held a special significance for Marlowe personally as Walsingham's agent in the scheming interplay of the political scene of his day. The subject touched a politically sensitive nerve in the French. As late as 1602 Sir Ralph Winwood, then English ambassador in Paris, had complaints voiced to him that the presentation of the murders of the Duke of Guise and of the French King Henry III on the English stage was offensive to them. Edward Alleyn was probably appearing in *The Massacre* at the Fortune that year. At the time of the Massacre of St Bartholomew's Eve there had been strenuous diplomatic efforts made to present this ghastly slaughter in an acceptable light to Queen Elizabeth as a cruel necessity to forestall an intended similar attack on the part of the Huguenots against the Catholics. Secondly, this play is the only work of Marlowe's of which a genuine Elizabethan manuscript page has survived, which is believed to be in Marlowe's autograph, and which throws valuable light on the kind of corruption of his texts which we might expect to find in assessing his other dramatic works from their available 'bad' quartos.* Thirdly, it is the most mutilated version of any of his plays to have survived in print, but despite its drastically truncated form, when presented on the stage, with actors breathing life into the brief scenes, a vivid theatrical experience emerges. When the Marlowe Society (of London) presented this play at the Chanticleer Theatre in Kensington, London, on 30th January 1963 as a 350th anniversary offering to mark its first performance at the Rose on 30th January 1593, it proved an unexpected, resounding success, although very short, running for only one and a half hours. John Bakeless similarly reports that there was a revival by the Yale Dramatic Association in October 1940, who apparently thought it worth performing.[27]

Amateur productions vary (as do professional ones) in their degree of success in interpreting dramatic works, and appraisal of the result is inevitably subjective, but for such an extremely mutilated version of any dramatic work to come across in performance with the impact, freshness and excitement which (in this experience) *The Massacre* did achieve, is in itself remarkable and shows that we have here lost what must have been a great play. We may be grateful that it has survived even if as an emaciated shadow of the original creation.[28]

Henslowe's Theatrical Finance

How Philip Henslowe's theatre had prospered before Alleyn joined him we do not know, for although presumably he had been in the habit of keeping accounts all his business life, none has survived. In his brother's old accounts book, which he adopted for his theatrical *Diary*, his first entry was a detailed list of his expenses for renovating the Rose in 1591/2. At the top of folio 4 he wrote:

> Jesus   1592
> A note of suche carges as I haue layd owt a bowte
> my playe howsse in the yeare of o^r lord 1592 as ffoloweth [29]

What follow are three pages of itemized lists of materials purchased for the rebuilding, including quantities of timber, deal boards, rafters, lathes, quarter boards, bricks, lime and sand, and 'naylles' by the

---

* See pages 120–121 for a comparison of these texts.

hundred and 'thowson' for hammering it all together, which he mostly bought from the ironmonger's shop called the Fryingpan which must have been in nearby Frying Pan Alley off Foul Lane. He pays also for wharfing and 'bryngen by watter' of his supplies. Some specific improvements are mentioned. He had the 'Rome ouer the tyerhowsse' ceiled, and specified a ceiling for 'my lords Rome', and he added a 'penthowsse shed at the tyeringe howsse doore'. He paid 'xjˢ' for 'payntinge my stage', and a mast cost him 'xijˢ'. This would have been for the flagpole. Like all Elizabethan theatres, the Rose was open to the sky, but the roof over the galleries and tyre-house was rethatched for he paid a thatcher and 'the thechers man' for several weeks' work. John Griggs was again employed, together with carpenters, painters, a plasterer, besides workmen and 'laborers'.[30] Altogether quite extensive renovations that cost him nearly £100.*

According to the terms of Henslowe's agreement with Cholmley the partners were to bear 'equal Cost and Chargis [to] repare...mantayne and vpholde the said playehowse', but no mention of Cholmley is made in Henslowe's costing of the above renovations to the Rose. Nor does his name appear in the *Diary* anywhere, apart from Henslowe's scribblings on the vellum wrappers and end pages of his book, where he noted proverbial sayings and other oddments, such as a medicinal 'simple' made from bryony root for curing a fit (elsewhere his medicinal concoctions reveal a superstitious mind typical of the age in which he lived). Cholmley's name is written here in the curious context of Henslowe's doodlings as though he were ruminating on Cholmley's fate?

> Cholmley when
> Clement Bowle   Bowle wᵗʰ owt mersey
> Chemley Chomley
> Bowghte wᵗʰ mersey [31]

What the significance of these incomplete jottings may be is a mystery, but they appear to reflect Henslowe's moods and emotions at times when things were not going smoothly for him. With regard to his partner Cholmley, who must be intended in the above, there seems to be a connection with one Clement Bowle. 'Bowle without mercy' Henslowe calls him. (Inclement Bowle?) Was he oppressing the grocer, Cholmley,

---

* The construction of the turret is not specified, although this must have been the time when this was added.

so that he was unable to pay his due instalment to Henslowe? And did Henslowe then buy him out? 'Bought with mercy' he scribbles. These strange doodlings are psychologically revealing of Henslowe, and merit our attention. Another curious fact is that, whereas all sorts of names from among Henslowe's theatrical and business associates, local trades people and his own relatives, Edward Alleyn and Joan, appear in the *Diary* as witnesses to his numerous small financial transactions, *not once* is John Cholmley's signature there. As Henslowe's partner living on the spot at the tenement where the refreshments were sold, one would have expected him to have been readily available for this friendly office. But it seems as if the grocer had disappeared from the scene without trace. In that case, to whom was the other share of the gallery takings paid? The most obvious candidate would be Edward Alleyn. Philip Henslowe would have shown typically shrewd judgement in linking Alleyn with himself in his theatrical venture from the start, and if so it was an alliance he chose to repeat throughout his life, in their joint Bear Garden partnership, and in building their grand theatre, the Fortune. Moreover, Alleyn's partnership would go some way to explain the mysteries of Henslowe's gallery recordings in 1597 and thereafter, when abrupt and puzzling changes occur, which we shall investigate.

After the brief ten days' playing of the joint Admiral's and Chamberlain's companies at Newington Butts from 3rd to 13th June 1594, Henslowe draws a line,[32] which has been interpreted as signifying the end of that season and the return to the Rose, although he writes no further headings from here on for the next four years – but it is clear from the repertoire given throughout all this long period that the company which is continuously in residence is the Lord Admiral's, and we may assume confidently that the theatre is Henslowe's own, the Rose. As before, the entries list the names of plays, tell us which are new, and record the gallery takings at each performance.[33]

The company settles down to a regular pattern followed year by year; after playing with hardly a break for the next nine months' season, from 15th June 1594 until 14th March 1595, always observing the Sunday rest day, and ceasing for Lent 1595 for thirty-two days. Then they reopen on Easter Monday, 22nd April 1595, playing 'the ffrenshe doctor', and continue until Thursday 26th June (Sundays excepted): there follows a break of almost two months, probably for summer touring, resuming at the Rose on 25th August with their first play of the long autumn-winter-spring season, which carries on without a break until Lent when they cease playing on 27th February until Easter Monday, 12th April 1596.

384

And so on. Henslowe's entries continue in this regular format. Apart from his introduction of a Henslowian squiggle at the beginning of each day's entry, the meaning of which is obscure, (Henslowe was fond of drawing and adorns some of his letters with sketches) these records are fairly similar to his first season with Alleyn and Strange's Men in 1592. His entries for these four years – preceded by a ƒ squiggle – now appear thus:

ƒ 25 of June 1594   Read at the masacer .... xxxvj^s
ƒ 26 of June 1594 ne— Rd at galiaso .... iij^{li} iiij^s
ƒ 27 of June 1594   Rd at cvttlacke .... xxxvj^s [34]

A new play invariably brought the reward of a larger box office. According to Henslowe's note we must assume that his financial record relates to the gallery takings. These remain remarkably constant when averaged over a four weekly period. For the four weeks from Easter Monday, 22nd April 1595, they total £44. 4s. giving a weekly average of £11. 1s. but whether this represents the whole gallery's takings is not known. Samples of receipts for four weeks' playing show that the average hovers steadily around £10 a week from 1592 to 1595/6 when there is a decline to £8–£9. But it is significant that when Henslowe later completely alters his style of recording with the announcement –

Here I Begyne to [th] Receue the wholle gallereys
frome this daye beinge the 29 of July 1598 [35]

– the weekly average instead of showing an increase, as might be expected were the takings now to be all his own, is still around £8. From this should we deduce that he had always recorded the entire gallery takings? From 29th July 1598 Henslowe no longer records the entries *daily*, but resorts to *weekly* totals, without showing what plays are being performed. This is disappointing. The *Diary* now becomes *solely a financial record*. As the box office takings are given for the week, we do not know whether they represent a full week's playing as before, and it is perplexing that the totals for the weeks now tend to fluctuate wildly from as low as £2.2s. (the week ending 1st April 1599) to as high as £16. 12s. (the week ending 3rd June 1599), but the *average* for a four weekly period tends to be around £8 as in 1596; by 1599 it has dropped to £5. 11s. 11d.[36] The Rose seems to be losing its appeal and dynamism as a theatre. Henslowe himself was apparently no longer present daily as before, and the fact that he no longer bothers to enter the names of the plays performed seems symptomatic of a loss of personal interest and involvement with his theatre. All this has, I suggest, to do with Edward Alleyn's retirement from the stage at some time during 1597, which must have been a sad event for Henslowe, who recorded this information in his *Diary*:

> A not of all suche goods as I haue Bowght for
> playnge sence my sonne edward allen leafte laynge [sic]*
>
> Bowght the 29 of desemb₃ 1597 j short vealuett ⎫ iij^{li} 37
> clocke embradered wth bugelles & a hoode cape ⎭

The list of costumes bought continues, but this extract gives us the year when Edward Alleyn decided to leave the profession in which he had become famous. We do not know his reason, but it seems to have had a profound effect on Henslowe, and would have been regretted by his company. Early in 1597 there is already a curious alteration in Henslowe's gallery recordings for which no satisfactory explanation has been found. As from 24th January 1597 he adopts five-figure columns for his gallery takings, and changes from 'Rd' to 'tt', which probably represents 'total'. He also makes use of the margin of the pages for adding notes.

			£	s	£	s	d
Janewary	24	Rd at that wilbe shalbe	0	17	00.	19 - 07	
1597	25	Rd at the blinde beagar	0	19	03.	08 - 00	
	26	tt at Nabucadonizer	0	09	02	00 - 03	
	27	ne--tt at womane hard to please	2	11	06	07 - 08	38

This now remains his format *throughout 1597* until 5th November. In these five-figure columns the gallery takings appear to have been split, although in a way that is inconsistent from day to day, sometimes one column being more than the other, sometimes less. The two sets of figures presumably relate to the gallery receipts. If so, how he calculates it is a mystery. But that these accounts are directly connected with Alleyn's retirement, which he would most certainly have discussed with Henslowe well beforehand, is, I believe, shown by the following entry which evidently records this important event.

Note the curious '0.' entry with no box office receipts against the performance of Marlowe's *Doctor Faustus*, shown in the extract from Henslowe's Diary for a date which is not recorded precisely between 11th and 19th October 1597 (see opposite).

---

* Henslowe obviously meant to write "playnge" (playing).

386

Octob͛ 1597	11	tt at Joroneymo	⟨...⟩2.	. ⟨...⟩	01 - 13 - 00	
In the name		tt at the comodey of vmers	⟨...⟩2.	..00	00 - 19 - 0	
of god a men		tt at docter fostes	.... 0.			
the xj octob͛		tt at				
be gane my lord		tt at				
admerals & my		tt at				
lord of penbrockes	19	tt at				
men to playe at		tt at hardicute	00	16	00 - 00 - 1 [39]	
my howsse 1597						

Was this Edward Alleyn's last appearance at the Rose in the role he had made his own and given as a benefit performance for him? It would have made a fitting dramatic finish to his career, this date conforming with Henslowe's note of 20th December on Alleyn's retirement, sadly recalling it as though it had been a fairly recent event which poor old Henslowe had not yet come to terms with. As we shall see in pursuing this line of inquiry further, Alleyn had been making most careful preparations for his retirement throughout July and August of that summer, leaving us in no doubt that this was a well-planned decision on his part, which culminated in this final benefit performance in his favourite role as Faustus on what seems to have been the 13th October – a date that Henslowe was probably too superstitious to enter and so left the last two days blank.

We can visualize a packed house attending for what must have been one of Alleyn's finest performances. With hushed breath the audience would have heard Faustus's moving heart-cry in that last great speech which Alleyn had performed so often, but never to more ardent applause surely than on this last occasion when the great actor would have given his all, living the role he loved with every anguished word –

> *Faustus.*   Ah, Faustus.
> Now hast thou but one bare hour to live,
> And then thou must be damn'd perpetually!
> Stand still, you ever-moving spheres of heaven,
> That time may cease, and midnight never come;
> Fair Nature's eye, rise, rise again, and make
> Perpetual day; or let this hour be but
> A year, a month, a week, a natural day,
> That Faustus may repent and save his soul!
> *O lente, lente currite, noctis equi!*

to his final despairing cry –

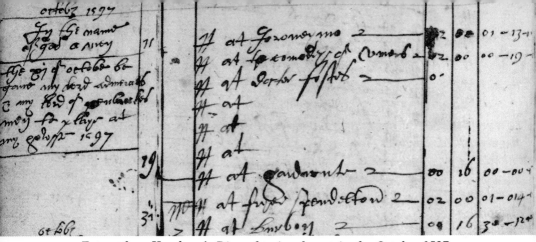

Extract from Henslowe's Diary showing the entries for October 1597.

By kind permission of the Governors of Dulwich College.

> My God, my God, look not so fierce on me!
> Adders and serpents, let me breathe a while!
> Ugly hell, gape not! come not, Lucifer!
> I'll burn my books! – Ah, Mephistophilis!

Not a dry eye in the theatre, followed by thunderous applause, is not too fanciful a conclusion to make. Another piece of suggestive evidence is that here, for the first time since the plague, we find recorded another company as playing at the Rose indicating a change – the end of the old order and a new beginning.

The blank 'tt at' entries show that Henslowe wrote these in advance down his page in readiness for filling in with the details on the day of performance. Evidently following *Doctor Faustus* there was a break of at least three days before playing was resumed. All this is suggestive of some radical new development taking place: what appears to have been a benefit performance of *Dr Faustus*, followed by three days of no playing, and then amalgamation with Pembroke's Men, all pointing to Edward Alleyn's retirement. This event must have entailed some kind of financial deal with Henslowe, involving much prior discussion for it is inconceivable that his retirement would have been a sudden decision, unless for reasons of sickness, of which there is no indication whatsoever. It must have been a conscious decision, for which Henslowe, however reluctantly, made his careful preparation.

It is, I suggest, significant that these five-figure accounts begin nine months *before* Alleyn's retirement, and then carry on to record only six plays *after* his last performance, when they cease as abruptly as they began, as though the financial transactions which they are recording had

388

by then been resolved. After an interim Henslowe announces (on 29th July 1598) 'Here I Begyne to Receue the wholle gallereys',[40] and he reverts to the form of his previous entries using Roman numerals – the only difference being that he now records *weekly totals as a lump sum*, omitting any reference to the plays performed as if now less personally interested. If we can first resolve what is meant by the 'wholle gallereys' we may have some hope of discovering what his five-figure columns represent.

Greg has given deep thought to the interpretation of Henslowe's accounting methods in his chapter on *Dramatic Finance*, and I agree with Foakes and Rickert in acclaiming his suggested solutions as brilliant, and far more logical than any put forward by other critics who have attempted an explanation. However, no one would claim that the last word has been said on the matter. First, to follow Greg's interpretation of the sums Henslowe entered as his gallery receipts, which average around £10 a week in the years 1592–1595, and thereafter tend to be marginally lower – despite Henslowe's comment that he now *receives* the whole galleries, what he *enters* on paper does not reflect this in any way. Greg has therefore argued (and here I agree that his solution is the only possible answer) that Henslowe entered only *half* the gallery takings *after* he had deducted his moiety, or half, for the rent of the house. It was a standard practice in theatrical management, as well by Burbage as by Henslowe, that half the galleries was due to the proprietor of the theatre as his rent. The sum of £10 for a six-day week yields two hundred tuppenny gallery seats sold daily* (a few more expensive special seats reducing the number). The groundlings paid 1d for their standing room below, the takings being divided among the players; the gallery takings reserved for the proprietor and sharers in the company. This is how Greg sees this transaction:

'I suppose Henslowe...to have been from the beginning to the end of his recorded career in receipt of one half of the takings of the galleries as rent for his house. As this was a constant payment there was no need to specify it, and as it was all profit there was no need to keep a record.'[41]

Foakes and Rickert comment on this: 'If there was no need for Henslowe to keep a record at this time (1598), it may be wondered why he should

---

* If this is only half the gallery takings then the true situation shows nearer four hundred gallery seats sold, testifying to the enormous popularity of theatre-going, for the Rose was only one of London's theatres.

have troubled to keep one earlier. A possible answer could have been provided by the contract Henslowe had made with Cholmley to build the Rose in 1586/7; this specified that receipts were to be divided equally between them. This contract, however, was due to expire in April 1595 and there is no evidence of its renewal'.[42] Precisely. But was Alleyn now the recipient? Greg points out:

> 'It is certainly strange that we should find no other deed or document of any kind, not even a stray acquittance mentioning Cholmley, and it is curious that the accounts for the spring of 1595 when the partnership would have expired are particularly regular and afford no indication of any change in the management of the Rose.'[43]

Greg himself suggests then, that a change in management would be reflected in *some alteration in the accounts*. This is precisely what we find in the abrupt change occurring in 1597, yet Greg completely overlooks the impending retirement of Alleyn as having any possible significance, and he hardly mentions him.

Turning now to an examination of the five-figure accounts, Greg has clarified these entries by demonstrating convincingly that the first two columns represent pounds and shillings only, while the last three represent £. s. d.: despite one or two discrepancies which may be attributed to Henslowe's human errors, as when he enters the figure 30 in the shillings column on 29th January as follows:

| Janewary 1597 | 29 | tt at long mege... | 0 | 07 | 01. 30 – 11 [44] |

Evidently he meant to write 03 instead of 30.* Greg states: 'The first two columns agree sufficiently closely with the sums previously entered to justify the supposition that they represent similar takings' (i.e. half the gallery receipts, which Henslowe has recorded ever since the *Diary* began). He then postulates that 'the remainder represents some quite novel payment', noting that the three columns recorded as £. s. d. vary from sums in excess of the takings in the first two columns, down to minimal amounts, or even nothing at all. From the strange fluctuation in the amounts recorded, Greg postulates a theory.

> 'My suggestion ... with regard to the mysterious figures which appear so erratically in the last three columns of the daily accounts

---

*In the old English currency 12d. = 1 shilling, 20s. = 1 pound.

is that these represent the sums which Henslowe was able every now and then to squeeze out of the company towards the repayment of the moneys advanced. This view is borne out by the fact that, as we shall see later on, when the practice had become systematized in the next century, the takings of a special portion of the house were actually earmarked for the repayment of advances.' [45]

At first sight this seems a very reasonable explanation, for there is indeed reference to part of the gallery money being allocated to the repayment of debts in the agreement Henslowe made with Nat Field, for instance, which is preserved among Alleyn's Papers at Dulwich. The vellum is so decayed that the date is obliterated, but it must be circa 1613, and it is just possible to make out 'that ther shalbe due accompte given Every night to any one that shall by the Company be appoynted ther vnto ⟨.....⟩ half of the galleries allo⟨w⟩ed towards the payment of the s⟨...⟩ hundred t⟨w⟩enty & fower pounds'[46] which was the debt owed. Again, in the 'Articles of Grievance and Oppression' that troubled the last year of Henslowe's life, being complaints by the actors brought against him in 1615, there is reference to an arrangement for the payment of 'the other halfe galleries towards his debt of 126^{li}: and other such moneys as hee should laie out for playe apparrell...'[47] But these arrangements apply to the future when Henslowe's inability to keep the actors' debts down to a reasonable figure, whether by policy or mismanagement (so that they were in the region of £600 at times and rarely less than one hundred) finally swamped him in the turmoil he created. But in the time of Alleyn's efficient co-management of the company we have no evidence of mounting debt. In the period 1596–7 leading up to and relating to the five-figure accounts, Alleyn's influence in the company was able to maintain borrowing at a low level, mostly under his personal supervision I believe, and mainly for essential company expenditure on building their stock of apparel and play-books, the sums being commonly between £20 and £50, which were never allowed to accumulate but were systematically paid off. For instance Alleyn's loan account 'for the company' to buy 'a new sewte of a parell' and other items, is meticulously paid off in daily amounts until settled, from 2nd May until 8th July 1596. The sum was £39. 10s. Having entered the loans, Henslowe casts up his account for repayment.

li	s	d	Receued agayne of my sonne EA of this
			deate abowe written as foloweth
39 - [ ] -		00	
	10		

			Rd the 10 of maye 1596	.... xxx^s
			Rd the 11 of maye 1596	.... xx^s
			Rd the 12 of maye 159[5]6	.... xxxxvjs
			Rd the 13 of maye 159[5]6	.... xxxxvjs
			Rd the 14 of maye 1596	.... xxvjs
			Rd the 15 of maye 159[5]6	.... xxiiijs
			Rd the 16 of maye 1596	.... xxxvjs
			Rd the 17 of maye 1596	.... 1s
			Rd the 18 of maye 1596	.... liijs
			Rd the 22 of maye 1596	.... xxviijs
			Rd the 23 of maye 1596	.... xxxxs
			Rd the 24 of maye 1596	.... xxijs
			Rd the 25 of maye 1596	.... xxv^s

li	s	d		
025 - 10 -		00	Rd the 11 of June 1596	.... iij^{li} iiij^s
			Rd the 23 of June 1596	.....................iij^{li} xiij^s
			Rd the 25 of June 1596	.... xxjs
			Rd the 26 of June 1596	.... xxx^s
			Rd the 27 of June 1596	.... xxjs

li	s	d		
36 - 07 -		00	Rd the 1 of July 1596	.... xxxxvijs
			Rd the 2 of July 1596	.... xxv^s
			Rd the 5 of July 1596	.... xxxiijs
			Rd the 6 of July 1596	.... xvijs
			Rd the 8 of July 1596	.... xxijs [48]

The foregoing shows the punctiliousness with which Edward Alleyn always paid his bills and debts. The £39. 10s. he had borrowed 'for the company' here reveals the relationship of Henslowe to the company as their financier and banker with Alleyn acting as the chief representative for the actors, handling and regulating the necessary moneys on loan. One cannot help concluding that with the disappearance of Alleyn from the scene, the happy-go-lucky philosophy of the actors prevailed, and Henslowe allowed them to get away with piling up debts, for it emerges from the later history of his theatrical ventures without Alleyn that he lacked the latter's authority with the actors and was relatively powerless to curb their indebtedness, both in mounting personal debts, as in company finances, which led to so much trouble from their recurrent insolvency.

It is in this later period that we have evidence of half the galleries being reserved as the fund to finance the company's loan account, but as we have no records to show how Henslowe kept his later accounts on paper, we cannot compare them with the five-figure accounts of 1597 which Greg believes represent some such loan account. However, there may be an indication of the introduction of the use of the half galleries for this purpose in the accounts running from 29th July 1598, when he announces that he begins to receive the 'wholle gallereys' (having cleared his debts following Alleyn's retirement and having no longer any partner with whom he had to share a part of the galleries). This account ends on 13th October 1599 when Henslowe, having cast up his reckoning with the company over the past fifteen month period, (in which there are gaps for August 1598, and March, July and August 1599 for Lent and summer touring or vacations) is retrieving a debt of £358! This figure, when averaged weekly, approximates to the normal half galleries of the preceding years of £8. 2s. 8d., and Henslowe specifically records that this sum of £358 was the debt the company owed to him.

Reconed wth the company of my lord of notinghame men to*
this place beinge the 13 of octob, 1599 & yt doth a peare
that I haue Receued of the deate w[ch] they owe vnto me iij hundred
fiftie & eyght pownds.[49]

So that Greg was therefore right in anticipating that Henslowe (later) used the galleries to reclaim the company's debts to him, but he was not right in claiming that this is what we see represented in the puzzling five-figure accounts. Firstly, the accounts of 1589 to 1599 are not kept in five-figure columns, but are Henslowe's normal accounting style with the difference that they only show weekly, and not daily receipts. I believe that Henslowe was not able to use this half gallery money, which he had always habitually recorded *because it was the part due to his partner*, who would originally have been Cholmley but who was succeeded by Alleyn, *until* he was in possession of the 'wholle gallereys', and it is from this time on that he records in the margin the amounts received in a running total -- and then at the end of the account on 13th October announces that he had received all the company's debt owed to him. That this debt was repaid *via* the receipts from the half galleries which now flowed from indebted sharers to him is borne out by the marginal running totals and his own announcement at the end of this lengthy account that the debt is now cleared. It is also obvious that this situation did *not* apply

---

*Nottingham's Men are the Lord Admiral's Men, for in 1596 he became Earl of Nottingham.

before the 29th July 1598. What financial resources Henslowe had used before to oil the wheels of the company we do not know – he had all his own rent money from the other half of the galleries, and he had other income. However, once he gained use of the whole galleries he floated his loans from the second half for his theatrical business. Thus Greg's theory is vindicated in 1598, but does not apply in 1597 before Alleyn's retirement to the five-figure accounts.

Secondly, to answer Greg further, if he had been right in assuming that the five-figure accounts represent Henslowe's records of moneys 'squeezed' out of the actors for repayment of their debts, we would expect to find such an accounting method to be continued afterwards, but it is *only* used in 1597, and ceases soon after Alleyn's retirement. This surely has some significance that has so far been unappreciated and unconsidered.

Thirdly, it is strange that Henslowe should keep separate loan accounts in addition to this five-figure account if this were also a loan account, and thus duplicate his work. In the *Diary* carefully kept loan accounts for itemized company purchases for play-books, apparel and so on, are a regular feature.

> A note of Suche money as I haue
> lent vnto thes meane whose names
> folow at seaverall tymes edward alleyn
> martyne slather Jeames donstall & Jewbey
> all this lent sence the 1596 14 of octobʒ

lent vnto martyne to feache fleacher .... vjs
lent vnto theme to feache browne .... xs
lent vnto my sonne for thomas honte .... vjs 8ᵈ
lent vnto them for hawodes bocke ....xxxs
lent vnto them at a nother tyme 1s
lent vnto marteyn at a nother tyme...xxxs
lent vnto the tayller for the stocke ....xxxs
lent vnto them to by a boocke ....xxxxs
lent the company to geue fleatcher
[sic] & the hauepromysed me payment who promysed me is marten donston Jewby ⎫ xxˢ
Rd in pt of payment the 29 of octobʒ 1596 .... xxs
Rd in pt of payment of al holanday 1596 .... xxs
Rd in pt of paymente the 13 of desembʒ 1596 ....xxxxs
[Some is vij^li] [viij^li xs] ttottalles. .... 31^li [0]15ˢ – 00ᵈ 50

The above is typical of Henslowe's separately kept loan accounts at the period prior to the commencement of his five-figure accounts. But now we come to the really interesting part. If Greg wanted proof of whether his hypothesis concerning the five-figure accounts really does represent Henslowe's record of such moneys as he was able to squeeze out of the actors – during 1597 – against clearing their debts to him, here it is. And I am afraid it is negative.

We have below a separate loan account for January 1597 for money Henslowe was able to squeeze from the actors as a result of certain more successful performances of which he gives the dates and the plays, so that we can compare his records of these performances and gallery takings with the money paid to him by the actors for their debts. The account begins concurrently with the last of the old style accounts, and here we can see that the money taken does not tally with the amount of debt recovered, excepting in the very first entry which I believe was merely fortuitous. The half galleries were, therefore, we may conclude not appropriated for debt repayments – at this period. The final proof comes when the performance on 27th January is actually recorded in his new style five-figure account. And here there is *no* relationship between the sums recorded in either of the five-figure account columns with the amount Henslowe was able to recover towards his debit clearance.

First the evidence of his loan account.

Rd at the second time of playinge that wilbe shalbe
the 4 of Janewary 1597 the some of .... xxxxs
Rd at Joronymo the 7 of Jane[y]wary 1597 in pte
of payment .... vij^{li}
Rd at elexsander & ladwicke the 14 of Janewarye the
fyrste time yt wasse playde 1596 in pte .... v^{li}
*Rd at woman hard to please the 27 of Janewary 97 .... iiij^{li} 51

It will be seen that Henslowe has made an error in writing the date of the play 'that wilbe shalbe' as on 4th January when it was actually 3rd January, as below in his gallery records.

♭ 3 of Jenewary 1597   – Rd at that wilbe shalbe .... xxxx^{s}

♭ 7 of Jenewary 1597 [n] – Rd at Joronymo .... iiij^{li}

♭ 14 of Janewary 1597 ne – Rd at elexsander & lodwicke .... lv^{s} 52

And now in the five-figure accounts:

Janewary 1597 27 ne–tt at womane hard to please .... |2 |11| 06 07 - 08 53

It will be seen in the above comparison of the sums recorded by Henslowe that his reimbursement for loans to the company do not approximate the gallery receipts at any of these performances excepting the first when at the play 'that wilbe shalbe' on 3rd (4th) January xxxx^{s}

or £2 exactly figures in both accounts. At "Joronymo" the gallery receipt was only £3 but Henslowe received fully £7; at "elexsander & lodowicke" they took £2. 15s. but Henslowe was repaid £5. Now if these figures were supposed to reflect the fluctuating last column of the five-figure accounts one might argue with Greg that these too bear no relation to the takings of their half galleries (assuming that the first columns are the half gallery receipts, as Greg suggests they are). But when we come to compare the receipts for 27th January at *"woman hard to please"* in the five-figure account, we see that Henslowe was reimbursed £4, which sum accords with neither the first column of £2. 11s. nor the second of £6. 7s. 8d. Greg argued that the second column would represent what Henslowe had been able to squeeze out of the actors, but on this evidence (admittedly only one solitary example) it falls to the ground.

Furthermore, according to Greg's hypothesis the first column of £. and s. represents the normal gallery receipts (due I have suggested to the partner, either the whole moiety, as agreed with Cholmley, or a sufficient proportion thereof); but the second three figures recorded as £. s. d. have no relation to the galleries at all, *if* as received from the actors' pockets - which is how Greg sees it. My belief is that they would, in that case, not have been entered here, but would appear in a separate loan account as was Henslowe's wont, and that these figures are despite their fluctuation and irregularity in some way connected with the gallery receipts. My proposition is that we have here, for the first and only time in Henslowe's accounts, a record of the whole galleries.

To test this I have totalled the two daily amounts recorded side by side, and then added these totals in order to arrive at a figure for a weekly or six–day average, which can then be compared with the weekly six–day averages of the half galleries in 1596, each over a ten week period. The correlation is amazingly close.

Half Galleries 1596[54]		£	s		Whole Galleries 1597[54]		£	s	d
Week beginning	12th April	8	8		Week beginning	24th Jan	25	19	5
"	"	19th April	4	19		"	"	31st Jan	27	1	6
"	"	26th April	8	8		"	"	11th April	15	15	4
"	"	2nd May	8	0		"	"	18th April	12	2	9
"	"	10th May	9	6		"	"	2nd May	11	4	3
"	"	17th May	11	19		"	"	9th May	12	14	0
"	"	1st Nov	6	11		"	"	16th may	14	17	10
"	"	8th Nov	5	5		"	"	6th June	18	18	0
"	"	10th Dec	7	4		"	"	27th June	12	8	1
"	"	27th May	12	15		"	"	4th July	20	9	8
			-----					---------	
		82	15				171	10	10
	Average	**£8 5s 6d**				**Average**	**£8 11s 8d**		

This is a satisfactory enough correspondence. Even the appearance of one abnormally large figure of £34. 1s. 3d. (or £17. 0s. 7½d expressed as a half gallery) for the week beginning 7th February 1597 (omitted from the averaging exercise above) can be balanced by the equally large receipt of 9th June 1595 of £17. 15s. 0d. (£35. 10s. 0d. as a whole gallery).[56] Such large sums are abnormal but not unique.

Any interpretation of Henslowe's curious and puzzling accounts of this period is necessarily conjectural. Nothing can actually be proved by citing the figures. But they must have a *reason*. If we put these five-figure accounts into their context we cannot omit note of the fact that Edward Alleyn was planning to retire at this time, and that he actually did so we know from Henslowe's entry of 20th December 1597, which tells us that Alleyn had already retired for he speaks of what costumes he has purchased *since* he had left playing, which implies that it was a fairly recent event.

All the activities and changes in the company reflected in the *Diary* prior to December 1597 point to the performance of *Dr Faustus* on 13th October as the date of Alleyn's retirement. Firstly, the sealing of bonds with the chief actors of the company binding them to play under the management at the Rose, which Alleyn busied himself with from July to October 1597. Secondly, the amalgamation with the Earl of Pembroke's players on the 11th October, which I believe to have been the handing over period. Thirdly, Greg argued that one would expect to find an indication of a change in the management of the theatre to be reflected in the accounts, and this is what we do find in 1597, the year of Alleyn's retirement.

Greg's explanation for Henslowe's habitual entry of only half of the gallery receipts was that the rent due to him of his own half was 'all profit', and it was therefore unnecessary to record it. According to the fifty-fifty arrangement made with Cholmley, the other half (which he records) is due to his partner. We find a single example of such a payment made to Edward Alleyn when he was Henslowe's partner in the Fortune, recorded under Henslowe's heading 'Begininge wth A new Reckynyng wth my lord of nothingames men the 23 daye of febreary 1601 as foloweth'.

> Itm pd vnto my sonne EAlleyn w^ch
> was after we had Reckneyd to geather
> the company & I wch after ou^r castyng   } xxvij^s vj^d
> dew to my sone owt of the gallery mony
> the some of...   57

397

The amount of 27s 6d is typical of one day's half gallery receipt, here recorded presumably because there had either been some query of the amount or Alleyn was absent on the day. This examples what Foakes and Rickert have in mind when they question why Henslowe should have bothered to record the half galleries, *unless* it had to do with a partnership arrangement. What is highly significant is the change in style *after* Alleyn has retired, from detailed daily accounts recording the plays performed, to a weekly sum from the time when he announces that he is now in receipt of the 'wholle gallereys'. Plainly before this time someone else was taking a share of the galleries, and in the total absence of Cholmley that person could only have been Alleyn. Henslowe's strange accounts in five-figure columns, which I have argued show the whole receipts for the first and only time in the *Diary*, occur only at this period of Alleyn's retirement, and therefore I conclude that they show Henslowe's gradual paying off his partner for his share in the business, which he is taking out of his own gallery share, or rent, to do so. It is a perfectly normal commercial practice to stagger payments out of assets in this way.

The reason the second group in the five-figure columns fluctuates so wildly may be explained when they are seen to be dependent on Henslowe juggling his financial commitments. At first sight they appear to bear no relation to the first group, which Greg has argued represent the half galleries as before. But totting up the totals and comparing them has shown that the averages are comparable to the figure of the whole galleries. If these figures had nothing to do with the receipts they would not have been included in Henslowe's daily theatrical accounts, but surely would have been entered separately, as in the pawnbroking and miscellaneous loan accounts. In the agreement with Cholmley the half gallery receipts recorded by Henslowe represented what would have been due to his partner; whether Alleyn also acquired a half share, we do not know, but at all events his share would have been calculated as a proportion of these regularly recorded galleries. And these figures remain constant, even when the five-figure accounts appear with their fluctuating second column of £. s. d. This answers Foakes's and Rickert's first point concerning the relevance of Henslowe's gallery records to a partnership share.

When Edward Alleyn joined Henslowe in 1591/2 the Rose was undergoing extensive renovations. There is some evidence in the *Diary* to support my hypothesis that Alleyn contributed a sum of money towards this expenditure and thereby bought himself into partnership at the outset, for he was man of some means.[58] If this had not already been effected so early, then it is very likely that an arrangement would have been concluded at the time of his marriage to Joan, perhaps in part as a marriage settlement from his 'father'.

Most significant of all is that at the conclusion of these five-figure accounts, Henslowe announces that he is in receipt of the whole galleries, yet he continues to record the half amount received as before, but irregularly, as a lump sum, as profits for his personal business record so that he knows what is coming in, the details being now no longer necessary because he is not accountable to anyone. Edward Alleyn as partner would have keenly followed the success or failure of the plays in his repertoire, in order to maximize the company's profitability. Under him the Lord Admiral's Men thrived. Henslowe's records highlight this, and thereby reveal his accountability to someone in a position of partnership with him – someone who was not merely a manager but was personally interested in the repertoire being performed. It is doubtful whether the grocer, Cholmley, would have been that interested.

The fact that Henslowe, left to play a solo hand, was no longer sufficiently interested to record the daily performances, would seem to confirm Fleay's view of him as a mere soulless businessman who 'regarded art as a subject for exploitation'. But this, I feel, is only partly true. Henslowe's letters at this time to Alleyn, who went with his wife to live in the country, show him anxious and depressed. Throughout his career it becomes increasingly evident, the more is revealed about these two who stood in the relation of 'father' and 'son', that it was Henslowe who was dependent on Alleyn's guidance and expertise, especially in the management of his theatrical business. We have no records to indicate how Henslowe fared before Alleyn came to join him at the Rose, but the theatre seems hardly to have made an impact before the season of 1592 when it burst into prominence, although it must, we assume, have been in use since 1586/7.

On the other hand, the total disappearance of Cholmley from the scene was not so much a loss to Henslowe, as a mystery to us. In fact, financially it could have been nothing but a gain to the proprietor once the theatre was operating.

The loss of Alleyn would have been a heavy one also for the company. It was customary, upon an actor's retirement, to give him a lump sum of money from the company's funds. I suggest that it is, therefore, a logical deduction to see the last performance of *Doctor Faustus* in October 1597, on a date between 11th and 19th of the month, for which Henslowe records no receipts, as Alleyn's farewell to the theatre at which time the entire box office was given to him personally, which would explain the puzzling *zero* entry in Henslowe's accounts. In other words, this occasion was his company's benefit performance for Alleyn's retirement.

It is interesting to note, too, that the opening of the five-figure accounts was launched with the performance on 24th January 1597 of the appropriately titled play, *That Will Be Shall Be*. It is, of course, no more than an amusing conjecture to suggest that this was possibly a whimsical choice expressing the company's resignation to the sad fact that Alleyn had decided to retire. Maybe one of the wits in the company, or Alleyn himself proposed that this is the piece that they would play, the die being cast? It is one of the most striking idiosyncracies of Alleyn's character that important dates and events in his life should always be significantly highlighted in some way, and this would have been a typical gesture on his part.

Further evidence of Alleyn's impending retirement may be seen in the bonds sealed in the autumn of 1597 binding actors to perform at the Rose under Henslowe and at no other theatre, thus stabilizing the company and ensuring that there were experienced and capable actors to carry it forward when Alleyn would no longer be there. On 10th August 1597 William Borne 'came & ofered hime sealfe to come and playe wth my lord admeralles mean at my howsse called by the name of the Rosse...for the space of iij yeares beginynge Imediatly after this Re straynt is Recaled by the lords of the cownsell'.[59] This was a reference to the closure of the theatres at the end of July as a punitive measure for the performance of Nashe's play *'the Ieylle of dooges'* as it is here written, which landed some of the actors in prison and all of them out of work for presuming to criticize the government in a play on the public stage. This rash venture had been performed by the Earl of Pembroke's company at the Swan on 28th July 1597. Unfortunately the play is lost, but evidently the 'very seditious and sclanderous matter' it contained, which so offended Her Majesty's Government, was strong satire in which witty Tom Nashe had overstepped the mark.

Meanwhile all through July and August 1597 Alleyn was busily drawing the company together on a secure basis for its future by signing bonds of fealty with the actors binding them to play with the Lord Admiral's Men at the Rose for periods varying from one to three years. On 27th July Thomas Hearne was signed up;[60] on 3rd August John Helle 'the clowne'[61] signed his bond; and on 6th August Richard Jones sealed the same, at the time also standing surety for Robert Shaa, binding him to play with 'my lordes admeralles men as he hath covenanted be fore',[62] presumably Shaa being absent at the time of executing the bond. On 6th

400

October 'Thomas dowten' or Downton, 'came & bownd hime seallfe vnto me in xxxx^{li} in [covenante]' for the space of two years.[63] Downton is particularly important for he became the leader of the Lord Admiral's Men after Alleyn's departure. The last bond witnessed by Alleyn was on 8th December for William Kendall.[64] All these bonds are made on the traditional payment of pence (2d or 3d was a normal token sum) in recognition of their bond, and all are signed and witnessed by Alleyn himself with members of the company. Alleyn was therefore actively involved in making provision for his succession and the continued wellbeing of the company. A note in Henslowe's *Diary* further records the purchase of a boy actor from his master, the actor who had nurtured, supported and trained him.

> Bowght my boye Jeames brystow of william agusten
> player the 18 of desemb₃ 1597 for viij^{li} [65]

After Alleyn's retirement the company was further strengthened when Richard Alleyn[66] bound himself for two years on 25th March 1598, and on the same day Thomas Heywood, the actor-playwright, also bound himself 'as a covenente searvante for ij years by the Receuenge of ij syngell pence acordinge to the statute of winshester'.[67] But now Edward Alleyn's name no longer appears as a witness and signatory.

On 16th November 1598 two more 'covenente Servantes Charlles massy & samewell Rowley', both actor-playwrights and close friends, bound themselves for one year.[68] All these are the first bonds of this kind recorded in the *Diary*, and the implication of their timing suggests that they are connected with Alleyn's retirement. While Alleyn was leader of the company his authority would have been the necessary cement holding the players together, but in his absence it was probably felt advisable to procure bonds of fealty from them.

A further piece of recorded evidence from Henslowe's *Diary* which points to the likelihood that Alleyn must have been a partner in the Rose is in the entries recorded with the book reversed of which folio 238 is mainly taken up with a list of miscellaneous items of building materials, which appear to relate to the repairs and renovations of the Rose in 1592. It is a lengthy list beginning as follows:

> A not what edward allen hath layd owt
> as foloweth
> Itm pd for ij thowsen & halfe of bryckes............. xxvijs vjd
> Itm pd for a mantell tre.. xijd

Itm pd vnto J gryges man John the 24 of novemb‡ 1592..xxxx[s] [69]

John Gryges (or Griggs) was the builder employed by Henslowe for the renovation of his playhouse in 1592, so this may be significant. He was also working on Edward Alleyn's own house nearby, however, so this may be connected with this job, excepting that immediately following the above list is another separate account of similar materials for building which is headed specifically as being for charges 'layd owt a bowt edward alenes howsse...........1592'.[70]

Henslowe then leaps into 1594 with a brief list of expenses for 'my Lorde Admeralle seruantes' for playing at Somerset House, which includes money for 'drinckinge wth the Jentellmen' on two occasions which cost him 4s. 8d. and 12d. and for 'goinge vp & downe to corte twise'.[71]

The next two folios 235 verso and 235 (we are going backwards in the book here) are particularly interesting being covered on one folio with long reckonings in Arabic numerals of fairly large sums, from £173 to £362, and the other is given over to a very lengthy itemized list of expenditures which cover a period from February 1593 to March 1597, and it is headed 'edward allenes Recknynge'.[72] This certainly looks like a totting up of all moneys owed for a final reckoning – the sort of final accounts which Henslowe whimsically terms casting up 'from the begininge of the world'! The old boy had a sense of humour. On folio 234 verso we find yet more reckonings in Arabic numerals:

> A note what money I owe vnto my
> Sonne edward allenne as ffolowethe & a
> notte what my sonne edward allen owes
> vnto me

	li	s	d
Itm I owe vnto my sonne........	0[2]45	– 08	– 00
Itm my sonne owes vnto me........	[0]060	– 00	– 00 [73]

Then continues a loan account involving Arthur Langworth, but it is not clear whether all these debts and loans are connected. There seems, however, to be a general clearing up of all outstanding financial commitments to June/July 1597.

Henslowe's *Diary* can, perhaps, tell us still more which has not been suspected. That Edward Alleyn stood in a business relationship to Henslowe in the management of the Rose over and above that of merely leading actor of the company, seems to me to be an inescapable conclusion, and the curious five-figure accounts of 1597 would appear to have some connection with the financial side of the dissolution of that relationship, which had for five years so happily ensured the smooth and successful running of the theatre. The Rose had seen its best days under the mutually supportive and harmonious partnership of Philip Henslowe and his 'sonne'. But the theatre was periodically showing signs of wear and tear and was nearing the end of its useful life. Following the major renovations of 1591/2 Henslowe recorded further repairs in 1595 in his *Diary*.

A nott what I haue layd owt abowt my playhowsse
ffor payntynge & doinge it abowt wth ealme bordes & other
Repracyons as ffoloweth 1595 in lent [74]

Wages to the carpenters and painters, and materials such as elm boards, nails and so on totalled £108. 19s. 0d. and an additional expense had been for 'mackinge the throne in the heuenes the 4 of June 1595...vij^{li} ijs'.[75] It was the last time he would spend money on the Rose. After this the theatre gradually fell into decay. In 1603, after he and Alleyn had together built the Fortune, Henslowe was no longer willing to renew his lease on the 'littell Roosse', and he expressed his opinion forcibly in a memo in the *Diary*.

Memorandom that the 25 of June 1603 I talked wth m^{r} Pope
at the scryveners shope wher he lisse consernynge the [lea]
tackynge of the leace a new of the littell Roosse & he showed
me a wrytynge betwext the pareshe & hime seallfe wch was
to paye twenty pound a yeare Rent & to bestowe a
hundred marcks vpon billdinge wch I sayd I would Rather
pulledowne the playehowse then I wold do so & (b) he beade
me do & sayd he gaue me leaue & wold beare me owt for
yt wass [h] in hime to do yt [76]

The demise of the Rose seems, however, to have been less dramatic, and Henslowe did not carry out his threat to pull down his playhouse, heavens and all.

The Rose faded gently. Henslowe's last records of its use as a theatre are for the Earl of Worcester's Men in 1602 and 1603. In August 1602 he lent 40s to the company 'to paye vnto thomas deckers for new A dicyons in owldcastelle',[77] and subsequently there was a play-reading, or some kind of convivial business meeting to discuss matters concerning the company, held at the Mermaid, for which Henslowe footed the bill for their supper.

> Layd owt for the company at the mermayd
> when we weare at owre a grement the 21 $\rbrace$ ix^s
> of aguste 1602 [s]toward ou^r sups the some of $\quad$ 78

It was almost a last supper for the players of the Rose, for the following June Henslowe expressed no further interest in his old playhouse and declined to spend any more money on doing it up; and it was allowed slowly to succumb to its rotting timbers.

404

XII *The Bear Garden and the Fortune*

After Edward Alleyn's retirement he and Joan went to live in the country, at Brill or Broyle in the parish of Ringmere in Sussex, where they seem to have been living in the home of Arthur Langworth, who was an old friend of Philip Henslowe. He and Arthur had probably known each other since boyhood, for Philip's father, a man of Devonshire descent, had settled at Lindfield nearby and held the position of master of the game at Broyle Park. This had probably been for wild game, but it may have been his father's professional involvement with the animal world that had inspired Philip's interest in becoming Master of the Royal Game of Bears and Bulls which was engaging him at this time.

Whether Alleyn was planning to move permanently to the country or not, they had evidently been away for some time when Henslowe wrote to his 'sonne' and 'dawghter' on 4th June 1598 to give them news of the progress of their suit to obtain the Mastership of the Royal Game which was likely to fall vacant. This office was granted by the Queen for life, and the current holder, Ralph Bowes, was feared to be on the point of death. Henslowe reported: 'the causse whie I writte vnto you is this m^r Bowes liesse very sycke & every bodey thinckes he will not escape'.[1] Henslowe and Alleyn were particularly anxious to obtain the patent for this office, which conferred favours on the holder over and above the lucrative fees and gate money at baiting displays, because they had already invested heavily in the Bear Garden, which was located conveniently near to the Rose on Bankside. In 1594 they had together purchased the lease of Paris Garden, as the baiting ground was called, for £200; and subsequently they negotiated a licence held under Bowes naming them as his deputies with the right to mount baiting displays at the Garden for which they paid him £40 annually, in quarterly sums, plus a tithe of 6s. 8d. to St Saviour's parish. It was the royal patent itself for which Henslowe and Alleyn were now angling, but Henslowe was not optimistic regarding their chances. As Groom of the Chamber he had contacts at Court, and he was doing his best to pull the right strings, but with little hope of success.

'I feare I shall losse alle for doctor seasser hath done nothinge for me', he writes, Dr Julius Caesar being then Judge of the Court of Admiralty and Master of Requests to whom application for royal patents had to be officially made. He had also approached their patron, the Earl of

Nottingham, '& he promyssed me that he wold move the quene a bowte yt & the next daye he Rides frome the corte to winser so that ther is nothinge ther to be hade but good wordes wch trvbelles my mynd very mvche'. Then he had moved Lady Edmonds to speak with the Queen on their behalf, but before she could do so 'm^r darsey of the previ chamber crossed hir & made it knowne to her that the quene had geven yt all Readey in Reversyon to one m^r dorington a pensener'. He sought out Dorrington, who confirmed this to be true. However, while Bowes clung to life there was hope. Henslowe tells Alleyn that Arthur Langworth will be able to inform him of 'what paynes & travell I haue tacken in yt...for I haue had his heallpe in yt for so mvche as In hime lyesse for we haue moved other great parsonages for yt but as yeat I knowe not howe yt shall pleasse god we shall spead for I am sure my lord admerall will do nothinge & this I comitte you bothe to god leavinge the wholle descord to be vnfolded to you by m^r langworth'.[2] And so he signs off.

Alleyn seems to have wanted the office badly for when Arthur Langworth returned to Brill and unfolded the story, he got it in the neck from Alleyn who apparently upbraided him for failing to promote their suit more actively at Court, which hurt Arthur's feelings and caused a slight *contretemps* in the friendship.[3] The patent was a lucrative monopoly in itself, and would have increased the financial interest derived from the investment they already held in the Bear Garden. Bowes lingered on, but despite string-pulling at Court the office eventually went as promised to John Dorrington. He was later knighted by King James who was as keen on the gruesome sport of the Royal Game as was Queen Elizabeth.

On 26th September Henslowe wrote again to Alleyn, a rather pathetic letter, urging him to return to London to discuss the problems of the Bear Garden. This is his excuse for pleading Alleyn's return, but it is evident that Henslowe is sorely missing his 'sonne' and feels lost without him.

sonne Edward alleyn I haue Rd you^r letter the wch you sent
vnto me by the careyer wher in I vnderstand of both you^r good
healthes wch I praye to god to contenew and forther I vnder
stand you haue considered of the wordes wch you and I had
betwen vs consernynge the beargarden & acordinge to you^r
wordes you and I and all over frendes shall haue as mvch
as we cane do to bring yt vnto a good eand therfore I wold
willingeley that you weare at the bancate for then wth our
losse I shold be the meryer therfore yf you thincke as I thinck
yt weare fytte that we weare both her to do what we mowgh⟨t⟩

& not as two frends but as two Joyned in one therfor ned
I love not to mack many great glosses & protestaciones to you
as others do but as a poor frend you shall comande me
as I hoope I shall do you therfore I desyer Rather to haue you^r
company & you^r wiffes then you^r leatters for ower laste talke w^{ch}
we had abowte m^r pascalle assuer you I do not for geatte now to
leat you vnderstand newes I will teall you some but yt is
for me harde & heavey sence you weare wth me I haue loste one
of my company wch hurteth me greatley that is gabrell for
he is slayen in [f]hoges den fylldes by the hands of benge⟨men⟩
Jonson bricklayer therfore I wold fayne haue alittell of you^r
cownsell yf I cowld thus wth hartie comendations to you &
my dawghter & lyckwise to all the Reast of our frends I eande
from london the 26 of septemb₃ 1598

You^r assured frend

to my power

Phillippe Henlowe ⁴

Henslowe's letters are very revealing of the man; his combination of the simplicity and shrewdness of the peasant, and his reliance on the more sophisticated judgement of Alleyn are there. But he was also a man with a heart. His distress over the death of Gabriel Spencer, one of the actors in the Lord Admiral's, which he calls 'my company', who crossed swords with the hot-tempered Ben Jonson and had the worst of it, is obviously sincere. This had landed Ben in prison only to escape the gallows by reading his 'neck verse' in Latin to prove himself an educated fellow although a bricklayer, as Henslowe calls him. This would have been no derogatory term in Henslowe's eyes, for he always designated himself as a dyer. Trades conferred respectability. Ben Jonson was, in fact, already well known to both himself and Alleyn as an actor and playwright, for the previous autumn, together with Gabriel Spencer and Robert Shaw, both of them now members of the Lord Admiral's Men, Jonson had sojourned in the Marshalsea for a space as a result of the performance of the seditious play *The Isle of Dogs*, in which Jonson had collaborated with Tom Nashe. The latter had made good his escape to Yarmouth while the actors, including Jonson, languished in prison, and the Privy Council expressed their extreme displeasure by closing all the theatres.

Henslowe had good cause to be once again feeling upset and angry with Ben Jonson, and whenever he is anxious or miserable he reveals himself pathetically dependent on Edward Alleyn for his guidance and succour. Feeling depressed about the lack of progress over their suit for the Mastership of the Game he seeks Alleyn's 'cownsell' and longs for his presence, if not to celebrate success then to give consolation in failure. A touch of poignancy is added by his drawing on the back of his letter of a man's head in profile, (is this a self-portrait?) and written under it the words 'Lamentation is ever remoued w^t ioy', and he adds quaintly, 'Hinchlowe is my name & w^t my pen I writt ye same'.[5]

Henslowe and Alleyn were eventually to become joint Masters of the Royal Game of Bears, Bulls and Dogs, but the time was not yet. This ancient sport, in which fierce mastiff dogs, bred for their fighting qualities, were pitted against a staked bear or bull, was popular all over Europe. The oldest extant plan of the Bankside baiting establishment, dated 1574, shows two separate arenas for 'The Bowll Baytyng' and 'The Beare Baytyng', which were later replaced by one baiting house on the site of the former, the Rose being built a little to the south of the old Bear house. Three ponds are shown lying between the two baiting houses. Their use is explained in an account of a visitor to the Dresden Bear Garden of the Elector of Saxony, published in 1685.

'In the hunting-house, in the old town, are fifteen bears, very well provided for, and looked unto. They have fountains and ponds, to wash themselves in, wherein they much delight: and near to the pond are high ragged posts or trees, set up for the bears to climb up, and scaffolds made at the top, to sun and dry themselves; where they will also sleep, and come and go as the keeper calls them.'[6]

It sounds an idyllic existence for the beasts. The truth was bestial cruelty. This crude entertainment was avidly sought by Londoners as well as by foreign visitors with well-lined purses, and drew crowds of pleasure seekers to Bankside where the theatre stood nearby. The site of Paris Garden itself was further to the west along Bankside near the Paris Garden Stairs giving access to the river, and presumably that is where the old bear baiting ground had been located. But it seems the Bear Garden had been moved, some time before 1540, to its present site near the Rose in the Liberty of the Clink – conveniently near for Henslowe and Alleyn – the name of Paris Garden adhering to the Royal Game itself, as well as applying to the Liberty of Paris Garden, the ancient traditional location of the bear garden.

Luckily Dorrington proved amenable to continuing the arrangement by which Henslowe and Alleyn acted as his deputies, and he renewed their licence on the same terms as before with Bowes.[7]

Verso of Henslowe's letter with the head of a man smiling. It depicts a sort of 'laughing cavalier' which may be a self-portrait sketch to show how happy he would be to have his 'sonne' back home with him at the Bankside. He has inscribed his drawing:

'Lamentation is euer remoued wth ioy'.

'Hinchlowe is my name & w^t my pen I writt y^e same'.

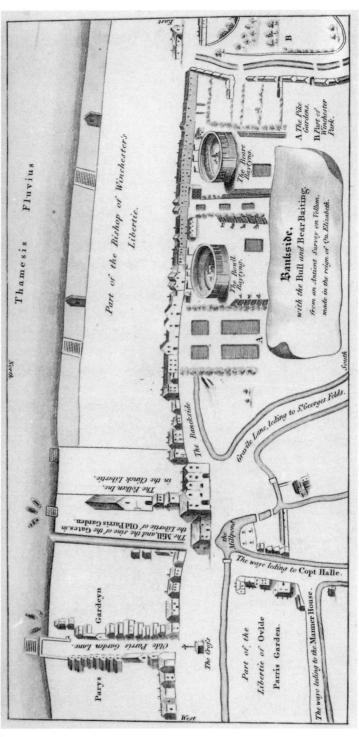

Map of the Bear Garden, Bankside, 1592.

410

The financial side in this partnership appears to have been handled by Henslowe, as in their theatrical association. Henslowe always seems to have preferred to take a subservient part in all their joint ventures, leaving the limelight to his 'sonne' Edward, who became known as the Master of the Bears. It seems that Alleyn from the first took the active part in the baiting displays, while the care of the beasts was in the charge of a keeper, Jacob Meade, a waterman, who probably plied his oars between feeding and tending the bears, bulls, horses, mastiff dogs and bitches, and apes, which formed this menagerie. Ned Alleyn was a big built man, and he was evidently good at handling animals; moreover, a considerable amount of showmanship was involved in presenting the baiting displays, at which he would have excelled, bringing his theatrical expertise to bear. Like most Elizabethans he must have had a strong stomach for it was a bloody and horrid spectacle.

The bears were valuable animals to be spared for fighting another day whenever possible, but a bull would often be advertised as destined to be baited to death at the stake by the fierce mastiff dogs set on it, the meat being afterwards sold for the butcher's trade. Betting, challenges and wagers were part of the excitement. Apes featured as comedy side-shows, as, for instance an ape riding a horse (being tied on) pursued by dogs. The famous blind bear, Harry Hunks, would provide another 'comic' interlude as he was whipped until the blood ran. The baiting of these fighting beasts was a 'royal' sport and a favourite Elizabethan and Jacobean pastime with the populace in general, from the Queen downwards, who relished this sickening bloody spectacle and did not consider it cruel; or if they did, then they openly enjoyed the cruelty. It was not a squeamish age.

Edward Alleyn and Joan were soon persuaded to return to London to resume residence near the Henslowes at their house on Bankside. We are not sure where this stood, but it must have been in the Liberty of the Clink, and it would have been a well-appointed, comfortable home for considerable improvements had been made to the house after their marriage preparatory to their moving in, including making a wainscoted hall.[8] Shortly after Alleyn's return plans were under way for a new theatrical partnership between him and Henslowe, not at the Rose, but to build a new and splendid theatre, which they would call the Fortune.

The decision to build the Fortune was prompted by two factors. In the winter of 1598 the Burbages arrived on Bankside. The lease for the site of their theatre in Shoreditch had run out. It was called simply the Theatre for it had been the first and only one in its day. James Burbage, who had

411

built the Theatre in 1577 in partnership with his brother-in-law John Brayne, quarrelled violently with Brayne's widow after his partner's death in 1593, and with her legatee, one Robert Miles, over their share of the profits from the playhouse; and he quarrelled with the ground landlord, Giles Allen (no relation of Edward Alleyn) over the renewal of the lease which expired in April 1597. In the midst of all this bickering the elder Burbage died, leaving his son and heir Cuthbert Burbage to continue the fight, and he decided not to renew the lease but instead dismantled the Theatre, lock, stock and barrel, and transported its timbers across the river to the Bankside. Here he had acquired a new site for his theatre on a thirty-one year lease, not far from the Rose, and proceeded to re-erect the old timbers anew, thus saving great expense in materials, to form a fine new theatre, which they called the Globe. Henslowe's main theatrical rival had therefore arrived on his doorstep. At the same time, the Rose was evidently beginning to look the worse for wear, and he was faced with the prospect of spending a further sum of money on it, while the lease of the site of the Little Rose where it stood was also due to expire in a few years' time.

These were doubtless some of the problems on which Henslowe urgently wanted Alleyn's 'cownsell'. After due discussion and deliberation they came up with a winner. Their reply to the Burbages was not to refurbish the Rose smartly in competition with the Globe, but to cross over to the North side of the river, now depleted of its main theatre, and seek a new site in which to invest their money with a brand new theatre. In suing for the requisite warrant from the Privy Council to build their new theatre, they were able to claim that the Rose had now fallen into 'dangerous decaye', and they described their former site on 'the Banck' as 'verie noysome for resorte of people in the wynter tyme'. Leaving all this noisomeness to the Burbages, they soon found just what they were looking for at Golding Lane (or Golden Lane) in St Giles without Cripplegate, where was a goodly piece of waste ground very suitable for their purpose. On it had once stood a royal nursery for the children of King Henry VIII 'whither they were sent out of town for the benefit of the air'.[9] It was a site shrewdly chosen, 'verie fitt and conuenient', being easily accessible from the Court as well as the Inns of Court, where the law students dearly loved to go to a play in the afternoon, and not too far from the residential district of the nobility on the North bank of the river. It was a neat turning of the table on their rivals, and it proved an advantageous and profitable move. After protracted negotiations over the lease, and the obtaining of a warrant from the Privy Council to build, in the teeth of opposition from

Puritan elements and local gentry who feared the disturbances associated with theatre audiences, with petitions and counter-petitions for or against the erection of a new playhouse in the vicinity, the permit was finally won on the promise of generous, regular contributions from the box office takings for the relief of the poor of the parish. Edward Alleyn built almshouses in the parish, thus modestly beginning his charitable acts.

Alleyn had received support for his project from the start from his patron, the Earl of Nottingham, Lord High Admiral, as well as from Queen Elizabeth who, like her royal father, loved the dramatic art. This is expressed in the two warrants licensing the erection of the Fortune theatre. The first is over the signature of 'Notingham' alone, dated 'att the Courte at Richmond the xij[th] of Januarye. 1599'.

Whereas my Seruant Edward Allen. in respect of the dangerous decaye of that Howse w[ch] he and his Companye haue nowe, on the Banck, And for that the same standeth verie noysome for resorte of people in the wynter tyme) Hath thearfore nowe of late, taken a plott of grounde neere Redcrossestreete london. verie fitt and convenient) for the buildinge, of a new Howse theare, and hath prouided Tymber and other necessaries for theffectinge theareof. to his greate chardge: fforasmuche as the place. standeth very convenient, for the ease of. People, And that her Ma[tie]. (in respect. of the acceptable Seruice, w[ch] my saide Seruant and his Companie. haue doen and presented before her Highenes to her greate lykeing and Contentm[t]; aswell this last Christmas as att sondrie other tymes) ys gratiouslie moued toward them. wth a speciall regarde of fauor in their proceedings:[10]

The second warrant, dated three months later, 8th April 1600, certifies the establishment of the new theatre on 'a plott of grounde, scituat in auerie remote and exempt place neere Goulding lane' after the complainants against its erection had been mollified, and is more forcefully issued over the signatures of my lords Nottingham, Hunsdon and Cecil, addressed:

'To y[e] Justices of Peace of y[e] Countye of Midds especially of S[t] Gyles. w[th]out Creplegate. And to all others. whome it shall Concerne.
    Whereas. her Ma[tie]. (haveinge been well pleased heeretofore. at tymes of recreaċon, w[th] the services of Edward Allen and his Companie. Servants to me the Earle of Nottingham. whereof, of late he hath made discontynuance:) Hath sondrye tymes signified her pleasuer, that he should revive the same agayne:' [11]

The warrant then goes on to elaborate 'the conueniencie' of the site of the new theatre and signifies that the Queen has given order 'to requier yo^u. to Tollerate the proceedinge of the saide New howse neere Goulding lane. And...To permitt and suffer the said Edward Allen to proceede in theffectinge and finishinge of the same Newehowse, wthout anie yor lett or interrupcõn, towarde him, or anye of his woorkmen'. This sealed the matter and the building of the Fortune went ahead. These warrants testify the high regard in which Alleyn was held by the Queen, certainly as an actor and probably also as a man. In deference to her Majesty's expressed wish, and in gratitude for her support, upon the completion of his new theatre Edward Alleyn did return to the stage to play on his own boards. Probably his intention to retire had been serious, for he sold his stock in the Admiral's Men while retaining a specially privileged share without liabilities in 1597, but in the warrants he is still named 'my Seruant Edward Allen' and 'Servante to me the Earle of Nottingham' and is recognised as the leader of 'his Companie' so the links had only been partially severed. He was as yet only thirty-three years old when his new theatre was being built.

Henslowe and Alleyn must have keenly noted the construction of the Globe, for the contract for building the Fortune was given to Peter Streete, Citizen and Carpenter of London, who had been responsible for building the Globe for the Burbages, with the proviso that the 'new howse and stadge for a Plaiehowse' was to be exactly like the design and arrangement of 'the late erected plaie-house on the Banck in the saide parishe of Ste Sauiour called the Globe'. The only difference was in size, for the dimensions given to Peter Streete exceeded those of any theatre heretofore. When finished the new theatre gave accommodation for three thousand people, Henslowe and Alleyn having no intention of turning anyone away for lack of room. This spaciousness doubtless added to the comfort of the new playhouse, which was to be set square 80 feet each way without, and 55 feet each way within, and three storeys high with each floor graded in ascending order, twelve feet, eleven feet and nine feet high, with twelve feet six inches of floor depth to the galleries with the two upper floors jutting out an extra ten inches. The roof was open (despite the vagaries of English weather this was doubtless an advantage for health reasons and safety), but the tiring-house at the back of the stage was roofed, and there was 'a shadowe or cover' over the stage for protection of the valuable playing apparel and properties from the elements, rather than for the actors one imagines. The stage was large – forty-three feet 'in length' (this must refer to what we would call its width) and extending to the middle

414

of the yard, which is where the groundlings would stand, 'And the saide Stadge to be in all other proporcōn Contryved and fashioned like vnto the Stadge of the saide Plaiehowse Called the Globe'. In the two upper floors there were four 'convenient divisions' for gentlemen's rooms, as also for two-penny rooms – the Elizabethan equivalent of modern theatre boxes; 'necessarie Seates' were provided in the rooms and throughout the galleries.

The contract to Streete contains the repeated injunction that he was to copy *exactly* what he had built in the Globe, in every detail, with the exception *only* of the shape of the 'maine postes' supporting the stage and frame of the playhouse, which had presumably been fashioned like pillars, that is round, but which Alleyn wanted to have square because he wanted carved satyrs (his favourite ornamentation) on the faces and on top of the square pillars. 'And the saide howse and other thinges beforemencoed to be made & doen To be in all other Contrivitions Conveyances fashions thinge and thinges effected finished and doen accordinge to the manner and fashion of the saide howse Called the Globe Saveinge only that all the princypall and maine postes of the said fframe and Stadge forwarde shalbe square and wroughte palasterwise wth carved proporcōns Called Satiers to be placed & sett on the Toppe of every of the same postes'.[12]

This instruction comes right at the end of the details listed in the contract, and obviously refers to a minor difference, that is, in the design of the posts or pillars. It has no bearing on the shape of the building, which is given at the start clearly and definitely as being square. Since the Fortune was to follow exactly the construction of the Globe, this means that the original Globe was also a square building and not a round playhouse as has always been asserted. When the Globe was burnt down in 1613 it was then rebuilt as a circular theatre, as also was the Fortune when it likewise rose from the ashes of its fire in 1622, round theatres again evidently having become the fashion. But nowhere in the entire contract is there anything that can be construed as indicating that this first Globe was a round theatre, whereas the Fortune was to be a square building. The only major difference between the two theatres is in size, not in shape, and this is again stated clearly: 'And shall alsoe make all the saide fframe in every poynte for Scantlings lardger and bigger in assize Then the Scantlinges of the Timber of the saide newe erected howse, Called the Globe'.

Since the belief that the Globe was always a round theatre from the first has been so constantly repeated and maintained as a fact, I append the complete contract with Peter Streete for those who doubt that it must have been square, like the Fortune, which was in all essentials as in most details an exact copy. Probably it is the power of Shakespeare's words that has mesmerized us, his invocation to 'this wooden O' combined with the name the Globe, inducing our minds to believe that the playhouse must always have been round. Not so. The famous prologue probably refers to a performance that took place in another theatre, not the first Globe. On the other hand, according to Norden's map or scenic depiction of London's Thames in 1593, the Rose *was* a circular building. Burbage's square Globe seems to have set a new fashion which was copied in the Fortune, and thereafter there was a *reversion* to circular theatrical construction when both these playhouses rose transformed from their burnt ashes. The Swan, like the old Rose, had always been a round theatre. Dewitt's sketch showing the round interior of the Swan has probably also contributed to our mental image of theatrical circularity. Visscher's map of 1616 shows only round theatres for by that time the Globe and the Hope had both been built in the round.

THIS INDENTURE made the Eighte daie of Januarye 1599 And in the Twoe and ffortyth yeare of the Reigne of our sovereigne Ladie Elizabeth by the grace of God Queene of England. ffraunce and Irelande defender of the ffaythe &ce Betwene Phillip Henslowe and Edward Allen of the pishe of Ste Savio^rs in Southwark in the Countie of Surrey gentlemen on thone pte And Peeter Streete Cittizen and Carpenter of London on thother parte witnesseth That whereas the saide Phillipp Henslowe & Edward Allen the daie of the date hereof Haue bargayned Compounded & agreed wth the saide Peter Streete ffor the erectinge buildinge & settinge upp of a newe howse and Stadge, for a Plaiehowse in and vppon a certeine plott or pcell of grounde appoynted oute for that purpose Scytuate and beinge nere Goldinge lane in the pishe of Ste Giles w^thoute Cripplegate of London To be by him the saide Peeter Streete or sōme other sufficyent woorkmen of his provideinge and appoyntem^te and att his propper Costes & Chardges for the consideraōon hereafter in theis pn̄ts expressed Made erected, builded and sett upp In manner & forme followeinge (that is to saie)

416

The frame of the saide howse to be sett square and to conteine
ffowerscore foote of lawfull assize everye waie square w^{th}oute
and fiftie fiue foote of like assize square everye waie w^{th}in, w^{th}
a good
suer and stronge foundacōn of pyles brick lyme and sand, both
w^{th}oute & w^{th}in, to be wroughte one foote of assize att the leiste
aboue the grounde And the saide fframe to conteine Three
Stories in heighth The first or lower Storie to Conteine Twelue foote
of lawfull assize in heighth The second Storie Eleaven foote of
lawfull assize in heighth And the Third or vpper Storie to conteine
Nyne foote of lawfull assize in height
All which Stories shall conteine Twelue foote and a half of lawfull
assize in breadth througheoute besides a Juttey forwards in eyther
of the saide Two
vpper Stories of Tenne ynches of lawfull assize, wth ffower convenient
divisions for gentlemens roomes and other sufficient and
convenient divisions of Twoe pennie roomes wth necessarie Seates
to be
placed and sett Aswell in those roomes as througheoute all the rest
of the galleries of the saide howse and wth suche like steares
Conveyances & divisions w^{th}oute & w^{th}in as are made &
Contryved in and to
the late erected Plaiehowse On the Banck in the saide pishe of S^{te}
Savio^{rs} Called the Globe wth a Stadge and Tyreinge howse to be
made erected & settupp w^{th}in the saide fframe, wth a shadowe or
cover
over the saide Stadge, wch Stadge shalbe placed & sett As alsoe the
stearecases of the saide fframe in suche sorte as is p^{r}figured in
a Plott thereof drawen And wch Stadge shall conteine in length
ffortie and Three foote of lawfull assize and in breadth to extende
to the middle of the yard of the saide howse, The same Stadge
to be paled in belowe wth good stronge and sufficyent newe oken
bourdes And likewise the lower Storie of the saide fframe w^{th}inside,
and the same lower storie to be alsoe laide over and fenced w^{th}
stronge yron pykes And the saide Stadge to be in all other
proporcōns
Contryved and fashioned like vnto the Stadge of the saide Plaiehowse
Called the Globe, wth convenient windowes and lights glazed to
the saide Tyreinge howse And the saide fframe Stadge and
Stearecases to be covered wth Tyle, and to haue a sufficient gutter

of lead to Carrie & convey the water frome the Coveringe of the
said Stadge to fall backwardes And alsoe all the saide fframe and
the Stairecases thereof to be sufficyently enclosed wthoute wth lathe
lyme & haire and the gentlemens roomes and Twoe pennie roomes
to be seeled wth lathe lyme & haire and all the fflowers of the
saide Galleries Stories and Stadge to be bourded wth good & sufficyent
newe deale bourdes of the whole thicknes wheare neede shalbe
And the saide howse and other thinges beforemencōed to be
made & doen To be in all other Contrivitions Conveyances fashions
thinge and thinges effected finished and doen accordinge to the
manner and fashion of the saide howse Called the Globe Saveinge
only
that all the princypall and maine postes of the saide fframe and
Stadge forwarde shalbe square and wroughte palasterwise wth
carved proporcōons Called Satiers to be placed & sett on the Topp
of
every of the same postes And saveinge alsoe that the said Peeter
Streete shall not be chardged wth anie manner of pay⟨ntin⟩ge in
or aboute the saide fframe howse or Stadge or anie pte thereof
nor
Rendringe the walls wthin Nor seelinge anie more or other roomes
then the gentlemens roomes Two pennie roomes and Stadge before
remembred nowe theiruppon the saide
Peter Streete dothe covēnnt promise and graunte ffor himself his
executo^{rs} and admistrato^{rs} to and wth the saide Phillipp Henslowe
and Edward Allen and either of them and thexecuto^{rs} and
admistrato^{rs} of them and either of them by theis p̄nts In manner &
forme followeinge (that is to saie) That he the saide Peter Streete
his executo^{rs} or assignes shall & will att his or their owne
propper costs & Chardges well woorkmanlike & substancyallie
make erect, sett upp and fully finishe In and by all thinges
accordinge to the true meaninge of theis p̄nts wth good stronge
and substancyall newe Tymber and other necessarie stuff All the
saide fframe and other woorks whatsoever In and vppon the saide
plott or pcell of grounde (beinge not by anie aucthoretie
Restrayned, and haveinge ingres egres & regres to doe the same)
before the ffyue & Twentith daie of Julie next Comēinge after the
date hereof And shall alsoe at his or theire
like costes and Chardges Provide and finde All manner of woorkemen
Tymber Joysts Rafters boords dores bolts hinges brick Tyle lathe

lyme haire sande nailes leede Iron Glasse woorkmanshipp and other thinges whatsoever wch shalbe needefull Convenyent & necessarie for the saide fframe & woorks & eu^rie pte thereof And shall alsoe make all the saide fframe in every poynte for Scantlings lardger and bigger in assize Then the Scantlinges of the Timber of the saide newe erected howse, Called the Globe And alsoe that he the saide Peeter Streete shall furthwth aswell by himself As by suche other and soemanie woorkmen as shalbe Convenient & necessarie enter into and vppon the saide buildinges and woorkes And shall in reasonable manner proceede therein wthoute anie wilfull detracċon vntill the same shalbe fully effected and finished In consideraċon of all wch buildings and of all stuff & woorkmanshipp thereto belonginge The saide Phillipp Henslowe & Edward Allen and either of them ffor themselues theire and either of theire executo^{rs} & admiŝtrato^{rs} doe Joynctlie & seu^rallie Covennte & graunte to & wth the saide Peeter Streete his executo^{rs} & admiŝtrato^{rs} by theis pñts That they the saide Phillipp Henslowe & Edward Allen or one of them Or the executo^{rs} admiŝtrato^{rs} or assignes of them or one of them Shall & will well & truelie paie or Cawse to be paide vnto the saide Peeter Streete his executo^{rs} or assignes Att the place aforesaid appoynted for the erectinge of the saide fframe The full some of ffower hundred & ffortie Poundes of lawfull money of Englande in manner & forme followeinge (that is to saie) Att suche tyme And when as the Tymberwoork of the saide fframe shalbe rayzed & sett upp by the saide Peeter Streete his executo^rs or assignes, Or wthin Seaven daies then next followeinge Twoe hundred & Twentie poundes And att suche time and when as the saide fframe & woorks shalbe fullie effected & ffynished as is aforesaide Or wthin Seaven daies then next followeinge, thother Twoe hundred and Twentie poundes wthoute fraude or Coven Prouided allwaies and it is agreed betwene the saide parties That whatsoever sōme or sōmes of money the saide Phillipp Henslowe & Edward Allen or either of them or thexecuto^rs or assignes of them or either of them shall lend or deliver vnto the saide Peter Streete his executo^rs or assignes or anie other by his appoyntem^{te} or consent ffor or concerninge the saide Woorks or anie pte thereof or anie stuff thereto belonginge before the raizeinge & setting upp of the saide fframe, shalbe reputed accepted taken & accoumpted in pte of the firste paym^te aforesaid of the saide some of ffower hundred & ffortie poundes And all such some & somes of money as they or anie of them shall as aforesaid lend or deliver betwene the razeinge of the saide fframe & finishinge thereof and of all the rest of the saide woorks Shalbe reputed accepted taken & accoumpted in pte of the laste paym^te aforesaid of the same sõme of ffower hundred & ffortie poundes Anie thinge abouesaid to the contrary notw^thstandinge

In witnes whereof the pties abouesaid to theis p̄nts Indentures Interchaun-geably haue sett their handes and Seales

Yeoven the daie and year ffirste abouewritten

P   S

Sealed and deliu^red by the saide Peter Streete in the p^rsence of me william Harris Pub Scr And me frauncis Smyth appr to the said Scr

[endorsed]
Peater Streat ffor the Building of the ffortune [13]

On the reverse of this document are various payments, acquittances and memoranda of accounts relating to the building of the Fortune in the hand of Henslowe for the most part.

According to his contract Peter Streete agreed to complete the building by 25th July 1600, but it seems builders were ever unreliable even in Elizabethan times, and by June only the foundations of brick had been laid, after which Streete apparently departed for the country. When he returned Henslowe did his best to expedite the construction of their theatre with an unprecedented mollification aimed at building good industrial relations: he frequently had 'brackefaste' with and dined Peter Streete, always at his own expense, sometimes in the company of his bailiff, Gilbert East, not forgetting the workmen who were similarly treated to drinks: 'geuen to the worckmen to drincke' is a recurring item.[14]

Under this treatment the work proceeded without further hiatus, and the new playhouse was completed only one month overdue in August 1600. It cost four hundred and forty pounds, with another eighty pounds

420

for painting and other embellishments, one of these being a figure of 'Dame Fortune' standing at the entrance. The flagstaff cost twenty-five shillings. The exterior of the building was wood and plasterwork in traditional Tudor style, and it must have looked very handsome.

The Fortune opened in December 1600, probably with the performance of Dekker's appropriately titled *Fortune's Tennis*, which one cannot help but suspect had been specially commissioned by Alleyn for the inaugural production at his new theatre. We do not know what the initial financial arrangements were between Alleyn and Henslowe in this partnership. Alleyn had purchased the lease of the Golding Lane site, and was later to buy the freehold outright. Henslowe doubtless contributed to the cost of building the theatre in the joint contract with Streete, Alleyn and himself. But the history of the theatre as it emerges shows it to have been very much Alleyn's theatre, rather more than Henslowe's. In the first instance Alleyn had returned to the boards as leading actor and a main sharer in the company, and Henslowe records an initial payment to him of an eleventh share in the profits of the first week's playing between entries dated 11th November and 14th December 1600.

> 'pd vnto my sonne alleyn for the firste
> weckes playe the xj parte of xvij^{li} ix^s
> wch came to therti & ij shellings I saye pd [15]

I take it that this would represent his share as an actor merely, for after his considerable investment in the project it is inconceivable that this modest sum would be his full return on the profits of the theatre. In his *Memorandum Book* Alleyn has noted his expenditure on the Fortune, beginning with the purchase of the lease[16] from Patricke Brewe, a London goldsmith, for £240, and in 1610 he was able to acquire the freehold from Daniel Gill the elder, who lived in the Isle of Man, for a further £340.[17] The total cost of building the playhouse was £520, (£440 to Streete plus £80 for painting etc.) and as he lists all this as *his* expenditure, not halved on a fifty-fifty basis with Henslowe, it would appear that Henslowe's relationship in this partnership was that of financial manager rather than proprietor of the theatre.

> What The fortune Cost me
> .... novemb̄ 1599
> first for ye leas to brew..............................240^{li}
> then for ye building ye playhowe................520^{li}

for other pruat buildings of myn

owne .... 120^{li}

so in all itt hath Cost me

for ye Leasse .... 880^{li}

bought the Inheritance of the land

of the gills of ye Isle of man w^{ch}:

is ye fortune & all the Howses in

whight crosstrett & gowlding Lane

in June 1610 for the some

of .... 340^{li}

bought in John garretts Lease

in revertion from the gills

for 21 years for .... 100^{li}

so in all itt Cost me .... 1320^{li}

Blessed be ye Lord god

      Euerlasting [18]

This is of course a retrospective statement of accounts. Doubtless Henslowe had originally advanced moneys for which Alleyn subsequently reimbursed him, for the contract with Peter Streete names Henslowe together with Alleyn and in his *Diary* he refers to the Fortune as 'owr new howsse', and he certainly took a great personal interest in ensuring that Peter Streete completed his contract for building it. Yet it is strange that the above statement of accounts, even if retrospective, does not mention Henslowe, as does Alleyn's retrospective account for the Bear Garden in the same *Memorandum Book*.

What The Beargarden Cost
me for my owne part
in december 1594

            li

first to m^r: burnabye 200

Then for the patten 250

      Some is 450

I held itt 16 year &

Rd [3]60^{li} p annum wch is .... 960^{li}

Sowld itt to my father

Hinchloe in februarie

1610 for .... 580^{li} [19]

His profit was therefore £1,090 over these sixteen years, and the lump sum he gained in 1610 was doubtless ploughed back into the properties he was investing in for the establishment of his college at Dulwich by then. But there is no such profit and loss account cast for the Fortune, so we are still in the dark as to how the dramatic finance, to coin Greg's apt terminology, of the theatre operated. It would appear, however, that the Fortune actually belonged to Alleyn for among the Alleyn Papers is an unexecuted assignment by Philip Henslowe's widow, Agnes, who was his executrix, stating that by a lease dated 4th April 1601, Alleyn had granted a moiety of the Fortune playhouse to Henslowe for twentyfour years at a rent of £8. Since this was in the grant of Edward Alleyn it must have been his property, and although no documentary evidence exists to show how the initial building of the theatre was financed, Alleyn must have become the recognised owner, Greg states that the above lease 'must clearly have been operative'.[20]

Henslowe played his part as before as banker to the company at the Fortune, as is seen from his entries in the *Diary* for loans to the actors and dramatists for apparel and play-scripts for their stock dating between 1601 and March 1604,[21] when his management would appear to have ended. He was also occupied during 1602 and 1603 with managing the Rose where the Earl of Worcester's Men were performing until the 1603 visitation of the plague closed the playhouses until the spring in 1604.

Henslowe noted the end of an era and the beginning of a new reign which brought a pause in theatrical entertainment until the companies could receive their licences from the new monarch, when he wrote:

Ther Reastethe dew vnto me to this daye beinge the
v daye of maye 1603 when we leafte of playe now
at the kynges cominge all Recknynges abated the
some of A hundred fowerscore & sevntenepownds &
thirteneshellyngs & fowerpence I saye dew   197^{li} – 13^s – 4^d
the fyftye pownds wch Jonnes & shawe had at ther goinge
a way not Reconed (as I tacke yt) [22]

Jones and Shaw had evidently retired. Early in 1604 playing resumed when the plague had finally spent its fury, and then Henslowe casts up his final account for what appears to be his farewell to the Fortune as manager, which he records almost dramatically with a touch of wry humour.

	li	s	d
totalles from ther hands is –	194 –	10 –	06

Caste vp all the acowntes frome the begininge
of the world vntell this daye beinge the 14 daye
of marche 1604 by Thomas dowghton & edward
Jube for the company of the princes men & I
Phillipe henslow so th^r Reastethe dew vnto me
P henslow the some of xxiiij^{li} all Reconynges con
sernynge the company in stocke generall descarged
& my sealfe descarged to them of al deats [23]

The portent of this is, as I take it, that Henslowe is settling his accounts 'frome the begininge of the world' with the company, now servants to young Prince Henry, on the eve of Edward Alleyn's second and final retirement from acting. The next day, 15th March 1604, the City of London was to present its magnificent entertainment for the accession of King James in which the entire City became transformed into a stage, and Edward Alleyn played the leading part as *Genius of the City*, which I believe to have been his final performance as an actor. Thus it would seem that 'father' and 'sonne' were bowing out together and handing over the company to its main sharers, who were headed by Downton and Juby. Henslowe and Alleyn retained their financial interest, but were relinquishing managerial control. Together they had launched a highly successful theatrical enterprise in the Fortune, but it was time for Alleyn to turn his energies to his greatest project, and Henslowe, being ever one to acquiesce to his son's wishes, prepared to step down too, albeit somewhat reluctantly.

The site on which the Fortune was erected had been in the possession of one William Gill, described as a gardener,[24] from whom it passed to Daniel Gill, the elder, who lived in the Isle of Man, who left it in trust to his four daughters. It was leased to the goldsmith, Patrick Brewe, from whom Alleyn first bought the lease,[25] but later he entered into complicated legal procedures to acquire the freehold from Gill's trust, which were finally successfully concluded in 1610.[26] The Fortune evidently meant a great deal to Alleyn as the symbol of his acting career, for in all his dealings in disposing leases to the actors, and other tenants of the tenements on the site – several of which he had built himself as an investment – he always stipulated that the Fortune should never be used for any other purpose except as a theatre. This proviso was also written into his bequest of the Fortune to his College.

The early arrangements for sharers in the company at the Fortune are obscure, as no documentation has survived. But in 1608 a lease was drawn up granting the leading actor of the company, Thomas Downton, of the parish of St Giles without Cripplegate, one thirty-second part of the net profits of the house for 13 years for the payment of £27. 10s. in hand, and an annual rent of 10s.; Downton also covenanting to pay his share of the charges of the house, and binding himself to play at the Fortune, and at no other place within two miles radius of the City of London. This complicated agreement never seems to have been executed.[27] But in 1618 Alleyn entered into a very straightforward legal transaction with the players whereby he simply leased the Fortune to them for 31 years as sharers at a rent of £200 per annum, plus two rundlets of wine of good quality (priced at 10s. a rundlet), one of sack and one of claret, to be delivered annually at Christmas.[28] The actors of the Fortune company thereby virtually owned their theatre. They were: Edward Juby, William Birde (alias Borne), Frank Grace, Richard Gunnell (or Gumnell), Charles Massey, William Stratford, William Cartwright, Richard Price, William Parr, Richard Fowler. Thomas Downton's name appears as witness, he evidently having retired by then. This deal is typical of Alleyn's generosity and conviviality. There is little doubt that the delivery of the rundlets of wine would have been the occasion for hospitable celebrations at Alleyn's house in Dulwich with his old friends, the players of the Fortune.

❖ ❖ ❖

In 1621 at midnight on Sunday, 9th December disaster befell the Fortune, as it had the Globe in 1613. Fire broke out and burned the theatre to the ground. The event was laconically recorded by Alleyn in his *Diary*, only the pointing finger indicating the importance of what he wrote with stoicism and a heavy heart.

 m̄d this night att 12 of yᵉ clock yᵉ fortune was burnt.[29]

In a letter written on 15th December by John Chamberlain to Sir Dudley Carlton we learn rather more.

'On Sonday night here was a great fire at the Fortune in Golden-lane the fayrest playhouse in this towne. It was quite burnt downe in two howres & all their apparell & playbookes lost, wherby those poore Companions are quite undone.'[30]

Alas for the irreparable loss of those play books which probably included many invaluable manuscripts of Marlowe's plays among others.

It must have been a bitter blow to Alleyn. Whereas at the Globe fire broke out during a performance of *King Henry the Eighth* when all the company were present to assist in a swift salvage operation, and all their properties and playscripts had been saved, only the playhouse being destroyed. This was a very great piece of luck, or perhaps the First Folio might have been a lot slimmer – a national loss of inconceivable proportions.

The Fortune was speedily rebuilt, the lessees contributing towards the cost of rebuilding in return for new leases extended to fifty-one years. Alleyn also provided most generous terms for a reduction of their rents by half after his death, and other such kind concern for his tenants at Golding Lane.[31] This generosity benefited these leaseholders at the eventual expense of his College, to which he bequeathed the Fortune as a source of College revenues. It had been rebuilt at a cost of one thousand pounds, and rose from its ashes as a round house this time, built of bricks, but it was demolished under the Protectorate in 1659, only a year before the Restoration which surely would have saved it. Its site is commemorated in the name Fortune Street which connects Golden Lane with Whitecross Street in London E.C.1. just north-east of the Barbican, today's great theatrical and entertainment centre in the City.

The Fortune must have offered very effective competition to the Globe and the Swan on Bankside (the Rose being by then in decline) for despite the Globe having its monopoly of Shakespeare's plays starring Richard Burbage, the Thames watermen felt the pinch. Their spokesman, John Taylor, the Water-poet, presented their grievances in a petition to King James lamenting the serious loss to their business in ferrying audiences across the river to the Bankside, owing to the attraction of the theatres on the north side of London, and begging that no more playhouses be licensed to be built north of the Thames, for the theatrical district on the south bank had once given a livelihood to a great number of watermen who were now in want.

Even the Bear Garden suffered a decline in the early years of King James's reign, by which the watermen also lost business. But this was equally to the detriment of Alleyn and Henslowe, who had finally acquired the royal patent for the 'Office of Cheefe Mr Overseer and Ruler of our beares Bulls and mastiffe dogges' under England's new monarch, which had eluded them under Elizabeth. But it had cost them dear.

On the accession of King James the patent for the Mastership of the Royal Game was confirmed to Sir John Dorrington, as he now became, but he died shortly afterwards. The patent was then immediately acquired by Sir William Steward, one of King James's 'greedy Scots', who was not interested in it for himself but wanted to make a quick profit by selling his patent at the highest price he could get.[32] This he achieved by flatly refusing to renew Alleyn's and Henslowe's licence to act as his deputies at the Bear Garden. Thus prevented from gaining any benefit from their investment in Paris Garden, Henslowe and Alleyn offered to sell the Scotsman their lease and their bears and dogs, which he again refused to do. By these tactics he forced them to buy the coveted patent from him at an exorbitant price, demanding 'ffour hundreth and fiftye poundes of lawfull money of England in full satisfaccon payment and discharge for the absolute bargayne, sale and assignment of a certen Patent to me made and graunted by o^r soueraigne Lord the Kinges Matie that now is, of the Mastership of his Matie games of Beeres, Bulls and doggs, and the ffees proffitts and app^{r}tences whatso eu^r to the same place of office belonginge or apptayninge.'[33]

By this document, signed by Sir William Steward, Knight, on 28th November 1604, Henslowe and Alleyn gained the patent which was theirs to hold 'duringe the naturalle lives of the said Phillipe Henslowe and Edward Allen and the life of the longer liver of them', which granted them 'full power comission and authoritie' to seek and take up any mastiff dogs and bitches, bears and bulls for the royal sport wherever they could find them in the King's realm or his dominions 'beyond the Seas'.[34] To this end they were empowered to issue warrants to their deputies to take up animals for them and to licence travelling bear-wards.

But they soon found that what should have been a lucrative monopoly was not quite such an 'absolute bargayne' as Sir William Steward had claimed. There was a small remuneration from the royal coffers of 'Tenn pence sterlinge by the daie, and for there deputie for exercisinge of the saide Rowme vnder them the fee and wages of fower pence by the daie' munificently to be paid yearly 'out of the Treasure of our Chamber' says the patent, but this was totally inadequate, the real profitability lying in the gate-money taken. Under Queen Elizabeth they had enjoyed liberty to bait at any time, the most profitable being always Sunday afternoon after divine service. But King James's government imposed restraint on baiting on Sundays, which was a serious loss, for these profitable displays had alone compensated for 'the smalnes of the fee in the Late quenes tyme',[35] as Alleyn and Henslowe bitterly pointed out in the petition to the King which they now presented in some distress, beginning with a rehearsal of the method by which Steward had obtained a large sum of money from them for the patent – a matter under which they still smarted.

By ill luck there had also been a high death rate among their most valuable beasts, especially in recent displays before the King of Denmark, father of Queen Anne, when they had lost a popular bear called George Stone, and as well in the last baiting before His Majesty and the Court four more bears were killed to the value of £300, being beasts of such quality as were not likely to be had again in the kingdom. Furthermore, their annual charges for running the Bear Garden now amounted to more than £200, so that they found that whereas formerly they could readily have let their office for £100 a year, 'now none will tacke it gratis to beare the charge wch is you^r pore servants vndoinge vnles yor m^{tie} of you^r gratious clemensey haue consideration of vs.' Their tale of woe continues, complaining that unlicensed bear-wards roamed the country competing illegally, and when challenged by their official deputies had often turned to violence. 'Thes cawses do in forse vs most humblie to be come sewters to you^r ma^{tie}': they request a relaxation of the Sunday baiting restraint, an increase in their daily fee of 10d to them and 4d to the keeper at the Bear Garden by the addition of 2s 8d daily, this allowance 'beinge never as yet incresed sence the firste fowndation of the office.' And they request powers to apprehend vagrant persons 'of losse and Idell liffe' who were found baiting without licence.[36]

Whether the King gave ear to their petition is not known but in view of the popularity of the sport at the Court, and especially as the traditional entertainment offered to important visitors from abroad, it seems unlikely that James would have allowed the Royal Game to suffer eclipse, and it was clear that there was an urgent need to replenish their stock of beasts.

English bears were famous and had on occasion been shipped across to France for displays before the French King. The finest mastiff dogs were also bred in this country, notably in Lancashire and Cheshire. Alleyn and his keeper, Jacob Meade, also engaged in the successful breeding of animals for use and for sale. In this connection they were in contact with owners of dogs, bears and bulls up and down the country from whom they bought stock, or sold it, and claimed their quota for the royal sport. Several curious letters relating to these transactions are extant among the Dulwich Papers.

Philip Henslowe has been much criticised, and even held to ridicule as an illiterate man on account of his strange spelling quirks, but by the standards of his day he was not unusual in this 'failing', which would not have been viewed as such by his contemporaries who happily spelt just as they fancied. It was only the printers who were gradually bringing in a modicum of standardization in the spelling of the printed word in English. Even the clerical quill-pushers whose profession it was to write used some whimsical spelling variants, as is clear from the documents quoted. Punctuation is also very curious, often it is simply ignored. Marlowe hardly uses it! The Elizabethans possessed no dictionaries by which spelling was standardized, and the emphasis in education was laid on developing a fair hand, not on correct spelling. Considering the implements of the day it is surprising how beautifully many Elizabethans wrote – they put the vast majority of twentieth century highly educated people to shame, of whom I know not a few of the highest degrees whose handwriting is almost illegible, and even some whose spelling is not so hot. It seems hardly fair to judge old Henslowe as ill-educated on the basis of his private *Diary* in which he sometimes wrote untidily or carelessly, and spelt like a typical Elizabethan – erratically and whimsically. He prided himself on his literacy and numeracy, and his addiction to cumbersome Roman numerals and quaint spelling may be seen as the indulgent expression of his individuality. But what shall we say of the very extraordinary spelling in the letters of one Sir William Faunte who corresponded with Alleyn on the sale and purchase of beasts for the game? Faunte was obviously a country squire and traces of a strong local accent are discernible in his spelling, particularly of the vowel sounds. Alleyn would not have had as much difficulty in reading and understanding his letter as we have, although he might have permitted himself a smile. Here he is writing to Alleyn describing the bulls he has to offer for sale:

'I vndersstoode bey a man which came with too beares from the gardeyne that you haue a deseyre to beyh one of mey boles. I haue three westerne boles at this teyme but I haue had verey ell loock with them, for one of them hath lost his horne to the queyck, that I think that hee will neuer bee to feyght agayne, that is mey ould Star of the West, hee was a verey esey bol.' [37]

Another bull he has to offer has lost an eye, but he still considers him a formidable beast, for this bull –

'would do you more hurt then good, for I protest I think hee would ether throo vp your dodges in to the loftes or eles ding out theare braynes agenst the grates,'

But he has another bull which he recommends unreservedly –

'if you so did leyck him you shall haue him. Of mey faith, hee is a marvilous good boole and coning and well shapte and but fore eyre ould feine come leine and shuch a on as I think you haue had but few shuch:'[38]

Some translation would be welcome to clarify 'fore eyre ould feine come leine'. This Sir William Faunte of Foston seems to have been a good customer in return, for he bought bear cubs from Alleyn requesting him to send him 'a cople of hee beare cobes the same to be black ones and shuch as you think will macke greate beares'.

The Bear Garden sometimes housed more exotic animals. In March 1611 Henslowe and Alleyn received payment of £42. 10s. and 12d. a day for keeping two white bears and a young lion.[39] Despite their complaints to King James about the unprofitability of their office the takings of the Bear Garden compare very favourably with the Fortune in the account Henslowe cast at Christmas 1608.

Rd at the bergarden this yeare 1608 begining
at Chrystmas holedayes as foloweth

Rd one monday S^t steuenes daye .... iiij^l

Rd one tewesday St Johnes daye .... vj^{li}

Rd one wensday beinge Chilldermas daye .... iij^{li} xiijs

Rd at the fortewne this yeare 1608 begenynge at
Crystmas holedayes

Rd one S^t steuenes daye .... xxv^s

Rd one St Johnes daye .... xxxxv^s

Rd one Chelldermas daye .... xxxxiiij^s ix^d [40]

Presumably these figures represent his moiety still paid on his investment in the theatre. The takings of £13. 13s. as compared with £5. 14s. 11d. are no cause for complaint. Bears and dogs were not shareholders in the Bear Garden, and only needed feeding, whereas the actors took their share of the profits from the box office at the Fortune.

Alleyn's financial account of the profits he made on the Bear Garden noted in his little Memorandum Book also shows that he made over a thousand pounds on the business, and he continued as Master of the Royal Game until the end of his life, even after selling his licence to Jacob Meade, and presented baiting displays whenever required at the Court of King James, attending to these in person.

Alleyn became known as the Master of the Bears in an equally famous capacity as he had been known as a great actor, and the Mastership carried more kudos. It was an office for which the holder might even expect to gain a knighthood, and probably Alleyn hoped for as much, but it was never realized.

XIII   *The End of an Era*

THE FORTUNE was one of the three theatres included in the licensing of the three main theatrical companies at the beginning of King James's reign, following the abatement of the plague that had given its baleful greeting to his accession in 1603. The warrant, dated 9th April 1604, issued by the Privy Council, licences –

> the three Companies of Plaiers to the King Queene and Prince publicklie to Exercise ther Plaies in ther severall and vsuall howses for the Purpose and no other vz the Globe scituate in maiden lane on the Banckside in the Cowntie of Surrey, the fortun in Golding Lane, and the Curtaine in Hollywell in the Cowntie of midlesex.[1]

Burbage's company now took precedence, for the Lord Chamberlain's had become the King's Men playing at the Globe, while the Lord Admiral's or Nottingham's Men became the Prince's Men at the Fortune, and the Earl of Worcester's as the Queen's Men were the resident company at the Curtain. The warrant is addressed to the Lord Mayor of the City of London and Justices of the Peace of Middlesex and Surrey, and it makes clear that the lifting of restraint on playing is conditional:

> Except there shall happen weeklie to die of the Plague Aboue the Number of thirtie w^thin the Cittie of London and the Liberties thereof. Att wch time we thinke it fitt they shall Cease and forbeare any further Publicklie to Playe vntill the Sicknes be again decreaced to the saide Number.[2]

It is issued over the signature of Alleyn's patron, the Earl of Nottingham, and five other lords. Alleyn had probably expressed his intention to retire finally from the stage for his name does not appear with the Prince's Men although he performed in the celebrations for King James's accession under the newly-licensed company, but he doubtless always saw himself as the servant of his old patron, the Lord Admiral, whom he had served so long and who had been such a good friend to him.

When the plague closed the theatres, the company from the Fortune had gone on tour, but Alleyn did not accompany them during the summer of 1603. Instead he left the plague-ridden city for a country holiday. As during the previous plague of 1593, Joan Alleyn bravely stayed behind in London to attend to her husband's business affairs. Fortunately, she seems to have had good immunity to the disease. Maybe it was feared that Edward, having mainly escaped to the country on tour while the plague raged at its peak before, might succumb to the infection if he remained on the Bankside. At all events, the wise precaution was taken to pack him off to stay with his friends, the Chaloners, in Sussex where he indulged in his favourite sport, hawking, as we learn from the letter sent to him by Joan.

Mistress Joan Alleyn was a most loving and solicitous wife, who put her husband's welfare and wishes before everything. Although of a good middle class background of some affluence, for she brought Alleyn a not inconsiderable dowry, possibly including property in Sussex, it seems she had not been educated to read and write, for the acquittances she sometimes witnessed for Henslowe in the *Diary* are signed with her mark. Her letters appear to have been written by the scribe, who was probably employed at the theatre for copying play-scripts. Her letter dated 21st October 1603 is nonetheless loving and intimate.

Jhesus

My Intyre & wellbeloued sweete harte still it Joyes me & longe I
pray god may I Joye to heare of yor healthe & welfare as you of ours
Allmighty god be thancked my owne selfe yor selfe, & my mother &
whole house are in good healthe & about vs the sycknes dothe Cease
& likely more & more by gods healpe to Cease. All the Companyes
be Come hoame & well for ought we knowe, but that Browne of
the Boares head is dead & dyed very pore, he went not into the
Countrye at all, and all of yor owne Company ar well at theyr owne houses.

She mentions Robert Browne (now leading actor of the company at the Boar's Head) who may be the Browne who went on tour with the Admiral's Men during the long plague when his wife and all his children died. Perhaps poor Browne had never got over the loss of all his loved ones and couldn't forgive himself for having left them in the plague-ridden city without him, so that this time he resolved to remain to face whatever fate might bring him. And it was Death.

my father is at the Corte but wheare the Court ys I know not
I am of your owne mynde, that it is needles to meete my father
at Basynge the Incertayntye being as it ys & I Comend your
discretion it were a sore Journey to loase yor labour besyd expenses

& Change of Ayre mighte hurte you therfore you are Resolued vpon
the best Course. for yor Cominge hoame I am not to advyse you
neither will I, vse yor owne discreation yet I longe & am very
desyrous to see you & my poore & symple opinion is yf it shall please
you you maye safely Come hoame, heare is none now sycke neare vs,
[sic.] vs, yet let it not be as I wyll but at yor owne best lykinge, I am
glad to heare you take delight in hauckinge, & thoughe you haue
haue worne your appayrell [the best ys] to Rags the best ys you knowe
[sic.] wheare to haue better, & as wellcome to me shall you be wth
yor rags as yf you were in Cloathe of gold or velvet, trye
& see. I haue payd fyfty shillings for yor Rent for the warfe
the Lordes Rent. m^r woodward my Lords bayly was not in towne but poynted
his deputy who Receaued all the Rents I had witnesses wth me
at the payment of the money & haue his quittance but
the quyttance cost me a groat, they sayd it was the baylives
fee, you know best whether you were wont to paye it, yf not
they made a symple woman of me. you shall Receaue a letter
from the Joyner hym selfe & a prynted bill. & so wth my
humble & harty Comēndations to yor owne selfe m^r Chaloners
& his wyfe wth thanckes for yor kynde vsage, wth my good
mothers kyndest Comēndations wth the rest of yor houshold
⟨...⟩ece is well but Can not speake I ende prayenge allmighty god
s⟨ti⟩ll to blesse vs for his mercyes sacke & so swete harte
once more farwell till we meete wch I hope shall not
be longe. this xxith of octobe⟨r 1⟩603 [3]

There follows more before she finally signs off, but it is on very worn
and fragmented paper, in which the egregious forger, J.P. Collier, in
publishing his *Memoirs of Edward Alleyn* had pretended that there was
a reference to Shakespeare ('and said he was known vnto you, and M^r
Shakespeare of the globe' etc...adding a reference to the actor 'Richard
Johnes' to colour it with a semblance of authenticity), but there is not
a word about either Shakespeare or Jones in the original. Collier made
efforts to erase traces of his forgeries in other manuscripts and the paper
here is sadly damaged.

Joan Alleyn's letter is a gem. It shows us a gentle, modest nature,
unselfish and devoted, an intelligent and capable lady who was a model
wife. Her tender concern for her husband's wellbeing is very touching,
and she expresses grateful thanks to their good friends for extending him
such 'kind vsage'. The Elizabethans valued courtesy highly. At the
accession of King James, Henslowe had become a Sewer of the Chamber
to the King, hence his presence at the Court. Her mention of 'm^r woodward

my Lords bayly' is most likely a reference to a relative, for this was Joan's maiden name, and her father too was a bailiff.

The Chaloners and the Langworths were both substantial Sussex families who were intimate friends of the Henslowes and the Alleyns, with whom they also had some business relations concerning property. The main branch of the Chaloner family lived at Lindfield on the edge of Ashdown Forest, where the Henslowes had their iron mining interests. The Langworths lived at Brill or Broyle in the parish of Ringmere, where Philip Henslowe was born and grew up, his father being master of the game at Broyle Park, all of which comes into the Ashdown Forest area of this lovely part of Sussex. The two families were not only close geographically but were linked by marriage. John Langworth, son of Henslowe's friend, Arthur Langworth, had married Mary Chaloner, sister of Thomas and Francis Chaloner who were the younger generation of the Chaloners of Kennards at Lindfield. It is probable that Edward Alleyn's host was Thomas Chaloner, who was then living at Bexhill, as far as may be tentatively adduced from the fragmentary remains of the address.[4] There is a copy of Arthur Langworth's will dated 19th February 1605/6 among the Alleyn Papers at Dulwich.

The death toll of the plague had been even greater than in the long plague of 1592 to 1594, but this time it had been a shorter, sharper visitation, more drastic in its culling of the population taking 30,000 dead in barely twelve months. It was a dreadful beginning for the new reign, but as soon as the virulence of the pestilence had passed, the arrangements for the proper celebration of King James's accession were finalised with such a burst of enthusiasm and vigorous activity as to dispel the clouds of gloom and horror and give full rein to the public love of spectacle and drama. London was soon in holiday mood, and Thomas Dekker's detailed description of the truly fantastic pageantry with which the people at last welcomed their King makes almost incredible reading to our eyes. Dekker entitled his pamphlet:

The Whole Magnificent Enterteinment:
Given To King James, Queene Anne his wife, and Henry
Frederick the Prince; vpon the day of his Maiestie's
Tryumphant Passage (ffrom the Tower) through his Honorable
Citie (and Chamber) of London, the 15, of March. 1603.

Tho. Dekker [5]

(The date was, of course, our year 1604, the anniversary of the King's accession.) His title was no euphemism for magnificent it was. No monarch in history could have received a more lavish tribute of loving welcome from his people. All that the Elizabethans had learned in the long reign of Gloriana, who encouraged the love of pageantry and drama, was brought together in this one great splendid effusion of loyalty to the crown. Whether King James really appreciated it is perhaps conjectural, but his people's delight in the occasion is not in doubt. It was in this glittering event staged on 15th March 1603/4 that the last known appearance of Edward Alleyn as an actor is recorded. Together with his friends, the dramatists Thomas Dekker and Ben Jonson, and probably also that superb architect of courtly masques, Inigo Jones, Alleyn was the leading theatrical figure most prominently involved in this presentation devised for the celebration of the royal accession. It was, in all likelihood, his theatrical swan song.

Dekker's reference in his title to the City as the King's Chamber gives the clue to what was devised. The streets of his royal route were completely transformed by the erection of huge wooden structures arching over them to simulate a Royal Court of many mansions. There were seven pageants on seven arches, and seven master craftsmen were chosen to direct the labour of construction, and they did this so well that their names are printed as an accolade at the end of the pamphlet. They employed 80 joiners, 60 carpenters, 12 sawyers, besides specialist artisans including turners, plumbers (a fully operational fountain was one of the wonders of the display) smiths, moulders, carvers, painters and artificers, besides some 70 labourers. All this on the construction side. To this were added the actors, musicians, theatrical costumiers – who excelled themselves in brilliant invention. Detailed descriptions of the costumes are given by the two authors of the script, Dekker and Jonson,[6] who were making their bid for royal patronage in which Jonson reaped a rich reward as the favourite creator of King James's court masques. The feverish activity culminated in bringing all to readiness on the 15th March, and happily the sun shone and it did not rain, and Dekker does not even mention whether it was cold. The Elizabethans were hardy. Several of the costumes were of extremely delicate, diaphonous materials and exposed bare arms and legs. Dekker tells us that the City had become 'a world of people. The Streetes seemde to bee paued with men; Stalles...were set out with children, open Casements fild vp with women. All Glasse-windowes taken downe, but in their places, sparkeled so many eies, that had it not bene daye, the light which reflected from them, was sufficient to haue made one.' Rails had been erected to keep back the throng, and 'a goodly ciuil order was obserued.' And at last the people 'haue their longing. And behold, A farre off they spie him, richly mounted on a white Iennet, vnder a rich Canopy, sustained by eight Barrons of the *Cinqueports*; the Tower seruing that morning but for his with-drawing Chamber, wherein he made him readie, from thence stept presently into his *Citie of London*, which (for the time) might worthily borrow the name of his *Court Royall*: His passage alongst that Court (offering it selfe for more State) through seauen Gates; of which the first was ereckted at *Fenchurch*.'[7]

Here was a great structure spanning the street with an arch '12 foote wide, and 18 foote hie' depicting 'true modells of all the notable Houses, Turrets' of the City, with many allegorical figures. At the highest level was a Personage representing 'The *Brittayne Monarchy*' and beneath her stood 'The *Genius of the Citie*, A man.' At his right hand was '*The Counsell of the Citie*', and at the next level lay a boy who represented '*Thamesis* the *Riuer*'. *Genius* had six daughters placed on either side of him 'on a spreading *Ascent*', personating *Gladness, Veneration, Promptitude, Vigilance, Loving Affection*, and *Vnanimity*: 'of all which personages *Genius* and *Thamesis* were the onely Speakers: *Thamesis* being represented by one of the Children of her Maiesties Reuels: *Genius* by M. *Allin* (seruant to the young Prince) his gratulation speech (which was deliuered with excellent Action and a well tun'de audible voyce) being to this effect.'[8]

Dekker then paraphrases Alleyn's speech because he did not write this. The two great orations spoken by *Genius* at the beginning and end of the spectacle were the work of Ben Jonson who shared the main honour with Dekker of writing the script for this fantastic royal show, several of the speeches being in Latin of which Jonson was an acknowledged master. And, as we shall discover to our surprise, Edward Alleyn also made his contribution to the script as the writer of one of the speeches relating to a subject of which he was an acknowledged expert – gardening, which he loved passionately – so that he emerges not only in his capacity as the chief actor, but as a dominant figure in the devising and creation and presentation of this royal pageant.

Jonson's describes Alleyn thus: '*Genius Vrbis*. A person attir'd rich, reuerend, and antique: his haire long and white, crowned with a wreathe of Plane tree, which is saide to be *Arbor genialis*; his mantle purple, and buskins of that colour: Hee held in one hand a Goblet, in the other a braunch full of little twigges, to signifie Increase and Indulgence.'[9]

Thus attired, the great actor's opening speech as '*The Genius*' greeted the King in the name of the Lord Mayor, Aldermen, Council, Commons and the Multitude, who tendered the heartiest welcome to his Majesty 'that euer was bestowed on any King &c.' Following *Genius's* gracious greetings, the boy's clear silvery voice spoke as the 'River Thames', – probably well rehearsed under Alleyn's direction.

The Waites and Hautboys of London were in attendance here, and the 'Banquet' of speeches 'being taken away with sound of Musicke,..his Maiestie made his entrance into this his *Court Royall*: vnder this first Gate, vpon the Battlements of the worke, in great Capitalls was inscribed, thus:

'LONDINIVM
And vnder that, in a smaller (but not different)
Caracter, was written,
CAMERA REGIA
The Kings Chamber"[10]

The next two displays encountered were presented by the Strangers of the City, the first being *The Italian Pageant*, which was an elaborate affair figuring Peace as the central female form, accompanied by 'Sea personages', including a Triton with a 'Trumpet at his mouth' appearing to utter the Latin tag 'Dum Calum stellas'.* The speech was also spoken in Latin by an anonymous orator, presumably an Italian. Jonson and Dekker each published only their own speeches in full, giving English translations alongside the Latin orations.

Next came *The Pageant of the Dutch-men* at the Royal Exchange, which Dekker describes as 'a royall and magnificent labour'. The large gate was adorned with Latin characters painted in gold on an azure ground, and was hung with long silken curtains which were drawn aside at the approach of the King by '17 yong Damsels (all of them sumptously adorned, after their countrey fashion)' who represented the '*17 Prouinces of Belgia*'. The central tableaux depicted the King in his 'Imperial Robes' with crown, sceptre and sword in his hands, elaborately attended by many mute symbolic personages. Groups of skilful artisans of the Low Countries were arranged plying their crafts, the men weaving, the women spinning and the children at their hand-looms, dressed in national costumes. 'The speaking instrument, was a Boy attyred all in white silke, a wreath of Lawrell about his Temples', who delivered a long Latin oration.[11]

Next encountered was *The Deuice at Soper-lane end*, which featured the wondrous 'artificiall Lauer or Fount', the theme being the five senses,

---

* "Calum" is presumably "Caelum": "Filling the sky with stars" – an incomplete quote.

438

Hearing, Sight, Feeling, Smelling and Taste as allegorical personages attended by the three 'Bright Hayrde Graces'.[12] The speech was spoken by a boy (one of the choristers of St Paul's) personating *Fame*, and was followed by a song 'to loude and excellent Musicke: composed of Violins and another rare Artificiall Instrument, wherein besides sundry seuerall sounds effus'd (all at one time)' in imitation of 'the chirping of Birdes' and which was 'by two Boyes (Choristers of Paules) deliuered in sweete and rauishing voyces'. Dekker rapturizes: 'Let vs follow King *Iames*, who hauing passed vnder this our thirde Gate, is by this time, graciously receiuing a gratulatorie Oration from the mouth of *Sir Henrie Mountague*, *Recorder* of the Cittie.'[13]

At the Conduit the next pageant presents something of a tour de force. It is a Garden made of Arbors on which flowers and fruit grow in profusion, all 'artificiall' but superbly created to resemble nature, and it is wreathed in 'the breath of musicall Instruments' and enlivened with a touch of dramatic dialogue. Dekker describes this interlude with enthusiasm and in great detail. It bears all the hallmarks of having been devised at Alleyn's inspiration, reflecting his personal taste and fancy.

Before the King reaches this Garden he is waylaid by an actor personating *Syluanus*, all 'drest vp in greene Iuie, a Cornet in his hand, being attended on by foure other *Syluans* in Iuie likewise, their Bowes and Quiuers hanging on their shoulders, and winde Instruments in their handes. Vpon sight of his Maiestie, they make a stand: *Syluanus* breaking foorth into this abrupt passion of ioy.

Syluanus
Stay *Syluanus*, and let the loudest voyce of Musicke proclayme it (euen as high as Heauen) that hee is come."[14]

'Alter Apollo redit, Nouus En, iam regnat Apollo',* he shouts. 'Which acclamation of his was borne vp into the ayre, and there mingled with the breath of their musicall instrumentes.' As the music dies away, *Syluanus* proceeds with his speech: 'Most happie Prince, pardon me, that being meane in habite, and wilde in apparence, (for my richest lyuorie is but Leaues, and my stateliest dwelling but in the woodes) thus rudely...I presume to intercept your royall passage. These are my walkes: yet stand I heere, not to cut off your way, but to giue it a full and bounteous welcome, beeing a Messenger sent from the Lady *Eirene* my

---

* "The one Apollo departs, and lo! a new Apollo is now reigning".

Mistresse....Many Kingdomes hath the Lady sought out to abide in, but from them all, hath she been most churlishly banished.....At last heere she ariued, *Destenie* subscribing to this Warrant, that none but this Land should be her Inheritance...Those that dwell far off, pine away with vexing to see her prosper....whilst all those that heere sleepe vnder the warmth of her winges, adore her by the sacred and Cœlestiall name of *Peace*: for number being (as her blessings are) infinite.'[15]

Syluanus then invites the King to 'deigne to walke into yonder Garden: the *Hesperides* liue not there, but the *Muses*', and the Lady *Eirene* (*Peace*) with her daughter, *Euporia* (*Plenty*) await his Majesty. As the King approached there sounded a 'florish from all their Cornets, that his Maiestie was at hand: whose Princely eye whilest it was delighting it selfe with the quaint obiect before it, a sweete pleasure likewise courted his eare in the shape of Musicke, sent from the voyces of nine Boyes (all of them Queristers of Pauls) who in that place presenting the nine Muses, sang the Dittie following to their Violls and other Instruments.' The fourth and last verses are:

> O this is Hee!
> Whose new beames make our Spring,
> Men glad and birdes to Sing
> Hymns of praise, ioy and glee.
> *Chorus:* Sing, Sing, O this is hee!
> And make heauen ring,
> His welcome showted loudlie,
> For Heauen it selfe lookes proudly,
> That earth has such a King.
> *Chorus:* Earth has not such a King.[16]

Dekker interposes: 'But, least leaping too bluntly into the midst of our Garden at first, we deface the beautie of it, let vs send you round about it, & suruey the Walles, Allies, and quarters of it as they lie in order.' The Garden has two gates 'arched and grated Arbor-wise' with 'Cowcumbers, Pompions, Grapes, and all other fruits growing in the Land, hanging artificiallie in clusters: Betweene the two gates, a payre of stayres were mounted with some 20 assents:' at the bottom of which '(on two pillars) were fixed two Satires carved in wood.'[17] These typically representing Alleyn's favourite decoration used prominently in his Fortune theatre. And – wait for it! 'The vpper part also carried the proportion, of an Arbor, being closde with their round tops, the midst whereof was exalted aboue the other two, *Fortune* standing on the top of it. The garnishments for the whole

Bower, being Apples, Peares, Cheries, Grapes, Roses, Lillies, and all other both fruits and flowers most artificially molded to the life. The whole frame of this Somer banqueting house, stood (at the ground line) vpon 4 feete, the *Perpendicular* stretching itselfe to 45 feete. Wee might (that day) haue called it the *Musicke roome*, by reason of the chaunge of tunes, that danced round about it; for in one place were heard a noyse of cornets, in a second, a consort, the third, (which sate in sight) a set of Viols, to which the Muses sang. The principall persons aduancde in this Bower were, *Eirene (Peace)* and *Euporia (Plenty)* who sate together.'[18]

In addition to the Nine Muses there were the seven Liberal Arts, each holding a shield identifying them as Grammar, Logic, Rhetoric, Music, Arithmetic, Geometry, and Astrology. Dekker describes all their costumes in detail.

> *Peace*: Was richly attired, her vpper garment of carnation, hanging loose, a Robe of White vnder it, powdered with Starres, and girt to her: her haire of a bright colour, long, and hanging at her back, but interwouen with white ribbands, and Iewels: her browes were encompasst with a wreath compounded of the Oliue, the Lawrell, & the Date tree: In one hand shee held a *Caducens*, (or *Mercuries* rod, the god of eloquence:) In the other, ripe eares of corne gilded: on her lap sate a Doue: All these being ensignes, and furnitures of *Peace*.

> *Plenty*: Her daughter sate on the left hand in changable colours, a rich mantle of Gold trauersing her bodie: her haire large and loosely spreading ouer her shoulders: on her head a crowne of Poppy & Mustard seede; the antique badges of *Fertilitie & Abundance*, In her right hand a *Cornucopia*, filde with flowers, fruits, & c."[19]

Just below them sat figures representing *Chrusos* (Gold) and *Argurion* (Silver) and *Pomona* (goddess of garden fruits) 'attirde in greene, a wreath of fruitage circling her temples, her armes naked: her haire beautifull, and long.' With her was *Ceres* 'crowned with ripe eares of Wheate'. This was not all.

In the Garden the King encountered the 'maister Gardener', husband to *Pomona*, dressed in a homely suit 'meete and fit for a Gardener: In steade of a Hat, his browes were bound about with flowers, out of whose thick heapes, heere and there peeped a Queene apple, a Cherie, or a Peare....A white head he had, & Sunne burnt hands: in the one he held a weeding hooke, in the other a grafting knife'.[20] He greets the King with a speech, which Dekker paraphrases only, and this was, I suggest, Alleyn's composition, for neither does it appear in Ben Jonson's contribution.

His Majesty was apparently delighted by all this for Dekker tells us:

'His Maiestie dwelt here a reasonable long time, giuing both good allowance to the song & Musick, and liberally bestowing his eye on the workemanship of the place: from whence at the length departing, his next entrance was, as it were, into the closet or rather the priuy chamber to this our Court royall, through the windowes of which he might behold the Cathedrall Temple of Sainte Paule: vpon whose lower batlements an Antheme was sung, by the Quiristers of the Church to the musicke of loud instruméts: which being finisht a latine Oratīo was *Viua voce* deliuered to his Grace, by one of maister Mulcasters Schollers, at the dore of the free-schole fownded by the Mercers.'[21]

The next 'Arch of triumph' was at the 'Conduit in Fleetstreete' where classical figures, headed by *Astraea*, greeted the King with many attendant symbolic virtues, and personifications of *England, Scotland, France* and *Ireland*, as also the four elements. Here another actor of Alleyn's company, the Prince's Men, performed the speech in the character of *Zeal*, who is named by Dekker as being '*W. Bourne*', or William Borne (alias Bird). His speech, written in heroic couplets, appears to make specific reference to the two rival theatres of London: the Globe, which is doubtless called to mind as a compliment to King James, whose company, the renamed King's Men, headed by Burbage and Shakespeare, were now possessors of the most important theatre on Bankside since the Rose was falling into decay, and theirs was the coveted patronage of the monarch, and the Fortune. In his verse Dekker glances at the two theatres using the favourite Elizabethan device of double meanings here for 'Globe' and 'Fortune', both the general sense and the specific as the names of the theatres:

> The populous *Globe* of this our English Ile,
> . . . .
> Our *Globe* is drawne in a right line agen,
> And now appeare new faces, and new men,

Then turning to –

> Mirror of times, lo where thy Fortune sits,
> Aboue the world, and all our humaine wits,
> But thy hye Vertue aboue that: what pen,

442

Or Art, or braine can reach thy vertue then?
At whose immortall brightness and true light,
Enuies infectious eyes haue lost their sight.[22]

This is hardly great poetry, but it is interesting historically. Clearly Alleyn's involvement in this grand royal entertainment is well to the fore. Only his company's actor, William Borne, and Alleyn himself and Sir Henry Montague are mentioned by name as having leading roles, and it is Alleyn's friend Ben Jonson, and not Shakespeare, who is the dramatist collaborating with Dekker in writing the speeches that were delivered; whilst one not insignificant passage of text, possibly in blank verse or heroic couplets, was, on the evidence, actually written by Alleyn himself as we shall presently see.

Astraea's pageant, writes Dekker, was a 'Towre of Pleasure'. *Astraea* (Justice) 'sitting aloft, as being newly descended from heauen' was 'gloriously attirde; all her garments being thickly strewed with starres: a crowne of starres on her head; a Siluer veile couering her eyes.' She is attended by *Invidia* (Envy).

The seventh and last pageant of the City again featured Alleyn as the *Genius* of the City. This was staged at Temple Bar, and appropriately took the form of an impressive Temple 'the height of the whole Aedifice...was 57 foote, the full bredth of it 18 foote: the thicknes of the Passage 12.' Within the Temple, the principal personification was again *Peace*, at whose feet 'lay *Mars* (War) groueling' and with her *Wealth*, and other allegorical personages. 'Within the Temple was an Alter, to which, vpon the approch of the King, a *Flamin* appeares, and to him, the former *Genius* of the Citie. The effect of whose speech was, that whereas the *Flamin* came to perform rites there, in honour of one *Anna*, a goddess of the Romanes' (this being probably a compliment to Queen Anne) 'the *Genius* vowes, that one shall doe Sacrifice there, but himselfe, the offring that he makes being, the Heart of the Citie, &c.'[23]

Edward Alleyn appears twice, at the beginning and end of this entertainment, and his performance as the *Genius* of the City of London is the dominant one. The most lavish of the spectacles is that presenting the Garden or 'Arbor', designed as a place of delectation with its realistic painted carvings of delicious fruit and flowers. Alleyn's influence is pervasive here, and is evident in the character of the 'maister Gardener', in which Alleyn with his love and knowledge of gardening would have been in his element. The speech of the 'maister Gardener', as already intimated, was, I believe, written by Alleyn himself, whose gardening expertise is reflected in his letter in which he gives instructions that his parsley bed must be resown in September with 'spinage for then is the tym', and this interest is further testified in his *Diary*. Such a passionate gardener would not have wanted to delegate the composition of this speech to the co-authors, Jonson and Dekker. Clearly neither of them wrote it, and the obvious author is therefore Edward Alleyn. In evidence I give below the complete paraphrase of the 'maister Gardener's' speech as given by Alleyn's good friend, Dekker, beginning –

'and this was the tenor of his speech. That he was bound to give thanks to heavē, In that the arbour and trees which growing in that fruitful Cynthian garden, began to droop and hang downe their greene heades and to vncurle their crisped locks, as fearing, and in some sort, feeling the sharpnesse of Autumnian malice, are now on the sudden by the diuine influence apparelled with a fresh and more liuely Verdure than ever they were before. The nine Muses that could expect no better entertainment than sad banishment, hauing now louely and amiable faces: Arts that were threatned to be trod vnder foot by Barbarisme, now (euen at sight of his Maiestie, who is the Delian Patrō both of the Muses & Arts) being likewise aduanced to most high prefermēt whilst the very rurall & Syluane troopes dancd for ioy: the Lady therefore of the place *Eirene*, (his mistris) in name of the Prœtor, Consuls & Senators of the City, who carefully pruine this garden, (weeding-out al hurtful & idle branches that hinder the growth of the good,) and who are indeede, *Ergatai Pistri, faithfull Laborers in this peice of ground, Shee doth in al their names, (& he in behalfe of his Lady) offer them selues, this Arbor, the bowers & walkes, yea her children (gold & siluer) with the louing & loyall harts of all those the Sons of peace, standing about him, to be disposde after his royal pleasure. And so wishing his happie Arriual at a more glorious bower, to which he is now going, yet welcoming him to this & praying his Maiesty not to forget this poore Arbor of his Lady, Musicke is commanded to carry all their praiers for his happie reigne, with the loud *Amen* of all his Subiects as hie as heauen.'[24]

This speech is followed by the song already quoted, 'O this is Hee' sung by the nine boys representing the Muses, which appears in Dekker's book, so was presumably composed by him. In the Gardener's speech

---

* If *Pistri* is *Pistrai* this is Greek: Hard working drinking cups"

we can again detect a certain quaintness of expression which I have associated with Alleyn's style, as in the 'Cynthian garden' and 'Autumnian malice'. Aware of King James's reputation as a scholar, the writer makes an effort to appear learned by using classical names and a bit of Greek(!) which would also fit in with Alleyn's approach. Since neither Dekker nor Jonson wrote this speech, it seems an irresistible conclusion that here we have a final piece of dramatic writing from the pen of Alleyn which is evidence that he was recognised as a writer by his contemporaries. Thus the testimony of Henry Chettle in 1592 acknowledging 'his facetious grace in writting, that aprooues his Art', is once more supported. And here the context was congenial. The whole concept of the fruitful Garden with its flowery arbours and bowers, and the great emphasis on delightful music, as well as the touch of dramatic entertainment in the encounter with Sylvanus, suggests that this interlude was largely the brain-child of Alleyn himself. He was undoubtedly a most skilful musician, and the detailed statutory provisions he made for the teaching and practice of music at his College in Dulwich underline the important place music held for him. This is also reflected in his *Diary*. Finally, the seal of Alleyn's as the master-hand in this device is seen in the introduction of carved Satyres and the figure of Dame Fortune topping it all. Interesting, and revealing too, is the inclusion of the seven Liberal Arts personified here, and the presentation of the choristers of St Paul's at the door of their free grammar school, which is given in conjunction with this horticultural-musical interlude, as a kind of postlude to it. For Alleyn's thoughts were already deeply engrossed with his plans for the founding of his college for the education of poor boys.

Dekker concludes his commentary of the royal progress through the City: 'And thus haue wee (lowely and aloofe) followed our Soueraigne through the seauen Triumphal gates of this his Court Royall, which name, as *London* receiued at the rysing of the *Sunne*; so now at his going from her (euen in a moment) She lost that honour: And being (like an Actor on a Stage) stript out of her borrowed Maiestie, she resignes her former shape & title of Citie: nor is it quite lost, considering it went along with him, to whom it is due: For such Vertue is begotten in Princes, that their verie presence hath power to turne a Village to a Citie, and to make a Citie appeare great as a Kingdome.'[25]

But all is not quite ended. As the King emerged from his City tour, he came into the Strand where the City of Westminster and the Duchy of Lancaster (not to be outdone by the City of London) had combined to present their tribute to his Majesty. This offering, which was termed 'A Monument of their affection', was in the form of a Rainbow, with the Sun, Moon, and seven stars of the Pleiades, one of whom hung suspended in the air between two 'Pyramides' (the Elizabethan term for pillars) in the figure of a Comet, who from this aerial position delivered a speech of welcome and loyalty to their new King – this also written by Jonson.

And so this 'Most happie Prince' was welcomed to his kingdom. After his departure doubtless the Londoners made a fine day of it clambering over the magnificent displays and oohing and aahing over the workmanship of each great triumphal arch, the beautifully painted lettering, the wonder of the fountain, the carved and painted artificial fruit and flowers of the garden, before it was all dismantled and taken away. Dekker tells us that sixteen committees had been set up by the citizens of London to devise this elaborate presentation, and they doubtless had the responsibility for levying the money to pay for it. None of the members is named, but it seems certain that Alleyn became involved early in the proceeding and was most likely a member of one of the committees, for his theatrical experience and expertise, his creative energy and organising ability would have been of great value. The high standard of commitment he brought to bear on any project would have contributed much to seeing it successfully through. One can visualize him in happy collaboration with his friends Dekker, Ben Jonson and Inigo Jones in an advisory role, organising, and harnessing their creative talents. Once the plans had been formulated, London must have become an absolute hive of activity for the few days in which the work of construction was in progress. Dekker tells us something of this at the beginning of his pamphlet: the seething activity in the City where erecting the wooden structures, pillars, arches to bear the devices of pageantry, the painting and decorating went on without ceasing. Until: 'The daye (for whose sake; these wonders of Wood, clymde thus into the cloudes) is now come' – and gone, leaving but a memory, and for us a historic record.

Alleyn's name is absent from the list of actors who are servants of the Prince in the Patent issued on 30th April 1606 to 'licence and auctorize Thomas Downton, Thomas Towne, William Byrde, Edward Iuby, Samuell Rowle, humfrey Ieffs, Charles Massey and Anthonie Ieffs Servauntes to our dearest Sonne the Prince and the rest of theire Associates to vse and exercise the arte and facultie of playing Comedies Tragedies Histories Enterludes Moralls Pastoralls Stage playes and such other like as they haue alreadie studied or hereafter shall vse or studie as well for the recreacion of our louing subiectes as for our solace and pleasure'.[26]

446

The leading actor named in the Patent is Thomas Downton, who had taken over as the head of the company on Alleyn's previous retirement in 1597.

There was an element of flamboyancy in Alleyn's character which would have found great satisfaction in finishing in splendid style at King James's accession celebration. He had resumed playing at Queen Elizabeth's request, and with the new monarch securely established he would feel no obligation to continue to exert himself in the public performance of plays when what he considered his life's work still lay ahead of him waiting to be accomplished. He was now aged thirty-eight and (praise be to God) still had his health and strength, but the span allotted to man was brief in his day, and with the recent plague in mind he would be only too well aware how slender was the thread of life. In all probability he had consciously planned to bow out as *Genius* when his stage was no less than the teeming City of London.

It would have been a typically theatrical gesture from the actor described as 'the onely Shake-scene in a countrey' to have chosen this magnificent conclusion to a magnificent career deliberately. There was no false modesty in Alleyn's make-up. He knew his worth; though he never forgot that he owed all he was to his Maker. He worked hard to develop the talents with which God had blessed him – in both senses of the word.

There is no doubt that Edward Alleyn was now contemplating in all seriousness a second career which would satisfy his deep religiosity: that as founder of a charitable institution which would commemorate his name, while giving glory to God, and to which he would contribute his personal talents as organiser, and his minted talents in the form of his accumulated worldly wealth. With these he would found his College of God's Gift in Dulwich, which to-day survives and thrives as one of the great public schools of England.

Dulwich College, circa 1903 with cricket in progress on the field.   *(By kind permission of the Governors of Dulwich College.)*

APPENDIX A

Alexander v. Tucker Brooke Concluded:
The X and Y Texts

Continuing his attack on Tucker Brooke's thesis, *The Authorship of the Second and Third Parts of 'King Henry VI'*, reviewed in Chapter IV, Peter Alexander proceeds to cast doubt on the value of versification tests and whether the frequency of double endings reveals anything at all.

'The basis on which these tests stand is still very uncertain', he states, and he then devotes several pages to disintegrating the value of such critical textual analysis.

'Metrical tests are difficult to apply in this instance, for the counting of double endings and similar verse phenomena on which they depend cannot be very reliable when one of the texts is admittedly corrupt. Professor Tucker Brooke recognizes this difficulty, but proceeds to count good and bad lines indifferently and to tabulate the results.'[1]

This sweeping claim is both exaggerated and unjust as anyone troubling to read Tucker Brooke's exposition can verify. Nothing is done 'indifferently' in this meticulously objective work. Here is what he himself says on this point.

'Rules relating to metrical tests are doubtless particularly subject to exceptions, and it may be, of course, that the irregularity here is only accidental. It is worth noting, however, that this apparent discrepancy lends weight to the inference, which on other grounds amounts to practical certainty, that the 1254 lines printed in *The Contention* give a much abbreviated and corrupted version of Marlowe's manuscript, whereas the large number of new and altered lines in *2 Henry VI* (2148) include not only Shakespeare's revisions, but also a very considerable amount of original matter not represented in *The Contention*.[2]

The drift of Alexander's criticism of metrical tests is that it is pointless to examine any text which is not perfect, and the best we can settle for with these 'bad' quartos is to dismiss all internal evidence and fall back on faith in the First Folio, thus the argument would be effectively closed.

This is an unduly pessimistic view and would rule out almost all of Marlowe's work from any valid textual examination, as well as that of most of his contemporaries. As Tucker Brooke has pointed out:

> 'The unusual excellence of the Folio text of Shakespeare's plays inclines us to estimate too lightly the accuracy of extant versions of the works of other dramatists of the period. Shakespeare's practical connexion with the company that acted his plays was productive to the poet of many benefits, both literary and temporal. Among others, it protected the acting version of his plays from outside interference, made sure that such changes as might from time to time become commercially desirable should during his life to be made by the poet himself, and after his death procured the careful editing of the genuine texts by those who knew most about them. With the dramas of Marlowe, Kyd, Greene, and other popular writers not connected with particular companies, the case is very different.'[3]

Finally, Alexander further clouds the issue by making great play with the importance of the putative existence of two slightly less corrupt scripts of *The Contention* and *The True Tragedy* which were presumably available to the printer Pavier, who brought out a later edition of both plays in 1619, which contains some slight corrections of the earlier 'bad' quartos, bringing them nearer to the Folio text in some respects, yet not in others. These putative scripts are peripheral to Tucker Brooke's thesis, but Alexander insists on treating them as of basic importance to Tucker Brooke's argument and he expends several pages in considering these X and Y scripts as he calls them (though Tucker Brooke does not so call them). His tactics serve to complicate the issue unnecessarily by elevating these X and Y scripts to a place of *paramount* importance, and by means of his convoluted argument he so confuses the unwary reader that one is easily misled. It is necessary to re-read this part of Alexander's argument several times in order to discover what he is driving at. On the surface it seems impressive and learned, but in substance amounts to very little, for Tucker Brooke merely discusses these putative scripts as a postlude to his thesis, *not* as an integral part of it as Alexander implies. However, it is important for this present investigation of the orthodox views, which have taken root on the basis of Alexander's work in apparently disintegrating Tucker Brooke's thesis, to examine this aspect in some detail. I have italicized and enumerated the points to be answered in the following passage from Alexander's attack on Tucker Brooke on these so-called X and Y texts.

'The unknowns, X and Y, enable Professor Tucker Brooke to offer *a solution to a further difficulty in the parallels with Marlowe.*[a] Since it is on these parallels he claims the quartos and their originals for Marlowe he is forced to make *this distinction between X and Y and the new matter of the 1623 versions added by Shakespeare:*[b] the Marlowe parallels he insists are peculiar to the originals, while *Shakespeare's part in the Folio shows an entirely different manner.*[c] *Professor Tucker Brooke actually finds some of the resemblances to Edward II (nos. 32-6) in those parts of the text first printed in 1623,*[d] but his hypothetical X and Y permit him to argue that these passages stood in Marlowe's originals of 1594-5 without finding their way into the quartos. Had the quartos been good texts of X and Y he would have found the additional parallels there beside the others.'[4]

Taking these points in order:

a.   *a solution to any further difficulty in the parallels with Marlowe* is Alexander's problem, *not* Tucker Brooke's who finds no difficulties. He has shown that these parallels exist, and he takes them for what they are - an indication of authorship by Marlowe by their very number.

b.   *this distinction between X and Y and the new matter of the 1623 versions added by Shakespeare*: these distinctions are seen as of 'little importance' by Tucker Brooke because they are so slight and they do not affect his thesis. The Pavier text of 1619 shows a few passages corrected to agree with the 1623 Folio text, while other discrepancies remain. Alexander does not offer any explanation for these discrepancies himself, and he implies that X and Y are a significant 'invention' of Tucker Brooke's to prove his case. This is frankly nonsense.

c.   *Shakespeare's part in the Folio shows an entirely different manner.* This is what one would expect in the writing of a mature dramatist compared with that of a young man, Marlowe as compared with the mature writer, Shakespeare, and should cause no surprise. Tucker Brooke makes the criticism that the youthful work as first conceived in these two early history plays is - in his opinion - fresher and more dramatically effective, even as apparent in these corrupt texts, than some of the altered and expanded writing which appears in the Folio versions, which he finds sometimes actually detracts from the original dramatic impact. It is a subjective view. Is it his appreciation of Marlowe's powers as a dramatist that presumably upsets Alexander? for here Tucker Brooke is expressing a preference for early Marlowe. This has nothing to do with his thesis, however, and in no way destroys the validity of the textual evidence of the Marlovian qualities intrinsic to the writing.

d. *Professor Tucker Brooke actually finds some of the resemblances to Edward II (nos. 32-6) in those parts of the text first printed in 1623.* Can Alexander be unaware of the fact that the texts of Shakespeare's plays bear significant testimony to Marlowe's all-pervading influence? And especially is this true of the early plays. How does one escape from the close verbal parallels between speeches in *The Jew of Malta* and *The Merchant of Venice* in the relationship of the two Jews with their daughters? Or the similarly close parallels between the deposition scenes in *Edward II* and *Richard II*?
Who was borrowing from whom here, Mr Alexander?

Alexander is loath to face up to any of the problems, and he seems to suggest that Tucker Brooke is the villain who has invented all these parallels:

'several repetitions that Professor Brooke particularly ascribes to Marlowe have been confidently cited as actors' interpolations' (by Alexander, that is, *not* by Tucker Brooke who never mentions actors' interpolations). 'No doubt Professor Tucker Brooke admits that certain repetitions are due to actors.'[5]

This must be Alexander thinking wishfully. He is attempting it seems to inject his own theory about the actors' responsibility for introducing lines from one play to another into Tucker Brooke's thesis, which is an impossibility as at *no* point is Tucker Brooke concerned with any such gratuitous hypothesis.
He continues his attack on Tucker Brooke as follows:
'His conclusions as to what belongs to the original of the 1594-5 texts, and what has been added in the Folio is framed to suit his hypothesis that the earliest version of *2 and 3 Henry VI* is Marlowe's.

X and Y are assumptions to make this hypothesis work, but it is impossible to take on trust from Professor Tucker Brooke what was or was not in these versions, till he can first prove that the hypothesis that demands them is itself necessary.'[6]

Thus, having with this extraordinary allegation given what he considers to be the *coup de grace* to Tucker Brooke, we will leave Alexander and turn to what Tucker Brooke himself has to say about these problematical X and Y texts which Alexander seems to think are so indispensible to Brooke's thesis that without them it would fall to the ground. Here is Tucker Brooke's authentic voice:

'There would thus seem, on *prima facie* evidence and on the testimony of parallels, a very good reason to believe that Millington's version of *The Contention* and *True Tragedy*, printed in 1594/5, gave a corrupt text of the plays and omitted certain passages belonging to Marlowe's original draft. This suspicion is rendered almost a certainty when we consider this intermediate version printed by Pavier in 1619. In the preceding pages there has been little occasion to mention Pavier's edition, which *inherently possesses very small importance.*' (My italics). 'No just ground exists for supposing either that this edition represents an independent recension of the plays or that it includes any of Shakespeare's alterations. Pavier doubtless used as basis for his printer's "copy" the text of Millington of which the copyright was in his possession. In the case of *The Contention*, he increased the total number of lines by some eight or ten; in the *True Tragedy* he added two new lines, but omitted, presumably by accident, two of the old ones. *In the main essentials, however, the text of Pavier is the text of Millington;*' [my italics] 'and the failure of the former to make use of the hundreds of new lines by Shakespeare, in spite of his fraudulent use of Shakespeare's name on the title-page, is conclusive evidence that he had no access to the Shakespearean version of the dramas.'[7]

We can now see that Alexander's convoluted discussion of his X and Y texts is so much hot air - a tactical way of sowing confusion. Tucker Brooke finds the Pavier edition on which rests the suppositious existence of Alexander's importantly named X and Y texts to possess 'very small importance' as the alterations made to the corrupt Millington text of 1594/5 were *absolutely minimal* and bear little relation to the Folio. So how can Alexander argue that '*X and Y are assumptions to make this* (Tucker Brooke's) *hypothesis work*'? Tucker Brooke has no need of X and Y to substantiate his thesis; it is Alexander who needs these texts, elevated to a position of prime importance, to attack Tucker Brooke. The chief interest for Tucker Brooke in the discrepancies between Millington's texts and Pavier's slightly variant edition lay in its curiosity value; particularly with regard to its correction of a historical omission in York's long recital of his claim through his lineage to the throne of England, and, thereby, in the implication that he had access to another script than the one Millington supplied. The existence of another text is evidence to Tucker Brooke's mind that these plays, even in their pre-Folio form, were originally much longer than these 'bad' quartos; otherwise it is difficult to account for the strongly Marlovian element in almost the *whole* of the Folio texts, which in Tucker Brooke's view show only slight evidence of revision, but rather addition by Shakespeare.

Pavier was a printer of dubious reputation, not noted for his care in preparing texts. His 1619 edition of *The Whole Contention* incorporates both plays under this one title, and binds it in a composite volume of corrupt texts of six plays in all, which he prints as being all by Shakespeare. Two of these are patently not his - *Sir John Oldcastle* and *A Yorkshire Tragedy*; and the others are very corrupt versions of *Pericles* and *Henry V.*

It will be seen from the foregoing that Peter Alexander has misinterpreted and deliberately misrepresented Tucker Brooke's arguments substantially in order to give the appearance of having refuted them. He invites us not to 'take on trust' what Tucker Brooke has stated. Rather, I suggest, we should not take on trust Alexander's claims as to what Tucker Brooke is supposed to have said. Those who still doubt this can do no better than to read or re-read Tucker Brooke's very impressive thesis for themselves.

APPENDIX B

Parallelisms

The following parallelisms from Marlowe's works and *The Contention* and *The True Tragedy* culled by Professor Tucker Brooke present an impressive display or similarities to substantiate his thesis on Marlowe's authorship:[1]

Oh fatall was this mariage to vs all	(Massacre, 203)
Ah Lords, fatall is this marriage...	(Contention, p.5. 79)
For this I wake, when others think I sleepe	(Massacre, 105)
Watch thou, and wake when others be asleepe	(Contention, p.8. 156)
As though your highnes were a schoole boy still, And must be awde and gouernd like a child.	(Edward II, 1336-1337)
But still must be protected like a childe, And gouerned by that ambitious Duke.	(Contention, p.12. 49-50)
Furies from the blacke *Cocitus* lake. Wherein the Furies maske in hellish troupes,	(I Tamburlaine. 1999)
Send vp I charge you from Sosetus lake.	(Contention, p.17. 15-16)
Nay, to my death, for too long haue I liued.	(Edward II, 2651)
Euen to my death, for I haue liued too long.	(Contention, p.25. 10)
A griping paine hath ceasde vpon my heart: A sodaine pang, the messenger of death.	(Massacre, 542)
For sorrowes teares hath gripte my aged heart.	(Contention, p.25. 17)
See how the panges of death doth gripe his heart.	(Ibid. p.42. 12)
How inlie anger gripes his hart.	(True Tragedie, p.21. 156)
Or looke you, I should play the Orator?	(I Tamburlaine, 325)
Our swordes shall play the Orators for vs.	(Ibid. 328)
Nay, I can better plaie the Orator.	(True Tragedie, p.12. 2)
To trie how quaint an Orator you were.	(Contention, p.39. 127)
Full well hath *Clifford* plaid the Orator.	(True Tragedie, p.29. 42)

For he hath solemnely sworne thy death.
Muge. I may be stabd, and liue till he be dead. (Massacre, 783-784)

Lord Say, Iacke Cade hath solemnely vowde to haue thy head.
Say. I, but I hope your highnesse shall haue his. (Contention, p.49. 6-7)

The sworde shall plane the furrowes of thy browes. (Edward II, 94)

Giue me a look, that when I bend the browes,
Pale death may walke in furrowes on my face. (Massacre, 158)

Deepe trenched furrowes in his frowning brow. (Contention, p.57. 53)

The wrinkles in my browes now fild with bloud
Were likened oft to kinglie sepulchers. (True Tragedie, p.68. 10-11)

Weaponles must I fall and die in bands. (Edward II, 1289)

And die in bands for this vnkingly deed. (True Tragedie, p.10. 177)

Here, take my crowne, the life of *Edward* too. (Edward II, 2043)

Off with the crowne, and with the crowne his head. (True Tragedie, p.19. 92)

Inhumaine creatures, nurst with Tigers milke. (Edward II, 2057)

But thou art sprung from *Scythian Caucasus*,
And Tygers of *Hircania* gaue thee sucke. (Dido, 1566-1567)

But you are more inhumaine, more inexorable,
O ten times more then Tygers of *Arcadia*. (True Tragedie, p.21. 139-140)

For which thy head shall ouer looke the rest
As much as thou in rage out wentst the rest. (Edward II, 1547-1548)

Off with his head and set it on *Yorke* Gates,
So *Yorke* maie ouerlooke the towne of *Yorke*. (True Tragedie, p.21. 164-165)

And we are grac'd with wreathes of victory. (Massacre, 794)

Thus farre our fortunes keepes an vpward Course,
And we are grast with wreathes of victorie. (True Tragedie, p.39. 30-31)

Your Lordship shall doe well to let them haue it. (Jew of Malta, 274)

Your highnesse shall doe well to grant it them. (True Tragedie, p.43. 9)

The royall vine, whose golden leaues
Empale your princelie head, your diadem. (Edward II, 1472-1473)

Did I impale him with the regall Crowne. (True Tragedie, p.52. 118)

..... I stand as Ioues huge tree,
And others are but shrubs compard to me. (Edward II, 2578-2580)

Whose top branch ouerpeerd Ioues spreading tree. (True Tragedie, p.68. 9)

456

Shaking their swords, their speares and yron bils,
Enuironing their Standard round, that stood
As bristle-pointed as a thorny wood.   (I Tamburlaine, 1397-1399)

See brothers, yonder stands the thornie wood,
Which by Gods assistance and your prowesse,
Shall with our swords yer night be cleane cut downe.   (True Tragedie, p.71. 35-37)

Frownst thou thereat, aspiring *Lancaster*?   (Edward II, 93)

Highly scorning, that the lowly earth
Should drinke his bloud, mounts vp into the ayre.   (Edward II, 2000-2001)

What? Will the aspiring bloud of *Lancaster*
Sinke into the ground, I had thought it would haue mounted.
                                                        (True Tragedie, p.76. 50-51)

Æneas no, although his eyes doe pearce.   (Dido, 1007)

Her lookes did wound, but now her speech doth pierce.   (Contention, p.4. 30)

The wilde *Oneyle*, with swarmes of Irish Kernes,
Liues vncontroulde within the English pale.   (Edward II. 966-967)

The wild Onele my Lords, is vp in Armes,
With troupes of Irish Kernes that vncontrold,
Doth plant themselues within the English pale.   (Contention p.33. 134-136)

And ride in triumph through *Persepolis*.   (I Tamburlaine, 755)

When thou didst ride in tryumph through the streetes.   (Contention, p.27. 6-10)

Sweet Duke of *Guise* our prop to leane vpon,
Now thou art dead, heere is no stay for vs.   (Massacre, 1122-1123)

Sweet Duke of *Yorke* our prop to leane vpon,
Now thou art gone there is no hope for vs.   (True Tragedie, p.23. 45-46)

The hautie *Dane* commands the narrow seas,
While in the harbor ride they ships vnrigd.   (Edward II, 970-971)

Commands the narrow seas   (True Tragedie, p.11. 210-211)

Tell *Isabell* the Queene, I lookt not thus,
When for her sake I ran at tilt in Fraunce,
And there vnhorst the duke of *Cleremont*.   (Edward II, 2516-2518)

I tell thee *Poull*, when thou didst runne at Tilt
And stolst away our Laidies hearts in *France*,
I thought King *Henry* had bene like to thee,
Or else thou hadst not brought me out of *France*.   (Contention, p.13. 59-61)

457

Marlowe's characteristic tendency to self-repetition within the same work is also amply demonstrated by the following examples from *The Contention* and *The True Tragedy*.

Till terme of eighteene months be full expirde.	(Contention, p.4 39)
Till terme of 18. months be full expirde.	(Ibid. p.5 60)

The common people swarme about him straight,
Crying *Iesus* blesse your royall exellence,
With God preserue the good Duke *Humphrey*,   (Contention, p.6. 98-100)

See you not how the Commons follow him
In troupes, crying, God saue the good Duke *Humphrey*,
And with long life, *Iesus* preserue his grace,
Honoring him as if he were their King.   (Ibid. p.30. 9-12)

Ile laie a plot to heaue him from his seate.	(Contention, p.6. 104)
Weele quickly heaue Duke *Humphrey* from his seate.	(Ibid. p.6. 111)

And put them from the marke they faine would hit.	(Contention, p.6. 108)
For thats the golden marke I seeke to hit.	(Ibid. p.7. 150)

Cold newes for me, for I had hope of *France*,
Euen as I haue of fertill England.   (Contention, p.7. 144-145)

Cold newes for me, for I had hope of France,
Euen as I haue of fertill England.   (Ibid. p.31. 34-35)

My mind doth tell me thou art innocent.	(Contention, p.23. 171)
My conscience tels me thou art innocent.	(Ibid. p.32. 70)

If our King Henry had shooke hands with death,
Duke Humphrey then would looke to be our King.   (Contention, p.33. 118-119)

As I bethinke me you should not be king,
Till our *Henry* had shooke hands with death.   (True Tragedie, p.19. 86-87)

You bade me ban, and will you bid me sease?	(Contention, p.40. 165)
Bids thou me rage? why now thou hast thy will.	(True Tragedie, p.20. 128)

Make hast, for vengeance comes along with them.	(Contention, p.62. 63)
Awaie my Lord for vengance comes along with him.	(True Tragedie, p.38. 61)

For strokes receiude, and manie blowes repaide,
Hath robd my strong knit sinnews of their strength,
And force perforce needes must I rest my selfe.   (True Tragedie, pp.33-34)

For manie wounds receiu'd and mani moe repaid,
Hath robd my strong knit sinews of their strength,
And spite of spites needes must I yeeld to death.   (Ibid., p.68. 25-27)

Her lookes are all repleat with maiestie.   (True Tragedie, p.45. 64)

Thy lookes are all repleat with Maiestie.   (Ibid., p.63. 19)

For I am not yet lookt on in the world.   (True Tragedie, p.47. 107)

For yet I am not lookt on in the world.   (Ibid., p.78. 22)

And free King *Henry* from imprisonment
And see him seated in his regall throne.   (True Tragedie, p.59. 52-53)

And pull false *Henry* from the Regall throne.   (Ibid., p.63. 58)

Awaie with him, I will not heare him speake.   (True Tragedie, p.65. 3)

Awaie I will not heare them speake.   (Ibid., p.72. 50)

My Lord, this harmefull pittie makes your followers faint. (True Tragedie, p.29. 55)

My gratious Lord, this too much lenitie,
And harmfull pittie must be laid aside.   (Ibid., p.28. 8-9)

...tell false *Edward* thy supposed king,
That *Lewis* of France is sending ouer Maskers
To reuell it with him and his new bride.
Bona. Tell him in hope heele be a widower shortlie,
Ile weare the willow garland for his sake.
Queen. Tell him my mourning weedes be laide aside,
And I am readie to put armour on.
War. Tell him from me, that he hath done me wrong,
And therefore Ile vncrowne him er't be long.   (True Tragedie, p.52. 135-143)

...tell false *Edward* thy supposed king,
That *Lewis* of France is sending ouer Maskers,
To reuill it with him and his new bride...
Tel him quoth she, in hope heele proue a widdower shortly,
Ile weare the willow garland for his sake...
Tell him quoth shee my mourning weeds be
Downe, and I am ready to put armour on...
Tell him quoth he, that he hath done me wrong,
And therefore Ile vncrowne him er't be long."   (Ibid., p.56. 64-79)

This is not an unconscious self-repetition for the ambassador is delivering the message he received at the French Court to the English King, but, as Bakeless points out 'only a dramatist with a strong tendency to repeat would give the report in words so closely resembling the original'.[2]

However, perhaps it is here intentional for dramatic purposes. Marlowe sensed that repetition has a dramatic value, and I believe he did not therefore view it as a fault; it is rather a part of his dramatic technique.

Notes and References

INTRODUCTION

Page	Ref.	
(ii)	1	J.S. Smart: *Shakespeare: Truth and Tradition* (1928, London) p.196

CHAPTER I   THE TRIUMPH OF *TAMBURLAINE*

Page	Ref.	
2.	1.	Thos. Fuller: *The Worthies of England (Vol. on Lancs & Wales)* (London, 1662) p.233
	2	Shakespeare: *A Midsummer Night's Dream*, Act I, sc. 1, 1.73
3.	3	Marlowe: *The Famous Tragedy of the Rich Jew of Malta* (1633) Sig. A^v
	4	*Henslowe's Diary* ed. R.A.Foakes & R.T.Rickert (Cambridge, 1961) p.60, fol. 27^v
	5	*Ibid*: p. 290 *Warrant from the Privy Council to the Justices of Middlesex*, d. 8 April 1600, Richmond G.F. Warner: *Catalogue of MSS and Muniments of Dulwich College* (1881) Article 29.
5.	6	William Wordsworth: 'My heart leaps up when I behold'.
	7	George Peele: 'The Honour of the Garter' (1593)
6.	8	John Bakeless: *The Tragicall History of Christopher Marlowe* (Harvard, 1942, Reprinted Connecticut, 1970) Vol. II, p. 183
	9	E.H.C. Oliphant: *Shakespeare and His Fellow Dramatists* (London, 1929) Vol. I, p. 32
	10	*Ibid:* p. 34
8.	11	Bakeless: *op. cit:* Vol. II, pp. 3-4
10.	12	Oliphant: *op. cit*: Vol. I, p. 33
12.	13	Bakeless: *op. cit*: Vol. I, pp. 225-6
13.	14	*Ibid*: Vol. I, p. 245
16.	15	Oliphant: *op. cit*: Vol. I, p. 32
17.	16	These 16th century editions are now in the Library of the Dean and Chapter of Canterbury Cathedral. They are not printed in the inventory of Dr Gressop's library in William Urry's *Christopher Marlowe and Canterbury* (London, 1988) posthumously edited by Andrew Butcher, at Appendix II; but Dr Urry informed me that he thought these volumes had come from Gressop's library. Urry has Loniceras's *Historia Turcorum* as a title, (see p. 48)
	17	Bakeless: *op. cit*: Vol. I, p. 220
	18	*Ibid*: Vol. I, p. 220
	19	*Ibid*: Vol. I, p. 225
	20	*Ibid*: Vol. I, p. 218 and pp. 234-36
	21	*Ibid*: Vol. I, p. 222 Bakeless quotes all these historians in the original Latin. English translations are by Michael Rowett.
19.	22	Wm. Oldys and Thos. Park: The Harleian Miscellany (1809) Vol. II, 'Fragmenta Regalia', p. 99 and p. 100

23   Eleanor Grace Clark: *Ralegh and Marlowe* (1941) p. 229
A.D. Wraight and Virginia F. Stern: *In Search of Christopher Marlowe*, (1965, London and N.Y.) pp. 134-36

20.   24   A.W. Ward: *History of English Dramatic Literature* (1875, 1899) Vol. I, pp. 362-63

25   Bakeless: *op. cit*: Vol. I, p. 223. Eng. trans. M. Rowett. This is echoed by Jovius, by Fulgotius, by Andrew Cambine, and by Pope Pius whose *Asiae Europae que elegantiss. descriptio.* was actually on the shelves of the library at Corpus Christi.

21.   26   *Ibid*: Vol. I, pp. 221-22. Eng. trans. M. Rowett.
Jovius, ed. 1578. fol. 3291, copy in *HCL*

22.   27   *Ibid*: Vol. I, p. 228. Eng. trans. M. Rowett.
Henricus von Efferhen: *XIII Homiliae in Caput XXXVIII et XXXIX. Prophetae Ezechielies de Gog & Magog, seu de Turcis* (1571) fol. i, 8^v

28   *Ibid*: p. 228

23.   29   Marlowe used the same technique in his *Edward the Third* in the ritual arming of the youthful Prince Edward, the Black Prince, before his baptism of fire in the battle of Crecy in which he won his spurs. (See pp. 71-72 where this play is discussed).

24.   30   Bakeless: *op. cit*: Vol. I, p. 223

31   *Ibid*: Vol. I, pp. 223-24. Eng. trans. M. Rowett.
Pope Pius: *Asiae Europae que elegantiss. descriptio.* pp. 85-87
Rough List of Parker Books, no. 251

25.   32   *Ibid*: Vol. I, pp. 219-221

33   *Ibid*: Vol. I, p. 234. Eng. trans. M. Rowett.
Antonius Bonfinius: *Rerum Vngaricum Decades Qvatvor*, 1581 ed. p. 457

27.   34   *Ibid*: Vol. I, pp. 233-34

35   *Ibid*: Vol. I, p. 235 Eng. trans. M. Rowett.
Bonfinius: *op. cit*: pp. 457-58

28.   36   *Ibid*: Vol. I, pp. 235-36 Eng. trans. M. Rowett.
Bonfinius: *op. cit*: p. 464

30.   37   *Ibid*: Vol. I, p. 204

38   See Ethel Seaton: 'Marlowe and His Authorities', *TLS*. 20, 388, 16 June 1921

39   Bakeless: *op. cit*: Vol. I, p. 236

33.   40   *Enc. Britannica*, Vol. XXVI, pp. 994-95, under Timur. Timur i Leng, the lame Timur, was, in fact, not low born. He was the son of Teragai, head of the tribe of Berlas, who, by right of inheritance, could have assumed a high military rank, but preferred to devote himself to study. The young Timur was well educated under his father's eye, both in religion, deeply read in the Koran. and in 'manly outdoor exercises'; c. 1358 he rose to become leader of the tribal armies. He eventually succeeded to the throne of Samarkand, the capital of his domains. His conquests finally stretched from the Irtish and the Volga (mentioned by Marlowe) to the Persian Gulf and, on the other side, from the Hellespont to the Ganges.

41   Bakeless: *op. cit*: Vol. I, p. 228-232

42   *Narrative of the Embassy of Ruy Gonzales de Clavijo to the Court of Timur at Samarkand, A.D. 1404-6*, trans. by Clements R. Markham

Hakluyt Soc. Publications. Also trans. by Guy de Strange (London, Routledge, 1928)

34.	43	Bakeless: *op. cit*: Voo. I, p. 226-230
35.	44	*Ibid*: Vol. I, p. 226 Eng. trans. M. Rowett.
		Petrus Perondinus: *Vita magni Tamerlanis* ed. 1556, p. 245
	45	*Ibid*: Vol. I, p. 229
	46	*Ibid*: Vol. I, p. 228
	47	*Ibid*: Vol. I, pp. 228-232
	48	*Ibid*: Vol. I, pp. 229-230
		Mir Khwand's *Rauzat-us-Safa* (Teheran, 1854) Vol. IV, fol. 15
36.	49	*Ibid*: Vol. I, p. 231
	50	Wraight: *Christopher Marlowe and the Armada* (to be published 1993) See Chap. III of the present work for a resumé of this research.

CHAPTER II   A GREAT THEATRICAL PARTNERSHIP

Page *Ref.*

38.	1	Thos. Fuller: *op. cit*: p. 224
44.	2	Oliphant: *op. cit*: Vol. I, p. 32
45.	3	Sir Edmund Chambers first noted this in *TLS*. 29; 683, 28 Aug. 1930. See *Elizabethan Stage II*, p. 135
46.	4	*Tamburlaine, Part II*, Act. V, sc. 1, 1.122
	5	Henslowe did not commence his *Diary* records until February 1591/2 but between 28 Aug. 1594 and 13 Nov. 1595 he recorded 23 performances of *Tamburlaine*. The long plague had intervened from June 1592 until the Summer of 1594.
	6	B.M. *Egerton MS* 2804, fol. 35
		Letters of Philip Gawdy, ed. I.H. Jeayes (1906)p. 23
47.	7	Bakeless: *op. cit*: Vol. I, p. 223
		See also his Chapter VII, 'Tamburlaine' in its sub-heading 'Influence', pp. 248-55
48.	8	George Gascoigne: *Jocasta*
		Complete Works of Gascoigne ed. J. Cunliffe (Cambridge Eng. Classics, 1907, 2 vols.) Vol. I, p. 246. Based on original ed. 1575.
50.	9	Thos. Lodge: *The Wounds of Ciuill War, or The most Lamentable and true Tragedies of Marius and Scilla* (1594) Act III, Sig. E^v and Sig. E2
	10	*Soliman and Perseda* and *The Troublesome Reign of King John* are both among the Marlowe apocrypha.
52.	11	*Selimus*: Temple ed. 11. 1748 ff.
		See C.F. Tucker Brooke: *The Reputation of Christopher Marlowe* (1922) pp. 367-8. Brooke has assembled the most comprehensive examples of allusions and quotations relating to Marlowe's works to date. I am indebted to him for the greater part of these citations.
	12	George Peele: *The Battle of Alcazar* (1594) Malone Soc. ed. 11.248-50
		Tucker Brooke: *op. cit*: p. 370
	13	A.H. Bullen ed. *Works of Middleton*, Vol. VIII, p. 25
		Tucker Brooke: *op. cit*: p. 366
53.	14	Dekker and Marston: *Satiromastix* (1602) ed. Penniman, IV, iii, 210 f.
		Tucker Brooke: *op. cit*: p. 369 and n.38

	15	*Satiromastix*, IV, ii, 38-40. Tucker Brooke, *op. cit*: p. 369
54.	16	*II Henry IV*, Act II, sc. 4 11.154-158
	17	Day and Chettle: *The Blind Beggar of Bednall-Greene* (1669) ed. Bang 1.1660. See Tucker Brooke: *op. cit*: p. 371 and n.46. He adds: 'This play was written in 1600, but first printed in 1659'.
	18	John Marston: *Antonio and Melida* (1602) Bullen ed. *Marston I*, 11. Tucker Brooke: *op. cit*: p. 370 and n.42 Bakeless: *op. cit*: Vol. I, p. 241
	19	Jonson, Marston, Chapman: *Eastward Hoe* (1605) Act 2. Sig. B3
55.	20	Samuel Rowlands: *The Life and Death of John Leyden, or Hell's Broke Loose* (1605) ed. Grosart, Vol. 1, p. 34 Tucker Brooke: *op. cit*: p. 367
	21	Edward Sharpham: *The Fleire* (1607) ed. Nibbe, p. 22 Tucker Brooke: *op. cit*: p. 370
	22	Beaumont and Fletcher: *The Coxcomb* (1612) Act II, sc. 1. Tucker Brooke: *op. cit*: p. 371 and n.44
	23	Beaumont and Fletcher: *Women Pleased* (1620) Act IV, sc. 1, ed. Dyce (1843) VII, 63. Tucker Brooke: *op. cit*: p. 371 and n.44 Bakeless: *op. cit*: Vol. I, p. 239
	24	Philip Massinger: *Believe As You List* (1631) Act III, sc. 3, Mermaid ed. p. 424 Tucker Brooke: *op. cit*: p. 363 and n.35
	25	John Ford: *Love's Sacrifice* (1633) Act II, sc. 1. Tucker Brooke: *op. cit*: p. 371. He comments that Ford 'puts it with ludicrous intention into the mouth of 'an old antic', Mauruccio.'
56.	26	William Rowley: *A New Wonder* (1632) 11. 1633 ff. Tucker Brooke: *op. cit*: p. 369 and n.40
	27	John Cooke: *Greene's Tu Quoque* (1641) ed. Hazlitt-Dodsley, XI, p. 186. Tucker Brooke: *Ibid*.
	28	W. Prynne: *Histriomastix* (1632) written c. 1598, Act V. Tucker Brooke: *op. cit*: p. 368
	29	Ford and Dekker: *The Sun's Darling* (1657) Act III, sc. 2 Tucker Brooke: *op. cit*: p. 371 and n.45
	30	Philip Massinger: *Maid of Honour* (1627) Act II, sc. 2 Tucker Brooke: *op. cit*: p. 369
	31	William Habington: *Queen of Aragon* (1640) Act V, sc. 1, ed. Hazlitt-Dodsley, XIII, p. 369 Tucker Brooke: *op. cit*: p. 368
57.	32	Abraham Cowley: *The Guardian* (1650) Act III, sc. 6 Tucker Brooke: *op. cit*: pp. 372-3 and n.48 He quotes Bullen's comment: 'From Cowley's *Guardian* it appears that *Tamburlaine* was revived at the Bull about 1650', which Brooke corrects to 1641, 1650 being the date of the play's publication by which time all the theatres were being closed down.
	33	Sir John Suckling: *The Goblins* (1648) p. 46 ed. Hazlitt, Vol. II. Tucker Brooke: *op. cit*: p.372. This seems to suggest that the two plays, *The Bold Beauchams* and *Englands Joy* were by Marlowe.
	34	1st Duke of Newcastle: *The Variety* (1649) Act V, sc. 1, p. 72

Tucker Brooke: *op. cit*: p. 371 and n.45

58. 35 Sir William Alexander, Lord Stirling: *Doomsday* (1637)
Tucker Brooke: *op. cit*: p. 368

36 John Taylor's *Works* (ed. 1630) 'The World runnes on Wheeles', Sig. Bbb.2. Tucker Brooke: *op. cit*: p. 371 and n.46

37 *Ibid*: in 'A Thiefe', Sig. L1.3.
Tucker Brooke: *Ibid*. p. 371. He cites a variant version of Taylor's poem.

38 Bakeless: *op. cit*: Vol. I, pp. 248-252.
Nikolai I. Storozhenko: 'Life of Greene' in *English Drama to the Death of Shakespeare: General History of Literature* ed. V.Th. Korsh and A. Kirpichnikov (St. Petersburg, 1888) Vol. III

60. 39 Robert Greene: *Perimedes the Blacke-Smith* (1588) Sig. A3-A3ᵛ
See *Works of Robert Greene* ed. A.B. Grosart (Huth Library, 1881-86) Vol. VII, pp. 7-8

61. 40 Thomas Nashe: 'To the Gentlemen Students of both Vniuersities', Preface to Greene's: *Menaphon, Camillas Alarum to slumbering Euphues, in his melancholie Cell at Silexedra* (1589)
ed. Grosart: *op. cit*: Vol. VI, pp.2-3

62. 41 Gabriel Harvey: *Pierces Supererogation* (1593)
ed. Grosart, Vol. III, p. 45

63. 42 A.C. Swinburne: 'Christopher Marlowe in Relation to Greene, Peele and Lodge' in *Letters on the Elizabethan Dramatists* (1914) bound with *Letters* (1910) p. 9

43 *Ibid*: p. 20

44 *Ibid*: pp. 16-17

CHAPTER III   AN 'ARMADA' ENGLISH HISTORY PLAY

Page   Ref.

66. 1 *Henry the Fifth*, Introductory Essay: 'The Mirror of Kingship': *The Folger Library General Reader's Shakespeare* (1960-) ed. Louis B. Wright & Virginia A. la Mar

67. 2 J.K. Laughton ed. *State Papers relating to the Defeat of the Spanish Armada* (Navy Records Society, 1894) Vol. II, p. 60
Letter from Howard to Walsingham, d. 8th August 1588, ccxiv. 50.

72. 3 *Ibid*: Vol. II, Appendix H. p. 390

4 *Ibid*: Vol. II, Appendix H. Ubaldino's MS (O.R.14.A.X) was discovered in the B.M. just as Laughton's Vol. I had gone to press, and he added a translation of Ubaldino's Dedicatory Epistle to Lord Howard in his Appendix to Vol. II. This entire document has been translated for inclusion in my *Christopher Marlowe and the Armada*, to be published shortly.

73. 5 *Transcript of the Stationers' Registers, 1554-1640*, ed. E. Arbor (London, 1876) Vol. III, f. 6

6 E.K. Chambers: *Elizabethan Stage*, Vol. IV, p. 104. At Richmond. 'Christmas. The Admiral's showed activities as well as plays this winter.'

74. 7 Greene's *Francescos Fortunes, or the Second Part of Neuer too Late* (1590) ed. Grosart, Vol. VIII, p. 132

75. 8 Greene: *Perimedes the Blacke-Smith* (1588) Sig. A3

9 Greene: *Menaphon* (1589) ed. Grosart, Vol. VI, p. 86

465

	10	Nashe: Preface to Greene's *Menaphon*, ed. Grosart, Vol. VI, pp. 26-27
76.	11	Nashe: *Pierce Penilesse, His Svpplication to the Diuell* (1592)
		Sig. B4, 1.12 ed. A.B. McKerrow, *Works of Nashe* (1958) Vol. I, p. 174
77.	12	Greene: *The Second Part of Neuer too Late* ed. Grosart, Vol. VIII, p. 132
79.	13	*Edward the Third* ed. G.C. Moore Smith (The Temple Dramatists, 1897)
		Preface, pp. xix-xx
		See 'The New Shakespeare Society's Proceedings', 1887-92, p. 58 for the article by Miss E. Phipson.
80.	14	*Ibid*: Preface pp. xii-xiii and p. xiv for a discussion of F.G. Fleay's opinions of the play *Edward the Third*.
	15	A.F. Hopkinson: *Shakespeare's Doubtful Plays* (1900) pp. 14-15
		Bakeless *op. cit*: Vol. II, p. 283
81.	16	*Ibid*: Vol. II, p. 282
	17	*Ibid*: Vol. II, p. 282. Bakeless is here citing Fleay's opinion with which he seems to be in agreement. See Fleay: *Outlines* (1883) p. 109; *Chronicle History of the life and work of William Shakespeare* (1886) p. 23 and pp. 118-19
	18	A.W. Ward: *History of English dramatic literature* (1875, 1899) Vol. I, pp. 352, 359-360. Vol. II, p. 223
	19	C.F. Tucker Brooke: *The Shakespeare Apocrypha* (1908) Introduction p. xxiii
	20	A.C. Swinburne: *A Study of Shakespeare* (1880) Appendix p. 234
		Swinburne embarks on an impassioned and lengthy critique of the play in which his opinion veers between extremes of eulogy and censure. Like other critics he totally fails to note its Armada connection.
82.	21	K. Warnke and L. Proescholdt: *Pseudo-Shakespearean Plays* (1886) Introduction, pp. xxx-xxxiv. Theirs is the first scholarly edition of this play based on the quartos of 1595 and 1596, and not merely referring to those of the 19th century scholars who copied each other's work based on Capell's collated edition of 1760.
84.	22	See Wraight: *Christopher Marlowe and the Armada* (to be published in 1993).
85.	23	Garrett Mattingly: *The Defeat of the Spanish Armada* (2nd ed. 1983) p.302
86.	24	*B.M. Cotton MSS. Julius* F.X. f.97^r
	25	Mattingly: *op. cit*: p. 269
	26	B.M. Cotton MSS Julius FX f.99^r
	27	Mattingly: op cit. p302
	28	J.K. Laughton: *op. cit*: Vol. I, pp. 279-280
		Letter, Fenner to Walsingham, d. July 17, *ccxii. 62*
88.	29	See Wraight: *Christopher Marlowe and the Armada* for a complete transcript of this MS. Julius FX f.99^r
89.	30	William Urry: *Christopher Marlowe and Canterbury* (1988) posthumously ed. Andrew Butcher. He does not give this information which was cited as appearing in Dr Urry's 'forthcoming book' in my *In Search of Christopher Marlowe* (1965) p. 26, n.10. Urry's book was long delayed by his struggle against his fatal illness.
90.	31	H.H. Hewitt: *The Organization of War under Edward III, 1338-62* (1966) N.Y. See pp. 63 and ff. He makes it clear that bows and arrows were the chief weapons of war of this time, and 'Great engines' mentioned

were devices for flinging stones. Cannon and guns were 'among English arms by 1346' and were employed at the siege of Calais.

	32	Raphael Holinshed: *The Chronicles of England, Scotlande, and Irelande* (London, 1577) 'King Edward the thirde' p. 909 (wrongly printed p. 915) top left-hand column.
95.	33	Bakeless: *op. cit*: Vol. II, Chapter XV, 'The Mighty Line', especially pp. 189-200
98.	34	Holinshed: *op. cit*: p. 924
99	35	William Armstrong ed. *Elizabethan History Plays* (1965) The World's Classics, O.U.P. Introduction: p. x
100.	36	*Ibid*: pp. ix-x
	37	Toby Robertson's production of *Edward the Third* (edited by Toby Robertson and Jeremy Brooks) opened 26th June 1987 at Clwyd Theatre, North Wales.
	38	For Zenocrate's lament see p. 17; Tamburlaine's famous threnody, p. 30
103.	39	*Edward the Third*, Act III, sc. 1, 11.73-76

CHAPTER IV   THREE PLAYS OF THE PEMBROKE PLAYERS

Page   *Ref.*

109.	1	Bakeless: *op. cit*: Vol. II, p. 207
112.	2	F.S. Boas: *Christopher Marlowe*, (1940) Appendix IX, p. 194
113.	3	Allison Gaw: *The Origin and Development of 1 Henry VI: In Relation to Shakespeare, Marlowe, Peele and Greene* (1926) Univ. of Southern California, p. 10
114.	4	Peter Alexander: *Shakespeare*, (1964) p. 77
116.	5	*Ibid*: p. 77
117.	6	*Ibid*: p. 73
	7	Alexander: *Shakespeare's Henry VI and Richard III* (1929) p. 95
118.	8	*Ibid*: pp. 70-71
120.	9	'Massacre at Paris Leaf' J.b.8. Folger Shakespeare Library, Washington D.C.
	10	See Wraight and Stern: *In Search of Christopher Marlowe* (1965) pp. 226 and 230-1 for photographic reproduction of this MS and discussion of its authenticity.
121.	11	*Ibid*.
	12	Alexander: *Shakespeare's Henry VI and Richard III*, p. 93
123.	13	*Ibid*: p. 102
124	14	Alexander: *Shakespeare*, p. 77
	15	*Ibid*: p. 76 Alexander gives no reference for this citation from Dover Wilson's works.
125	16	Bakeless: *op. cit*: Vol. II, pp. 242-3
126	17	*Ibid*: Vol. II, pp. 242-3
127	18	*Ibid*: Vol. II, pp. 230-1
129	19	Alexander: *Shakespeare's Henry VI and Richard III* p. 116

Page	Ref.	
131	1	Robert Greene: *The Repentance of Robert Greene Maister of Artes* (1592) Sig. D2ᵛ
132	2	See Greene's *A Quippe for an Vpstart Courtier* (1592) and Gabriel Harvey's *Foure Letters and certain Sonnets* (1592) 'The Second Letter'
	3	*Greenes Groats-Worth of witte* (1592) Sig. Fᵛ
135	4	*First Folio* (1623) Norton Facsimile ed. (1968) p. 9
136	5	J. Churton Collins. ed. *The Play and Poems of Robert Greene* (1905) Oxford, Vol. I, pp. 11-14
	6	*Ibid*: p. 14. *Dictionary of National Biography*, Vol. XXIII, p. 66
137	7	*The Repentance of Robert Greene*, Sig. C-Cᵛ
	8	*Ibid*: Sig. C3
138	9	Greene's *Farewell to Folly* (1591) 'Preface to the Gentlemen Students of both Vniuersities'
	10	Greene's Repentance, Sig. Bᵛ
139	11	Gabriel Harvey: *Foure Letters*, 'The Second Letter', Sig. B2ᵛ
	12	Greene's *Repentance*, Sig B2
140	13	*Ibid*: Sig. Bᵛ
	14	*Ibid*: Sig. C4ᵛ
	15	Thomas Nashe: *Strange Newes, of the intercepting certaine Letters* (1592) Sig. E4ᵛ See McKerrow, Vol. I, p. 287
141	16	Sir E. Brydges ed. *Archaica* (1814) Privately printed. Preface, Vol. II.
142	17	Greene: *Francescos Fortunes or The Second Part of Greenes Neuer too late* (1590) See Grosart, Vol. VIII, pp. 128-9
143	18	*Ibid*: Grosart, p. 129 and pp. 132-3
147	19	*Greenes Groats-Worth of witte* (1592) Sig. B-B4
	20	*Ibid*: Sig. B4
150	21	*Ibid*: Sig. D4-E
	22	*Ibid*: Sig. Eᵛ
	23	*Ibid*: Sig. E2
	24	Nashe: *Strange Newes*, Sig. E4ᵛ 11.34-38 McKerrow, Vol. I, pp. 287-8
	25	*Greenes Groats-Worth*, Sig. E2
151	26	*Ibid*: Sig. E2ᵛ-E3
152	27	Nashe: 'Preface' to Greene's *Menaphon*. Grosart, Vol. VI, pp. 26-27
154	28	Nashe: *A Countercvffe giuen to Martin Ivnior by the venturous, hardie and renowned Pasquill of England. cavaliero, from Gravesend Barge, the eight of August, the first and last yeere of Martinisme*, (1589) Sig. A4ᵛ 11.22-23 McKerrow, Vol. I, p. 64
	29	Richard Simpson: *The School of Shakspere* (1878) Vol. II, p. 355
158	30	Greene's *Groats-Worth*, Sig. E4ᵛ-F2ᵛ
159	31	Francis Meres: *Palladis Tamia* (1598) p.286ᵛ 'As *Anacreon* died by the pot, so George Peele by the pox.'
160	32	Allison Gaw: *op. cit*: p. 157
	33	Ivor Brown: *Shakespeare*, (1949) p. 172
161	34	*Henslowe's Diary* ed. R.A. Foakes and R.T. Rickert (1961, Cambridge) p. 94 fol. 48
162	35	W.W. Greg ed. *Henslowe Papers* (1907, London) pp. 64-5

G.F. Warner: *Catalogue of MSS and Muniments of Dulwich College* (1881) p. 36 MSS.I, Article 67.

I have followed Greg in his interpretation of the partly obliterated words in this much worn paper.

163   36   See *The Defence of Conny-catching by Cuthbert Cunny-catcher*, (1592) Sig. C3 for the contemporary reference to Greene's double-dealing.

        37   See pp. 170 ff. of the present work.

164   38   *Henslowe's Diary* ed. R.A. Foakes and R.T. Rickert and Greg's edition of the *Diary* (1908) in his Part 2, *Commentary* are the sources to be consulted for references to all these acquittances in the transactions concerning these plays of the Lord Admiral's company.

165   39   Henry Chettle: *Kind-Harts Dreame* (1592) Sig. B3

        40   *Ibid*: 'To the Gentlemen Readers'

CHAPTER VI   THE CASE FOR 'SHAKE-SCENE' PRESENTED BY THE NEW ORTHODOXY

Page   *Ref.*

168   1   Greene's *Groats-Worth*, Sig. F^v

        2   *Ibid*: Sig. F2-F2^v

169   3   *Ibid*: Sig. F2-F2^v

170   4   D. Allen Carroll: 'Greene's 'Vpstart Crow' Passage: A Survey of Commentary', p. 111; *Research Opportunities in Renaissance Drama, XXVIII*, (1985) Univ. of Kansas, ed. David M. Bergerson

        5   *Ibid*: p. 112

171   6   *Ibid*: p. 113

        7   *Ibid*: p. 113. Smart: *Shakespeare: Truth and Tradition* (1928) p. 196

        8   *Ibid*: p. 113. Smart: *op. cit.* and Alexander: *Shakespeare's Henry VI and Richard III* (1929)

172   9   *Ibid*: pp. 113-114

           Greene's *Francescos Fortunes, or The Second Part of Neuer too late* (1590) Sig. B4^v-C1

        10   *Ibid*: p. 114. Alexander: *op. cit*: p. 48

        11   *Ibid*: p. 114. Smart: *op. cit*: pp. 196-7

173   12   *Ibid*: pp. 114-115. Alexander: *op. cit*: pp. 43-44

174   13   *Ibid*: p. 115

        14   *Ibid*: p 117

175   15   Nashe: *Pierce Penilesse* (1592) 'A priuate Epistle of the Author to the Printer', Sig. C2 11.19-20 McKerrow, Vol. I, p. 153

        16   Harold Jenkins: *The Life and Work of Henry Chettle* (1934, London) p. 19

176   17   H. Chettle: *Kind-Harts Dreame* (1592) 'To the Gentlemen Readers'

177   18   Carroll: *op. cit*: p. 116

        19   S. Schoenbaum: *William Shakespeare: A Compact Documentary Life* (1977) p. 155

        20   Carroll: *op. cit*: p. 116

        21   *Ibid*: p. 116

178	22	Harold Jenkins: *op. cit*: pp. 20-21
	23	Carroll: *op. cit*: p. 116 Dover Wilson: *TLS*, 29 June, 1951, p. 405
	24	*Ibid*: p. 118 *Introductions to Shakespeare* (New York, Norton, 1961) pp. 124-127. Published originally as *Collins Classics Shakespeare* of 1951
	25	*Ibid*: p. 118. E.A.J. Honigmann: 'Shakespeare's 'Lost Source Plays'', *Modern Languages Review, 49* (1945) p. 295
	26	*Ibid*: p. 119
	27	*Ibid*: p. 121
180	28	*Ibid*: p. 122
	29	*Ibid*: p. 117. Janet Spens: *TLS*, 15 June, 1951, p. 373
	30	*Ibid*: p. 117 Andrew S. Cairncross: Introduction, *The Second Part of Henry VI*, (1957, London) p. xliii
181	31	Lewis Carroll: *Alice Through the Looking Glass* (1902 edition) Chapter VI, pp. 113-115
182	32	Allison Gaw: *op. cit*: p. 150, n.22
	33	*Ibid*: p. 150, n.22
	34	Schoenbaum: *op. cit*: p. 151
	35	Gaw: *op. cit*: p. 152, n.22
183	36	F.E. Halliday: *A Shakespeare Companion* (1952) pp. 162-3
	37	Carroll: *op. cit*: p. 123
	38	Nashe: *Pierce Penilesse*, 'A priuate Epistle of the Author to the Printer', Sig. C2ᵛ 11.10-11. McKerrow, Vol. I, p. 154

CHAPTER VII   JOHANNES FACTOTUM AND HIS WORKS

Page	Ref.	
186	1	Gabriel Harvey: *Foure Letters*, 'The Third Letter' Grosart: Vol. I, p. 194
187	2	J.C. Jordan: *Robert Greene* (1915) Columbia Univ. Studies in English and Comparative Literature. pp. 77-8 Jordan suggests he married in 1585-1586.
189	3	Muriel Bradbrook: *The Rise of the Common Player* (1962) pp. 85-6
	4	Richard Simpson: *op. cit*: Vol. II, p. 355
	5	*Ibid*: p. 355
190	6	W.W. Greg ed. *Fair Em* (1928, Malone Soc. Reprint) Introduction, p. viii
191	7	*Greenes farewell to Folly* (1591) Preface 'To the Gentlemen Students of both Vniuersities' (No pagination)
	8	*Ibid.*
192	9	*Martin Mar-sixtus* (1591) Sig. A3ᵛ
193	10	Meres: *op. cit*: p. 286ᵛ
194	11	Wm. Young: *History of Dulwich College* (1889) Vol. pp. 45-6 Young places Adlington in Cheshire, but there is an Adlington in Lancs, south of Preston. See Warner: Cat. pp. 62-3
195	12	E. Arbor ed. *Transcript of the Stationers' Register, 1554-1640*, Vol. 2 '2nd March 1581: Henry Carre: Lycensed vnto him vnder th[eh]andes of ye wardens A Ballad/Intituled, The Millers daughter of Manchester.'
	13	Alwin Thaler: *Faire Em & Shakespeare's Company?* in *Lancashire*, Publications of the Modern Languages Assoc. of America, Vol. XLVI, No. 3, Sept. 1931

14 *Derby Household Books* by William Ffarington, ed. F.R. Raines, *Chetham Society Remains*, XXXI (1853)

15 *Ibid*: p. 22

196 16 *Ibid*: pp. 34, 35, 36, 37, 63

197 17 Thaler: *op. cit*: pp. 651-653

18 Dasent: *Acts of the Privy Council, New Ser.* XIII, p. 184

19 *Greenes farewell to Folly*, Preface 'To the Gentlemen Students..'

198 20 *Chetham Society Remains*, LXVII, p. cclxxxi.

21 E. Baines: *History of the County Palatine and Duchy of Lancaster*, (1836) Vol. III, p. 235

22 Thomas Hearne: *Discourses of British Antiquaries* (1771) Vol. I, p. 262

199 23 Thaler: *op. cit*: p. 648

24 Warnke and Proescholdt: *Pseudo-Shakespearean Plays* (1883)
Faire Em: Introduction, p. x

25 Tucker Brooke: *Shakespeare Apocrypha*, Introduction p. xxxix

26 Richard Simpson: *op. cit*: Vol. II, p. 397
Simpson sees these as being Shakespeare's qualities. His views on this play and its authorship are very inconsistent.

27 Thaler: *op. cit*: pp. 648-9

203 28 Simpson: *op. cit*: p. 396

205 29 Greg ed. *Faire Em*, Introduction, p. viii
Greg gives an excellent resumé of the evidence supporting this dating.

30 Thaler: *op. cit*: p. 652, n.38
Chetham Society Remains, LXVII, p. ccclxxxi

206 31 William Ffarington: *Derby Household Books*, p. 34

32 *Ibid*: p. 34

33 *Ibid*: pp. 36-37

34 *Dictionary of National Biography*,
In January 1587/8 the Earl of Derby was made chief commissioner to treat for peace with Spain at Ostend.

35 *Derby Household Books*, p. 43

207 36 *Ibid*: p. 46

37 Thaler: *op. cit*: p. 658

38 *Derby Household Books*, p. 46

39 *Ibid*: p. 50

208 40 40 *Ibid*: pp. 56-57

41 *Ibid*: p. 56

42 *Ibid*: p. 58

209 43 *Ibid*: p. 62

44 *Ibid*: p. 65

45 *Ibid*: p. 63

46 *Ibid*: p. 66

47 Thaler: *op. cit*: pp. 654-655 and n.62

48 *Ibid*: p. 655, n.62

211 49 *Henslowe's Diary* ed. Foakes and Rickert, p. 187 fol. 96

212 50 *Henslowe's Diary* ed. Greg, *Part II, Commentary*, pp. 170-1, *The French Doctor*; p. 176, *Crack Me this Nut*.

51 *Diary*, ed. Foakes and Rickert, p. 103, fol. 53

52 *Diary, Part II*, ed. Greg, p. 197

Greg comments: 'This was evidently an old play belonging to Alleyn revised by Chettle on the occasion of its revival. 'The Vaivode', says Hazlitt, 'was possibly founded on the current incidents in the war between Transylvania and Austria'. Vaivode, or Voivode, is a title equivalent to general or governor in certain Slavonic countries.'

Chettle received xx^s. (£1) 'ffor his playe of vayvode' (29 Aug. 1598, fol. 49^v Foakes and Rickert, p. 97) Alleyn had sold the play to the company for £2 as an old play. As it was his property and no other author is known, it is the logical conclusion that he had written it, which Greg obstinately refuses to countenance as even a possibility. He does not argue the point; he simply does not admit it.

213	53	*Diary*, ed. Foakes and Rickert, p. 187, fol. 96
	54	*Diary, Part II*, ed. Greg, p. 220
	55	*Diary*, ed. Foakes and Rickert, p. 180. fol. 93
	56	*Diary, Part II*, ed. Greg, p. 167
214	57	*Diary*, ed. Foakes and Rickert, p. 181, fol. 93^v
	58	*Diary, Part II*, ed. Greg, p. 172
	59	*Ibid*: p. 172
	60	*Diary*, ed. Foakes and Rickert, p. 276
		Warner: *Catalogue*, MSS Vol. I, Article 11
	61	*Ibid*: p. 184, fol. 95
	62	*Ibid*: p. 49, fol. 22^v
215	63	*Diary, Part II*, ed. Greg, p. 181
	64	*Diary*, ed. Foakes and Rickert, p. 185, fol. 95
	65	*Ibid*: p. 185, fol. 95^v
	66	*Ibid*: p. 186, fol. 95^v
216	67	*Ibid*: p. 199, fol. 105; p. 208, fol. 109^v
	68	*Diary, Part II*, ed. Greg, p. 296
	69	*Ibid*: p. 296
	70	*Diary*, ed. Foakes and Rickert, p. 208, fol. 109
217	71	*Ibid*: p. 211, fol. 112

Diary, Part II, ed. Greg, p. 309. Greg merely comments that this play 'may have been an old one'. He does not consider Shaa's obvious literacy as a factor which combined with the other evidence cogently argues that he was selling his own play to the company.

	72	*Diary*, ed. Foakes and Rickert, p. 204, fol. 107
	73	*Diary, Part II*, ed. Greg, p. 176
	74	*Ibid*: pp. 223-4
218	75	*Diary*, ed. Foakes and Rickert, p. 205, fol. 108
	76	*Ibid*: p. 217, fol. 116^v
	77	*Diary, Part II*, ed. Grge, pp. 155-156

On *Tamar Cam* (as Greg calls this play) his commentary is brief and non-commital, expressing no opinion on its authorship.

Malone's *Variorum*, iii, p. 414, prints 'The plott of the *First parte of Tamar Cam*, giving the entrances and exits of actors, including some who are named, (e.g. 'H. Jeffs: Mr. Allen & Mr. Burne. exit') with sound effects &c. It is obviously a stage manager's play-plot. It has since been lost, but Greg reprints the 'plott' in his *Henslowe Papers* (1907) pp. 145-148 as '*Tamar Cam, 1602*', this being the date assigned to the plot on the basis of the actors named. Greg comments: *'Tamar Cam'* appears...to have belonged, not to the company, but to Alleyn, and he brought it with him when he rejoined the Admiral's men [on their return from their Continental tour when they were reunited with Alleyn]. These revived it as a new play, acting the first part 6 May and the second 11 June 1596. Finally, 2 Oct. 1602, the company bought the 'Boocke' of Alleyn for £2. This was the usual payment for an old play, and therefore probably only included Pt. I, though this is not specified.' (p. 144)

| 221 | 78 | See William Young: *The History of Dulwich College* (1889) Vol. II for his transcript of the whole of Edward Alleyn's *Diary*, dating from 29 Sept. 1617 to 1 Oct. 1622. Warner: *Cat.* MS. IX |

79   *Transcript of the Stationers' Register*, ed. E. Arbor, Vol. 2, f. 314

80   *Diary*, ed. Foakes and Rickert, p. 54, fol. 25

230   81   W.W. Greg: *Two Elizabethan Stage Abridgements: The Battle of Alcazar & Orlando Furioso: An Essay in Critical Bibliography* (1923, Oxford) Chapter VII, p. 138

82   *Ibid*: p. 139

83   *Ibid*: The MS begins at p. 168; the following are selections from parts of it.
Warner: *Catalogue*, MS.I. item 138.
This whole MS is reprinted by Greg in his *Henslowe Papers* (1907) at pp. 155-171

234   84   *The Defence of Conny-catching by Cuthbert Cunny-catcher, Licenciate in Whittington Colledge* (1592) Sig. C3

85   Greg: *op. cit*: pp. 127-8

235   86   *Diary, Part II*, ed. Greg, p. 336, Section V: 'Court Performances by the Various Companies During the Years 1583 to 1603'.
He gives 29 Dec. and 11 Feb. 1588/9 as dates for the Lord Admiral's Men. There is some uncertainty regarding the Queen's Men as both dates on 26 Dec. and 9 Feb. 1558/9 are listed by Greg with a question mark against the name of the company performing.

236   87   *Ibid*: p. 153

CHAPTER VIII   A NEW PLAY AT THE ROSE WITH ITS NEW LOOK

Page   *Ref.*

239   1   *Diary*, ed. Foakes and Rickert, p. 16, fol. 7

2   *Ibid*: p. 16, fol. 7

240   3   Nashe: *Pierce Penilesse*, Sig. F3 McKerrow, Vol. I, p. 212

243   4   Allison Gaw: *The Origin and Development of 1 Henry VI*, p. 64

244   5   *Ibid*: p. 54

6   *Ibid*: p. 56

7   *Ibid*: pp. 36-37

249   8   *Ibid*: pp. 56-58

9   *Ibid*: pp. 58-59

250   10   *Ibid*: p. 59

251   11   *Ibid*: p. 15

A.W. Ward: *History of English Dramatic Literature*, (1899, London) Vol. II, pp. 71-74

12   J.Q. Adams: *A Life of William Shakespeare* (1923, Boston) pp. 136, 214
C.F. Tucker Brooke ed. Yale edition of *Henry VI*, 138 ff.

13   F.G. Fleay: 'Who wrote 'Henry VI'?' *Macmillan's Magazine XXXIII*, Nov. 1875. pp. 50-62

14   Fleay: *Chronicle History of the Life and Work of Shakespeare* (1886, London) pp. 259-263. Amplifying the hypothesis announced in his Macmillan's Magazine article.

254   15   Gaw: *op. cit*: p. 68

16   *Ibid*: pp. 64-65

17   *Ibid*: p. 88

255   18   *Ibid*: p. 91

256   19   *Ibid*: pp. 72-73

257   20   *Ibid*: pp. 82-83

21   *Ibid*: pp. 106-107

22   *Ibid*: pp. 104, 105

260   23   *Ibid*: p. 106

24   *Ibid*: p. 60

25   *Ibid*: p. 107

26   *Ibid*: p. 88

261   27   *Ibid*: p. 129

262   28   *Ibid*: p. 137

263   29   *Ibid*: p. 137

30   *Ibid*: p. 140

31   *Ibid*: p. 141

264   32   *Ibid*: p. 108

33   *Ibid*: pp. 116-117

34   Jordan: *Robert Greene*, (1915) pp. 41-42

265   35   Gaw: *op. cit*: p. 111

36   *Ibid*: p. 116

37   *Ibid*: p. 117

38   *Ibid*: p. 121
H.D. Gray: 'The Purport of Shakespeare's Contribution to *1 Henry VI*' *Publications of the Modern Languages Association, XXXII*, 367-82 (Sept. 1917) p. 382

39   *Ibid*: pp. 110, 111

268   40   *Ibid*: pp. 122-123

41   *Ibid*: p. 108

269   42   *Ibid*: pp. 141-142

270   43   *Ibid*: pp. 144-145

271   44   *Ibid*: p. 143

275   45   *Ibid*: pp. 141-143

46   *Ibid*: p. 120

47   *Ibid*: p. 60

277   48   Gabriel Harvey: *Foure Letters*, 'The Second Letter' (1592)
Sig. B2 and B3

Page	Ref.	
282	1	*Diary*, ed. Foakes and Rickert, p. 19, fol.8
	2	Nashe: *Pierce Penilesse*, Sig. F4ᵛ 11. 13-15
		McKerrow, Vol. I, p. 215
	3	Hanspeter Born: *The Rare Wit and the Rude Groom: The Authorship of A Knack to Know a Knave in Relation to Greene, Nashe & Shakespeare* (1971, Francke Verlag, Bern) p. 5
		See Paul E. Bennett: 'A Critical Edition of A Knack to Know a Knave' pp. 4-6. (Univ. Microfilms, Ann Arbor, Michigan, 1952)
		Pietro Ubaldino: *Le Vite delle Donne Illustre* (1591) pp. 29-30
284	4	Born: *op. cit*: p. 7
		Born cites this in his Notes. Arthur Freeman: 'Two Notes on 'A Knack to Know a Knave'.' *Notes and Queries, IX*, N.S. (1962) 326-7. p. 327
285	5	*Ibid*: p. 37
		See Grosart, Vol. XI, p. 209.
	6	*Ibid*: p. 35
		Greenes Vision (1590) Grosart, Vol. XII, p. 281
286	7	Born: *op. cit*: pp. 35-36
	8	*Ibid*: p. 35
	9	*Ibid*: p. 35
	10	*Ibid*: p. 35
287	11	J.C. Collins: *Plays and Poems of Robert Greene*, Vol. I. 'General Introduction', p. 33
	12	*Ibid*: p. 34. 'The Black Booke' in which Greene intended to publish the names of those underworld villains known to him was never completed before his death. Collins tells us: 'It was the first thing...which he meant to publish after his recovery'. 'General Introduction' p. 34.
	13	*Ibid*: p. 34
288	14	Born: *op. cit*: p. 36
289	15	*Ibid*: p. 33
		Waldo F. McNeir: 'Robert Greene and 'John of Bordeaux'.' *PMLA, LXIV* (1949) 781-801, p. 789
	16	*Ibid*: p. 38
	17	McKerrow: *op. cit*: Vol. 5, Notes pp. 80 and 102
290	18	Born: *op. cit*: p. 4
	19	*Ibid*: p. 5
		The same topical conditions pertain as for *harey the vj* (see previous chapter p. 174) where the military aspect is reflected in the dramatized prominence given to Rouen. These plays emphasize the relevance of news-worthiness to the Elizabethan drama.
	20	*Ibid*: p. 5
		Dasent XXI, p. 391
291	21	*Ibid*: p. 5
		Dasent XXII, p. 392
	22	*Ibid*: p. 5
		Dasent XXII, pp. 411-2
	23	*Ibid*: p. 3
		See Bennett: *op. cit*: p. 56

	24	*Ibid*: p. 33
292	25	*Ibid*: pp. 28-29

Born gives these parallels from *Bacon* and *A Knack* and he adds many more to make an impressive case showing Greene's tendency to self-repetition throughout his canon of works. See pp. 29-30.

	26	*Ibid*: p. 30
293	27	*Ibid*: p. 30
	28	*Ibid*: p. 24
	29	*Ibid*: p. 46
294	30	*Ibid*: p. 51. See also pp. 48-51 for copious examples from Greene's works and discussion of this stylistic trait.
297	31	*Ibid*: p. 63. Born writes: 'Nashe's cruel streak is disagreeably revealed by the ending of his *Unfortunate Traveller*'.
	32	*Ibid*: p. 22
	33	*Ibid*: p. 22
	34	*Ibid*: p. 54
298	35	*Ibid*: p. 55
	36	*Ibid*: p. 20
		Bennett: *op. cit*: p. 89
	37	*Ibid*: p. 53
299	38	*Ibid*: p. 22
	39	Nashe: *Haue with you to Saffron-walden* (1596)
		McKerrow, Vol. III, p. 132
	40	Born: *op. cit*: p. 64 and Note 26.

He is referring to Proudfoot's unpublished ms. in which he points out that Nashe 'wrote satires on upstart gentlemen, the decay of hospitality, the strange ways of Puritans', and that he was also 'well acquainted with the history of King Edgar as recorded in Holinshed's *Chronicle*.'

300	41	*Ibid*: p. 73
	42	*Ibid*: p. 75
301	43	*Ibid*: p. 75
	44	Gabriel Harvey: *Pierces Supererogation* (1593)
		Grosart, Vol. III, p. 45
302	45	Richard Lichfield: *The Trimming of Thomas Nashe by Don Richardo de Campo* (1597)
		McKerrow, Vol. V, p. 9 and p. 107

Lichfield was the barber to Trinity College, Cambridge, to whom Nashe dedicated *Haue with you to Saffron-walden*.

	46	Born: *op. cit*: pp. 78-79
303	47	*Ibid*: p. 78
	48	*Ibid*: p. 59

See Edwin Haviland Miller: 'The Relationship of Robert Greene and Thomas Nashe (1588-92)': *Philological Quarterly, XXXIII*, (1954) 353-67. p. 359

See also H.C. Hart: 'Robert Greene's Prose Works', *Notes & Queries Xth Ser. IV*, (1905) and V, (1906).

304	49	*Ibid*: p. 75
305	50	Wraight: *Scanderbeg, the Young Marlowe* (Forthcoming publication)
	51	Born: *op. cit*: p. 102

	52	*Ibid*: pp. 102-103
		Kenneth Muir: 'Robert Greene as Dramatist' in *Essays on Shakespeare and the Elizabethan Drama in Honor of Harden Craig*, ed. Richard Hosley (1963, Columbia) pp. 45-54
307	53	Thomas Middleton: *The Black Book*. See A.H. Bullen ed. *The Works* of Thomas Middleton (1886, London) Vol. VIII, p. 25
	54	*Ibid*: p. 118
	55	*Ibid*: p. 119
	56	*Ibid*: p. 119
308	57	*Ibid*: pp. 119-120
		A.F. Falconer: *Shakespeare and the Sea* (1964, London) p. 124
	58	*Ibid*: p. 119
309	59	Nashe: *Haue with you to Saffron-walden*, Sig. D2^v
		McKerrow, Vol. III, p. 20, 11. 15-19 and 11. 23-24
310	60	*Ibid*: McKerrow, Vol. III, pp. 21-22
311	61	*Ibid*: Sig. F4^v-G1^v
		McKerrow, Vol. III, pp. 39-41
312	62	*Ibid*: Sig. G2^v 11. 35-37
		McKerrow, Vol. III, p. 42
315	63	Born: *op. cit*: p. 95
	64	*Ibid*: p. 95
	65	Harry Levin: *The Overreacher: A Study of Christopher Marlowe* (1952, London) p. 25
316	66	Born: *op. cit*: p. 135
	67	*Ibid*: p. 134
	68	*Ibid*: p. 139
	69	Bakeless: *op. cit*: Vol. II, Chapter XV, 'The Mighty Line', pp. 193-199
317	70	Born: *op. cit*: p. 139
	71	*Ibid*: p. 144
318	72	*Ibid*: p. 145
		Dover Wilson ed. *The First Part of Henry VI* (1952, Cambridge) p. xiv
	73	*Ibid*: p. 85
	74	*Ibid*: p. 85
	75	*Ibid*: p. 85
320	76	See Bakeless: *op. cit*: Vol. II, pp. 43-44
		Bakeless writes: 'The elegy is mentioned by Bishop Thomas Tanner (1674-1735) and by Thomas Warton the younger (1728-1790), but it does not appear in any of the three known copies of the play. There seems no doubt, however, that it once existed - perhaps in the fourth copy of the 1594 quarto, now lost, which is listed among the books of the early nineteenth century comedian, William E. Burton.'
		Bibliotheca dramatica. Catalogue...of William E. Burton, no. 1291, p. 95. Copies in NYPL, Yale, Columbia University, and Grolier Club.

CHAPTER X THE GREAT 'SHAKE-SCENE'

Page *Ref.*

| 322 | 1 | William Young: *The History of Dulwich College* (1889) Vol. II, p. 45 |
| | | Warner: *Catalogue* MS.I. Articles 135 & 136. |

In Ben Jonson's hand a translation of Martial's epigram, '*Vitam quae faciunt beatiorem*' (The things that make life happier are these), and Sir Henry Wotton's poem, 'How happy is he born and taught'.

    2   *Ibid*: Vol. II, p. 41.
Written on the back of a letter from Thomas Bowker about a mastiff whelp - 'a book Shaksper Sonetts - 5^d'.
Warne: MS.II.f.44^v

326   3   Thomas Fuller: *The Worthies of England: Lancashire and Wales* (1662, London) p. 223

        4   *Skialethia, or the Shadow of Truth* (1598) Sig. B2b

327   5   Thomas Nashe: *Pierce Penilesse*, Sig. F4^v
McKerrow, Vol. I, p. 215

        6   Ben Jonson: *Epigrammes* (1616) Epigram LXXXIX
The Poems of Ben Jonson, ed. Bernard H. Newdigate (1936, Oxford) p. 28

328   7   Warner: *Cat. MUN.* no. 80

        8   Alleyn's Pedigree, Copy in *B.M. Addit. MSS* 24487, f. 166.b
His paternal descent is borne out by the Visitation of Buckingham, 1634.

        9   Warner: *Cat. MUN.* no. 82. The Will is dated 10 Sept. 1570.
J.P. Collier prints it in Appendix I: *Memoirs of Edward Alleyn* (1841) p. 197

     10   Wm. Young: *op. cit*: Vol. I, Pt. 1, p. 41.
Warner: *Cat.* MS. V. Article 31 and MUN. no. 584, The Letters Patent for the foundation of Edward Alleyn's College of God's Gift.

     11   Young: *op. cit*: Vol. II, p. 2
Warner: *Cat. MUN.* no. 84

329   12   G.L. Hosking: *The Life and Times of Edward Alleyn* (1952) p. 17

     13   Warner: *Cat. MUN.* no. 106

     14   *Ibid*: MS.I, Article 2.
Diary, ed. Foakes and Rickert, p. 273

330   15   *Borough of Leicester: Hall Papers*, Vol. I, pp. 38-42 under date 6th March 2583/4
Young: *op. cit*: Vol. II, p. 3

     16   *Ibid*.
Young: *op. cit*: Vol. II, p. 4

     17   *Ibid*.

331   18   *Ibid*.

     19   *Ibid*.
Young: *op. cit*: Vol. II, pp. 4-5

333   20   Young: *op. cit*: Vol. II, p. 244. He gives a transcript of the entire *Diary*.
Warner. *Cat.* MS.IX *Alleyn's Diary*.

     21   Albert Cohn: *Shakespeare in Germany in the Sixteenth and Seventeenth Centuries* (1865) p. xxxvii

334   22   Warner: *Cat.* MS.I. Article 15
Diary, ed. Foakes and Rickert, Appendix I, p. 282

336   23   *Ibid*: p. 6, fol. 2

339   24   Nashe: *Summer's Last Will and Testament* (1600)
McKerrow: Vol. III, pp. 282-4 11. 1574-1615

342   25   Warner: *Cat.* MS.I. Article 11

		Diary, ed. Foakes and Rickert, pp. 276-77
343	26	*Ibid*: MS.I. Article 12
		Ibid: pp. 277-78
344	27	*Ibid*: p. 278
	28	*Ibid*: MS.I. Article 13
		Ibid: pp. 278-79
345	29	*Ibid*: MS.I. Article 13
		Ibid: pp. 279-80
	30	*Ibid*: MS.I. Article 14
		Ibid: pp. 280-81
348	31	Young: *op. cit*: Vol. II, p. 58 and n.
		The book is no longer in Dulwich College Library.
		G.F. Warner notes that it was probably *The General Practise of Physicke &c. translated from the German of Christopher Wirtzung by Jacob Mosan* (1605, London)
	32	Catherine Drinker Bowen: *Francis Bacon: The Temper of a Man* (1963, Boston, Toronto) p. 221
349	33	Warner: *Cat.* MS.I. Article 30
		Greg: *Henslowe Papers*, p. 52. Foakes and Rickert omit the forged entries.
350	34	*Diary*, ed. Foakes and Rickert, p. 35, fol. 15.
		This is followed by a record of weekly repayments of 'vs.' by Jones until the debt is settled.
	35	*Ibid*: p. 37, fol. 16
	36	*Ibid*: p. 37
351	37	Greg: *Henslowe Papers*, Appendix I, pp. 113-123.
		Documents now lost. Reprinted from Malone (1790) Vol. I, Pt. 2, p. 300 and *Variorum'* (1821) Vol. III, p. 309
	38	J.P. Collier: *Memoirs of Edward Alleyn*, (1841) p. 21
354	39	Young: *op. cit*: Vol. II, p. 49
355	40	*Ibid*: Vol. II, p. 137
		Warner: *Cat.* MS.I. Edward Alleyn's *Diary*
356	41	*Ibid*: Vol. II, p. 78 MS. IX fol. 11^v
	42	*Ibid*: Vol. II, pp. 79-80 MS. IX fol. 12^v
	43	*Ibid*: Vol. II, p. 80 MS. IX fol. 12^v
	44	*Ibid*: Vol. II p. 116 MS. IX fol. 26
358	45	Young: *op. cit*: Vol. II, p. 53. Warner: *Cat.* MS. I.
	46	*Ibid*: Vol. II, p. 69. *Ibid*.
359	47	*Diary*, ed. Foakes and Rickert, p. xli and pp. 299-300

CHAPTER XI   THE ROSE

Page	*Ref.*	
363	1	Warner: *Cat.* MUN. no. 15
		Greg: *Henslowe Papers*, p.1
	2	*Henslowe's Diary* ed. Greg. Part 2, pp. 43-45
366	3	Warner: *Cat.* MUN. no. 16
		Greg: *Henslowe Papers*, pp. 2-4
		Diary, ed. Foakes and Rickert, pp. 304-306
368	4	*Diary*, ed. Foakes and Rickert, p. 19, fol. 8

369	5	*Ibid*: p. 20, fol. 8
	6	*Ibid*: p. 20, fol. 8^v
370	7	Warner: *Cat.* MS.I. Article 18
	8	*Henslowe's Diary*, ed. Greg, Part 2, pp. 50-51
		W. Rendle: *Southwark* (1878) p. 8
	9	B.M. *Lansdowne MSS 71*, ff. 28 and 32
371	10	Greg: *op. cit*: pp. 51-52
		Acts of the Privy Council, 1591-2, xxii, p. 549
372	11	Warner: *Cat.* MS.I. Article 16
		Diary, ed. Foakes and Rickert, pp. 283-284
373	12	*Ibid*: MS.I. Article 17
		Ibid: pp. 284-285
		See also Greg: *Henslowe Papers*, pp. 42-43
374	13	*Henslowe's Diary*, ed. Greg. Part 2, p. 50
		Acts of the Privy Council, 13 August 1592
376	14	*Diary*, ed. Foakes and Rickert, p. 21, fol. 9
	15	*Ibid*: p. 21, fol. 8^v
	16	George Chapman, *Shadow of Night* (1594)
377	17	B.M. *Harleian MSS 6849* fol. 218
378	18	*Henslowe's Diary* ed. Greg, Part 2, p. 79
	19	E.K. Chambers: *Elizabethan Stage*, Vol. II, pp. 92-96
	20	F.S. Boas: *Works of Kyd*, p. 1xiv
	21	Tucker Brooke: *The Life of Christopher Marlowe and the Tragedy of Dido Queen of Carthage* (1930) pp. 46-47
	22	Bakeless: *op. cit*: Vol. II, p. 258 and n.119
380	23	*Diary*, ed. Foakes and Rickert, p. 21, fol. 9
	24	*Ibid*: p. 21, fol. 9
	25	*Ibid*: p. 21, fol. 9
381	26	*Ibid*: p. 187, fol. 96
382	27	Bakeless: *op. cit*: Vol. II, p. 91

| | 28 | The press reviews give overall support to the view that *The Massacre at Paris* must originally have been an impressive, contemporary, and indeed unique political drama that dared to present a critical appraisal of a recent political event. |

The Guardian, Thursday Jan. 31 1963, by Christopher Driver (excerpt): 'Marlowe's account of the massacre of the Huguenots written 20 years after the event and four years after the Spanish armada is an essay in Protestant McCarthysim touched up à la James Bond. It survives in an apparently truncated version which yet provides a part which Bernhardt once thought worth playing, and one or two speeches of which Faustus might not have been ashamed. Racy stuff. There is one particularly Bondish episode, in which a playful lecher called Mugeroun cuts off a man's ear for stealing his gold buttons off his hose at a levée, makes love to the pregnant wife of the Duc de Guise (the villain of the massacre), and is consequently shot by the most comical, bawdiest and least competent hired assassin on the English stage....The true villain in the author's eyes was not Catherine de Medici nor the Duc de Guise but religion itself. The dramatic blood bath is only fashionable anti-popery. The cast of the Marlowe's Society's devotees at the Chanticleer Theatre died their deaths with notable aplomb, and Michael Ferguson's production, neatly alternating off-stage drum taps with on-stage heel taps, should do something to instil a sense of proportion into contemporary Anglo-French relations.

Daily Telegraph and Morning Post, Thursday Jan. 31 1963:
Christopher Marlowe's 'The Massacre at Paris' is such a stage orgy of murder that almost the first qualification for those taking part is an ability to be killed and dragged across the stage in a convincingly lifelike manner. This qualification was amply met...but it was a pity that the most gruesome touch - the tolling of a bell calling 'the Devil's Matins' was not audible. The action, taken at a brisk pace, was matched by the eager malice of John Sheppard as the Duke of Guise, leader of the massacre. A special word of praise to Dolly Wraight for her delicious sketch of the Duchess of Guise. Producer: Michael Ferguson, M.M.S.'

The Times Thursday Jan. 31 1963:
(Commenting on the truncated text) 'The company brought a kind of competence, springing from a thorough familiarity with the text and from pleasure in their association with the enterprise, to their delivery of the lines. Their performance was smoothly orchestrated. It was no reflection upon them or the director Mr. Michael Ferguson that the play constantly let them down, that in the massacre at Paris, while practically everyone was stabbed, not blood came out but sawdust. Guise's first soliloquy, almost alone in the play, sounded as though some of the lines were straight from Marlowe. As for the rest, they were from Marlowe by way of - whom? One felt that last night's players served him, whoever he was more intelligently than he served the poet.'

The Stage and Television Today, February 7 1963:
'The play was well directed by Michael Ferguson...and the first entrance of the Duke of Guise was a stroke of theatrical ingenuity. He delivered his terrifying monologue while leaning nonchalantly on the side of the stage, presenting a picture of extreme ruthlessness. The set was simple but effective, thanks to excellent use of lighting. R.W.S.'

	29	*Diary*, ed. Foakes and Rickert, pp. 9-13, ff. 4 and 5^v
383	30	*Ibid*: pp. 10, 11, ff. 4, 4^v
	31	*Ibid*: p. 3, fol. 1
384	32	*Ibid*: pp. 21-22, fol. 9
	33	*Ibid*: pp. 22-37, ff. 9-16
385	34	*Ibid*: p. 22, fol. 9
	35	*Ibid*: p. 94, fol. 48
	36	*Ibid*: pp. 12-121, fol. 62^v
386	37	*Ibid*: pp. 83-84, fol. 43
	38	*Ibid*: p. 56, fol. 26
	39	*Ibid*: p. 60, fol. 27^v
389	40	*Ibid*: p. 94, fol. 48
	41	*Henslowe's Diary*, ed. Greg, Part 2, p. 134

See Greg's chapter on 'Dramatic Finance' pp. 127-137, which is still the most authoritative contribution we have on this subject.

390	42	*Diary*, ed. Foakes and Rickert, 'Introduction', p. xxviii
	43	*Henslowe's Diary*, ed. Greg, Part 2, p. 45
	44	Foakes and Rickert: *op. cit*: p. 56, fol. 26
391	45	Greg: *op. cit*: p. 131
	46	Greg: *Henslowe Papers*, p.24
		Warner: *Cat*. MUN. no. 52
	47	*Ibid*: pp. 87-88
		Ibid: MS.I. Article 106
392	48	*Diary*, ed. Foakes and Rickert, pp. 139-140, fol. 71^v
393	49	*Ibid*: p. 96, fol. 48^v
394	50	*Ibid*: pp. 50-51, fol. 23
395	51	*Ibid*: p. 51, fol. 23
	52	*Ibid*: pp. 55-56, fol. 25^v
	53	*Ibid*: p. 56, fol. 26
396	54	*Ibid*: pp. 36-37, fol. 15^v and pp. 54-55, ff. 25 and 25^v
	55	*Ibid*: pp. 56-59, ff. 26, 26^v and 27
397	56	*Ibid*: p. 56, fol. 26 and p. 30, fol. 12^v
	57	*Ibid*: p. 199, fol. 105
398	58	*Ibid*: pp. 232-233, fol. 238 and pp. 236-237, ff. 235, 234^v
400	59	*Ibid*: p. 240, fol. 232
	60	*Ibid*: p. 238, fol. 233
	61	*Ibid*: p. 239, fol. 233
	62	*Ibid*: pp. 239-240, fol. 233^v
401	63	*Ibid*: p. 240, f. 232
	64	*B.M. Egerton MSS* 2623, fol. 19
		See W.W. Greg: *Collections*, Vol. IV, pp. 27-28 (1956. Malone Soc.) Discovered by Greg, identified as belonging to fol. 231 in Henslowe's *Diary*. See Foakes and Rickert: *op. cit*: pp. 268-9
	65	*Diary*, ed. Foakes and Rickert, p. 241, fol. 23
	66	*Ibid*: p. 241, fol. 231
	67	*Ibid*: p. 241, fol. 231
	68	*Ibid*: pp. 241-2, fol. 230^v
402	69	*Ibid*: p.232, fol. 238
	70	*Ibid*: p. 233, fol. 237
	71	*Ibid*: p. 234, fol. 236
	72	*Ibid*: p. 236, fol. 235
	73	*Ibid*: p. 237, fol. 234
403	74	*Ibid*: p. 6, fol. 2^v
	75	*Ibid*: p. 7, fol. 2^v
	76	*Ibid*: p. 213, fol. 114^v
	77	*Ibid*: p. 213, fol. 115
	78	*Ibid*: p. 214, fol. 115

CHAPTER XII   THE BEAR GARDEN AND THE FORTUNE

Page	*Ref.*	
405	1	Greg: *Henslowe Papers*, pp. 97-98
		Warner: *Cat*. MS.II. Article 1.
406	2	*Ibid*: p. 98

		Ibid: MS.II. Article 1.
3		*Ibid*: pp. 99-100. Greg prints Langworth's letter showing his ruffled feelings.
		Ibid: MS.II. Article 2.
407	4	*Diary*, ed. Foakes and Rickert, p. 286
		Warner: *Cat*. MS.I. Article 26.
408	5	*Ibid*: p. 286 MS.I. Article 36^v
	6	*Brown's Travels* (1685) p. 108
		Robt. Wilkinson: *Londina Illustrata* (1819) Vol. I (2) p. 176^v
	7	Warner: *Cat*. MUN. no. 25
	8	*Diary*, ed. Foakes and Rickert, p. 6, fol. 2 and pp. 233-4, fol. 237
412	9	Robt. Wilkinson: *op. cit*: Vol. II, p. 141
413	10	*Diary*, ed. Foakes and Rickert, p. 288
		Greg: *Henslowe Papers*, pp. 49-50
		Warner: *Cat*. MS.I. Article 27
		Redcross Street is no longer extant unless this is a misnomer for Whitecross Street near Golding (or Golden) Lane.
	11	Warner: *Cat*. MS.I. Article 29
		Diary, ed. Foakes and Rickert, p. 290
		Greg: *Henslowe Papers*, p. 51
415	12	*Henslowe Diary*, ed. Greg, Part 2, p. 62
		Greg also rejects the view that the Globe was round.
		'In all points unspecified the house was to be exactly similar to the Globe, which it would seem had been built by Streete...except that all the chief supports were to be square and wrought pilaster-wise with 'carved proporcōns Called Satiers'.'
420	13	Warner: *Cat*. MUN. no. 22
		Diary, ed. Foakes and Rickert, pp. 306-315. Including the accounts written on the reverse.
		Greg: *Henslowe Papers*, pp. 4-7
	14	*Diary*, ed. Foakes and Rickert, pp. 191-192, ff. 98^v-99
421	15	*Ibid*: p. 137, fol. 70^v
	16	*Ibid*: p. 302
		Warner: *Cat*. MS. VIII, fol. 6^v: MUN. no.20
	17	Young: *op. cit*: Vol. II, p. 256
		Warner: *Cat*. MUN. nos. 36 and 38
422	18	*Diary*, ed. Foakes and Rickert, p. 302
		Warner: *Cat*. MS. VIII, fol. 6^v
	19	*Ibid*: p. 301
		Ibid: MS.VIII, fol. 5^v
423	20	*Henslowe's Diary*, ed. Greg, Part 2, pp. 63-64
		Warner: *Cat*. MUN. no.53 dated 15 Feb. 1615/16
	21	*Diary*, ed. Foakes and Rickert, pp. 196-209, ff. 102^v-110
	22	*Ibid*: p. 209, fol. 109^v
424	23	*Ibid*: pp. 209-210, fol. 110
	24	Warner: *Cat*. MUN. no.2
		Henslowe's Diary, ed. Greg, Part 2, pp. 56-57.
		Greg gives details of these transactions.
	25	*Ibid*: MUN. no.20

	26	*Ibid*: MUN. no.38, MS.I. Article 57
		Young: *op. cit*: Vol. II, pp. 258-9
		Greg: *Henslowe Papers*, pp. 17-18
425	27	*Ibid*: MUN. no.33
		Young: *op. cit*: Vol. II, p. 258
		Greg: *op. cit*: pp. 13-14
	28	*Ibid*: MUN. no.56
		Greg: *op. cit*: p. 28
	29	*Ibid*: MS.IX
		Young: *op. cit*: Vol. II, p. 225 and f-n.2
	30	*B.M.Addit.MSS* 4174, f. 225ᵛ
		Court and Times of James I, Vol. II, p. 280
426	31	Greg: *Henslowe Papers*, p. 30 and f-n.
		See his Addendum, p. 112 re: these leases
		Warner: *Cat.* MUN. nos. 58, 59, 60, 62, 63, 64
427	32	*Cal. State Papers Dom. 1603-1610*, p. 154. Dated 20 July 1604.
	33	Warner: *Cat.* MS.II, Article 6
		Young: *op. cit*: Vol. II, pp. 19-20
	34	*Ibid*: MS.II, Article 5
		Greg: *Henslowe Papers*, p. 101
	35	*Ibid*: MS.II, Article 9
		Greg: *op. cit*: p. 104
428	36	*Ibid*: MS.II, Article 9
		Greg: *op. cit*: p. 105
429	37	*Ibid*: MS.II, Article 38
		Young: *op. cit*: Vol. II, p. 26
	38	*Ibid*: MS.II, Article 39
		Young: *op. cit*: Vol. II, p. 26
	39	*Cal. State Papers Dom. James I, 1611-1618. Vol. LXII*, p. 17. d. March 20, 1611, *Warrant. Bk.ii*, p. 198 2nd series 1611-18, p. 17
		Young: *op. cit*: Vol. II, p. 27
	40	*Diary*, ed. Foakes and Rickert, p. 264, ff. 127 and 126ᵛ

CHAPTER XIII THE END OF AN ERA

Page *Ref.*

432	1	Warner: *Cat.* MS.I. Article 39
		Greg: *Henslowe Papers*, p. 61
	2	*Ibid*: pp. 61-62
434	3	*Diary*, ed. Foakes and Rickert, pp. 297-298
		Warner: *Cat.* MS.I. Article 38
435	4	*Henslowe's Diary*, ed. Greg, Part 2, pp. 13-14
436	5	Thomas Dekker: *The Whole Magnificent Enterteinment..* B.M. edition printed 'at London by E. Allde for Tho. Man the yonger. 1604.'
	6	Ben Jonson: *'B.JON. His Part of King James his Royall and Magnificent Entertainment...15 of March. 1603.'*
437	7	Dekker: *op. cit*. No pagination in early pages.
	8	*Ibid*: Sig. B4ᵛ-C
438	9	Jonson: *op. cit*: Sig. A3; Speech for *Genius* B2ᵛ; for *Tamesis* B4ᵛ

APPENDIX A   ALEXANDER v. TUCKER BROOKE CONCLUDED: THE X AND Y TEXTS

APPENDIX B   PARALLELISMS

Index

Adams, J.Q., 251

Adams, Robert, 71

Alexander, Peter, x, xi, 111–3, *Shakespeare's Henry VI and Richard III* (1929), 113; *Shakespeare* (1964), 114–25, 171–4, 183, 184, 244, 278, 317; Appendix A, 449–54

Alexander, Sir William, Lord Stirling, 57

Allen, Giles, 412

Alleyn, Edward, ix-xiv; actor, 2–3, 48, 65,75–7, 153–5; see also under *Tamburlaine, Jew of Malta, Dr. Faustus*; early acting career, 2, 186–7, 330–2; career reviewed, 322, 326–8, 376; playing with other companies, 376; first retirement from the stage, 385–7, 432–47; loyalty to Marlowe, 381; actor-manager, 159, 164, 213, 250; efficient co-management of the Rose, 391–2; association with Strange's Men, 333–48; handing over of management of the Rose, 400–1, 424; return from retirement to build own theatre, 411–26

Books owned, 322–4

Charity, xiv, 162–3, 220, 275, 322, 335; almshouses built, 413; planning his College of God's Gift, 424, 445, 447

Chettle, anxious to please, 184–5

Crack Me This Nut, 217

Diary, 210, 216, 220, 325, 333, 348, 352; shopping and tailoring accounts, 355–8; the Fortune burnt, 425; musical education for his poor orphans, 445; comment on the weather, 358

Dekker, his friend, 435–46

Dr. Faustus, 2–3, 64, 76, 158; probably owned playscript, 211, 380–1; benefit performance at first retirement, 386–8, 399–400

Education, 2, 88, 188, 210, 228, 324–5

Edward the Third, lampooned by Greene and Nashe, 65, 72–7

Faire Em, 190–9; Lancashire connection, 194, 205; possible première at Lancashire mansion of the Earl of Derby, 208; association with the Windmill, 190, 210; stylistic characteristics of Alleyn's authorship, 219–20, 224–8

Family: early life, 328–32; see also under names of members of his family

Fortune Theatre, 384, 411–32

French Doctor, The, 211–2, 217

'Genius of the City', 424, 437, 443, 447

Greene, Robert: envious of Alleyn, his *bête noire*, xiii, 60–2, 64, 65, 72, 74–7, 152–5, 159–61, 190, 198; see also under *"Shake-scene"*; business connections with, 161, 184, 229, 236; double dealing over *Orlando Furioso*, 234–6; head-on clash in writing of *harey the vj*, 269–79; timing of Greene's scandalous attack, 337; accuses Alleyn of heartless exploitation, 159–60, 184–5; Alleyn smitten with remorse, 320

harey the vj, 239, 241, 243; playing Cardinal Winchester, 250; as collaborative Author C, 266–7, 269–72, 274–6

Henslowe, xi, xii-xiii, 169, 184–5; joined him at the Rose, 236, 240; becomes step-father-in-law, 335,

486

337; both diarists, 358,361; letters to, 342–8, 406–7; business partnership, 384–399; loss of Alleyn heavy blow, 400–3; Bear Garden collaboration and building of the Fortune, 405–32; personal relationships, xiii, 406–7

Heywood's accolade, 327

Inventories, 348–51, 355–7

Jew of Malta as Barabas, 2–3, 44, 64, 76, 211; famous in the role, 327–8, 339; performed at Newington Butts, 369, 376; playscript owned, 380–1

Jocasta, 48–9

"Johannes Factotum", 186, 190–1, 322, 354

Jonson, Ben, 327 407

A Knack to Know an Honest Man, 220–9

A Knack to Know a Knave, 220–1, 229, 281–4

Knighthood aspired to, 164

Lancashire connections, 194

Landowner/Landlord, 344, 354, 355, 402, 411, 421–33

Letters: to wife, 340–2; from wife, 433–5

Longshanks, 217

Lord Admiral's Men, xii-xiii; script of *Tamburlaine* read, 39; *Tamburlaine* performed, 46, 58; played at Court, 73; Alleyn the company's leading actor, 155, 186–8; company's playscripts, 211–9, 351; go on Continental tour, 340; amalgamation with Strange's Men, 332–3; return from Continent, 380; Alleyn's retirement, 399–401, 414

Lord Strange's Men, 187, 238–76, 332–3

Love of Ceremony, 220, 241

Mahomet (Mahemett), 213, 217

Marlowe, 2–3; theatrical partnership, 38–40, 47–52, 72–3, 76, 237, 238–9;

collaboration in *harey the vj*, 241, ff; lampooned together by Greene and Nashe, 60–1, 64, 76–7; admired Marlowe, 202, 233, 381; bought/ owned his plays, 211, 219, 381; see also under *Tamburlaine* and other plays

Marriage, xiii, 166–7, 221, 228 335, 337–8, 384; his second marriage, 210

Massacre at Paris, playscript owned/ sold by Alleyn, 211, 219, 381; first performance, 369, 379

Massey, Charles, 216

Master of the Bears, 408, 411, 422, 426, 430–1

Medicine, herbal remedies, 340, 348, 354

'*Memorandum Book*', 421–2

Money-lender, 159, 161–3, 166, 168–9

Musician, 329, 445, 449

Nashe, satirises him, 57, 60–2, 72–3, 74–6, 80; changed attitude, praising him, 283

Orlando Furioso, 229–39; sold to the Lord Admiral's and the Queen's Men, 180, 234–6

Patron, Lord Admiral, Charles Howard, 284, 332–3, 372, 413, 432

Philip of Spain, 217

Physique, 2, 250, 322, 326, 411; and personality, 212, 277, 342, 353–5, 358, 447

Plague, 336–48, 369–75, 432–5; Henslowe's letter giving data, 343

Playwright, xii-xiii; as the playwriting Player in the *Groatsworth* tale, 149–51, 164–6; acquittances for plays in Henslowe's *Diary*, 211–9; lampooned as author of *Faire Em*, 191–210; *A Knack to Know an Honest Man*, 220–9, 236; *harey the vj*, 269–79, 443–5; see plays listed separately

(1971), 283–4, 289–91, 297–8, 301–9, 315–9

Borne, (Bird), William (with Rowley), *Judas*, 164, 215, 400, 425, 442–3, 447

Boswell, James, 352

Bowes, Ralph, 405–7, 411

Bowle, Clement, 383

Bradbrook, Muriel, 188

Bradstreit, John, 333

Brayne, John, 412,

Brewe, Patrick, 421, 424

Brill or Broyle, Ringmer, Sussex, 405, 406, 435

British Museum, 70

Brown, Ivor, *Shakespeare* (1949), 160

Browne, Edward, 330, 332

Browne, John, 328, 329

Browne, Robert, 329, 330, 332, 333, 343, 433

Bruno, Giordano, 202

Bryan, George, 238

Brydges, Sir Edward, 141

Brystow, James, 401

Burby (or Burbie), Cuthbert, (printer) of *The Reign of King Edward the Third* (1595), 73, 221, 337

Burbage, Cuthbert, 412

Burbage, James (elder), 241, 333, 366, 411–4

Burbage, Richard, 110, 169, 183, 238, 278, 324, 326, 366, 411, 414, 416, 426, 432, 442

Burbage's Company, xii

Burgundy, Duke of, 274

Burghley, Lord, 70, 108, 370

Caesar, Dr. Julius, 405

Caine, 132

Cairncross, Andrew S., 180

Caldewall, Rev., 208

Cambine, Andrew, *Turkish Affares*, 18; *Two Very Notable Commentaries* (1562) 18

Cambridge University, 6, 7, 38, 60, 136, 186, 189, 301, 305, 324

Campion, Father, 197

Canterbury, 5, 7, 8, 33, 45, 46, 67, 270 339, 378

Canterbury, Archbishop of, 5, 220, 338, 353

Canterbury Cathedral, 5, 67, 68

Canterbury, Raph, 356

Carey, George, 379

Carlton, Sir Dudley, 425

Carroll, D. Allen, *Green's 'Vpstart Crow' Passage: A Survey of Commentary* (1985) 170–4, 177, 180, 183

Cartwright, William, 425

Cecil, Lord Robert, 413

Chaderton, Bishop of Chester, 197, 205

Chaloner, Francis, 433, 435

Chaloner, Mary, 433, 435

Chaloner, Thomas, 433, 435

Chamberlain, John, 425

Chambers, 378

Chanticleer Theatre, 382

Chapman, George, 377, 378; *The Shadow of Night* 377; (with Jonson) *'Eastward Hoe'* 54

Charles I, King of England, 56

Charles II, King of England, 199

Charles VI, King of France, 33

Chettle, Henry, 165, 166, 174–6, 178, 180, 184, 212, 218, 219, 445; *Kind Hart's Dream* 165, 175; *Reply or Apology* 165, 174, 180, 184

Cholmley, John, 363–6, 383, 384, 390, 393, 397–9

Clare Hall, Cambridge, 136

Clarke, Eleanor Grace, 19

Clavijo, Ruy Gonzales de, 33

Clink, Liberty of, 336, 340, 371, 408, 411

Cockpit, The (Theatre), 2, 327

East, Gilbert, 420
Edmonds, Lady, 406
Edward, The Black Prince, 65, 67, 68, 72, 102, 153
Edward II, King of England, 127
Edward III, King of England, 66, 68, 82, 89–90, 95, 98, 108
Edward the Second, Marlowe, 1, 80, 109, 112; parallelisms with *The Contention* and *True Tragedy*, 114, 117, 123, 124; compared to *Richard II*, 125–6; historical transposition for dramatic effect, 127–8; 256; Appendix B, 455
Edward the Third, 65, 68–72; Armada reflections in the text, 82–90; launch of English historical drama, 66, 108; Greene and Nashe identify author and actor, 72, 74–7; modern critics, 79–82; stylistic comparisons with *Tamburlaine*, 79, 91–5; the love episode, 80, 82, 91–9, 104, 105–6; the *"Nonpareille"*, 70, 71, 86–7, 89; Marlowe's Armada report, 67, 70–2, 82, 86–9; ritual arming of the Prince, 101; basic theme, the education of princes, 99–100, 106–7; use of rhyme, 105–6; a 'first' in Marlowe's canon, 108; 235, 309
Efferhen, Heinrich von, *Book of Sermons* (1571), 22
Elizabeth I, Queen of England, 1, 3, 66–7; performance of play at court, 74; her own company, 234–5, 332, 242; her admiration for Alleyn, 325, 413–4; enjoyed bear baiting, 381, 406, 427
Elizabeth II, Queen of England, 1
Essex, Earl of, 37, 242, 290

Fabian, 274–5
Faire Em, performed in London, 185; authorship considered, 190–7;

Lancashire connection, 194, 197–200; Alleyn's hand detected, 201–4; first performance in patron's home, 205–9; Greene's satirical attack on author, 191–4; comparison with *A Knack to Known an Honest Man*, 227–8
Falconer, A.F., *Shakespeare at Sea* (1964), and *A Glossary of Shakespeare's Sea and Naval Terms including Gunnery* (1965), 307
Farewell to Folly, Greene, 138, 187, 190, 192, 197, 285
Farmer, Richard, 116
Faunte, Sir William of Foston, 429, 430
Faustus, Doctor, Marlowe, 1–2; Marlowe's most personal creation, 3; Marlowe an essentially religious thinker, 44; play imitated, 56; Alleyn famous in the role, 64, 76; probably owned by Alleyn, 211, 381; 105, 109; written probably 1589 and revised 1592, 158; imagery personalising the elements, 308–9; chosen by Alleyn for his final performance, 386–8, 397–8
Fenner, Thomas, Captain of the *"Nonpareille"*, 70, 86, 89
Ffarington, William, 195, 205–9
Field, Nathaniel, 391
First Folio, The, 82, 113–6, 119, 128, 134–5, 240, 243, 245, 251–4, 273, 379, 426
Fleay, F.G., 80, 194, 199, 213, 214, 219, 251–2, 254, 267–9, 366
Flowers, *Visitation of Lancashire* (1567), 198
Foakes, R.A. (with Rickert, R.T.) *Henslowe's Diary* (1961), ix, 359, 364, 366, 389, 398
Folger, The Library, 66, 70
Ford, John, *Love's Sacrifice*, 55, 56;

(with **Dekker**), *The Son's Darling*, 56

Forte Del Ore, Seige of, 19, 36

Fortesque, Thomas, *The Foreste*, 17

Fortune Theatre, The, 52, 211–2; *The Massacre at Paris* performed, 381; partnership in building, 384, 397, 403; decision to build, 411–5; contract to Peter Streete, 416–20; belonged to Alleyn, 423; licensed under James I, 432, 442; burnt to ground, and rebuilt, 425–6

Fortune's Tennis, Dekker, 52–3, 421

Fowler, Richard, 425

Francesco's Fortunes, Greene, 74, 141, 152, 154, 171–2, 186

Free Thinkers, The, 202

Freeman, Arthur, *Two Notes on 'A Knack to Know a Knave'* (1962), 284

Friar Bacon & Friar Bungay, Greene, 131, 198, 235, 239, 264, 268, 284–6, 292–3, 305, 380

Froissart, 264

Frying Pan Alley, 383

Fulgotius, Baptista, *Exemptiorum Libri IX* (1578), 17, 21, 25, 39

Fuller, 2, 38, 326, 329

Garnier, Robert, 376

Gascoigne, George, *Jocasta* (1566), 48–50

Gaw, Allison, *The Origin and Development of I Henry VI*, ix, xi, 111–3, 135, 160, 181–3, 237, 241–4, 248–54, 256–269, 271, 275–280, 307

Gawdy, Philip, 46

Geoffrey of Monmouth, 274, 275

Gill, Daniel, 421, 424

Gill, William, 424

Globe, The, 412, 414–6, 421, 425–6, 432, 434, 442

Golden Lane, 412–3, 425

Grace, Frank, 425

Gravelines, The, 67, 86

Gray, H.D., 266

Grays Inn, 48

Greg, W.W., *Henslowe's Diary* (1908); *Henslowe's Papers* (1907), ix, 162, 164, 190, 194, 205, 211–9, 221, 229–30, 364, 366, 370–1, 374, 378–90, 393–8, 423

Greene, Robert, x, xi; autobiography, 130–43, 150; allegorical/ autobiographical *Groatsworth* story, 144–49; his Letter, 156–8; author B in *harey the vj*, 263–68, 272–4; historical importance in shedding light on contemporary scene, 61–2, 65–6, 72, 74–7, 276–9, 320, 354

Alleyn his *bête noire*, xiii, 61–4, 65–6, 72, 74, 76; business association with, 163, 229, 236, 242–3; collaboration in *harey the vj*, 238, 242–3, 270–9; *Faire Em* identified by, 191–7; the Windmill, 190, 203–4

Alphonsus, King of Aragon, 50, 58–9, 63, 131, 138, 187, 213, 236, 266, 284, 286, 292, 293

Cambridge, 136

Ciceronis Tamor, 198

Cony-Catchers, 140, 234, 287, 291, 303

Faire Em, 190–202, 219, 221, 227–8, 233

Farewell to Folly (1587), 138, 187, 190, 192, 197, 285; *Preface 'To the Gentlemen Students'*, 191;

Francesco's Fortunes, 74, 141,152, 154, 171–2, 186

Friar Bacon & Friar Bungay, 131, 198, 238, 268, 284–6, 292–3, 305, 380

Greene's Mourning Garment, 192, 198

Greenes Vision written at the instant of his death, 131, 285, 294, 314

George a Greene, 131

Groatsworth of Wit, 129–167, 169, 170, 175–8, 181–5, 187, 190–1, 194, 199, 210, 219, 221, 228, 276, 295–7, 289; see also main heading below

Habington, *Queen of Aragon* (1640), 56

harey the vj, ix; première at the Rose, 239; identified by Nashe as *1 Henry VI,* 239–40; most unevenly written of *Henry VI* trilogy, 240; topicality of the play in 1591/2, 241–2; Dr. Gaw's examination of First Folio text, 243, 251–4; novelty of turret exploited, 241, 244–50, 278; Alleyn as director/ planner of production, 241, 243, 250; consensus on hybrid nature of play, 251, 279; irreconcilable inconsistencies in text, 260; spelling idiosyncracies basis of identification of collaborative authorship, 252–4; Author A, 255–60; Author D, 260–3; Author B, 263–8, 272–3; Author C, 296–72, 274–6 (in B's part), 266–7; origin of Groatsworth attack identified, 276–80

Harris, William, 420

Harryson, William, 348

Hart, H.C., 303

Harvey, Gabriel, 57, 62–3, 74, 132, 139, 150, 158, 277, 301, 315

Harvey, Dr. William, 348

Hathaway, Anne, 110; children, Susanna, Hamnet, Judith

Haughton, 218, 219

Hearne, Thomas, *Discourses of English Antiquaries* (1771), 198, 400

Helle, John, the clown, 400

Heminge, John, 110, 114, 238, 324

Henry of Navarre, 37, 242

Henry III, King of France, 381

Henry III, King of Spain, 33

Henry IV, King of England, 33

Henry VI, King of England, 66, 240, 241, 261

2 and 3 Henry VI, compared with *The Contention* and *True Tragedy* 110–2, 113–5; theory of actors' responsibility for parallelisms with Marlowe's works, 116, 118–23; Shakespeare's alleged connections with Pembroke's Men, 114, 124–9; 240, 244, 251, 254, 257, 259, 261, 263–4, 317–8; "tiger's heart" line, 134, 160–1, 180, 182; see also Appendix B, 455

Henry VIII, King of England, 412

Henslowe, Agnes, formerly **Woodward,** wife of Philip, 166, 333, 359, 423; see also under Letters below

Henslowe, John, brother of Philip, 359

Henslowe, Philip,

Alleyn, his "sonne", their relationship, xii-xiii, 116, 161, 174, 184–5, 250, 278, 335, 337–8, 361, 367, 371; joint petition on behalf of watermen, 372–3, 375; partnership reflected in gallery accounts, 384, 393–403; close association in Bear Garden and the Fortune, 405–31; his dependence on Alleyn, 392

Banker, 161, 169, 174, 178, 184, 423

Bankside, xii, 336–40, 359; riots affecting the Rose, 370–4; 405–8, 412, 426

Bear Garden, 405–8, 426–31

Chettle, Henry, 178, 212

Cholmley, John, 363–6, 383–4, 390, 393, 397, 398–9

Education and character, xiii, 342, 343, 367, 383–4, 399, 405–9

Family, 166–7, 333, 335, 340, 359, 405, 423, 435; see also under names of members of family

Fortune Theatre, 412–32; warrants for the site, 413–14; building of theatre, 420; casting up his final account for the theatrical season, 423

Gentleman of the Sewer, 359, 433

Groom of the Chamber, 359, 405

harey the vj, 239, 243

494

Inventories, 350, 351, 382–3, 386

Jonson, Ben, 407

A Knack to Know a Knave, 283, 291

Langworth, Arthur, 405, 406

Letters to Alleyn, 116, 342–8, 399, 406–9

Lord Admiral's Men, 380–91, 211–8, 402; see also under **Henslowe's** *Diary*

Lord Strange's Men, 238–40, 282, 333, 339, 342; two warrants, 369–76

Marriage, 333, 359

Master of the Royal Game jointly, 405, 408, 426, 427–30

Money-lender, pawnbroker and small businessman, 344–5, 359

Plague, 342–8

Proprietor of theatre, xii, 363–404, 420, 421–2, 423–4

Rose Theatre, xiii, 238–9, 241, 333, 335; building of, 363, contract with Cholmley, 364–6; renovations, 368, 382–3; petitions re closure of theatre, 369–74, 376; theatre allowed to rot, 404; see also under **Henslowe's** *Diary*

Henslowe's *Diary*, ix, xii, begins 238; described, 359–61; Elizabethan dates recorded idiosyncratically, 360, 367–8; step-daughter Joan Woodward marries Edward Alleyn, 334; expenditure on the Rose, 382–3, 401, 403, 404; performances recorded, 238–9, 282, 368–9, 376, 380, 385, 386–8, 390, 395–6; changes of recording method of box-office takings, 385, 386, 393–6; loan accounts, 392, 393, 394, 395; settlements with Alleyn and the company, 393, 397, 402, 421, 423–4, 430; sale of costumes, 350; Henslowe's sketches, 346–7, 409; Henslowe's doodlings, 383–4; Alleyn's first retirement re-

corded, 386; acquittances for plays sold/bought for company stock, 161, 211–8; Henslowe overwhelmed by debt when managing the theatre without Alleyn, 392

Herbert, Lord Edward, 4th Earl of **Worcester,** 332

Hero and Leander, Marlowe, 328

Herod, 48

Hewitt, H.J., *The Organisation of War under Edward III,* 89

Heywood, Thomas, 218–9, 327, 401; *Book of Oserecke* (1602), 2, 184; *The Prologue to the Stage at the Cockpit,* for *The Famous Tragedy of the Rich Jew of Malta* (1633), 327

Hitler, Adolph, 34

Hogg, Ralph, 359

Holinshed, '*Chronicles*', 66, 84, 89–91, 96, 98 244, 250, 261, 264, 274–5

Holy League, The, 70

Honigman, E.A.J., 179

Hope, The, 416

Hopkinson, A.F., 80

Horace, *Ars Poetica,* 59

Hosking, G.L., 329

Howard, Charles, Lord Admiral, 2nd Baron of Effingham, then 1st **Earl of Nottingham,** 67, 70–2, 74, 84, 167, 185, 187, 332, 372, 413

A Brief Abstract of Accidents, 86

Howard, Frances, Countess of Kildare, 333

Hughes, 118

Huguenots, 37, 242, 270, 381

Hunks, Harry, (A Bear), 411

Hunsdon, Lord Henry, Lord Chamberlain, 377, 379, 413

Ignatius, Baptista, *De Origine Turcarum Libellum,* 17, 25

Ingleby, *Complete View of the Shakespeare Controversy* (1861), 352

Inns of Court, 48, 412
"Iohannes Fac Totum", xiii, 132, 138, 155, 166, 174, 186–90, 274, 354
Isabel, Queen, 127
Isle of Dogs, Nashe, 315, 400, 407
Italian Pageant, 438
Iuby, Edward, see Juby
Iudas, 132
Iulian, 132
Iuuenall, 132, 170
Ives, Paul, *Practise of Fortification*, 36

James I, King of England, xiv, 3, 406, 426–8, 430–48
James IV, Greene, 131, 236, 268, 284–6, 292–3, 304
Jeffes (or Jeffs), Anthony, 447
Jeffs, Humphrey, 447
Jenkins, Harold, 178
Jesuits, The, 197
Jew of Malta, The, Marlowe, 2–3, 44, 48, 56, 64, 76; ship 'The Flying Dragon', 89; 104, 106, 109; Alleyn's ownership of play, 211, 255–6, 294; Alleyn's fame in role, 327; Alleyn playing the part, 339, 376, 380–1
Joan of Arc, 242, 254, 274
John a Kent, John a Cumber, 214
John, King of England, 66
Johnes, Ryc, 330
Jones, Inigo, 446–7
Jones, Richard, 282, 329, 332, 333, 350, 400, 423, 434
Jonson, Ben, 322, 407, 436–8, 443–6; as actor, 135, 184
Epigrams (1616), 327
Joronymo, 381
(with Chapman) *Eastward Hoe* (1605), 54
Jordan, J.C., 150, 264, 266
Jovius, Paulus, 18, 20; *Turcicarum Rerum Commentarii*, Shorte Treatise upon the Turkes Chronicles (1546),

17; *Elogia virorum bellica virtute illustrium* (1578), 18
Juby, Edward, 424, 425, 447
Julian, Cardinal, 27

Keats, 80
Kempe, William, 110, 135, 183, 238
Kemps Nine Daies Wonder, 110, 135, 183, 238
Kendall, William, 401
Kinwelmarshe, Francis, 48
King James' Accession Celebration, 436–46
King's Men, The, 427, 432, 442
King's School, Canterbury, 6, 8, 17, 68
Kipling, Rudyard, 63
Knack to Know an Honest Man, A, attributed to Alleyn, written as riposte to *A Knack to Know a Knave*, 220–1; the play analysed, stylistically compared with *Faire Em*, 222–8
Knack to Know a Knave, A, apocryphal, attributed to Greene, 131; played by Ed. Alleyn & his company, 281–2; authorship considered, 283 ff; cf. *A Quip for an Upstart Courtier*, 285, 289; moralizing, 286–8, 290–1; Greene's faults and virtues present, 291–3, 298; his love of exotica, 294; cf. *Groatsworth*, 295–6; evidence of Nashe's collaboration, 299–303, 306–7, 309–13; not Shakespeare's hand, 303–5, 307–9, 316–8; Greene and Nashe in close collaboration, 313–4; 319
Knowsley, 196, 205, 206, 207
Kyd, Thomas, 5, 6, 32, 176, 179, 234, 251, 376–9
The Spanish Tragedy, 5, 32, 62, 234, 379–80
Titus Andronicus, 376–80
Hamlet, 62

496